Desperate Journeys,
Abandoned Souls

Desperate Journeys, Abandoned Souls

True Stories of Castaways and Other Survivors

EDWARD E. LESLIE

Foreword by Sterling Seagrave

HOUGHTON MIFFLIN COMPANY · BOSTON

For information about permission to reproduce selections from this book, write to Permissions, Houghton Mifflin Company, 2 Park Street, Boston, Massachusetts 02108.

Library of Congress Cataloging-in-Publication Data

Leslie, Edward E.

 Desperate journeys, abandoned souls : true stories of castaways and other survivors / Edward E. Leslie ; foreword by Sterling Seagrave.

 p. cm.

 Bibliography: p.

 ISBN 0-395-47864-2. ISBN 0-395-43608-7 (pbk.)

 1. Survival (after airplane accidents, shipwrecks, etc.) 2. Castaways. I. Title.

G525.L58 1988   88-644

910.4'53—dc19   CIP

Printed in the United States of America

FFG 12 11 10 9 8 7 6 5 4 3

Book design by Robert Overholtzer

The author is grateful for permission to quote from the following sources: Elizabeth Boyer, *A Colony of One*. Reprinted by permission of Elizabeth Boyer. Don M. Campbell, "Nightmare on Missinaibi," *Outdoor Life*. Reprinted by permission of *Outdoor Life* and Don M. Campbell. Lauren Elder with Shirley Streshinsky, *And I Alone Survived*. Reprinted by permission of Lauren Elder and Shirley Streshinsky. Peter Foley, "We Ditched at Sea." Reprinted from The Saturday Evening Post © 1966 The Curtis Publishing Co. Scott Jeffrey, "When the *Pride of Baltimore* Sank, Eight Sailors Got a Crash Course in Ocean Survival," *People Weekly*. Reprinted by permission of *People Weekly*. H. R. Kabat, "Bare Fists Against the Shark." Reprinted from The Saturday Evening Post © 1944 The Curtis Publishing Co. Paul Madden, "Tragic Voyage." Reprinted from The Saturday Evening Post © 1944 The Curtis Publishing Co. William Laird McKinlay, *"Karluk": The Great Untold Story of Arctic Exploration*. Reprinted by permission of Weidenfeld & Nicolson, Ltd. Archibald MacLeish, *J.B.: A Play in Verse*. Copyright © 1956, 1957, 1958 by Archibald MacLeish. Copyright © renewed 1986 by William H. MacLeish and Mary H. Grimm. Reprinted by permission of Houghton Mifflin Company. Roger Lewis and Denise Harris, as told to Jim Rearden, "We Nearly Froze to Death," *Alaska, The Magazine of Life on the Last Frontier*. Reprinted by permission of *ALASKA*® magazine. C. J. Rosebert, "Only God Knew the Way." Reprinted from The Saturday Evening Post © 1944 The Curtis Publishing Co. Antoine de Saint-Exupéry, *Wind, Sand and Stars*. Copyright © 1939 by Antoine de Saint-Exupéry; renewed 1967 by Lewis Galantière. Reprinted by permission of Harcourt Brace Jovanovich, Inc. Karl Shapiro, "Crusoe." Reprinted by permission of Wieser and Wieser. Louis Zamperini, *Devil at My Heels*. Reprinted by permission of Louis Zamperini.

 The author has made every effort to locate all owners of photographs and copyrighted material and to obtain permission to reproduce them. Any errors or omissions are unintentional and corrections will be made in future printings if necessary.

*This book is dedicated with love and gratitude to
Dr. James E. Carver
of St. Andrews Presbyterian College.
Although they have long since left his classroom,
many of his students still struggle to live up to
the extraordinary example he set.*

---

*This book is also respectfully dedicated to
the memory of
Steven Frederick Geisz
1946–1975.
The certain knowledge that he was dying did not
daunt or defeat him; instead it gave him a
purpose and a resolve. To the last days of his
life he worked on behalf of those whom society
has discarded and forgotten, and he grew
spiritually even as he declined physically.
Rest in Peace.*

I am most entertained by those actions which give me a
light into the nature of man.

—Daniel Defoe

Contents

PART II · THE DELICATE QUESTION WHICH

PART III · LORDS OF THE FOWL AND THE BRUTE

PART IV · THE CHARMS OF SOLITUDE

Foreword
by Sterling Seagrave

All we may ask of some books is to be a good read, but there is a great deal more to this one. By bringing together for the first time scores of horrific misadventures that we usually hear about only in bits and pieces, Edward Leslie reveals some dark truths about human nature, the limits of courage, and the fragility of life itself.

Seen separately, survival stories can be oddly misleading: we are swept along by the unique circumstance, by the exceptional personalities, by the agonizing suspense, or by the skills of the narrator, and often miss the dark side completely. This applies whether we are reading a news report on the harrowing ordeal of a young woman who, stranded in the Alaskan wilderness, endures a week of being mauled and chewed repeatedly by a maddened grizzly, or rereading a picaresque account of the marooning of an eighteenth-century Jack Nastyface. It is difficult to see what these extraordinary sufferings have in common until you bring them all together.

The overly familiar adventures of *Robinson Crusoe* and *The Swiss Family Robinson* are sugar-coated tablets whose simple message is the virtue of ingenuity and courage in the face of adversity. That was all well and good for the age in which they were written, a gaslight age when courage and ingenuity were adornments that the middle class put on each morning with their boiled collars and corsets. The real story of Alexander Selkirk, on whom Daniel Defoe based his novel, like the similar story of Pedro de Serrano 168 years earlier and many others in this book, is much truer to our eve of nuclear winter. How they persevered, while many others among them died, is much more pertinent to us than to anyone before; for the question of individual and group survival has never been so

urgently considered since the Black Death. After a century of enjoy-
ing the roller coaster ride of the Industrial Revolution, we face the
bleak prospect of it all ending so suddenly that there's no time to
don a life jacket, grab a parachute, or find a pack of matches. The
fact that many people imagine they will survive Armageddon if they
stock underground shelters with freeze-dried foods and paramilitary
weapons is not a psychiatric aberration; the sober governments of
Switzerland and Sweden have spent great sums preparing and
stocking vast disaster shelters in the Alps and along the rocky coast
of the Baltic, some designed for thousands of long-term inhabitants,
to increase the odds of someone being around to pick up the pieces.
Assuming, of course, that there is sufficient advance notice to get
into the shelters.

The fact that most humans are hopelessly unprepared for the
ultimate crisis was driven home for me several years ago when a
survey of boating accidents on Chesapeake Bay produced a curious
detail: most of the male corpses fished out of the bay over the years
had their flies open. The inescapable conclusion reached by the
authorities was that all these people had met their end while blithely
peeing over the side. Their last thought, I'm sure, was astonishment.

The next most common emotion (for those who do not die immediately) is a deep, sometimes suicidal melancholy, eventually
pushed aside by hunger, panic, and — in many cases — temporary
insanity. The mysterious disappearance not long ago of solo yachtsman Donal Crowhurst is a case in point. One fascinating aspect of
Leslie's book is the dawning awareness that when survivors get
back to civilization, they carefully hide much more than they reveal.
For the brutal truth, we have to look for clues between the lines.
Some of these stories ring more true than others, and it is entertaining to see the lengths to which the scoundrels go to paint themselves
in noble hues. One comes away with the nagging suspicion that nice
people usually do not survive being stranded, and when they do, it
is often through freak accident or divine intervention. The real survivors in this world are few and far between. And if they are the
fittest to survive, God help us, indeed.

Much of this book, as you would expect, has to do with food.
How many of us, unexpectedly tumbled onto an alien shore, would
silently give up the ghost rather than face the reality of drinking
iguana urine, chewing up grubs, or gagging down raw turtle liver?

Lord Byron's grandfather, shipwrecked in the Straits of Magellan, saw his dog killed and eaten by his shipmates, Leslie tells us, then became so starved himself that he dug up and devoured the dog's paws. We are all too far removed — even from the rural farms of our immediate ancestors and the prosaic hardships they faced — to know what is really put in sausage meat or scrapple, or how to wring a bird's neck. Our soldiers have to be given months of training in jungle survival to prepare them for only a few days of commando operations in rain forests where barefoot people happily raise babies. It is all in your point of view.

Certainly it helps to be marooned with somebody else, for you can commiserate, quarrel, and feud like newlyweds, and when things really get difficult, you can always eat him, or vice versa. Leslie clearly demonstrates that when the going gets tough, the tough get eaten. Cannibalism, like so many other customs, is merely a state of mind. Over the centuries famine repeatedly drove Europeans and Asians alike to eat everything, including each other. The culinary genius of the French and the Chinese, working with nothing more than a few spices and a bit of garlic, turned famine food into such delicacies as snails, sea slugs, and stewed bats, garnished with larvae, pupae, and spawn — all, like escargot, under more elegant names. And while doughboys in the trenches of World War I were driven insane by body lice and other vermin, political prisoners, POWs, and castaways savor them in their gruel as if they were herbs from Provence. One culture's famine food is another's caviar.

In the case of survival cannibalism, society seasons its judgments with something akin to garlic by conveniently applying certain criteria: Was the main course already dead of natural causes? If not, was a lottery properly conducted before the murder, and are the culprits suitably pious, making analogies to Holy Communion? In this way, the survivors of a plane crash in the Andes could make a group decision to eat some of their number, and walk away heroes. It is only a short distance from the Andes to Soylent Green. But what is customary is comforting. Cannibalism is a social affair. Solitary survival is not.

Solo survivors are a breed apart. Confronted by extreme solitude, by starvation, and by no prospect of rescue, they do not sit around long pining in self-pity but set about urgent practical matters. In some cases this reveals strength of character, tenacity, and the will to live. In others it reveals only animal cunning and stubbornness.

Sensitivity and imagination are terrible disadvantages in the crunch. Unusual among these tales because of its painful and pathetic revelations is the diary of a nameless castaway on Ascension Island. Unlike other classical accounts, in which the survivor returns to civilization to enlarge endlessly on his ingenuity, this victim was much too sensitive for his own good. He kept a diary frankly revealing his misery, his mistakes, his melancholy, his weakness of character, and his hallucinations. The diary is singularly lacking in excuses. Perhaps because he was overly absorbed in his own failings and inadequacies, his struggle failed, and the diary was found beside his bones.

Women also play their role as survivors here. In addition to Marguerite de la Rocque, marooned off Canada for the crime of fornication, and WACs lost in the jungles of New Guinea, there is the puzzling account of Ann Saunders, who took charge of carving up the dinner guests aboard the derelict *Francis Mary,* insisted on eating the lion's share when her fiancé gave up the ghost beside her, and vindicated herself by publishing her tragic story. Others challenged her version, painting her as a demon who went about her dreadful chores with unnecessary vigor, and we are left wondering which version to accept. Leslie chooses to believe her, but I am not so convinced.

While several of these stories may be familiar to some readers, the great majority will be new, because Leslie has gone to extraordinary lengths to search the archives, to find accounts that are long out of print, to locate their corollaries, and to track down the most obscure and fascinating details. As a literary detective, he has that rare gift of being able to find things. This is by no means as easy as it sounds. The foolhardy may venture into the underground catacombs of the Library of Congress, for example, and never be heard from again, but Leslie has an uncanny knack for finding his way in and out alive and in the process locating what he is seeking. It is this that enables him to find the original version of so many of these stories, to determine if such a vessel actually plied those waters in the year 1713, to discover the real background of the castaway, and to find contrary testimony of other survivors from the same disaster. I first enlisted his help years ago in researching the use of obscure biological poisons through the centuries, an exercise that also involved comparing the properties of the most exotic toxins with the results of autopsies from remote parts of the world, including Ethiopia, Laos, and Afghanistan, and examining the sorry history of America's secret involvement in chemical weapons. Later, at my request, he followed the cold trail of a young Chinese runaway, Charlie Soong, from Boston to North Carolina in the years following the Civil War, and in the course of resolving many riddles even came up with a string hammock the boy had made a hundred years before.

In *Desperate Journeys, Abandoned Souls,* he has produced a gem.

might be interested y to try.

← LITERARY DETECTIVE

Introduction

This book was inspired by an incident in the life of an eighteenth-century mariner by the name of Alexander Selkirk. While on a voyage to the Americas, Selkirk, an able but argumentative sailing master, quarreled with his captain, a man considerably less competent than he was, if equally bad-tempered. Selkirk believed that the ship on which they sailed was not being maintained properly and was in danger of sinking. The captain, of course, felt otherwise, and the heated disagreement that followed was only concluded when Selkirk demanded that he be put ashore on the nearest island. He had expected to be joined in voluntary exile by at least some of his fellow sailors, but few men of his day would have preferred the unknown dangers of life on some remote isle to the hazardous but familiar existence on board a vessel — however leaky — and so in the end he was marooned alone.

As it happened, his fears were well founded: the ship did sink, and the crew was picked up by Spaniards and languished for many years in a colonial prison. This would have been of little comfort to Selkirk, because it was nearly five years before he was rescued and returned to the Scottish fishing village of his birth.

These facts are not controversial and are attested to by several authoritative, contemporary sources. In 1830, however, Walter Wilson, writing in the *Life and Times of Defoe,* added a curious detail to the Selkirk canon. He claimed that when the former maroon came home after having been so long alone, he found that he could not abide the presence of other human beings. He therefore dug a cave in his parents' yard and lived in it until he gradually became acclimated to the society of his own kind.

Some readers may be made a bit uncomfortable by this. Their response seems to me inappropriate. For reasons that will be enumerated later, the cave anecdote is almost surely apocryphal. But if it is true, what Selkirk did was therapeutic: he rid himself of a crippling phobia, something not too many of us have been able to accomplish even with expensive and far more time-consuming treatments.

What intrigues me about the story is not its remedial angle but rather the questions it raises about the personality of the survivor. What traits, for instance, enable one person to come through a life-threatening crisis while others in the same or similar circumstances die? What psychological changes does the survivor undergo while in solitude? And what lasting psychological effects does he continue to experience long after his rescue and return to civilization?

These questions are often not easily or comprehensively answered, especially with regard to those cases that occurred before the twentieth century. The writers of survivor narratives in earlier times were less preoccupied with such matters than we are, and more concerned with theological ones. Nonetheless, it is sometimes possible to draw certain inferences or reach conclusions based on the later lives of particular individuals.

Although my curiosity about the mental states of survivors caused me to do the research that resulted in this book, and although I do make references to such matters in it, the reader should not expect it to bear any resemblance to a psychology text. It contains a collection of true stories, some inspiring, some harrowing, and a few even humorous. I hope that they are also diverting and, just now and again, perhaps, insightful.

EDWARD E. LESLIE

Desperate Journeys, Abandoned Souls

Prologue
Found Alone

The beginning is not history and fact; it is legend and fantasy. The legend is of a man who really did live and who accomplished great things in his lifetime, while the fantasy is borne of the fears of his age and profession. It is a dream of compelling dread in the minds of men.

The man whose legend we recall is a privateering captain by the name of Woodes Rogers. He was a daring man, a resourceful and shrewd plyer of the Sweet Trade. A contemporary of the pirates Morgan, Kidd, and Teach, he was as fearsome a fighter as any of them and a far greater seaman.

He was a resolute man, indisputably wise and immensely courageous. Once, as the young commander of a small fleet caught in a fierce sea battle with the Spanish enemy, he was struck in the face with a musket ball that shattered his jaw and lodged in his throat. Although he was in excruciating pain, he refused to leave the deck to seek medical aid. Unable to speak, he continued to direct the fighting by writing down his orders, his blood spurting onto his uniform and flecking the pages of his messages. Six weeks after the victory he had won, Rogers, it is said, had a sudden spasm of coughing — and *coughed, coughed, coughed* the bullet up.

He was a hero cut from a pattern that has long since been lost, one whose life would have once been studied by school pupils, as indeed his was — a century or more ago. A life to be admired by such children not only at the ending of each day, to be read about as an escape from the wretched puzzles of Latin and geometry, but a life for the classroom as well: decades before his vanquishing of the buccaneers at New Providence and his death on a Caribbean shore, Rogers, at the mere age of twenty-nine, led a successful expedition to circumnavigate the globe. His was not the first to do so — Ferdinand Magellan's crew had made a circling 180 years earlier, although the captain general himself was killed by natives before its completion. A few other circumnavigations took place in the interim, but in absolute contrast to his predecessors, Captain Rogers came home with all of his ships and most of his crew intact. In addition, he wrote about the adventure in an account so vivid and lucid that it remains highly readable two and a half centuries after its composition.

Yet despite his achievements and the admiration he once received, he is largely forgotten today. Romantic historians and their readers prefer such as Captain William Kidd, a man of decidedly lesser attainments, whose fame rests chiefly on dubious legends of his sea robberies and on the folk tales of the treasure he is supposed to have buried and whose sulking, furious ghost is said to guard it still.

Indeed, except for a cursory mention of his subjugation of the West Indian pirates and his own days as a privateer, Woodes Rogers might be ignored by the modern chroniclers of his age — were it not for what he found on that circumnavigation and wrote about thereafter and what became of the story.

A man whose great accomplishments might be lost save for a brief moment at a point off the western coast of South America, beyond Cape Horn, below the Tropic of Capricorn, perhaps only a third of the way on the serpentine line between Bristol and London, via Cape St. Lucas and Guam, the Sunda Strait and the Cape Verde Islands.

Just a single moment to keep a man's name remembered, one that took place before he captured the Spanish towns and ships, while his beloved brother was yet alive and his own jaw whole, and the subduing of the cutthroats of all nations was a task for the far and unknowable future. When all he had to worry about was mutiny and starvation, French corsairs and Spanish soldiers, gales and scurvy and plague, cannibals and the minions of the very Devil himself.

South of the Islands of Wolves, floating on that tranquil and treacherous sea.

He brought the *Duke* and *Duchess* to the island of Más á Tierra and searched its bays for enemy ships. When he found none, he sent eight armed men in a yawl to the shore to collect supplies. While they were gone he kept a good watch for sails.

He was an Englishman and a Protestant in waters that lapped on shores that Catholic Spain claimed as part of its empire. Years before, Pope Alexander VI, who had bribed his way to the papal throne and was the father of several illegitimate children, turned his attention from these scandals long enough to divide the Unknown World between Portugal and Spain. It was not a division that was likely to be respected by Protestant nations, whose merchants desired sea trade and colonies in the New World.

So the Spaniards jealously guarded their decreed territories (which included nearly all of Central and South America), prophetically fearing that if other Europeans became familiar with these waters, alliances with disgruntled local inhabitants would follow — and thereafter trading relationships, settlements, and perhaps ultimately the loss of colonies. They therefore sought diligently to discourage curious foreigners with the fate of those whom their diligence netted.

Notwithstanding the Spanish threat, there were Frenchmen in these waters, and England was in the midst of a protracted conflict with that nation as well. Such wars were often long, and the periods of peace between them seemed brief and few.

The yawl had not yet returned. Rogers was becoming uneasy.

He was what was known as a privateer. It was the custom of the monarchs of the mercantile countries to grant commissions to adventurers, giving them permission to capture the ships and towns of their enemies. In return for such a hunting license, the privateer presented the crown with a share of the spoils and agreed not to molest the vessels of his sovereign's allies. To attack without such discrimination was piracy, and pirates belonged to no nation and could be hung by any without recrimination. Thus the risk in the privateer's bargain: the voyages took him far from home and lasted for years, and he might return to find that he had become a diplomatic embarrassment to his government, which could resolve the matter most easily by having him executed as a pirate.

The yawl had now been gone a very long time. Rogers was worried and impatient. He had a party of armed men put in a pinnace and sent them after the yawl.

No doubt the men in the yawl felt the need for caution, too.

They had been sent to bring back vegetables and game. Privateers had planted crops at the higher elevations of this island and had released herds of goats in the hope that without natural enemies they would reproduce abundantly.

But on the shore could be creatures considerably less benign: a troop of soldiers, for instance, might be lying in ambush to capture interlopers. The men of the yawl knew as well as Rogers did what would happen to them in Spanish hands: the gibbet rope or a slow death in a colonial prison — or torture by the ecclesiastical authorities of the Inquisition.

The Spaniards posed an indirect threat as well. The appearance of their warships in a number superior to their commander's own forces might cause him to sail away hastily, leaving them to be taken prisoner or to exist as maroons until their gunpowder ran out, and they slowly starved to death.

"Civilized" men did not constitute the only danger. Many islands were inhabited by hostile natives or were visited by war parties of them. The Englishmen surely knew of Magellan's death on the sands of a remote isle. Two hundred and fifty-eight years later, Captain James Cook would die in a similar fashion, murdered by tribesmen who had but a short time before worshiped him as a god.

The behavior of even initially friendly natives would be undecipherable to these men; treachery could come suddenly and unpredictably. An even more dreadful knowledge was that some of the inhabitants of the South American coast and of the South Sea islands practiced cannibalism. Francis Drake had encountered such cannibals on his circumnavigation; from their ships his crews had watched helplessly while on the beach some of their hapless, captured fellows were literally eaten alive.

One more possibility, one last threat might await them on the approaching shore. Sailors were a superstitious lot. So much at the whim of uncontrollable and inexplicable forces, they sought refuge in arcane beliefs. They were certain of the existence of a great many extraordinary creatures, a whole bestiary of mythical beings and monsters.

Their religion abetted this creation, greatly augmenting its size and fearsomeness. By the fourteenth century, church authorities were conducting witch hunts. In Catholic countries, the hunters used witchcraft encyclopedias that effectively functioned as torture manuals. Catholics were not alone in seeking worshipers of the Devil and the practitioners of his magic — nor in devising excru-

ciating ways to get the accused to confess. The ferreting out of
Satan's followers and the consequent spread of witch and demon
lore was nearly universal in the West.

Under prolonged and terrible pain, victims not only denounced
friends and members of their own families as Devil worshipers but
also supplied their tormentors with all manner of delusions regarding Satan's dominion, his ability to assume the shape of men and
animals as well as other, wilder guises. He also gave his demons
such powers, it was said. They, like their master, could assume
recognizable forms or strange ones as befitted their purpose.

Demons walked the earth, then, able to take on the appearance
of men while retaining all their own diabolic capabilities. So, too,
on the globe moved Satan himself, and with him his witches and
sorcerers with their conjurings and familiars. There were also cruel
apparitions — not invisible or transparent, but corporeal and indis-
tinguishable from human beings save for the coldness of their flesh.
In addition to all of these malevolent forces, there was that fantast-
ical catalogue of diverse creatures rarely seen by man . . . monsters
awful to look on, ferocious, unrelenting, unmerciful. . . .

The yawl was approaching the beach. The men worked the oars and
searched the shoreline with their eyes, seeking a place to land.

Suddenly there burst from the bushes onto the sand a wild thing,
a grotesque beast bellowing and screeching at them, racing upright
on two legs faster than any human being could move, covered in fur
of all colors from the top of its pointed head to its feet. It had no
face at all, only eyes, staring. They fought to bring the boat about,
bent their backs to pull her from the island, away from that thing,
their rasping breaths and curses mixing with its roaring in their ears.

They expected to see the creature plunge into the surf and swim
in boiling water after the yawl or to soar on dragon's wings and
swoop down on them, claws extended — but it did not. It stopped
at the edge of the land, and its cries became high, pitiable.

Still they worked the oars for their lives, for the sake of their
souls, even as they began to discern words in the monster's pleadings, sounds of their own language. But demons possessed the
power of speech, they knew, the better to delude men about their
true nature.

So on they rowed undeceived . . . until . . . the words they heard
made them hesitate . . . gradually fall to rest upon their oars listen-

ing in wonder . . . to names they as Christians were certain that
neither Devil nor demon was permitted by God to say:

> I believe in God the Father Almighty,
> Maker of Heaven and Earth,
> And in Jesus Christ,
> His only Son, our Lord. . . .

What they encountered on that island was not a demon but a man.
A man who had been marooned in that place for more than four
years. His experiences would inspire the creation in his own lifetime
of the first great English novel, *The Life and Strange Surprising
Adventures of Robinson Crusoe*.

And his name was Selkirk — Alexander Selkirk.

PART I

MONARCHS

I am monarch of all I survey,
  My right there is none to dispute;
From the centre all around to the sea,
  I am lord of the fowl and the brute.
Oh, solitude! where are the charms
  That sages have seen in thy face?
Better dwell in the midst of alarms,
  Than reign in this horrible place.

  — William Cowper, "Verses Supposed to be Written by
    Alexander Selkirk, During His Solitary Abode in the
    Island of Juan Fernández"

The man frequently bewailed his return to the world, which
could not, he said, with all its enjoyments, restore to him the
tranquility of his solitude.

  — Richard Steele on Alexander Selkirk

CHAPTER 1

His Hair Was Weedy and His Beard Was Long

Pedro de Serrano off the Coast of Peru

The survivor's predicament is a very old one, well documented in our history and literature. It is a subject of perennial fascination, one of which we never tire. Look up from the mending of your nets, pause in your whittling, put aside the oily rag, and begin a tale . . . and we will listen as rapt as children.

The sheer adventure of the story holds us, it is true, but there is an element of gawking in our obsession. Ours is the stare of bystanders after an automobile accident, watching with studied indifference, arms folded, while the ambulance drivers kneel on the asphalt and work deliberately over still bodies. The sunlight glinting on the chunks of windshield glass does not hurt our eyes — or cause us to turn away.

At our best in such moments we are dry-mouthed, thinking, *There but for the grace of God go I.* At our worst we are relieved and triumphant: *It didn't happen to me! I'm still invincible, invulnerable!*

Another reason the old stories of the island or the longboat are retold and passed on is because, I believe, like folk tales, they offer instruction. They warn fishermen and sailors of genuine dangers that await and provide practical directions on what to do when the worst occurs. On some deeper level, again like myths and folk tales, they inform us about ourselves. They offer, as Defoe posited, "light into the nature of man."

Indeed, I suspect we remain captivated by these accounts because we *sense* that they describe our psychological state, if not our spiritual one. Those of us who are battered by our tribulations feel as if we are alone in a barren place with no hope of rescue and no means of escape. The waves roar all around us, and to preserve ourselves a little while longer, we do things that we know we should not do. With enormous effort and damning action, we continue the most elemental kind of existence, and we are appalled at what it takes to maintain us in our confinement, never mind to set us free.

There are relatively few survivor situations. An island may have more foliage or less, the sea may be choppy or calm, the climate moderate or severe, but these are just variations. Such dramas can play in only so many theaters. There are, however, an almost infinite number of performers who can assume the roles. Thus what does vary — and this considerably — is the individual actor's interpretation of his part . . . the extraordinary diversity of human response to exigent circumstances.

Some survivors — often professional military or naval personnel — will deal with chaotic situations by imposing over themselves a rigid and, on the face of it, slightly absurd order. It is as if they expect to stave off madness and disaster by regimentation.

One of these is the first man whose story we learn, a Spaniard called Pedro de Serrano. In 1540, Serrano was sailing in the Pacific when, for unknown reasons, his ship sank. He plunged into the sea wearing only a shirt and girdle, a knife tucked in at his waist. He swam alone, the only survivor of the wreck, until he reached an island and was able to drag himself onto the shore.

When he found the strength to look about his new dominion, he may have felt at least a moment's despair. This was not the isle of lush vegetation and plentiful fresh water so often conjured up by eighteenth- and nineteenth-century romantic writers, nor was it the happy embodiment of such fantasies in the Juan Fernández chain. This was a true desert island, and Serrano found it not at all idyllic. Granted, it was large enough to live on (he estimated it two leagues in compass), but it was devoid of trees, so there was no shade and no wood to build fires and huts. It entirely lacked grass and had neither pools nor streams. Rather there was only sand that reflected the cruel sunlight and stored up its heat and too quickly absorbed the rain that fell during the brief, ferocious storms.

It was on this desolate place that Serrano would have to live until a passing ship might find him. His great enemies would be hunger and thirst, and he would struggle constantly, daily, just to survive. He knew what fate awaited him if his efforts were insufficient or his luck bad: slow starvation and dehydration would have been to him, says his chronicler, a "languishing manner of death . . . much more miserable than . . . a speedy suffocation in the waters."

Serrano comprehended his predicament well enough that first night to pass it with "sad thoughts . . . lamenting his affliction with as many melancholy reflections as we may imagine capable to enter into the mind of a wretch in like extremities." But in the morning he put aside his lamentations and went about the business of staying alive. At first light he arose and went exploring. He found along the beach cockles, shrimp, and other small sea creatures that had washed up at the water's edge. These he ate raw.

Serrano remained by the beach because whatever the ocean might give was all the resource he had. So he patrolled the sand, walking back and forth, back and forth, always looking, searching: "With this small entertainment he passed his time, till observing some turtles not far from the shore he watched until they came within his reach." He then seized several of them and turned them over on their backs. Having found no source of drinkable water and already being quite thirsty, he cut their throats one at a time and drank their blood.

His thirst slaked, he set about dressing the reptiles by cutting the flesh out of the shells, slicing it into pieces, and leaving the strips in the sun to cure. He carefully cleaned out the shells and let them dry. He would employ them to store rainwater: using the smaller shells to scoop up the puddles that formed during the "great and sudden rains," he would pour the water into the larger shells, which acted as his storage tanks, some of these holding eleven or twelve gallons.

In the days that followed he killed as many turtles as he could, both for their meat and shells. He soon learned which of them to attack and which to leave alone: he could go after even those as large as "targets or bucklers" (small shields), but the really enormous ones he did not molest. These were too unwieldy for him to flip over.

Having solved these two most elemental problems of fresh water and food, Serrano next set out to build a fire. He had neither flint nor steel to strike sparks, so he went over the whole island looking for two pebbles to use as flints against which his knife would serve as the steel. But though he searched carefully, thoroughly, he could find none that were suitable. In this bleak, dry world there was only "dead sand."

So Serrano swam out into the sea, "and diving often to the bottom, he at length found a couple of stones fit for his purpose, which he rubbed together until he got them to an edge." He tested them with his knife, and seeing that they would strike sparks, he pulled threads out of his shirt, "which he worked so small that it was like cotton and served for tinder."

He collected from the beach a "great quantity" of seaweed and seashells along with some planks from the ships that "had been wrecked on those shoals." Striking sparks with his knife and the pebbles, he ignited the thread and fueled his fire with seaweed and driftwood. Now he could warm himself against the night air and cook his meals — but more important, he could signal to passing vessels. Sometimes the heavy rain would threaten to extinguish the flames, but he would put a cap over them, using larger turtle shells to form a "small hut . . . taking care that his fire should not go out."

Pedro de Serrano's determination and resourcefulness are remarkable, even considering the desperation of his circumstances. In similar situations others would have given up and died. The human will is unfathomable; one man perseveres despite an endless set of obstacles while another collapses after expending only the slightest effort. The chronicler in praising Serrano's inventiveness attributes it to the man's profession: "Seamen are much more ingenious in all times of extremity than men bred on land."

Serrano would need all of his resourcefulness and perseverance. The heat and humidity of the island's climate spoiled his food supplies quickly, so that much of his energy was spent constantly searching for cockles and dragging turtles onto the shore. The winds and storms battered him. The sun burned down fiercely on him. When his shirt fell apart he had "neither clothes to cover him nor shadow for shelter," so he felt he was being broiled by the sun and could find relief only by diving into the ocean.

His hair and beard grew so long that they reached his waist. This way at least some of his skin was covered. The hair on his body grew out as well (the chronicler attributes this to his exposure to "all weathers"), so that he was "covered all over with bristles."

In this misery and care he passed three years, during which time he saw several ships at sea and as often made his smoke; but none turned out of their way to see what it meant, for fear of those shelves and sands which wary pilots avoid with all imaginable circumspection. So that the poor wretch, despairing of all relief, esteemed it a mercy for him to die.

One night near the end of the third year, a vessel was wrecked in the area. The lone survivor clung to a plank until the current carried him to Serrano's shore. In the morning he saw the smoke of the signal fire and made his way toward it, expecting it to have been made by a shipmate, another castaway from the same vessel.

Imagine the surprise of the two men when they suddenly saw each other. Serrano had been over and over his little habitat and absolutely knew himself to be its only human occupant. Yet here was something in the form of a man, having the appearance of a man, which seemed to have come up right out of the ground, to have magically materialized. Looking at Serrano, and having expected to see one of his own fellows, the mariner newly cast away saw instead a "wild and savage creature," naked, covered with fur, an immense mane and beard hanging to his waist — knotted, matted, and encrusted with sand, salt, bits of shell, and turtle meat — skin burned red and peeling in great strips, and those strips enmeshed in the hair on the face and form.

For a moment each man was speechless and still. Then both of them concluded at the same instant what the other one was, what he could only be: the very Devil himself! The newcomer was face to face with Satan "in his own proper shape and figure, being covered over with hair and beard." Serrano, too, was confronting the Father of Lies, who had taken on the aspect of a man in order to "tempt him to despair."

Panic and terror seized them both. They fled screaming in opposite directions.

Serrano cried, "Jesus, Jesus, deliver me from the Devil!"

The other man, hearing the words and believing that Satan was not permitted to speak Christ's name, realized the truth. He turned around and began chasing Serrano, shouting for him to stop: "Brother, Brother, don't fly from me, for I am a Christian, as thou art!"

But Serrano could not be tricked. The Devil was pursuing him and calling to him in his own language! He ran all the faster.

Meeting for the first time, two startled maroons each take the other to be the Devil. Pedro de Serrano is on the left. (Copy print courtesy of Special Collections, Lehigh University Libraries)

So the absurd footrace continued until the pursuer, having searched his mind frantically for convincing evidence of his humanness, began to bellow the Apostles' Creed for his quarry to hear:

> I believe in God the Father Almighty,
> Maker of Heaven and Earth,
> And in Jesus Christ,
> His only Son . . .

Serrano stopped running, and the two men came together. "They embraced each other with sighs and tears, lamenting their sad estate without any hopes of deliverance. Serrano, supposing that his guest wanted refreshments, entertained him with such provisions as his miserable life afforded. And, having a little comforted each other, they began to recount the manner and occasion of their sad disasters."

Forced to exist side by side in such a small place under such difficulties, the two men imposed a strict regimen on themselves, ordering their behavior "for the better government of their way of living." At a specified hour they fished; at another they gathered seaweed and other fuel for the fire. They took turns standing watch so that the horizon might always be scanned for ships, and they relieved each other's watches exactly at the prescribed hours.

For a short time this artificial orderliness enabled them to get along without dispute, but before their first month together was out, they quarreled. The argument began when one accused the other of being less than diligent in doing his chores, and it became so heated that they very nearly came to blows.

Rather than make a peace between themselves, these two maroons, victims of severe weather and an inhospitable environment who were seemingly fated to a lifetime of hardship, allowed their private furies to rage and grow until, incredibly, they decided to separate from one another! They moved to different parts of the island, neither being willing to see or have anything to do with the other.

How long this stubbornness lasted is not known, but eventually the harshness of their existence and the rigorous efforts required just to survive caused them to put aside their differences: "Having experienced the want of that comfort which mutual society procures, their choler was appeased. And so they returned to enjoy converse and the assistance which company and friendship afforded."

Thus the years passed for them, one after the other, with the days so painfully alike. During their four years together they saw and attempted to attract many ships. "Yet none would be so charitable or curious as to be invited by their smoke and flame."

Their despair and desperation increased at these sightings, with the attendant false hopes and terrible letdowns. Finally they reconciled themselves to the likelihood of living out their lives on those barren sands.

They became as similar as their days. The newcomer's clothes fell away, and his hair and beard grew, and his skin burned until he could not be distinguished from Serrano. They must have looked like nothing so much as two brothers out of some predator's litter.

At last one day a vessel came sailing on a course that brought her nearer to the island than the others had come. The captain, having been apprised of the smoke and correctly intuiting its meaning, ordered a boat hoisted out and sent ashore to pick up any shipwrecked survivors.

When Serrano and his companion saw the craft approaching, they raced to the water's edge to the place where she would land. But when the sailors drew close enough to the beach to see what the two men looked like, they were terrified — and began rowing back to their ship!

The two men cried out for the mariners to *come back! come back!* But they would not. The maroons then shouted out the Creed in unison, and when they had finished it, they cried out over and over again the name of Jesus. The words proved talismanic, as they had years before, when Serrano had heard them, and the seamen turned back toward the maroons.

In this fashion were the two men saved and taken aboard the vessel "to the greatest wonder of all present, who with admiration beheld their hairy shapes, not like men but beasts, and with singular pleasure heard them relate the story of their past misfortunes."

Pedro de Serrano, along with his fellow maroon, sailed for Spain, but unfortunately the other man died on the voyage. Serrano lived, however, and made his way from his own country to Germany. He did not cut his hair and beard during all this time, but rather "nourished [them] to serve as an evidence and proof of his past life. Wheresoever he came the people pressed as to a sight, to see him for money. Persons of quality, having the same curiosity, gave him sufficient [money] to defray his charges."

In this way Serrano arrived at the royal court, having enriched himself to a degree by receiving the payments of peasants and noblemen who shared the same human impulse to stare open-mouthed at one displaying himself as a freak might show his affliction at a fair. Taken before His Imperial Majesty, he told his by now well-rehearsed story about those seven long years, with his hirsuteness as evidence of his veracity. His Majesty paid as surely as the other viewers had, though in a greater amount, bestowing "a rent upon him of 4,000 pieces of eight, which make 4,800 ducats in Peru," where he was to receive it.

Serrano sailed back toward the Americas to collect the first of these annual sums, no doubt serenely contemplating his future as an idle, wealthy man with silver chalices instead of turtle shells from which to drink wine, not rainwater. Alas, it was never to be: along the way, near the coast of Panama, Pedro de Serrano died of causes unknown and without, as his chronicler says, "further enjoyment."

If Serrano could take no more pleasure in his life, the same cannot be said of those who came after him. His story has been regularly anthologized and retold since the seventeenth century.

One of the more curious retellings of his experience, or at least one aspect of it — the quarrel with his island companion — is "Etiquette," the witty poem by the librettist and playwright Sir William S. Gilbert. Like any number of nineteenth-century authors, Gilbert developed in his youth what was to be a lifelong fascination with sea lore, especially that involving shipwrecks, castingsaway, and maroonings. His early works contain a number of references to such incidents, and the text of "Etiquette" shows that he was aware of Selkirk's story as well as Serrano's, albeit that he transformed the latter into a Victorian comedy of manners.

The *Ballyshannon* foundered off the coast of Cariboo,
And down in fathoms many went the captain and the crew;
Down went the owners — greedy men whom hope of gain allured:
Oh, dry the starting tear, for they were heavily insured.

Besides the captain and the mate, the owners and the crew,
The passengers were also drowned excepting only two:
Young Peter Gray, who tasted teas for Baker, Croop, and Co.,
And Somers, who from Eastern shores imported indigo.

These passengers, by reason of their clinging to a mast,
Upon a desert island were eventually cast.
They hunted for their meals, as Alexander Selkirk used,
But they couldn't chat together — they had not been introduced.

For Peter Gray, and Somers too, though certainly in trade,
Were properly particular about the friends they made;
And somehow thus they settled it without a word of mouth —
That Gray should take the northern half, while Somers took the south.

On Peter's portion oysters grew — a delicacy rare,
But oysters were a delicacy Peter couldn't bear.
On Somers' side was turtle, on the shingle lying thick,
Which Somers couldn't eat, because it always made him sick.

Gray gnashed his teeth with envy as he saw a mighty store
Of turtle unmolested on his fellow-creature's shore:
The oysters at his feet aside impatiently he shoved,
For turtle and his mother were the only things he loved.

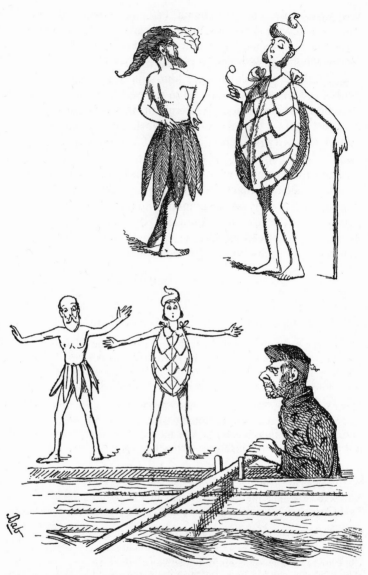

Sir William S. Gilbert's illustrations for his poem "Etiquette." Two marooned English gentlemen refuse to acknowledge each other's existence because they have not been formally introduced; they are dismayed to discover that their rescuer is their old friend Robinson, now a convict. (Copy prints by Larry Rubens, Audio-Visual Services, Kent State University)

And Somers sighed in sorrow as he settled in the south,
For the thought of Peter's oysters brought the water to his mouth.
He longed to lay him down upon the shelly bed, and stuff:
He had often eaten oysters, but had never had enough.

How they wished an introduction to each other they had had
When on board the *Ballyshannon!* And it drove them nearly mad
To think how very friendly with each other they might get,
If it wasn't for the arbitrary rule of etiquette!

One day, when out a-hunting for the *mus ridiculus,*
Gray overheard his fellow-man soliloquising thus:
"I wonder how the playmates of my youth are getting on,
M'Connell, S. B. Walters, Paddy Byles, and Robinson?"

These simple words made Peter as delighted as could be,
Old Chummies at the Charterhouse were Robinson and he!
He walked straight up to Somers, then he turned extremely red,
Hesitated, hummed and hawed a bit, then cleared his throat, and said:

"I beg your pardon — pray forgive me if I seem too bold,
But you have breathed a name I knew familiarly of old.
You spoke aloud of Robinson — I happened to be by —
You know him?" "Yes, extremely well." "Allow me — so do I!"

It was enough: they felt they could more sociably get on,
For (ah, the magic of the fact!) they each knew Robinson!
And Mr Somers' turtle was at Peter's service quite,
And Mr Somers punished Peter's oyster-beds all night.

They soon became like brothers from a community of wrongs:
They wrote each other little odes and sang each other songs;
They told each other anecdotes disparaging their wives;
On several occasions, too, they saved each other's lives.

They felt quite melancholy when they parted for the night,
And got up in the morning soon as ever it was light;
Each other's pleasant company they so relied upon,
And all because it happened that they both knew Robinson!

They lived for many years on that inhospitable shore,
And day by day they learned to love each other more and more.
At last, to their astonishment, on getting up one day,
They saw a vessel anchored in the offing of the bay!

To Peter an idea occurred. "Suppose we cross the main?
So good an opportunity may not occur again."
And Somers thought a minute, then ejaculated, "Done!
I wonder how my business in the City's getting on?"

"But stay," said Mr. Peter: "when in England, as you know,
I earned a living tasting teas for Baker, Croop, and Co.,
I may be superseded — my employers think me dead!"
"Then come with me," said Somers, "and taste indigo instead."

But all their plans were scattered in a moment when they found
The vessel was a convict ship from Portland, outward bound!
When a boat came off to fetch them, though they felt it very kind,
To go on board they firmly but respectfully declined.

As both the happy settlers roared with laughter at the joke,
They recognized an unattractive fellow pulling stroke:
'Twas Robinson — a convict, in an unbecoming frock!
Condemned to seven years for misappropriating stock!!!

They laughed no more, for Somers thought he had been rather rash
In knowing one whose friend had misappropriated cash;
And Peter thought a foolish tack he must have gone upon
In making the acquaintance of a friend of Robinson.

At first they didn't quarrel very openly, I've heard;
They nodded when they met, and now and then exchanged a word:
The word grew rare, and rarer still the nodding of the head,
And when they meet each other now, they cut each other dead.

To allocate the island they agreed by word of mouth,
And Peter takes the north again, and Somers takes the south;
And Peter has the oysters, which he loathes with horror grim,
And Somers has the turtle — turtle disagrees with him.

CHAPTER 2

Among the Cruelest Savages
Peter Carder in the Brazils

The task of the survivor is to keep himself alive until he is rescued. For the maroon this means locating reliable sources of water and food and securing the means to build a fire. The list is deceptively simple, as the story of Serrano shows, and as we shall see again and again.

The castaway at sea has the same needs, but there are no wells upon the ocean and, unless he has a fishing line and bait, few means of procuring food. To reach a shore before he dies from lack of water or food, he must keep an oftentimes leaky and damaged craft afloat while trying to navigate her in the general direction of land. No one lives in a longboat or even a crippled hulk for one year, much less seven. To survive a hundred days in one is an amazing accomplishment.

In the course of a single adventure Peter Carder was cast away once and marooned twice. His experiences were not typical at all, however. His boat was sound and contained seven other mariners who were able to sail her where they wished. The island of his first marooning was utterly devoid of fresh water, it is true, but his second marooning took place on the continent of South America, where the presence of hostile Indians, not the lack of nourishment, would be the greatest threat.

Most survivors have lived because they persevered. Maroons held on until help happened by; the vessels of castaways fortuitously drifted in the right direction. But Carder had more than perseverance; he had pluck and cleverness. Others might get by on determination alone, but he used his wits.

■ ■ ■

They were not too long on the Pacific Ocean in their shallop, those eight mariners, just fourteen days. Long enough to grow thirsty and hungry but not to start dying. Most of those who came to die did so of causes considerably more sudden and violent.

They were men lost at sea from the expedition of Sir Francis Drake on his circumnavigation of the globe. His voyage would earn Drake — a man born in obscurity and poverty — wealth, a knighthood from his grateful queen, the adoration of his countrymen, and the enduring hatred of his Spanish enemies. Their participation in the historic venture would earn all but one of these men nothing more than ignoble death upon the sands of a strange land. Not that Francis Drake is to blame for their fate. The cause of their misfortune was a sudden storm, a routine hazard of the sailor's trade. The expedition's two ships had recently passed through the dangerous Straits of Magellan when they became separated. Drake, in the *Golden Hind,* expected to meet the *Elizabeth* later at the prearranged rendezvous, but her captain, John Winter, paid heed to her unnerved and disheartened crew and turned her toward home. While Drake struggled against storms, the *Elizabeth* was being sailed back to the safety of England. While he took prizes and sacked towns and made new discoveries, Winter was situated comfortably in London, trying to ruin his superior's reputation.

How could Drake know this? To reconnoiter the unfamiliar coast, he put eight men into a five-ton shallop. There was Peter Carder of Cornwall, Richard Burnish and William Pitcher, both of London, Paschie Gidie of Saltash, and a Dutch trumpeter named Artyur, as well as John Cottle, Richard Joyner, and one other servant. The boat held an oar for each man, but she entirely lacked navigational equipment, having neither charts nor compass. Also lacking were provisions — not even "one day's victuals." But why should any such things as these be put into the shallop when the crew would be on the sea no more than a few hours?

The storm came up suddenly and drove them from sight of the *Golden Hind.* After two days they made landfall somewhere on the southwest coast of South America. They fed on mussels, oysters, and crabs, and on roots they dug out of the woods. Then they went back onto the ocean, hoping to find their ship. Their comrades in the *Hind* sought them as well, but to no avail.

Realizing after fourteen days that they were on their own, the men in the boat decided to set a course for England. They went into the Straits, where much larger, more seaworthy vessels with far bigger crews had been wrecked. Twice they put into bays to gather food and fill their *barricoes* with fresh water, and "in one of these places," Carder writes, "we found savages, but they fled from us."

They landed on Penguin Island, near the mouth of the eastern side of the passage, where they slaughtered large numbers of the marine bird for which the island was named, drying and salting the meat as provision for the ensuing portion of the voyage.

Their next destination was known to them as Point St. Indian. It was here that earlier in the circumnavigation Francis Drake had dealt with a suspected mutineer, Captain Thomas Doughty, by trying him and securing a conviction from a jury of forty members of the expedition. Captain Drake then dined with the condemned man, toasting him and treating him with all cordiality, even kneeling beside him to take communion with him, before walking him to the killing ground, having his head cut off, and then seizing it to hold it aloft, ritualistically crying out, "Lo, there is the end of traitors!"

Perhaps the memory of the deed made some of the eight castaways uneasy. They stayed only a day or two, fishing for mackerel and bream.

After sailing north for two more weeks, they arrived at another small island not far from the continent. This place was populated with seals, which they slaughtered in abundance. They roasted the flesh and found that the younger seals tasted best.

Beyond the wide Río de la Plata, they discovered a much narrower river into which they sailed and then they beached their craft.

Since leaving the Straits, where they knew the natives carefully avoided white men, they had apparently gone ashore on the mainland only the one time, at Point St. Indian. If this is fact, it seems certain that the men were trying to avoid the continent's indigenous Indian populations by moving from island to island. The reason for such caution is obvious, but why now would they chance coming onto land? Had their food supplies been utterly exhausted, and were they unable to secure more? Or had the lack of trouble so far on this long, extraordinary journey made them too bold and confident?

Two men were left to guard the boat while six others went into the woods, seeking food.

What they found was a war party of some seventy Tapine braves, howling and shooting arrows and rushing at them. In the ensuing fight and retreat all the whites were seriously wounded, and four of them were captured. The other two were able to reach the shallop, and with the help of the men who had been on guard duty, they held off their pursuers long enough to push her frantically into the water and get her away from the shore. While the boat was being launched, both guards were wounded as well.

Three leagues from the mainland, they found an island about three miles in circumference. Here they treated each other's wounds and "cured ourselves as well as we might." Without medicine or the ministrations of skilled surgeons, however, two of the four succumbed.

Now only Peter Carder and William Pitcher were left, and the desperation of their circumstances was compounded by their having been stranded: a storm had dashed the boat upon the rocks, utterly destroying her.

In some respects the isle was habitable enough. "Creeping" upon the beach were white crabs, which could be easily caught and eaten, along with eels dug out of the sand. There was also a fruit that grew in tall trees with small, aspenlike leaves; Carder thought it resembled an orange.

What the place did not contain was fresh water, not even rain caught in the crevices of rocks. In fact, during all the time they stayed there, it never rained at all. It mattered little: they lacked the means to collect or store any significant quantity of it, having neither barrels nor whole jars.

Eventually they were forced to drink their own urine, catching it in pieces of jars that they had salvaged from the wreckage of the shallop and leaving it to cool overnight.

Carder and Pitcher passed two months in this fashion until their urine, "being drunk often and often voided," had become very red. They knew they were dying and sought a way to get back to the continent, choosing to risk their fate at the hands of such as the Tapines, or even drowning in the sea, rather than die passively in that arid place.

When a log floated in on the surf (all the way from the Plate River, they thought), they used it for the center beam of a raft, binding to it other pieces of wood with withes (supple twigs). Having gathered crabs, eels, and fruit to use as provisions and having prayed fervently, they pushed off with the setting in of the tide.

Using two poles for oars, they took two nights and three days to travel to the coast. Their joy was immense when immediately after landing they found a stream of "very sweet and pleasant water." It was the first they had had to drink for eight weeks or more, the last having been drunk while their comrades were still alive.

William Pitcher lay down at the stream's edge and gorged himself upon it. Carder tried to stop him, of course; he knew better. But Pitcher would not be dissuaded. "Being pinched with extreme thirst," he just kept drinking and drinking until, said Carder, "my only comfort and companion, to my unspeakable grief and discomfort, died." Without a shovel to dig a proper grave in the woods, Carder was forced to bury him as well as he could in the sand.

He was a solitary alien in this strange country with its hostile natives and its other innumerable, unknown dangers.

The *I Ching,* the ancient book of Chinese wisdom, teaches that in moments of danger all that matters is going forward. For Peter Carder forward was north toward Brazil. The day after he buried Pitcher, he armed himself with a sword and target and began marching along the beach. Before that day was over he encountered a party of Indians, thirty armed men and women. They were Tuppan Basse, members of a warrior tribe of moon worshipers who practiced ritualistic cannibalism upon their prisoners.

So here was Peter Carder, who had been through so much and was now alone in the Unknown World, outnumbered thirty to one by savages who were dancing before him to the rhythms of music they made with tabrets and large rattles.

The plucky Carder resumed his march, heading right for them. They danced away. He strode forward. They fell back. As this odd cotillion went on, it became clear that they were endeavoring to keep a constant distance between him and themselves — just over the length of a musket shot, as he judged it, which suggests they had met up with Europeans before. After a while the natives halted long enough to hang a piece of white netting on a stick, and then, shaking their rattles and resuming their dance, they re-established their distance. Carder approached the material and took it down. He had the presence of mind to decide as he examined it that the netting was made of a "cotton-wool," and he hung it up again.

He would not know until later that the hanging up of the net was a Tuppan Basse gesture of friendship. So now the tribesmen and women stopped and waited for him to come up to them, and then they greeted him. After this, Carder reports that

> they friendly led me along some half a mile, all the way dancing, as
> well men as women . . . until we came to another riverside, where
> they hanged up their beds, tying them fast to a couple of trees, being

a kind of white cotton netting, which hanged two feet from the ground, and kindled fire of two sticks, which they made on both sides of their beds for warmth and for driving away of wild beasts, and having fed me with such as they had, we took our rest for that night.

In the morning the Indians "trussed up" their hammocks, and "crying *tiasso, tiasso,* which is to say, *away, away,*" they set off on what proved to be a twenty-mile hike, which brought them to their town before nightfall.

The settlement was built on the design of a square and contained four buildings to house a population of four thousand people. Each of these structures was quite long ("two bowshot in length") and was covered with palm leaves. The buildings did not have windows, but each had thirty to forty doors for the use of the families who dwelled therein.

The leader of this tribe was the forty-year-old "chief lord" known as Caiou, whom Carder referred to as "the governor." Caiou proved to be a hospitable fellow: the day after Carder's arrival, he sent out many food gatherers to collect examples of the edibles of the region. These he offered to the Englishman for him to sample "to see which of them I liked best, among which there was great store of fish, many sorts of fowls, many sorts of roots and divers land beasts, as armadillos, which afterward I found to be very good meat."

Of this plenitude, Carder nibbled at only one bird and a few fish. Astutely he gave the rest of the feast to the children of the village. The gesture won him wide popularity.

Carder dedicated himself to learning the language and customs of his hosts. Most men, he discovered, were permitted only one wife, although each of the most valiant warriors was allowed two — one to accompany him on campaigns to see to his needs while the other stayed in the town to care for his children. The notable exception to this pattern was Caiou himself, whose princely privileges included having *nine* wives. The dreadful burdens of leadership must always have some, albeit inadequate, compensation.

The war parties often consisted of four hundred or more warriors, and they were armed with only bows and arrows. Victory initiated an elaborate ceremony requiring the bringing back of at least one captive, and once he was at the settlement, the celebration began. Women gathered a root Carder knew as the "I.P.," which they "seethed" (boiled) before chewing it and spitting it into a long trough. Water was added, and the mixture was allowed to set for two or three days, gathering yeast on it and fermenting like "our ale." The resulting spirits were then collected in wide-mouthed earthenware jars.

The prisoner was brought forth and tied to a post. The dancing and drinking commenced. Both men and women participated, moving around the captive and imbibing until they were all "drunk as apes." Finally one of the stronger men of the tribe approached him, and with a massive redwood club cracked his skull, taking care to split it at one blow. The victim's corpse was then roasted and eaten.

Carder found the Tuppan Basse to be irreligious except for a marked "reverence and worship" of the moon, especially the new moon, the appearance of which occasioned much dancing, leaping, and hand clapping. He noted that the "merchantable commodities" of their land were Brazil wood, tobacco, red pepper, and the much-utilized cotton wool. They also had "great stores of apes, monkeys, armadillos, hogs without tails as big as ours; their birds are parrots, parraketos, black fowls as big as doves, and ostriches as high as a man."

At the end of his first half year among the Indians, Peter Carder was given the opportunity to participate in their war-making. The king invited him to go along on a raid against the tribe's enemies, the Tapwees. He was willing, but before the party started out, he prevailed upon Caiou to let him show them how to make shields like Europeans used, so that they might have protection from their adversaries' arrows. (Apparently, this defensive device was unknown in the region.) A hundred two-foot-long targets were constructed of tree bark, along with twice that number of clubs.

This new materiel having been issued, Carder marched with Caiou and seven hundred of his followers. The journey took three days. Before approaching the Tapwee town, the king's troops, following another suggestion of the assertive Englishman, each painted one leg below the knee with red balsam as a kind of uniform, enabling them to distinguish themselves from the foe during the sudden desperate moments of battle.

At about four A.M. the attack was launched against the town, which was built along the same fortresslike design as the Tuppan Basse's own. The attackers were met with showers of arrows, which their new targets readily withstood. Breaching the defenses and rushing the defenders, the red-legged warriors quickly clubbed

to death two hundred of their enemies and captured twenty more
hapless souls alive. The rest of the villagers fled into the woods.

It is a small, curious moment in the history of an obscure people.
The intrusion of European civilization with its superior technologi-
cal (if not cultural or spiritual) development, represented in the
person of Peter Carder, had just changed the ancient equation of
war between two fierce tribes. Heretofore, while the number of
combatants might be unequal, the contest was essentially evenly
matched in terms of weapons (solely offensive ones) and the tactics
they dictated. The attackers, charging a fortified settlement whose
defenders would have been shooting arrows from the doorways and
perhaps the roofs, would have expected to take heavy casualties.
But Carder's shields enabled them to reach the walls while sustain-
ing few if any losses, and the use of clubs in tandem with the targets
meant they could strike against their foes with relative impunity.
The result was a rout.

For a day the victors rested in the village, foraging for plunder
and broiling the carcasses of the slain over coals. Flesh was more
plentiful than spoils, for the Tapwees did not value or collect gold
or silver. Only tobacco, cotton bedding, and liquor were to be had,
and these commodities could be found in the Tuppan Basse settlement. Why, then, did Caiou's warriors travel this distance and risk
their lives? Undoubtedly they were motivated by tradition, long-
standing enmity, and the prospect of a ghastly feast.

The next day the march home began. The conquerors brought
with them the twenty prisoners who, after arrival in Tuppan Basse
land, met the usual fate.

Despite his intense interest in Tuppan Basse life and his precision
in recording it, Peter Carder has left a few intriguing gaps in his
account. Some of these seem unintentional, but others may be attributable to a certain disingenuousness. So careful to describe the
ritual of the cannibalistic celebrations, he omits the matter of
whether he joined in or declined to eat, and, if he did refuse, how
he managed to do so without giving offense and becoming an inad-
vertent and even more unwilling participant in the next grisly meal.
As accepted as he was in the tribe — evidenced by his participation
in the Tapwee raid — he was presumably eligible to take a wife,
possibly two, but of his relations with Indian women he is utterly
silent.

A less curious omission is his failure to calculate just how long he remained with the Tuppan Basse, although it seems likely to have been at least several years. Certainly he does not depict himself as having been discontented to stay with these hospitable people, at least until an incident occurred that caused him profound uneasiness and motivated him to attempt to return to England.

A party of Portuguese had come into the jungle, bringing with them some Brazilians and blacks. They may have been slavers — Carder says they wanted to see "whether they could surprise any of our savages" — but they were definitely after intelligence. A rumor had reached them that some of Drake's company had been "cast ashore amongst the savage people." Thus these Portuguese were seeking crewmen of the hated *El Draque*. A man like Carder, trusted by and able to communicate with an aboriginal people, would be a particular threat to the Portuguese. Such rapport readily converted into alliances between the indigenous inhabitants and Protestant interlopers, who could turn the natives into trading partners or even into guides and scouts to lead them in raids against Catholic settlements.

Carder had already shown an ability to ingratiate himself with the tribe, and he had been careful to note the resources of the territory. His return to Europe with this type of information could cause a great deal of mischief.

So the Portuguese were hunting for any of Drake's castaways, and as it happened, they nearly discovered the only one. They had come within ten leagues of the town when they ran into Tuppan Basse warriors, and in the clash that followed, two Portuguese and an unspecified number of blacks were taken alive. These unfortunate captives confessed to "the intent of their coming thither" before the ritual club fell.

Though they were disposed of, some of their comrades got away. They might return with other chastened and more careful parties.

Thinking over the unhappy prospect of falling into their hands, Carder "became a suitor to the king to give me leave to depart his country and to go to some river of Brazil not planted by the Portuguese, to see if I could spy out any English or French ship to pass me into my country." Caiou was reluctant to see him go but in the end was persuaded.

He assigned four warriors to act as the white man's guides and to procure birds, fish, and roots for him while on the trail. For ten weeks Carder and the tribesmen marched toward the line. Five

miles south of the town of Bahia de Todos os Santos, they encountered a Portuguese man named Michael Jonas, to whom Carder
unaccountably decided to give himself up, confessing in Portuguese
that he was a Briton and asking whether any of his fellow countrymen lived nearby.

Apparently there were none, because Jonas led him to the house
of one Antonio de Pava, an Anglophile. Taking pity on the stranger,
Antonio, who spoke English, counseled him to pretend ignorance
of the Portuguese language. In this way, when he dealt with the
authorities, Carder could eavesdrop on their deliberations and think
carefully about his responses to their inquiries while de Pava made
a show of translating them. De Pava would also be able to advise
Carder in English on what replies he thought he should make, while
the unsuspecting officials stood waiting.

So they went before the governor, who was named Diego Vas.
Carder learned through his sham interpreter that because "I was
found in the inland of their country westward, being a stranger,
contrary to their laws, [Vas] could do no less than to commit me to
prison and send me into Portugal to be committed to the galleys for
[a] term of life."

To live out the remainder of his days as a galley slave!

Peter Carder and Antonio de Pava conferred. Then the Briton
argued that he had not willingly intruded into Governor Vas's do-
minions but had been forced there by circumstance. He also pointed
out that he had voluntarily surrendered himself into their hands,
"laying down my weapons at one of their national's feet."

It was a telling argument that had the virtue of being true, but it
had no immediate effect: the governor sent Carder off to jail. Antonio and some of his friends saw to it that he was comfortably situated, and then they set to work behind the scenes to gain his freedom.

It was two weeks before their efforts caused him to be brought
before Vas and his advisers again. A fortnight in the dungeon had
given Carder a chance to reshape his argument along more appealing, if somewhat disingenuous, lines: he might have remained in the
jungle or tried to circumvent the settlement, he suggested. "Yet of
my own free will I made a long journey with great hazard of my life
through countries of savages, being man-eaters, which favored me
to seek the Portuguese Christians out and peaceably to put myself
into [your] hands."

The governor consulted with his counselors and reversed his

judgment; he was willing to refer the matter to the king of Portugal for a decision, but in the meantime there was no need for the Englishman to languish in the jail. He was committed to the house of none other than Antonio de Pava until they could learn from Portugal what "the King's pleasure" was regarding him.

So Peter Carder was able to enjoy the hospitality of this good man for nearly a year, at which time the decision of the distant monarch was made known. The outcome was never really in doubt, for Catholic King Philip of Spain, an absolute foe of Britain's Protestant Queen Elizabeth, had only recently made himself the ruler of Portugal as well. The Englishman was to be sent to his court upon receipt of an order authorizing his transportation.

The order would be long in coming. In the meantime the prisoner was inexplicably allowed to remain free. For the next year and a half he worked in the fields of his friend, de Pava, acting as an overseer for "Negroes and savages" as they planted ginger and dressed sugar cane.

But Peter Carder was not a farmer. He was a sailor who had been "brought up to the sea," and Antonio could use him on his bark, which carried trade goods from port to port and transported sugar to the docks, where it was loaded on ocean-going vessels. So Carder sailed up and down the coast from Bahia to Ilhéus, touching at Porto Seguro, Espírito Santo, Saint Vincent, and "River Jenero," exchanging sugar and cotton wool for linen, wine, and oil.

When he returned from one excursion, de Pava was waiting with bad news. Word had reached him that in a short time a ship would come to carry Carder back to Portugal as a prisoner. De Pava was helpless to prevent it. He told Peter that he must "look to" himself, but he promised to aid in the escape.

The deception used to mask the Englishman's flight was that he was going to sea to fish. He took along four blacks without telling them his true purpose, and he sailed all the way to Pernambuco. Here the slaves were questioned by the authorities about why the bark had docked in the port, and they were able to say only what Carder had told them, that the detour had been caused by bad weather. Since Antonio de Pava was their master, they were well treated, and when the next fair wind arose, they were allowed to sail home.

The white man was not with them, of course. He had disappeared.

Within a few months there arrived in Pernambuco a ship with a twenty-one man crew, the majority of whom were Portuguese but eight of whom were British. For three months the vessel remained until at last she was laden with goods, including some belonging to the "worshipful merchants of the city of London." When the ship finally cleared the harbor, she carried one more man than had been aboard when she arrived. He was an Englishman who had long been away from home.

He was not in Cornwall yet, however.

The ship, in convoy with four other Portuguese vessels, had passed the Isles of the Azores and was within sight of the Isle of Pike, when she was hailed by a squadron of British warships. The peace between Queen Elizabeth and King Philip having been broken a year before, the English meant to take the convoy's vessels as prizes of war. The Portuguese had a choice: they could make a fight of it or they could surrender. These were merchants; they chose the latter course "without any resistance."

Peter Carder was in the hands of his countrymen.

But still he was not home.

Approaching Ireland they encountered "contrary weather," which forced them to seek shelter in the port of Baltimore. When the storm finally subsided, they dashed the last little distance to Britain and so "arrived in the narrow seas in the haven of Chichester" at the end of November 1586.

A haven, indeed: Carder made his calculations and decided that it had been a full "nine years and fourteen days after my departure out of England with Sir Francis Drake in his voyage round the world."

Drake had scattered other men in his wake. (One of these had been sent ashore near the start of the expedition to bargain with suspicious Moors, only to be detained by them just long enough for Drake to feel forced to go on without him. The poor fellow missed the entire adventure.) Of those who made it home, Peter Carder was the last to come in.

The Lord High Admiral, the Right Honorable Lord Charles Howard, came to hear of Carder's "strange adventures and long living among cruel savages," and he let Her Majesty know of them. Thereupon Elizabeth had the Lord Admiral bring mariner Peter Carder into her presence at Whitehall, "where it pleased her to talk with me a long hour's space of my travails and wonderful escape

. . . and afterward bestowed twenty-two angels [gold coins] on me, willing my Lord to have consideration of me. With many gracious words I was dismissed, humbly thanking the Almighty for my miraculous preservation and safe return into my native country.''

Francis Drake came home from the voyage a wealthy man. He had the pleasure of kneeling before his monarch and being knighted with a gilded sword. His joy could only have been increased by the fact that the Spanish king had been demanding that he be beheaded as a pirate.

Drake went on to have an illustrious career harassing his Catholic enemies in their colonies and on the high seas, further enriching himself with their gold and ships. Among his achievements, he is given much of the credit for the defeat of the Spanish Armada in 1588. So implacable a foe of Philip II was he that for many generations after his death, Spanish women still threatened their naughty children with a visit from *El Draque*.

Many privateers and explorers fell afoul of their governments: Columbus was taken home in chains from his third expedition to the New World; Captain Kidd was hanged; and Sir Walter Raleigh, once a favorite of his queen, spent thirteen years in the Tower of London and was beheaded. But Drake, though he at least once mightily annoyed his monarch, never suffered such a fate. Perhaps he was just too fierce a fighter in a Protestant nation so often at war with Catholic adversaries. The crowds never stopped cheering him. In between expeditions and battles he served in the House of Commons and busied himself establishing a water supply system for Plymouth that lasted three hundred years. He became a mill owner and country squire, having married ''a good-looking young woman of gentle birth and ample property.''

But Francis Drake, who was one of twelve children in a family so poor they were forced to take up residence in an abandoned hulk, did not die in a country manor attended by a devoted, attractive wife. There was one last voyage against the Spanish in Honduras and Panama. Near an island off the Panamanian coast, fever struck the ships' companies. Drake, who had been through epidemics before without becoming seriously ill, this time contracted dysentery. He was at first optimistic about recovering. ''It matters not, man,'' he told an aide, referring to the disease. ''God hath things in store for us and I know many means to do Her Majesty good service and

make us rich." When his true fate became clear to him, he made
out his will, writing that he was "now in service for the West Indies,
being perfect of mind and memory thanks be therefor unto God,
although sick in body."

As his condition worsened, he suffered periods of delirium. Did
he in this state of hallucination see himself capturing treasure vessels or sacking Philip's cities? Or did he kneel once more on the
deck of the *Golden Hind* and feel the weight of the sword on his
shoulders while the solemn words of knighthood were intoned?

In the final hours of his life he struggled to his feet and demanded
that his armor be put on so that he could meet death as a soldier,
but his compatriots whispered soothing words and eased him back
onto his pallet, where he soon died. The date was January 28, 1596.

On an earlier voyage, yellow fever had at one point raged among
the crews. One of the victims was Drake's beloved brother, Joseph,
who expired in his arms. Nevertheless, Drake ordered the ship's
surgeon to dissect the corpse in order to learn more about the disease, in the hope of providing better treatment for its other victims.
The gravity of the deed is suggested by the intonation of Drake's
nephew: "This was the first and last experiment that our captain
made of anatomy on this voyage." George Malcolm Thomson, a
recent biographer, adds that the act "spoke of a spirit of vehement,
not to say ruthless, enquiry in the man."

On that sad day in 1596, there was no one left alive with such a
hunger for knowledge or so absolute a concern for the welfare of
his men. Drake's body, which had so often been pierced by arrows
and swords and bore so many old scars in consequence, was not cut
by the surgeon's knife.

Instead, the new leader of the expedition directed the vessels to
a point three miles from the Panamanian shore, where Drake's lead
coffin was released into the ocean while "trumpets in doleful manner [echoed] out this lament for so great a loss, and all the cannons
in the fleet were discharged according to the custom of all sea funeral obsequies."

Given the extraordinary accomplishments and richness of his commander's later life, one wonders what happened to Peter Carder.
Most likely he quickly went back to the sailor's trade and spent Her
Majesty's twenty-two angels in taverns, regaling besotted listeners
with tales of Governor Caiou and his nine wives. But from his own

account he seems a sensible fellow, and considering all that he had been through, it is just possible to conceive of his working a little patch of ground and dying peacefully on a cot in a hut in Cornwall. The latter is a conjecture for those who do not care to see him in their mind's eye wheezing out his last few breaths in the dank air below decks or washed overboard into the freezing sea.

A variety of speculations are possible according to the sentimentalism peculiar to the imagination of the speculator. All are equally permitted since none can be contradicted by banal reality, for when Peter Carder left the presence of the queen, he disappeared from history.

CHAPTER 3

To Live Upon This Barren Shore
The "Poor Englishman"
off the Coast of Scotland

We now come to the most ele-
mental story to be found in these pages. The man we know only as
the "Poor Englishman" had nothing to ameliorate his predicament,
no sea chest like Alexander Selkirk had and certainly no friendly
tribe of cannibals such as Peter Carder encountered. His only shelter was a slab of stone and a few pieces of wood. The birds he
caught in his hands were his only food. The clothes fell off his back,
leaving him naked against the elements. To make matters worse,
his home was not an isle in the temperate Pacific; it was hardly more
than a boulder in the north Atlantic, butting out of the bitter ocean
above the fifty-eighth parallel.

Yet whatever he lacked, he had the one thing that a survivor
needs more than a fire, a weapon, or a stream of fresh water. He
had the will to live.

Not all bleak and empty islands were to be found in the uncharted
waters of the Unknown World. In 1615, two men were cast away
on a desolate isle quite near the coast of Scotland. They had been
among the occupants of a passenger boat sailing from England to
Dublin, Ireland, when the craft was captured by French pirates. A
storm struck suddenly, and to keep their own vessel afloat, the
corsairs were forced to abandon the small prize and the three passengers they had left in her. The wind and waves buffeted the boat
and drove her into the open sea.

Their only provision was some sugar, their chronicler tells us.

Upon this they lived, and drank their urine till their bodies were so dried up that they could make no more.

In this doleful condition one of the company, being quite spent with fatigue and misery, died and was heaved overboard by the remaining two. After a while the second grew so feeble that he laid himself along in the boat, ready to yield up the ghost.

Before he could die, however, his fellow castaway "providentially descried" a small isle on the horizon. Although it was a very great distance away, he used its promise to instill hope in the other man, to keep him alive until at last they reached it. Their craft was broken in two against a rock, but the men managed to crawl up on the shore unharmed.

What they found there — or, more exactly, what they did *not* find there — surely must have dampened their spirits and tempered their rejoicing. For the island had neither springs nor streams and was utterly devoid of vegetation: no grass, plants, or trees

or anything else by which a man could procure subsistence, nor any shelter from the weather except about the middle of the island, where there were two long stones pitched in the ground and a third laid upon them, like a table, which they judged to have been so placed by some fishermen to dry their fish upon; and under these they slept at night.

They now judged themselves to be in a more wretched condition than if, being swallowed up by the sea, they had been delivered from the extremities they were in for want of meat and drink.

They did have a knife, and they managed to catch some seals and gulls. Lacking the means to make a fire, they dried the flesh in the sun. They also found birds' eggs in the rock crannies. Their only sources of water were pools that formed in crevices when it rained; but these were sometimes contaminated by salt water when stormy weather caused the size and fury of the waves to increase dramatically and wash over much of the dismal little isle.

In this precarious fashion they lived for six weeks, somewhat protected against the "rain and injuries of the wind and weather" by a lean-to they clumsily erected without tools, using boards from the boat, at the same time "comforting one another and finding some ease in their common calamity." But one morning the Poor Englishman, who had been the stronger of the two and had encouraged the other to go on living, awoke to find himself alone. Not only

The Poor Englishman and his fellow maroon find shelter beneath a stone table; (OPPOSITE) the Poor Englishman begs to be rescued. (Copy prints courtesy of Special Collections, Lehigh University Libraries)

was his fellow maroon not in the shelter, he had disappeared from the island entirely.

The Briton searched and called, but the man was gone.

He would never know what happened to his companion — whether he committed suicide by jumping into the ocean or accidentally fell into it when wandering about in the darkness. Eventually the Poor Englishman concluded that the man must have slipped while looking for eggs along the cliff above the sea. After all, he reasoned, he had discerned no distraction in him, neither could he imagine that he "should, on a sudden, fall into that terrible despair against which he had so fortified himself by frequent and fervent prayer."

In his new solitude the Briton experienced a severe depression. He often resolved to drown himself "and so put a final period to that affliction of which he had endured but one half, while he had a friend to divide it with him." Yet he always managed to dissuade

himself from it, believing that committing suicide would cause him to be damned eternally.

Soon he was given a further affliction: his knife, which he had used for cutting up gulls and seals, also disappeared. Since it had been wrapped in a bloody piece of cloth, he deduced that a bird of prey had snatched it up and carried it off.

If he was to survive he must eat, and to do so he needed to be able to kill and prepare the gulls. He painfully worked a nail out of one of the boards of his lean-to and then sharpened it on rocks in order to use it as a substitute for the lost blade.

In the harsh, wet weather his clothes rotted and fell apart, and the sun burned his body black. When winter came, snowstorms frequently struck the island, leaving it so blanketed in snow that he could not go out of his makeshift hut. Once more he was faced with the prospect of starvation, and once more he responded resourcefully: he took a long sliver of wood, rubbed the end of it with fat from a seal, and then, using it as bait, stuck it through a crack in the shelter's wall. When a bird approached the stick he slipped his hand under the wall and up through the snow to seize it.

For nearly a year he existed alone and gradually became resigned to living the rest of his life in this fashion, when, according to the chronicle, "the gracious Providence of God sent a ship thither, which delivered him out of as great a misery as perhaps any man was ever in."

The master of the vessel was a Flemish trader named Picman or Pickman. Apparently he was an accomplished salvager of wrecks since in Britain and Holland he was celebrated for his "art and dexterity in getting out of the sea the great guns of the Spanish Armada, which was driven upon the coasts of Scotland and Ireland."

In 1616 he was sailing from Drontheim, Norway, with a cargo of lumber, when he was "overtaken by a calm." Without wind his ship drifted on the current that carried her to the island. Fearing his vessel would be wrecked upon the rocks, Pickman put some of his men into a shallop and had them tow her out of danger. Afterward they went ashore to look for birds' eggs. It was while they were among the boulders that they glimpsed at a distance the figure of a man. They assumed that he was one of a party of ambushers or that he had escaped from pirates who might still be lurking in the area, and so they fled from him back to their shallop and raced to the ship.

By this time the current was again moving her too close to the shore, and it was necessary to tow her off once more. As they completed that chore they saw the man, who had come to the edge of a cliff, making

> signs with his hands lifted up, entreating them to come nearer; sometimes falling on his knees and joining his hands together, begging and crying to them for relief.
>
> At first they made difficulty about going to him; but at length, being overcome by his lamentable signs, they went nearer the island, where they saw something that was more like a ghost than a living person: a body, stark naked, black and hairy, a meagre and deformed countenance with hollow and distorted eyes, which raised such compassion in them that they endeavored to take him into the boat. But the rock was so steep thereabout that it was impossible for them to land. Whereupon they went about the island and came at last to a flat shore, where they took him on board at the same rock where he had been cast ashore. They saw neither grass nor trees on the island, nor any shelter except the hut which the poor man and companion had built.

A curious, almost magical happening occurred just as the Briton was saved. The sun had already set when they brought him back to the ship, and as soon as he got on her deck the wind, which had been so long and fortuitously still, rose up strongly and carried her from the isle. The coincidence was so remarkable that the crew immediately wondered, considering his wild appearance, if he were a man at all and not some supernatural being, and they hurriedly questioned him about who he was and how he came to be in that place.

The story he told reassured them and no doubt amazed them as well.

The chronicle of the adventures of this nameless man ends in this way:

> The master of the ship, commiserating his deplorable condition, treated him so well that within a few days he was quite another creature. He afterwards set him ashore at Londonderry and sometime after saw him again at Dublin; where such as had heard of his singular affliction gave him money to enable him to return to England, his native country.

The story of the Poor Englishman was first told in *The Voyages and Travels of J. Albert de Mandelslo,* published in 1662. It contains two other anecdotes about maroonings. The first concerns a French pirate who arrived with six of his comrades at Maurice Island. Their vessel had been wrecked in the East Indies, and they were forced to make a precarious voyage in a small canoe to reach the island. Two of the pirates died there, and four of the others elected to sail on, but the Frenchman declined to go further. He lived in solitude for twenty months, subsisting solely on raw tortoise. When found by Dutchmen in September of 1601, he was in good health physically, although he was stark naked and deranged: "burning fever which heightened into a degree of madness" had caused him to rip off all his clothing.

The other story is that of a Dutch mariner who was marooned on St. Helena (where Napoleon would later be exiled) as a punishment for some malefaction. Terrified and "representing to himself the horrour of that solitude much beyond what it really was, [he] fell into a despair that made him attempt the strangest action that was ever heard of." He frantically disinterred the corpse of a comrade so that he could use the coffin as a canoe in which to paddle after

A man marooned as punishment used a coffin as a canoe to pursue his fellows.
(Copy print courtesy of Special Collections, Lehigh University Libraries)

his fellows. Their ship had been becalmed a league and a half from
the island, and "seeing so strange a kind of boat floating on the
water, [they] imagined they saw a spectre." When they finally recognized him, they "were not a little startled at the resolution of the
man, who durst hazard himself upon that element in three boards
slightly nailed together, which a small wave might have overturned,
though he had no confidence [he would] be received by those who
had so lately sentenc'd him to death." Some of the sailors wanted
to leave him in the sea, but others so pitied him that they took him
back on board.

   Voyages and Travels was widely read in the decades after its
publication, and the particular material in it that seems to have most
interested contemporary readers was that concerning the Poor Englishman. The story was retold a number of times by other writers,
and it was always used to illustrate God's love for mankind.

   There is something a little disquieting about this theological viewpoint, since, after all, the other two men in the boat with the Briton died. The discomfort grows as one examines the use made of that tale and similar if more horrendous ones by writers of the sevententh century. Increase Mather, in *An Essay for the Recording of Illustrious Providences* (1684), describes one tragedy after another, a whole litany of grief: an entire ship's company lost in a storm except for a single man; a castaway father who watches helplessly as his children grow sick and die; whole families wiped out save for one or two members who live to search the shore for the bodies of their loved ones. Yet Mather presents these sorrows as proof of the Almighty's *loving care* for his believers.

One wants to ask, What about those who died? What about the children? How can a story in which they drown in dark waters be touted as an instance of the benevolence of God?

Mather was far from alone in looking on large or small calamities as illustrations of the love of God. At least two other religious tomes that predate his own recount the Poor Englishman's ordeal. The titles of still other books relating numbers of similarly harrowing adventures, often with long casualty lists, include William Johnson's *Sermon and Narrative of the Dangers and Deliverances at Sea* (1664), James Janeway's *Legacy to His Friends, containing twenty-seven famous instances of God's Providence in and about Sea-Dangers and Deliverances* (1675), and Jonathan Dickinson's *God's Protecting Providence Man's Surest Help and Defence in the Times of greatest difficulty and most imminent Danger* (1699). Even as late as 1800, Isaac James published a volume from which several of the tales told in these pages have been taken; his title: *Providence Displayed*.

When issues concerning divine justice and mercy are raised, one thinks of the story of the "blameless and upright man" set forth in the Book of Job. In the thirty-eighth chapter, God's voice comes out of the whirlwind to silence the painful questions and plaintive complaints of Job and to drown out the babble of his comforters.

> "Where were you when I laid the foundation of the earth?
>   Tell me, if you have any understanding.
> Who determined its measurements — surely you know!
>   Or who stretched the line upon it?
> On what were its bases sunk,
>   or who laid its cornerstone,

> when the morning stars sang together,
>   and all the sons of God shouted for joy?

> "Or who shut in the sea with doors,
>   when it burst forth from the womb;
> when I made the clouds its garment,
>   and thick darkness its swaddling band,
> and prescribed bounds for it,
>   and set bars and doors,
> and said, 'Thus far shall you come, and no farther,
>   and here shall your proud waves be stayed'?

> "Have you commanded the morning since your days began,
>   and caused the dawn to know its place,
> that it might take hold of the skirts of the earth,
>   and the wicked be shaken out of it?"

In *J.B.*, Archibald MacLeish's modern rendition of the story, J.B.'s wife, Sarah, tells him, "Cry for justice and the stars/ will stare until your eyes sting." MacLeish's protagonist finds solace not in the awesome majesty of the Lord of Creation, but in the simplicity of human love — as God and the Devil exit the stage. At the end of the drama, when J.B. complains of the darkness all around him, Sarah articulates the playwright's theme:

> Then blow on the coal of the heart, my darling.
> Blow on the coal of the heart.
> The candles in the churches are out.
> The lights have gone out in the sky.
> Blow on the coal of the heart
> And we'll see by and by . . . we'll see where we are.
> The wit won't burn and the wet soul smoulders.
> Blow on the coal of the heart and we'll know . . .
> We'll know . . .

In the Book of Job, however, the blameless and upright man willingly disregards the death of his children, repents of his demands for an explanation for his suffering, and concludes with a blind submission to divine will which reflects the attitude of Mather and those who wrote about the Poor Englishman as surely as *J.B.* reflects the much-scorned humanism of some of us. Job acknowledges to his Creator that

> "I know that thou canst do all things,
>   and no purpose of thine can be thwarted.

. . . .
Therefore I have uttered what I did not understand,
    things too wonderful for me, which I did not know.

. . . .
"I had heard of thee by the hearing of the ear,
    but now my eye sees thee;
therefore I despise myself, and repent in dust and ashes."

The Island
Juan Fernandes

good Fishing

good Fishing

A Draught of part of the Island of Juan Fernandes,

Dute 6.   Baye   Depth6

A map of Más á Tierra as drawn by Edward Cooke, who visited there
with Woodes Rogers (Permission of the Folger Shakespeare Library)

CHAPTER 4

A Singular Naval Man

William Dampier: Adventurer, Author, Survivor

Heretofore the people we have seen marooned have fallen into that circumstance by accident. Oh, their predicaments were indisputably by-products of their seafaring way of life or their decision to travel on the ocean, and undoubtedly they knew — or should have known — the risk of the wreck and the island, but it was just that for them: an unpleasant, remote possibility. This will also be true of one of the two men we will shortly meet, an Amerindian known as Will; but the other man, William Dampier, set himself into several survival situations by *choice*.

When one recalls the hardship that awaited the Poor Englishman — or Peter Carder on an isle outside the mouth of the Plate River — one wonders why anyone would decide to be left on an island or to climb into a longboat when it was not absolutely essential, when there was any alternative at all. The answer is temperament. If Carder's personality had aspects that saw him through moments of danger, if other survivors found within themselves the will to live, something in Dampier caused him to put himself in jeopardy unnecessarily.

The life of the privateer was a difficult one, to be sure, but not everyone who lived it became so irascible as this man. We will never know just what forces shaped his personality. But the consequences of his disposition will shortly become clear.

Alexander Selkirk was not the first man to be marooned on the island of Más á Tierra. At least two men preceded him, and the experience of one of them, the Miskito Indian Will, is if anything more extraordinary than Selkirk's own.

William Dampier knew the story. He had been a part of it and told of it in his highly successful book, *A New Voyage Round the World,* published in 1697. No other volume and certainly no other author has been more closely associated with the literature of the survivor.

Daniel Defoe read *A New Voyage* as well as Dampier's other works and was profoundly influenced by them. He borrowed liberally from them for *Robinson Crusoe.* Even Defoe's prose style shows a great debt to the privateering captain.

Jonathan Swift was influenced by Dampier's writings, too. He had his most famous creation, the much-marooned Lemuel Gulliver, claim kinship with "Cousin Dampier," and he used the captain's description of the Australian aborigines as the basis for the most unsettling beings Gulliver met, the Yahoos. Furthermore, as Christopher Lloyd, Dampier's biographer, has argued, Swift also seems to have written into *Gulliver's Travels* a thinly disguised depiction of Dampier himself in the character of Captain Pocock, who was "an honest man, and a good sailor, but a little too positive in his opinions, which was the cause of his destruction." *

In a later age William Wordsworth took details from Dampier for his poetry, as did Samuel Taylor Coleridge for that greatest of all works of survivor literature, "The Rime of the Ancient Mariner." It was Coleridge, after all, who affectionately referred to the privateer as "Old Dampier, rough sailor, but a man of exquisite mind," and recommended that all writers of naval and military matters read and imitate him.

Yet William Dampier was linked with more than the literature of survival; he was also intimately connected to its reality. For a time he was Selkirk's commanding officer on the voyage during which that bad-tempered Scotsman would put ashore, and he was present at his rescue. He found Will and told the world of him. And, of course, he lived through two maroonings and two dangerous voyages in open boats.

■   ■   ■

* In putting together the biographical sketch of Dampier for this chapter, I have drawn from his own writings, but I have also relied quite substantially on Lloyd's research as presented in his *William Dampier* (1966) and his and P. K. Kemp's *The Brethren of the Coast* (1960).

He is perhaps the most enigmatic human being to be found in these pages. Where some men seem to grow in stature according to the challenges they meet, Dampier was diminished by them. A man of insatiable curiosity, he felt compelled to wander through the world. In his youth this clear-eyed, eager observer abhorred men who were dissolute or lacking in self-discipline, yet later in life he turned into the very sort of man he had once despised, becoming a weakling and a drunkard. His relations with his fellow mariners were often strained, and his subordinate officers particularly suffered under his command. Although he was indisputably brave, as a leader he was sometimes hesitant and indecisive, traits that led his crewmen to charge him with cowardice. Always a sensitive man, easily wounded, he would become rancorous and was subject to wild outbursts of temper. His accomplishments were many, but apparently he felt his failures more acutely.

Although he served his country with distinction for all his adult life, first as a wartime sailor and afterward as an explorer and privateer, the Admiralty had him court-martialed on dubious charges, and the judges recommended that he be barred from commanding any of Her Majesty's ships. This episode seems to have been the turning point in his life, to have embittered him, making him temperamental and irresolute. Hereafter, he would write no more books. While he would sail again (and, indeed, be a commander of a privately funded expedition) and make impressive profits for others, he would find wealth elusive and would die deeply in debt.

He was the greatest explorer of the Age of Observation. He discovered the strait between New Britain and New Guinea which now bears his name. He was the first Englishman to visit Australia. He charted the wind system of the Southern Hemisphere and made other important contributions to the science of hydrography. His wind map of the Pacific was "the first of its kind," and was, according to Christopher Lloyd, "an amazingly comprehensive compilation by one man, unassisted by the multifarious aids of a modern meteorological office."

Always fascinated by the inhabitants, flora, and fauna of the places he visited, he made careful and vivid notes and brought back valuable botanical specimens, some of which have been preserved to this day in the herbarium at Oxford. (Among the plants botanists have named for him are the *Clianthus dampieri* and the *Beaufortia dampieri*.)

Even near the end of his days, after the humiliating court-martial, he was chosen to be the navigator on Woodes Rogers's circumnavigation, and his skills in performing those duties contributed enormously to the success of that triumphant voyage.

What is most memorable about him, however, is his obsessive curiosity, that fierce inquisitiveness.

He was apprenticed at the age of eighteen to a Weymouth shipmaster, "complying with the inclination I had very early of seeing the world." A few years later he enlisted to serve in the Third Dutch War, fighting in two battles and witnessing another from the deck of a hospital ship, after which he "languished a while" in a naval hospital.

He next sought an advantageous position at a Jamaican sugar plantation, but the owner tried to trick him into indenturing himself, and after a brief stint as a laborer, he set out for Honduras to join the Brethren of the Coast. In the company of such raffish fellows he would spend most of the rest of his days. (He did shortly thereafter return to England just long enough to marry a woman and live with her a few months; he left her childless and may never have gotten back home while she lived.)

A seaman's life was a harsh one. Crews encountered many dangers, not the least of which were storms and vessels that sank because their planks were worm-eaten and rotten. Scurvy and dysentery (the "bloody flux") were as pervasive hazards of the profession as musket balls and cannon shot and very often as lethal. Officers were frequently incompetent or cruel or both, and mutiny was a constant possibility. (On a voyage Dampier commanded, the sailors would become so unruly and disrespectful that he thought it wiser not to sleep below but to lie down on deck each night, a brace of pistols by his side.)

An acquaintance of Dampier's, Edward Barlow, who had gone to sea for the same reason as Dampier — "a wandering mind" — had no illusions about the trade:

I was always thinking that beggars had a far better life of it and lived better than I did, for they seldom missed of their bellies full of better victuals than we could get; also at night to lie quiet and out of danger in a good barn full of straw, nobody disturbing them, and might lie as long as they pleased; but it was quite contrary with us, for we seldom in a month got our bellyful of victuals, and that of such salt as many

beggars would think scorn to eat; and at night when we went to take
our rest, we were not to lie still above four hours; and many times
when it blew hard were not sure to lie one hour, yea, often we were
called up before we had slept half an hour and forced to go up into
the maintop or foretop to take in our topsails, half awake and half
asleep, with one shoe on and the other off, not having time to put it
on; always sleeping in our clothes for readiness; and in stormy
weather, when the ship rolled and tumbled as though some great
millstone was rolling up one hill and down another, we had much
ado to hold ourselves fast by the small ropes from falling by the
board; and being gotten up into the tops, there we must haul and
pull to make fast the sail, seeing nothing but air above us and water
beneath, and that so raging as though every wave would make a
grave for us.

It is no wonder that men who lived in this fashion were given to
rowdiness and inebriation. Yet even making allowance for the hardness of their lot, they were a scurrilous bunch, and Dampier was
not being prim when he at various times characterized them as
drunkards, madmen, and aimless, unthinking rabble. Near the end
of one arduous journey, as the food supply ran low, the crew secretly agreed that when it was gone they would eat their captain and
Dampier. "Ah! Dampier," the captain joked after the crisis was
past and the plot uncovered, "you would have made them but a
poor meal," for, added Dampier in explanation, "I was as lean as
the captain was lusty and fleshy."

Though he said he "did ever abhor drunkenness," the companionship of such dissolute souls offered the best opportunity to satisfy his hunger for knowledge. He explained that he joined one company "more to indulge my curiosity than to get wealth" and that
he remained with another "mad crew" because "the further we
went the more knowledge and experience I should get, which was
the main thing I regarded."

His first circumnavigation certainly would have effected the cure if
anything would have. He embarked in 1680 and was gone about a
dozen years, sailing on nearly as many vessels under a bewildering
variety of captains. (It was on this voyage that he was contemplated
for supper.) He was seriously ill a number of times: with scurvy;
with dropsy, which he cured by having himself buried in the sand
and sweating the illness out of his system; and with dysentery,
which he tried to treat with a more harrowing and universal remedy

Captain William Dampier (Permission of the National Portrait Gallery, London)

— he sought to bleed himself, but the knife was too dull to make a success of it. As Lloyd observes, he was lucky not to have contracted blood poisoning from the attempt.

In the Indian Ocean, Dampier lost all patience with the recently installed captain (the last one having been deposed and left in the Philippines) and his loutish followers. He begged to be put ashore on one of the Nicobar Islands. The captain was quick to oblige him and then just as quick to change his mind, sending an armed party to retrieve him. Eventually Dampier was able to convince the officer to maroon him and three other white men, all of whom were as anxious to get away from the captain as he was; four Malays were also put ashore. Still, the first night on the beach Dampier felt it necessary to patrol the sands with an ax that had been secretly smuggled away from the vessel in case the captain changed his mind once more.

The next day Dampier traded the ax to some natives in return for a canoe. When it proved unseaworthy, the Malays fitted it with outriggers to make it into a catamaran. Dampier then navigated the craft nearly two hundred miles through choppy seas and monsoon winds, despite heavy clouds at night which prevented his taking a sighting of the stars, and the alternating tropical downpours that soaked them and the brutal sun that burned them.

At least once during the journey he lost heart. On a stormy night with the sea "roaring in a white foam" all around the catamaran

> I had a lingering view of approaching death, and little or no hopes of escaping it; and I must confess that my courage, which I had hitherto kept up, failed me here, and I made very sad reflections on my former life, and looked back with horror and detestation on actions which before I disliked, but now I trembled at the remembrance of. I had long before repented me of that roving course of life, but never with such concern as now. I did also call to mind the many miraculous acts of God's Providence towards me in the whole course of my life, of which I believe few men have met the like. For all these I returned thanks in a peculiar manner, and thus once more desired God's assistance, and composed my mind as well as I could in the hope of it, and as the event showed, I was not disappointed of my hopes.

When they finally reached Sumatra, the white men were feverish and exhausted; they suffered from ague (malaria) and the "bloody flux." It was at this juncture that Dampier tried to cure his fever by bleeding himself.

Even though ailing, he was off again, this time on a tangential visit to Tonkin (North Vietnam). He set out on foot, accompanied by a guide whose services he had purchased for a silver dollar, despite the fact that they had no language in common. It was not always the best arrangement: Dampier tried to bargain for meat at what he took to be a market stall but which was, in fact, a sacred funeral pyre. He was surrounded by angry mourners who tore off his hat, ripped his clothing, and pommeled him. His guide managed to pull him free, but the mob chased them for quite a distance.

He suffered from dysentery for more than six months (unknowingly aggravating it by eating citrus fruit), but he would not rest: "However, though I was but weak, yet I was not discouraged from this journey, but weary of lying still, and impatient of seeing [something] that might further gratify my curiosity."

He made his way home by slow stages with side trips to smuggle a load of opium to Malacca and to visit the South African mainland. He was not back in England until mid-September 1691.

He had nothing to show for the dozen years he had been gone except for two possessions that he hoped would make his fortune. One of these was his journal and the other was his "painted Prince," Jeoly. Jeoly, a slave boy, had been given to Dampier by a sea captain. He was covered from head to foot with tattoos of ornate and intricate design. These were, thought his new owner, "very curious, full of great variety of lines, flourishes, chequered work, etc., keeping a very graceful proportion, and appearing very artificial, even to wonder, especially that upon his shoulder blades."

Dampier intended to exhibit the boy in a "raree" show, but his need for money was so acute that on his first day in London he was forced to sell half his interest in Jeoly to "some eminent persons." Before long he had sold them the other half as well.

They promptly advertised the attraction:

> This admirable Person is exposed to publick view every day, during his stay in town, from the sixteenth of this instant June at his lodgings at the Blew Boar's Head in Fleet Street near Water Lane: where he will continue for some time, if his Health will permit. But if any Persons of Quality, Gentlemen or Ladies, do desire to see this noble Person at their own Houses, or any other convenient place in or about this City of London, they are desired to send timely notice, and he will be ready to wait upon them in a Coach or Chair any time they please to appoint, if in the day time. VIVAT REX ET REGINA.

As it turned out, Dampier may have gained more by selling his shares in the enterprise than he would have by keeping them. Either way he profited a great deal more from the venture than did the poor admirable Person, for his health did not permit an extended exhibition: lacking immunity to Western diseases, he contracted smallpox after only a few months and died at Oxford.

While Dampier was not enriched by *A New Voyage Round the World* any more than he was by the painted Prince, the book (an improved version of his journal) did attract the attention of the First Lord of the Admiralty, who invited him to propose a voyage of discovery. He chose to go back to New Holland (Australia).

It was not a propitious undertaking. Like the men with whom he served in his youth, many of the expedition's crew were undisciplined drunkards who proved inclined to mutiny. Their officers were hardly more reliable. Dampier had particular difficulty with First

Lieutenant George Fisher, an arrogant, insubordinate man who seemed forever to be challenging his authority; he also made disparaging remarks about Dampier's past, suggesting that he was nothing more than a traitorous pirate. Worse, Dampier came to believe that the man was fomenting an insurrection.

Finally, after having been much goaded, the furious Dampier fell on the lieutenant and beat him with a cane. He then had him confined to his cabin in irons for the three weeks it took to reach Brazil. There Dampier got the Portuguese governor to jail Fisher until a ship could carry him back to England. The lieutenant would remain incarcerated for three months in unrelieved misery because his captain had left him no money with which to bribe his guards. Dampier did leave him a servant, however, and provisions from the ship.

Even if Dampier's sending Fisher home was just punishment, it was a tactical error which enabled his adversary to arrive in Britain nearly two years before he himself returned. Fisher used the time well to build his case against his superior officer, blacken his name, and prejudice his judges.

Among Dampier's adventures while Fisher was home slandering him was a second marooning. In trying to repair a leak in the hull, an incompetent carpenter's mate so enlarged the hole that the ship could not be kept afloat. Dampier did manage to bring her close enough to Ascension Island for his men to reach shore on a raft, carrying with them much of their gear, including even the sails from which tents could be made.

The site of a number of maroonings, Ascension, rocky and forbidding, was a thousand miles from the nearest mainland. Still, fresh water and turtles kept the men alive for a few months until a convoy of vessels passed close enough for their frantic signals to be seen.

The court-martial was held on board the H.M.S. *Royal Sovereign* on June 8, 1702. The judges found Dampier's treatment of Fisher to be "notorious and past dispute." They dismissed his concerns about mutiny, fined him all the pay he had earned in the three years he was at sea, and, most humiliating of all, added their opinion that "the said Capt. Dampier is not a fit person to be employed as commander of any of Her Majesty's ships."

If his government had no use for this rare and troubled man, British merchants did. The War of the Spanish Succession having broken out shortly before the trial, Thomas Estcourt spent four thousand pounds refitting the two-hundred-ton *Nazareth* as a privateering vessel, which he renamed the *St. George*. He gave the command to William Dampier. It was to be his second circumnavigation of the globe.

Although the expedition encountered a number of early setbacks, including the separation of the *St. George* and the expedition's other ship, the *Cinque Ports,* Dampier ultimately had some success. Unfortunately, his behavior on the voyage showed a marked deterioration. While not a coward, he tended to avoid engaging the enemy, and thus opportunities to take prizes were lost; many of his men attributed this reluctance to abject fear. Dampier's lack of resolve extended to his dealings with his underlings; he was unable to maintain discipline among the crewmen, and despite the recent rebuke of the queen's admirals, he continued to mistreat his officers. The "modest naturalist and resolute explorer" had degenerated into a bully. Among the traits he now adopted was the one about which he had once been most scathing: he became a drunkard. In fact, it would be claimed that in some moments when his vessel was in peril, he was incapacitated by drink.

After Stradling, the captain of the *Cinque Ports,* departed for Juan Fernández to pick up stores he had left behind (and to maroon Alexander Selkirk, as it turned out), Dampier's luck seemed to change. Prizes were taken, and the town of Puná fell to his privateers. He sailed back to England to receive that special mark of distinction that frequently comes with success and fame, one that was often bestowed on those involved in profitable privateering ventures: he was sued.

The suit came to nothing, although the various litigations over Dampier's final circumnavigation (under Woodes Rogers's command) dragged on so long that many of the crew were thrown into jail for debts, Rogers was ruined, and Dampier died two thousand pounds in debt.

However, unlike Daniel Defoe, who died while in hiding from his creditors, Dampier was able to live out his last days in comfort. So certain were his friends that he would ultimately collect his due that they freely loaned him money (which they were never repaid).

Alexander Selkirk was marooned while Dampier was on his second circumnavigation, and he was found while Dampier was making his third. The Amerindian Will, on the other hand, was both marooned and rescued while Dampier was trying to return to England from the New World the very first time.

On March 22, 1684, two ships anchored in a southern bay of Más á Tierra, which was sometimes known as Greater Land or John Fernando's Isle. They were the *Bachelor's Delight* and the *Nicholas*. As was so often the case, the crews were sick with scurvy and in need of fresh supplies. On March 23, lookouts scanning the shore spotted a man frantically waving his arms. Dampier recognized him at a distance: he was the Miskito who had previously been part of the expedition.

About three years before, the privateers had spent Christmas at Greater Land. The season did not instill feelings of love and forgiveness in these hard men: after the last of the holiday wine had been drunk, they mutinied, deposing their captain, Bartholomew Sharp, in favor of John Watling. On January 14, 1681, Watling sent a party of men ashore, including Will, who was to hunt goats. (Privateering expeditions usually had several Miskitos along; the Europeans valued these Indians highly, crediting them with unusually sharp eyesight and superior hunting skills.) Three Spanish vessels were descried while the foraging party was still on the island; Watling managed to collect all but one of the men before ordering that his ships set sail. Will, who had been in the woods by himself, was left behind. He returned to the beach in time to see his comrades sailing away. He had been marooned with nothing more than a knife, a gun, a small horn of powder, and a few shot.

When Watling was killed not long thereafter in an attack on the town of Arica, the majority of the sailors voted to restore Sharp, but a minority of forty-four men refused to accept his authority. Among these was Dampier, who doubted the captain's courage. He and the other dissenters, along with three Indians and five black slaves, climbed into three open boats and made a six-hundred-mile journey to the Isthmus of Darien.

Sharp would capture a Spanish prize and then sail for Barbados and home. Since the prize contained a valuable collection of charts of the Pacific, the British government was happy to exonerate him of piracy charges and awarded him a commission in the Royal Navy. Will, meanwhile, would maintain himself in solitude on Greater Land for three long years.

Dampier went ashore to rescue the Indian but took the precaution of bringing with him another Miskito named Robin. Will had been left alone in an uncivilized environment for quite a while; there was no telling what effects such prolonged, enforced isolation might

have had on a man who belonged to a race of savages. Would he
have regressed? Better to have him meet one of his own first and
gauge at a distance his mental state.

What Robin met, in fact, was a man who had remained eminently
civilized. Having seen the vessels arrive the day before and rightly
believing they were British, Will hospitably killed three goats in the
morning and prepared an English-style feast — with cabbage! —
for his deliverers.

As Dampier's boat came in, Will was waiting on the beach "to
congratulate our safe arrival." At a calculated distance the cautious
Dampier was able to witness the scene that followed:

> And when we landed . . . Robin first leaped ashore and running to
> his brother Moskito man, [Robin] threw himself flat on his face at his
> feet, who, helping him up, and embracing him, fell flat with his face
> on the ground at Robin's feet and was taken up by him also. And
> when the ceremonies of civilities were over, we also drew near, each
> of us embracing him we found here, who was overjoyed to see so
> many of his old friends come hither, as he thought purposely to fetch
> him.

Tall, raw-boned, "long-visaged, hard-favour'd," and lank-haired,
Will had survived his marooning with little difficulty. This was not
surprising since his was a nation of hunters who had existed for
generations in an environment far more forbidding than this one.
The hardness of their lot required that they be extremely adaptable
and inventive.

Will had displayed these qualities from the start. Once he exhausted his supply of powder and shot, he notched or serrated his
knife blade with a rock and used it to saw his gun barrel into lengths.
These he smithed into harpoon heads, lance points, fish hooks, and
another long knife blade, "heating the pieces first in the fire, which
he struck with his gunflint and a piece of the barrel of his gun, which
he hardened, having learnt to do that among the English. The hot
pieces of iron he would hammer out and bend as he pleased with
stones and saw them with his jagged knife or grind them to an edge
by long labour and harden them to a good temper as there was
occasion." Until he built these "instruments," he had been forced
to eat seal, which he found to be "very ordinary meat," but after
he had spears, harpoons, and fish hooks, he would kill seals only to
obtain their skin for making tackle and thongs.

He built a hut a half mile from the sea and lined it with the hides

The Miskito Indian Will *(standing, left)* is greeted by Robin while white privateers look on. (Copy print courtesy of Special Collections, Lehigh University Libraries)

of goats he had brought down with his spear and skinned with his new blade: "his couch or 'barbacue' of sticks, lying about two foot distant from the ground, was spread with [goatskin as] was all his bedding." When his European clothes fell apart, he fashioned a loincloth from the hide as well.

Several times parties of Spaniards came ashore to hunt him, but he was so wily and cunning in eluding them that they at length gave up, having come to believe he was an apparition.

Dampier's contact with Miskitos must have been limited strictly to those who signed on to white men's ships, because he explains Will and Robin's having European names by saying that their tribe was too poor for its members to have names in their own language. Walter de la Mare perpetuates this condescending attitude toward Miskitos, writing that they were a "minute nation of Amerindians, civil, good-natured and monogamous, only a hundred men strong.

A prudent people too, for when its men-folk enjoyed a carousal, the women used to hide their weapons.''

This is delightful and quaint, but it is not accurate. It is wrong in nearly every particular as well as in the general impression that it gives.

The Miskitos were a fierce and valiant race of warriors, acknowledged by the privateers to be skillful hunters, clever scouts, and fearsome fighters. In a harsh, unforgiving land (non-Indians would never seek to settle in it, even in the twentieth century), they existed and prospered by their willingness to adapt and to absorb the customs and technologies of other nations. They changed in order to survive, but they never forsook their identity. They might adapt, but they never surrendered. They might absorb, but they refused to be absorbed.

They would remain distinct and proud in the home of their ancestors.

To this very day.

CHAPTER 5

On a Piece of Stone

Alexander Selkirk on Greater Land

As a result of Alexander Selkirk's stay on Más á Tierra, his island has become absorbed into our common imagination. Even if you have never heard of Más á Tierra, when you think of being marooned or speak mistakenly of a *desert* isle, Selkirk's dwelling place is probably what you have in mind. The shore you see yourself on is not a rock off the coast of Scotland, where the bitter wind blows the snow around, nor one north of the Straits of Magellan, where there is no fresh water; neither is it Ascension, where food is difficult to find. No, the island you dream of has a temperate climate and is surrounded by a warm, calm sea. Wood is plentiful, as are herbivorous animals. There are no carnivores to stalk you, and the ocean teems with easily caught fish. Storms never threaten, and tall trees offer shade. It is a place, in short, without danger or cause for serious anxiety, and it is never visited by evil men in warships. With the exception of this last, then, you are talking about Greater Land. If there ever was a shore to be stranded on, it is this one.

Just how even those of us who have forgotten the names of Más á Tierra, Woodes Rogers, and Alexander Selkirk should have come by the conception is not entirely clear. It may result, however, from the fact that a number of writers who were aficionados of sea lore and did know Selkirk's story depicted Greater Land in their creations, which continue to be read or performed today. Daniel Defoe was the first, of course, and after him followed a host of imitators including Johann David Wyss, the obscure army chaplain from Switzerland who wrote *The Swiss Family Robinson,* and Robert Louis Stevenson, who conceived of *Treasure Island* when he idly

Captain Woodes Rogers *(seated)* and his family. Painting by William Hogarth.
(Permission of the National Maritime Museum, London)

drew a pirate map one rainy afternoon to entertain a small boy.
(This map bears an interesting resemblance to drawings made of
Más á Tierra by two of Dampier's shipmates and published in books
Stevenson might have seen.) Then, too, there was the Scottish playwright, Sir James M. Barrie, the author of *Peter Pan*. Poets as
diverse as William Cowper, William S. Gilbert, Walter de la Mare,
and Karl Shapiro have also etched the image of Más á Tierra in our
consciousness.

A curious thing happens when artists address themselves to the
survivor motif. Not content with plunking down their protagonists
in the most ideal of settings, the fanciful creators usually employ
some device to ease the plight of their heroes. Most often, following
the lead of Defoe, this takes the form of the hull of a wrecked ship
from which can be salvaged a wealth of tools and supplies. Defoe,
in fact, has the wreck remain conveniently offshore for *thirteen days*
while Robinson ferries back and forth on a raft between it and the

beach. Remembering that most maroons crawled up on the sand literally naked and that those who, like Selkirk, were marooned intentionally had only the contents of their sea chests, consider a partial list of what Crusoe retrieves and brings to his new home: a hogshead of bread, a barrel of fine flour, rice, barley, tobacco, sugar, three Dutch cheeses, corn, dried goat meat; several cases of the skipper's liquor, three large rundlets of rum, and about six gallons of rack (wine); all the men's clothing; the carpenter's chest ("which was indeed a very useful prize to me, and much more valuable than a ship-loading of gold would have been at the time") and tools, including two saws, an ax, a hammer, two or three bags of nails and spikes, crowbars, several dozen hatchets, a grindstone, and a great jackscrew; several razors, a dozen knives and forks, an enormous kettle, and a large pair of scissors; pens, ink, paper, three Bibles, and a number of books, including several Catholic prayer books; at least three compasses, mathematical instruments, perspectives and several perspective glasses (spy glasses), and charts and books of navigation; a hammock and some bedding; three seamen's chests; the mizzenmast, spritsail, foretopsail, all the other sails, and spare canvas; rigging, cables, a hawser, small ropes, and twine. He also has money, however useless it may be to him: thirty-six pounds as well as some European coins, pieces of eight, and some gold and silver. He takes ashore the ship's dog (which will live with him for many years) and two female cats.

Finally — and crucially — there are the weapons that Crusoe is able to collect: seven muskets and two barrels of musket bullets, two "very good" fowling pieces and one other besides, two pistols and three barrels of powder, as well as assorted powder horns, bags of shot, and rusty swords.

No wonder Crusoe says that "the most covetous griping miser in the world would have been cured of the vice of covetousness, if he had been in my case; for I possessed infinitely more than I knew what to do with. I had not room for desire, except it was of things I had not, and they were but trifles."

Possessed of such wealth, Alexander Selkirk and many another real maroon might well have been reluctant to give up a life in seclusion to return to the risks and poverty of the sailor's trade.

Of course, Daniel Defoe and most of the old masters of survival literature were not attempting to draw an entirely factual portrait of a maroon's predicament. Quite the contrary — for them the island

The survivor in literature: Robinson Crusoe shipwrecked and as a benevolent colonist (Courtesy of Special Collections, Kent State University. Copy prints by Larry Rubens, Audio-Visual Services, KSU)

experience was an allegory of the human condition, and they used it to show the psychological transformation of their protagonists. Thus they relieved them of the true and desperate burdens of elemental existence in order to work an internal alteration. Given the time, in other words, to meditate and remember, the fictional characters undergo profound change.

In this century, few authors have written of maroonings, perhaps because the event has become so rare and unlikely that we no longer fear it. American and European filmmakers, however, have sometimes returned to the desert isle, and not only to make and remake such classics as *Robinson Crusoe, The Swiss Family Robinson, Treasure Island,* and *Peter Pan.* Yet they have been no more interested in representing authentic situations than were artists of earlier times. What the camera sees is the lush and unthreatening Más á Tierra, but psychological transformation has been dispensed with: on Selkirk's residence are now most often played out silly comedies of social role reversal and sexual combat.

Where the masters of our most realistic medium decline to depict reality, shall the poets be faulted for lyricism? In 1944, Karl Shapiro wrote these lines about Crusoe:

> For he has outwitted nature and shipwreck;
> Some day the tapering mast will fill the west,
> The castaway once more upon the deck
> Gaze at two worlds, and set sail for the best.
>
> Gladly he gives this isle to all mankind
> To tread the hills and shores with countless feet.
> Henceforth the globe itself swims in his mind,
> The last unknown and insular retreat.

This is quite lovely, but it is radically removed from the experience of the man who inspired it all, that irascible eighteenth-century privateer, Alexander Selkirk.

Actually his name was Selcraig, but he seems to have changed it when he went to sea. Perhaps the alteration was an accident, the mishearing of the name by a shipowner's clerk putting it down in the book. More likely it was the bearer's own act of defiance: he was declaring his independence from the repressive fishing village of his birth, with its severe, pious elders.

A difficult man was Alexander Selkirk. Much given to the vices of sailors — strong drink, loose women, and brawling — he had a personality perfectly suited to such diversions: impulsive and hot-tempered with little respect for authority, quick to speak his mind and just as quick to fight.

Still, despite these traits, he was a skillful, hard-working mariner. He went to sea early, against his father's wishes though with the blessings of his mother, who may have felt less need to test wills with him and was the more willing to rid her house of such a disruptive, ungovernable boy. He signed on with privateers and from them took his instruction in the sailing of ships and the working of the Sweet Trade. He learned his lessons so well and progressed so quickly that by the summer of 1704, the young man was the "sailing master" on the *Cinque Ports,* a vessel that was part of an expedition making a circumnavigation of the globe.

The completion of Selkirk's own circumnavigation would be delayed some four years by the events of that summer, triggered by his own bad temper. His fate, though, was not as unhappy as that of many of his shipmates, whose corpses would sink beneath the waves or be carted out of Spanish jails.

His misfortune began with the death of the *Cinque*'s captain, Charles Pickering. The sailing master had been able to get along with Pickering, but his successor was Thomas Stradling, a man as quarrelsome and temperamental as Selkirk himself. In addition, the leader of the expedition, Captain William Dampier, was of the same volatile type as Stradling and Selkirk. Strife was impending, inevitable.

The first conflict arose between the two captains. The voyage had not been going well. Several prizes had eluded or outrun them. They had failed to take the Peruvian town of Santa María, said to be rich with gold. In fact, the greatest success to date had been the capture of a vessel laden with food. In the Bay of Panama, Stradling and Dampier had it out. The result was that the *Cinque Ports* separated from Dampier's ship, the *St. George,* and sailed south alone down the western coast of South America.

Next Stradling quarreled with the members of his crew. The nature of this disagreement is not known, but the captain patched it up haphazardly — as haphazardly as he had the *Cinque Ports* patched when she leaked. A residue of bad feeling remained.

Finally and most calamitously for both men, Stradling and Selkirk squared off. The sailing master had long felt that repairs to the ship were being made poorly and that as a result the *Cinque Ports* was dangerously leaky. If time was not taken to go over her carefully and do the necessary work properly, he predicted disaster.

The captain responded as an insecure man would, by asserting his authority.

The argument grew heated.

Selkirk shouted that if Stradling was determined to continue on without making the repairs, then the *Cinque Ports* could go to the bottom without him. It was a foolish thing to say, a statement borne of the angry moment, but Selkirk was too proud to withdraw it.

The captain for once was obliging. Actually, he seized on the rash demand as a means of removing a thorn from his side, the most obdurate and rebellious of the crew: *Very well, if that was what the sailing master wanted, he would be accommodated.*

The island of Más á Tierra was at hand. Stradling dispatched a boat to carry his defiant subordinate to the shore. Selkirk hoped that other sailors would choose to stay with him, but none did. Standing by himself on the sand with his sea chest beside him, watching his fellows struggle to relaunch the boat, he glimpsed the enormity of what he had done and lost his nerve.

To be marooned was a terrible fate. It usually meant death by slow starvation or dehydration. Even if it were possible to preserve one's life, prolonged isolation could drive a man mad.

Perhaps more than privateers, pirates had a special appreciation for the horrors of solitude, and they so regularly condemned people to it that they came to be known as "marooners." That many of the victims of this practice were from among the ranks of the buccaneers themselves is an ironic result of the fact that these rough men formed themselves into societies that were surprisingly democratic. As part of the process they often drew up constitutions for all to agree to, and the laws they promulgated were specific, the penalties for violations exact. The most heinous offenses they punished not with the noose or the plank but with marooning. The offender was put on shore with only his sea chest, a pistol, and a single ball. Many tales were told of one landing party or another coming upon a rotting chest and a skeleton with a shattered skull, a rusted pistol in one bony hand.

This was the fate to which Selkirk had so impetuously doomed himself.

Woodes Rogers, who heard the story from the man himself, described his change of heart: "A difference betwixt him and his captain . . . together with the ship's being leaky, made him [more] willing to stay [on the island] than go along with him at first; and when he was at last willing the captain would not receive him."

Here Rogers may be indulging in characteristic understatement. As his former comrades rowed back to the *Cinque Ports,* Selkirk, it is said, plunged into the ocean, thrashing after them until the water was up to his chest. He stretched out his arms toward them and cried out that he had changed his mind, pleading pitifully to be taken back on board. But the only reply was the captain's jeer: "*Well, I have not changed mine!*" came his words across the water. "*Stay where you are and may you starve!*"

As soon as the small boat reached the *Cinque Ports,* the ship's sails were unfurled, and she sailed away.

Alone upon the beach, Selkirk watched the *Cinque Ports* until she disappeared from view. He should then have gone inland to survey the unfamiliar terrain for springs, edible plants, and animals and to locate a suitable shelter or the materials to build one. These first days for a maroon were crucial to survival. While he was at his strongest he had better prepare for the desperate struggle to stay alive. Once strength began to ebb, searching would become more difficult. Better to find what was needed before weakness and panic set in.

But Selkirk did not immediately seek the means to sustain himself in the coming weeks and months. Instead, according to Defoe biographer Thomas Wright, he hugged the shore in alternating moods of false optimism and despair:

> Unable to abandon the hope that Stradling would relent and come back for him, the unhappy Selkirk found himself chained to the beach; and even when gnawed with hunger, rather than go in search of fruits and other products of the woods, he contented himself with shellfish and seal's flesh, and whatever else he could obtain without moving inland. He hated even to close his eyes. Often he cursed the folly that had brought him to this terrible solitude, and sometimes, starting up in agony, he would resolve on suicide. Voices spoke to him both in the howlings of the sea in front and in the murmur of the woods behind. The shore was creatured with phantoms. Then — cooling his fevered brain — came sweet visions of his childhood, the home at Largo, his mother, the fields he had rambled in, the words he had heard in the old kirk, thoughts of God.

This last image of the Scotsman, devout and meditating lovingly on the memories of his mother, is surely nineteenth-century lyrical sentimentality, or else solitude and the howlings of the sea were making wonderful changes in the volatile mariner. Undoubtedly, though, the miserable man did think back on the course of his life.

He was from the fishing village of Largo in the county of Fife, Scotland. Like the hero of many a folktale, he was the seventh son of a cobbler, having been born to John and Euphan Selcraig rather late in his mother's childbearing years.

He was a stubborn, unruly boy. One scholar says that he was so "wild and restless [that he] daily kicked against the authority of the home, and elsewhere his conduct was equally wild."

His father resisted the boy's early ambition to go to sea, until his behavior would seem to have forced him to relent. Late in the summer of 1695, Alexander was ordered to stand before the kirk session and answer to having made a disturbance in church. On August 27, his name was duly called out, but he did not answer to it. As the elders noted in the record, he "did not appear, having gone to sea."

For six years he stayed away, learning the sailor's trade and, not incidentally, avoiding the confinement of Largo and the disapproval of its kirk, only to return if anything "more reckless and boisterous than ever." After no time at all the community again had cause to chastise him, but this was for something more than making rude noises in a house of worship. His "half-witted" brother, Andrew, had given Alexander a can of salt water to drink, instead of fresh water, and had compounded the offense by laughing at his brother's reaction. Selkirk fell on him and began to beat him; worse, when his father and older brother John interceded he fought them as well. John's alarmed wife went to the assistance of her husband, and in the confusion of the melee, she, too, was struck.

On November 30, 1701, in obedience to a decree from the kirk session, Alexander Selkirk stood up in front of the pulpit in church and made an "acknowledgement of his sin in disagreeing with his brothers, and was rebuked in the face of the congregation for it, and promised amendment in the strength of the Lord, and so was dismissed."

That was enough humiliation for this seething young man. The winter held him in Largo, but when spring came he was gone again. Within a year he was serving under William Dampier on a privateering voyage round the world.

Stradling left him provisions enough for two days, and after that, as Wright says, he ate mainly shellfish. (Greater Land's crawfish, Rogers would note happily, were "as large as our lobsters and very good.") Although fish were abundant, Selkirk found he could not eat them because he had no salt or bread and because they gave him, as Rogers decorously put it, "a looseness" of the bowel.

He did catch great quantities of turtles and gorged himself on their "extremely delicious" flesh until it began to upset his stomach, after which he could eat it only in jellied form.

Gradually his attention turned from the sea's horizon to the land at his back. In at least one respect he was very fortunate: the island on which he was marooned, the one that happened to be closest to the point where he had lost his temper with his captain, was a virtual paradise. In absolute contrast to so many other shores on which other luckless souls had found themselves, Más á Tierra offered a very hospitable environment.

It was one of three in a cluster collectively known as the Juan Fernández Islands, lying four hundred miles west of the coast of Chile. Only Greater Land, the largest of the three, was truly habitable; it was more than twelve miles long and nearly four miles wide at its broadest point, and it rose to a height of three thousand feet above sea level. Más Afuera (Further Out), some one hundred miles to the west, was a rocky mass marked by deep ravines with swift water flowing through them. The last of the group, Santa Clara, was a rocky, steep-sloped islet sometimes referred to as Goat Island, presumably because only such a contrary beast could clamber over it.

The first known discoverer of the group was the Spanish navigator Juan Fernández, who chanced upon it in about 1570 and, with inspiring modesty, named it after himself. His intention was to found a colony. Using Indian slaves, he built thatched and timber huts on Greater Land, and he set about breeding herds of cattle and sheep, the progenitors of which he had brought with him. He also tried to set up a trade in sea lion oil and salted fish.

The enterprise was not a success, and Fernández abandoned the little chain, giving it to a friend who conveniently bore the same name as himself. The second Juan Fernández bequeathed it to the order of Jesuits. After a time the Crown of Spain laid claim to the group, taking fish from its waters and timber and sandalwood from Más á Tierra. But by the latter part of the seventeenth century, the Spanish had abandoned the islands, and Greater Land was a stopover for their enemies.

For privateers who had been raiding the coast, the island was a convenient haven and a critical source of resupply. It was of no less value to European adventurers and explorers who had just come around the harrowing Cape Horn. It was the first landfall offshore where fresh vegetables, fruits, and meat could be procured for crews whose supplies were often desperately low and many of whose number were suffering from potentially fatal cases of scurvy.

The climate was so good, observed Woodes Rogers, who had just traced the journey through the treacherous seas and braved the Horn, and fifty of whose men were down with the disease, that "the trees and grass are verdant all the year. The winter lasts no longer than June and July and is not then severe, there being only a small frost and a little hail, but sometimes great rains. The heat of summer is equally moderate and there is not much thunder or tempestuous weather of any sort.''

Black plum trees grew in the high elevations in the rocky, difficult terrain. Lower down were cabbage, palm, pimento, and cottonwood trees in abundance. (During his brief visit, Rogers saw some pimento that reached a height of sixty feet and a thickness of two yards; the cottonwood trees were taller and "near four fathom round in the stock.")

There were no "venomous or savage" creatures on the island or its beaches, only turtles and sea lions, as well as goats, rats, and cats. Privateers had put the goats on the isle, hoping they would breed sufficiently to be a source of fresh meat to any marauder who stopped there. The rats had swum ashore from ships or had been brought there inadvertently in the barrels of foraging parties. They had bred so prolifically that the Jesuits released cats to control their population; the clerics had also turned loose dogs with the intention that they decimate the goat herds and thus deny sustenance to the foes of the Spanish crown.

The priests' plan was a failure. The cats did multiply fruitfully, but their prey reproduced in even greater numbers. The dogs, on the other hand, died off: the goats were merely driven to the higher elevations, and the canines starved or plunged off precipices while chasing their nimble quarry.

The goats proved crucial to Selkirk's survival. Not only was the animal's flesh a staple of his diet, but he would use its hide for clothing and for lining the interior of his huts and the sinews for sewing thread and fishing line.

At first he hunted goats with the firelock, gunpowder, and bullets that he had brought from the *Cinque Ports*. Before too long, however, his ammunition ran out. His only other weapon being a knife, he was compelled to pursue the animals on foot. Eventually he was able to run down even the fleetest of them, having first chased them up the steep, rocky slopes and through the dense undergrowth. The forced restriction of his diet — no alcohol, tobacco, or salt-preserved meats — along with the present availability of fresh meat, fruits, and vegetables had made him exceptionally healthy. Cleansed of poisons, he developed an extraordinary agility, an inhuman speed that he would later demonstrate for Woodes Rogers

Three nineteenth-century illustrations depicting Selkirk's life on Greater Land. At the moment of his marooning, he pleads to be taken back on board. He reads his Bible to become a better Christian (in the background is his smokehouse), and he chases a goat. (Courtesy of the Albin O. Kuhn Library and Gallery, UMBC. Copy prints by Alan M. Scherr)

and his men. Rogers made approving mention of it: "His way of living and continual exercise of walking and running cleared him of all gross humors, so that he ran with wonderful swiftness through the woods and up the rocks and hills, as we perceived when we employed him to catch goats for us."

His prowess was such that he came to hunt the animals for sport as well as sustenance: those adults and kids that he did not need he released after notching their ears as a brand, a sign of ownership.

Even excepting the island's resources, he was far better off than most maroons. Since he was here by choice, he had been able to bring with him all of his possessions. In addition to his bedding and his firearm and knife, these included the contents of his sea chest: a hatchet, kettle, flint and steel, a flip jar (however useless where there were no taverns), a Bible, devotional books (as well as some on navigation), and his mathematical instruments.

No mention is made of his having carpentry tools, but by the onset of winter he had managed to build two huts of pimento logs covered with long grass. The interiors he lined with goat fur, a lining chosen surely for its insulating properties against the cold rather than for its pleasant aroma. He burned pimento wood for heat and cooking, finding that it was nearly smokeless and "refreshed him with its fragrant smell."

The smaller of the two huts he used as a smokehouse and kitchen. He built it some distance from the other, larger one, which served as his study and sleeping quarters. Here he read the Bible, prayed for rescue, and fervently repented of his sins, becoming, as a contemporary paraphrased his remark, "a better Christian while in this solitude than ever he was before, or than, he was afraid, he should ever be again." Sometimes he prayed or read aloud, seeking not only to become a good man and bring about God's intercession in his plight but also to maintain his grasp of language. (Back in civilization he resumed his profligate ways, and when he was brought before Rogers on the *Duke,* he was barely able to make himself understood. He croaked more than talked.)

He cured goat meat and made from it a "very good broth," as Rogers judged, "for [the island's goats] are not so rank as ours." In addition, he ate jellied turtle, boiled or broiled crawfish, "with a very cordial and grateful smell resembling that of a balm," parsnips, cabbage palm, radishes, watercress, parsley, purslane, and turnips. (This last, one of the crops the privateers had planted, had become so profuse, Dampier was pleased to observe, that turnips now covered acres of ground.)

For a man who had stayed so long on the beach hoping for quick rescue, Selkirk was now becoming acclimatized, relatively at ease in his environment.

During the worst of his early depression the dreadful howling of the "monsters of the deep" had terrified him, their voices seeming "too terrible to be made for human ears." But he now took a certain pleasure in the noise, and when he ventured forth to explore his domain, he found that the clamorous creatures who had been so hideous in his imagination were merely sea lions that had crawled up on the sand. Despite his relief and amusement he wisely remained cautious of their tails and their jaws which

> were capable of seizing or breaking the limbs of a man if he approached them. But at the time his spirits and his life were so high that he could act so regularly and unconcerned that merely from being unruffled in himself he killed them with the greatest ease imaginable. For observing that though their jaws and tails were so terrible, yet the animals being mighty slow in working themselves round, he had nothing to do but place himself exactly opposite to their middle and as close to them as possible, and he dispatched them with his hatchet at will.

Their whiskers, he thought, were "stiff enough to make toothpickers." Each November the sea lions came ashore to "whelp and engender." He could hear their roars and bleatings a mile inland.

Moving about Greater Land, Selkirk carved his name into tree trunks so that if he died in this place, his having once lived there might be known. He also notched tree limbs to mark the passing of his days. Apparently on these walks he enjoyed observing nature. He was particularly interested in a dark bird with a red breast which he thought resembled a blackbird, and a multicolored hummingbird "no bigger than a large humble bee."

So he became adjusted to this solitary life, mastering with reason and discipline much of the fright and depression that at first enfeebled him. He read the scriptures and studied his navigational books and by degrees reconciled himself to his fate. This reconciliation took about one and a half years. After its completion, wrote journalist Richard Steele, who interviewed Selkirk in a tavern after his return to England, the vigor of his health, disengagement from the world, a constant, cheerful, serene sky and a temperate air made his life one continual feast, [it] being much more joyful than it had before been irksome. He, now taking delight in everything, made the hut in which he lay, [using as construction materials] ornaments which he cut down from a spacious wood, on the side of which it was situated, the most delicious bower fanned with continual breezes and gentle aspirations of wind, that made his repose after the chase equal to the most sensual pleasures.

This image is far too picturesque, of course. When Rogers's ships appeared, the marooned man was so anxious to leave Steele's delicious bower that he was willing to surrender to French corsairs rather than continue where he was, albeit fanned by continual breezes. (At the same time he decided not to give himself up to the sailors if they were Spanish: better to experience the wind's gentle aspirations than breathe the dank air of a gold mine or a jail.)

No, Alexander Selkirk's life on Más á Tierra was not an idyll. As he came to be aware, he would live only so long as he was healthy. An illness or disability that would mean temporary inconvenience in a more civilized setting would here incapacitate him and keep him from hunting and gathering food and thus prove fatal.

The precariousness of his situation was brought home to him by an incident that occurred after he had begun pursuing goats with a knife. He chased an animal up a steep hill to the edge of a precipice hidden by dense bushes. Leaping into the undergrowth to seize the beast, he toppled over the edge, the goat falling before him. They dropped a great distance, the one above the other, and the impact with the ground killed the goat.

Selkirk landed directly on the animal, the carcass cushioning his fall and saving his life. Nonetheless, he was knocked unconscious and lay in that state for at least one full day. (By the time he met Steele five or six years later, imagination and the application of flip had stretched it to three days.) When he came to his senses, he found he was unable to stand or walk. He crawled painfully the mile or more to his hut, and he was unable to leave it for ten days.

Thereafter he became obsessed by the fear that injury or illness would disable him, leaving him unable to catch goats or to hike to the distant parts of the island where vegetables grew. So that a source of food would always be at hand, he captured very young kids and took them back to his compound, where he lamed them to keep them from wandering away.

Selkirk dancing with his cats and kids (Copy print by Larry Rubens, Audio-Visual Services, Kent State University)

Selkirk tamed kittens as well. The numerous and bold rats would enter his shelter at night while he slept and would gnaw at his clothing and bite his naked feet. The felines fed off the rodents, of course, but they were every bit as wild as their prey. He could do nothing with the adult cats, but he captured some of the young kittens and raised them on goat meat and milk. In time, dozens of these furry creatures lounged about the hut and lay on his bed, keeping the rats away.

For diversion he taught the cats and some of the kids to dance. "Thus best we picture him," writes the twentieth-century poet Walter de la Mare, "praying aloud, singing and dancing with his kids and cats in the flames and the smoke of his allspice wood, and the whole world's moon taunting and enchanting him in her seasons."

If he was not moonstruck, at least he was alive. When his clothes fell apart he made new ones out of goatskins — cap, coat, and pants — using a nail for a needle and threading it with goat sinew and the yarn of a worn-out sock he had unraveled. With his legs protected by fur and leather, he was, says Steele, "inured to pass through the woods, bushes and brambles with as much carelessness and precipitance as any other animal."

His shoes fell apart as well, but his feet grew tough and calloused. (Aboard Rogers's ship, he would have difficulty getting used to wearing shoes.) More seriously, he wore his knife down to its back, but he was able to make others from discarded iron barrel hoops, which he beat thin and ground on rocks.

Two fears haunted him. One was that after his death his pet cats would devour his corpse. The other was that he would be captured by the Spanish, and twice he chose to remain a maroon rather than give himself up to them.

On the first of these occasions he saw a ship anchored close to shore and went to the beach to determine her nationality. When he realized she was Spanish, he raced away while the soldiers fired at his fleeing form.

The second incident was more harrowing. The Spaniards landed before he knew it, and they very nearly caught him. Once again he was able to sprint away from them, and their shots went wide of the mark. They hunted him, but he scrambled up one of the tall trees. High in its branches, hidden by its leaves, he watched while they killed several of his goats and "made water" at the base of his refuge. Frustrated, unable to locate him, his would-be captors at last gave up and returned to the sea.

Had they been Frenchmen, Selkirk assured Rogers, he would have surrendered to them, but he preferred a lonely death to the fate of a Spanish captive. They would have killed him outright, he was certain, or worked him to death as a slave in their mines. He was too dangerous to spare, for he could lead still more Europeans into these waters.

So he kept his watch and hunted goats and enjoyed the company of his cats until the day when the *Duke* and *Duchess* appeared, four years and four months after he had so arrogantly confined himself in this prison with breakers for bars. He scouted these ships as he had the ones before them and this time concluded they were friendly. In the night he built a signal fire on a hill, but when Rogers saw it he worried that there might be enemy troops garrisoned on the island or French corsairs nearby.

Still, supplies were low, and many of Rogers's men were suffering

The rescued Selkirk *(seated, right)* being taken aboard the *Duke*. Drawing by Robert C. Leslie (c. 1859). (Copy print courtesy of Special Collections, Case Western Reserve University Libraries)

from scurvy. He chanced sending the yawl ashore and waited anxiously for its return.

Brought on board, the rescued maroon could not at first speak, so overcome was he with joy, but after a time he was able to tell his tale, struggling to make himself understood. Some of the sailors may have been skeptical of his account despite the evidence of his costume and wild appearance, but Dampier came forward and, recognizing his former crewman, confirmed what part of the story he could.* He also recommended Selkirk to Rogers, as the best man to sail on the *Cinque Ports;* Rogers in turn offered him a position as mate.

Selkirk accepted, of course, although he may indeed have harbored some few regrets over leaving Más á Tierra. Alone he had

* Edward Cooke, who was a member of the expedition, wrote an account in which he claimed that Dampier was so irascible that Selkirk, learning his former commander was aboard the *Duke,* at first declined to be rescued, preferring to remain marooned rather than sail with him.

Rogers makes no mention of such an inclination, however, and the anecdote is probably apocryphal.

become self-reliant and introspective, and the place seemed to have come to represent for him — or came to represent for him *in retrospect* — a forfeited serenity.

By the time he talked to Richard Steele, the island dream had intoxicated Alexander Selkirk as surely as it would those who had not lived it, who would only read of it in books. Now that it was at a safe remove, he could desire it right along with the rest. No longer was he the man who had greeted his rescuers with speechless rapture. Instead, as Steele reports Selkirk's recollection, "when the ship which brought him off the island came in he received them with the greatest indifference with relation to the prospect of going off with them, but with great satisfaction in an opportunity to refresh and help them. [He] frequently bewailed his return to the world, which could not, he said, with all its enjoyments, restore him to the tranquility of his solitude."

Having related the Scotsman's experiences to the readers of his publication *The Englishman,* Steele drew this conclusion:

> This plain man's story is a memorable example that he is happiest who confines his wants to natural necessities, and he that goes further in his desires increases his wants in proportion to his acquisitions; or to use his own expression, "I am worth eight hundred pounds, but shall never be so happy as when I was not worth a farthing."

The money Selkirk referred to was his share of the booty from the rest of the voyage. But that glorious enterprise would be delayed temporarily: Captain Rogers was not ready to embark because of the fifty diseased sailors. Some of them were able to totter on "trembling legs" to the boats waiting to take them ashore, while others "who could not, stared feebly as they were hoisted up through the hatch and lowered over the side in a canvas sling."

To these invalids Selkirk played host. He fed them turnips, wild cabbage, shellfish, and young seal. They picked their teeth with sea lion whiskers and slept in tents strewn with fragrant leaves. They gained strength "at marvelous speed" on goat meat broth mixed with greens.

While they rested, Selkirk, whom the men jokingly addressed as "the Governour," displayed his incredible agility. When asked by Captain Rogers to hunt for animals for the crew to eat, Selkirk made a contest of it, chasing after the goats with the most athletic of the sailors and leaving them all far behind. (He also raced against a bulldog, with the same result.) While the other contestants lay panting, the fleet maroon would return carrying a goat on his back. That he was able to perform this feat over and over again was especially amazing to those who witnessed it.

Like Richard Steele, Woodes Rogers was compelled to draw a lesson from Selkirk's sojourn:

> Solitude and retirement from the world is not such an insufferable state of life as most men imagine, especially when people are fairly called or thrown into it unavoidably, as this man was; who in all probability must otherwise have perished in the seas, the ship which left him being cast away not long after and few of the company escaped. We may perceive by this story the truth of the maxim that necessity is the mother of invention, since he found means to supply his wants in a very natural manner, so as to maintain his life, though not so conveniently yet as effectually as we are able to do with the help of all our arts and society. It may likewise instruct us how much a plain and temperate way of living conduces to the health of the body and the vigor of the mind, both [of] which we are apt to destroy by excess and plenty, especially of strong liquor and the variety as well as the nature of our meat and drink; for this man, when he came to our ordinary method of diet and life, though he was sober enough, lost much of his strength and agility.

It was true. As Selkirk readjusted to wearing shoes, having recovered from the initial, painful swelling of his feet, and as he overcame an early revulsion toward salted meat, he found that his astounding prowess waned. The poisons of society had been reintroduced into his system and had diminished his abilities.

For almost two weeks Rogers let his crew linger on that peaceful shore. Nearly all recovered fully under Selkirk's ministrations; in just two of the men had scurvy progressed so far as to be fatal. On a day when the wind was strong, the sails were unfurled, and the ships sailed north. Ahead of them lay towns to be sacked and vessels to be taken, but that was all to come in the days and months ahead.

This was only the thirteenth of February, and their destination was the coast of Peru.

It would prove to be a long and momentous voyage. A number of prizes were captured, cargoes appropriated or sold, aristocrats ransomed or carried back to England as prisoners; even the inland

Ecuadorian town of Guayaquil was taken with very light casualties.*

So it was a grand triumph when, on October 14, 1711, the treasure-laden flotilla sailed up the Thames. The English privateers had accomplished what relatively few had before them — the circumnavigation of the globe. And Rogers had done what none of his predecessors had: he brought back his original ships and most of his crew.

In his journal he noted the end of "our long and fatiguing voyage." But in a sense it had not ended. Even before the arrival of the *Duke* and *Duchess,* the wrangling had begun. The officers of the East India Company claimed that the privateers had interfered with their crown-granted monopoly on trade in Asian waters, and they obtained a declaration of seizure. After the vessels docked, the Company of Silk Throwers filed suit. Many of Rogers's men had already joined together to hire a barrister to protect their interests, and the expedition's investors hired their own lawyer to sue the officers and crew.

Untangling the legal snarls took five years, nearly twice as long

* The behavior of another man who served under Rogers would come to serve as a source of inspiration for quite a different literary masterpiece about a survivor. He was the third mate of the *Duchess,* Simon Hatley.

Shortly after the capture of Guayaquil, the small English convoy was scattered by a storm. All of the vessels rendezvoused except one, a prize bark with eleven men in her. The ships searched for her, signaling with lanterns and gunfire, but the bark could not be located. The privateers delayed resuming the voyage as long as they could, but they were pressed by several problems: they were low on water and medicine; a dozen of their comrades were dead and many more were sick with a plague contracted when some of the men sacking Guayaquil had, against Rogers's wishes, dug up the graves of recently interred fever victims in the search for gold and jewelry. Reluctantly the privateers set sail.

Simon Hatley was in charge of the bark. He ran her toward the continent. One of the crew died before they could reach landfall, and the rest, including Hatley, became prisoners of the Spanish in Peru. Hatley was not released until 1713. He subsequently sailed around the Horn with Captain George Shelvocke. A series of violent storms struck, causing Hatley to become afflicted with melancholia. He fixated on the "disconsolate black albatross" that hovered near his vessel, and he eventually shot it. Shelvocke reported the deed in his book *Voyage Round the World* (1726).

Some seventy years later, Samuel Taylor Coleridge was describing to William Wordsworth his idea for a poem about a mariner condemned to sail with a crew of ghosts. He was baffled by the problem of what deed the character could commit to warrant such a ghastly fate. Wordsworth, who had been reading Shelvocke, had a suggestion: " 'Suppose,' I said, 'you represent him as killing one of these birds on entering the South Sea, and that the tutelary spirits of these regions take upon them[selves] to avenge the crime.' "

as the actual journey. Before it was over, the sailors had twice petitioned the House of Lords for relief, complaining that they were "perishing for want of bread and daily thrown into the gaol." The sale of the prizes and cargoes brought £147,975, of which the investors were to receive two thirds; court costs, customs duties, warehousing fees, and bribes reduced their profit by half. Most seamen received less than £50, and Dampier did not live to be paid all that was owed him.

Rogers's final share was not large, and the debts accrued by his family while he was gone took all of it. He had been bankrupted; he had lost a beloved younger brother in a sea battle; his jawbone had been shattered and his health damaged — and for all of this he received no financial reward.

Yet it had been an extraordinary experience for a young merchant from Poole. Following a tradition of adventurers, he sat down to write an account of all that had happened to him. He used what he called "the language of the sea," by which he meant not profanity but a plain, readable prose without literary flourish or pretension. The resulting volume, *A Cruising Voyage Round the World,* was published in 1712. It proved to be popular with the public and valuable to later circumnavigators, who carried it on their journeys for its "seamanly hints." (Among others, Lord Anson and Captain Shelvocke used it.) When the book was reissued in 1718, Daniel Defoe obtained a copy, and the passage about Selkirk's marooning had a profound influence on the creation of *Robinson Crusoe.*

We know very little about Selkirk's later life.

Walter Wilson, author of *Life and Times of Defoe* (1830), wrote that after he returned home from the voyage, the Scottish maroon, having been for so long alone, was unable to bear the company of other human beings. He dug a cave behind his parents' house and lived in it until he managed to adjust to being among people. As Wilson put it, "His parents, who were still living, received him with great joy; but his recluse habits induced him to shun the haunts of men, and he constructed a cave in their garden, where he sought repose in solitude."

This remarkable anecdote is hardly creditable. For, after his isolation on Más á Tierra, Selkirk lived in close quarters with a hundred or more men during the rest of the expedition — a period of more than two years! It is difficult to see how he could bear the company of so many within the confines of a ship only to become oppressed by the presence of strollers on the streets of Largo.

In any case, before long he was back to his old self. Richard Steele found him in a pub and obtained an interview during which, as we know, Selkirk expressed a longing for the serenity of his island and the purity of his Christianity while he was marooned there. Steele observed the effects of Selkirk's isolation in his countenance and bearing:

> When I first saw him I thought, if I had not been let into his character and story I could have discerned that he had been much separated from company, from his aspect and gesture; there was a strong but cheerful seriousness in his look, and a certain disregard to the ordinary things about him, as if he had been sunk in thought.

Here again we must beware the romanticizers. Anyway, if the stress of seclusion was written on the sailing master's features, it soon faded.

> Though I had frequently conversed with him, after a few months' absence he met me in the street, and though he spoke to me I could not recollect that I had seen him; familiar converse in this town had taken off the loneliness of his aspect and quite altered the air of his face.

Selkirk stayed for a time in Largo. One day he happened on a girl named Sophia Bruce, who was tending a cow. They ran off to London, where they married. But Selkirk was a wandering man. He left his wife in the city and appeared again in Largo. Some new conflict caused him to be on his way, and he drifted about the ports of England for a time before going to sea once more.

He died in 1721, still a sailor by occupation and spirit. De la Mare tells us that he "bequeathed his effects to 'sundry loving females' — including two who claimed to be his widows. But of this episode Defoe made no practical use."

While the novelist declined to include Selkirk's reputed womanizing in his book, he happily borrowed his goatskin outfit. He also appropriated his dwelling place, although he lifted it out of the Pacific Ocean and transported it over the continent of South America, putting it in the Atlantic off the coast of Brazil, some 3,500 miles northeast of its actual location. Ironically, in this more temperate climate there would be no need for a fur suit. This did not deter Defoe, and despite it being absurd for the warm locale, the attire remains one of the most memorable and widely known features of *The Life and Strange Surprising Adventures of Robinson Crusoe.*

In Largo a small statue has been erected in memory of its famous native son. And in the Pacific, two of the islands of the Juan Fernández chain, now possessions of Chile, have undergone name changes. Greater Land, on which Will and Selkirk were marooned, has been renamed in honor of . . . Robinson Crusoe. Further Out, on which, so far as we know, the Scottish sailing master never set foot, is now officially dubbed the Isle of Alexander Selkirk.

Both the captain and his mate have been dead for centuries. Like so many others we have met, their lives were hard. They routinely took grave risks — their trade required it — and suffered greatly when the wagers were lost. They are gone now, and though their stories are not often retold, there is a note for each name in history. Unlike nearly all whom they worked beside, fought against, or loved, their names are recorded and recalled. And will continue to be after most of ours are forgotten.

How, then, shall we grieve for them?

CHAPTER 6

The Occupation of Mischief
Philip Ashton on Roatán Island

Alexander Selkirk and William Dampier marooned themselves as the result of conflicts with their commanding officers. Philip Ashton chose island solitude rather than remain among such men as the youthful Dampier abhorred. Yet Ashton was not being prudish when he deplored the behavior of his captors; he had fallen into the hands of one of the bloodiest bands ever to sail under the black flag.

Heretofore we have seen only privateers, but with Ashton's story we encounter authentic pirates. The former were anxious that a clear distinction be made between themselves and the latter. Sir Francis Drake and William Dampier, for example, were both extremely sensitive about being thought of as pirates. The desires of these long dead men to the contrary, some modern historians are inclined to lump the two occupations together. The French historian Philip Gosse includes accounts of the deeds of Drake, Dampier, and Woodes Rogers in his books on sea robbers. This is nonsense, of course. Daniel Defoe, who avidly followed the exploits of Dampier and Rogers and whose *A General History of the Pyrates* is still one of the basic sources on the subject, would have asserted that men like them differ significantly from men like Blackbeard or Bartholomew Roberts.

Defoe also would have dissented from the trend of twentieth-century historians to downplay the viciousness and criminality of buccaneers. Reading some recent works about them, one gets the impression that they were hardly more than playful, slightly ribald businessmen or ocean-going entrepreneurs. The author of *Robinson Crusoe* knew better. He wrote, for example, a condemnation of

Edward Low and his men (who are featured prominently in this chapter) that, if only slightly moderated, might be made to stand for his estimation of all such villains:

> Thus these inhumane wretches went on, who could not be contented to satisfy their avarice only, and travel in the common road of wickedness; but, like their patron, the Devil, must make mischief their sport, cruelty their delight, and damning of souls their constant employment. Of all the pyratical crews that were ever heard of, none of the English name came up to this, in barbarity. Their mirth and their anger had much the same effect, for both were usually gratified with the cries and groans of their prisoners; so that they almost as often murdered a man from the excess of good humour, as out of passion and resentment; and the unfortunate could never be assured of safety from them, for danger lurked in their very smiles. An instance of this had liked to have happened to one Captain Graves, master of a Virginia ship last taken; for as soon as he came aboard of the pyrate, Low takes a bowl of punch in his hand, and drinks to him, saying, *Captain Graves, here's half this to you.* But the poor gentleman being too sensibly touched at the misfortune of falling into his hands, modestly desired to be excused for that he could not drink; whereupon Low draws out a pistol, cocks it, and with the bowl in t'other hand, told him he should either take one or the other. So Graves, without hesitation, made choice of the vehicle that contained the punch and guttled down about a quart, when he had the least inclination that ever he had in his life to be merry.

On another occasion Low cut off a man's ears and split his nose. There seems to be something of a fixation here: the deranged captain once sliced off a victim's lips and required him to watch them being broiled. This psychopath's history, in fact, is filled with mutilations, disembowelings, decapitations, and slaughter. On a day when he became annoyed with the master of a seized prize, he massacred him and his entire crew of thirty-two men.

While the degree of Ned Low's cruelty may have been uncommon, it was the custom of pirates when a ship resisted them to slaughter everyone on board. It could be argued that this policy was pragmatic since it discouraged opposition, but pirates also routinely tortured prisoners for sport. Thus, while from a safe distance we go about the business of demythologizing history, judiciously weighing and reappraising, it is well to remember that the epithets of "bloodthirsty" and "cutthroat" were attached to the names of sea robbers by their contemporaries — that is, by their victims, past or potential.

The behavior of pirates, then, was in marked contrast to that of privateers like Woodes Rogers. He endeavored to keep the casualties of his crews and those of his enemies to a minimum, and he dealt with his captives quite humanely. He would not allow his men to rape women prisoners and cautioned them against debauchery, even forbidding them to take advantage of captured female slaves.

Pirates would make the same claim to the decent treatment of female prisoners. Their constitutions generally forbade rape. For instance, the ninth article to which Captain John Phillips's men subscribed stated that "if at any time we meet with a prudent woman, that man that offers to meddle with her without her consent shall suffer present death." We should be suspicious, however, of the virtuousness of brigands. Such rules were regularly honored in the breach. Captain Bartholomew Roberts had a similar regulation, but Defoe debunks the suggestion of rectitude on the part of his men — whenever a female "fell into their hands . . . they put a sentinel immediately over her to prevent ill consequences from so dangerous an instrument of division and quarrel; but then here lyes the roguery: who shall be sentinel, which happens generally to one of the greatest bullies, to secure the lady's virtue, will let none lye with her but himself."

Rogers, in explaining to his crew the severe orders he was issuing against the mistreatment of women, remarked that proper conduct was "both for our own benefit and the future reputation of ourselves and our country." Yet when privateers insisted on the distinction being made between themselves and sea robbers, it is unlikely that they were often motivated by anxiety over how much esteem they were held in by the public. Theirs was not a concern over image, but over fate. They knew the ends that buccaneers often came to, and if they needed a reminder, they could sail into many a port and see the decomposing corpses hanging up at dockside.

If pirates were cruel and brutal, so were the fates many of them suffered. The death of Blackbeard, who died with twenty-five wounds in his body, sounds like that of the victim of a modern gangland slaying. Still, at least his was a true pirate's end — in the midst of a last desperate sea battle, he led a boarding party onto a sloop's deck and had a duel of pistols with a young British naval lieutenant, followed by a sword fight. An enviable death, perhaps, but one not every brigand was lucky enough to experience.

More than a few died miserably in jail cells of disease and hunger.

Antonio Mendoza had a particularly hard time of it: the authorities of St. Christopher's Colony cut off his ears, burned his tongue with a red-hot iron, chained him in a dungeon, and left him to rot.

At least as many pirates seem to have stretched a rope as expired in battle. Captain William Kidd died with his neck in a noose, but then his corpse was cut down and hung up again, suspended in chains alongside the bodies of six of his cohorts. This educational exhibit remained "for many years," presumably to serve as a deterrent to honest sailors who might have idle thoughts of hoisting the Jolly Roger. The public display of the cadavers of pirates and other nefarious criminals was a common practice, and evidently English authorities were reluctant to see such edifying and cautionary spectacles collapse too soon. At Newgate Prison, when Daniel Defoe was incarcerated and William Hogarth was doing sketches of its inmates, there still existed "Jack's Kitchen," in which the heads and torsos of executed criminals were boiled and treated as a means of preserving them.

Hanged men often died not of broken necks but of strangulation, as they slowly kicked and struggled. Captain John Smith, alias John Gow or Goffe, pleaded not guilty to murder and piracy but was convicted. This hapless fellow had been hanging for four minutes when the rope broke. He had the strength to climb the ladder a second time, and after he died, his body was hung in chains.

Erasmus Peterson cautioned his executioner that he was a strong man and pleaded with him to make a quick end of him. Pedro Nondre was also a man of size and strength, but he had a problem much like that of Captain Smith: he was so heavy that his rope snapped. Here again, a second rope proved sufficient for the task.

Such cheerful prospects as these guaranteed that public executions drew large, festive crowds. The entertainment value of justice can hardly be underestimated. Governor Woodes Rogers once hanged eight piratical backsliders before a huge mob of their former cohorts. Two of the condemned, festooned in red and blue ribbons, mounted the stage. Each was dressed as gaily as if he were a "Prize-Fighter," athletes apparently then as now being extremely fashion-conscious. Since it was the tradition of buccaneers to die with bravado, one of these colorfully attired fellows shouted that there was a time when those looking up at him would not have allowed him to die like a dog. Then he kicked his footwear into the crowd, explaining that he had promised not to die with his shoes on.

Referring to Rogers, another man announced that "we have a new governor, but a harsh one." He added that had he known it sooner, he would have been an even greater plague to the region.

A third fellow wished to die drunk and called for wine but was scolded by a fourth man, who suggested that where they were about to go water was what they would need.

At the last moment Rogers had a ninth man taken down off the scaffold. He was not yet twenty years old, hardly more than a boy, but the governor may have saved him less for the tenderness of his years than as a gesture to please the crowd.

Youth was not reliable protection against condemnation. John Walden was known to his shipmates as Miss Nanney, an odd nickname that the *General History* explains his being given due to the "hardness of his temper." Whatever his friends intended by the silly name, Walden was a violent, dangerous man, who, during his brief career, lost a leg in a sea battle. He was hanged at the age of twenty-four. William Davis and Abraham Harper met the same fate at twenty-three, Benjamin Jefferies and Marcus Johnson at twenty-one, John Jessup and Robert Hays at twenty, and Joseph More at nineteen.

At the other end of the spectrum, Captain John Calles was quite elderly when he tried to escape the noose by promising to help hunt down his former confederates. Authorities, alas, were unwilling to make a bargain with the old man.

Courts and governors were no more swayed by sudden religious conversion. William White was accompanied to the gallows by two solemn preachers. That his soul was on the way to heaven must have been of great comfort to those watching his heels kick spasmodically in the air.

Peter Scudamore, a surgeon, was taken prisoner when his ship was boarded by pirates. It was not the usual practice to force a doctor to join the band; when one was captured, he was held only until another physician could be seized to replace him, probably because even buccaneers were reluctant to be operated on by a surgeon with a sharp blade and a deep resentment. Scudamore, however, *insisted* on signing the articles and boasted that he was the first of his profession to do so. The degree of his skills at sawing and sewing is unknown, but he was an accomplished linguist, braggart, and scalawag. When it came time to die, however, he spent the three days between sentencing and execution in constant prayer and Bible reading. On the gallows he sang a solo rendition of Psalm 31. He might have given a whole, lovely concert of sacred music if the hangman had not been strict in his duty.

A man known only as Armstrong spent his last hours on board the H.M.S. *Weymouth* lamenting his sinful past and exhorting everyone within earshot to live an honest life. He just had time to lead the spectators in the singing of a few verses of Psalm 140 before he was pulled up the foreyard by the neck.

Domingo Eucalla may not have had such a melodious voice as these last two because he contented himself with giving a speech that drew tears to the eyes of many who heard it. He ended with a prayer and died with such dignity that of the ten pirates executed that day, he was accounted as having shown "the greatest courage."

It should not be concluded from this recitation that buccaneers were summarily executed. They were not. They were tried according to the legal conventions of the time, although these hardly fit our notion of impartial jurisprudence. Captain Kidd had a commission to take enemy prizes, but British authorities suspected that he was cheating the Crown of its full share of the proceeds. Kidd was therefore arrested on charges of piracy and murder and put through a series of trials that were grossly unfair. He was denied the opportunity to be defended by competent counsel; witnesses offered perjured testimony against him; judges were biased; and documents which he had handed over to the state — documents that would have exonerated him of at least some charges — conveniently "disappeared" until long after his death.

Judges in buccaneers' trials were sometimes naval officers or, as in the courts Rogers set up, reformed pirates. These were not men, therefore, inclined to be overly sympathetic to the accused. Boatswain John Upton produced as evidence at his trial a journal he kept while among brigands; it showed he had been forced to sign the articles and had escaped the bad company at the first opportunity. The written proof did him no good: he went to the gallows proclaiming his innocence.

Some pirates were acquitted, of course, but others never made it to trial; reflecting on their likely fate at the hands of the authorities, they chose to commit suicide instead.

Considering the miserable ends of those who sailed under the black flag, it is not surprising that privateers would be sensitive to being thought of as buccaneers. Indeed, it is amazing that anyone was willing to hoist the Jolly Roger. That many were is attributable to hard times, mental illness, a craving for adventure, or, most of all, a desire for riches.

The lives and deaths of real pirates, then, were very different from the image we have of them. This distortion began even while some of them were sailing on the main. Romantic novelists and play-wrights took them as their subjects, and after a time pirate kings came to be depicted as noblemen cheated of their rightful inheri-tances. Gilbert and Sullivan followed this line, portraying them as kind-hearted dimwits, the cowardly lions of the sea.

Hollywood embraced these notions, and cinematic sea robbers were usually shown to be lusty, athletic adventurers or were played for laughs. Such actors as Douglas Fairbanks, Sr., Charles Laugh-ton, Errol Flynn, Tyrone Power, Gilbert Roland, Burt Lancaster, Gene Kelly, Yul Brynner, Robert Shaw, Tommy Lee Jones, James Mason, Orson Welles, Robert Newton, Peter Ustinov, Kevin Kline, Walter Matthau, and, perhaps inevitably, Bud Abbott and Lou Cos-tello have assayed the role. It is doubtful that very many leading men would want to be seen in a part that called for them to cut off a man's ears or lips or execute a whole crew of helpless prisoners.

The behavior of Edward Low and his band, as seen through the eyes of Philip Ashton, is at first consistent with the false image we have of pirates. All these blackguards seem to do is bluster, make ineffectual threats, and call everyone a dog. You know by now, however, that there was a much darker side to Low than is repre-sented by these fulminations.

Ned was born in Westminster, England, and went to school there, although he failed to learn how to read and write. "Nature seem'd to have designed him for a pyrate from his childhood," for he took up thievery early on, learning to rob other boys of their farthings. Those who resisted were beaten.

As Ned grew older he took to gambling, at which he was a noto-rious cheat. Anyone who caught him at it and spoke up was in for a thrashing. Having reached his majority, Low immigrated to Boston, where he found work as a rigger. This honest labor may constitute the only blot on an otherwise unblemished record. Anyway, it was not for him — he was too inclined to argue with his employers —

and he signed on the crew of a sloop bound for Honduras to steal logwood. Returning to the vessel from a pilfering expedition late one afternoon, Ned and his captain fell into disagreement over what time supper should be served. Debates over such fine points of etiquette tend to be convoluted and drawn out, marked by soaring rhetoric and appeals to obscure precedents, but Low sought to bring this one to a quick conclusion by firing a musket at his commander. His aim was slightly off, and he blew out the brains of a bystander. Perhaps realizing that the incident might affect his superior's opinion of him, Ned hurriedly departed in a boat with a dozen comrades. The next day they took their first ship, and having made and hoisted a black flag, they "declared war against all the world." Edward Low had found his true vocation at last.

For a while he sailed in concert with Captain George Lowther, a quarrelsome but clever and successful brigand who eventually marooned himself to avoid capture and then committed suicide. When the two commanders parted company, Lowther's quartermaster, Francis Farrington Spriggs, joined Ned Low. Spriggs, in the estimation of Gosse, was an "uninteresting and bloody pirate without one single redeeming character[istic]." Ambitious, treacherous, and vicious, Spriggs could not stay with Low for long without coming into conflict with him. At the time Master Philip Ashton was captured, however, the two men were still together and with their bloody crews were having no small amount of success.

Ashton's schooner was taken by these blackguards on Friday, June 15, 1722. Disguising themselves, they slipped among the fishing vessels harbored in Port Rossaway. Four of their number climbed onto the deck of Ashton's schooner, whereupon they pulled out pistols and cutlasses and demanded the surrender of all those on board. (They would use the same strategy over and over again that day to capture more than a dozen vessels.)

The prisoners from the schooner — five men and a boy — were brought back to the buccaneers' brigantine, where their captors immediately demanded that Ashton sign their articles of agreement. In other words, they wanted him to formally join their band; a commitment in writing would ensure his loyalty and dedication in a fight. If the ship was taken, the articles would be proof that he was on board voluntarily, and thus he could be hanged for his willing participation in piracy. Ashton refused and "suffered much bad

Ned Low offers the captain of a captured prize a choice between being shot or having a drink with him. The terrified prisoner emptied the cup. (Copy print courtesy of the Library of Congress)

usage in consequence.'' When he continued to be obdurate, he was led with other prisoners to the quarter-deck to be . . . *interviewed* by the captain.

This was the infamous Ned Low himself, and he came at the captives with a pistol in each hand. He shouted at them, ''Are any of you married men?'' It was such an unexpected question that none of them knew how to answer: would saying yes get you set free — or murdered? In their alarmed uncertainty, all stood dumb. Their silence infuriated Low, who cocked a pistol and put its barrel against Philip Ashton's head.

''You dog,'' he raged. ''Why don't you answer?'' He swore that he would fire unless he got a response.

Ashton had no choice. He said that he was single.

The reply calmed Low — he took the pistol from his prisoner's skull and walked away — but it was the wrong answer. As it happened, he was willing to release those men who had families.

Low was resolved to take no married men whatever, which often seemed surprising to me until I had been a considerable time with him. But his own wife had lately died before he became a pirate, and he had a young child at Boston for whom he entertained such tenderness, on every lucid interval from drinking and reveling, that, on mentioning it, I have seen him sit down and weep plentifully. Thus I concluded that his reason for taking only single men was probably that they might have no ties such as wives and children to divert them from his service and render them desirous of returning home.

The prisoners were not alone long. Soon their captors were back to recruit them, temporarily putting aside threats in favor of flattery and persuasion. They described to Ashton all the spoils he would gain as one of their number, but when he remained steadfast, the mercurial Low became incensed once more and again swore to shoot him through the head. In the end, one of the villains forged Ashton's signature in the book.

On June 19, the buccaneers moved their belongings to a newly seized schooner, and they allowed most of their prisoners to sail for Boston in the brigantine. The rest, who were only eight in number, they kept with them. Among those in that unfortunate company was Philip Ashton, who had knelt before Low and begged to be set free.

The first time Ashton tried to escape, he climbed into a boat with two other captives who were going ashore to retrieve Low's dog — the animal had inadvertently been left behind. Before the craft could be pushed off, the quartermaster seized him by the shoulder and pulled him back on deck. When the other two men deserted, the quartermaster accused Ashton of being a party to their plot, and Ashton's denial so infuriated him that he aimed a pistol at the prisoner and snapped it, but it misfired. This only fueled the man's rage, and three more times the weapon misfired as he tried to kill his victim. When, in total frustration, he drew his cutlass, Ashton was able to save himself only by leaping into the hold.

While Low sailed about the Caribbean, taking nearly a dozen prizes in the process, Ashton watched for another chance. He thought it had come when the brigands talked of returning to New England for provisions and the recruitment of more men. He and

seven others planned to seize the pirates' vessel when she was off
the coast and the pirates were in drunken stupors. Francis Spriggs
learned of the plot and informed Low of it. Luckily the captain
discounted the accusation, but Spriggs was furious. He threatened
to shoot the would-be mutineers, adding, "You dog, Ashton, you
deserved to be hanged for designing to cut us off." Nothing came
of these fulminations, despite their ferocity.

Philip Ashton would remain with this disreputable company for
nine months before his opportunity finally came. They were visiting
an island north of the Honduran coast when the cooper and six men
went ashore to fetch water. At first they did not want to take him
along, but he managed to talk them into it. On the beach he put
them off guard by being very energetic in helping to get the casks
out of the boat and rolling them to the stream.

He took a deep drink of water and then strolled along the sand,
nonchalantly picking up stones and shells as he drifted away. Once,
when he was nearly out of musket range, the cooper shouted after
him asking where he was going. "For coconuts" was Ashton's
reply, and he headed for the woods. As soon as he was out of sight,
he began to run.

As the others were preparing to depart, they called out for him,
but he "lay snug" and silent in a thicket. They said to each other,
"The dog is lost in the woods and cannot find the way out again."
They hallooed some more. The cooper said, "He has run away and
won't come to us." They searched the nearby trees and bushes.
The cooper, a man with some kindness in him, cried, "If you do
not come away presently I shall go off and leave you alone." This
was a warning to Ashton that he was about to be marooned, but he
would not heed:

> Nothing . . . could induce me to discover myself, and my comrades,
> seeing it vain to wait any longer, put off without me.
>
> Thus was I left on a desolate island, destitute of all help and remote
> from the track of navigators; but, compared with the state and society
> I had quitted, I considered the wilderness hospitable and the solitude
> interesting.

The foraging party having rowed away, Ashton came out of the
thicket and sat down by a stream to keep a watch on the pirate
vessels. Five days later, to his great joy, they departed, and only
then did he examine his situation realistically. The cooper's implicit
warning had had merit:

I was on an island which I had no means of leaving; I knew of no human being within many miles; my clothing was scanty and it was impossible to procure a supply. I was altogether destitute of provision, nor could tell how my life was to be supported. This melancholy prospect drew a copious flood of tears from my eyes; but as it had pleased God to grant my wishes in being liberated from those whose occupation was devising mischief against their neighbors, I resolved to account every hardship light. Yet Low would never suffer his men to work on the Sabbath, which was more devoted to play; and I have even seen some of them sit down to read in a good book.

He began exploring his new Caribbean home. It was known as Roatán, and he estimated it to be eleven leagues long and thought it lay at about 16° 30′ north latitude. No human beings lived on it, but he found shards of earthenware belonging to its former Indian inhabitants. It was very hilly and had numerous fig and coconut trees. Another tree he did not recognize bore an oval fruit with brownish skin and red pulp. He was afraid to eat these until he saw wild hogs feeding on them without being sickened, and then he found them to be quite delicious.

The hogs were plentiful, as were tortoise and deer, yet though the "store of provisions abounded," he could avail himself of "nothing but the fruit." This was because he lacked a knife or any other weapon, and he did not have the means of starting a cooking fire. He dreamed of trapping the hogs and deer by digging pits and covering them with branches but had no shovel. No matter what his desires, it seemed he would have to be satisfied with fruit.

Eventually Ashton managed to locate tortoise eggs that had been buried a foot or two down in the sand. He did this by poking a stick into the ground repeatedly until the end came out with part of an egg adhering to it. He scooped out the sand with his hands and found about 150 unspoiled eggs, some of which he ate immediately; the rest he strung up on a strip of palmetto. He hung them in the sun until the insides became "thick and somewhat hard, so that they were more palatable. After all they were not very savory food, though one who had nothing but what fell from the trees behoved to be content."

There were snakes on Roatán, too. The most intimidating grew to a length of twelve to fourteen feet and had a circumference as large as a man's waist. When lying stretched out, these serpents had the appearance of moss-covered tree trunks, and the first time

Ashton came upon one of them unawares, it "opened its mouth wide enough to receive a hat and breathed on me." After that Ashton was at pains to avoid them.

The enormous numbers of small black flies were more of a problem. During his first months on the island he built several huts; the frames were constructed of branches bound together with split palmetto palms over which he laid coverings of larger leaves. Most of these shelters he built near the beach, facing the ocean, so that he could be cooled by the sea breeze and at the same time keep watch for ships. But if these open structures worked well to defend him "against the heat of the sun by day and the heavy dews at night," they afforded no protection from the pesky flies. The insects were such an annoyance that Ashton became determined to reach adjacent islands in the hope of finding some relief, even though he was a poor swimmer and lacked a canoe or raft or the means of building one.

The only life preserver he could find was a hollow piece of bamboo with which he experimented, sticking it under his arms and across his chest and kicking his feet in the water until he felt confident enough to make a try for a small key a gunshot's distance from Roatán.

Buoyed by the bamboo, he reached his destination without difficulty. He found that though it lacked trees and was less than four hundred feet in circumference, it had an overriding attraction: the wind passing unobstructed over it kept it free of flies. Even without food sources or shelter, it was for Ashton "a new world, where I lived infinitely more at ease. Hither I retired, therefore, when the heat of day rendered the insect tribe most obnoxious; yet I was obliged to be much on Roatán to procure food and water, and at night on account of my hut."

He swam back and forth between the two islands with his jersey and trousers tied to the top of his head. The journeys were not without danger, since alligators and shovel-nosed sharks hunted in these waters. At least once a shark attacked him, striking his thigh, but this occurred just as he had gotten close enough to shore to stand, and in the shallows his assailant became grounded and unable to make a second pass. Ashton had not been bitten, but his leg ached for some time afterward from the blow.

On another occasion the bamboo slipped from under his arms, and he had to fight for his life in the powerful current. Gradually his swimming improved, however, to the point where he was able to visit still other islands in the archipelago.

His shoes having fallen apart, his feet were constantly being injured. The hot sand burned them, and sticks, stones, and broken shells cut them.

Often, when treading with all possible caution, a stone or shell on the beach or a pointed stick in the woods would penetrate an old wound and the extreme anguish would strike me down suddenly as if I had been shot. Then I would remain for hours together with tears gushing from my eyes from the acuteness of the pain. I could travel no more than absolute necessity compelled me in quest of subsistence and I have sat, my back leaning against a tree, looking out for a vessel during a complete day.

Once, while faint from such injuries, as well as smarting under the pain of them, a wild boar rushed towards me. I knew not what to do, for I had not the strength to resist his attack. Therefore as he drew nearer I caught the bough of a tree and half suspended myself by means of it. The boar tore away part of my ragged trousers with his tusks and then left me.

In his weakened condition, subsisting on little more than figs and grapes, he sometimes fell into a trancelike state from which "I thought I should never wake again, or rise in life. Under this affliction I first lost count of the days of the week. I could not distinguish Sunday, and as my illness became more aggravated I became ignorant of the month also."

He was depressed. He had no "healing balsam for my feet nor any cordial to revive my drooping spirits." He was unable to enlarge his diet, and although wood was plentiful on Roatán, he was still unable to start a fire: he rubbed sticks together without producing a spark until he was utterly weary.

Earlier in his marooning he had been able to accept his lot with a certain equanimity:

One day after another was lingered out, I knew not how, void of occupation or amusement except collecting food, rambling from hill to hill and from island to island and gazing on sky and water. Although my mind was occupied by many regrets I had the reflection that I was lawfully employed when taken, so that I had no hand in bringing misery on myself. I was also comforted to think that I had the approbation and consent of my parents in going to sea, and I trusted that it would please God in his own time and manner to provide for my return to my father's house. Therefore I resolved to submit patiently to my misfortune.

A few pages later in his narrative, however, we see Philip Ashton losing his composure:

> While passing nine months in this lonely, melancholy and irksome condition my thoughts would sometimes wander to my parents; and, I reflected that, notwithstanding it would be consolatory to myself if they knew where I was, it might be distressing to them. The nearer my prospect of death, which I often expected, the greater my penitence became.

One day in November his melancholia was interrupted by the appearance of a man and a dog in a canoe. At first Ashton did not react to the sight: he had no hope that the stranger would befriend him, and if he had hostile intentions, Ashton had no means of resisting him. While still in the water, the canoeist, who was startled to see a man on what he thought would be an uninhabited shore, cautiously called out to him. Ashton assured him it was safe to land, "for I was alone and almost expiring. Coming close up, he knew not what to make of me; my garb and countenance seemed so singular that he looked wild with astonishment. He started back a little and surveyed me more thoroughly; but, recovering himself again, came forward and, taking me by the hand, expressed his satisfaction at seeing me."

He was an elderly Englishman "of grave and venerable aspect and of a reserved temper," who had lived for twenty-two years among the Spanish. He was in flight from them now because for an unspecified reason they had decided to burn him at the stake. He had paddled twenty leagues in his canoe to Roatán, seeking sanctuary, intending to live out his days there, subsisting on what he could shoot; he had brought along his dog, a gun and ammunition, and a supply of pork.

For two days these men lived together, and on the third day the stranger announced that he was going to make a hunting expedition to other islands. Ashton could not go along; the condition of his feet would not allow it. This did not seem to matter because the Englishman would be gone only a short time, and there was no danger; the sky was clear, with no signs of a storm. . . .

An hour after the old fellow had set off, a sudden, violent tempest arose, and Ashton never saw him again.

Thus, after having the pleasure of a companion almost three days, I was reduced to my former lonely state as unexpectedly as I had been relieved from it. Yet, through God's goodness, I was myself preserved from having been unable to accompany him, and I was left in better circumstances than those in which he found me; for now I had about five pounds of pork, a knife, a bottle of gunpowder, tobacco, tongs, and flint, by which means my life could be rendered more comfortable. I was enabled to have fire, extremely requisite at this time, being the rainy months of winter. I could cut up a tortoise and have a delicate broiled meal. Thus, by the help of the fire and dressed provisions, through the blessing of God I began to recover strength, though the soreness of my feet remained. But I had, besides, the advantage of being able now and then to catch a dish of crayfish, which, when roasted, proved good eating. To accomplish this I made up a small bundle of broken sticks, nearly resembling pitch-pine or candle-wood; and having lighted one end, waded with it in my hand up to the waist in water. The crayfish, attracted by the light, would crawl to my feet and lie directly under it; when, by means of a forked stick, I could toss them ashore.

Three months later, Ashton found a small canoe at the water's edge. At first he thought it was the Englishman's, but a closer examination proved otherwise. The craft would, he thought, make him "admiral of the neighboring seas as well as sole possessor and chief commander of the islands." Laying in it a stock of figs, grapes, and tortoise, he set off for the isle of Bonacco, six leagues away.

Arriving there, he spied a sloop anchored near the eastern coast. Unable to tell whether or not she belonged to pirates, he paddled around to Bonacco's western side. He would creep overland until he was close enough to get a look. He dragged the canoe ashore and undertook a trek that, because of the condition of his feet, would take two days and two nights to complete. At the end of this painful journey, during which he had often crawled on his hands and knees through dense undergrowth, he eased himself up to the edge of the beach to study the vessel, while at the same time being careful to keep himself concealed from those on board her — and found that she had sailed away.

Utterly weary, Philip Ashton slumped against the stump of a tree and immediately fell asleep. He awoke to the sound of musket fire. Leaping up, he saw in the sea before him nine periaguas (long canoes) filled with Spaniards taking aim at him. He spun and hobbled into the bushes as bullets perforated leaves and severed twigs all around him. The marksmen bellowed, "O, Englishman, we will give you good quarter!"

He thought later that had he not been so startled, he might have accepted the offer. As it was, he lay out of range in a dense thicket for several hours until he heard the Spaniards leaving. Creeping to where he could observe the departure, he noted that the sloop was flying British colors. She had been just recently captured in the Bay of Honduras, he was certain.

The next day he returned to the stump where he had fallen asleep and found that it had been struck six or seven times by musket balls, all of which had landed within a foot of where his head had been resting. For a moment he had been an unmoving target, yet the marksmen had missed. It showed, he thought, the wonderful goodness of God.

The walk back to his canoe took three days. Though he felt quite exhausted, he was glad to push off for Roatán, with which he was now more contented. Bonacco had proved to have even less to offer in the way of food, and it harbored insects "infinitely more numerous and harassing than at my old habitation." In fact, Roatán was, he thought, "a royal palace to me compared to Bonacco."

For the next four months he occupied his time by hunting and visiting the adjacent islands. One day in June 1724, while on the small key, hiding from the flies and mosquitoes, Ashton saw two canoes heading for the harbor. When the occupants glimpsed the smoke of his fire, they paused. Ashton was also hesitant: the memory of the Spaniards' attack was still fresh in his mind. He chose to slip away to his canoe and paddle to Roatán, where he had "places of safety against an enemy and sufficient accommodation for any ordinary number of friends."

The sight of him racing for the island did not comfort the visitors. They were in flight from Spaniards, as it turned out, and were not anxious to run into a pirates' ambush. So they approached the shore with great caution.

Screwing up his courage, Ashton walked out into the open. The men stopped rowing and called out, asking who he was and where he had come from. His answer brought them closer to the beach. Now they wanted to know how many men were with him. Ashton replied that he was by himself, and then he asked questions of his own. At last he invited them ashore, and they accepted — although they landed a safe distance from him and sent only one of their company toward him. The maroon went to meet this delegate, who "started back at the sight of a poor, ragged, wild, forlorn, miserable object so near him. Collecting himself, however, he took me by the hand and we began embracing each other, he from surprise and wonder and I from a sort of ecstasy of joy. When this was over he took me in his arms and carried me down to the canoes, where all his comrades were struck with astonishment at my appearance; but they gladly received me and I experienced great tenderness from them."

Ashton told them of his adventures — his capture by Low and his escape and his sixteen months alone. His story amazed them.

Observing me very weak and depressed, they gave me about a spoonful of rum to recruit my fainting spirits. But even this small quantity, from my long disuse of strong liquors, threw me into violent agitation and produced a kind of stupor, which at last ended in [the] privation of sense. Some of the party, perceiving a state of insensibility come on, would have administered more rum, which those better skilled among them prevented; and, after lying a short time in a fit, I revived.

The leader of the group was John Hope, an elderly man known as Father Hope. He had come with seventeen men from the Bay of Honduras; they had left their homes after learning that a Spanish raid was imminent. They knew of Roatán because Hope and another of their number, John Ford, had once hidden themselves for four years on a neighboring island. On that isle, named Barbarat, Hope and these Baymen had just established two "plantations," having brought with them provisions, firearms, hunting dogs, nets for tortoises, and an Indian woman to prepare their food. Actually they would be spending much of their time on a key near Barbarat, which they called the Castle of Comfort because, since it had no trees or bushes, the wind swept over it unimpeded and drove away "pestiferous mosquitoes and other insects."

The barrenness of the Castle of Comfort forced them to travel to surrounding islands for water, firewood, and materials with which to build their huts. It was while on such an errand that they found Ashton.

They took him to Barbarat and fed and clothed him. They even gave him a large wrapping gown to protect him from the dew at night while they finished constructing their shelters. They treated him with "a great deal of civility in their way," Ashton admitted gratefully, although his puritanism qualified his admiration for them.

Yet after all they were bad society; and, as to their common conversation, there was little difference between them and pirates. However, it did not appear that they were now engaged in any such evil design as rendered it unlawful to join them or be found in their company.

In any case, while among them he mended well enough to hunt with them. (Much of what they killed was smoked as a means of maintaining a "ready supply at all times.") Perhaps more important, being in the presence of so many constantly armed men gave Ashton a feeling of security. This confidence would soon prove to be misplaced.

The assault on the plantations came seven months after Ashton had been brought to Barbarat. He and three other men were returning to the island from a hunting trip one evening when, upon entering the mouth of the harbor, they saw a great flash and heard the boom of a swivel gun. It came from a large periagua floating close offshore and was followed by a volley from about twenty small arms. Hope's settlers fired back.

Ashton and the men with him, caught in the open, decided to try to slip away to another island. They took down their mast and sail and endeavored to row quietly out of the harbor. But the large periagua pursued them and was soon closing the distance between them. Ashton and the others rowed with all their might. The enemy fired, but the shot passed over their heads. When the canoe ground ashore, the Barbaratists leaped out and raced for cover while bullets cut the air around them. Their pursuers called out that they had nothing to fear — they were buccaneers, not Spaniards.

No attempt at reassurance could have been less comforting to Philip Ashton: "I had the utmost dread of a pirate; and my original aversion was now enhanced by the apprehension of being sacrificed [for] my former desertion." He and the others fled deeper into the woods.

The cutthroats contented themselves with taking the canoe and its contents and marooning the four men. This did not dismay Ashton, "who had known both want and solitude." At least this time he had companions, and they had weapons.

Ashton's fear proved to be well founded. These brigands had once held him prisoner. They were commanded by Spriggs, who had broken with Low and gone off on his own. The cause of their parting had been an argument over whether or not to hang a crewman who had murdered another man in cold blood. Low had been against the execution, and so Spriggs, who had wanted the killer to die, slipped away under the cover of darkness in the *Delight*. Eighteen men went along with him in the appropriated prize, which had formerly been the man-of-war *Squirrel*. They held an election and, not surprisingly, chose Spriggs to be their commander. They also made a Jolly Roger with the same design that Low used: a white skeleton in the middle of a black background, holding in one hand an hourglass and in the other a long dart that pierced a bleeding heart. "When this was finished and hoisted," Defoe tells us, "they fired all their guns to salute their captain and themselves and then looked out for prey."

In the West Indies they captured a Portuguese bark, and in her they found

> valuable plunder, but not contented with that alone, they said they would have a little game with the men, and so ordered them a sweat, more for the brutes' diversion than the poor men's healths; which operation is performed after this manner: they stick up lighted candles circularly round the mizzenmast, between decks, within which the patients one at a time enter; without the candles the pyrates post themselves, as many as can stand, forming another circle, armed with penknives, tucks [swords], forks, compasses, etc., and as he runs round and round, the musick playing at the same time, they prick him with those instruments. This usually lasts ten or twelve minutes, which is as long as the miserable man can support himself. When the sweating was over, they gave the Portuguese their boat with a small quantity of provisions and set their vessel on fire.

These blackguards then sailed about taking other ships, forcing sailors to sign their articles and administering beatings with cutlasses and whips whenever they felt the least inclination. The mate of one sloop, being a "grave, sober man," declined to join the band and asked to be cast away. They told him they would give him a discharge — but instead of issuing him papers, they would write it on his back. He was given ten lashes by every man on the ship, which amounted to a total of well over two hundred strokes.

The pirates continued on in this fashion — drinking, firing their cannons, and shouting huzzas when they were not engaged in bloodier work — until they arrived at Roatán. They came in two vessels

(the largest of them being a well-armed ship with twenty-four guns),
seeking to replenish their water supplies, but when they found the
neighboring island populated, they sent some of their men in a periagua to capture the residents.

In the process of defeating the Englishmen, Spriggs and his men
killed one of them, threw his body into a canoe containing tar, and
then set fire to it. After this they "shamefully abused" the Indian
woman. One of the settlers chose to join the ranks of the victors
and immediately revealed to his new confederates that John Hope
had hidden valuables somewhere in the woods. This intelligence
resulted in the old man being beaten until he revealed the location
of his treasure.

For five days Spriggs kept his prisoners aboard his ship before
finally deciding to let them go. They were put into a flat, which they
were welcome to try to sail the seventy leagues to the Bay of Honduras. Spriggs refused to give them any provisions and made them
swear not to go near Ashton and the other marooned men.

As soon as Spriggs's vessels were out of sight, Father Hope,
"little regarding the oath extorted from him," came to find his comrades in hiding. They had lived for the five days without lighting a
fire, for fear of disclosing their whereabouts, and so had been subsisting on raw victuals.

All but one of Hope's company had had enough of island existence: they elected to return to their homes on the Bay. Ashton
wanted to go with them, but the old leader counseled against it. The
journey would be very risky in an overloaded flat that had not been
designed to sail in rough seas. Then, too, the Spaniards might be
waiting at the far end of the precarious voyage. Better that Ashton
remain where he was — even in solitude — than gamble with his
freedom and his life.

Besides, he would not be alone. One individual, a man named
John Symonds, was not leaving. Symonds saw the opportunity to
make money trading with the colonists on Jamaica, and he urged
Ashton to stay and assist him. Ashton, he argued, was more likely
to get passage for New England on a ship bound from Jamaica than
any he could find in the Bay of Honduras. Since Ashton's only
desire now was to get home, he allowed himself to be persuaded.

Hope gave them a canoe, firearms, and two dogs, and then he
sailed away. For a few months the men "ranged" among the is-

lands, eventually accumulating a supply of tortoise shells that could be used as trade goods.

When the "season for the Jamaica traders approached," they went to Bonacco. One day a number of vessels arrived, but a furious storm kept their crews from coming ashore. The weather eventually improved enough for some men from a brigantine to be dispatched in a boat to search for fresh water.

Ashton studied the three occupants of the cask-laden craft as she approached the beach. Concluding from their appearance that they were Englishmen, he stepped from his hiding place and walked onto the sand, where they could get a look at him. Symonds stayed out of the way so as not to make them fear an ambush.

As so often seems to have happened at these moments, they stopped rowing at the sight of him and demanded to know who he was. He answered and then asked the same question of them. They were indeed British, and their vessel was part of a convoy bound for Jamaica under the protection of a man-of-war named the *Diamond*. By chance the brigantine was commanded by a man Ashton knew, a Captain Dove, and her home port was Salem, which was just a few miles from the house of Ashton's father. Ashton assured the sailors that they could safely land, and they did so: "A happy meeting it was for me."

The next day, the water casks having been filled, the ships set sail. Symonds wept at Ashton's leaving.

Captain Dove treated Ashton with courtesy and kindness and not only promised to take him home but, being short-handed, took him on as a crewman. Thus Ashton would not be returning to his family utterly destitute.

They left the island at the end of March 1725 and reached Salem Harbor on the first of May. Ashton calculated the time he had been gone: it was "two years, ten months and fifteen days after I was first taken by pirates, and two years and nearly two months after making my escape from them on Roatán Island. That same evening I went to my father's house, where I was received as one risen from the dead."

The *History of the Strange Adventures and Signal Deliverances of Mr. Philip Ashton* was published in Boston in 1725. Some scholars would come to argue that it was not a factual account at all, but a novel that owed a substantial debt to *Robinson Crusoe*. Philip Ashton was a real person, however. Born in Marblehead in 1702, he married twice and fathered six children. He is listed in the *Boston News-Letter* of July 9, 1722, as being one of those captured by Edward Low.

As for Francis Spriggs, he continued his plundering for a time, sailing up and down the coasts of the Americas. On one occasion he captured a ship from Rhode Island with a cargo of horses. Some of his men entertained themselves by riding these animals up and down the deck until the horses bucked them off. Eventually Spriggs's vessel was sighted by a British man-of-war that gave chase. The villains were forced to abandon ship to avoid capture, marooning themselves on Roatán Island, of all places. Their frustrated English pursuers burned their vessel and left them there. That is the last we hear of Spriggs.

Low also managed to continue his atrocities for some time longer. Despite the horrible nature of his deeds, there is often an element of bizarre humor associated with him. Once, for instance, when one of his men was threatening a prisoner with a cutlass, he accidentally struck Ned across the face, slicing open his cheek and exposing his teeth. The surgeon was sent for and stitched up the wound, but as he was "tollerably drunk" at the time, "as it was customary for everybody to be," Low was unhappy with the job and said so. The affronted doctor thereupon struck the captain "such a blow with his fists, that broke out all the stitches and then bid him sew his chops himself and be damned; so that the captain made a very pitiful figure for some time."

Eventually Low encountered and gave chase to the H.M.S. *Greyhound,* a man-of-war that both he and Captain Charles Harris mistook for a merchant vessel. In the short fight that followed, Ned unaccountably lost his courage and sailed his ship away, leaving Harris to fight alone or surrender. Harris chose the latter course and was hanged with twenty-four of his men.

> This narrow escape of Low and his companions, one would have thought, might have brought them to a little consideration of their black and horrid crimes, and to look upon this interval as an opportunity put into their hands by providence to reconcile themselves to God by a hearty and sincere repentance. But alas they were dead to all goodness and had not so much as one spark of virtue to stir them up to be thankful for such an eminent deliverance. But, instead thereof, [they] vented a million of oaths and curses upon the captain of the *Greyhound,* vowing to execute vengeance upon all they should meet with afterwards for the indignity he put upon them.

They kept these promises and in the process committed some of their most heinous crimes. Like modern terrorists, they often took reprisals against innocent victims, bystanders who had no part in their conflict with society. It is easier to slaughter sheep in their folds than to hunt wolves in the wilderness. There is no glory in cutting the throats of the helpless — no glory that is not perverse, at any rate — but neither is there risk.

There is no need to further catalogue their crimes. The few you already know are enough.

In July 1723, Ned took a new prize, which had ironically been named the *Merry Christmas,* and refitted her to make a proper pirate vessel, mounting thirty-four guns. At the same time he began to style himself grandly as *Admiral* Low. He also adopted a new flag, this one having a red skeleton on a black background. We see him for the last time skulking among the Azores and the Canary Islands.

Just how his life ended is uncertain. At the time Defoe published his *General History,* the admiral had only just recently captured the *Squirrel.* "We have no news concerning him come to England," the novelist added, "but I have heard that he talk'd of going to Brazil; and if so, it is likely we may too soon hear of some exploit or other; tho' the best information we could receive would be that he and all his crew were at the bottom of the sea."

Philip Gosse, in his delightful *The Pirates' Who's Who,* ignores this speculation but has nothing new to add: "What the end was of this repulsive, uninteresting, and bloody pirate has never been known."

Howard Pyle reported a rumor of the monster's death in "Buccaneers and Marooners of the Spanish Main," an article he wrote in 1887 for *Harper's New Monthly Magazine.* He stated that eventually Ned Low's own "vile crew of cutthroats" grew sick of the smell of the blood their commander spilled and refused to obey his orders to disembowel a harmless captive. Low could do nothing but offer the appearance of a hideous grin as he gnashed his teeth in impotent rage. "The end of this worthy is lost in the fogs of the past: some say that he died of a yellow fever down in New Orleans; [that] it was not at the end of a hempen cord, more's the pity."

Captain Edward Low was certainly bloody, as Gosse would have it, and he was indisputably repulsive, but he was hardly uninteresting. There is not one dull thing about the man. He compels the same unwavering, dry-mouthed attention as any modern mass murderer. Those who move among us, however, all seem to have prosaic, banal personalities; except in their moments of monstrosity, there is nothing vivid about them.

But there is something searingly bright and vivacious (albeit maniacally so) about Ned Low. In his rage he burns like a great fire moving across a landscape, leaving nothing but devastation behind.

That he did not die of one of the childhood diseases that took so many of his generation is a cause for profound regret. That he was not confined at Newgate or Bedlam early enough in his life to keep him from doing great harm is another such cause. Given that he did live and stay free to do what he did, his not winding up at the end of a rope, and a weak one with a poorly tied knot at that, is rank injustice.

But the *pity* is that he was not born two centuries sooner. What a play Shakespeare or Ben Jonson could have made of his life! The steam from the blood in which he steeped himself would have driven the wheels of their verse to whirl wildly, spinning wide ribbons of glowing colors.

If we must have horror, then at least we might have the comfort of poetry.

CHAPTER 7

Heaven's Gracious Justice
An Unknown Man on Ascension Island

William Dampier had been marooned for a time on Ascension Island. One has the impression that his stay there was not too arduous, but perhaps the lack of a detailed report is misleading. While the isle is fairly large, its terrain is bleak and its supplies of food and water difficult to locate. However, Dampier landed there with a whole ship's company; he had plenty of men to form foraging and hunting parties and to fan out in coordinated, systematic searches for springs. For one person, prolonged confinement on the island would have been much more strenuous—and alarming.

His story would have been lost to us as surely as his name has been had he not kept a journal after having been put on Ascension by order of the commodore of the Dutch Fleet on May 5, 1725. That he did not identify himself is regrettable; one wishes to know just who went through all of that agony. The man who comes through the diary's pages seems very human: deceived, uncertain, self-deluding, and bedeviled by his fears and guilt.

The cause of his marooning is at first unclear. A contemporary wrote that he had been put ashore because he was guilty of "a most enormous crime," one of the "blackest dye." This is puzzling when one considers the brutality of the age and the rough, worldly lives of mariners in the early eighteenth century. What could be so heinous to tough men such as these that they would abandon one of their fellows on a desolate isle? Mutiny? Murder? Treason?

On that Saturday in May he was dropped on the beach with seemingly adequate supplies: some clothing, a tent, a tarpaulin, a hatchet, a knife, an old frying pan, a fowling piece, a tea kettle, two buckets, a water cask, and some very small amounts of edible provisions (onions, peas, rice, and chick peas, which he knew as calivances).

He left the large, cumbersome water cask where he had been put ashore and walked along the sand for about a mile until he found a good spot to pitch his tent. The next day, he began to hunt for food, climbing a high cliff to look for game or vegetation to satisfy his already "raging hunger." He found none, to his "great sorrow and confusion." Immediately he began to brood over his misspent life and the "justice of the Almighty, who had thought it fit to punish me in so exemplary a manner for the foul crimes I had committed; and [I] sincerely wished that some unforeseen accident would put a period to those days which my malpractices had rendered miserable."

This is the first indication of a behavior pattern he was to display frequently during his ordeal: seeking food or water and not finding it, he would give up the search too quickly and fall into lamentation and self-accusation. Later he would sometimes spend days at a time praying for the redemption of his soul and the preservation of his life. However efficacious this may have been for his spiritual salvation, it was a dangerous error in terms of bodily survival. For though the island was inhabited by species of birds, turtles, and goats, it was necessary for him to hunt them diligently. Too often in the early days of his marooning his religious fixation kept him from searching for food.

That second evening, prayerful and melancholy, he returned to his shelter — having first had difficulty locating it — empty-handed and discouraged. He busied himself covering it with the tarpaulin and fortifying it with stones. Before the sun went down, he also managed to shoot three boobies, but in doing so he expended all his powder and shot. Hereafter he would have to trap the birds. (His captain had not provided him with much ammunition, having assured him that it would be unnecessary since ships regularly passed the island, and he would soon be rescued.)

On the third day he climbed a hill overlooking the ocean and put up a distress signal, using a white shirt for a flag and the now useless fowling piece as a pole. He also went to retrieve his water cask from the place where he had first come ashore, but while hauling it to his camp he broached it, spilling much of its contents before he could turn it on its head. It would prove a costly bit of clumsiness.

He moved his flag to the other side of the isle on the next day. Along the way he encountered a huge turtle, the first he had seen, and killed it with the butt of his musket. The reptile was too large for him to carry, so he left it and returned later with his hatchet, splitting its shell and taking along some of the flesh of the forefin to be salted and dried in the sun. He would come back for the rest of the turtle the next day.

He managed to trap several boobies, and he moved his tent to the most "commodious place on the whole island . . . which was no small satisfaction to one who labored under such deplorable circumstances."

On May 10 he walked across part of Ascension, seeking a suitable location for a garden, "looking carefully all the way on the sand in order to discover a rivulet of water or the footsteps of some beast, by whose track I might in time find out the place where they drank." (His thinking was correct: herds of wild goats roamed about, drinking from small streams, pools, and the crevices in boulders where rainwater collected, but he would not learn that for some time to come.) He came across some purslane, "part of which I ate for my refreshment."

He continued his search the next day, finding some "roots which had a taste not unlike that of potatoes," but he was apprehensive about eating them. He went back to his shelter that night, "almost choked with thirst" and feeling disconsolate, "being much disordered in mind and body."

It was Friday. He had been there just one week.

By now there was something of a routine to his solitary existence. He would eat birds and turtle eggs and flesh, mixing the meat with rice and other of his provisions. (He fished but never caught anything.) He would make it his "usual custom to walk out every day in hopes of a distant view of ships upon the ocean, forced by stress of weather to make towards this desolate island to repair their damages." At times he could find no game for days and would know terrible hunger. He was easily dispirited by the arduousness of his life and by loneliness. He tried to keep a booby for a pet, but it soon died.

His prayers and Bible study seem to have agitated more than comforted him. For instance, after he had carelessly left a tinder box on his quilt, causing a fire that did minor damage to some of his possessions, he spent the whole day in admiring the infinite goodness of Almighty God, who had so miraculously preserved the small remainder of my worldly treasure; and sometime tortured myself with the melancholy reflection of the inexpressible punishment my crimes deserved, well knowing the wages of sin was inevitable death and that my crime was of the blackest dye; nor could I possibly form an idea in my mind of a punishment that could make the least atonement for so great an offence.

If he was physically uncomfortable and psychologically disturbed, he was still surviving, and he would continue to be able to do so — as long as all the elements in the fragile equation held.

The first crisis began on June 8. He was running out of fresh water, and what little he had left was going bad. It was so thick that he was obliged to strain it with his handkerchief. Thirsty and panicky, he went to the middle of the isle and dug a hole seven feet deep but found no water at the bottom. He went back to his camp and dug another well there, going down a fathom without finding moisture: "My grief was inexpressible to find no water to relieve me from this desolate island, where there is nothing left that can long subsist a human creature."

Now he had genuine cause to be afraid. Since the last week in May he had sighted neither bird nor turtle, and his provisions would soon give out. There would be no food except for a few roots of uncertain edibility, and the water would be gone, too. . . .

He slept little that night, kept awake by his "meditations and dismal reflections on my unhappy state."

On the ninth he was once more unable to discover food or water, and the next day he tried to prepare himself to die. Then he remembered once having heard that somewhere on Ascension was a well, and he set out with new hope to locate it. He resolved not to give up without searching every inch of ground.

Despite his thirst and the terrible heat, he kept looking until he grew very faint and believed himself near death. At the end of his strength and in complete despair, he found a hollow place in a boulder, from which flowed a stream of clear, cool water. His joy was immense; his spirits soared. He gorged himself, drinking to "that excess as to almost hurt myself." His thirst slaked, he rested beside the stream for some time and then drank again.

He returned to his tent and the next day came back; although he lacked the energy to bring his buckets, he did carry a little firewood, his tea kettle, and some rice, which he boiled beside the stream. The day after that, "with much trouble" he lugged two full buckets back to camp.

The second crisis was already building. His shoes had fallen apart, and he walked barefoot with great difficulty. The rocks slashed his feet and tripped him; carrying the buckets, he became afraid he would fall and smash them. Without them he was sure he could not live.

The obsessions with getting off the island on the one hand and saving his soul on the other mounted and merged in his distressed mind, feeding his panic. Early in June he wrote that

> it would be useless to relate how often I strained my eyes, misled with distant objects, which the earnest desire of my delivery made me believe to be some ships approaching. The roaring torrent of the ocean, intermixed with the sun's bright rays, presented to my view a yellow gloom, not much unlike the moon when part obscured. The streaks of the element and every cloud seemed to me as a propitious sail. But reflect how dreadful was the shock when from my tired eyes the object flew and left behind sad scenes of black despair.

He continued to walk the beach daily, scanning the horizon and reminding himself that his captain had told him that during this season vessels passed Ascension. He still had a few dried provisions and some salted meat, but now he was eating weeds and roots that he had formerly shunned. Hysteria was growing.

On June 16, after he had made his shoreline patrol and returned to his tent

> to repose myself, where in the solemn gloom and dead of night I was surprised by an uncommon noise that surrounded me, of bitter cursing and swearing mixed with the most blasphemous and libidinous expressions I ever heard. My hair stood on end with horror and cold sweat trickled down my pallid cheeks. Trembling I lay, fearful to speak, lest some vile fiend more wicked than the rest should make a prey of me, food fit for devils after my revolt from the just laws of Heaven. For no man living but would have thought the Devil had forsook his dark abode and come attended by infernal spirits to keep his hell on earth, being very certain that there was not a human creature on the island except myself, having never observed the footsteps of a man since being there.

Their discourse and their actions [were] such that nothing but
devils could be guilty of, and one more busy than the rest kept such
a continual whisking of his tail about my face that I expected nothing
less than to be instantly torn to pieces by them. Among the rest I
imagined to have heard the voice of a friend of mine, with whom in
this lifetime I was very conversant. Sometimes I imagined myself to
be agitated by an evil spirit, which made me apply to the Almighty
for succor and forgiveness of my sins. I believe it was near three
o'clock in the morning before this hellish tumult ceased; and then,
being quite weary and spent, I fell asleep.

He arose at seven in the morning, thanking God for the with-
drawal of his tormentors, but immediately he heard piercing shrieks
outside his shelter. So he took up his prayer book and read those
selections "proper for a person in my condition." Even as he did
this, however, a demonic voice whispered the accusation of the sin
of which he was guilty, that great offense, that most enormous crime
requiring his being cast out of the company of men: "*Bugger!*" it
hissed. "*Bugger!*"

The man prayed on, yet still the hoarse persecution came. *Bugger! Bugger!*

The wretched soul concludes his account of the incident by saying
that he could not "afford paper sufficient to set down every particular of this unhappy day."

The next day, Sunday, he took his buckets to the stream and
brought them back, all the while dreading the night to come and
pleading with God to prevent his further haunting. He was spared
that night, but in the light of day he was visited by another apparition, this one in the shape of a man he thought he "perfectly knew";
apparently he had once been his lover. "He conversed with me and
touched so sensibly in exposing the diabolical life of Nature, for
which I was then a sufferer and fiercely repented of, that I wished
the shock would have ended my miserable life."

His wish not having been granted, on Monday he crossed Ascension, taking along his hatchet. He found no food, but he did discover
a tree that had washed up on shore. He chopped it into pieces and
carried as much of the wood on his shoulders as he could. Halfway
back to his camp he stopped to rest, and when he did so, the specter
again appeared before him, filling him with horror. It was indeed
the ghost of the fellow he had known. Before his death he had been
a soldier in Batavia. "His name I am unwilling to mention," writes

the diarist, "not knowing what the consequence may be. He haunted me so long that he began to be familiar with me."

Somehow the maroon managed to get back to his shelter, and for several days there were no further visitations ("which made me hope the damned had resumed their dismal caves"). But then one night they returned, redoubled in their rage and fury, "tumbling me up and down so in my tent that in the morning my flesh appeared like an Egyptian mummy." They played other poltergeists' tricks on him, too, tossing his saucepan in the air, putting out his light, and leaving his meager possessions in great disarray.

The ghost of the friend was with them and spoke to him several times; the beleaguered man "could [not] think he meant any harm, for when he was living we were as friendly as brothers."

The man began to hope that his enduring these torments would be considered by heaven to be an atonement for "my heinous crimes, in making use of man to satisfy my hellish and ungovernable lust, despising woman, which his hand had made a far more worthy object. My death begins to draw near, my strength decays and life is now become an insupportable burden."

At this juncture he managed to resume his routine for some days. He traveled barefoot over rocky ground, carrying his buckets, looking for water and food. He prayed, giving up four precious days to plead for mercy, salvation, and rescue. He checked on his flag. He despaired.

> [I] found the hand of Providence withdrawn. Insuperable grief and care oppressed my anxious soul. My senses were overwhelmed in depth of thought and every moment threatened my destruction. What pangs, alas!, do wretched mortals feel who headstrong tread the giddy maze of life and leave the beauteous paths of righteousness, pleased to increase the number of the damned.

The third crisis he brought on himself. He hauled his tent, bedding, and "necessaries" to the center of the isle so that he could be close to the stream on which his survival depended. Moving so far away from the shore was at least a tacit admission that rescue was not imminent, that he might dwell here until he died. But he had not gone back to check the rivulet of water before making the trek, and when he arrived, lugging his goods, he discovered to his "great astonishment" that it had dried up. The labor had been for naught. He consoled himself with turtle eggs boiled in a little water he had brought along and with purslane that he gathered late in the day from the tops of high, rocky hills.

With his water supply running low and his skin scorched by the sun, he once again gave in to a feeling of hopelessness.

Yet there was hope. Standing on top of a hill the very next day, scanning the sea for ships, he spied on the beach a piece of wood embedded in the sand; from a distance he took it to be a tree. Coming close to it, however, he found it was a cross, and he embraced it. The cross proved to be a grave marker and, therefore, confirmation that vessels did indeed visit here, if only so crews could bury the dead. The same day he discovered further proof in the form of a broken glass bottle.

Elements of hope and despair intermingled. On the day he found the cross, his feet were severely lacerated by sharp stones. Arriving at his tent with a bundle of wood, he heard the apparitions again; this time, instead of shrieking, they made a "dreadful noise, resembling many coppersmiths at work."

This was on the twenty-ninth of June. That evening he drank the last of his water.

The next day he resumed his search for food and water but could locate nothing, encountering instead a new and ominous manifestation: a "ghastly skeleton" with one hand raised and a bony finger pointing at its throat. He took it for a grim prophecy of his fate: he would die of thirst.

On Sunday, July 1, having thought for so long that no large animals lived on the isle, and being absorbed in a fantasy that his corpse would be eaten by carrion birds, he was startled to see from a hilltop a huge herd of goats "a-grazing in the distance, which I chased with all the speed I was able, but to my sorrow found they were too swift for me." He tracked them, hoping to discover their watering place. What he found was a pit six fathoms deep into which he climbed; the bottom of it was dry. He decided that the animals frequented it because it would collect water after a rain. He marveled at "how the goats keep themselves alive in a dry season, since water is so scarce throughout the whole island."

He gave up following them and wandered to another part of Ascension. Here, to his amazement, he came upon a second herd even larger than the first: "As there were so many on the island it is surprising I had not discovered them sooner, but believe they give their young ones suck in the holes of the rocks, till the sun has drawn the moisture thence, then sally out abroad in search of more."

The tracking of this group was more fruitful. He found about two gallons of water in a boulder's crevice. On August 3, he found a little more water "that goats had left in the hollow of a rock." He carried it back to his tent in his bucket. It was the last he would find. The prophetic vision was coming true. "Tongue can't express nor thought devise the wretched torments I endured."

The following day he sighted what he thought was a house. He raced toward it, only to discover that it was a hollow white boulder. Again his hopes were dashed; he found that it contained not men but only the refuse of their visit — a cache of nails and glass — which were "of little service to me; therefore I took my wood and went home."

Certain that he would soon be dead, he endeavored to prepare himself "for that great and terrible change which I was sufficiently convinced was near at hand, begging for salvation through the merits of my blessed Lord and Savior Jesus Christ, who shall change our vile bodies and make them like unto his."

He had prayed for a ship, but no sail appeared on the horizon. He had prayed for rain and watched the sky for clouds; no rain fell. He had asked God to deliver him as He had Moses and the Israelites, by causing "water to gush out of the rock." The stones did not give up moisture, rather the stream and pools had gone dry. His suffering, he was sure, was even greater than that of the Chosen People, in that he was "banished from all human society and left to be devoured by the birds of prey, who infest this desolate island."

Even the demons seemed to recognize his plight and turn away. They had appeared only twice in early August, cursing him, making a loud noise, and causing a flock of birds to block out the sun. This was poor magic compared with their earlier performances. By the middle of the month they had altogether forsaken him, gone skulking back to their caves in hell, no doubt muttering in muted fury.

Without their perverse presence, he was utterly alone on Ascension. One day he went to the garden he had planted and was delighted to see that three or four calivances were coming up, but a closer look showed that "vermin had devoured all the rest, which dampened my former joy." The culprits were probably rats that he would encounter for the first time one evening two weeks later.

Having wandered far from his camp, he lay down between two
boulders for the night. In the darkness the rodents came in such
enormous numbers that he feared they would eat him alive.

They did not. His agony was not at an end, but he was reaching
his lowest point. It came on August 21, his 108th day in solitude;
his thirst being extreme, his lips stuck painfully together, he was
faced with the necessity of taking in *some* moisture and chose
the only alternative to sea water: "I was forced to make water in
my scoop and drank my urine, thinking it wholesomer than salt
water."

The next day, August 22, while walking along the strand, he
discovered a turtle, which he promptly killed, and he drank a gallon
of its blood. The blood sickened him even while failing to "quench
my raging thirst, so that I was forced to drink a large quantity of my
urine."

He let the remaining blood "settle" overnight in the hope that it
would become more digestible, but in the morning he felt compelled
to add urine to it and to boil tea in the mixture. Later in the day,
having drunk more raw blood, he was "taken so violently with the
flux . . . that I could hardly stand. This was rather a satisfaction to
me than a shock, hoping the sooner to end my miserable days,
desiring nothing more."

He felt ill all the time now. His feverish thoughts were almost
exclusively on death, and his fervent prayers beseeched the Almighty to bring it on him.

On August 28 he killed a turtle and drained its blood into his
bucket, then drank the contents of its bladder, the urine "being
much better than the blood." It proved no more digestible, however: shortly thereafter he vomited.

He could not sleep for thirst, and his head swirled with dizziness.
In his extremity he expected to go mad. Instead, retaining his sanity, he resumed the search for water and continued writing in his
diary:

> On the thirtieth I prayed to be dissolved and be with Christ, for the
> most part of the day thinking my suffering exceeded that of Job, I
> being debarred the pleasure of human conversation, sick and had no
> clothing; my actions unjustifiable, my torments inexpressible and my
> destruction unavoidable. I tried to compose myself after I had prayed
> to the Almighty for rain or that I might die before morning. In the
> afternoon I endeavored to get out of my tent but could not walk, I

was so weak; therefore dressed some turtle eggs. I had some turtle flesh in my tent but it was not sweet, but was in such agony for want of water that tongue can't express. I caught three boobies and drank the blood of them.

On the last day of the month, still unable to walk, he crawled on the sand. Coming on a turtle, he chopped off its head and "then laid myself on my side and sucked the blood as it ran out; afterwards put my arm into the body and plucked his bladder out, which I crawled away with to my tent."

Painfully he came back again to cut up the meat and retrieve the eggs. In the process he broke the helve of his hatchet. He barely noticed this misfortune — it occasioned no bitter lamentations. He could think about nothing except getting back to his shelter with the eggs, which he then cooked and ate along with tea boiled in his urine. The drink at once nauseated and revived him.

Without the use of his hatchet, he was forced to crush the shell of the next turtle he killed. In the process he inadvertently broke the gallbladder, making the blood bitter, but he drank it anyway, certain he would die if he did not.

He expressed his ambivalence about dying by remarking that his "ardent desire to meet approaching death both cherished and tortured my departing soul." Wanting his life to end, he yet sought to prolong it. On September 2, he drank a quart of salt water, expecting to expire immediately as a consequence; instead he slept fitfully and awoke feeling stronger.

During this remission, he fitted a new helve to his hatchet and fed upon turtle meat, eggs, and blood.

He ran out of food on Saturday, September 8, which was his 127th day on Ascension. One week later he inscribed this passage into his journal:

I am become a moving skelton, my strength is entirely decayed, I cannot write much longer. I sincerely repent of the sins I committed and pray, henceforth, no man may ever merit the misery which I have undergone. For the sake of which, leaving this narrative behind me to deter mankind from following such diabolical inventions. I now resign my soul to him that give it, hoping for mercy in

Here the diary ends. The harrowing journey had been completed. The longed-for release had been attained. The burden he had borne sometimes querulously but always with agony and perverse pride had been lifted from him at last.

He had not been deceived after all. Ships did visit the island. The lookout of one such, the *Compton*, saw the signal flag. Captain Mawson sent men ashore, and they brought back the diary that they found lying near the skeleton of its author.

If the sailors who discovered his remains buried them, they left no record of it, and the site has been lost as surely as his name. What lingers is the extraordinary record he made, one that preserves his torment and touches the reader and gives him cause to wonder.

CHAPTER 8

A Country Peopled with Christians

Marguerite de la Roque on the Isle of Spirits

The story of that wretched man on Ascension Island, with its demons and marooning as punishment for sexual transgression, recalls another tale. This one concerns a Frenchwoman by the name of Marguerite de la Roque, who was betrayed by her cousin and left by him to die on an island off the eastern coast of Canada.

In both cases the marooning resulted not from an accident or disagreement but because of a violation of social norms. Of course, in a society more ostensibly and severely religious than our own, the Ascension diarist's offense was considered to be tremendous. Since the thirteenth century, homosexuality had been a capital crime in much of Europe, and had come to be associated in the popular as well as the ecclesiastical mind with those several perceived great threats to society and the individual soul: witchcraft, heresy, and Judaism. Persons accused of any one of these were often persecuted for the others as well, and homosexuals were put to death just as surely as witches and heretics were. (There is a reluctance on the part of the state to abandon even such extreme expressions of prejudice: in the American colonies, homosexuals were still being executed as late as 1625 or possibly 1646, although the few who were put to death here seem always to have been convicted of the rape or seduction of minors. The French continued executions until 1789, and British authorities put to death four sodomite crewmen of the H.M.S. *Africaine* in 1816.)

Marguerite's marooning is as appalling as that of the nameless homosexual. Her cousin may have exiled her because he was puritanical or feared that she would bring down God's disfavor on the enterprise he led, or perhaps — and this is the only explanation comprehensible to us — he was greedy for the wealth that he stood to inherit if she died. Whatever the true reason, her experience has fascinated a good many writers and historians. She has been the subject of plays, novels, and scholarly studies almost from the time she was returned to civilization.

In her own lifetime, three chroniclers set down her tale (one of them repeating it in two different tomes); they disagreed on some matters, and each supplied certain information the others did not include. The first to report the story was another Marguerite — Marguerite d'Angoulême, the queen of Navarre. Her recitation, published in L'Heptaméron in 1558, begins with the intention of a French explorer by the name of Jean-François de la Roque, sieur de Roberval, to colonize the Canadian wilderness:

> In order to people the country with Christians, he took with him all sorts of artisans, among whom there was one who was base enough to betray his master, so that he was near falling into the hands of the natives. But it was God's will that the conspiracy should be discovered; and so did no harm to Captain Roberval, who had the traitor seized, intending to hang him as he deserved. He would have done so but for the wife of this wretch, who, after sharing the perils of the sea with her husband, was willing to follow his bad fortune to the end. She prevailed so far by her tears and supplications, that Roberval, both for the services she had rendered him and from compassion for her, granted what she asked. This was that her husband and herself should be left on a little island in the sea, inhabited only by wild beasts, with permission to take with them what was necessary for their subsistence.

This passage, however touching, is inaccurate. Her Majesty was writing of events that occurred only fifteen years earlier, and two of the principals of the case were still living when she set it down. She was compelled to disguise the identities of all of the actors in the drama and to be disingenuous about their parts in it. After all, the marooned woman had suffered greatly, and there was no need to add to her burden now — especially since she was an aristocrat, as were the two men. Her "husband," in fact, far from being a skilled laborer, was apparently so well born that none of the early historians were willing to identify him, and so his name has been lost to us. As for Roberval, he was a powerful and ambitious man at the court of the queen's brother, King Francis I of France, and had been selected by His Majesty to lead the expedition on which the marooning took place. No, it was far wiser to say that the young couple was from the class of skilled workers and to hold up Roberval as a compassionate, disinterested commander rather than show him to be the furious, vengeful, and cruel man he was.

It is true that Roberval meant to found a colony. He was a spendthrift deeply in debt, and his creditors were hounding him; the "great revenues" of a prosperous New World settlement would relieve his financial plight, and he had willingly sold at least one of his own estates to underwrite the enterprise. (He gathered additional monies for it by committing piracy against Portuguese and English merchants with some of his fleet, while his subordinate, Jacques Cartier, went ahead to Canada with the rest of the expedition.)

Yet founding a colony was only the first part of Roberval's plan. Once established, the colony would function as a kind of base camp from which he could probe at leisure for the fabulous kingdom of Saguenay. Believed to be inhabited by a fierce race of pale-skinned warriors who wore wooden armor, Saguenay was said to be incredibly rich in gold and silver, diamonds and precious stones. This mythical realm was the invention of Indians, who excited the greed of French explorers by touching the white men's silver chains and gilt dagger handles and then, pointing north, cried, *"Saguenay! Saguenay!"*

A kingdom of such worth must be located and its treasure brought back to France before other Europeans could exploit it. Cartier had made a voyage to discover the place, and his failure to do so might have been the reason that, on the next try, he was demoted in favor of Roberval. The sieur had an immense monetary stake in the venture and would have had no desire to serve as second-in-command on the *third* expedition to Saguenay. Nothing would be allowed to jeopardize the success of this enterprise or detract from its glory — certainly not the love interests of a woman, even one very close to him.

One obstacle that had to be overcome before the voyage could get underway was a notable lack of volunteers for the colony. Roberval managed to recruit a few aristocrats, including his cousin, but commoners did not rush to join up. Establishing a settlement in the New World was a hazardous undertaking, and the high mortality rate among settlers was well known. (Besides the dangers present in all colonies, in Canada scurvy was as common and as deadly as on shipboard.) Roberval was hardly able to enlist the variety of dedicated artisans mentioned by Queen Marguerite, but he was very successful at securing large numbers of convicts, many of whom, both men and women, arrived at the embarkation site manacled and in chain gangs.

Were Marguerite and the young nobleman lovers before they embarked? The answer is probably not. The second contemporary chronicler, François de Belleforest, a writer of sometimes fanciful imagination, describes him as a "gentleman, young, lusty, hale, handsome and gracious . . . who perhaps undertook the voyage for no other occasion than to insinuate himself into the good graces of [Marguerite]."

The suitor — a man with the proper social refinements and accomplishments, as Belleforest depicts him — entertained the ship's company with his *citre* (a lutelike instrument), playing and singing clever and passionate verses of his own composition. What he was really about was the wooing of the damsel. He won her heart at last with a long and plaintive love song written especially for her.

André Thevet, the third chronicler and author of the most comprehensive account, was less interested in courting rites, saying only that the gentleman approached her "so privately that in spite of the perils and dangers which are offered to those who travel at the mercy of the winds, they played their games together so well that they went beyond promises or mere words."

A sixteenth-century sailing vessel offered little opportunity for secret trysts, but the lovers were aided in their assignations by Marguerite's old servant, a native of Normandy, named Damienne. She "stood sentinel" outside the place of rendezvous, watching to see that they were not surprised or interrupted. Thevet, who was a friend of Roberval and had been a Franciscan friar, reflects the captain's judgment that Damienne bore responsibility for the immorality beyond that of just being a guard: he calls her a bawd (a procuress or madam), as if she had arranged the whole affair.

Even with the watchfulness of the old woman, the secret could not be kept for long. Several people went quietly to Roberval with reports. He was indignant, furious. Marguerite had betrayed him.

She was more than his cousin and charge, she was his confidante; he had trusted her above all others with his secrets. She had violated the precepts of his religion as well: he was a Calvinist who feared God and believed that "this offended Him." But Roberval would not act against his cousin yet. He would bide his time and wait for the right moment to strike against both of them — but particularly against her, who had violated his trust and brought shame on him.

Elizabeth Boyer, author of *A Colony of One,* a new and exhaustive study of the case, suggests a baser motive for Roberval's plan. As Marguerite's guardian, he had charge of her financial holdings. If she married, he would be forced to give the groom's family a very thorough accounting of her finances. He was not a careful man with money, and he was in debt. Had he misappropriated her funds, her wedding would mean his exposure. If, to the contrary, she were to die before she could marry — and not by his hand — he would be safe.

In his rage, which he "discreetly and wisely dissembled . . . and harbored," he decided to maroon Marguerite on the Isle of Spirits in the Gulf of St. Lawrence off the coast of Quebec. The island, which appeared on old charts and was also known as the Isle of Demons, had been named for the apparitions that were said to dwell there. These included shades "which visibly show themselves and make attempts to lead men astray, and principally appear as remembered figures which have been drowned in some violent adventure and appear to those who will recognize them, showing thus openly that which was not at all known of their deaths." These "homeless and tortured ones" made terrible noises and played terrifying tricks. Their reputation was so fierce that no one had ever settled on their island, and no white people would even go ashore there.

It was a wild place inhabited by bears and other carnivores and occasionally visited by Indian war parties. The climate and soil were not conducive to planting. To maroon his young cousin here was to sentence her to death, and this is exactly what Roberval did. He also cast onto the beach Damienne, the servant who had conspired with the lovers. He gave them four arquebuses (soldiers' weapons, which the women probably did not know how to use), some ammunition, and supplies. He told them, according to Thevet, that "this was the place he had ordained for their punishment for the scandal which she had brought upon him."

Roberval made a mistake, however, which foiled his design. He had intended marooning the lover on a separate island but had failed to put him in irons. Now here the young man came, bringing with him his arquebus. Despite the terrible reputation of the isle, he chose to share his mistress's fate.

He is sometimes pictured as leaping over the side of the ship and swimming ashore, but Boyer argues that he was an experienced military man who would be unlikely to risk getting the arquebus wet. She believes he used it to threaten Roberval, forcing him to load a boat with supplies and ferry them and him to the beach. Certainly the arquebus in the hands of a trained combatant was a fearsome weapon — rather like a hand-held cannon — and its discharge on a crowded deck would have been devastating; the flame from its barrel might even have set the vessel on fire. Thevet would seem to offer support for such conjecture, reporting that the provisions the lover brought onto the land included clothing, several bushels of biscuits, his citre, canvas, tools, a fusil (a light weapon or a device to ignite fires), and some other supplies. This would be too great a load for even a strong young man to bear on his back as he swam to shore.

Roberval could not resist taunting his victims. Belleforest, who has it that Marguerite was already pregnant (and that she was the captain's sister), tells us that he shouted this speech across the water:

> As for you (said he to the Gentleman) since I hear that you string rhymes together rather passably, you will find ink and paper to write and compose virelays and ballades, to gain the grace of your gentle Goddess, since it is with songs that you won her. Live joyfully and be of great cheer until I come by here again to visit you and see how you are managing in your household and with what diligence you will nourish and instruct this little nephew, whom you have made, without advising me as to your intentions in this gallant project.

Her tears and pleadings did not weaken his resolve, and he gave orders that his ships were to set sail immediately, for fear that the sight of her weeping on the shore might cause his subordinates to pity her and go to her aid.

Those left behind had no time for the composition of rhymes. They built a small log cabin and made beds of branches. "When the lions and other wild beasts approached to devour them, the husband with his arquebus, and the wife with stones, defended themselves so well that not only the beasts durst not approach them but even they often killed some of them which were good to eat.'' Eventually they became quite expert hunters — "with her lover in the reckoning they made a terrible slaughter" — and they supplemented their diet of meat with herbs and fruits.

The evil shades came to attack their dwelling, assuming the shapes of horrible creatures. The maroons responded by repenting of their sins and reading the *New Testament,* and so the assaults diminished. Yet they did not cease: the apparitions would no longer come in daylight but waited until after dark to begin their torment. Damienne, Marguerite, and her lover lay upon their leafy pallets and listened to "cries so loud that it seemed to them as though they were made by more than a hundred thousand men, making them together.''

Many months after they landed, when Marguerite was near term with child, her lover died. The cause may have been the stress and sorrow of their island life, as André Thevet claims, or diet, as the queen of Navarre would have it:

> They drank such unwholesome water that he became greatly swollen and died in a short while, having no other service or consolation than his wife's, who acted as his physician and confessor; so that he passed with joy from his desert to the heavenly land. The poor woman buried him in a grave which she made as deep as she could; the beasts, however, immediately got scent of it and came to devour the body, but the poor woman firing from her little dwelling with her arquebus, hindered her husband's body from having such a burial. Thus living like the beasts as to her body and like the angels as to her spirit, she passed the time in reading, contemplation, prayers, and orisons, having a cheerful and contented spirit in a body emaciated and half dead.

Although Marguerite grieved, she could not be idle during her mourning. She needed to protect herself and the child she carried from the bears, wolves, and wolverines. Thus she became a "female warrior [fighting] against these beasts which did not cease to attempt to surprise and devour her and her child also." She and her servant hunted together, using firearms and the dead man's sword. It was Marguerite, however, who had the deadliest aim: in one day alone she shot three bears, one of them "white as an egg."

The child was born, and his mother baptized him. She had been the priest to her lover, and now she played the priest to her son.

In the sixteenth month of their marooning, Damienne died. She

Marguerite de la Roque hunts wild animals on the Isle of Spirits. To the left is her hut and her infant wrapped in swaddling clothes; to the right, the carnivorous beasts and a palm tree, showing that the sixteenth-century illustrator had some fanciful ideas about Canadian flora. (Copy print courtesy of the Library of Congress)

had been well past sixty when their ordeal began, and no doubt the deprivations she had suffered since had worn her out. There remained one last tragedy for Marguerite: "A little time afterward, the child followed the path of the two who went before."

In Marguerite's torment, the apparitions returned with a vengeance. She experienced horrible visions, though these passed when she prayed. Parts of her body became swollen — hands, arms, torso, and feet — and then numb. Her plight was made more desperate when the gunpowder, because of dampness or age, lost its combustibility. The carnivorous animals seemed to sense that she was alone and boldly hunted her day and night.

> This poor desolate one was assailed from without and within and daily the rampant beasts did not fail to give her alarms rampaging

. . . to devour her, because they felt that even she, alone, was worth visiting and devouring as their prey. Always they showed that they scented out their advantage. She was a real plum for them; their best desire was to pick her off. She retired at night, overthrown and enfeebled by work to awaken to even harder days, among enemies not to be conquered by lead, against whom arms have no power.

Far worse to her than all these afflictions was her isolation. She longed for someone to talk to. Yet her ordeal was nearly done. One day in the late summer or fall of 1544, more than two years after her cousin had condemned her, boats appeared offshore. These belonged to cod fishermen from Brittany. They saw the smoke signal she made, saw her at the water's edge, crying out to them for help. They did not believe that she was human, however, and thought that they were suffering from the "illusions [created by] demons who beguiled travelers, knowing that the island had never been inhabited by living men but only by fierce beasts, birds and smaller beasts." Still they did not flee from her but eventually maneuvered a craft closer to get a better look.

When they had finally convinced themselves that she was one of their race, they came ashore for her. "After thanking God for their arrival, she took them to her poor little hut and showed them on what she had subsisted during her melancholy abode there. They could never have believed it had they not known that God can nourish his servants in a desert as at the finest banquets in the world."

She gathered up her few possessions, including the citre of her deceased lover. Having erected a cross at the little graveyard, she departed from the Isle of Spirits. On board the fishing boat, the disconsolate Marguerite looked back and, "torn by sorrow as she was," felt an overwhelming desire not to leave at all but to remain there in solitude until she died, just as those she loved had died before her. But the fishermen took her away, putting aside the exigencies of their livelihood to sail straight to France.

Roberval's colony failed, and he was forced to return home without so much as even one small, authentic Saguenay diamond to console him. He lived for another sixteen years, during which time he made one more futile attempt to colonize New France. He died in Paris in 1560, murdered in a riot that resulted from a conflict between Protestants and Catholics.

After Roberval's death, his friend André Thevet tried to rename the Isle of Spirits in his honor, but the name did not stick. More appropriately, the group of islands to which it belongs came to be called, for a time, the Isles de la Demoiselle. The isle itself is now known as Hospital Island. Its small population is made up mostly of fishermen, and if you visit the place, it is possible to induce one of them to tell you legends of Marguerite and to point out such sites as a cave wherein the lovers are said to have dwelled for a time.

So far as we know, Marguerite never confronted her cousin or brought him into court seeking justice. She settled in Nontron, became a schoolmistress, and lived for many years. As the royal Marguerite concludes her tale, when the Brittany fishermen brought her back to France and told the inhabitants of the town the story of

the fidelity and perseverance of this woman, the ladies paid her great honor and were glad to send their daughters to her to learn to read and write. She maintained herself for the rest of her days by that honorable profession, having no other desire than to exhort everyone to love God and trust in Him, holding forth as an example the great mercy with which He had dealt [with] her.

CHAPTER 9

The Calming Effect of Rum and True Religion

John Byron on the Shores of Patagonia

All our dead heroes have been done in by Marxist historians and psychoanalytic biographers. We now know that valiant deeds and wise policy have always sprung from the baser motives of greed and avarice or the heated urgings of the libido. And we are grateful for the knowledge. It is hard, nevertheless, to relate some deeds without a note of admiration. Men like Drake and Rogers struggled against terrible odds in fragile ships on crushing seas, won great battles and treated the vanquished with kindness, and returned home despite misleading charts and surly crews. How can these exploits be recalled without a fragment of respect?

Yet many such men came from a profession that was hardly removed from brigandism, and their victims viewed them as nothing more than legitimized robbers. While the victorious leader watched the plunder being loaded, corpses lay at his feet. And somewhere far in his wake were those lost from his expedition — frantic, scattered men greedy only for their own safety and the way home.

Such a tale is that of George Lord Anson and Midshipman John Byron. The former was a rather traditional, upright hero, while the latter would become, in time, a new, slightly raffish one. Look for a moment on all that the commander achieved and remember it as you read of what became of his young junior officer. You may be reminded momentarily of Peter Carder, but you will find that this is a very different tale. Here men in isolation will act badly and selfishly. It is the first whisper of darker insights to come.

■ ■ ■

George Lord Anson entered the British navy in 1712, when he was about fifteen years old, and was made a captain at age twenty-six. It was in September of 1740 that his great opportunity came. War with Spain having broken out again, Anson was given charge of six ships and the rank of commodore and was ordered to the Pacific; he was to "annoy and distress the Spaniards" by plundering their possessions and, if possible, capturing one of the treasure vessels that sailed from Acapulco to Manila.

It was an undertaking fraught with problems, not the least of which was that his crews included a considerable number of "Invalids" or pensioners who had been retired from duty because of disease, disability, or age and who had been released from a hospital in order to make the voyage.

Still, Commodore Anson was particularly well suited for the task. A resolute leader, he was above all a rational man who remained unflappable and unafraid, no matter how perilous his situation. He also had a goodly amount of luck: at the very end of the journey his last remaining vessel would have been ambushed and captured by a French fleet had she not been hidden by a sudden and fortunate fog.

The circumnavigation proved to be an extraordinary triumph despite early setbacks. Near its beginning, storms dispersed Anson's squadron in the vicinity of Cape Horn; two of the ships were wrecked, and a third sailed back to England. The commodore's *Centurion* reached Más á Tierra, and while he waited for a rendezvous with the two other vessels, he went ashore and saw signs of Alexander Selkirk's sojourn there more than thirty years before. When what was left of his squadron reassembled, he visited his wrath on the South American coast, plundering settlements, capturing ships, and spreading alarm and panic throughout the colonies.

On June 20, 1743, the *Centurion* encountered the treasure ship *Nuestra Señora de Cabadonga* near the Philippine Islands. The engagement lasted just ninety minutes, and the victorious Anson found among the *Señora*'s cargo 1,313,843 pieces of eight and 35,682 ounces of pure silver. He sold the *Señora* to Chinese merchants at Canton.

Upon his return to England in June 1744, Anson paraded his plunder through the streets of London in a procession of thirty-two overloaded wagons while his countrymen cheered. His portion of the spoils made him an extremely wealthy man, and this and later actions won him a peerage, political position, and military power, as well as the opportunity to marry the rich daughter of the lord chancellor of England.

Still, success was not without its price. While, incredibly, only four of his crew were lost in combat, of the 2,000 sailors who began the undertaking, more than 1,300 died of disease — many of them from scurvy. Then there was the matter of what happened to the men of one of the wrecked vessels that went down near Cape Horn, the storeship *Wager*. . . .

The Wager was actually a man-of-war that had once been an Indiaman; thus she came from that great line of the finest sailing ships ever made in the West. On this expedition, however, Anson was using her rather ignominiously as a floating warehouse, and he had her so deeply laden with naval and military materiel, bale goods, and trade goods that she sailed with difficulty. The crew, in the evaluation of seventeen-year-old John Byron, "consisted of men dispirited by the prospects before them and worn out with past fatigues." The *Wager*'s captain confirmed their gloom when, in the final moments before his death, he prophesied disaster for her.

After the *Wager* became separated from the squadron, her new commander, Captain Cheap, set a course for the island of Socorro, intending to make a raid on nearby Valdivia. He wanted to deliver a quick and devastating blow to the Spanish before they knew Englishmen were in the area, and then he would rejoin Anson's forces. Young Byron had a certain, albeit ambivalent, admiration for Cheap: a sense of duty produced in the captain a "rigid adherence to orders, from which he thought himself in no case at liberty to depart [and] begat in him a stubborn defiance of difficulties and took away from him those apprehensions which so justly alarmed all [those who] from an ignorance of the orders had nothing present on their minds but the dangers of a leeshore."

Ever since separating from the *Centurion,* the *Wager* had run into one gale after another. The sailors fought against the weather, repaired the damage as best they could, and strained to keep the ship afloat. In the process, most of them were injured or became ill, until only a handful were left to carry on. It was at this moment that the *Wager* would wreck.

The mariners had known for some time that they were approaching the continent: they saw land birds in the sky and weeds in the water.

Admiral John Byron in a painting attributed to Sir
Joshua Reynolds (Permission of the National Maritime Museum, London)

Finally some of them thought they glimpsed mountains in the far
distance, but others scorned them for imagining things.

They were fighting against hurricane-force winds when the straps
of the fore jeer blocks broke and the foreyard came down. Immediate repairs were required, but only twelve men were fit for duty.
The few who could be spared had been put to work on the fore jeer
blocks when to the northwest, on the larboard beam, they saw land
upon which the ship was being driven. The captain shouted orders
to sway the foreyard up and set the foresail, and the sailors scrambled to obey. When this was accomplished, they desperately attempted to beat the ship to the south, away from the land and the
rocks.

But the relentless wind continued to push the *Wager* toward the
shoals. Night fell, and the mariners set their topsails to claw away
from the shore, but these were immediately ripped from the yards
by the wind.

At about four o'clock in the morning, the vessel struck a rock. The men felt the shock but did not recognize it for what it was. After the battering they had experienced, they told themselves that this was just another heavy blow of a powerful wave. When the ship struck again, this time with much greater force, they were "undeceived." The impact laid the *Wager* on her beam-ends, and the waves broke violently over her.

> In this dreadful situation the ship lay for some little time, every soul on board looking upon the present minute as his last, for there was nothing to be seen but breakers all around us. [At length] a mountainous sea heaved [the *Wager* off the rock], but she presently struck again and broke her tiller.
>
> In this terrifying and critical juncture, one [man] in the ravings despair brought on him was seen stalking about the deck, flourishing a cutlass over his head and calling himself king of the country and striking everybody he came near, till his companions, feeling no other security against his tyranny, knocked him down.
>
> Some [men], reduced before by long sickness and scurvy, became on this occasion as it were petrified and bereaved of all sense, like inanimate logs, and were bandied to and fro by the jerks and rolls of the ship, without exerting any efforts to help themselves.
>
> So terrible was the scene of foaming breakers around us, that one of the bravest men we had could not help expressing his dismay at it, saying it was too shocking a sight to bear and would have thrown himself over the rails of the quarter-deck into the sea, had he not been prevented.
>
> But at the same time there were those who preserved a presence of mind truly heroic. The man at the helm, though both rudder and tiller were gone, kept his station, and being asked by one of the officers if the ship would steer or not, first took time to make a trial by the wheel, then answered, with as much respect and coolness as if the ship had been in the greatest safety, and immediately after applied himself with his usual serenity to his duty, persuaded it did not become him to desert it as long as the ship held together.

Another fellow who kept his head was Jones, the first mate, who tried to give his comrades heart with this little speech: "My friends, let us not be discouraged. Did you never see a ship among the breakers before? Let us try to push her through them. Come, lend a hand. Here is a sheet, and here is a brace. Lay hold. I don't doubt but we may stick her near enough to the land to save our lives."

A sufficient number of the sailors heeded his words to run the *Wager* through an opening between the breakers, steering by sheets and braces, until she was "providentially . . . stuck fast between two great rocks, that to windward sheltering us in some measure from the violence of the sea." Yet the force of the storm was such that the men were certain their vessel would not hold together very long, and some of them raced to hoist out the boats. Others, in despair, fell to their knees on the deck and prayed to God to have mercy on them. In their panic, too many men jumped into the first craft away and very nearly sank her. They managed to reach the shore of what proved to be a large island, although for some time they would be uncertain as to whether they had been cast up on the mainland itself.

Byron went to the captain's cabin, where Cheap lay, having dislocated his shoulder the day before in the rush to get the foreyard swayed up. The midshipman inquired of his superior if he would now go ashore. Cheap declined; he held to the tradition that the captain should be the last to abandon ship. He instructed Byron to assist the crew in getting away as quickly as possible.

By the time the midshipman made his way back to the deck, the scene had changed incredibly. Most of the men had disembarked with alacrity, but it had become evident to the dozen or so sailors who were still on board that the *Wager* would not soon break up. This knowledge made them "very riotous," and to celebrate, they had rifled every chest and box in easy reach, looking for spoils. Further, they had brought up to the hatchways casks of wine and brandy. When Byron came back on deck, they were proceeding to get drunk. Soon they would be so inebriated that several of them would actually drown in the 'tween decks, where the water flowed in, and the corpses would be left by the other celebrants to float there.

Disgusted, Byron went to the bulkhead of the wardroom where his own chest was stored, intending to take out of it whatever could be of use on land. Before he could remove anything, however, the waves "thumped [the hull] with such violence, and the water came in so fast, that I was forced to get upon the quarter-deck again without saving a single rag but what was upon my back."

He went to the captain's cabin once more, this time telling him that the boatswain and some of the others would not be leaving as long as any liquor remained. Hearing this, Cheap "suffered himself to be helped out of his bed, put into the boat, and carried on shore."

The storm did not let up that night. The weather was cold, the wind fierce, and the rain heavy. Nearly 150 maroons searched along the edge of the beach for some sort of shelter. Finding nothing, they moved into the woods beyond, where they discovered a hut built by Indians. As many as could fit crowded into it, for once making no distinction of rank. It was a temporary democracy of desperation.

During the night, one lieutenant died in that "miserable hovel," and two other men who had not been able to fit in also succumbed. These deaths would be a harbinger of things to come: in the months and years ahead many more men would die of fever, exposure, accident, hardship, and want.

On that first morning, having had nothing to eat for forty-eight hours or more, the survivors felt quite hungry:

> It was time, therefore, to make inquiry among ourselves what store of sustenance had been brought from the wreck by the providence of some, and what could be procured upon the island by the industry of others. [The former] amounted to no more than two or three bags of biscuit dust, and all the success of those who ventured abroad, the weather being still exceedingly bad, was to kill one sea gull and pick some wild celery.

These were meager provisions indeed. The men debated forming forage parties but feared that savages were lurking about, just waiting for them to split into small groups. In the end, despite their apprehensions, they did send out squads, but these did not stray far from the shelter and were disheartened to find the "country very morassy and unpromising."

Meanwhile an officer was dispatched in the yawl to the *Wager* in an effort to persuade the rest of the sailors to disembark. He found them belligerent, disorderly, and inclined to rebellion, and he returned alone. That night the force of the gale increased, and the sea ran so high and wild that the ship seemed once more about to sunder. The drunkards

> then were as solicitous to get ashore, as they were before obstinate in refusing the assistance we sent them; and when the boat did not come to their relief the instant they expected it, without considering how impracticable it was to send it [to] them in such a sea, they fired one of the quarter-deck guns at the hut. The ball just [barely] passed over the covering of it, and was plainly heard by the captain and us who were within. Another attempt, therefore, was made to bring these madmen to land; which, however, by the violence of the sea and other impediments . . . proved ineffectual. This unavoidable

The wreck of the storeship *Wager*. On her decks may be seen the drunkards who refused to come ashore while the liquor supply lasted. (Courtesy of the Archives and Rare Books Dept., University of Cincinnati Libraries)

delay made the people on board outrageous. They fell to beating every thing to pieces that [they could lay their hands on], and, carrying their intemperance to the greatest excess, broke open chests and cabins for plunder that could be of no use to them.

In the fights that started over the spoils, one man was killed. When the weather improved and they had spent themselves in thievery and combat, these outlaws condescended to be taken off the wreck, having first thoughtfully collected every weapon they could find

in order to support them in putting their mutinous designs in[to] execution, and asserting their claim to a lawless exemption from the authority of their officers, which they pretended must cease with the loss of the ship. But of these arms, which we stood in great need of, they were soon deprived, upon coming ashore, by the resolution of Captain Cheap and Lieutenant Hamilton of the marines. It was scarcely possible to refrain from laughter at the whimsical appearance these fellows made, who, having rifled the chests of the officers' best suits, had put them on over their greasy trousers and dirty checked shirts. They were soon stripped of their finery, as they had before been obliged to resign their arms.

Now that everyone was on the beach, the officers sought to restore discipline and to organize the men for the common good. The first task was the erection of a larger shelter, and this assignment was given to the carpenter, the gunner, and a few others; they created one by turning the cutter over and propping her up on legs. Other dwellings would soon be under construction, but in the meantime, since an observation post was wanted and the nearby mountain was too steep to be climbed easily, a team of sailors cut steps to its peak and named it Mount Misery. Other men had the duty of carefully and constantly scouring the sand for food, and they had good results: they were able to procure some sea birds, limpets, mussels, and other shellfish in "tolerable abundance; but this rummaging of the shore was now becoming extremely irksome to those who had any sensibility, by the bodies of our drowned people thrown among the rocks, some of which were hideous spectacles from the mangled condition they were in by the violent surf that drove in upon the coast."

Not only corpses floated in from the *Wager*, but also small quantities of cargo, especially cloth and clothing. Some men slipped away from the hut at night in order to seize and conceal these items so that they would not have to share them with their comrades.

Despite the officers' efforts to direct and coordinate the men in procuring the essentials of survival, in the first weeks ashore the number of dead continued to rise. It was clear, therefore, that another crucial task was to salvage from the wreck as many supplies as could be gotten out of her. This was very difficult since nearly all of her was submerged except for the quarter-deck and part of the forecastle. The sailors were forced to fish through the hatches for whatever floated within reach, using long poles with hooks fastened to their ends. Here again, those of delicate sensitivities were "much incommoded" because floating between decks were bloated, water-logged bodies.

As the quantity of goods increased, Cheap ordered a store tent put up near his hut; his immediate subordinates were to issue its contents as they saw fit. Since some of the crew had already shown themselves inclined to mischief and thievery, the petty officers — who spent their days hunting for food — were instructed to give over their nights to "defend this tent from invasion. . . . Yet notwithstanding our utmost vigilance and care, frequent robberies were committed upon our trust, the tent being accessible in more than one place."

Some of the maroons continued to put up shelters for themselves, until they had a little village with several streets. At the same time, the officers turned their attention to discovering more about their location. The view from Mount Misery was partially blocked by other high hills, and so to make a reconnaissance it would be necessary to explore the coast by boat. Since the cutter was still being used for shelter, a party of men was sent out to the *Wager* to free the longboat and barge. While these fellows were working at this task, there paddled into view three canoes of Indians. At first the Indians were shy and unwilling to approach, but the sailors managed to allay their fears with friendly gestures and dumb-show promises of gifts in the form of bale goods. At last they came forward and accepted the offering. They allowed themselves to be conducted to the captain, who gave them still more presents; these were the inevitable trinkets with which European voyagers always seemed to arm themselves for encounters with "primitive" peoples. The Indians had not met whites before, however, and were entranced by the baubles: "They were strangely affected with the novelty of [them], chiefly the looking-glass. The beholder could not conceive it to be his own face that was represented, but that of some other person behind it, which he therefore went round to the back of the glass to find out.''

In return, the visitors gave Cheap some mussels, and then they left, but they were back in two days, bringing with them several dogs and three sheep. The Englishmen were astonished to see the latter, since the nearest Spanish settlement was a vast distance away. Byron does not tell us what became of these animals, but presumably they shared the same fate as the dogs, which were bartered for, roasted, and eaten.

A few of the maroons adjusted well to their lot. John Byron, for one, built a shelter just big enough for himself and "a poor Indian dog I found in the woods, who could shift for himself" by getting limpets along the shore at low tide. "This creature grew so fond of me and so faithful that he would suffer nobody to come near the hut without biting them."

Their predicament was taking its toll on the morale of many other men. They had become ill humored and discontented. They chafed at the rule of the officers, and they were obsessed with the fear that they might be confined in this place for many years.

Some of these men withdrew from the larger company, erecting shelters at a distance from the village, but ten others decided to make a trek through what they believed was the Patagonian wilderness. Byron thought that their leaving would constitute no great loss, feeling that they were "a most desperate and abandoned crew." It was an estimation they confirmed when, as they were setting out, they put a barrel of gunpowder beside the captain's dwelling and laid a train to it, with the intention of blowing up both the hut and its occupant. They were just preparing to ignite the explosives when one of their number — the only one "who had some remorse of conscience left" — managed to dissuade them from it.

These raffish fellows wandered through the woods until they became disheartened and correctly concluded that they were on an island. They went back to the camp not the least bit chastened. They put up new huts a sullen league from the settlement, and then they set about building a punt. When this boat was finished and they had made a canoe out of one of the ship's masts, they put to sea — and were never heard from again. Few of those who stayed behind regretted their going: they "did not distress us much by their departure, but rather added to our security."

Shortly after they left, there appeared in the lagoon a party of fifty Indians who had decided to settle among Cheap's men. The group included a number of women and children. Once ashore, they set about building wigwams and seemed to Byron to be "much reconciled to our company."

Midshipman Byron was exceptionally glad to see them: the white men were often hungry, and the aborigines' knowledge of the environment would be of immeasurable value in gathering food. Unfortunately they did not stay long enough to impart their learning. The sailors, "now subject to little or no control, endeavored to seduce [the Indian] wives, which gave the Indians such offense that in a short time they found means to depart, taking every thing along with them; and we, being sensible of the cause, never expected to see them return again."

Byron soon had a personal reason to lament the breakdown of order and the disregard of authority.

> One day, when I was at home in my hut with my Indian dog, a party came to my door and told me their necessities were such that they must eat the creature or starve. Though their plea was urgent, I could not help using some arguments to endeavor to dissuade them from killing him, as his faithful services and fondness [made him dear to me]; but, without weighing my arguments, they took him away by force, and killed him.

Yet hunger was having its effect on the young midshipman, too. The murder having been committed, he went to where the body of his pet was being eaten, and "thinking that I had at least as good a right to share as the rest, I sat down with them and partook of their repast." Indeed, a measure of his own desperation is in this: "Three weeks after that I was glad to make a meal of his paws and skin, which, upon recollecting the spot where they had killed him, I found thrown aside and rotten."

Deprivation brought out ingenuity and perseverance in a few of the maroons. One of these was Phipps, the boatswain's mate, who emptied a water puncheon (a cask) and, lashing a log on either side of it, went out into the lagoons after sea birds. None but the worst of weather kept him on the beach, and during these daylong forays he was able to catch enough to keep himself alive by means of his "extraordinary and original piece of embarkation." On one such trip, his little craft went down in a particularly heavy sea; Phipps, even though a poor swimmer, managed to reach a rock. He dragged himself up its sheer face, and he was forced to stay on it for two days, until some of his fellows who were out in a boat, also after birds, happened to see him; they brought him back to the island.

The experience did not deter him. He took a piece of ox hide, known as gunner's hide because it was used to sift the explosive powder, and from it he made a kind of canoe with pieces of barrel hoops as ribs. In this odd craft he went out on the ocean again.

Other men had his determination if not his cleverness. Since thirty or forty of their comrades had already perished on the isle, many of those still alive were convinced that if they were not soon away, they would die, too. The carpenter had been lengthening the longboat, and they proposed that when he finished they sail her through the Straits of Magellan, up the eastern coast of South America, and then home. Cheap had his own plan for the craft, however: he intended to use her to find and capture an enemy ship so that he could rejoin Anson's expedition.

To this end, he sent Byron and thirteen men in the barge to reconnoiter the mainland coast and islands to the south. The voyage began well enough: the first night they put into a good harbor and found a large bitch with puppies — "we regaled upon them." But by the third day the weather had turned bad again, and they had found little to eat. They entered an inlet and, having secured the barge, went ashore to camp for the night. The tent they had been issued proved to be too small for the whole party, and so Byron led some of them on a two-mile hike in the downpour to the skeleton of an Indian wigwam. They partially covered it with seaweed to keep out the weather, built a fire, and

> laid ourselves down, in hopes of finding a remedy for our hunger in sleep. But we had not long composed ourselves before one of our company was disturbed by the blowing of some animal at his face, and upon opening his eyes was not a little astonished to see, by the glimmering of the fire, a large beast standing over him. He had presence of mind enough to snatch a brand from the fire, which was now very low, and thrust it at the nose of the animal, who thereupon made off. The man then awoke us and related with horror in his countenance the narrow escape he had of being devoured.

The coast was dangerous, they decided. The strong gale and heavy seas were keeping them from making any discoveries in the barge. All they could do was go back to their dispirited comrades on "Wager's Island."

In their absence, the situation at the settlement had changed markedly. Cheap's ordering of the reconnaissance mission had given the crew convincing evidence that he really meant to find Anson. The vast majority of them had had enough adventure without making war on the Spanish or going around the world; they just wanted to get back to Britain, and they insisted on going through the Straits. When Cheap remained firm in his resolve, they took by force the longboat, the cutter, and all of the food and supplies, and they sailed away. (Of the eighty men who set out, thirty survived to reach the Rio Grande on the coast of Brazil three and a half months later.)

The men under Cheap's command now totaled only twenty. Since it was nearly midsummer and the days were at their longest, they wasted no time in preparing for the northern journey. The yawl and the barge were made ready and the wreck was visited, the happy result being three casks of beef.

Having feasted on the meat, they set off on December 15. Cheap, Byron, and the surgeon, Mr. Elliot, went with nine men in the barge, while Lieutenant Hamilton, a midshipman named Campbell, and six men were in the yawl.

After they had been on the ocean for just two hours, the wind shifted to the west and began to blow very hard. The sea ran high, and they were driven off course. They were forced to lighten the load by throwing their provisions overboard. As night came, they were running very fast on a lee shore, the waves breaking on it

> in a frightful manner. Not one among us imagined it possible for boats to live in such a sea.
>
> In this situation, as we neared the shore, expecting to be beat to pieces by the first breaker, we perceived a small opening between the rocks, which we stood for, and found a very narrow passage between them, which brought us into a harbor . . . as calm and smooth as a mill-pond.

They secured the boats and ascended a rock. They spent the night without a fire, shivering in the cold. In the morning, they realized they would find no food where they were, and so they set sail again. Outside the tranquil harbor, however, the ocean was raging, and they could make little progress.

This was the pattern of their days: while the light lasted, they struggled against the churning sea and the bellowing wind. As darkness came on, they put into whatever coastal cove or bay they could find and then landed to look for food and firewood. Occasionally they found groves of trees, built fires, and were fortunate enough to kill a goose or a seal. More often the terrain was swampy, and they hunched against the cold, eating seaweed.

[While in one small bay] we were so pinched with hunger that we ate the shoes off our feet, which consisted of raw seal-skin. In the morning we got out of the bay, but the incessant foul weather had overcome us, and we began to be indifferent to what befell us. This, by some of our accounts, was Christmas-day; but our accounts had been so often interrupted by our distresses that there was no depending upon them.

A few days later, the weather was so bad that they did not even try to leave the cove where they had taken refuge. Two men were delegated to stay in each craft while the rest went ashore. After dark Byron, who was on the barge, fell asleep. He awoke to men screaming. The barge was rolling violently, and the roaring of the breakers was all around. He looked out and saw the yawl canted bottom up by a wave; the cries had come from the men in her. The yawl sank. One of the men was drowned, and the other was flung ashore by the surf with such force that he landed head first, buried to his neck in the sand. His compatriots managed to pull him out before he had suffocated.

Byron and the other man in the barge struggled for a long time to pull her away from the breakers, eventually succeeding. All the next day they lay "in a great sea," contending with the weather and expecting at every moment to have their boat go down as the yawl had. "To add to our mortification, we could see our companions in tolerable plight ashore, eating seal, while we were starving."

The weather moderated sufficiently on the following day for them to take the barge near enough to the beach for their fellows to throw them some seal's liver. They wolfed this down and were soon violently ill. Their reaction was so severe that "our skin peeled off from head to foot."

The men on shore were busy killing what creatures they could. Mr. Hamilton came upon a huge sea lion. He approached him from behind and shot him twice. The animal merely turned on him, openmouthed. Hamilton hurriedly fixed a bayonet to his musket and thrust it far down the sea lion's throat. The creature bit the gun barrel in two as easily as if it "had been a twig. Notwithstanding the wounds he had received, he eluded all further efforts to kill him and got clear off."

The loss of the yawl had a terrible implication: the barge was too small to hold all the men, and so some of them would have to stay behind. Four marines were selected. They raised no objection. Indeed, "so exceedingly disheartened and worn out were they with the distress and dangers they had gone through" that they were indifferent to their fate. In this they were not alone; everyone felt the same numbing weariness and disregard of whether they got back into the boat or were left behind.

Captain Cheap issued firearms, ammunition, and "a few other necessities" to the marines. When the sea was calm enough to permit the others to set sail again, they piled into the barge. Standing on the beach, those who were being abandoned bravely gave their departing compatriots three cheers and called out, "God bless the king!" As the boat pulled away, those in her looked back to see the four slowly climbing a sheer cliff, each man pausing to help his brothers. Despite this spirit of camaraderie, Byron was certain that their trying to walk to civilization was nothing more than a "forlorn hope": the woods were so thick as to be "impenetrable," and everywhere there were deep swamps. "It is probable they all experienced a miserable fate."

Cheap's crew headed the barge back to Wager's Island. On the voyage out they had been optimistic, but they were returning utterly discouraged. They thought of how during their previous stay they had depleted the supply of shellfish, which was the only reliable food source on the isle. Further, the Indians had shown themselves to be "little affected by the common incitements of compassion" and "had already refused to barter their dogs with us for want of a valuable commodity on our side." Yet there was nothing else to do but return to the island.

One day a sudden squall nearly capsized and swamped the barge. They bailed frantically with their hats and hands, and at long last they managed to empty the boat. Badly shaken, the men brought the vessel into a cove, where they lingered until they had regained their courage. This rehabilitation took too long: foul weather set in and held them there for three days. They found a few seals to kill and then they waited, reflecting on the precariousness of their circumstances. Without the seals, they might have starved to death.

They set a course for Montrose Island, which they had previously visited. On it a bush grew, the fruit of which was a kind of a black berry that resembled English gooseberries. They reached the island

and ate these berries in abundance, along with the remainder of the seal meat, resting until the supply ran low. They attempted to set off again several times, but on each occasion tempests drove them back. When all the seal was eaten and the berries devoured, they knew they must get away or die. In a gale only slightly less fierce than the one that had wrecked the yawl, they recklessly set out.

In three days they reached Wager's Island. When they had left it two months before, they could not have imagined a more miserable spot, but their misadventures in the interim had made them almost sentimental for the place. Since leaving Montrose, they had eaten nothing but seaweed. They were starved, weary.

They carefully secured the barge and went into their village. In their absence, Indians had been there. The Englishmen were surprised to find that the visitors had boarded up one of their huts. They tore away the lumber and found that it had been used as a storehouse for ironwork and nails. The Indians had painstakingly collected the metal from the pieces of the wreck that had been flung up on the beach by storms. (These scavengers would not have belonged to the tribe with which the maroons had had earlier dealings, because the latter had had no previous contact with Europeans, while the former's assignment of value to metal indicated a trading relationship with Spaniards.) The discovery set Byron to ruminating over the nature of aborigines in the Americas: "Thieving from strangers is a commendable talent among savages in general, and bespeaks an address which they greatly admire; though the strictest honesty with regard to the property of each other is observed among them."

Several weeks later Indians arrived in two canoes; they seemed surprised to find that the whites had returned. One of them was a cacique, or chief, of a tribe of Chonos from the large island of Chiloé. This place was within the Spanish dominion, and so he was a Catholic convert, calling himself Martín and carrying with him "the usual badge and mark of distinction" that Spaniards conferred on chiefs — a cane with a silver head.

None of the whites were fluent in Spanish, but Mr. Elliot, who was "master of a few Spanish words," stepped forward to try to communicate with the cacique. The physician had a proposition for him: the Englishmen were so desperate to reach civilization that they were willing to go to a Spanish settlement, but they had no idea what the shortest and least hazardous way was. If he would guide them, they would give him their barge as soon as they were safe.

Martín was reluctant to undertake the trip. Elliot struggled to understand his objections — the fellow was speaking "Spanish . . . with that savage accent which renders it almost unintelligible to any but those who are adept in that language." Elliot cajoled and flattered the chief and at last persuaded him to help them.

The journey, undertaken in the barge and at least one canoe, proved to be a long and arduous one. Several of the white men collapsed and died while working the oars. Mr. Hamilton became so sick and disabled that he was left behind at an Indian village. Mr. Elliot, whose fatigue was "infinite," lay down and died. His death was a particular blow because when they departed from Wager's Island, he had been "a very strong, active young man" and had seemed the most likely of any of them to survive; not only would they suffer for lack of his medical knowledge, but he was the best marksman in the group and, of course, the only one who could communicate with the cacique.

At some point in all of this misery, the remaining common seamen and marines decided that they had had enough. One day while the officers were ashore, they seized the barge, took an Indian for use as a guide, and sailed away.

The cacique had been promised the vessel in return for his help, and now it was gone. Using sign language, the white men offered him the few pathetic possessions they had, but he was not impressed. Hereafter, while he would continue to show them the way, he would not share his food with them nor do anything to assist them. Wherever they landed, they would have to search the shore for shellfish and hope to shoot an occasional seal. They would have died had not some of the Indians they met along the way fed them, taken them into their wigwams, and given them blankets.

It was late one night when they finally reached Chiloé. The next day it snowed heavily. They were certain they would lose their feet to frostbite, being without stockings and having already eaten their homemade shoes. All were wretched, but Captain Cheap was in the worst shape. Were he to continue in this extremity for much longer, Byron was sure that he would die.

This is not to say that either Byron or Campbell was much better off:

It is impossible for me to describe the miserable state we were reduced to. Our bodies were so emaciated that we hardly appeared [to
be] men. It has often happened to me in the coldest night, both in hail
and snow, where we had nothing but an open beach to lay down
upon, that in order to procure a little rest, I have been obliged to pull
off the few rags I had on, as it was impossible to get a moment's sleep
with them on for the vermin that swarmed [in] them. I used to take
my clothes off and putting them upon a large stone, beat them with
another, in hopes of killing hundreds at once, for it was endless work
to pick them off. What we suffered from this was ten times worse
than the hunger. But we were clean in comparison to Captain Cheap.
I could compare his body to nothing but an ant hill with thousands of
those insects crawling over it. For he was now past attempting to rid
himself in the least from this torment, as he had quite lost himself,
not recollecting our names . . . or even his own. His beard was as
long as a hermit's, and that as well as his face was covered with dirt
and train-oil, from having accustomed himself to sleep upon the bag
in which he kept the pieces of seal, by way of a pillow. This prudent
method he took to prevent our getting at it while he slept. His legs
were as large as mill-posts, though his body appeared nothing but
skin and bones.

While the Englishmen lay scratching in their infested rags, the
cacique busied himself burying most of the articles they had given
him, for if the Spanish learned of his new-found wealth, they would
take it all away, leaving him not even so much as "a rusty nail."

In the evening the party pushed off again and made their way to
the outskirts of a small settlement where Martín was known. He
wanted to announce his presence dramatically. He had Byron load
his new fowling piece (which until recently had belonged to the
midshipman) and show him how to discharge it. He stood up in
the canoe and, craning his neck so that his head was as far from the
piece as possible, fired it. The recoil knocked him flat on his back.

The inhabitants were unused to the sound of firearms. Instead of
coming out to stand in proper awe while the regal cacique disembarked, they fled into the woods. It was some time before the brav-
est of them was willing to emerge from his hiding place and halloo
the strangers from a hilltop. When Martín had identified himself,
the other natives came out of the woods and down to the canoe,
bringing with them some fish and a large quantity of potatoes. "This
was the most comfortable meal we had made for many long
months," Byron recalled. After it was over, they paddled about two
miles to a village.

Here again, the cacique proudly discharged his weapon, and this time it had the desired effect. He theatrically flourished his silver-headed cane before the dutifully amazed crowd, and they led the Englishmen into a shelter, where a large fire was made. The Indians crowded around the visitors and heard with great pity Martín's recitation of what he knew of their history. They proved to be a gentle, kindly people:

> These good-natured, compassionate creatures seemed to vie with each other who should be the most [attentive to] us. They made a bed of sheepskins close to the fire for Captain Cheap and laid him upon it; and, indeed, had it not been for the kind assistance he now met with, he could not have survived three days longer. Though it was about midnight, they went out and killed a sheep, of which they made broth and baked a large cake of barley meal. Anyone may imagine what a treat this was to wretches who had not tasted a bit of bread or any wholesome [food] for such a length of time.
>
> After we could eat no longer, we went to sleep about the fire, which the Indians took care to keep up. In the morning, the women came from far and near, each bringing with her something. Almost everyone had a pipkin [earthenware pot] in her hand, containing either fowls or mutton made into broth, potatoes, eggs, or other eatables. We fell to work [eating] and employed ourselves so for the best part of the day.

Yet for all their hospitality, the Indians were Spanish subjects, and they dared not offend the colonial administrators. They therefore sent a messenger to the *corregidor* at Castro, informing him of the presence of their white guests. After three days, the messenger was back with an order from this magistrate that the foreigners be brought before him.

They were carried to Castro by canoe and then escorted by a squad of Spanish soldiers with drawn swords to the corregidor's house. It was filled with people who had come to stare at this pitiful remnant of Anson's crew. The magistrate received them with ceremony. A man of great height, he added to the impression his stature made by wearing a long cloak and a tie wig and by keeping a gigantic *spado* (a cut-and-thrust sword) at his side. He asked many questions of the strangers, but unfortunately, without Mr. Elliot to act as interpreter, they could not comprehend anything he said and stood dumb before him.

Their silence notwithstanding, the corregidor had a table spread for them with cold ham and fowl. They sat down to eat and quickly devoured "more than ten men with common appetites would have done. It is amazing that our eating to that excess we had done from the time we first got amongst the kind Indians had not killed us. We were never satisfied, and used to take all opportunities for some months after of filling our pockets when we were not seen, that we might get up two or three times in the night to cram ourselves. Captain Cheap used to declare that he was quite ashamed of himself."

After the supper, the Englishmen were led to a Jesuits' college in a procession that included the magistrate and a detachment of soldiers followed by all of the rabble of the town. This place would be their prison until the governor at Chaco decreed what should be done with them.

The corregidor and Father Provincial conferred while the foreigners were led away. Ushered into their cell, they found that sleeping mats had been placed on the floor and on each one lay a garment. These were ragged but clean and "of infinite service to us; nor did eating, at first, give me half the satisfaction this treasure of an old shirt did."

In the morning, Cheap was taken to the Father Provincial. The night before, the magistrate had asked the priest to look into the state of the strangers' souls: what religion were they, and if they were not Catholics, could they be converted? The father conversed with the British captain in the only language they had at all in common, which was Latin. It was not the best arrangement since neither man had much fluency in it, but "they made shift to understand each other." The Jesuits turned out to be far more interested in the prisoners' wealth than in their salvation. During this and subsequent conversations over the next several days, the priest harped on the question of where their valuables were: had they concealed them about their bodies? If so, they would be wise to give them up.

The Jesuits reported to the corregidor that their charges were nothing more than heretics. He wanted them to undertake their conversion, but the good fathers demurred: it would be a mere joke to attempt it now, they told him. The Englishmen had no reason to convert while they remained at Chiloé. Once they got to "Chili" and saw the wealth and glory of that place "where there was nothing but diversions and amusements, [they] should be converted fast enough."

Meanwhile the prisoners were settling into the routine of life among the clergy. The college was large but contained just four Jesuits, who were the only members of their order on the island. Even more curious to the Protestants was their vow of silence:

> We kept close to our cell till the bell rang for dinner, when we were conducted to a hall, where there was one table for the fathers and another for us. After a very long Latin prayer, we sat down and ate what was put before us, without a single word passing at either table. As soon as we had finished there was another long prayer, which, however, did not appear so tedious as the first, and then we retired again to our cell. In this manner we passed eight days without ever stirring out, all which time one might have imagined oneself out of the world: for, excepting the dinner-bell, a silence reigned throughout the whole as if the place had been uninhabited.

The tranquility was shattered on the eighth evening by a "violent" banging at the front gate. When it was swung wide, a young officer strode in, boots pounding, spurs jingling. After a week of unnatural quiet, he had the impact of a marching band. This self-important fellow announced that he was the governor's emissary, sent to conduct the captives to Chaco.

They traveled by canoe and then on horseback with an escort of thirty cavalrymen. The people of the city treated them with great hospitality. When the governor sought to show them off by taking them (and Hamilton, whom the governor had sent for) on a tour of his province, they found that their fame had preceded them. Thus they were able to glimpse the kind of inducements the Jesuits had been certain would cause them to deny their faith; everywhere they went they were invited into the homes of the wealthy. One of those which Byron eventually visited was that of a rich young woman. A lady of refinement and education, she quickly became infatuated with him. To his discerning eye she did not lack for a certain attractiveness: "Her person was good, though she could not be called a regular beauty."

This lady told her uncle, who was also her guardian, of her sudden but true love for the *Inglés*. The uncle happened to be a priest, although his vocation had not kept him from becoming one of the most affluent men in the colony, and his niece's desire seemed calculated to appeal to him: she wanted to convert Byron and then marry him.

The old man doted on his charge and had taken great care with her upbringing and instruction. How could he deny her now? The very next time the Inglés came to call, the uncle took him aside, leading him into the family treasure room for a little chat. (The conversation was facilitated by the fact that Byron had been diligently studying Spanish. How could one be a great lover in New Spain if one could not speak the ladies' lingo?) The room contained a vast number of large boxes and chests, and as he spoke, the priest opened one or another of these to make his point. He impressed Byron with the great quantities of fine clothing that belonged to his niece. He awed Byron, who was something of a dandy and had been dressed in rags for several years now, with his own luxuriant wardrobe, swearing that he would leave it to him in his will. He displayed other finery and riches, and then he brought out the last inducement, which would surely clinch the bargain and convince any sensible British gentleman to marry:

> He produced a piece of linen, which he said should immediately be made up into shirts for me. I own this article was a great temptation to me. However, I had the resolution to withstand it and made the best excuses I could for not accepting the honor they intended me.

John Byron soon had reason to regret his refusal. The captain general of Chile, Don José Manso, wanted to interview the officers of Anson's command himself, and he sent for them to be brought to "St. Jago." Captain Cheap and Mr. Hamilton had managed to preserve their commissions and so went on their way, but Byron and Campbell had long since lost theirs. Without this proof they were thrown into jail, and once Cheap and Hamilton were gone, they were treated very badly by their guards.

How long they remained incarcerated is unclear, but eventually Cheap was able to prevail upon Don José to release them and have them brought to Santiago. Mule trains transported goods from the port to the capital, and General Manso ordered one of the mule drivers (known as master-carriers) to bring the Englishmen with him. The fellow was bold enough to ask to be paid in advance, but the general refused to let him have even "a single farthing"; he hinted consolingly that the muleteer might be able to wring something out of those he was to escort.

The trip took five days, the route winding over several mountains and across wide plains. At night they slept out under the stars in open fields wherever there was water and good pasture for the animals. There were a hundred of them in the train, each carrying two heavy bales. Byron thought that their lot was a hard one but that the mules of Chile were the finest in the world: "Though they are continually upon the road and have nothing but what they pick up at nights, they are as fat and sleek as high-fed horses in England." In gratitude for the master-carrier's kindness, the midshipman helped him drive the animals, going after those that strayed as they moved over the plain. This service endeared him so much to the muleteer that on the morning of the last day, with the capital in sight, the fellow tried to convince Byron to shun the corruption of the city in favor of his own wholesome life:

> [He] advised me very seriously not to think of remaining at St. Jago, where, he said, there was nothing but extravagance, vice, and folly, but to proceed with him as a mule-driver, which he said I should soon be very expert at, [adding] that they led an innocent and happy life, far preferable to any enjoyment such a great city as that before us could afford.

In the capital, however, were fine linens and wealthy señoritas: "I thanked him and told him I was much obliged to him, but that I would try the city first, and if I did not like it, I would accept of the offer he was so good to make me."

Delivered to the palace gate, Byron and Campbell were taken before Don José, who treated them with civility. They were housed with Cheap and Hamilton at the home of a long-time resident of the capital, a physician and native Scotsman known as Don Patricio Gedd. This gentleman treated them as if they were his own brothers, "and during [the] two years that we were with him [it] was his constant study to make everything as agreeable to us as possible. We were greatly distressed to think of the expense he was at upon our account; but it was in vain to argue with him about it. In short, to sum up his character in a few words, there never was a man of more extensive humanity."

John Byron did experience at least one moment of extreme discomfort early on in his stay. He and the other Britons were invited to dine with General Manso, Admiral Pizarro, and his officers. "This was a cruel stroke upon us, as we had not any clothes fit to appear in and dared not refuse the invitation." Their terrible dilemma was resolved the next morning by the visit of one of Pizarro's officers, who wanted to give them two thousand dollars, an offer made "without any view of ever being repaid but purely out of a compassionate motive of relieving us in our present distress. We returned him all the acknowledgments his uncommon generous behavior merited and accepted of six hundred dollars only, upon his receiving our draft for that sum upon the English consul at Lisbon. We now got ourselves decently clothed after the Spanish fashion; and as we were upon our parole, we went out where we pleased to divert ourselves.''

It is comforting to know that during their long stay in Santiago, Anson's officers were not forced to hide in Dr. Gedd's house for want of fashionable attire.

After two years of sampling the local wines and flirting with the ''remarkably handsome'' women, it was time to go. General Manso arranged for Cheap, Hamilton, and Byron to be put aboard the French frigate *Lys*. (Midshipman Campbell had succumbed to the wiles of Chile: he converted to Catholicism and sailed with Admiral Pizarro to Spain, where he applied for a commission in that country's navy. When he was refused, he had the effrontery to return to England and apply for reinstatement in the British navy; he was bluntly rejected.) The *Lys* stopped at Más á Tierra and then sailed to the Bay of Concepción, where, on January 6, 1745, she joined a convoy of three other French ships.

On the *Lys*, the Englishmen were often treated with hostility, particularly by the senior officers. France was now at war with Britain, and the *Lys* was carrying a large amount of money, which made her an enticing target. (Indeed, in the course of the run, the other three French ships would all be captured; only the *Lys* escaped.) In one port, the prisoners were left on board while almost the entire crew went ashore. The weather was extremely cold, and the Englishmen were wearing only lightweight clothing. They could not warm themselves because vessels in the harbor were forbidden to have a fire or even a lighted candle for fear that one of them might be set ablaze and the conflagration spread to the port's magazines, which were located in the dock yard. Those in charge of the *Lys* so neglected Cheap and his subordinates that they did not send food out to them, and the three would have gone hungry had not a few of the junior officers taken it upon themselves to feed them. ''From five in the evening we were obliged to sit in the dark; and if we chose to have any supper, it was necessary to place it very near us before that time, or we never could have found it.''

After eight days they were put in with some captured British privateers and taken to a town where they spent three months, until word came from the Spanish court that they could be sent home on the first ship that would take them. This proved to be one from Holland, the captain of which they paid in advance to land them at Dover on the English coast.

The passage was a long and uncomfortable one. They finally sighted Dover one evening just before sunset, but in the morning they awoke to find their vessel off the coast of France, where the Dutch captain now proposed to set them ashore. As his passengers "complained loudly of this piece of villainy," an English man-of-war appeared, and when her captain had heard their tale, he dispatched a cutter to take them to Dover.

They started out for London on horseback that very afternoon, but by the time they arrived at Canterbury, Cheap was too weary to go further. A night's sleep hardly revived him. It was clear that he would not be able to reach the city astride a horse. The three of them pooled what little money they had — enough to hire a post chaise for Cheap to ride in and for Hamilton to accompany him. But what of Byron? With the money that remained, he could just pay for horses to get him to the city, but nothing would be left for food or even to pay the tolls at the toll stations on the turnpikes. "Those I was obliged to defraud by riding as hard as I could through them all, not paying the least regard to the men who called out to stop me."

Once in London, although utterly destitute, he took a carriage to the house of his family on Marlborough Street, expecting to pay for the ride with funds given him by his relatives when he got home.

But when I came there I found the house shut up. Having been absent so many years, and in all that time never having heard a word from home, I knew not who was dead or who was living, or where to go next, or even how to pay the coachman. I recollected a linen-draper's shop not far from thence which our family had [patronized]. I therefore drove there next, and, making myself known, they paid the coachman. I then inquired after our family and was told that my sister had married Lord Carlisle and was at that time in Soho Square. I immediately walked to the house and knocked at the door. But the porter, not liking my [attire] which was half French, half Spanish, with the addition of a large pair of boots covered with dirt, he was going to shut the door in my face, but I prevailed upon him to let me in.

I need not acquaint my readers with what surprise and joy my sister received me. She immediately furnished me with money sufficient to appear like the rest of my countrymen. Till that time I could not properly be said to have finished all the extraordinary scenes which a series of unfortunate adventures had kept me in for the space of five years and upwards.

John Byron's later career was hardly less illustrious than that of Lord Anson. In 1764, he made a rapid circumnavigation of the globe in search of the mythical continent of the Pacific, Terra Australis Incognita. The books he wrote about his experiences on that voyage and the earlier one aboard the *Wager* achieved great popularity. He subsequently served as governor of Newfoundland, and then, having been promoted to the rank of rear admiral, he commanded a fleet in the War of American Independence.

But common seamen were less concerned with a leader's rank than with his luck, and among them Byron developed the reputation of being something of a Jonah. His frequent encounters with severe storms caused him to be given the nickname Foul Weather Jack.

In his personal life he was a rake and libertine, traits presaged in the narrative of his marooning. In such vices he carried on an old family tradition. Yet his son, who earned the sobriquet Mad Jack and went through the fortunes of the two heiresses he married, so outdid his father in the familial profligacy that the affronted old man felt compelled to disown him.

The most famous and outrageous member of the family, however, would be Mad Jack's son, a young fellow who combined his grandfather's love of martial adventure and inclination to literary expression with his father's roguery. Once lionized by society, he would make himself its outcast by conducting an affair with his half sister. Club-footed athlete, swimmer of the Hellespont, incestuous lover, passionate pursuer of British choir boys and Venetian drapers' wives, he was one of the great poets of the English language, George Gordon, Lord Byron.

CHAPTER 10

The Utility of a Fashionable Hat

The Sloop *Betsy* Adrift Near Tobago

Captain Cheap and Midshipman Byron were not the first officers nor the last to have subordinates who, during a shipwreck, were more inclined to resort to liquor than to hard work. Indeed, as Byron's grandson once observed in a poem, "Even the able seaman, deeming his / Days nearly o'er, might be disposed to riot, / As upon such occasions tars will ask / For grog, and sometimes drink rum from the cask." When he wrote those lines, Lord Byron had in mind not only his grandfather's experience on the *Wager* but also a certain incident that took place during the sinking of the *Earl of Abergavenny*.

The *Earl* was run aground on rocks only two miles from land on February 5, 1805. She was freed, but not before her hull was damaged, and she soon began to leak. The pumps were manned and signal guns fired, but after several hours it became clear that the ship would go down. Two boats were hoisted out for passengers and some of the officers who were seeking the aid of the nearby shore's inhabitants.

The crew had not had time to think about the straits they were in while they worked the pumps or bailed or rushed to hoist out the boats, but soon after the departure, a huge wave struck the *Earl*. The impact terrified them, and from that moment their officers lost all control over them. "Everyone seemed assured of his fate," a contemporary account states, and it was not long before some of the seamen begged for an additional ration of liquor. When their request was refused, they attacked the spirit room, but they were repulsed by officers, "who never once lost sight of their character, or that dignity so necessary to be preserved on such an occasion, but continued to conduct themselves with the utmost fortitude to the last.''

One of the *Earl*'s officers, anticipating that the men might follow their baser instincts, had early on stationed himself with his back against the spirit room door. He held a brace of pistols "to guard against surprise in so critical a moment,'' and he remained at his post even as the vessel began to sink. With the sea pouring in on all sides, this extraordinary fellow was "importuned" by one persistent sailor to let him have some liquor. The thirsty man argued that "it would be all one with them in an hour hence,'' and since it did not matter whether they died drunk or sober, they might as well be drunk. The stalwart officer refused to accept the compelling logic of the argument: if it was God's will that they should perish, he thought they "should die like men.''

The *Earl* sank with great loss of life. Whether the courageous fellow with the pistols got off is not known, but the captain, John Wordsworth, was among those who drowned. He was warned that the waters were rising, "that all exertions were now in vain,'' and he had better get off, but he declined to do so. Instead he turned to Mr. Baggot, the man who had warned him, and looking at him steadily with the expression of "a heart-broken man,'' softly whispered, "Let her go! God's will be done!'' They were his last words. He stood stock-still as the water rose around him and made no effort to save himself. Some of his crewmen did try to rescue him from the sea, but they could not, and so he went down with the ship.

'' 'Silence!' the brave commander cried,'' his younger brother, William, would write.

> To that calm word a shriek replied,
> It was the last death-shriek.
> — A few (my soul oft sees that sight)
> Survive upon the tall mast's height;
> But one dear remnant of the night —
> For Him in vain I seek.
>
> Six weeks beneath the moving sea
> He lay in slumber quietly;
> Unforced by wind or wave
> To quit the ship for which he died,
> (All claims of duty satisfied;)
> And there they found him at her side;
> And bore him to the grave.

John Wordsworth's death was a terrible blow to William, and during the next year he pored over every report of the wreck and composed at least three poems about it.

Other verses of interest to us were written by Wordworth's contemporary, George Gordon, Lord Byron. For the second canto of *Don Juan,* Byron drew details not only from a narrative of the loss of the *Earl* and from his grandfather's account of the *Wager*'s sinking but also from a number of other survivor stories, including that of Philip Aubin. These stories did not show people acting as bulwarks against distress, and he unflinchingly if lyrically depicted this reality. Thus, when the leaky, storm-tossed *Trinidada* seems about to sink, the poet has the sailors, thirsty for drink, rush the storeroom. It is the young Don Juan "who, with sense beyond his years," uses a pair of pistols to hold off those "who, ere they sunk; / Thought it would be becoming to die drunk.''*

Byron understood that castaways in an open boat on the stormy sea faced dangers at least as great as those to be found in a leaky hulk with an inebriated crew. He knew what deprivation could do, even if he expressed it humorously.

> But man is a carnivorous production,
>   And must have meals, at least one meal a day;
> He cannot live, like woodcocks, upon suction,
>   But, like the shark and tiger, must have prey;
> Although his anatomical construction
>   Bears vegetables, in a grumbling way,
> Your laboring people think, beyond all question
> Beef, veal, and mutton, better for digestion.

Lord Byron continues the poem with a mixture of whimsy and grim truth as the ranks of the castaways are thinned by deprivation, and they turn to cannibalism.

> At length one whispered his companion, who
>   Whispered another, and thus it went round,

*Byron's hero facing down the villains recalls an incident from his own life. One day, while visiting Greece, he was daydreaming on a beach. He saw a half dozen soldiers carrying a large sack down to the ocean. When he asked what they were doing, he was told that they had caught a young Turkish girl in the midst of an act of illicit love; as punishment they had sewn her up in the sack, which they were now about to throw into the water. . . . The poet produced a pistol. The leveled piece and his appeal to sweet reason convinced these guardians of morals that they should turn her over to the Turkish governor instead. Byron then persuaded the *Waiwode* to release the girl, and he spirited her out of the area.

> And then into a hoarser murmur grew,
> An ominous, and wild, and desperate sound;
> And when his comrade's thought each sufferer knew,
> 'Twas but his own, suppressed till now, he found;
> And out they spoke of lots for flesh and blood,
> And who should die to be his fellow's food.

In the end only Don Juan is left alive to crawl up on a convenient shore. At this point the poet gives in completely to fancy and has him found by a sweet resident of the place — a seventeen-year-old nubile nymph who nurses him back to health and whom he seduces.

Captain Philip Aubin, like Midshipman Byron, had a dog, but he killed him himself and, having done so, was quite willing to eat him. He was never reduced to murdering his fellows, and his adventure ended only slightly less cheerfully than Don Juan's — he was found and cared for by kindly islanders.

Near midnight on the evening of August 4, 1756, the *Betsy* lay at anchor far north of the coast of Surinam. Captain Aubin had not yet gone below for the night because of a sudden change in the weather. The wind's velocity was increasing with the rising of the moon, and his heavy-laden vessel was laboring excessively in the ocean. He therefore thought it wiser not to retire until conditions moderated. He sat on a hen coop, drinking beer and swapping sea stories with a mate named Williams, passing the hours in this time-honored "custom of mariners of every country."

Below deck was a full cargo of goods taken on at Carlisle Bay in the island of Barbados four days before. The most valuable commodities the *Betsy* held were horses: a shortage of the animals in Surinam had led the colonists to pass a law forbidding any English ship from entering the harbor unless her cargo was at least partially composed of them. "The Dutch were so rigid in enforcing this condition," Aubin wrote, "that if the horses chanced to die on their passage, the master of the vessel was obliged to preserve the ears and hoofs of the animals, and to swear upon entering the port of Surinam, that when he embarked they were alive, and destined for that colony."

Suddenly the sloop swung broadside to the wind and then swung back with her head to the sea and plunged, her head filling with water "in such a manner that she could not rise above the surf." Now a huge wave struck, and all who were on deck were up to their

necks in water. The sea rushed into the hull, and the crewmen
sleeping there drowned in their hammocks without so much as a cry
or a groan.

> When the wave passed, I took the hatchet that was hanging up near
> the fireplace, to cut away the shrouds to prevent the ship from upset-
> ting, but in vain. She upset, and turned over again, with her masts
> and sails in the water. The horses rolled one over the other and were
> drowned, forming altogether a most melancholy spectacle.
>
> I had but one small boat, about twelve or thirteen feet long. She
> was fixed, with a cable coiled inside of her, between the pump and
> the side of the ship. Providentially for our preservation there was no
> occasion to lash her fast; but we at this time entertained no hope of
> seeing her again, as the large cable within her, together with the
> weight of the horses, and their stalls entangled one among another,
> prevented her from rising to the surface of the water.

Aubin held on to the shrouds with one hand and stripped off his
clothing with the other so that he might swim without hindrance.
He looked for a plank or an empty box to cling to as a life preserver
but saw none, spying instead the only other survivors of the wreck
— the mate and two sailors; they were hanging on to a rope and
imploring God to receive their souls. "I told them that the man who
was not resigned to die when it pleased the Creator to call him out
of the world was not fit to live." Having thus dispensed with theol-
ogy, he advised them to undress as he had and use whatever buoy-
ant objects they could find to keep themselves afloat.

Williams alone obeyed. A short time before, he had been drinking
beer with the captain and telling lies; now he swam naked in the
stormy ocean. It was he who found the keel of the submerged boat
and called out to Aubin, who swam to his side. Together they struggled to turn her over and finally succeeded, but of course she was
filled with water.

> I got into her and endeavored by means of a rope belonging to the
> rigging to draw her to the mast of the vessel. In the intervals between
> waves the mast always rose to a height of fifteen or twenty feet above
> the water. I passed the end of the rope fastened to the boat once
> round the head of the mast, keeping hold of the end. Each time that
> the mast rose out of the water it lifted up both the boat and me. I then
> let go the rope and by this expedient the boat was three-fourths
> emptied; but having nothing to enable me to disengage her from the
> mast and shrouds, they fell down upon me, driving the boat and me
> again under water.

Nearly all the *Betsy* was submerged, with only a small part of her stern above the surface of the water. After repeatedly trying to empty the boat, the captain put her rope in his teeth, dove into the water, and swam to the mate and the two disheartened sailors who were clinging to the stern. They took the rope from him, and then all four labored to drag the craft up over the stern and thus empty her. They succeeded, but in the process a hole was torn in her bottom.

One of the sailors had stripped naked, but the other was still wearing his clothes — pants, a coarse shirt with a knife in its pocket, and a large hat "in the Dutch fashion." All of these items would prove extremely useful.

The man got into the boat, cut off a piece of his shirt, and stuffed it into the hole. As Aubin climbed in after him to supervise the repair, he saw his dog come running along the gunwale. He reached down and scooped him up, at the same time ominously thanking Providence "for having thus sent provision for a time of necessity." It was food, not affection, that the captain and his crew would be needing.

The *Betsy* shifted suddenly, and the rope that held the boat snapped under the strain. The craft began to drift away. Aubin called to the mate and the other man, who still clung to the stern, and they came swimming, the mate bringing with him a small, spare topmast to use as a rudder. The captain helped the men in, and they soon lost sight of the "ill-fated" sloop.

At dawn they found floating about them boxes of provisions. The captain was particularly delighted to see one that belonged to him; it contained clothes, linen, bottles of orange and lime water, sugar, and a few pounds of chocolate. It was too big to wrestle into the boat, and the men tried unsuccessfully to pry off its lid. In the effort they nearly swamped their craft.

Of the relative richness around them, they were able to garner only thirteen onions. Lacking water or other food (except the dog), they would have to subsist on the onions until they reached land. They were without the most elemental sailing devices — no canvas, oars, or proper mast — while facing a journey of fifty leagues or more. The only tool they had was the one man's knife, and the only material was his clothing; they spent the first part of the day cutting his shirt into strips, which they twisted for rigging. Then they took turns cutting around all the nail heads of the planks that lined the

boat and painfully worked them loose. They tied the planks to a
bench to form a mast and used a board for a yard and two pieces of
the seaman's trousers for sails. In this fashion they ran before the
wind, steering with the topmast Williams had saved.

When the waves ran high, water lapped over the gunwales. Two
men were forced to lie down along them with their backs to the
ocean "and thus with our bodies . . . repel the surf, while [another
man], with the Dutch hat, was incessantly employed in bailing out
the water; besides which the boat continued to make water at the
leak, which we were unable entirely to stop."

The first night they made progress at a rate of one league an hour.
The following day the naked survivors sat in the craft, eating onions
and feeling melancholy. That night the wind grew violent and vari-
able, often blowing from the north and forcing the captain to steer
to the south. This made him very anxious since he was certain that
the closest land lay to the west.

> The third day we began to suffer exceedingly, not only from hunger
> and thirst but likewise from the heat of the sun, which scorched us in
> such a manner that from the neck to the feet our skin was as red and
> as full of blisters as if we had been burned by a fire. I then seized my
> dog and plunged the knife in his throat. I cannot even now refrain
> from weeping at the thought of it; but at the moment I felt not the
> least compassion for him. We caught his blood in the hat, receiving
> in our hands and drinking what ran over. We afterwards drank in turn
> out of the hat, and felt ourselves refreshed. The fourth day the wind
> was extremely violent and the sea ran very high, so we were more
> than once on the point of perishing. It was on this day in particular
> that we were obliged to make a rampart of our bodies in order to
> repel the waves. About noon a ray of hope dawned upon us but soon
> vanished.

This hope was in the form of a sloop seen at a distance. Aubin knew
her to be out of Barbados bound to Demerara, under the authority
of Captain Southey. This man was his friend, one who would surely
make every effort to save them, and they came so close to the sloop
that they could actually see the crew moving about on her. But the
shouts of the castaways could not be heard in the gale, and the
seamen, intent on keeping their vessel afloat, never saw the little
craft.

The disappointment was too terrible for the two sailors. They
refused to do anything more to keep the boat afloat. Aubin desper-

ately pleaded with them and gradually brought one of them around, but the other remained obdurate, refusing even to bail with the hat. The water was filling the bottom of the craft. It took two men to lie on the gunwales and one to steer. If she was to stay afloat, it was crucial that the fourth man scoop out the water. The captain knelt before him and begged for his help, yet he would not bestir himself.

Aubin and Williams conferred theatrically in shouts along these lines: *"If this fellow will not help us we are lost. We shall drown miserably in this sea." "Why should we not put a quicker end to it? Let us bash his head in with the topmast and then open our veins with the knife."*

The sailor took up the hat and began to bail.

Their hunger was increasing, but they had been without water for such a long time that their throats had closed, and all of them were reluctant to eat the flesh of the dog. The captain set an example for the others by chewing on a piece with some onion. He found it difficult to swallow even a few mouthfuls, but no matter how repugnant, the food was nourishing: after only an hour he felt stronger. Williams was able to eat a larger amount, and one of the seamen tried a bite. The fourth man, however, "either would not or could not swallow a morsel."

At dawn on the fifth day, the wind became calm and the ocean smooth. They awoke to find a flying fish in the bottom of the boat and a gigantic shark, as large as their craft, in their wake. They cut the fish into four parts and chewed on the pieces to draw out the moisture, and they watched the shark follow them for several hours, as if they were prey "destined for him."

Eventually the shark turned away, but their relief was short-lived. Before the day was over, they had become so desperate for food that, "pressed with hunger and despair, my mate, Williams, had the generosity to exhort us to cut off a piece of his thigh to refresh ourselves with the blood and [so] to support life." Philip Aubin does not say whether this offer was accepted, but since he makes no further reference to it or to a consequent disability on the part of the mate, it seems certain that no surgery was performed.

That night there were showers. They took the trousers down from the mast, caught rain in them, and then wrung them out above their open mouths. Unfortunately, the cloth was so impregnated with salt that they thought they might as well be drinking sea water. They lay on their backs and let the drops fall on their tongues. When the clouds passed, they rehung the trousers.

On the sixth day the two seamen, notwithstanding all my remonstrances, drank sea water, which purged them so excessively that they fell into a kind of a delirium and were of no more service to Williams and me. Both he and I kept a nail in our mouths and often sprinkled our heads with water to cool them. I perceived myself the better for these ablutions and that my head was more easy. We tried several times to eat of the dog's flesh, with a morsel of onion; but I thought myself fortunate if I could get down three or four mouthfuls. My mate always [ate] rather more than I could.

The seventh day was fine, with a moderate breeze, and the sea perfectly calm. About noon the two men who had drunk the sea water grew so weak that they began to talk wildly, like people who are light-headed, not knowing any longer whether they were at sea or on shore. My mate and I were so weak too that we could scarcely stand on our legs, or steer the boat in our turns, or bail the water from the boat, which made a great deal at the leak.

On the morning of the eighth day one of the sailors died, and by afternoon the other was gone as well.

At sunset Aubin sighted in the distance the high cliffs of the island of Tobago. "Hope gave us strength," he remembered later, and so they held the craft on a steady course in the darkness of that awful evening. "Williams and I were that night in an extraordinary situation, our two comrades lying dead before us, with the land in sight, having very little wind to approach it, and being assisted only by the current, which drove strongly to the westward."

In the early light of the morning, Aubin was able to estimate that they were now only five or six leagues from the shore. The wind picked up, and all through the day, too weak to stand, they sat in the boat and held their course. As darkness fell the wind died, yet the current pushed them on. At about two o'clock the keel of the craft ground against the high shore of Tobago, widening the hole in her bottom. The two men crawled out and struggled up the steep slope on their hands and knees. Reaching the summit, three hundred feet above the beach, they found the ground covered with leaves. They pushed them together in piles and lay down on them to wait for morning.

At dawn they rose to search for water and discovered a little in the crevices of rocks, but it was brackish. They gathered several kinds of shellfish, and they broke these open with a stone and chewed them for moisture.

Sometime between eight and nine o'clock, they saw a Carib Indian swim around the point of a projecting rock in the sea and make his way to the boat. When he reached her and saw the corpses inside, he turned back and shouted to two natives who were following him, "making signs of the greatest compassion. His comrades instantly followed him and swam towards us, having perceived us almost at the same time."

The three Caribs approached the castaways. They wept as they got a close look at their condition. Aubin attempted to talk with them, but they knew no English and only a few words of French. Resorting to hand signals, the captain managed to communicate that he and Williams had been at sea for nine days and were "in want of every thing." The oldest of the men signed back that they would fetch a canoe to carry the Europeans to their huts; then he took a handkerchief from his head and tied it around the captain's head, and one of the young men followed suit by giving the mate his straw hat.

The other [Carib] swam around the projecting rock and brought us a calabash of fresh water, some cakes of cassava, and a piece of broiled fish, but we could not eat. The two others took the corpses out of the boat and laid them upon the rock, after which all three of them hauled the boat out of the water. They then left us, with marks of the utmost compassion, and went to fetch their canoe.

About noon they returned in their canoe, to the number of six, and brought with them, in an earthen pot, some soup which we thought delicious. We took a little, but my stomach was so weak that I immediately cast it up again. Williams did not vomit at all. In less than two hours we arrived at Man-of-War Bay, where the huts of the Caribs are situated. They had only one hammock, in which they laid me, and the woman made us a very agreeable mess of herbs and broth of *quatracas* and pigeons. They bathed my wounds, which were full of worms, with a decoction of tobacco and other plants. Every morning the man lifted me out of the hammock and carried me in his arms beneath a lemon tree, where he covered me with plantain leaves to screen me from the sun. There they anointed our bodies with a kind of oil to cure the blisters raised by the sun. Our compassionate hosts even had the generosity to give each of us a shirt and a pair of trousers, which they had procured from ships that came from time to time to trade with them for turtles and tortoise shell.

After they had cleansed my wounds of vermin they kept me with my legs suspended in the air and anointed them morning and evening with an oil extracted from the tail of a small crab, resembling what the English call the soldier crab, because its shell is red. They take a certain quantity of these crabs, bruise the ends of their tails and put them to digest in a large shell upon the fire. It was with this ointment that they healed my wounds, covering them with nothing but plantain leaves.

After three weeks of such care Aubin was able to move about on crutches.

From all over the island natives came to see the white men, and they invariably brought gifts of food "which were given with pleasure, and accepted with gratitude." When visitors began arriving from Trinidad, the captain hit upon the idea of carving his name into pieces of wood and distributing them to various Indians. He thought that if a European ship sailed into the area, the wood might be shown to her crew and thus bring about his and Williams's deliverance.

Finally a sloop with a cargo of mules came by the west side of Tobago, and her sailors were given a carved plank. They did not turn out of their way to find the *Betsy*'s survivors, but the message was passed from ship to ship until it reached Aubin's employers. They immediately dispatched a small vessel, which arrived nine weeks after the castaways had come ashore.

When the captain and the mate were ready to embark, the Caribs brought them many gifts: bananas, figs, yams, fowl, fish, lemons, and oranges. Aubin had nothing to give in return but the boat, which his hosts had long since repaired and were using for turtle hunting. "Of this I made them a present and would have given them my blood." When he lamented his inability to reciprocate more generously, the rescue vessel's captain let him have some goods that he gratefully gave away: seven or eight bottles of rum, shirts and trousers, sail cloth, needles, rope, and assorted knives and fishhooks.

And then it was time to go.

> At length after two days spent in preparations for our departure, we were obliged to separate. They came down to the beach to the number of about thirty men, women and children, and all appeared to feel the sincerest sorrow, especially the old man, who had acted like a father to me. When the vessel left the bay the tears flowed from our eyes, which still continued fixed upon them. They remained standing in a line upon the shore till they lost sight of us. As we set sail about

nine o'clock in the morning, steering north-east, and as Man-of-War Bay is situated in the north-east point of the island, we had a long last time in sight of each other. I still recollect the moment when they disappeared from my sight, and the profound regret which filled my heart. I feared that I should never again be so happy as I had been among them. I love them and will continue to love my dear Caribs as long as I live; I would shed my blood for the first of those benevolent savages that might stand in need of my assistance, if chance should ever bring one of them to Europe or my destiny should again conduct me to their island.

For all the kind ministrations of the Indians, Philip Aubin was not fully recovered from his ordeal. When he arrived at Barbados after a three-day voyage, he was still having trouble speaking and breathing, felt "a violent oppression" on his chest, and continued to have to use crutches. Two doctors, including one who had authored a book on island diseases, treated him, prescribing a variety of remedies, but none proved effective. After all their efforts, his condition remained unchanged.

Williams was in only slightly better shape, but he had a stronger constitution and so would more easily recover. He chose to remain behind when Aubin decided to follow the advice of his physicians and return to Europe to seek further remedy.

During his first week in London, Aubin was treated by three doctors and, when their cures had little effect, by a number of others who were among "the most celebrated physicians of that metropolis." It was all for naught. At last Dr. Alexander Russell returned to the city after a stay in Bath. As soon as he heard of this famous patient, he hurried to test his skills. He offered to undertake his rehabilitation without fee but warned him that the treatment itself would be expensive — and tedious.

Money was not the castaway's concern: for the people on Barbados he had been an object of "the most tender interest and the most generous compassion," which included their giving him gifts of money.

As [Russell] had practiced for a long time at Aleppo, he had there seen great numbers afflicted with the same malady as myself, produced by long thirst in traversing the deserts of Africa. He ordered me to leave town to enjoy a more wholesome air. I took a lodging at Homerton, near Hackney; there he ordered me to be bathed every morning, confining me to asses' milk as my only food, excepting a few new-laid eggs, together with moderate exercise and a ride on horseback every day. After about a month of this regimen he ordered a goat to be brought every morning to my bedside. About five o'clock I drank a glass of her milk, quite hot, and slept upon it. He then allowed me to take some light chicken broth, with a morsel of the wing. By the means of the diet my malady was in great degree removed in the space of about five months, and I was in a state to resume any occupation I pleased.

Captain Philip Aubin never did completely recover. His constitution remained extremely delicate, and his stomach was ever after very weak. So far as is known, he never saw Tobago or any of its kindly inhabitants again.

PART II

THE DELICATE QUESTION WHICH

This case, in order to embrace all its horrid relations, ought to be decided in a long boat, hundreds of leagues from the shore, loaded to the very gunwale with forty-two half-naked victims, with provisions only sufficient to prolong the agonies of famine and thirst. . . . Decided at such a tribunal, nature, intuition, would at once pronounce a verdict not only of acquittal but of commendation.

— David Brown, attorney for Alexander Holmes

CHAPTER 11

The Pleasure of God

Richard Clarke in the *Admiral*'s Boat

The severest dilemma faced by victims of shipwrecks concerns the value of life itself: whether to sacrifice one or more of their number so that the rest might live at least a while longer. Put simply, if you are in an overcrowded lifeboat on a stormy ocean, do you have the right to eject some of her occupants — even though to do so means their immediate and certain death — in order to make her more seaworthy? If you are dehydrated or starving (and most commonly both), do you have the right to kill one of your companions to obtain nourishment? And keep in mind that the murder may prove futile or unnecessary. A gale that will sink your craft may come up in an hour, or a sail or landfall may be just over the horizon; safety may be only a few hours away, so there is no need for anyone to die. Or, having eaten the first victim, you may have to kill again and again and again. How many people are you willing to murder just to cling a brief time longer to your own miserable existence? And what assurance have you that, having committed the terrible deed, you will not die, anyway?

Even now your self-examination is not at an end, for once you have decided in favor of sacrifice, you must answer corollary questions: by what criterion and method do you determine who is to be the victim? These are matters of no small consequence, since you would not want to be rescued only to be charged with murder, and you would want your chances of being eaten to be no greater than those of your comrades.

A poem by Sir William S. Gilbert brings these issues nicely into relief.

The Yarn of the *Nancy Bell*

'Twas on the shores that round our coast
    From Deal to Ramsgate span,
That I found alone on a piece of stone
    An elderly naval man.

His hair was weedy, his beard was long,
    And weedy and long was he,
And I heard this wight on the shore recite,
    In a singular minor key:

"Oh, I am a cook and a captain bold,
    And the mate of the *Nancy* brig,
And a bo'sun tight, and a midshipmite,
    And the crew of the captain's gig."

And he shook his fists and he tore his hair,
    Till I really felt afraid,
For I couldn't help thinking the man had been drinking,
    And so I simply said:

"Oh, elderly man, it's little I know
    Of the duties of men of the sea,
But I'll eat my hand if I understand
    How you can possibly be

"At once a cook, and a captain bold,
    And the mate of the *Nancy* brig,
And a bo'sun tight, and a midshipmite,
    And the crew of the captain's gig."

Then he gave a hitch to his trousers, which
    Is a trick all seamen larn,
And having got rid of a thumping quid,
    He spun this painful yarn:

" 'Twas in the good ship *Nancy Bell*
    That we sailed to the Indian sea,
And there on a reef we come to grief,
    Which has often occurred to me.

"And pretty nigh all o' the crew was drowned
    (There was seventy-seven o' soul),
And only ten of the *Nancy*'s men
    Said 'Here!' to the muster-roll.

"There was me and the cook and the captain bold,
    And the mate of the *Nancy* brig,
And the bo'sun tight, and a midshipmite,
    And the crew of the captain's gig.

"For a month we'd neither wittles nor drink,
    Till a-hungry we did feel,
So we drawed a lot, and accordin' shot
    The captain for our meal.

"The next lot fell to the *Nancy*'s mate,
    And a delicate dish he made;
Then our appetite with the midshipmite
    We seven survivors stayed.

"And then we murdered the bo'sun tight,
    And he much resembled pig;
Then we wittled free, did the cook and me,
    On the crew of the captain's gig.

"Then only the cook and me was left,
    And the delicate question, 'Which
Of us two goes to the kettle?' arose
    And we argued it out as sich.

"For I loved that cook as a brother, I did,
    And the cook he worshipped me;
But we'd both be blowed if we'd either be stowed
    In the other chap's hold, you see.

" 'I'll be eat if you dines off me,' says Tom,
    'Yes, that,' says I, 'you'll be,' —
'I'm boiled if I die, my friend,' quoth I,
    And 'Exactly so,' quoth he.

"Says he, 'Dear James, to murder me
    Were a foolish thing to do,
For don't you see that you can't cook *me*,
    While I can — and will — cook *you!*'

"So he boils the water, and takes the salt
    And the pepper in portions true
(Which he never forgot), and some chopped shalot,
    And some sage and parsley too.

" 'Come here,' says he, with a proper pride,
    Which his smiling features tell,
"Twill soothing be if I let you see,
    How extremely nice you'll smell.'

"And he stirred it round and round and round,
    And he sniffed at the foaming froth;
When I ups with his heels, and smothers his squeals
    In the scum of the boiling broth.

Two drawings by Sir William S. Gilbert illustrating "The Yarn of the *Nancy Bell*." Tom and James debate the "delicate question which"; having won the argument, James, like the ancient mariner, feels compelled to wander the world telling his woeful tale. (Copy prints courtesy of the Library of Congress)

> "And I eat that cook in a week or less,
> And — as I eating be
> The last of his chops, why, I almost drops,
> For a wessel in sight I see!

> . . . .

> "And I never grieve, and I never smile,
> And I never larf nor play,
> But I sit and croak, and a single joke
> I have — which is to say:

> "Oh, I am a cook and a captain bold,
> And the mate of the *Nancy* brig,
> And a bo'sun tight, and a midshipmite,
> And the crew of the captain's gig!"

For the whimsical Gilbert, then, as for many real survivors, the *method* of determining who was to die was the drawing of lots, and where it was not brought into play, the *criterion* for choosing the imminent occupant of the pot was often based, theoretically, at least, on who had the greater survival skills. On a practical level, the outcome of the debate might be decided, as it was between Tom and James, on the basis of who sized up the situation most quickly, seized an opportunity (in this case, literally), or had the greatest physical strength.

While Gilbert poses the dilemma humorously, its true nature is more appropriately expressed by Walt Whitman, who wrote that when he sat by his window and considered all the sorrows of the world, "I observe a famine at sea, I observe sailors casting lots / who shall be kill'd to preserve the lives of the rest, / . . . all the meanness and agony without end I sitting / look out upon, / See, hear, and am silent."

Even where the drawing of lots to preserve the lives of some men at expense of others did not involve cannibalism, not all those in peril were willing for any selection to be made, for any sacrifice to take place. One of these was Richard Clarke of the *Admiral*, which was run aground and lost in 1583 through the stubborn foolishness of Clarke's commanding officer.

Sixteen men climbed or were hauled into a boat that had very few

provisions and only one oar. Her occupants did not expect to live
very long. They sought, said Clarke,

> to prolong their lives as long as it pleased God, and looked every
> moment of an hour when the sea would eat them up, the boat being
> so little and so many men in her, and so foul weather that it was not
> possible for a ship to brook half a course of sail. Thus while we
> remained two days and nights and that we saw it pleased God our
> boat lived in the sea (although we had nothing to help us withal but
> one oar, which we kept up the boat withal upon the sea, and so went
> even as the sea would drive us). There was in our company one [Mr.]
> Hedely that put forth [a] question to me the master.

Clarke may have been willing to accept their plight and trust in
the will of God, but Hedely wanted to intervene, to affect their
common fate and alter it for the good of . . . those lucky in the
draw. Behind Hedely's question was a realistic appraisal of their
situation and a cold-eyed proposition. Their craft had too many men
in her to stay afloat much longer; he asked that fifteen lots be made
and the men who drew the four short ones be cast overboard.
Hedely added the sweetener: of course, *Clarke,* being the master,
would not have to take a lot. He alone would be *exempt* from the
drawing; *his* preservation was assured.

No doubt Hedely thought this would win Clarke over. No doubt
it would have — had Clarke been a man like Hedely.

Richard Clarke refused to allow it. He insisted that they would all
live or die together.

Hedely persisted. He wanted to know how good the master's
memory was. Did the master recall how far they were from shore?

Richard Clarke praised God for the clarity of his memory and
proceeded to lie to the men in the boat: land was only three score
leagues away, he said, and would be reached in two or three days.

For the next two days the wind continued to blow them south,
just as it had the first two. They remained without "any sustenance,
save only the weeds that swam in the sea, and salt water to drink."
On their fifth day, two men died. (Those who see little justice in life
or history will find comfort in this: one of the dead was the hard-
eyed Mr. Hedely.)

> Then we all desired to die, for in all these five days and five nights
> we saw the sun but once and the stars but one night, it was so foul
> weather. Thus we did remain the sixth day. Then we were very weak

and wished all to die saving only myself which did comfort them and promised they should soon to land.

He did more than that: he swore that if they did not reach shore on the seventh day, they should cast *him* overboard.

The sailors did not have the chance to take him at his word. Late in the morning on that seventh day they sighted land, and they reached it four hours later. They were so feeble that they had to help each other out of the boat, and then they knelt together in thankful prayer. Afterward the stronger assisted the weaker to a stream, where they drank fresh water and ate berries that grew nearby.

On this day they witnessed an unusual occurrence that must have reinforced the belief of the more religious in the intervention of divine providence. For the past week the wind had blown in a constant southerly direction, but shortly after they came on the beach, it shifted clear around and blew to the north. Had it shifted at any time during their voyage, they all would have perished on the ocean.

For three days and nights they rested, eating berries and peas and drinking clear, fresh water. Then they put their craft back out to sea and sailed along the line of the coast, going ashore whenever they were hungry or thirsty.

Eventually they encountered a ship from St. John de Luz, and her master kindly took them aboard. The castaways experienced one more dangerous moment when Spanish authorities boarded the vessel and demanded to know their nationality. The master of the ship was able to convince the officials that these were poor Newfoundland fishermen.

That night he set them ashore near the French border, and from there they were able to make their way back to England.

CHAPTER 12

The Carpenter's Remains
John Dean on Boon Island

Survivors who did not have to answer "the delicate question which" still sometimes had to face the horrendous decision of whether or not to eat the bodies of those who had died natural deaths. The present example involves men marooned on an island, but this is an unusual case. More frequently the setting was a longboat or a disabled hulk. There such factors as injuries suffered in battling storms, continued exposure to intemperate weather, age, health, and at the very least a reduced rations of food and water would cause some individuals to die more quickly than others, their corpses providing a means of sustenance for those still breathing.

However desperate the circumstances, the eating of human flesh requires overcoming an ancient and powerful taboo. Anthropologists have found evidence that prehistoric nomadic hunters sometimes made quarries of their own kind. The taboo presumably fell into place as soon as people became pastoral and settled into communities. Thus we are very far from caves containing blade-scarred human bones — until our ship or plane goes down, until we become lost in a frozen land, until our city is besieged by enemy troops. Then, with our food supplies dwindling or gone and famine wasting our bodies, we are transported back to those caves, and we are faced with the same bleak choices our ancestors had. Most often we make the decision they did, and newly scored bones soon litter the campsite or the deck or accumulate in the bottom of the boat. The dead are not always wholly interred when the burial party is starved.

Survival cannibalism where the victim has died naturally is cer-

tainly less repugnant than the commission of murder to obtain nourishment. The English law professor and maritime writer A. W.
Brian Simpson has observed that "though disagreeable and distressing, it is difficult to see any moral objection to this." Yet the practice does violate that deeply ingrained taboo and therefore makes
some of us distinctly uncomfortable. Since several of the stories
that follow involve such violations, it may be useful to examine our
attitudes toward cannibalism, for they are slightly more complex
than Simpson's remark might suggest. The best way to bring them
into relief is to digress briefly on a rather recent example, that
involving the famous Andes plane crash.

On October 13, 1972, a Uruguayan Air Force C-47 was transporting the members of a rugby team and some of their families and fans
from Montevideo to a match in Santiago. The athletes were alumni
of a Roman Catholic college run by an order of Christian Brothers
who had encouraged their charges' interest in rugby as being "morally uplifting," and the young sportsmen called their team the Old
Christians Club.

The aircraft, a Fairchild F-227, crashed among snow-covered
peaks at an elevation of 11,500 feet. Those who did not die on
impact waited seventy days for a rescue that came only after two of
their number walked out of the mountains and guided helicopters
back in. In the meantime, the survivors ate the bodies of those who
had died. They were convinced to take this step by Roberto Canessa, a nineteen-year-old medical student who told them that otherwise they all would perish. He spoke of human flesh in terms of
protein, and the discussions he led caused some of them to compare
cannibalism to a heart transplant, in which the organ of a deceased
donor is removed in order to save a recipient's life.

Antonio Vizinting, a law student who was the same age as Canessa, later gave an interview in which he reflected this attitude in
his rationalization for what had transpired in the Andes. "It was
done, and so be it," he told a *Newsweek* reporter.

> I don't think I have anything to regret and I don't think it was some
> thing evil. I think we used something without movement, without
> life, something completely material, with which sixteen human beings
> can continue to live, perhaps aid their fellow men, and who knows
> what paths God has prepared for them. . . .
> I don't think I'll suffer a trauma or anything of the sort. I'll remem
> ber this with a great deal of affection and love toward all those beings

or persons who died, because thanks to them I am alive at this moment. . . . The subject must be approached as something elevated, as a sort of communion. We were entering into communion with a human body. Instead of doing it with the body of Christ, we were doing it with the body of a comrade in order to prevail.

Concerned that those who had not been on the mountain might fail to think of the cannibalism in such inspirational terms, he added,

It must be remembered that we're not cannibals or brutal about this. That would hurt me, if people were to think that, if the press were to say we acted like animals. We were completely conscious of what we were doing, in full possession of our faculties. We never lost our rationality to [the] environment. We never turned into animals devouring another being or grabbed a piece of leg. We always did it with respect. In little bits.

This description is somewhat at odds with the macabre scene the rescuers found and the ghoulish pranks some of the survivors played in front of them. Still, both the jokes and the uplifting rhetoric may be part of the phenomenon of "psychic numbing," which cannibalism authority Reay Tannahill explains this way: "Behavioral scientists are only just beginning to study the 'psychic numbing' effect of air crashes on the survivors, but it is clear that some people react by adopting an attitude of insensitivity that is subconsciously designed to conceal, as much from themselves as from others, the full extent of the emotional damage they have suffered."

More than *sub*conscious concealment went on in this case, however. The crash victims initially made a pact not to reveal the truth about their actions. Instead they maintained for a time the pleasant fiction that they had subsisted on chocolate and cheese from the plane and on fish they caught in a lake and roots they found under the snow. They said they kept up their morale by organizing work teams and holding prayer meetings at night.

When rumors of cannibalism circulated in Montevideo, the survivors' spokesman steadfastly denied them. Continuing press reports of the allegations infuriated their disbelieving relatives. One insisted to journalists that such behavior "would have been impossible for these boys, who were brought up with deep Christian devotion." The mother of another of the survivors complained, "They were in the mountains for seventy days and nobody made an effort to save them. Now they are trying to draw morbid statements from them. They want to deny the greatest miracle in aviation history."

While the Old Christians were still issuing denials in Uruguay, church authorities in Rome rushed to their defense. On December 27, a prominent Catholic theologian, the Reverend Gino Concetti, wrote in the Vatican newspaper *L'Osservatore Romano* that "if the facts took place as narrated by the survivors, even from the theological and ethical point of view the action cannot be branded as cannibalism. . . . The action is only apparently cannibalistic: the necessity and the priority right to survive deprive it of any negative element."

The "greatest miracle in aviation history" was finally debunked when photographs of the crash site were published in Latin American newspapers. One, which made the front pages, was of the broken fuselage of the C-47; it showed a human leg stripped of all flesh above the ankle lying in the snow, near the fuselage.

The intricate pattern of denial and justification went on. At a press conference on December 29, one Andes survivor claimed that "if Jesus, in the Last Supper, offered his body and blood to all disciples, he was giving us to understand that we must do the same." Another insisted to a reporter that "we did things that in other circumstances could seem to be morbid or macabre. They were unspeakable things that could never be told. Yet what we did was really Christian. We went right back to the very source of Christianity." A third young man continued the religious theme: "We swallowed the little bits of flesh with the feeling that God demanded it of us. We felt like Christians."

Our fascination with cannibalism is such that some survivors who resorted to it have been granted a bizarre celebrity. In the 1880s, for instance, so many people visited the jail cell of Alfred G. Packer, the infamous "Colorado Man-Eater" who had killed and devoured five men, that he was considered something of a tourist attraction. (The entrepreneurial Packer turned a tidy profit selling to the rubberneckers the horsehair watch chains and belts he made.) In 1884, the *Mignonette*'s dinghy, in which a teenage boy had been murdered and cannibalized to sustain the lives of three other castaways, was displayed in a show to raise money for the legal defense of the murderers; a photograph of the craft was later made into a postcard. Other nineteenth-century cannibals made money putting themselves on display at fairs and carnivals. (The conditions of Packer's parole seem to have forbidden such flagrant capitalism.)

The Andes survivors, educated and from well-to-do families, exhibited considerable shrewdness regarding their notoriety. Apparently they agreed among themselves to give the whole story exclusively to one book writer; thus they arranged to tell the "unspeakable things that could never be told," and in the process they controlled how their actions would be depicted. The resulting book, *Alive!*, by British author Piers Paul Read, became an international best seller and earned such ironic accolades as THUNDEROUS ENTERTAINMENT and EXCITING AND HUGELY ENTERTAINING from the *New York Times*, ONE IS STRUCK WITH JOY from the *Village Voice*, THIS BOOK WILL EXCITE YOU from *John Barkham Reviews*, AN ADVENTURE BOTH PHYSICAL AND SPIRITUAL from the *New Yorker*, and, finally, INSPIRATIONAL — SPIRITUAL IF YOU WILL from, of all magazines, *Playboy*.

Accompanying Read on a publicity tour of the U.S. and Europe were the two Old Christians who had walked out of the mountains to get help, Fernando Parrado and Roberto Canessa. Parrado, who had lost "my mother and sister and three of my best friends" in the Andes, had since become quite a luminary in Montevideo, having found that his fame "opened many doors" for him. When the movie rights to the book were sold, Parrado and Canessa were hired as the film's consultants.

In June 1975, Parrado, a handsome bachelor, told *Newsweek*'s "Update" reporters that he was hoping to meet Raquel Welch when he went to Hollywood, but Canessa was giving serious thought to how their experiences would be depicted cinematically. "We, and what we did, will be judged by how our situation is portrayed in the movie. It is important that even little details, such as the position we slept in at night in the fuselage, are correct." More important and more riveting details — those involving cannibalism — he hoped would not be shown onscreen. "To us, now, it is nothing. We have done it and we know why we have done it. The families of our dead comrades understand. But for the world at large it is difficult."

We have already seen that when the ship goes down, some sailors are more inclined to raid the liquor stores than to save themselves or others. Both John Byron and Richard Clarke struggled to keep some of their men from stupid or cruel behavior. To these names we now add that of Captain John Dean, who saw deprivation bring out the worst in some of those under his command. The Andes survivors claimed they never became irrational, but this could not be said for all of those who swam away from the wreck of the *Nottingham Galley*. Dean was at pains to prevent his men from "grabbing a piece of leg," as young Vizinting would have it; that is, he recognized the danger of fights breaking out, of men squabbling and killing one another over trifles, of gluttony resulting in murder. Like Master Clarke, he would seek to preserve order and discipline and to keep his men conscious of their humanity. Unlike Clarke, however, Captain Dean would fail.

Late in the fall of 1710, the *Nottingham Galley* departed for Boston from London, England, with a cargo of butter and cheese. East of Piscataqua, she encountered a "hard gale" that drove her off course and wrecked her off the coast of Maine on a boulder known as Boon Island. Dean had seen the breakers ahead, but the crew had been unable to turn the ship away from the hazard.

With the sea battering the *Nottingham* and waves washing over her, no man could stand on deck. It was so dark and the storm so severe that they could not see the island on which they had wrecked, and the captain ordered everyone below to pray. Believing that "prayers without endeavors are vain," he soon directed his crew back topside to try to cut away the masts. Not all seamen complied: some had such guilty consciences that they remained below, praying. The effort to cut away the masts proved unnecessary, for the force of the wind and the waves broke them off.

Dean allowed several of the crew's best swimmers to plunge over the side. If they found a place safe from the tempest and the ocean, they were to call out and direct the others to it.

Meanwhile the captain raced below to grab his papers, money, and what supplies he could carry, especially ammunition and brandy. This effort was also futile — the *Nottingham*'s back had been broken and the beams were giving way; the decks were splitting and the stern was sinking. Dying was all he could do down there, so he hurried topside once more.

No shouts had been heard from the swimmers, but the remaining sailors went over the side, anyway. Captain Dean did, too: "I cast myself with all the strength toward the rock, and it being dead low water and the rock exceedingly slippery I could get no hold but tore my fingers, hands and arms in the most lamentable manner, every wash of the sea fetching me off again, so that it was with the utmost peril and difficulty that I got safe on shore at last.''

He was amazed to find that his entire crew had managed to get off the wreck. They tried that night to find shelter from the wind, rain, and snow on the leeward side of the rock but could find none. In the darkness they huddled together, hungry and miserable in the bitter cold.

In the morning the ship was gone. The cargo had disappeared, save for a little cheese that they found among the rockweed. They were able to collect some planks, timber, sails, and canvas that had washed up on the shore, but the wood was too wet to ignite. That night they used the canvas to cover themselves as they lay beside and on top of one another for warmth — ''stowed'' like ballast or cordwood, as the captain described it.

The weather lifted a little, and the next morning John Dean was able to see the mainland in the distance. It was, he estimated, four leagues away, and he used its proximity and promise of deliverance to motivate his dispirited crew to search for more planks with which to build a proper shelter and a boat.

Some of the men were already too disabled to perform even these chores. Several of them, said Dean, had been ''seized'' by the frost, and one, the cook, was complaining of feeling starved. One look at his face and the captain knew he was not malingering. Within a few short hours he had died, and Dean had his body put in a ''convenient place for the sea to carry him away.''

No one suggested eating the corpse at the time, but several of the men would later admit that the thought had occurred to them. They had not been ashore two full days and had been deprived of full rations for only a little longer, yet already they were entertaining thoughts of cannibalism. There would be no waiting until the last extremity for these fellows.

The immediate problem was the cold, which benumbed and discolored their hands and feet to such a degree that they feared what the captain referred to as ''mortifications,'' by which he meant gangrene, which would result from frostbite. Lacking fire to dry their footwear, ''we pulled off our shoes and cut off our boots, but in getting off our stockings many whose legs were blistered pulled off skin and all and some the nails of their toes. We wrapped up our legs as warm as we could in oakum and canvas.''

Dean set the men to building a tent. A triangular form was made of wood (with each leg being eight feet long) and then covered with canvas. To the top of the shelter they attached a staff with a piece of cloth to serve as a distress signal. The tent itself was so small, however, that the fourteen men could fit into it only if they all lay on their sides. Once they were packed in, they had to choreograph their actions: every two hours someone would announce a movement and they all would turn in unison.

Next they constructed a boat. Their tools were a hammer, a caulking mallet, and a saw they had made from a cutlass blade. The planks they hammered together using nails they had worked out of the sheathing or found in the clefts of rocks. They used oakum to caulk the seams, plugged up larger holes with pieces of canvas, and affixed a short mast and a square sail. They had seven oars for rowing and an eighth, longer than the rest, for steering.

The boat was built with painful slowness, as fewer and fewer men were able to crawl from the tent. The rest lay enfeebled; among these was the ship's carpenter, who was so ill he was barely able to give them instructions. At the last only the captain and two others were able to work, and even they were so affected by the cold that they could go outside for no more than four hours at a stretch — when they could go out at all.

One day about a week after their arrival, someone spotted three vessels a few leagues southwest of the isle. Dean made all the men creep out of the shelter and "hullo together so well as our strength would allow, making also the signals we could; but alas, all in vain, they neither hearing nor otherwise discovering us."

Far from disheartening them, this incident raised their spirits. They told themselves that the wind had blown the *Nottingham* in a southwesterly direction, ultimately driving her ashore on the coast. When the wreck was found, a search party would be sent out. "Thus we flattered ourselves in the hopes of deliverance though in vain."

Still, they would not wait passively for rescue. They completed their boat, intending to send several of their number to the mainland for help. (The last stages of their labor had been made easier by the finding of the carpenter's ax, which had been "cast up on the rock.")

The weather on December 21 was clear and the sea relatively calm. The maroons discussed who should attempt the voyage. Dean volunteered; he had remained the strongest, and so he was accepted. Another man volunteered, and five more were chosen, including the captain's brother.

They all prayed together for the success of the journey, and then those who were able struggled to launch the boat. The surf was running so high that the men were required to wade very far out. While the others steadied her, two men clambered into the craft — just as a swell came and tore her out of the hands of those in the water. The force spilled her occupants back into the sea, where in their weakness they nearly drowned, and then hurtled their painstakingly constructed boat against the rock, smashing her to pieces.

John Dean was able to discern the benevolent intervention of God in every occurrence. When the carpenter's ax was found, he knew that Providence had "ordered" it. Now their only hope of escape had been dashed by a wave, an action he himself described as one "totally disappointing our enterprise and destroying all our hopes at once," and this calamity was compounded by the fact that when the wave tipped the craft, it spilled into the sea their means of making another one, the ax and hammer. One waits for him to find the beneficence of his deity in this fresh catastrophe, and the captain does not disappoint: "Yet had we reason to admire the goodness of God in overruling our disappointment for our safety" because that afternoon a wind came up; it blew so hard that Dean was certain it would have sunk their "imitation of a boat" and caused the drowning of those in her.

Dean's religiosity did not blind him to the reality of their plight, however:

> We were now reduced to the most deplorable and melancholy circumstance imaginable, almost every man but myself weak to an extremity and near starved with hunger and cold, their hands and feet frozen and mortified, with large and deep ulcers in their legs, the very smell offensive, and nothing to dress them with but a piece of linen that was cast on the shore. No fire, and the weather extreme cold; our small stock of cheese spent and nothing to support our feeble bodies but rockweed and a few mussels, scarce and difficult to get (at most not above two or three for each man a day). So that we had our miserable bodies perishing and our poor disconsolate spirits overpowered with the deplorable prospect of starving, without any appearance of relief. Besides, to heighten if possible the aggravation, we had to apprehend lest the approaching spring tide (if accompanied with high winds) should totally overflow us. How dismal such a circumstance must be is impossible to express: the pinching cold and

hunger, extremity of weakness and pain, racks and horror of conscience (to many) and foresight of certain and painful but lingering
death, without any (even the most remote) views of deliverance.

In such a situation an air of universal dejection might be expected,
but at least one besides the captain remained undaunted. He was
Swedish, a "stout brave fellow," according to Dean. Although he
had "lost the use of both his feet by the frost," he fervently argued
for another escape attempt, this time, lacking the tools to make a
boat, on a raft. As persistent as he was courageous, the Swede
continually urged the building of such a craft, volunteering to accompany Dean on the voyage or, if he was unwilling to go, to
undertake it alone. Against his insistence the others gave way.
"After deliberate thoughts and consideration," says Captain Dean,
as if to deny that *he* could be swayed to a foolhardy course by
obsessive determination, "we resolved upon a raft but found abundance of labor and difficulty in clearing the foreyard (of which it
was chiefly to be made) from the junk, by reason our working hands
were so few and weak."

But clear the yard they finally did, and then they split it and fixed
lightweight planks four feet in width to the pieces. They attached a
mast and used as a sail two hammocks that had washed ashore. A
paddle was provided for each of the two crewmen in case the wind
failed, and a third was stowed as a spare.

Throughout the construction, the Swede had constantly pestered
the captain about whether or not he intended to make the voyage.
If not, the Swede had already lined up another volunteer "ready to
embrace the offer." In the end, probably so that he could care for
the other men, Dean chose not to go. It would prove a fortunate
decision.

The preparations were interrupted by the sighting of another sail
"come out of the Piscataqua River about seven leagues to the westward." Again the maroons tried to attract the mariners' attention,
and again their effort was futile: the vessel sailed away without
noticing them, "which proved a very great mortification to all our
hopes."

In the middle of the next afternoon, a propitious breeze came up,
and the raft being at last finished, the two men were anxious to set
off. The mate raised his voice in opposition — it was too late in the
day, he thought — but the two men were determined: night would

not hinder them, and they wanted to begin. Reluctantly the captain gave his approval. He called for God's blessing on the undertaking and then helped get the raft into the water.

John Dean's prayer notwithstanding, the venture was an unlucky one. The first swell capsized the raft. The Swede easily swam ashore, but the other man floundered. He was under a long time before he finally broke the surface; when he did, Dean managed to catch hold of him and pull him to safety.

One dunking proved enough for this man. He was unwilling to make a second attempt, but the Swede was as resolute as before. Although the captain sought to talk him out of another launching that day, he was adamant. The choice was simple: Dean could come with him or he would go alone. All he needed was help getting away. Another sailor stepped forward to volunteer, and this time the captain succeeded in pushing them off.

He watched their progress while the light lasted. At twilight they were halfway to the mainland, and he estimated that they would reach it by two A.M. Who can blame him if he crawled into the tent that night elated and rejoicing?

Two days later, some Maine fishermen found the raft on the beach. Some distance from it was the body of the nameless volunteer, a paddle still fastened to his wrist. The ocean that had washed up so little of use to the marooned men had readily given up their dead — one of them, at any rate: the valiant Swede was never found. John Dean would later conclude that the man had drowned with his companion when their raft was overturned in "some breakers, or the violence of the sea overset them and they perished." The discovery of the raft did not lead to the immediate creation of a search party. The fisherfolk apparently felt no urgency about looking for possible survivors.

Captain Dean kept up his patrol of the little island (it was barely one hundred yards long and half that wide), seeking anything edible. The men often saw birds, but these never landed when humans were nearby. They had seen seals upon the rock when they had first been wrecked, but these proved elusive, too. Dean even went out at midnight in the hopes of surprising the beasts, but to no avail.

The creatures being close at hand but unobtainable was a great frustration, a disappointment that, as the captain put it,

was grievous and still served to irritate our miseries, but it was more especially afflicting to a brother I had with me and another young gentleman, who had never either of 'em been at sea or endured any severities before, but were now reduced to the last extremities, having no assistance but what they received from me.

When a piece of green hide washed ashore, Dean carried it to the tent, where the men were crying for it, and they "minced it small and swallowed it down."

After this, Dean busied himself shoring up the shelter against the weather. But there was no shoring up against what was now at hand.

The ship's carpenter, who had been quite ill ever since the wreck and who had long since lost the use of his feet due to frostbite, now complained of terrible back pain and a stiffness in his neck. He had so much mucus in his lungs that his companions thought he might drown from it, and he lacked the strength to cough it up. He was roughly forty-seven years old, and Captain Dean described him as a fat man with a "dull, heavy, phlegmatic constitution and disposition." He was dying, and his comrades could do little for him except pray and use "our utmost endeavors to be serviceable to him in his last moments." Though the man remained conscious to the end, he lost his ability to speak. Late one evening he died, but the men were too weary or dispirited to remove his corpse from the tent.

In the morning, John Dean ordered his crew to put the body outside the shelter and then crawled out to go on his patrol. But when he returned, he did not see the corpse, and he called to his men, demanding to know why they had not complied with his command. They were unable to, they told him. Very well, then; Dean himself tied a rope around the body and coaxed them to help him drag it outside. Once in the open, however, the captain was overcome by fatigue and grief. Feeling faint, he crept back into the tent . . . and immediately his men began beseeching him to let them devour the corpse.

This, of all I had met with, was the most grievous and shocking to me, to see myself and company, who came thither laden with provisions but three weeks before, now reduced to such a deplorable circumstance as to have two of us absolutely starved to death, the other two we knew not what was become of, and the rest of us at the last extremity and though still living yet requiring to eat the dead for support.

After abundance of mature thought and consultation about the lawfulness or sinfulness on the one hand and absolute necessity on the other, judgment, conscience, etc., were obliged to submit to the more prevailing argument of our craving appetites, so that at last we deter-

mined to satisfy our hunger and support our feeble bodies with the
carcass in [our] possession.

Dean, clinging to formalities, told his subordinates that certain
parts of the carpenter were to be given a sea burial: the head, hands,
feet, bowels, and skin. He then stipulated that they were to quarter
the corpse so that it would dry properly. The men replied that they
were unable to do these chores and begged him to perform them. It
was not a task he relished; in fact, it was one that so distressed him
that only their "incessant prayers and entreaties" compelled him to
do it at all. In the end, though, he gave in and set to work.

The dreadful chore took him the rest of the day.

In the evening he brought them thin slices of flesh washed in salt
water, along with rockweed to eat in place of bread. Three men
refused to partake of the food that evening, but by morning they,
too, "earnestly desired" to eat.

All of the men quickly became so voracious that Dean felt it
necessary to carry the quarters of the carcass far from the shelter.
He recognized that overeating would not only pose a danger to their
health but also quickly deplete their "small stock." When the provisions were gone, a new set of dangers would arise, for already he
was having to protect the men from one another. Cannibalism, not
deprivation, had changed their personalities, in his estimation.

I also limited each man to an equal proportion, that none quarrel or
entertain hard thoughts of myself or one another, and I was the more
obliged to this method because I found in a few days that their very
natural dispositions changed, and that affectionate, peaceable temper
they had all along discovered totally lost, their eyes staring and looking wild, their countenances fierce and barbarous, and instead of
obeying my commands as they had universally and readily done before, I found all I could say, even prayers and entreaties, vain and
fruitless, nothing now to be heard but brutish quarrels, with horrid
oaths and imprecations, instead of that quiet, submissive spirit of
prayer and supplication we had before enjoyed.

This, together with the dismal prospect of future want, obliged me
to keep a strict watch over the rest of the body, lest any of 'em should
be able to get to it, and this being spent we be forced to feed upon
the living.

As he crawled out of the tent one morning, Dean saw a shallop
halfway between the mainland and the isle — and she was sailing

straight toward them! It was as if in that moment he had been brought back to life from death.

But the *Nottingham*'s company was not delivered yet. The boat could come no closer than a hundred yards offshore because of the swell. There her crew dropped anchor and waited for a smoother sea. Across the water Dean shouted an account of the calamities he and his men had suffered, omitting the lack of provisions and the resultant cannibalism. He was afraid that if the fishermen knew the truth, they would not dare to land for fear that a sudden shift in the weather would cause them to be marooned, too, and left to starve with those they had come to help. The captain did make it known that they had no fire and asked for the means to build one if the fishermen could not immediately take them away.

One man was dispatched in a canoe, and with an "abundance of labor," he got ashore. As soon as he landed, Dean urgently asked him about the fire, but the poor man was so appalled by the captain's appearance that he had difficulty answering. He was even more aghast when he saw the men in the tent: "So many of us [were] in so deplorable condition, our flesh so wasted and our looks so ghastly and frightful that it was a very dismal prospect."

The fire finally made, Dean climbed into the canoe with the stranger. His intention was that the men should be ferried out to the shallop one or two at a time, but a wave took the craft and dashed her against a rock; the two men spilled out, and John Dean was barely able to save himself and crawl up on the shore. The canoeist managed to swim out to the boat, undoubtedly relieved to be alive and away from that island.

The crew of the shallop elected to sail for home, intending to come back the next day. The maroons watched in great anxiety as she sailed away. Yet as it turned out, they were better off where they were: that night the boat was sunk in a sudden storm. Hearing of it later, Dean would find yet another affirmation of God's benevolence toward his company — had they been in the shallop, they would surely have drowned because they were so feeble.

Once they got home, the would-be rescuers sent word of the maroons' plight to Portsmouth. The citizens of that town were unable to act immediately, however, because the gale raged all the next day.

On Boon Island, realizing that their rescue would be delayed by the weather, the hungry men vehemently demanded more of the carpenter's flesh. Dean gave them a large ration, but they were not satisfied. "They would certainly have eat up the whole at once had I not carefully watched 'em, designing to share [the] rest the next morning if the weather continued bad."

It did not. On that morning, a shallop arrived with a five-man crew. Carrying the maroons from the tent to the water's edge and ferrying them to the boat in a long canoe, they were able to get them all on board in two hours.

The first bite of bread and drink of rum nauseated most of the *Nottingham Galley*'s men, but their sickness "cleansed our stomachs and [after we had] tasted warm, nourishing food we became so hungry and ravenous that had not our worthy friends dieted us and limited the quantity for about two or three days we should certainly have destroyed ourselves with eating."

All of the rescued maroons lived and recovered completely, with the exception of the cabin boy, who lost part of a foot to frostbite.

The story of John Dean raises two questions that deserve brief consideration. The first concerns the role of officers in survival situations; the second has to do with Dean's veracity in depicting his own actions.

A. W. Brian Simpson, in *Cannibalism and the Common Law,* his engaging and thorough study of the *Mignonette* case, observes that "the chance of survival of castaways was enormously increased if they had a competent officer to lead them." One obvious reason for this is that only men of rank had instruction in navigation. The value of an officer to castaways for this reason among others is aptly illustrated by the example of Captain William Bligh's open-boat voyage after the *Bounty* mutiny. His little craft was so laden with men that the gunwales were only inches above the sea's surface, but in forty-seven days he managed to guide her 3,600 miles across the ocean. Despite the burning sun, storms, the attacks of savage islanders (the castaways had no firearms), and a daily ration of little more than an ounce of bread and a few ounces of water per man, Bligh lost only one of his company, and that was in a skirmish with natives. His accomplishment surely remains one of the most extraordinary feats in the history of navigation.

A good officer could improve the odds of his crew's survival by maintaining discipline and keeping his men from each other's throats. Unfortunately, not all officers behaved in an exemplary manner — they could be cruel, cowardly, incompetent, and just as drunken and venal as any who served under them. The captain was not always the last off the sinking ship; sometimes he was the first, taking with him the soundest boat and most of the provisions. Where an officer was not self-serving, however, he could hold down the casualty rate. He could make a difference, as John Dean did.

Again one thinks of the *Bounty* mutiny. After getting rid of Bligh and his supporters, the rebels sailed back to Tahiti. Seventeen of their number elected to stay in paradise and risk being found by the Royal Navy (as indeed they were), in the unlikely event that any of Bligh's party lived to inform the authorities of what had transpired aboard the ship. Eight of the mutineers sailed on with Fletcher Christian in search of a secret haven, taking with them nineteen natives — six men, twelve women, and a baby girl. They eventually happened on the uncharted Pitcairn Island and went ashore on January 18, 1790. No other vessel descried the isle until the American trading ship *Topaz* visited it in February of 1808. By then only one of the fifteen males who had come on the *Bounty* was still alive. One had died of illness, one had jumped off a cliff while drunk on homemade alcohol, and the other twelve had killed each other in squabbles over the women or had been murdered by the vengeful widows of the men who had been killed. Among those who died such ignoble deaths was Fletcher Christian.

There were eighteen men with Bligh in a little boat, yet only one of them was lost. There were fourteen men with Christian, but they — the white men, at least — were, in the words of essayist Milton Rugoff, "of dubious character . . . and found themselves on an island, without responsibility, free of law and restraint, beset by sensual temptation, and, most corrupting of all, without hope of ever returning to civilization." Only one of them survived. To Rugoff's catalogue one more factor, then, must be added: the men had no competent leader to keep them under control. They killed and were killed only *after* they had rid themselves of the hated William Bligh.

How ironic that Bligh has come down to us as the villain of the incident, while the syphilitic Christian and his band of pocked murderers are the romantic heroes.

Considering the aftermath of the *Bounty* mutiny, it is hardly surprising that officers often come across as heroes in survival narratives.

Of course, skeptics might point out that most narratives were written by officers, since they were literate, and sailors rarely were. Were there more versions available of particular cases, the logic of this proposition runs, we might have a very different view of the general conduct of officers in survival situations.

As a matter of fact, a dissenting account of the tragedy on Boon Island does exist. Released late in 1711, not long after Jasper Dean put together and published his brother's story, it is based on the depositions made in New Hampshire and London by three of the crew: mate Christopher Langham, boatswain Nicholas Mellon, and seaman George White. Their title indicates their bias and their argument: *A true Account of the Voyage of the Nottingham Galley of London John Dean Commander from the River Thames to New England, Near which Place she was castaway on Boon-Island, 11 December 1710 by the Captain's obstinacy, who endeavoured to betray her to the French, or run her ashore; with an Account of the Falsehoods in the Captain['s] Narrative.*

Langham et al. allege that Dean had overinsured the *Nottingham,* implying that he was more interested in collecting on the policy than in seeing his ship safely to her destination. According to their testimony, early in the voyage they encountered privateers, and the captain would have surrendered his vessel to them had not Langham prevented it; off the coast of Newfoundland, Dean sighted what he took to be another privateer and again prepared to give up the *Nottingham* — but she proved to be an English ship, the *Pompey Galley.*

As to the wreck, John Dean had attributed it to navigational error, but the deponents related that the mate had warned the captain that it was impending. They argued, and Dean shouted to Langham that "he would not take his advice though the ship should go to the bottom." He threatened to shoot him and then knocked him cold with a periwig block. (Thus John Dean wrecked the *Nottingham* because he was arrogant in his incompetence, or he did it intentionally — the act of a madman in the midst of a New England winter — in order to collect the insurance.)

It was not *these* men who suggested eating the carpenter but Dean himself, of course, who explained, as they paraphrased him, that "it was no sin, since God was pleased to take him out of the world, and that we had not laid violent hands upon him." The three men at first primly refused to participate in the cannibalism, and after they gave in, they never became "brutish," as their captain had claimed.

And so on.

What are we to make of these contradictions? We have the word of the Dean brothers and Miles Whitworth, another maroon who stood with them, against that of Langham and his friends. Since we were on neither the ship nor the shore, how are we to decide? A close reading of both narratives leaves one convinced of John Dean's honesty and equally dubious of the veracity of his antagonists. They are just too virtuous, too prescient, and too right.

History has come down on Captain Dean's side as well. His reputation was so little damaged by the scurrilous charges against him that he went on to become the British consul for the ports of Flanders, residing at Ostend. He held the post for many years and eventually died in that city on August 19, 1761.

His narrative proved popular enough to have been brought out regularly in new editions, the last being released in 1762, a year after his death. Since then, it has been anthologized widely in collections of shipwreck tales. The account of Langham and company, on the other hand, fell into such disrepute and obscurity that for a period of time in this century all copies were thought to have been lost.

In 1956, the masterful historical novelist and Maine resident Kenneth Roberts became interested in the story. In the resulting novel, *Boon Island,* Roberts, who had earlier written of survival cannibalism in *Northwest Passage,* defended John Dean with great vigor. The fictionalized captain appears far more heroic than the man ever laid claim to being. (Roberts even lays the blame for the wreck on "Langman's" dereliction of duty.)

Near the end of *Boon Island,* Miles Whitworth, the narrator, remarks that "God, if we are fortunate, is good to us. How many of us have our Boon Islands? And how many have our Langmans?" We can only hope that the answer to both questions is very few indeed.

CHAPTER 13

The Ownership of a Plank

David Harrison on
the Wreck of the *Peggy*

Where a party of survivors lacked the convenience of a carpenter with a respiratory weakness, it was necessary to select a victim. The usual recourse was a lottery. Since theoretically, at least, a game of chance meant that the participants were all at equal risk and were willing players, the drawing of lots took the onus from the winners. They would not be ostracized from their communities if they finally managed to return to them, and civil authorities would be reluctant to prosecute them. The cannibals could rejoin society in good conscience — they were not murderers; after all, they had taken their chances, too.

Difficulties were more likely to occur for those who found some other means, however rational, of determining who would die. The case of the *Mignonette* is instructive. In the summer of 1884, the yacht went down in a storm in the South Atlantic, and her crew abandoned her for a dinghy in which they drifted for nearly a month with little food and water. At a moment near the end of their ordeal, it was clear that they would all soon die if one of them was not sacrificed. An eighteen-year-old lad named Richard Parker was in far worse shape than the three others. Despite the warnings of the older men, he had drunk a large quantity of sea water, a practice they felt would bring on certain madness and death. He was alternating between states of delirium and semiconsciousness, and there was no doubt that he would be dead within some hours. Rather than put at risk men who could exist at least a while longer, the master, Tom Dudley, decided that Parker's death should be . . . hurried. It was a reasonable decision, one difficult to fault from this distance, and Dudley carried it out himself.

Cannibalism at sea was so widely practiced and accepted in the latter part of the nineteenth century that after the *Mignonette*'s men were found, they made no effort whatsoever to conceal their actions and did not imagine that they would be prosecuted. Dudley in particular incriminated himself repeatedly. While on board the rescue ship, he wrote no fewer than eight drafts of a letter to the Board of Trade, in which he described Parker's death. He told his rescuers and a pilot who came aboard the vessel what he had done, and his volubility continued ashore as he talked to a policeman (readily handing over the murder weapon, a small knife) and gave a deposition to authorities.

At first popular feeling ran high against the survivors precisely because they had not drawn lots, but as the details of their suffering became known, it swung radically in their favor. Government officials were less willing to overlook the lack of a lottery than the general populace was. As the criminal proceedings began, the dead man's brother made a point of being seen shaking hands with the defendants in the courtroom, and community support for them was so strong that it was thought that the judge's life might be in danger if they were convicted. Two of them were found guilty nonetheless (the third man having been made a witness of the Crown) and were sentenced to death.

Although the condemned men were soon pardoned, the lesson was clear: where survival cannibalism took place, the ritual of a lottery must be performed.

The association of the lottery with shipwrecks is quite ancient. An early reference occurs in *De officiis,* by Marcus Tullius Cicero. Written in the summer of 44 B.C., while its author was engaged in a power struggle with Mark Antony, *De officiis* is perhaps Cicero's most important work. In it, he poses a series of what were for him increasingly difficult choices.

Suppose, he began, it was necessary to jettison something from a ship in distress in a stormy sea. Should a "high-priced horse" be thrown overboard, or a "cheap and worthless slave"? Without stating a conclusion, Cicero notes, "Here, self-interest and human feeling pull in different directions." (One doubts that European slavers felt any such conflict: when their vessels were threatened by bad weather, they would have had no scruples about throwing cargoes of blacks over the side or leaving the slaves on a sinking hulk while they rowed away in longboats. When it became necessary to eat someone, a slave was the first to fall under the knife.)

Another example involves two shipwrecked survivors in the water with a single plank big enough to support only one of them. Does the wise man have the right, wondered Cicero, by virtue of his superior intellect, to push a foolish man off the board and save himself? This was a problem of considerable weight for the Roman philosopher since he valued wisdom above all else. Nonetheless, his answer is no, because such an action would be *unjust* — a rationale that did not always hold with castaways.

What if the man not in possession of the plank was the vessel's owner? Could he be justified in pushing off the other man because he owned the lumber that once made up his ship? Again the answer is no, since by purchasing passage on the vessel the passengers had chartered her; thus *they* became the owners until she reached her destination.

The last dilemma that Cicero offers involves two men, equally wise. If one must die to save the other, by what criteria shall the choice be made? He concludes that "the one whose life is more valuable either for his own sake or that of his country" should have the board. If both lives have equal worth, Cicero advises the method that would be employed by survivors centuries later: "One will give place to the other, as if the point were decided by lot or by a game of [chance]."

The first mention of a lottery in an actual survival situation appears to be in Richard Clarke's narrative of 1583; the losers in the proposed lottery would be thrown overboard to make the craft more seaworthy. The first known instance in which death and cannibalism resulted from the drawing of lots is reported in *Observationem medicarum,* a 1641 medical text by Nicholaus Tulpius: seven Englishmen, adrift for weeks after a storm, have a lottery, and the one who proposes it loses; he is "by his own consent killed."

In the eighteenth century, as sea trade, passenger travel, and immigration increased, the number of such incidents escalated dramatically. Indeed, by the Victorian period, survival cannibalism on the ocean had become so nearly routine and almost universally accepted that it was referred to simply as "a custom of the sea."

Sailors had long been aware of the predicament of the plank, of course. They told one another stories of murder and cannibalism, and they sang of the deeds in song and chantey.

> A merchant ship, under Divers, captain,
>   long time had been bound to sea,
> The weather being so uncertain,
>   we were drove to great extremity!
> Nothing was left these poor souls to cherish,
>   for the want of food most feeble grown,
> Poor fellows, they were almost perish'd,
>   nothing was left but skin and bone.
>
> Their cats and dogs, O, they did eat them,
>   their hunger for to ease, we hear,
> And in the midst of all their sorrow,
>   Captain and men had equal share;
> But now a scant has come upon us,
>   a dismal tale, most certainly,
> Poor fellows they stood in torture,
>   Casting lots to see who should die.
>
> Now the lot fell on one poor fellow,
>   Whose family was very great,
> Which did the more increase his sorrow,
>   for to repent it was too late:
> I'm free to die, but, messmate brothers,
>   unto the top mast head straightway,
> See if you can a sail discover,
>   whilst I unto the Lord do pray.

The unlucky mariner in "The Ship in Distress" manages to forestall his fate with prayer just long enough for a sail to be descried to windward, and so he does not die. Such a reprieve was rarely granted, and other songs faithfully depicted acts of cannibalism, many of them based on fact.

The public came to be just as well informed of the risks of ocean travel. Penny ballads, poems, newspaper stories, broadsheets, and books all catalogued recourses to that "custom of the sea," and these varied accounts are often surprisingly consistent: the lottery is always fair, and the one selected meekly accepts his fate; he never struggles or accuses anyone of trickery. Certainly some lotteries were conducted honestly, but there are a number of instances where the impartiality of the proceedings is suspect. One way to preserve your own life, after all, would be to rig the game against someone else, and you might meet little resistance from fellow castaways if you perpetrated the fraud on an outsider — a foreigner, say, or a slave.

The *Euxine* was about 850 miles southwest of St. Helena on August 8, 1874, when, her cargo of coal having spontaneously ignited, she was abandoned by her crew. The crew climbed into three boats, one of which contained second mate James Archer and seven other men. That craft became separated from the others the first night, and Archer attempted to navigate to St. Helena. After failing to find it, he headed the boat toward Brazil. Struck by bad weather, she capsized several times, resulting in the drowning of two men and the loss of the navigational instruments and all the food and water.

Two days later, a sailor named August Muller, who had been drinking sea water, became delirious. Archer would later claim that in the midst of his suffering, Muller "offered his body to serve as food for the others and entreated the others to kill and devour him." Instead of taking him up on this generous proposal, at least some of the men agreed to a drawing. Just whose idea this was is unclear — in retrospect no one wanted to take credit for it, and everyone sought to attribute it to someone else. The assertion by one survivor that it came from the victim, one Franco Gioffey, is unlikely, especially given the fact that he spoke little or no English.

Archer later said that

> Having no other means to make a lottery we hit upon using small sticks of different sizes, deciding that the one who drew the smallest should be the victim. After having made the sticks ready I held them in my hand while the others drew. On comparing them together [we] found that the Italian Francis Shufus held the smallest stick.

The men were sports and did not immediately kill "Shufus," or "Gioffous," as they corrupted his name. Instead they repeated the lottery. In describing what followed, Archer is careful — perhaps too careful — to stress the formality and honesty of the game.

> Having also agreed that the lottery should be thrice repeated and that when it should then prove that either two or three of us had drawn the shortest stick, these should cast lots amongst themselves, so that the victim should be singled out, we found that the same man had for the second time picked out the same object.

Despite the language barrier, it was by this time quite obvious to Gioffey that he was being "singled out."

> Francis Shufus, when his turn came for the third drawing, hesitated to join and would not draw, upon which the man [Victor] Sandström

proposed he would do it for him. This he did, and the shortest stick was found in Sandström's hand.

The stories the *Euxine* survivors told following their rescue contain enough discrepancies to suggest they may have been casually manufactured after the fact. Archer, true to the convention of survival cannibalism, thought "Shufus" bore up under the threat of being eaten "with great calmness and showed the utmost resignation." Alexander Vermoulin saw the lad as being more subdued than accepting: "The Italian, from the few words he said and gesture he made, said he would undergo his fate." Only Sandström hinted at the truth, noting that the "Italian appeared to be a little agitated."

Estimates by the castaways as to how long they waited before they killed Gioffey range from ten minutes to two hours. During at least part of that time, according to Archer, "We stood upon the thwarts [while] Shufus prepared himself to meet his fate by praying and speaking in Italian. He gave us no parting message to be sent to his friends, most probably as he hardly knew more English than to say 'yes' and 'no.' His bearing was that of a man whose mind was made up." Archer even included the detail that Muller charitably offered to be sacrificed in the young man's place, but "this Shufus refused, and laying himself down in the bottom of the boat gave himself up to be tied. . . . He did not struggle or scream."

This information only serves to raise our suspicions. What, for instance, was Gioffey saying in Italian? Was he by chance making protests or leveling accusations or just cursing his murderers, perhaps? And why was it necessary to tie him up? I know of no other instance of voluntary sacrifice that required the binding of the victim. Last, why did Archer feel it necessary to give assurances that the Italian did not *"struggle or scream"*? Was it because this was exactly what he did?

In public, the rescued sailors tried to maintain a more or less united front, but rumors spread, apparently based on their private conversations. It was said that after the second lottery, Gioffey jumped into the sea, obviously preferring to have his body feed the fishes rather than sustain such dishonest and cruel men as those with whom he had shipped out. He was dragged back into the boat, and his throat was cut with such violence that he was decapitated. "This story," wrote Captain G. H. Harrington, who reported the allegations in a letter to a newspaper, "is told from their own lips, and horrifying to relate, they seem to consider that they were justified in committing the atrocious murder for the sake of appeasing their own wants."

Despite the furor and indignation the affair aroused, it was not brought to a satisfactory conclusion. Some British authorities were at first inclined to prosecute Archer and the others, and the officials debated and corresponded a good deal over whether and how to do it. (One fear was that an acquittal in the case might be seen by sailors everywhere as a seal of approval on murder and cannibalism in survival situations, with a resultant reduction in the "life expectancy of ship's boys.") The accused were transported to England and jailed for a time. In the end, the case was dropped because of the complexities of the legal issues, the embarrassingly illegal detention of the accused, and the political problems that might result from their prosecution. The defendants were allowed to go back to sea, but only after most of them had signed pledges not to sue the *Euxine*'s owner or officers.

From this we can conclude that even when chicanery and callous murder were at issue, authorities remained reluctant to claim jurisdiction over what took place on the high seas or to punish those who participated in a certain custom thereon.

Perhaps it was the sheer number of men on board the sloop *Peggy* or the cargo they hauled or the slow, maddening ordeal they experienced — or the combination of these — that made them base.

They had sailed from the island of Fyal, bound for their home port of New York, on October 24, 1765. Five days out, they encountered rough weather, heavy seas, and violent winds. In the month that followed, the *Peggy* was struck by one terrible gale after another, and her sails were gradually torn away until only one remained.

David Harrison's assessment of the situation was bleak. There was, he felt,

no prospect whatever before us but what was pregnant with the bitterest distress. For the conflict which our vessel had so long maintained against waves and winds had by this time occasioned her to leak excessively, and our provisions were so much exhausted that we found it absolutely necessary to come to an immediate allowance of two pounds of bread a week for each person, besides a quart of water and a pint of wine a day. The alternative was really deplorable, between the shortness of our provisions and the wreck of our ship. If we contrived to keep the latter from sinking we were in danger of perishing with hunger, and if we contrived to spin out the former with a rigid perseverance of economy for any time, there was but little probability of being able to preserve our ship. Thus on either hand little less than a miracle could save us from inevitable destruction. If we had an accidental gleam of comfort on one hand, the fate with which the other so visibly teemed gave an instant check to our satisfaction and obscured every rising ray of hope with an instant cloud of horror and despair.

Several times they saw other vessels, but the weather was so bad that they could do nothing more than exchange signals with them. These tantalizing sightings only increased their misery.

Harrison lessened further their daily rations, but inevitably the food ran out. The liquor supply was depleted as well, and only two gallons of "dirty water remain[ed] in the bottom of a cask."

It was now nearly the end of December. The men, emotionally exhausted and experiencing the fatigue of an advanced state of starvation, were compelled to work frantically, incessantly, merely to keep their ship afloat and themselves alive.

In this desperate condition, it was not unnatural for them to seize the bulk of the *Peggy*'s cargo, which happened to be a large quantity of wine and brandy. The liquor was the last thing they had in the world, they told the captain, and they might have added that it was possibly the last they ever would have. They drank it in copious amounts, cursing and blaspheming continually. Witnessing this sudden breakdown of discipline and self-control, Harrison became increasingly uneasy. A dedicated officer who took seriously his responsibility for the safety of his crew, he could only view their behavior with trepidation.

So it must have been with an extra measure of relief that on Christmas morning Captain Harrison descried a sail to leeward. The sight of it

suddenly transported [us] with the most extravagant sensations of joy. . . . Distress generally inspires the human mind with lively sentiments of devotion, and those who perhaps dispute or disregard the existence of a Deity at other times are ready enough in the day of adversity to think every advantageous turn in their affairs a particular exertion of the Divine benignity. It was, therefore, but natural for some of the people to think that the twenty-fifth of December was appointed for their preservation. Our thanksgivings, however, to Providence, though profoundly sincere, were not offered in any general form.

Instead the men crowded upon the deck and hung out the distress signal. Before noon they had the "unspeakable satisfaction" of seeing the ship approach. Harrison quickly informed the captain of their plight: the *Peggy* was wrecked, and her sailors, "every moment exposed to the mercy of the waves, as our leaks continually increas[ed]," declined "in their strength in proportion as the necessity grew urgent to employ them at the pumps." Harrison asked if the captain would take them off the *Peggy*. He would not. Even after Harrison swore that neither he nor any of his company would eat so much as a single morsel of his provisions, the captain remained obdurate. All he was willing to do for them, in fact, was to give them a little bread. Harrison was grateful nonetheless: "The promised relief was but small; [yet] the smallest to people in our circumstances was inestimable."

The intractable captain promised to have the meager food passed over as soon as he completed his noon nautical observation. Gullible in his optimism, David Harrison went below to lie down. He was weary, emaciated, and suffering from a severe flux. The malnourishment had considerably impaired his vision and aggravated his rheumatism.

He had barely lain down when some of his men burst into his cabin. They were so excited that he had trouble understanding them, but their faces bore expressions of profound despair. Their purported provider was sailing away from the *Peggy* as fast as he could.

Harrison tried to make his way up on deck and found himself so feeble that he could only crawl. Topside, he saw his crew transfixed by the sight of the departing vessel as she was propelled away by a favorable wind.

> As long as my poor fellows could retain the least trace of him they hung about the shrouds or ran in a state of absolute frenzy from one part of the ship to the other. They pierced the air with their cries, increasing in their lamentations as he lessened upon their view and straining their very eyeballs to preserve him in sight, through a despairing hope that some dawning impulse of pity would yet induce him to commiserate our situation and lead him to stretch out the blessed hand of relief.
>
> But alas! to what purpose did we exhaust our little strength in supplicating for compassion, or aggravate our own misfortunes with a fruitless expectation of such a change? The inexorable captain pursued his course without regarding us and steeled, as he undoubtedly

must be, to every sentiment of nature and humanity, possibly valued himself not a little upon his dexterity in casting us off.

Yet for all the animosity Harrison felt toward his "barbarous" colleague, he would not "hang him up to universal detestation or infamy by communicating his name to the reader. If he is capable of reflection his own conscience must sufficiently avenge my cause and God grant that the pungency of that conscience may be my only avenger."

As joyous as the sailors had been at the prospect of deliverance, they were now to the same degree dejected. Their captain saw desperate gloom on every face.

On board the *Peggy* were two pigeons and a cat. The birds went for Christmas dinner that very afternoon. The next day the men drew lots for parts of the cat. Harrison's draw was the head. Though he had pitied the creature, he was forced to admit that "in all my days I never feasted on anything which appeared so delicious to my appetite. The piercing sharpness of necessity had entirely conquered my aversion to such food, and the rage of an incredible hunger rendered that an exquisite regale which on any other occasion I must have loathed with the most insuperable disgust."

When the last of the cat's bones had been picked clean, the men went back to their drinking. Drunk, they cursed their fate with torrents of excoriation. In the steerage this rough crew heated their wine, while in his cabin their captain lay nauseated by the odor of the cooking spirits. He was trying to distract himself from their blasphemy and his own desire to give up, to die and experience the "moment of dissolution," by focusing on the memory of his wife and children.

When the reader comes to consider our total want of necessaries, that my vessel had been for some time leaky, that I myself was emaciated with sickness and had but one sail in the world to direct her; when he considers that the men were either too weak or too much intoxicated to pay a necessary attention to the pump; when he likewise considers the severity of the season, that it blew 'black December,' as Shakespeare phrases it; and is told that we had not an inch of candle or a morsel of slush to make any, having long since eaten up every appearance of either which could be found; when the reader comes to consider all these things and is moreover informed that the general distress had deprived me of all command on board my own ship, he will scarcely suppose that I could sustain any new misfortune.

Such a supposition would be incorrect. On December 28, the *Peggy* was struck by the worst storm yet, and it tore away the last of her canvas, the mainsail. Now, thought Harrison, she had truly become a wreck. "Death became so seemingly unavoidable that even I gave up hope, that last consolation of all the wretched, and prepared for an immediate launch into the dreadful gulf of eternity."

Yet he did not die. He was so weak that he could no longer hold the pen he had been using to make journal entries, but he was still alive on January 13, when, with the *Peggy* being "tossed about at the discretion of the sea and wind," the entire crew filed into his cabin.

Most probably he knew why they had come before a word was said. But even if he did not, their facial expressions, so "full of horror, . . . indicated the nature of their dreadful purpose."

The cabin would have been damp and dark and its atmosphere thick with the odor of their bodies and the liquor on their breath.

Archibald Nicolson, who was the first mate and their designated leader, spoke up. Their tobacco was "entirely exhausted." They were starving. They had eaten the buttons off their jackets and all the leather they could find in the ship, including that which was part of the pump. They could hold out no longer. Their only chance was to cast lots and sacrifice one of their number for the "preservation of the rest."

Knowing they were drunk, Harrison tried to "soothe them from their purpose," to stall them, begging them to get some rest and bring the matter back to him in the morning.

They were furious. They told him that what needed to be done could not wait, and they did not care if he disapproved of the plan: they had been kind enough to inform him of what would take place and, having done so, would "oblige me to take my chance as well as another man, since the general misfortune had leveled all distinction of persons."

The captain, because of the "excesses of their intoxication," had been expecting the drunkards to attack him, and he had prepared for it by keeping his pistols close at hand. Bitterly he realized that his forethought had merely been an "idle precaution": there were just too many of them for him to make a fight of it. Having failed at persuasion, he told them that even if they pursued this course he would not order any man's death, and neither would he "partake by any means of so shocking a repast."

Belligerently they replied that they were not asking his consent, and as to eating or not eating, why he could follow the "bias of my own inclination." Then they filed out of his cabin and into the steerage — but very soon they returned. Not surprisingly, the lot had fallen on a black slave who was part of the cargo.

Considering how little time it had taken to perform the ceremony and that it had been done carefully out of his sight, Harrison was more than suspicious that the draw had been fixed against the "poor Ethiopian." He was surprised that they had even bothered with the subterfuge.

When the black man saw the pistol being loaded, he ran to the captain and begged for his life, but Harrison could only watch helplessly as they dragged him away to the steerage, where he was shot through the head. He was hardly dead before some of the sailors had gutted him and built a large cooking fire. One of the foremastmen, James Campbell, was too ravenous to wait, and he tore out the liver and ate it raw. He would die three days later, a raving madman, having "paid dear for such an extravagant impatience," and his body would be thrown overboard immediately rather than eaten, since the men feared that devouring his flesh would make them insane, too.

They stayed up most of the night of the murder, David Harrison noted with disdain, feasting on the slave whose body afforded them "a luxurious banquet." In the morning the mate came to the captain to ask mockingly what his orders were relative to the pickling of the corpse. Weak as he was, Harrison grasped a pistol, leveled it at his tormentor, and offered to send him "after the Negro" if he did not instantly quit the cabin.

The man left, muttering that the captain was no longer in charge of the ship and that he would call a council of the crew. Its unanimous vote was to cut the body into slices, which the cannibals thereafter referred to as steaks.

Harrison heard one man say, "Damn him, though he would not consent to our having any meat let us give him some." Immediately the speaker entered the cabin with a portion and an invitation to dine, but the captain still had his pistol. He pointed it at the bearer and expressed a desire to hear him make the offer a *second* time.

Harrison would later freely admit that principle was not the only motivation for his refusal to eat:

In fact, the constant expectation of death, joined to the miserable state to which I was reduced through sickness and fatigue, to say nothing of my horror at the food with which I was presented, entirely took away my desire of eating. Add also to this that the stench of their stewing and frying threw me into an absolute fever and that this fever was aggravated by a strong scurvy and violent swelling in my legs. Sinking under such an accumulated load of afflictions and being, moreover, fearful, if I closed my eyes, that they would surprise and murder me for their next supply, it is no wonder that I lost all relish for sustenance.

The suspicion that he would be their second victim was well founded. He frequently heard them speculating over who would be the next "supply" and agreeing that they should kill their captain before putting any of themselves at risk.

"Notwithstanding the excesses into which my people ran, they nevertheless husbanded the Negro's carcass with the severest economy and stinted themselves to an allowance which made it last for many days." Even so, the time for another lottery was drawing close, and his awareness that the number of steaks was diminishing kept David Harrison from sleeping very much. He found that in "proportion as the Negro grew less, so in proportion my apprehensions were increased, and every meal which they sat down to I considered as a fresh approach to destruction."

In the end, his subordinates declined to murder him brazenly. (This refusal may be attributable to the vestiges of the old discipline they had once worked under, or to the captain's readiness to flourish his pistol, depending on your estimation of human nature.) Again the mate came leading a procession of the famished to propose casting lots. The Negro had been all eaten up days before, he told Harrison, and they preferred to die one at a time from a pistol shot rather than from starvation. They knew the captain must be hungry, too, Nicolson conciliated, but added that he would have to take his chances with the rest.

Again Harrison tried to dissuade them. Another death would be futile since killing and eating the black had done them no good: now that he was devoured they were as "greedy and as emaciated as ever." Submit to Providence, he counseled them, offering to pray with them for a quick rescue or a quick death.

They would not listen. Brusquely they dismissed his piety. There was no time for prayer; they were hungry *now,* and they would cast lots with or without his consent.

Seeing how stubborn they were, and having just cause to think that if he did not oversee the lottery it would certainly select him, Harrison got out of his bunk, tore pieces of paper into slips, and marked one with ink. Ever a man for doing things properly, he followed the procedure used at the Guildhall lottery drawing.

This time the loser was a foremastman named David Flatt, the only man of the crew the captain thought at all reliable. He was respected by his fellows as well, and when he drew the marked slip they fell into a long, unhappy silence broken only by Flatt himself.

"My dear friends, messmates and fellow sufferers," he said to them, "all I have to beg of you is to dispatch me as soon as you did the Negro and to put me to as little torture as you can." He then appointed James Doud as his executioner, as Doud had been for the black.

The fire was burning in the steerage and the pistol was loaded, yet they hesitated. When Flatt asked for a few minutes in which to prepare himself for death, they readily agreed. Harrison thought, in fact, that they were in a mood to spare Flatt altogether — until they resumed their drinking. "A few draughts of wine, however, soon suppressed all these dawnings of humanity." Well, not entirely: they regarded Flatt so highly that they agreed to put off his execution until eleven o'clock the next morning, in the hopes that in the interim "the Divine Goodness" would provide a rescuer. For now they asked — *begged* — Harrison to read prayers, which they joined in with the "utmost fervency."

As he read, he had the satisfaction of seeing his men behaving for the first time in a long time with "tolerable decency." He led them in religious observance while his strength lasted, and then he fell back on the bed, utterly wearied by those slight exertions. Yet even in a semiconscious state he heard the sailors trying to comfort the wretched Flatt with hope. Although they had been singularly unsuccessful at catching fish, they promised that at dawn they would put their hooks into the water and try once more to pull something in and thus "mitigate their distresses [and] avert the severity of his sentence."

There could be no solace for this unlucky man. He who at his selection had asked only that he not be tortured found the stress of waiting unbearable. By midnight he had become completely deaf. By four A.M. he was raving.

Lying on his bunk, David Harrison heard the men debate whether

or not to put Flatt out of his misery *immediately* as an act of humanity. In the end they decided to keep to the agreed timetable.

It was eight o'clock the next morning when two men burst into
the captain's cabin. Without a word they seized his hands. Their
faces were contorted. He knew instantly why they were there: they
were going to murder him. They would not risk insanity by devouring Flatt. They would kill and eat him. He wrestled one hand free
and snatched up a pistol. He would sell his life as dearly as he could.
But before he shot either one of them, they managed to blurt out
that a sail had been descried. There was a ship to leeward! Here
came the rest of their comrades, crowding in to jubilantly confirm
the sighting.

> It is impossible to describe the excess of my transport upon hearing
> that there was a sail at any rate in sight. My joy in a manner over-
> powered me and it was not without the utmost exertion of my
> strength that I desired them to use every expedition in making a signal
> of distress. Our vessel, indeed, itself was a most striking signal; but
> as there was a possibility for the ship in view to suppose that there
> was not a living creature on board I judged it absolutely expedient to
> prevent the likelihood of so dreadful a mistake.

Now that salvation was at hand, discipline began to return. The
crew followed their captain's instructions with alacrity. He heard
the men cry, "She nighs us . . . she nighs us . . . she is standing
this way!"

For a moment while they waited they spoke of Flatt, of how sad
it was that they could not communicate to him in his unhearing
madness that they were saved. But he was forgotten when someone
proposed — and all the sailors agreed — that they break out more
liquor to drink to their imminent release. It took all of Harrison's
powers of persuasion to stop them; he argued that if they appeared
in "any way disguised with liquor the ship might probably decline
to take us on board, and [I] endeavored to convince them that their
deliverance in a very great measure depended upon the regularity
of this moment's behavior. My remonstrances had some effect and
all but my mate, who had for a considerable time abandoned himself
to the brutality of intoxication, very prudently postponed so un-
timely an instance of indulgence."

They watched the vessel approach with a feeling of excruciating
suspense, "a most tumultuous agitation." In this hour the wind
died, and the sea became calm. With two miles still separating her

from the *Peggy*, the rescue ship was unable to come closer. A boat was hoisted out and was rowed vigorously toward the wreck. Their apprehension grew: so often thwarted and disappointed in these last months, they feared that even with help so close something would interfere and plunge them back into distress. Life and death seemed to sit on every stroke of the oars, "and as we still considered ourselves tottering on the very verge of eternity, the conflict between our wishes and our fears may be easily supposed by a reader of imagination."

When the boat finally reached them, her occupants were so astonished at the ghastly, inhuman appearance of the *Peggy*'s men that they rested upon their oars and demanded to know *what* they were looking at. After they had been convinced that the wretched castaways were indeed human, they scrambled aboard and urged them to hurry into the boat lest another gale strike before they could return to their vessel. The *Peggy*'s sailors hastened to comply, but their captain was so weak that he had to be lowered by ropes. They were about to push off when someone remembered the demented Flatt, still below deck and unaware of what had happened. "In the general hurry every man's attention was engaged by the thought of his own preservation and it was almost a matter of wonder that anybody remembered the absence of the mate."

Flatt was gone after and eventually led to the rail, holding in his hand a "can of joy with which he had been busy, having completely erased every idea of the preceding occurrences from his recollection." He appeared to be absolutely amazed to see strangers before him, but they managed to get him into the boat.

The passengers and crew had gathered on the deck of the rescue vessel, the *Susanna*, curious to see the castaways. A close look at their "hollow eyes, shriveled cheeks, long beards and squalid complexions" appalled them. Even the captain, Thomas Evers, shook with horror as he assisted David Harrison to his own cabin. Before Harrison allowed himself to be led to luxury — indeed, as soon as he was brought on board — he dropped to his knees on the deck and, propping himself against a hen coop for support, prayed fervently with "sincerest gratitude to the great Author of all things for the abundance of his mercy, and in the fulness of my heart began also to express my sensibility to the captain for his readiness to assist the distressed."

■ ■ ■

Harrison had no appetite for four days and found when he tried to eat that he could not taste the food. By taking small amounts of broth and solids, he gradually began to improve, until one day

> having an occasion for a particular indulgence of nature, I thought I should have expired performing it. The pain it gave me was excruciating to the last degree and the parts were so contracted, having never once been employed for a space of thirty-six or thirty-seven days, that I almost began to despair restoring them to their necessary operations. I was, however, at last relieved by the discharge of a callous lump about the size of a hen's egg, and enjoyed a tranquility of body, notwithstanding all my disorders, with which I was utterly unacquainted for some preceding weeks.

Soon he was able to eat well enough that he gorged himself on turkey and threw himself into a fever. It was an odd, dangerous triumph of sorts.

Even now, safely aboard the *Susanna* and under the care of a solicitous and generous captain, the former castaways were dogged by bad luck. A gale that had struck the ship earlier in her voyage had resulted in the loss of a large quantity of stores, including, noted the long-famished Harrison in a litany of mourning, "four hogs, four or five hogsheads of fresh water, forty or fifty head of fowl, and twenty or thirty geese and turkeys." With the added drain caused by the seven survivors now on board, Captain Evers was forced to institute rationing: two and a half pounds of bread per week along with a quart of water and eight ounces of salt provisions per day. A long series of storms battered the vessel and made her so leaky that the pumps had to be manned continually, and all on board hoped to encounter *another* ship that might provide them with help. To the *Peggy*'s men it must have seemed that the dreadful nightmare had begun again.

Yet it was not so. Eventually they sailed into Dartmouth and were able to go ashore.

> The next day my inconsiderate mate, Mr. Archibald Nicolson, who had so long wallowed, as I may say, in every mire of excess, having reduced himself by a continued intoxication to such a state that no proper sustenance would stay on his stomach, fell a martyr to his inebriety. Having a watch and some trinkets about him, which defrayed the expense of his funeral, he was decently interred.

It is here that the pious and stalwart Captain David Harrison ends the narrative of his travail. Most of his men were still weak, although he himself had recovered. In this respect there is a moral underpinning to the story, clear and strong enough to please any eighteenth-century gentleman: the officer who had steadfastly refused to descend to bestiality makes a complete and speedy recovery, while the villainous leader of the disobedient rabble dies of his own excesses after reaching safety.

One feature would seem to mar the symmetry of this conclusion. David Flatt, respected by Harrison and so loved by his comrades that they were reluctant to kill him, remained quite out of his mind.

The object of this study has not yet been fully examined; other surfaces remain to be seen. In tracking the human heart one must always go deep into the darkness of the wood, where the lamentations are heard more loudly and the guttural growls come from too close by.

The word "pathetic" is often used to characterize inadequacy, but this is its second meaning. Its first pertains to the arousing of pity, sympathy, or tenderness. Comes forward now a gentle, pious woman . . . a woman of great strength and faith. She is Miss Ann Saunders, and her tale is most pathetic. You will not soon forget her.

CHAPTER 14

The Weaning from All Vain Enjoyment

Ann Saunders on the Wreck of the *Francis Mary*

It is easy for us to condemn the captain who sailed away from David Harrison and his crew. We should keep in mind, however, that rescuing castaways entailed risks and offered no tangible rewards; indeed, taking survivors on board would deplete already limited supplies of food and water. Under the best of circumstances supplies were never more than just adequate, since they took up room that might be profitably employed housing cargo or passengers. So the consumption of supplies by rescued castaways could have catastrophic results if their benefactor's ship was subsequently becalmed or so delayed by storms that her progress to port was significantly delayed.

A squint through the spyglass at the skeletal occupants of a distant, crowded longboat could be enough to inform a would-be Good Samaritan of what the terrible consequences might be to him, his passengers, and crew if some happenstance were to make his otherwise admirable charity go awry. The realistic fear of starving might govern kindly impulses. Thus Alexander William Holmes acted wisely when he had the castaways of the *William Brown* lie down in the bottom of their boat as a ship appeared, so that those on board the rescue vessel would not immediately see how many people were to be saved — and provided for.

Sailors did not earn high wages to begin with, and they were not paid at all if the cargo was not delivered to its destination. Thus, seamen whose vessels went down might struggle through months or even years of terrible hardship as castaways or maroons and then, having finally been rescued, arrive home with nothing to show for what they had endured. Meanwhile their families would have been driven into destitution. No wonder such survivors were so quick to sell their stories or to display themselves before whoever would pay, even if it meant being a sideshow exhibit in a fair.

Understanding why captains might choose to ignore castaways does not mean they should not be judged for their actions. People in communities where mariners and their families lived were far better qualified to be judges than most of us could ever be. They were certainly aware of the perils of the main, and they were not intolerant: we have seen that they accepted survival cannibalism so long as the proprieties were observed. They opposed the prosecution of the cannibals and raised money for their benefit; amazingly, this leniency was sometimes endorsed by the victims' kin.

The refusal of sailors to help distressed comrades was another matter altogether. Every schoolchild knows the poem by John Greenleaf Whittier that commemorates the punishment of a certain skipper named Ireson.

> Body of turkey, head of owl,
> Wings a-droop like a rained-on fowl,
> Feathered and ruffled in every part,
> Skipper Ireson stood in the cart.
> Scores of women, old and young,
> Strong of muscle, and glib of tongue,
> Pushed and pulled up the rocky lane,
> Shouting and singing the shrill refrain:
>   "Here's Flud Oirson, fur his horrd horrt,
>   Torr'd an' futherr'd an' corr'd in a corrt
>   By the women o' Morble'ead!"
>
> Wrinkled scolds with hands on hips,
> Girls in bloom of cheek and lips,
> Wild-eyed, free-limbed, such as chase
> Bacchus round some antique vase,
> Brief of skirt, with ankles bare,
> Loose of kerchief and loose of hair,
> With conch-shells blowing and fish-horns' twang,
> Over and over the Maenads sang:
>   "Here's Flud Oirson, fur his horrd horrt,
>   Torr'd an' futherr'd an' corr'd in a corrt
>   By the women o' Morble'ead!"

Small pity for him! — He sailed away
From a leaking ship in Chaleur Bay, —
Sailed away from a sinking wreck,
With his own town's-people on her deck!
"Lay by! lay by!" they called to him.
Back he answered, "Sink or swim!
Brag of your catch of fish again!"
And off he sailed through the fog and rain!
   Old Floyd Ireson, for his hard heart,
   Tarred and feathered and carried in a cart
   By the women of Marblehead!

. . . .

Sweetly along the Salem road
Bloom of orchard and lilac showed.
Little the wicked skipper knew
Of fields so green and the sky so blue.
Riding there in his sorry trim,
Like an Indian idol glum and grim,
Scarcely he seemed the sound to hear
Of voices shouting, far and near:
   "Here's Flud Oirson, fur his horrd horrt,
   Torr'd an' futherr'd an' corr'd in a corrt
   By the women o' Morble'ead!"

"Hear me, neighbors!" at last he cried, —
"What to me is this noisy ride?
What is the shame that clothes the skin
To the nameless horror that lives within?
Waking or sleeping, I see a wreck,
And hear a cry from a reeling deck!
Hate me and curse me, — I only dread
The hand of God and the face of the dead!"
   Said old Floyd Ireson, for his hard heart,
   Tarred and feathered and carried in a cart
   By the women of Marblehead!

Then the wife of the skipper lost at sea
Said, "God has touched him! why should we!"
Said an old wife mourning her only son,
"Cut the rogue's tether and let him run!"
So with soft relentings and rude excuse,
Half scorn, half pity, they cut him loose,
And gave him a cloak to hide him in,
And left him alone with his shame and sin.
   Poor Floyd Ireson, for his hard heart,
   Tarred and feathered and carried in a cart
   By the women of Marblehead!

The poet's depiction of the indignation of the port's residents is realistic enough, but since he was inspired by a bit of doggerel heard in childhood, his creation is inaccurate in some respects. The doomed vessel went down not in Chaleur Bay but off Cape Cod, in a gale on the night of October 28, 1808. The schooner *Active* was of Portland rather than of Marblehead, which makes the townsfolks' outrage all the more pure: they were punishing the abandonment of *strangers* in distress rather than the betrayal of friends and neighbors. Furthermore, those on the *Active* were not even fishermen — they were passengers and sailors.

Benjamin Ireson (his nickname was Flood, one common enough wherever people lived in close proximity to water) had not mocked those on the storm-battered vessel at all. He had, in fact, tried to rescue them, but in the darkness and the heavy seas his men were unwilling to risk their lives. His was a fishing boat, not a navy ship, and he was more an employer than what we would think of as a captain; thus he could not force his crew to obey in this matter. He instructed the watch to lie by the wreck all night, intending to save those on the schooner in the morning, when the weather had improved and it was light.

Once Ireson had gone below and fallen asleep, however, the watch sailed the *Betty* back to Marblehead. By the time they reached port, the men had given considerable thought to how the residents might react to their perfidy, and as soon as they were ashore they spread the word that Flood Ireson and Flood Ireson alone was responsible for the flight from Cape Cod.

On a bright moonlit night, a mob of men and boys came for him. They tarred and feathered him and put him in a dory, which they dragged through the streets until his body broke through the bottom. After that he rode in a cart. They took him as far as Salem, but the town officials would not allow the strange parade to march through their streets, and so the ruffians took him home again.

Throughout his ordeal, Ireson had remained silent, not once protesting his innocence. Why should he have? Who would have listened, much less believed? When at last he was allowed to climb down from the cart, he thanked the *gentlemen* kindly for the ride. Then he added that they would live to regret it.

And so they did, and quickly, too. As it happened, some of those on the *Active* were saved by a Provincetown whaleboat. It is unclear whether they corrected the misunderstanding as soon as they got ashore or whether, once Ireson had been humiliated and tempers had cooled, one of the *Betty's* men allowed that things were *just a little* different from how they had seemed at first. . . . Either way, a new story spread through Marblehead. This one was as accurate as the other was false and self-serving, and thus the old skipper's true role in the event came to be known.

To the "credit of the town," wrote Samuel Roads, Jr., in 1879, "[this] is one of the few incidents in its entire history that its citizens have any reason to regret." Roads uncovered the facts concerning Ireson while compiling a chronicle of the port. When it was done, he sent a copy to Whittier. The poet replied from a place with a name as wonderful as his own — Oak Knoll, Danvers. "I heartily thank thee for a copy of thy *History of Marblehead*," the gentle old man began. "No town in Essex County has a record more honorable than Marblehead . . . and certainly none has given such evidence of self-sacrificing patriotism." About his poem he added,

> I have now no doubt that thy version of Skipper Ireson is the correct one. My verse was solely founded on a fragment of rhyme which I heard from one of my schoolmates, a native of Marblehead.
>
> I supposed the story to which it referred dated back at least a century. I knew nothing of the participators, and the narrative of the ballad was pure fancy. I am glad for the sake of truth and justice that the real facts are given in thy book. I certainly would not knowingly do injustice to anyone, dead or living.

Very well, then, we have a delightful poem and an authentic history. We have truth, in other words, but what of justice?

It is easy to act in anger as part of a mob raging through the darkness. It is hard to offer apology and redress singly in the light of day. There is no record that the people of Marblehead ever made individual or collective amends to Benjamin Ireson.

As for the skipper himself, a man named John W. Chadwick once asked a Marblehead contemporary of Ireson's what lasting effect the ride had had on Flood. "Cowed him to death," was the reply, "cowed him to death." Despite this testimony, it seems doubtful that the tough old salt who quietly endured the tar, the dory, and the cart and came down still in full possession of his sarcasm could be broken afterward by the memory of the ordeal.

We do know, however, that he "went skipper" only one more year — that is, out into the ocean in a boat with other men under him. Thereafter he fished in the bay alone in a dory, and he sold each day's catch from a wheelbarrow. He lived on for many years, and when failing eyesight finally kept him from fishing at all, he had his dory hauled up to his house, and he left it by the wall for the weather to rot.

Long after his death, people continued to point out his modest little home, which was in one of the "queerest corners of town." Many who paused before the house knew only the verses and not the truth, and so they spat and cursed his name.

The story of Ann Saunders concludes with a rescuer being put in jeopardy because of his charity. It is one of the most moving sea tales I know. Saunders's travails are touching not only because of their nature but also because a genteel young woman experienced them. One doubts that she really grasped the risk she was taking when she booked passage. She sailed out of her hometown of Liverpool, bound for St. John, New Brunswick, on November 10, 1825. A young woman of limited means, she had undertaken the voyage as companion to the wife of the captain, John Kendall. She had never been to sea before, and she expected her passage to be pleasant and uneventful. Her optimism proved well founded — on the crossing to New Brunswick.

On the return trip, the *Francis Mary* was struck by a fierce gale that quickly destroyed many of the spars and injured some of the crew. When it was over, Mrs. Kendall and Miss Saunders nursed the hurt men while the uninjured ones cleared the deck of the broken spars and made repairs as best they could. The journey was then resumed, with the women still having, as Saunders characterized it, the "pleasing hope that they should encounter no more boisterous and contrary winds to impede their passage."

Four days later, the vessel ran into an even more ferocious storm that raised the waves, so it seemed, to the height of mountains. One great wave alone swept every movable object from the decks and carried a hapless sailor over the side. Hardly had his fellows managed to get him back on board when the ocean stove in the whole of the *Mary*'s stern.

The officers gathered around the captain and argued about the best course of action. While they shouted over the roar of the gale, the two women knelt on the quarter-deck and prayed.

Their prayers were not efficacious: that night the storm doubled in its intensity. In the morning, with the *Mary* taking on water, the crew was forced to relocate the provisions that had not been contaminated by salt water. The sea was reaching up for them from below as the wind hammered them from above.

Ann Saunders understood that their prospects were grim.

> The night approached with all its dismal horrors. The horizon was obscured by black and angry-looking clouds, and about midnight the rain commenced falling in torrents, attended with frightful peals of thunder and unremitting streams of lightning.
>
> Daylight returned, but only to present to our view an additional scene of horror. One of the poor seamen, overcome by fatigue, was discovered hanging lifeless by some part of the rigging. His mortal remains were committed to the deep. As this was the first instance of entombing a human body in the ocean that I had ever witnessed, the melancholy scene made a deep impression on my mind, as I expected such eventuality would be my own life.

At this juncture they saw a vessel sailing toward them, but though she remained in company with them for the next twenty-four hours, the sea was too rough to permit her crew to aid the *Mary*. The gale showing no sign of abating, the ship's captain resumed his course, and those on the wreck watched the departure of their would-be deliverer with emotions Ann Saunders could not describe. (Not long thereafter they would encounter a brig that came near enough for her men to inquire about their situation, but again the storm was too terrible to allow a boat to be put into the water, and they were once more left alone.)

They were all living on the forecastle now, in a tent made of spare canvas. On the sixth of February, their provisions nearly depleted, they went on a ration of a quarter biscuit per day per person. Such a paltry amount could hardly ward off starvation, and it lifted their spirits not at all. Crowded in their flimsy hovel, battered by the rain and wind, their vessel filling with water and buffeted on the turbulent ocean, famished and seeing no possibility but a slow and certain death, they became utterly disconsolate.

This mood was not improved by the sight of yet another ship nor by her steady progress on her course, despite their distress signal.

The first man died of starvation the day after that last sighting, February 12. He was a sailor named James Clarke. Prayers were read over his body before it was slipped over the side.

The next victim, John Wilson, died ten days later, by which time their predicament had become truly desperate. Food had been mea-

ger since about the first week of February, and although the Saunders account does not make clear exactly when the supplies were
exhausted, they certainly were gone by the day James Clarke died.
Saunders does not say when they ran out of water or whether they
rationed it, but run out they did. So by the time Wilson died, the
eighteen people still alive had not eaten at all for ten days and had
had only a biscuit and a half each during the six days before that.

They did not commit to the deep the body of John Wilson. They
cut it into slices, which they washed in salt water and dried in the
sun. Then they divided it among themselves, partaking of it as a
"sweet morsel," Ann would remember, though she herself held off
for another twenty-four hours before eating that "revolting food."
After that, she wrote, "we eyed each other with mournful and melancholy looks" appropriate to those who were beyond human help
and utterly dependent on the "mercy of the Almighty, whose ways
are unsearchable."

Despite what had happened and what was to come, Saunders
would never lose the piety that she couched in the effusive, sentimental rhetoric of the nineteenth century:

> Many of the seamen were married men and had left in Europe nu-
> merous families dependent on them for support. Alas! poor mortals,
> little did they think, when they bid their loving companions and their
> tender little ones the last adieu, that it was to be a final one and that
> they were to behold their faces no more in this frail world! But we
> must not charge an infinitely wise and good God foolishly, who can-
> not err, but orders every event for the best.

The deaths came more rapidly now. A sailor named Moore died
the day after Wilson; his corpse was dropped into the ocean —
minus its liver and heart. In the following twelve days, seven more
people succumbed: two cabin boys, the cook, and four crewmen.

> The heart-piercing lamentations of these poor creatures dying for the
> want of sustenance was distressing beyond conception. Some of them
> expired raving mad, crying out lamentably for water. [John] Hutch-
> inson, who, it appeared, had left a numerous family in Europe, talked
> to his wife and children as if they were present, repeating the names
> of the latter, and begged of them to be kind to their poor mother,
> who, he represented, was about to be separated from him forever.
> [John] Jones became delirious two or three days before his death and
> in his ravings reproached his wife and children as well as his dying
> companions present with being the authors of his extreme suffering

by depriving him of food and in refusing him even a single drop of water with which to moisten his parched lips. And, indeed, such now was the thirst of those who were but in a little better condition that they were driven to the melancholy distressful horrid act (to procure their blood) of cutting the throats of their deceased companions a moment after the breath of life had left their bodies!

Deprivation abolished all class distinctions on the wreck. What was the value of Mrs. Kendall's superior financial and social position when, before this ordeal was over, the lady would eat the brains of one of the seamen and find them, she would declare, the most delicious thing she had ever tasted? The irony of this seaman's fate was not lost on Saunders: he had been shipwrecked no less than three times before, once being confined on a wreck for twenty-two days; this time he would live for twenty-nine days before becoming "food for his surviving shipmates!"

When the *Francis Mary* departed St. John on January 18, 1826, twenty-one persons were on board. Only eleven now survived.

While all were feeble, the two women had remained far stronger than the men. This may have been in part because, being females and passengers, they had not had to exert themselves in the earlier battles against the storms and heavy seas. Of the two, Ann Saunders had held up better than Mrs. Kendall.

This was not a completely happy fact for Saunders. True, with the men lying about so weak that they could not stand, she was able to move among them performing spiritual ministrations, exhorting them to pray together and reminding them to prepare their souls for eternity, but at the same time her relatively good health caused her to be elected to a dreadful office as well. It was she who carved up the corpses and daily distributed the rations. It was she, too, who had to cut the throats of the recently deceased and, no doubt, push the unused portions of their bodies overboard.

Although Ann Saunders's life before this voyage had not been without sorrows, it had been a fairly sheltered and refined one. Certainly nothing had prepared her for the dreadful tasks she now routinely performed. Yet she never turned away: beneath the sentimentality and pious interjections, her narrative is remarkably frank and unflinching, even as she describes the death of young James Frier, her fiancé:

Judge then, my female readers (for it is you that can best judge), what must have been my feelings, to see a youth for whom I had formed an indissoluble attachment — him with whom I expected so soon to be joined in wedlock and to spend the remainder of my days — expiring before my eyes for want of that sustenance which nature requires for the support of life and which it was not in my power to afford him. And myself at the same moment so far reduced by hunger and thirst as to be driven to the horrid alternative to preserve my own life to plead my claim to the greater portion of his precious blood as it oozed half congealed from the wound inflicted upon his lifeless body! Oh, this was a bitter cup indeed! But it was God's will that it should not pass me — and God's will must be done. O, it was a chastening rod that has been the means, I trust, of weaning me forever from all vain enjoyments of this frail world.

Near the end of the month an event occurred that further dampened their spirits, if that was possible. An English brig came in sight, but despite their frantic signals and relatively calm sea, she sailed on without ever approaching the wreck.

Our longing eyes followed her until she was out of sight, leaving us in a situation doubly calamitous from our disappointment in not receiving the relief which appeared so near. Our hopes vanished with the brig and from the highest summit of expectation they now sunk into a state of most dismal despair. Nature indeed now seemed to have abandoned her functions. Never could human beings be reduced to a more wretched situation. More than two thirds of the crew had already perished and the surviving few — weak, distracted, and destitute of almost everything — envied the fate of those whose lifeless corpses no longer wanted sustenance. The sense of hunger was almost lost, but a parching thirst consumed our vitals. Our mouths had become so dry for want of moisture for three or four days that we were obliged to wash them every few hours with salt water to prevent our lips gluing together.

Still they held out, endured, delaying death and hoping for rescue, and at last their perseverance was rewarded. On the seventh of March, a sail was descried to windward. Saunders managed to signal their distress. She was helped in this by several of the seamen, who mustered up a small measure of strength for the effort. This time their signals were seen — and heeded.

The survivors — there were only six — felt such elation at the approach of H.M.S. *Blonde* that although until this moment they had been able only to crawl about on their hands and knees, when they were able to move at all, now they managed to pull themselves to their feet and, no doubt at Ann's urging, lift their hands high in praise of God for their deliverance.

The captain of the *Blonde* dispatched a lieutenant with a small relief party. They climbed aboard the *Mary* and looked about the quarter-deck. The lieutenant's gaze fell on the few remaining slices of the last of the dead, which were drying in the sun. Before he could be told by the castaways what extremity they had been driven to, and failing to comprehend what he was seeing, he blurted out his satisfaction at their not as yet having run out of fresh meat. . . .

Informed of the *source* of the meat, he was horrified, the more so when he learned that this supply had been dwindling so rapidly that the living had begun to ration it.

On the *Blonde,* coarsened sailors who felt, Saunders was sure, no fear of death, wept at the sight of the feeble, emaciated castaways and at the tale they told.

The rest of their voyage was uneventful.

On April 5, Ann Saunders returned home to the embrace of her mother. She had been gone less than six months, yet she was extraordinarily changed. Her faith was undiminished, but no longer could she find joy in life. Looking back on all she had been through, she had only this reflection: "I think I can say I had witnessed and endured more of the heavy judgments and afflictions of this world than any other of its female inhabitants."

Truly, who was there to dispute her claim?

The derelict *Francis Mary* drifted on after the *Blonde* sailed away. (Because of the buoyancy of their cargoes, wrecked timber ships "were unsinkable so long as they held together.") Some months later the crew of an English vessel boarded her and then towed her to Jamaica, where she was refitted and sent back to sea.

The following year, in 1827, a Providence publisher brought out *The Narrative of the Shipwreck and Suffering of Miss Ann Saunders.* The young woman's story won the sympathy of her contemporaries, but at about the same time, a second, somewhat dissenting account appeared bearing the name of Captain John Kendall. While Saunders writes with occasional flights of rhetoric consistent with her grief and distress, Kendall's style is taciturn and cynical. He lists the string of disasters that befell his vessel with hardly a pause to give weight to particular details or revelations. This, for instance, is how he introduces the death of the first casualty:

> At ten P.M. another heavy sea struck us, which stove in our stern. Cut away our foremast and both bower anchors, to keep the ship to

the wind. Employed in getting what provision we could, by knocking out the bow-port; saved fifty pounds of bread and five pounds of cheese, which we stowed in the maintop. Got the master's wife and female passenger up, whilst we were clearing away below, lightening the ship; most of the people slept in the top. At daylight, found Patrick Conney hanging by his legs to the cat-harpins, dead from fatigue; committed his body to the deep.

As for Saunders, he has high praise for her strength, of which she had more "in her calamity than most of the men." Yet he is duplicitous in his commendation. Twice in his short memoir he stops to tell readers how literally bloodthirsty she was and with what alacrity she rushed to bleed the corpses of the recently deceased, including that of her own "late intended husband." He goes on to depict a scuffle between Ann and a sailor over Frier's blood, before "the heroine got the better of her adversary, and then allowed him to drink one cup to her two."

The origin of the captain's animosity toward the young woman will never be known. Perhaps he was one of those who early on was laid low by want. If so, he would have watched his wife's servant assuming authority that should have been his. Then, too, he had watched over five weeks as the *Mary* was destroyed piece by piece in storms. He had seen fourteen crewmen, including three boys, starve to death: "They became foolish, and crawled upon their hands round the deck when they could, and died, generally, raving mad!" Before his eyes his own wife, the mother of his small son, became emaciated and was reduced to the most dreadful behavior just to keep herself alive. Four times vessels came near and could have helped, he was sure, but each sailed away instead. In the end he lost both cargo and ship.

All that had happened to him was then brought before the public, first in newspapers immediately after the rescue and then again in more lasting fashion with the publication of Miss Saunders's account. In such circumstances it is hardly surprising that he might — however unjustly — lash out at a woman who had found it within herself to perform those deeds that had to be done.

CHAPTER 15

The Cruel Death I Did Sustain

The Wreck of the *William Brown*

Chicanery was not the only means survivors employed to protect themselves from the democratic risks of the lottery. An easier way to accomplish the same end was to avoid participation entirely — to limit, in other words, who was required to reach a trembling hand into the hat. Mr. Hedely suggested that Richard Clarke be exempt from the drawing by virtue of his position as master; in some other boats all officers were so privileged. The rationale for this special treatment was that without their knowledge of navigation, no one would reach safety, and so they should not be put in jeopardy.

A similar line of reasoning justified giving immunity to all the sailors in a longboat. The handling of small craft in heavy seas was a demanding task that required the experience and skills of professional mariners. If the boat capsized and could not be righted, everyone would drown. Therefore no sailor could be sacrificed. . . .

By this point in the discussion, passengers and cabin boys might have begun exchanging nervous glances. Such conversations did take place, and limited lotteries were held. The reasoning that lay behind them was logical, but it is unsettling nonetheless. It violates our sense of fair play and makes us suspect that all too often it was used as a convenient rationale for murder.

Images of passengers being bullied out of longboats by more numerous and muscular seamen are disturbing, and positively harrowing is the thought of an apprentice, blindfolded and on his knees on the deck of a drifting hulk, calling out the names of his young friends while an older man draws lots. "All we got from out the wreck was three bottles of Port Wine," explains the anonymous author of

"The Sorrowful Fate of O'Brien," an Irish ballad based on the true story of the *Francis Spaight*.

And every time that we got weak, we took a drop each time.
We had not water for to drink but what fell from the sky,
And no dry spot then could be got to either sit or lie.

On the third day of December, it being on the ninth day,
Without tasting any kind of food; the hunger upon us did prey
Our captain cried: "Cheer up, my boys; let those four boys cast lots
They have no wives: to save our lives one of these four must die."

While lots they were preparing, these poor unfortunate boys
Stood gazing at each other with salt tears in their eyes
A bandage o'er O'Brien's eyes they quickly then did tie
For the second lot that was pulled up said O'Brien was to die.

He said unto his comrade boys: "Now let my mother know
The cruel death I did sustain, when you to Limerick go."
Then John O'Gorman he was called to bleed him in the vein
Twice he tried to take his blood, but it was all in vain.

Our captain cries: "Cheer up, my boys, this work will never do;
O'Gorman, you must cut his throat, or else you will die too."
The trembling cook, he took the knife, which sore did him
    confound,
He cut his throat and drank his blood as it flowed from the wound.

Early the next morning the weather it got clear,
And the American *Aginora* [*sic*], in sight she did appear
Providence sent her that way for to protect our lives
We're safe once more on Limerick's shore with our children and our
    wives.

What really happened aboard the wreck was even more terrible. Fourteen-year-old Patrick O'Brien protested the four ship's boys alone having to draw lots but gave up when he realized that if he continued to object, the lottery would be dispensed with and he would be murdered. That the lot fell on him, the one dissenter, is a cause for skepticism, the more so since he was sightless during the proceedings. The blindfold was a rare and suspect accessory in the custom of the sea. True, it was Patrick who called out names as the lots supposedly were being drawn, but if the drawing had been an honest one, why could not the boys select their own sticks from a sailor's fist? And why was not O'Brien permitted to witness the drawing?

Nonetheless, O'Brien bared his arm, and the cook, who, to his credit, did indeed refuse the task until his own life was threatened, attempted to open a vein. It was only after this hapless fellow failed and the captain spoke of cutting young Patrick's throat that the boy grew panicky and put up a fight. One survivor paraphrased O'Brien as warning the others that "the first man who lays hands on him would be the worse for him: that he'd appear to him at another time; that he'd haunt him after death." Only well-fed men safely on land have the luxury of fearing ghosts: the poor lad was seized, and the still-protesting cook was forced to kill him.

The ballad's greatest inaccuracy is in the quick end to the suffering of the *Spaight*'s sailors. The derelict drifted on for four or five days longer before being found, during which time the drinking of sea water brought on madness and death, and the veins of at least one more boy were opened. Only eleven of the original eighteen-man crew were taken off by the *Agenora,* three fatalities having occurred in the storm that wrecked the ship and the other four during the twenty days she drifted.

Before we leave this unhappy episode, one point should be stressed. This concerns the argument for a drawing confined to apprentices. Captain Timothy Gorman's opinion, as one witness later recalled it, was that "the lots should be drawn between the four boys, as they had no families, and could not be considered so great a loss to their friends, as those who had wives and children depending upon them." It is true that before the twentieth-century advent of the social welfare system and the widespread availability of life insurance for the working poor, the loss of a wage earner was an enormous catastrophe for a family. Destitution was certain and the breakup of the family likely. In one age the loss of the wage earner might end in his dependents being thrown into debtors' prison; in another they might experience the cruelties of the workhouse or the orphanage.

Thus Captain Gorman and other family men had some grounds for excusing themselves from lotteries. Their reasoning was a refinement of the notion that in moments of crisis some lives can be found more valuable and worth saving than others. Cicero was reluctant to make such an evaluation, but men in a longboat or on a wreck were too pressed and desirous of life to be so philosophically disinterested.

Put another way, once you have determined that *someone* must be sacrificed for the good of the rest, you have opened the door, and all that we have seen and feared may enter in. If you can hasten the death of a man who is clearly dying, you can hold a lottery. If you can exempt one officer, you can exempt them all. If you can excuse the officers, you can excuse the crew. In the end, if you make rational and pragmatic choices to limit the damage in a disaster, you may find yourself looking on while children roll up their sleeves.

It was such an eventuality, in addition to the descent into brutishness, that some officers tried to forestall. They knew that once a single departure from a higher code of conduct was made, all control would be gone. This insight, and not just knowledge of the compass and the sextant, made the officer valuable in survival situations.

Cabin boys were so often the victims of lotteries because, being young and small, they were easily subdued. This explanation is implicit in the story of Patrick O'Brien. O'Brien and his friends were forced into a drawing because they were four youths against eleven adult males; when Patrick became frightened and tried to resist, he was immediately overcome and could do no more than threaten to haunt his killers.

Passengers, like the apprentices, were often at a physical disadvantage, and as a result, where they were present, the lottery might be dispensed with altogether. Few passengers would have been a match for seamen who were renowned for their frequent brawls and who had spent many years performing strenuous labor. Furthermore, in the days of sail, mariners routinely carried knives as essential tools of their trade. We have seen a case of a seaman who swam away from a wreck only half-clothed — but with his knife tucked in at his waist. Faced with such armed, strong, practiced fighters, a passenger could do little more than hope that death could be forestalled until, just in the nick of time, a sail appeared on the horizon.

Too often, unfortunately, it did not.

The *William Brown* struck several times against an iceberg on the evening of April 19, 1841, at a point some 250 miles southeast of Newfoundland. She immediately began to leak, and the pumps were manned, but it was soon clear that there was no hope of keeping her afloat.

Eighty-three persons were on board, including eighteen officers and crewmen and sixty-five male and female passengers, most of whom were Irish immigrants bound for the *Brown*'s home port of Philadelphia. The captain, the second mate, seven sailors, and one lucky passenger appropriated for themselves the better of the only two "lifeboats." This was known as a jollyboat; it had a sail and a fairly deep draft. The other craft, a longboat, which could be propelled only by oars, was left for the remainder of the crew and as many of the passengers as could fit into her; this number came to some nine of the former and thirty-three of the latter.

These figures indicate that about half of the passengers were left behind, and they stood on the deck, "shrieking and calling on the captain to take them off on his boat." First mate Francis Rhodes's benediction for them was realistic: "Poor souls! you're only going down just before us." At about 11:20 P.M., less than two hours after the *Brown* had encountered the ice, an "eerie silence" fell, and the ship sank.

The weather was stormy and the sea rough. The longboat, which leaked badly enough to require constant bailing, had lost her rudder and was terribly overcrowded. Indeed, she was so weighed down that her gunwales were only four or five inches above the water. Despite this alarming fact, Captain George L. Harris would not permit any of her occupants to transfer to the jollyboat, in which he was more or less comfortably ensconced. The two craft were roughly the same size and had about the same capacity, but the one held forty-two people and the other only ten. Nonetheless, Harris was adamant about not accepting anyone else in the jollyboat.

The captain contented himself with giving Rhodes, whom he had placed in charge of the longboat, a chart, a watch, a compass, and a quadrant, and he told him that they were 250 miles from land. How much good the information and instruments would be is questionable, since the mate was a poor navigator at best. Why Harris even bothered to hand over a compass and the rest is a bit puzzling: he would later say that he had been certain that the craft was "not manageable," and even had she many fewer people in her, "it would have been impossible to row her to land; and . . . the chances of her being picked up, were ninety-nine to one against her." Surely the experienced sailors in the longboat must have shared his opinion and understood that they were being sentenced to death. In any case, from his gesture it would have been evident to everyone that Harris did not intend to keep the jollyboat beside the longboat but planned to go off and leave the passengers and crew to their fate.

The two craft did remain moored together through the night. In the morning, however, Captain Harris prepared to sail away. Rhodes asked him to "keep company with us today," but he would not.

It was probably at this juncture that the mate told his superior that unless he took some of the passengers into the jollyboat, it would be necessary to have a lottery and eject some several occupants of the longboat. Once again we see how familiar men who made their living on ships were with that custom of the sea: Rhodes and Harris spoke in a kind of shorthand yet understood each other perfectly. Someone heard the mate say simply, "Captain Harris, we will have to draw lots." The officer's reply has been variously reported. One witness thought he said only, "I know what you mean." A second insisted his comment was "I know what you'll have to do. Don't speak of it now. Let it be the last resort." Yet a third had Harris speaking in a way that certainly was consistent with his actions: "I know what you mean. I don't want to hear anymore about it."

Shortly thereafter he sailed away. . . .

After some hours of trying to follow the captain's course for Newfoundland, the mariners in the longboat headed her south in the hope of reaching temperate latitudes. This decision may have been based partly on the difficulty of making progress toward shore and partly on the cold weather. It had hailed the day before and was raining now. They had encountered icebergs yesterday and would shortly do so again. Few if any of those in the craft were dressed for lengthy exposure to the harsh weather. Quite a number of passengers did not have overcoats, and many more, having gone to bed before the wreck, were wearing only night clothes. They were later described variously as being "half-naked," "half-clothed," and "practically naked," and as Captain Harris himself put it, "all crowded up together like sheep in a pen." Prolonged exposure to the cold would kill them all, and so they navigated toward warmer waters and hoped to be picked up by a ship.

The boat was not seaworthy. She had been leaking from the start. She had to be bailed constantly; the passengers took turns at this fatiguing chore. Despite the problems, those rowing managed to make three miles an hour.

By nightfall, however, the wind had picked up, a second leak had developed, and they were again among floes. Rhodes would recall that when he realized the boat was "surrounded by small and large masses of ice, and that the water was gaining upon her, I thought it improbable that she should hold out, unless relieved of some of her weight. I then consulted the sailors, and we were all of the opinion that it was necessary to throw overboard those who were nearly dead, until we had room enough to work the boat and take to our oars."

The captain had been careful not to approve a lottery. Now the mate was picking his words cautiously, speaking in a way that objectified the subject and not incidentally kept the blame from falling on his shoulders: it was a *unanimous* decision to remove *weight,* and, anyway, those to be ejected were nearly dead.

The killing did not begin right away. Eventually Rhodes, who was taking his turn bailing, gave up this chore in despair and cried, "This work won't do. Help me, God. Men, go to work."

No one moved.

He tried again: "Men, you must go to work, or we shall perish." This time his henchmen stirred, and the killing began.

Five sailors acted as executioners, but Rhodes was not among them. He took no part in what happened during those hours of darkness, and, indeed, having announced the commencement of the atrocity, he seems to have had very little to say for the rest of the night.

The first death was that of James Riley. When he was told to stand up, he called out, asking several of the women to intercede for him. They tried. One of them moaned, "Good God, are they going to drown the man?"

They did just that, and a second fellow followed soon after him. This may have been George Duffy, who entreated them to let him live for the sake of his wife and three children, "who were on shore." The murderers were not moved.

James MacAvoy asked for five minutes to say his prayers and prepare himself for death, and this was granted him. When his time was up, he rose, buttoned his coat, intoned, "Lord, be merciful to me, a sinner," and jumped into the ocean.

Frank Askins refused to accept his fate with similar resignation. He resisted with such determination that his attacker, Alexander William Holmes, had his shirt torn in the struggle and had to shout for assistance. Askins, realizing that he could not win against so many, tried an appeal to reason, sweetened with a bribe: "I'll not go out," he told Holmes. "You know I wrought well all the time. I'll work like a man till morning, and do what I can to keep the boat clear of water; I have five sovereigns, and I'll give it for my life till morning, and when morning comes if God does not help us we will cast lots, and I'll go out like a man if it is my turn."

"I don't want your money, Frank," Holmes replied, and threw him into the sea.

Holmes is something of a puzzle. A twenty-six-year-old native of Finland, he was a dedicated and skilled mariner "who had followed the sea from youth, and his frame and countenance would have made an artist's model for decision and strength." It was he who suggested turning the longboat away from Newfoundland toward the temperate latitudes, and he had already stopped a major leak by cutting a plug with an ax. He was not a brute by any means: he was so diligent in saving passengers at the time of the wreck that some described him as being self-sacrificial and "generous" in the extreme. After the two craft were away and the *Brown* sinking, he returned to the doomed vessel alone, pulling himself up a rope hand over hand, to bring off an ill child. He put her on his back and, holding on to her with one arm, slid down the "falls of the ropes by which the longboat was lowered." The girl's widowed mother and sisters were already in the longboat, and presumably he did not want to separate them. At the time, however, another woman stranded on the deck with her several children offered him a year's pay to save her, but the craft was too full as it was. He refused, saying he was not after money and wanted only to save lives. Still, he had gone back for the invalid at "great peril of his life" and for no gain at all, becoming in the process "the last man to leave the sinking ship." Despite the bitter cold, he gave away his coat and other warm clothing.

Thus his being among the executioners is confusing. Perhaps fear had changed him, as it did so many men. More likely, he genuinely believed that the boat was going to sink unless she was lightened, and he set about keeping her afloat for the sake of the majority — twenty-six people — who would be left in her when the others were at the bottom of the sea. This would explain why, when Askins offered him the sovereigns, his reply was the one he had given to the woman on the *Brown:* he was not after money; he wanted to save lives.

All of this makes what happened after Askins was gone the more disturbing. While he was still in the boat, his two sisters begged for his life. The younger of them offered to die in his stead. What is more, she declared that if he was thrown into the ocean, she wished to share his fate — a heartfelt sentiment but, under the circumstances, surely not a wise one to express. . . . Thus it was that *both* the sisters were drowned, too.

The younger one, Mary, seems to have jumped in voluntarily, but the other did not. Her name was Ellen, and she did not want to go over the side. She pleaded that she not be thrown into the cold sea because she had no cloak — and she was promptly given one. It would not have kept her warm long. It only would have weighed her down and pulled her under sooner. Perhaps that was a blessing.

The deaths of the Askinses seem to have touched Holmes. By some accounts he thereafter tried to put an end to the killing, decreeing that "no more shall be thrown over. If any others are lost, we shall be lost together." The other murderers ignored him.

James Black was seized, and his wife insisted she would die with him. Black asked that she be allowed to do this. They were given a reprieve when Francis Rhodes's voice was heard in the darkness, ordering that they be left alone.

Another man was also permitted to live because his wife was with him, but this clemency was not extended to men with families to support at home . . . or to uncles whose nieces were in the craft . . . or to the sole guardian of an orphaned girl . . . or to the last surviving member of a family of fifteen. After pleading their cases, they all went in. Some struggled and some did not; at least one more jumped in unassisted, but they all went in.

The dreadful business continued on through much of the night. After dawn, two men who had been hidden by the women were discovered. The murderers cursed this duplicity and went back to work. (At this, Rhodes, who appears to have been sickened by what he had initiated, cried, "Lord! cruel, cruel!")

Later some of the killers would claim that their victims were dying or dead. One would even insist that, after praying, each victim had voluntarily leaped over the side. Many of the passengers, of course, would tell a different tale.

The last head had hardly disappeared beneath the waves when the *Crescent,* an American ship, appeared. Holmes, the only one among the "passengers and crew . . . whose energies and whose hopes did not sink into prostration," was alone in descrying the vessel's mainmast. While everyone else lay in the bottom of the boat, "exhausted and despairing," he raised a distress signal; thus he saved them all. When he told them that their craft had been sighted, some of them began to pull themselves up to get a look at the *Crescent,* but he shouted that they were to stay out of sight, and he shoved one woman down as she tried to stand. "Lie down, every soul of you, and be still," he told them. "If they make out so many of us on board, they will steer off another way, and pretend they have not seen us."

As it turned out, deception was not necessary. The vessel's captain was a compassionate man who maneuvered her "at some considerable risk" through the icebergs to pick them up, and he would later go so far as to burn his longboat to provide warmth for them. Since he is the only officer or sailor in this whole story who behaved with consistent honor and humanity, let us recall his name: Captain George T. Ball.

For a time the *Crescent* was trapped in the ice, but eventually, on May 12, she arrived at Le Havre, France. Both the British and American consuls investigated the matter and took statements. Some of the passengers, including the men who had been allowed to live, actually spoke favorably of Holmes and the others and affirmed the necessity of what they had done. Despite a furor in England and the United States over the incident, the authorities in both countries decided no prosecution was warranted.

Some of the passengers were less charitable. When they reached Philadelphia in mid-July, they told stories that excited emotions in the Irish community there, its members believing that Irish Catholics had been left behind on the *William Brown* or sacrificed at sea, while Scottish Protestants had lived unmolested until rescued.

Some of the officers and crew unwisely made their way to the port city, which, you will recall, had been their ship's destination. Despite the anger of Irish residents, in the end only Holmes was tried, and then just for the death of Frank Askins. The trial lasted more than a week, beginning on April 13, 1842, and concluding on April 23. In summing up the case, one of the prosecutors sought to refute the defense's contention that Askins and the other victims had been killed to preserve Holmes's life and the lives of the other people in the boat:

Peril, even extreme peril, is not enough to justify a sacrifice such as this was. Nor would even the certainty of death be enough, if death were yet prospective. The law regards every man's life as of equal value. It regards it, likewise, as of sacred value.

The prosecutor, whose name was George M. Dallas, then turned to an argument that Cicero might have recognized:

Admitting, then, the fact that death was certain, and that the safety of some persons was to be promoted by the early sacrifice of the others, what law, we ask, gives a crew, in such a case, to be arbiters of life and death, settling for themselves both the time and extent of the necessity? No. We protest against giving to seamen the power thus to make jettison of human beings, as of so much cargo; of allowing sailors, for their own safety, to throw overboard whenever they may like whomsoever they may choose. If the mate and the seamen believed that the ultimate safety of a portion was to be advanced by the sacrifice of another portion, it was the clear duty of that officer, and of the seamen, to give full notice to all on board. Common settlement would, then, have fixed the principle of sacrifice, and, the mode of selection involving all, a sacrifice of any would have been resorted to only in the dire extremity. Thus far the argument admits that, at sea, sailor and passenger stand upon the same base, and in equal relations. But we take a third, stronger ground. The seaman, we hold, is bound beyond the passenger to encounter the perils of the sea. To the last extremity, to death itself, must he protect the passenger. It is his duty. It is on account of these risks that he is to be paid. It is because the sailor is expected to expose himself to every danger that, beyond all mankind, by every law, his wages are secured to him. It is for this exposure that the seamen's claims are a "sacred lien," and "that if only a single nail of a ship is left, they are entitled to it."

What did Alexander Holmes think of this logic as he sat in that safe, dry courtroom? The *William Brown* had gone down, and he had not even a nail to show for it. He had heard the mate tell the captain that if he did not take some of the passengers into his boat, it would be necessary to throw some people overboard. He had heard the captain tell the sailors in the longboat that they were to obey Rhodes as they would him. Rhodes had "twice imperatively given" the command to jettison, and five men had taken part . . . but here was Holmes in the dock alone.

Holmes's lawyers argued that he and the other seamen had been given an order by their superior and that because of their trade they had been conditioned to follow orders instantly and without question. The chief defense counsel, David Paul Brown, asserted, "It is no part of a sailor's duty to moralize and to speculate, in such a moment as this was, upon the orders of his superior officers. The commander of a ship . . . 'gives desperate commands. He requires instantaneous obedience.' The sailor . . . obeys by instinct." Holmes and the other four were acting in the only feasible manner.

[The prosecution says] that lots are the law of the ocean. Lots, in cases of famine, where means of subsistence are wanting for all the crew, is what the history of maritime disaster records; but who has ever told of casting lots at midnight, in a sinking boat, in the midst of darkness, of rain, of terror, and of confusion? To cast lots when all are going down . . . is a plan easy to suggest, rather difficult to put in practice. The danger was instantaneous . . . and . . . there [was] no time for deliberation. The sailors adopted the only principle of selection which was possible in an emergency like theirs — a principle more humane than lots. Man and wife were not torn asunder, and the women were all preserved. Lots would have rendered impossible this clear dictate of humanity.

The jury found the defendant guilty of manslaughter but recommended mercy. He was sentenced to six months of hard labor and fined twenty dollars. Since he had already been in jail longer than that, he was released, and the fine evidently was remitted. An appeal to President John Tyler for pardon was denied.

As for Captain George L. Harris, his jollyboat was picked up six days after he abandoned the longboat. Although everyone in her had suffered from frostbite, they had all survived. Harris was not charged in the case because, after all, nothing he had done had violated the law.

CHAPTER 16

The Headhunter's Casket

A Caesura

The lottery would seem to be fixed in our psyches as part of a deeply rooted impulse to gamble. In situations where benign games of chance have no place it nonetheless crops up — even where the circumstances are odd or unlikely. In the fall of 1864, for example, the Confederate guerrilla John Singleton Mosby captured twenty-seven Yankee soldiers. Six of his men having been executed by Union general George Armstrong Custer, Mosby was determined to retaliate in kind, but he was unwilling to choose among the prisoners. Therefore a hat containing slips of paper was passed around. A recent and if anything more horrific instance occurred in the summer of 1985, when a group of Brazilian prisoners sought to protest the conditions of their confinement by beating to death, one at a time, selected fellow inmates. The victims were chosen, of course, by lot.

The occurrence of murder in survival situations — for the purpose of cannibalism or lightening the boat — has virtually ceased. Modern ships and aircraft are equipped with adequate numbers of well-stocked lifeboats. Where supplies are lost or exhausted, the passenger capacity of twentieth-century transport is usually so large that, as in the case of the Andes crash, there are more than enough bodies available to obviate the necessity of any person's life being extinguished.

So with the end of this section we will hear no more of lotteries and no more of cannibalism. Indeed, except for passing references to them in this chapter, the lesson is concluded. The "delicate question which" is one that we may relievedly cease to ask.

We will soon make a substantial departure from all that has gone before, forsaking the sea entirely for land, solid land. Before we disembark, however, two issues should be examined and resolved. The first involves an individual's responsibility or guilt for actions taken to ensure his survival. The second has to do with the lasting effects of ordeals.

We might expect the murderer or cannibal to be hounded by guilt once he is back to safety. We imagine him keeping to the shadows, starting at the sound of his name, and feeling compelled to move from place to place as his identity and crimes become known.

This is nonsense, of course. Most survivors forced to commit horrible acts to survive wisely seem to have looked back on their behavior as being inextricably linked to the situations in which they found themselves. Consider the case of Tom Dudley, the master of the yacht *Mignonette*. It was he who decided that one man must be sacrificed to preserve the other three, and it was he who made the selection and then hastened the death of young Richard Parker. Apparently Dudley was so untroubled by what he had done that a short time afterward he readily told his story to anyone who would listen.

After their release from prison, both Dudley and his codefendant, Edwin Stephens, were issued new Board of Trade certificates so they could resume their occupations. Stephens and the third cannibal, Ned Brooks, who had been a witness for the Crown, went back to making their living on the sea. As for Dudley, he had been planning to emigrate before he ever set sail in the *Mignonette*, and he and his family left for Sydney, Australia, soon after he was freed. He established himself as a tent and tarpaulin maker, and the business may have been expanded to include sail-making and yacht chandlery.

One author has claimed that once in Australia, Dudley changed his name and was at pains to conceal his identity. Many years later, overcome by guilt, he tried to re-enact the tragedy of 1884: he set off on a voyage with a woman companion who sometimes masqueraded as a man, and he intended while at sea to cut off a portion of his buttock and feed it to her. The truth, alas, is more mundane.

Tom Dudley retained his name and, in fact, called his business T. R. Dudley and Company. The firm became quite successful and expanded accordingly. Its owner prospered and seems to have attained a degree of social prominence. He died on February 22, 1900, the first Australian to succumb to a pandemic of bubonic plague that had begun in China in 1894 and had been spreading around the world ever since, via the fleas of ship rats.

Dudley's willingness to return to a sea-related occupation is consistent with the reactions of other survivors detailed here. In nearly every instance, in fact, they went back to the very employment that once almost cost them their lives. This is true not only of those whose ordeals we have been examining in recent chapters but also of the men described in the first part of this book. Having been forced to dwell for four years on an island, Selkirk continued to sail the sea and, for that matter, died there. Dampier, despite repeated maroonings and open-boat voyages, never gave up his trade. John Byron, an eighteen-year-old midshipman when he was wrecked off the coast of Chile, stayed in the navy and attained the rank of admiral. And so on.

What would cause men who had been through such dreadful events to step back on the deck voluntarily?

One explanation lies in a denial mechanism: they told themselves that what had happened to them once could never happen to them again. Then as now, such a notion was expressed in terms of electrical storms. In 1822, in a vessel off the Ecuadorian coast, a twenty-four-year-old midshipman named Charles Wilkes met Captain George Pollard, Jr. Two years before, he had been cast away with six other men in a boat for about three months. By the time of the rescue, four of the seven had died, including one by lot to feed the others.

Young Wilkes, who had just read an account of the tragedy, asked Pollard if he was by chance related to the man in the story, and was thereupon treated to a recital of its details. The youth was then bold enough to ask, as he subsequently paraphrased it, how the captain "could think of again putting his foot on board ship to again pursue such a calling, or hazard another voyage." Many years later, Wilkes noted the captain's serene reply: "He simply remarked that it was an old adage that lightning never struck in the same place twice." Whether or not such a notion is scientifically valid in the natural world, less than three years after his first ship, the *Essex*, went down, Pollard would suffer a second shipwreck, albeit one with considerably less horrendous consequences.

A second, related theory for why survivors went back "board ship" is that trauma had relieved them of fear. They had traveled to the furthermost corner of a place of terror and come back alive.

What was there left to be afraid of? At least a few survivors held to this idea, but they are in a distinct minority.

A third possibility has to do with what is sometimes referred to as "the romance of the sea." Wilkes asked the precise question many of us would ask — how can you ever go on the ocean again? — but it is one scorned by sailors and aficionados of sea lore alike. Thomas Farel Heffernan, who is an authority on the *Essex* tragedy, is astonished to find what is so obviously a "landlubber's " question coming from "the mouth of a seaman."

Many modern sailors feel that the ocean has changed them forever. No matter what has happened to them while they were aroving, they assert, they could never be content to stay on shore. The sky is so much more immense, so much deeper where there are no city lights, they say, that no one who has worked beneath it can be at ease for very long on land.

This view is not new, of course. In *Moby Dick,* Herman Melville expresses it with a special beauty as he praises a tall mariner named Bulkington, who, a few days after returning to New Bedford from a lengthy voyage, signs on for another one. The character has realized, as Heffernan has it, that only in the storm can he survive the storm. Melville, being a novelist instead of a scholar, is far less succinct, far more enchanted.

> When on that shivering winter's night, the *Pequod* thrust her vindictive bows into the cold malicious waves, who should I see standing at her helm but Bulkington! I looked with sympathetic awe and fearfulness upon the man, who in mid-winter just landed from a four years' dangerous voyage, could so unrestingly push off again for still another tempestuous term. The land seemed scorching to his feet. Wonderfullest things are ever the unmentionable; deep memories yield no epitaphs; this . . . is the stoneless grave of Bulkington. Let me only say that it fared with him as with the storm-tossed ship, that miserably drives along the leeward land. The port would fain give succor; the port is pitiful; in the port is safety, comfort, hearthstone, supper, warm blankets, friends, all that's kind to our mortalities. But in that gale, the port, the land, is that ship's direst jeopardy; she must fly all hospitality; one touch of land, though it but graze the keel, would make her shudder through and through. With all her might she crowds all sail off shore; in so doing, fights 'gainst the very winds that fain would blow her homeward; seeks all the lashed sea's landlessness again; for refuge's sake forlornly rushing into peril; her only friend her bitterest foe!
>
> Know ye, now, Bulkington? Glimpses do ye seem to see of that

mortally intolerable truth; that all deep, earnest thinking is but the intrepid effort of the soul to keep the open independence of her sea; while the wildest winds of heaven and earth conspire to cast her on the treacherous, slavish shore?

But as in landlessness alone resides the highest truth, shoreless, indefinite as God — so, better it is to perish in that howling infinite, than be ingloriously dashed upon the lee, even if that were safety! For worm-like, then, oh! who would craven crawl to land! Terrors of the terrible! is all this agony so vain? Take heart, take heart, O Bulkington! Bear thee grimly, demigod! Up from the spray of thy ocean-perishing — straight up, leaps thy apotheosis!

These sentiments might be dismissed as mere fancy or hyperbole coming from another author. Had Defoe or Poe or any of a hundred other landlocked writers who attempted to depict shipboard life expressed themselves thus we might hoot and close the book on them. Melville, however, was an experienced sailor who knew the darker side of the seaman's trade. He first signed on to a crew (that of the merchantman *St. Lawrence*) at the relatively late age of nineteen, because his family was in difficult financial straits and he had been unable to secure suitable employment on land. This voyage left him so far from being entranced that it was a year and a half before he sought a berth on a second vessel, the whaler *Acushnet*. After eighteen months he jumped ship on Nuku Hiva, one of the Marquesas Islands, having become thoroughly disgusted with living conditions aboard the vessel and the cruelty of the captain.

He and a companion had intended to find sanctuary with the cordial Happar tribe but wandered instead into the territory of the cannibalistic Typee, who made them their "guests." Melville's leg became seriously infected, and his friend was allowed to go after medical assistance for him — and did not return. After a period of increasing anxiety over what his hosts intended for him, he was rescued by the crew of another whaler, the *Lucy Ann*. He signed on and was down for a 120th share of the profits. This might have netted him some money if the enterprise had been a success, but it was not. Eventually he joined in a rather tame mutiny that was promptly thwarted. Jailed in Tahiti, he escaped without much difficulty and spent a few weeks drifting around Polynesia.

In early November 1842, he signed on the *Charles and Henry* as a harpooner. Six months later he was without a ship again, this time in the Hawaiian Islands, where, by setting pins in a bowling alley, he earned a little money and the lasting scorn of local missionaries.

Melville embarked on the last journey of his youth on August 17, 1843, as an ordinary seaman aboard the frigate *United States.* Again a stern disciplinary code was harshly enforced: over 160 floggings were administered to sailors and apprentices before they reached Boston. Melville was discharged in October 1844.

He gave up life on the sea at the age of twenty-five. From now on he would attempt to support himself and his family in a more cerebral fashion. His first book, written not long after his return to America, was a fanciful depiction of his adventures among the Typees, and it was a critical and popular success. When in later years his popularity diminished and his earnings from writing declined, he sought meager financial security by working as a customs inspector on the docks of the port of New York.

We may believe Melville's rhapsodic invocation of the seaman's life, then, because he knew of its unglamorous aspects as well: cruel, drunken officers, vicious punishments, brutal press gangs, injustices of every sort, mutinies, and inhuman exploitation. He recognized and lauded the brotherhood of mariners even while being aware of the corruption and savagery of some of its members. Add to this list the dangers he either experienced at first hand or reliably heard of — storms, leaky ships, and disabling or fatal accidents — and you realize that when he sings of the romance of the sea, the song must be true.

Call me Ishmael. Some years ago — never mind how long precisely — having little or no money in my purse, and nothing particular to interest me on shore, I thought I would sail about a little and see the watery part of the world. It is a way I have of driving off the spleen, and regulating the circulation. Whenever I find myself growing grim about the mouth; whenever it is a damp, drizzly November in my soul; whenever I find myself involuntarily pausing before coffin warehouses, and bringing up the rear of every funeral I meet; and especially whenever my hypos get such an upper hand of me, that it requires a strong moral principle to prevent me from deliberately stepping into the street, and methodically knocking people's hats off — then, I account it high time to get to sea as soon as I can. This is my substitute for pistol and ball. With a philosophical flourish Cato throws himself upon his sword; I quietly take to the ship. There is nothing surprising in this. If they but knew it, almost all men in their degree, some time or other, cherish very nearly the same feelings towards the ocean with me.

Denial and the romance of the sea can explain the willingness of a number of survivors to resume their old occupations, but I suggest that often something far more mundane was at work: economic necessity. What else could a man do who had been apprenticed as a boy and had worked for fifteen or twenty years at the sailor's trade? Most seamen had nothing to offer an employer but their two hands, a specialized knowledge, and a set of skills they had begun developing in childhood.

The lot of working men and women is difficult in any age. In the nineteenth century, economies often swung in abrupt cycles from boom to bust. The ranks of the poor were beyond number. Immigrants were exploited by employers and flung aside. The labor pool was considerably larger than the number of jobs available. The sailor may have returned to the sea because he loved it — but also because he had no choice.

The wreck of the *Essex* has achieved lasting fame because, like the story of Selkirk, it was incorporated into a literary masterpiece. In "The Affidavit," chapter 45 of *Moby Dick,* Melville departs from fictionalizing to relate the true story of the *Essex.* More important, he adapts its most memorable and salient feature into the climax of his novel: the destruction of the *Pequod* by the malevolent white whale.

On the morning of November 20, 1820, at a point in the Pacific approximately halfway between the Hawaiian Islands and the Galápagos, the whaleship *Essex* came upon a shoal of her prey. All boats were lowered and manned, and the hunt commenced. By the time three of the whales had been killed, one of the craft had been brought back to the vessel and hoisted in for repairs. First mate Owen Chase was in the process of patching a hole when a very large sperm whale, eighty-five feet long, broke the surface of the sea twenty rods from the *Essex.* The mate was not alarmed at first, but as he watched, the whale came full speed at the ship and rammed her side.

The "appalling and tremendous jar" nearly knocked all the men on board off their feet. The *Essex* immediately began to take on water. In the frantic moments that followed, as the sailors manned the pumps and lowered a boat, the whale repeatedly butted the vessel. That the rammings were intentional there was no doubt. In fact, the mate was sure the whale was attacking in retribution for the murder of the other whales. Between two of the rammings,

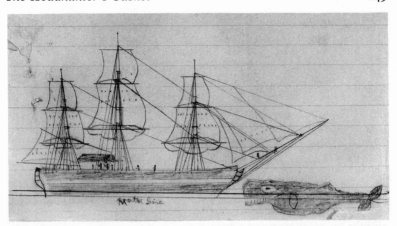

As an old man, Thomas Nickerson, who had been a cabin boy on the *Essex,* drew from memory this illustration of the whale's attack. (Courtesy of the Nantucket Historical Association)

Chase saw the animal lying on the surface a hundred rods to leeward: "He was enveloped in the foam of the sea, that his continual and violent thrashing about in the water had created around him, and I could distinctly see him smite his jaws together, as if distracted with rage and fury."

In the midst of this extraordinary crisis, a signal had been fired to call the other boats back to the *Essex,* but before they arrived, she filled with water and started going down on her beam-ends. Hardly had the mate and the other men climbed into a boat than she "fell over to windward, and settled down in the water." According to Chase,

> Amazement and despair now wholly took possession of us. We contemplated the frightful situation the ship lay in, and thought with horror upon the sudden and dreadful calamity that had overtaken us. We looked upon each other, as if to gather some consolatory sensation from an interchange of sentiments, but every countenance was marked with the paleness of despair. Not a word was spoken for several minutes by any of us; all appeared to be bound in a spell of stupid consternation; and from the time we were first attacked by the whale, to the period of the fall of the ship, and of our leaving her in the boat, more than ten minutes could not certainly have elapsed!

The other whaleboats arrived, and their occupants cried out in horror at the sight of the *Essex.* Only Captain George Pollard was silent. He had, remembered Chase, "no power to utter a single syllable: he was so completely overpowered with the spectacle before him, that he sat down in his boat, pale and speechless. I could scarcely recognise his countenance, he appeared to be so much altered, awed, and overcome, with the oppression of his feelings, and the dreadful reality that lay before him."

The captain roused himself to supervise a salvage operation. The lanyards were cut loose and the masts cut away with small hatchets, and so the ship "came up about two-thirds of the way upon an even keel." The men cut a hole through the planks and brought out supplies, including casks of bread and fresh water, boat nails, a musket, two pistols, and a bit of powder.

They tethered their craft to the wreck and stayed by her that night. One or two of the whalers slept complacently, but most suffered from a feverish anxiety. Some, in Chase's opinion, "were like sick women; they had no idea of the extent of their deplorable situation." Others whispered incessantly of their predicament. The first mate himself kept reviewing over and over again in his mind the moments during which the *Essex* had been destroyed, until he managed to convince himself that what had happened was an illusion:

> After many hours of severe reflection . . . I was able to discard the idea of the catastrophe as a dream. Alas! it was one from which there was no awaking; it was too certainly true, that but yesterday we had existed, as it were, and in one short moment had been cut off from all hopes and prospects of the living! I have no language to paint out the horrors of our situation. To shed tears was indeed altogether unavailing, and withal unmanly; yet I was not able to deny myself the relief they served to afford me.

The following day they climbed onto the wreck and wandered about her absently, searching for useful supplies. They could find none. They stripped off the light sails, collected the spars and masts for use in the voyage to come, and outfitted the boats as best they could. Still they were emotionally attached to the *Essex* and unable to bring themselves to abandon her.

On the second night the wind blew hard and the sea became rough. The men, who had managed to distract themselves during the day with searching the wreck and readying the boats, were now forced to confront the reality of their circumstances. As a result, "they passed to a sudden fit of melancholy, and the miseries of their situation came upon them with such force, as to produce spells of extreme debility, approaching almost to fainting."

In the morning Chase took a work party back on the *Essex*. There was nothing more to be taken from her, however, and she was showing signs of breaking up. He reported this to the captain and suggested they shove off, but Pollard was unwilling to leave the wreck just yet. He went back on board one more time to survey her and to take a nautical observation with what instruments he had. Then he called a council of officers; they decided that without charts their best hope lay in sailing a course first to the south and then eastward until they encountered the coast of either Chile or Peru.

They set off in three whaleboats shortly after noon on November 22. The crew did not lose sight of the ship for three and a half hours. "Many were the lingering and sorrowful looks we cast behind us," Chase recalled. "It has appeared to me often since to have been, in the abstract, an extreme weakness and folly, on our parts, to have looked upon our shattered and sunken vessel with such an excessive fondness and regret; but it seemed as if in abandoning her we had parted with all hope, and were bending our course away from her, rather by some dictate of despair."

They fought gales, heavy seas, and strong, contrary winds. Day after day they huddled in the incessantly rocking, fragile boats and endured continual soaking by the ocean's spray. Their clothes were never dry except when the sun burned down on them, dehydrating their bodies. They rationed their water and food from the beginning. Much of the bread had become contaminated with sea water during the shipwreck. They first ate this portion, which made their thirst rage, taking about two weeks to consume it. They were able to catch only a little rain in a bucket and eventually were compelled to rinse their mouths with sea water and drink their own urine. When flying fish dropped into the craft, they ate them raw. Calms retarded their progress and forced them to drain their strength rowing. They made headway with painful slowness.

Whaleboats were not designed for long ocean voyages. The three craft had been used on many hunts, had sustained much damage, and had been crudely repaired. As a result, leaking was an ongoing problem and bailing a constant necessity. Serious breaches required immediate attention. On one occasion a man had to tie a rope around his waist, swim under the boat, and reattach a board onto the bottom by holding his hatchet against a nail that was "driven through from the inside for the purpose of clenching it." On another, all the men in one boat leaned against one side so that the other side rose out of the water; a man in a different boat then hammered on a piece of lumber.

In the rough weather and at night, one craft or another was always becoming separated from the other two. By mutual consent, the two still together would heave to immediately and signal with lights and firearms until the missing one rejoined them. Obviously this slowed their progress and increased the risk of everyone dying, but Chase tells us that no one was willing to forgo the "consolation which each other's presence afforded."

> Strange as the extraordinary interest which we felt in each other's company may appear, and much as our repugnance to separation may seem to imply of weakness, it was the subject of our continual hopes and fears. It is truly remarked, that misfortune more than anything else serves to endear us to our companions. So strongly was this sentiment engrafted upon our feelings, and so closely were the destinies of all of us involuntarily linked together, that, had one of the boats been wrecked, and wholly lost, with all her provisions and water, we should have felt ourselves constrained, by every tie of humanity, to have taken the surviving sufferers into the other boats, and shared our bread and water with them, while a crumb of one or a drop of the other remained. Hard, indeed, would the case have been for all, and much as I have since reflected on the subject, I have not been able to realize, had it so happened, that a sense of our necessities would have allowed us to give so magnanimous and devoted a character to our feelings. I can only speak of the impressions which I recollect I had at the time.

They sighted land on December 20, exactly one month after the *Essex* went down. This was Henderson Island, located at latitude 24° 20' south and longitude 128° 18' west. While they were now on a line with the coast of Chile, they had been carried *west* of their point of embarkation.

What is more, Henderson is one of four isles that make up the Pitcairn group, and had they been lucky enough to arrive just a little farther west and south, they would have struck Pitcairn itself, where they would have received help: the last surviving *Bounty* mutineer still lived there, along with the women and children of his deceased shipmates. Furthermore, Pitcairn was eminently habitable, while Henderson was not. The problem, as they soon discovered, was a scarcity of both food and water. At first they could find no water at all, but eventually, after several days of increasingly desperate searching, they located a spring in a cliff on the beach; it was accessible, however, only at low tide. They were able to catch nothing more than a few crabs and birds, and so they were forced to subsist almost entirely on birds' eggs and peppergrass.

After a week it was evident that the eggs and grass would not long support twenty men, and some of them were already complaining of hunger. It was time for most of them to push off. Three sailors chose to stay behind, and when the others left on December 27, these few were building a "habitation" out of tree branches.

The new destination was Easter Island, but on the fourth of January, they estimated that they had drifted south of it and decided to make for Más á Tierra. The first man died on January 10. His body was sewn up in his clothes and committed to the deep in a solemn ceremony.

On the night of January 12, in the midst of a gale, Owen Chase's whaleboat became separated from the other two. He stood on the course they had agreed upon, expecting to meet up with the others, but he never did.

On January 14, with his crew growing weaker, Chase estimated that they had traveled only nine hundred miles from Henderson. The sun continued to burn them . . . there were storms . . . rough seas . . . contrary winds. A shark attacked the boat.

Chase had begun to fear that someone would steal food, and he tried to keep the lid of the "provision-chest" secured, but one sailor managed a theft. The first mate confronted the thief, threatening to shoot him. The man confessed, pleaded that "hard necessity [had] urged him to it," and repented.

> I could not find it in my soul to extend towards him the least severity on this account, however much, according to the strict imposition which we felt upon ourselves, it might demand it. This was the first infraction [by anyone]; and the security of our lives, our hopes of redemption from our sufferings, loudly called for a prompt and signal punishment; but every humane feeling of nature plead in his behalf, and he was permitted to escape, with solemn injunction, that a repetition of the same offense would cost him his life.

On January 20, the second man died. His body was also thrown into the ocean.

On February 9, the third man died. His body was eaten.

The rescue of survivors from Henderson Island (Courtesy of the Nantucket Historical Association)

On February 18, a sail was descried. The brig *Indian* picked them up not far from Más Afuera. Captain William Crozier fed the three survivors tapioca and nursed them back to health.

The men in the other two boats fared even worse. Six died of want, and most or all of the bodies were cannibalized. It was not enough, and a lottery was held. The cabin boy, Owen Coffin, was chosen. He was sixteen years old and happened to be Pollard's first cousin. The captain shouted to him, "My lad, my lad, if you don't like your lot, I'll shoot the first man that touches you." We may doubt such sentiments in other instances, but by all reports this officer was a man of great honesty, gentleness, and integrity. Anyway, as Pollard recalled, "The poor emaciated boy hesitated a moment or two; then, quietly laying his head down upon the gunnel of the boat, he said, 'I like it as well as any other.' "

At some point in all of this sorrow, the two boats parted company. On February 23, when George Pollard's was discovered by the *Dauphin* very near the coast of Chile, only he and sixteen-year-old

Charles Ramsdell were still alive. The three men on Henderson Island were saved, but of the third boat, which held two living souls when last seen by the captain, nothing more was heard.

If ever there was an instance to cause men to give up the sea and find another calling, this was it. Yet neither Owen Chase nor George Pollard did.

Thomas Farel Heffernan, who has thoroughly researched the later lives of both men, tells us that the first mate arrived back in Nantucket on June 11, 1821, and the captain, a few weeks later. Chase spent the summer and early fall with his wife and infant daughter — whom he had never seen. During this time he wrote or dictated a narrative of his experiences. "It was my misfortune," he explained to the reader,

> to be a considerable, if not principal, sufferer in the dreadful catastrophe that befell us; and in it, I not only lost all the little I had ventured, but my situation and the prospects of bettering it, that at one time seemed to smile upon me, were all in one short moment destroyed with it. The hope of obtaining something of remuneration, by giving a short history of my sufferings to the world, must therefore constitute my claim to public attention.

The book having been completed by the end of October, he sailed as first mate on the whaler *Florida* in the latter part of December. On all his subsequent voyages, he served as captain.

For the next nineteen years, he was a Bulkington. Gone for two or three years at a stretch, he would return home for as little as seven months or, in one case, thirty days. He was ashore just long enough, it seems, to pay his debts, arrange his personal affairs, and impregnate his wife, and then he was gone again. If he stayed longer, it was generally because his whaler was being refitted and repaired or a new one on which he was to be master was being constructed. Save for these interludes, his children grew up without him. His first two wives died while he was away, both of them shortly after giving birth. His third wife had a child sixteen months after he had last been home, and so he divorced her as soon as he returned to Nantucket. (Curiously, though, he raised the illegitimate child in his household.) Two months after the divorce was final, he married for the fourth and final time. He was then almost forty-five years old and ready to retire from the sea. Thereafter he took the wealth he had accumulated through successful voyages and in-

Captain Owen Chase, who had been first mate on
the *Essex* (Courtesy of the Nantucket Historical
Association)

vested it in real estate, bonds, banks, railroads, and mills. Thus his
remaining on land could be attributed to advancing age, lack of
economic necessity, or family tragedy and scandal — but not to
what he experienced when he was a twenty-four-year-old castaway
in one of the *Essex*'s boats. Neither did it influence his four brothers, all of whom hunted whales long enough to obtain the rank of
captain. Nor did it deter Chase's own son from following in his
father's footsteps.

None of this should surprise us. The end of his life might, however, because during his last years Owen Chase went insane. His
family was forced to hire an attendant for him and to contemplate
committing him to an asylum. His first cousin, Phoebe B. Chase,
wrote to a relative that when she visited him, the deranged captain
mistook her for someone else and "held my hand and sobbed like a
child, saying *O my head, my head* it was pitiful to see the strong

man bowed, then his personal appearance so changed, didn't allow himself decent clothing, fear's he shall come to want."

The last phrase, having to do with Chase's anxiety about the future, recalls a Nantucket oral tradition reported by Heffernan, that in his madness Chase was terrified he would starve to death. As a consequence, he "hid food in the rafters of his house." Heffernan also recounts a Chase family story that has Owen insisting food be bought in "double quantities — not a ham but two hams, and so on. Certainly if fantasies of starvation are going to come back after almost fifty years, there are few people whom they should so reasonably trouble."

George Pollard went back to sea almost as quickly as his first mate had. He became captain of another whaler, the *Two Brothers*, which sailed for the Pacific hunting grounds before the year was out. On February 11, 1823, the vessel was struck by a gale west of the Hawaiian Islands and driven onto a reef that stove in her bottom and sank her. Two boatloads of survivors were picked up before too long by another Nantucket whaler, the *Martha*.

Two months later, in the harbor of Raiatea, in the Society Islands, George Bennet met Pollard, who was then a passenger on the U.S. brig *Pearl*, and heard from him the story of the *Essex*. The miserable captain concluded his tale with this lamentation: "After a time I found my way to the United States, to which I belonged, and got another ship. That, too, I have lost by a second wreck off the Sandwich Islands, and now I am utterly ruined. No owner will ever trust me with a whaler again, for all will say I am an *unlucky* man."

Indeed they did. Pollard was only thirty-one or thirty-two when he made this prophetic utterance, but thereafter he was forced to earn his living on land. He became a nightwatchman in Nantucket, where, in 1852, some thirty-two years after the *Essex* went down and one year after *Moby Dick* was published, he met Herman Melville. The humility and nobility of the captain made a profound impression on the novelist. Later in life, when he had become a customs inspector, Melville turned from fiction to poetry and left us this portrait of the man:

> 'A Jonah is he? — And men bruit
> The story. None will give him place
> In a third venture. Came the day

> Dire need constrained the man to pace
> A night patrolman on the quay
> Watching the bales till morning hour
> Through fair and foul. Never he smiled;
> Call him, and he would come; not sour
> In spirit, but meek and reconciled;
> Patient he was, he none withstood;
> Oft on some secret thing would brood.
> He ate what came, though but a crust;
> In Calvin's creed he put his trust;
> Praised heaven, and said that God was good,
> And his calamity but just.
> So Sylvio Pellico from cell-door
> Forth tottering, after dungeoned years,
> Crippled and bleached, and dead his peers:
> "Grateful, I thank the Emperor." '

By all accounts George Pollard accepted his fate throughout his life with remarkable equanimity. He expressed sorrow that he was considered a Jonah, but not bitterness.

Recent survivors' attitudes toward danger are no different. Whether their distress has resulted from occupation or, at least as often now, recreational pursuit, they are loath to give up what carried them into peril. They learn from their ordeals to appreciate the "little things in life" and to live "from moment to moment" and "one day at a time." In this respect they are distinct from survivors in previous centuries who found the beneficence of God in the midst of their crises. Selkirk embraced true religion on Greater Land, even if he left it there when he departed. But today, on other islands, in other boats, we find only that familiar message of our popular culture: there is nothing beyond the moment, beyond immediate feeling, sensation, and gratification.

The pattern of survivors' lives from the sixteenth century on consistently indicates that no matter what the individual has been through, he will not undergo a radical transformation. Perhaps the explanation for this can be found in the reasons why one person survives and another does not. Over and over again in disaster accounts, the individual who is overwhelmed and gives up very quickly dies, while the one who refuses to be defeated lives until rescued. So the narrowly focused individual who does not lift his eyes from the task at hand to see the enormity he faces may prevail, but his myopia will continue to permit him to stumble into danger.

Herman Melville saw something of this stubborn steadfastness in George Pollard. Although he altered some details of the captain's tribulations, his verses accurately depict the qualities that brought the man through them.

> 'Him they picked up, where, cuddled down,
> They saw the jacketed skeleton,
> Lone in the only boat that lived —
> His signal frittered to a shred.
>   ' "Strong need'st thou be," the rescuers said,
> "Who hast such trial sole survived."
> "I *willed* it," gasped he. And the man,
> Renewed ashore, pushed off again.'

The most salient feature of the survivor's personality is resilient, absolute determination. It is purposeful resolve, not the skills of seamanship or woodsmanship, that saves the lost soul. This trait is manifest in nearly every survivor narrative — just as surely as psychological metamorphosis is absent.

To see transformation, we have to turn from fact to fiction. Spiritual alteration is a constant theme of nearly all the poetry and prose of survival. Nowhere is it better expressed than in Samuel Taylor Coleridge's "The Rime of the Ancient Mariner." In this, the greatest work of the genre, an uncaring, melancholy man kills an albatross, a bird of good omen, and causes the death of two hundred of his shipmates. His penance is to wander the world, telling his story to those who need to hear it.

> Since then, at an uncertain hour,
> That agony returns:
> And till my ghastly tale is told,
> This heart within me burns.
>
> I pass, like night, from land to land;
> I have strange power of speech;
> That moment that his face I see,
> I know the man that must hear me:
> To him my tale I teach.

What the ancient mariner has learned is to love and revere his fellow earthly creatures and to love and worship God as well.

> O Wedding-Guest! this soul hath been
> Alone on a wide, wide sea:

So lonely 'twas, that God Himself
Scarce seemèd there to be.

O sweeter than the marriage-feast,
'Tis sweeter far to me,
To walk together to the kirk
With a goodly company! —

To walk together to the kirk,
And all together pray,
While each to his great Father bends,
Old men, and babes, and loving friends,
And youths and maidens gay!

Farewell, farewell! but this I tell
To thee, thou Wedding-Guest!
He prayeth well, who loveth well
Both man and bird and beast.

He prayeth best, who loveth best
All things both great and small;
For the dear God who loveth us,
He made and loveth all.

Shakespeare maroons Prospero for twelve years, and Defoe leaves Crusoe on his island for a daunting twenty-seven years. Coleridge casts away the mariner for a much more realistic period of time, and yet he makes his character's ordeal radically more searing than that endured by either Prospero or Crusoe. Not incidentally, the mariner's metamorphosis is commensurately more dramatic and lies at the very heart of the poem. Indeed his tribulation is of such power that those, like the wedding guest, to whom he tells it are themselves deeply affected.

The Mariner, whose eye is bright,
Whose beard with age is hoar,
Is gone: and now the Wedding-Guest
Turn'd from the bridegroom's door.

He went like one that hath been stunn'd,
And is of sense forlorn:
A sadder and a wiser man
He rose the morrow morn.

Whether we read the creations of literary artists or the recollections of real survivors, it is possible for us to claim a distant kinship to the wedding guest. For it just could be that these stories change *us* in some slight, subtle fashion. We learn from them that adversity can be overcome by perseverance and ingenuity; that however terrible our situation, we can endure and even triumph. These lessons may be absorbed in moments of serenity and contemplation and lie dormant until they are needed. Then they buoy us up, like Queequeg's coffin, as we float above the solemn, still, and boundless void.

Until our *Rachel* comes seeking her lost children and finds only one last orphan, chastened and adrift.

PART III

LORDS OF THE FOWL AND THE BRUTE

Nature never did betray
The heart that loved her; 'tis her privilege,
Through all the years of this our life, to lead
From joy to joy. . . .
— William Wordsworth

Naked and without a man-made thing, I depend on Nature,
who, if we will but realize it, is our friend and protector.
Why should a white man lost in the woods in winter lie down
and freeze, when a savage will live on the fat of the land?
— Joseph Knowles

But go out on the great ice field of the Arctic, out of sight of
land, and any man's chances of "living off the country" are
just about equal to his chances of finding a gold mine on the
top of an iceberg.

It is difficult for men living in comfort in civilized countries
to realize the harshness of the Arctic, so the "Friendly Arctic" has given to many an entirely wrong impression of the
care, experience, equipment, and planning necessary to
merely stay alive in the far North. I have had men express
astonishment at the elaborate preparations made by me to
carry abundant food in concentrated form for use on my
expeditions. They have been led to believe that a march to
the North Pole is little more than a light-hearted hunting
expedition, upon which one leisurely advances across the
ice, stopping occasionally to kill something to eat and wandering on his way with no cares about to-morrow's food.
— Roald Amundsen

CHAPTER 17

"He Wouldn't Oblige by Dying"

Hugh Glass on the Great Plains

For much of this century science teachers have been taxing the brains of students with a conundrum: if a tree falls in the forest and no one hears it, does it make any noise? Survivors care not for the motion of molecules; their minds are focused on haven and rescue. But if noise requires ears, morality in survival situations requires a crowd. The solitary abandoned soul has no ethical dilemmas. It is only when he is among other men that we may have cause to chastise him.

The preceding stories, ones that raise "the delicate question which," have an inevitable moral cast. They cause us to wonder about the value of individual human lives and the ethical implications of actions taken to preserve some lives at the expense of others. In the tale that follows, several mountain men will choose to forsake a seriously injured, comatose comrade deep in Indian country, leaving him to be found by hostiles or carnivorous beasts rather than endanger themselves by remaining at his side until he dies. Yet their decision is not the sort we dealt with in Part Two: they did not violate the cannibalism taboo, after all, and they did not murder him to save themselves. Given what they knew — that they could not move him, that his death was inevitable, and that they were in jeopardy — they would appear to have had no other choice.

As it happened, the comatose man, Hugh Glass, did not die. When he returned to consciousness, his rage at his friends' betrayal gave him the determination to live when he really should have died. He set out on an arduous journey, a two-thousand-mile trek for revenge.

Even after we have completed that astounding odyssey, we will not have abandoned matters of morality. Yet with Hugh Glass we move among the lords of the fowl and the brute, men afoot on terra firma, lost in wildernesses and deserts. The underlying themes of their stories have to do with heroism as often as with ethics. In the more than one hundred years between the time when Glass crawled across the Great Plains and Antoine de Saint-Exupéry staggered across the Libyan desert, the popular cultures of America and Europe offered up at least four distinct heroic archetypes. The first was the mountain man, foul smelling, irascible, and autonomous. The second was the northern explorer, a reserved aristocrat, cultivated, observant, and brave. The third was the twentieth-century woodsman who left effete, technocratic civilization for the university of nature. The fourth was the aviator, hard drinking, taciturn, and self-reliant.

What the individuals represented by these archetypes had in common are the harsh locales into which they went and the perils that awaited them there. Furthermore, the remoteness of those locales conferred on them a special aura of independence. The very nature of their callings seemed to condition them to be especially capable of dealing with crises. They were, in other words, ideal survivors — or so you might think.

The stories that follow are of human beings, of course, not of mythic archetypes. Still, Hugh Glass was a mountain man, and it is worthwhile to begin with what we imagine such a one to be, instead of what he actually was.

In our mind's eye we see the mountain man framed against the immense sky as he rides his horse up a steep slope, stubborn pack mules following close behind. He is a big man with a bushy beard, deep-voiced, unwashed, his buckskin clothing greasy and reeking. A Hawken rifle rests across the crook of his arm as he watches the trail ahead for signs of game — or one of those Indian war parties that are perpetually after his scalp. He is a difficult fellow, solitary but never lonely, afflicted by claustrophobia whenever mischance takes him into even the smallest town. He has a deep and abiding contempt for store clerks, farmers, and everyone else tied to one place by occupation, family obligations, or — most horrifying of all — timid inclination. The mountains are to him what cathedrals are to city folk, and he knows God walks over the same ground he does.

He has taken an Indian wife to facilitate trading with her tribe, but she stays with her people, and he neither wants nor needs anyone beside him as he sits before his campfire at night. Once a year he goes to a rendezvous and spends a few days getting drunk and swapping lies with men like him, who live by the same few, spare rules he does. Then, filled with enough talk to last him twelve months and anxious to be alone again, he strikes out for some place he has never been before, confident he can deal with whatever awaits him. To him the Rockies mean freedom, and the settlements on the plains below are for self-domesticated serfs. He is as free as the hawk that flies above him, as wily as the prey he hunts, and as dangerous as the bear and mountain lion that share his habitat. When he dies, his body ripped by claws or punctured with arrows, his spirit will continue to roam among the peaks just as though nothing has changed — as indeed it has not.*

So lasting and cherished is our image of the mountain man, perpetuated even now in literature and film, that it is remarkable that scholars took so long to assault it. They love nothing better than to demythologize our idols and knock out from under them the pedestals we set them on. With their little hammers and their short, exacting blows they put first hairline cracks and then wide fissures into the granite faces of our heroic statuary and leave us only rubble and a few sad, evocative remnants.

The first cruel whack seems to have been delivered in 1963, by William H. Goetzmann, writing in *American Quarterly*. Other historians and sociologists quickly rushed in for the kill. They posited that, far from being at the higher elevations out of a love of freedom, the mountain men were nothing more than entrepreneurs after in-

---

* The image has an amazing resiliency. In 1972, Sydney Pollack directed *Jeremiah Johnson,* starring Robert Redford. In the movie, farmers are spoken of with disparagement. Johnson goes into the wilderness as a young man, unfrightened by "ghosty stories." His motivation for leaving the comforts of civilization is never made clear, but an old mountain man pointedly remarks that "many's the child journeys this high, seeking something their natures can't get them below." What Johnson gets is war with the Crow nation. Braves are sent one at a time to kill him. The repeated, single combats batter him psychologically as well as physically. Near the end of the film, as he sits shuddering and hollow-eyed, another mountain man gently suggests that he should leave the Rockies and go to a town. "I've been to a town, Del," is his simple reply, and no further explanation is necessary. Eventually realizing they will never be able to succeed in bumping off a movie star, the Crows make peace with him. In the last line of the picture the narrator tells us, "Some folks say he's up there still."

vestment capital, and once they got it (in the form of pelts), they hurried back to the banks and brothels of town as quickly as they could.

Alas, some evidence supports this theory. John Johnston, whose adventures are rather loosely retold in *Jeremiah Johnson,* made his peace with the Crows, left the mountains, and became the marshal of Red Lodge, Montana. He did not die on a jagged peak but in bed in a California veterans' home. The famous John Colter, who got his start on the Lewis and Clark expedition of 1804, also eventually grew weary of fighting Blackfeet and did what was supposedly unthinkable for a mountain man: he married a *white* woman and bought himself a *farm* in Franklin County, Missouri. Jim Bridger, the most renowned and arguably the greatest of the mountain men, used the capital he accumulated from beaver skins to build a trading post, where, until furious Mormons drove him out, he did a brisk business selling supplies to immigrants traveling along the Oregon Trail. He did marry a Shoshone woman, but the money he earned as a guide for drunken European aristocrats went to buy a Missouri farm, where he raised his family and where he, too, died old and in bed.

It may be, as one aficionado of western exploration has recently suggested, that the mountain man is thought of as an entrepreneur because that is exactly what the most famous of them were. For those looking for backers in a trapping company or hiring themselves out as guides and scouts, a sizable reputation, albeit one salted with tall tales, was an invaluable advertisement. On the other hand, those who were on the frontier because they loved it or wanted solitude would not have returned to civilization to boast of their exploits. They would have been content to stay in the wilderness — let the braggarts and the city folks be damned. Not surprisingly, the names and deeds of these men were never recorded.

What motivated Hugh Glass to stay on the frontier for so long will never be known. Probably he had the same affliction Jedediah Strong Smith had: a "natural roving disposition." Or he may have been one of those mountain men who genuinely could not stand to be around other people; life in the wilderness with all its hazards and hardships was vastly preferable to nosy neighbors and trivial conversation. Undoubtedly he was irascible, a character trait that got him into trouble on more than one occasion — but it also got him back out again. Like William Dampier, he had a personality suited to survival: he was so ornery that he would not give up no matter how menacing the situation or poor the odds, and so he nearly always came through.

He waits just ahead of us on the trail, and with him is a beast as bad-tempered as himself. It was his worst enemy and the nemesis of every woodsman. Indians could sometimes be bought off, evaded, or outfought, but once that huge monster was alarmed or angered, either a man found something tall to climb, or he died.

In our time we have come to think of the great white shark as nature's perfect eating machine, with its sharp teeth, gaping jaws, and incredible determination. For the frontiersman, the same description could be applied to the grizzly bear. The earliest western explorers gave him that name because at a distance — which was as close as they wanted to get — his silver-tipped fur looked as gray and grizzled as an elderly man's beard. The mountain men dubbed him Old Ephraim and avoided him if they could. The taxonomists labeled him *Ursus horribilis* to describe not his appearance but his disposition.

His meanness is now a matter of dispute. Scientists argue that he is courageous but not ferocious and is dangerous only if wounded, attacked, or cornered. Beginning in 1959, Frank and James Craighead and the members of their research team spent thirteen years studying grizzly bears in Yellowstone National Park. They were always armed but never had to kill one of their subjects, although frequent practice must have made them highly adept at climbing trees. "The grizzly," said Ernest Thompson Seton, "according to all the best authorities, never attacks man, except when provoked. That is, he is a harmless, peaceful giant, perfectly satisfied to let you alone if you let him alone." Perhaps — but the animal's notion of provocation seems broader and more liberal than our own.

In any case, the grizzly's temper and aggressiveness are legendary. These traits make him more difficult to tame than even the tiger or the lion. Old Ephraim does not fear the whip or the chair. James Capen "Grizzly" Adams was one of the few people ever to have any success training them. He used a grizzly, which he named Benjamin Franklin, as a pack animal on hunting expeditions, and on one occasion Ben fought another, wild grizzly to protect Adams. In 1860, Adams took three of his bears to New York to appear in a P. T. Barnum show; they and he paraded down Broadway and up the Bowery; two of the grizzlies were chained, but the third, General Fremont, was unfettered and carried Adams on his back. When Adams retired, he opened a small museum in San Francisco and charged children a dime for a ride on the aging Ben.

It would be something to see one of these massive creatures nonchalantly strolling down a city street with a man on his back, or ponderously moving in a circle to entertain a child. Before we wax sentimental, however, we should recall that when Adams died in middle age, the cause was attributed to a blow to the head from one of his domesticated pets or to the accumulated injuries he had sustained in working with them.

No frontiersman got to see Old Ephraim from the same perspective that Barnum's customers did. Kit Carson shot an elk, and before he had time to reload his rifle, he heard something crashing through the bush. "Two grizzlies bounded toward me, flashing fiery passion, their pearly teeth glittering with eagerness to mangle my flesh." The redoubtable Indian fighter turned on his heels and, throwing away his useless gun, raced for the nearest tree. The grizzly has been clocked at speeds in excess of forty miles per hour, which is faster than a man can run, but Carson had a head start and pulled himself up on a limb as powerful paws swept through the air where his legs had hung just an instant before. He remained high in the tree for a long time, until the bears finally became discouraged. He said later that he had never been so badly scared in his life.

The determination of these creatures is fact as well as legend. Captain Ezekiel Williams had tethered a canoe on the Arkansas River some twenty feet from shore one night to protect himself from animals and Indians, when he heard swimming toward him what proved to be a grizzly. He seized an ax and stood. The bear put both forepaws on the "hind end" of the craft and started to climb in. Williams brought the ax down on one paw, chopping off some of the claws. The grizzly, who was after a deer carcass in the canoe, still held on with the other paw. This time the captain brought the ax squarely down on the beast's skull, and the bear released his hold. Williams kept the claws for many years, "as a trophy which he was fond of exhibiting."

James O. Pattie saved the claws of the "white bears" he killed. He knew the claws to be of "considerable value among the Indians, who wear them around the neck, as the distinguishing mark of a brave. Those Indians who wear this ornament view those who do not as their inferiors.'' Undoubtedly they did: to kill a grizzly with spear or bow and arrow was no mean feat and took substantial courage.

In 1810, David Thompson and his men were fleeing through the snows of Athabasca Pass, pursued by a band of Piegans. These Indians were intent on murder until three grizzlies wandered onto their quarries' tracks, and then they immediately broke off the chase. "They were fully persuaded that I had placed the bears there to prevent any further pursuit,'' Thompson wrote. He may have been right; it would be better not to tangle with a man who had power over those fierce animals, but in that rough country the grizzlies easily could have run down the Piegans' ponies, and that may have been the reason the warriors went the other way.

Old Ephraim has twenty claws, four to seven inches in length. Large and slightly curved, they are excellent for digging and turning over rocks and logs. They can also tear a man apart. "The claws are formidable weapons in combat," noted F. M. Young, "cutting like razors and strong as steel."

The grizzly's paw is huge, and his legs are immensely powerful. Indeed, with his distinctive ridge of shoulder muscle and short, thickset body, the bear is generally considered the strongest land mammal in North America and one of the strongest animals in the world. An explorer told of seeing a grizzly strike a caribou in the muzzle, break its jaw, and send the bone sailing more than twenty feet. Few men have survived a blow to the head from Old Ephraim.

In the 1850s, Major Horace Bell, a California newspaper correspondent, witnessed a number of staged sporting contests between species of bears and other powerful animals. The grizzly bears always seemed to win. In one such brave spectacle, a grizzly was pitted against five wild long-horned bulls, one after another. Although his movements were restricted by a short chain that tethered him to a post, he managed to kill the first four bulls. He had received several serious wounds from the horns of his victims, and the fifth gored him in the neck and then put a horn into his heart. Even so, the grizzly fought on until the horn struck home a second time.

Before the advent of the repeating rifle and the modern high-powered rifle, Old Ephraim was uncommonly hard to dispatch. More than one hapless hunter approached the carcass of a fatally shot animal, one certainly dead, and was mauled. "The hunter of the grizzly bear,'' Washington Irving informed his readers, "must be an experienced hand and know where to aim at a vital part; for of all quadrupeds he is the most difficult to kill. He will receive repeated wounds without flinching, and rarely is a shot mortal unless through the head or heart." The third vital spot is through the center of the shoulder spine, but hitting any of these places on an animal charging forward in fifteen-foot bounds would not be easy. "I try to hit in the right spot," a bear hunter named Messalino told Captain John Gunnison in 1831, "but if I miss it I have to run."

A man finding himself in close quarters with Old Ephraim and unable to escape could thrust his rifle barrel into the animal's mouth in hopes of putting a bullet into his brain. This was possible if the bear reared up on his hind legs, at which point he stood about nine feet tall and was not, therefore, approachable by the faint of heart. A wild grizzly does not lumber toward his victim on two legs as a trained circus bear does, but he will rise up if he is startled, senses danger, or, apparently, is in the midst of combat — the California bear that Major Bell watched stood to fight the charging bulls. So a man might ram his gun into that fearsome mouth and pull the trigger, but if the weapon misfired, as sometimes happened, he would then be in Old Ephraim's fatal embrace.

Grizzly bears have forty-two teeth, including incisors, canines, premolars, and molars. The canines, long and sharp, are for piercing and ripping. The bear's jaws are extremely powerful, and the molars have broad, flat crowns for crushing tree branches and bones.

So an embrace with those jaws, teeth, and claws is a frightful thing. Old Ephraim might hold you "with one arm, while clawing and striking with the other and biting at the same time." The worst damage might come from the hind legs; the bear can stand on one and rip with the claws of the other.

James O. Pattie dispatched a grizzly that was busily mauling a hunter. The fatal shot came too late: the man "was literally torn in pieces. The flesh on his hip was torn off, leaving the sinews bare, by the teeth of the bear. His side was so wounded in three places that his breath came through the openings; his head was dreadfully bruised, and his jaw broken. His breath came out from both sides of his windpipe, the animal in his fury having placed his teeth and claws into every part of his body. No one could suppose that there was the slightest possibility of his recovery" — and indeed there was none. The poor fellow lingered for some days, cared for by his friends, and then died.

In 1821, Lewis Dawson was one of a group who stumbled on a grizzly in what is now Colorado. All the men ran, with the bear in pursuit. He pulled down Dawson. A man known as Colonel Glanns tried to kill the animal, but his weapon misfired. With the party was a large female dog, and she attacked the grizzly with such fury that the bear left off mauling Dawson and chased her. Dawson jumped up and ran, but the bear gave chase and easily caught up with him. Colonel Glanns again raced to the grizzly to kill him, but once more his rifle misfired. Here came the valiant bitch . . . the bear was distracted . . . Dawson ran . . . and was dragged down. The colonel's weapon misfired a third time, which seemed to unnerve him because, fearing he would be next in the jaws, he headed for a tree. The dog, being unafraid, went after the bear, and Dawson was able to make a run for the same tree, with the grizzly close behind. Since Dawson was the second man scrambling up the trunk, he was the one to be caught by the leg and pulled down. Glanns sharpened his flint, primed his gun, and shot the bear, which collapsed. He soon rose up again, but by this time several men with more reliable firearms had arrived, and they finally killed him. Dawson was carried to camp, where his wounds were examined. According to Jacob Fowler, who gawked at the damage along with everyone else,

> It appears his head was in the bear's mouth at least twice and that when the monster gave the crush that was to mash the man's head (it being too large for the span of his mouth) the head slipped out, only the teeth cutting the skin to the bone wherever they touched it so that the skin of the head was cut from about the ears to the top in several directions. All of which wounds were sewed up as well as could be done by men in our situation, having no surgeon nor surgical instruments. The man still retained his understanding, but said, "I am killed that I heard my skull break." But we were willing to believe he was mistaken as he spoke cheerfully on the subject, till in the afternoon of the second day when he began to be restless and somewhat delirious.

Dawson was re-examined, and a hole was found in his temple, out of which his brains were leaking. His friends were now convinced that his skull was broken, and they watched over him another day until he died.

Grizzlies have a thick hide and layers of fat and muscle to absorb bullets. Prince Maximilian of Wied was traveling on the Missouri River in the early 1830s when he saw a huge "white bear" shot at by fifteen hunters without being noticeably affected. F. M. Young reports a grizzly which was shot twenty-three times before dying — and another an incredible fifty-four times.

Nevertheless, it was possible even in the days of the frontier to dispatch Old Ephraim with fewer shots than those listed above, and to do so quickly enough to save yourself or a comrade. Jedediah Smith was traveling near the Black Hills with a party of trappers when a grizzly raced out of the bushes and seized Smith's head in his "capacious mouth." The other men's fire killed the beast or at least drove him off. Several of Smith's ribs had been broken, one eyebrow had been ripped away, his scalp had been lacerated and his skull exposed in a line across the crown from his left eye to his right ear; in addition, "one of his ears was torn from his head out to the outer rim." He sat on a rock and calmly instructed James Clyman in the fine art of wilderness stitchery. Although Clyman had never performed such surgery before, he did a passable job on the worst of the damage, but "I told him I could do nothing for his ear. 'O, you must try to stitch [it] up some way or other,' he said. Then I put in my needle, stitching it through and through and over and over laying the lacerated parts together as nice as I could with my hands." Despite Clyman's earnest attention to detail, the ear never did look quite right after that, and Jedediah considerately grew his hair long to cover it so as not to scare wolves or ruin the appetites of Comanches.

Smith was attacked in 1823. That same year — in fact, just a few weeks earlier — Hugh Glass had encountered *his* grizzly, with less happy results.

That Hugh Glass never set down the particulars of his tribulations is regrettable. We know that he was literate because he once wrote, at the request of a dying lad, a letter of condolence to the boy's father, and thus he could have told his own story. If he would not take the time to do that, at least he might have related it to a journalist, but he did not. Without his testimony, then, it is necessary, as it was with Marguerite de la Roque, to piece together the tale from the accounts of contemporaries. There is no shortage of these; his ordeal intrigued a number of writers of his age, and they recorded detailed if sometimes conflicting versions.

The exact circumstances of his meeting with the bear are a matter of dispute. Some say he and a black man named Moses Harris had wandered away from Major Andrew Henry's party, "in search of wild fruit, which in that region in this season is said to be most delicious." Henry had specifically forbidden such excursions, but the "commands of the leader of an expedition to the Rocky Mountains are not observed with quite the punctiliousness of a military corps."

A variation has Henry sending two scouts ahead and Glass going with them despite the major's orders to the contrary: he was showing his independence, showing that he would do pretty much what he damned well pleased. He did not remain with the scouts, it goes without saying, but set out on his own course. Fellow mountain man George C. Yount characterized Hugh as "bold, daring, reckless and eccentric to a high degree." He added that Glass "was nevertheless a man of great talents and intellectual as well as bodily power. But his bravery was conspicuous beyond all his other qualities for the perilous life he led."

The sources agree that what Glass met up with was a female grizzly and her two cubs. Mountain men held that this was the most hazardous way to meet a grizzly; in their estimation, mother grizzlies, extremely protective of their young ones, perceived almost any movement by human beings as a threat and acted accordingly. This one would have given the distinctive *koff! koff!* warning and charged. Glass had time to level his rifle and get off a single shot, which wounded but did not kill the sow. Rufus Sage and George Frederick Ruxton, both writing in the 1840s, report that he next pulled out a pistol or brace of pistols, which he discharged, but this seems both theatrical and a waste of time. A grizzly was not going to be slowed down, much less stopped, by such puny weaponry. Glass turned and ran, and as the beast closed in on him, he pulled out his knife. The bear struck him twice, knocking him down and opening "ghastly wounds, the claws literally baring of flesh the bones of the shoulder and thigh." The fight did not last long. Glass drove the blade in where he could, rolled and struggled and screamed, and was subjected to fangs and claws.

Ruxton, writing in *Life in the Far West,* gives us an unusually specific description of the bear's attack. He says that Glass was running for a steep bluff a hundred yards from the thicket where he had shot the bear. He had nearly reached safety when he tripped over a rock and fell. He leaped to his feet, but the grizzly was beside him, standing on her hind legs, blood streaming from her nose and

Charles M. Russell depicts Glass being attacked by the grizzly. (Courtesy of Historical Times, Inc., publisher of *American History Illustrated*)

mouth. Glass produced his pistol and fired it; the bear then knocked it from his hand with a swat of her paw and, fixing her "claws deep into his flesh, rolled with him to the ground." Hugh struggled "manfully," plunging his knife over and over into the beast, "which, ferocious with pain, tore with tooth and claw the body of the wretched victim, actually baring the ribs of flesh and exposing the very bones. Weak from the loss of blood, and blinded with blood which streamed from his lacerated head, Glass dropped his knife and sank down insensible and apparently dead." The bear, stabbed twenty times and shot two or three, fell across Hugh's body and died.

The other members of the expedition had been alerted to Glass's distress. His cries were so terrible that, hearing them at a distance, they thought an Indian war party was about to attack them. When the howling savages failed to arrive and the shouts became discernible as calls for help, they went to investigate.

Did the grizzly really fall across Hugh's body? This sounds like something from a nineteenth-century melodrama: the hero lies before the footlights; the villain, whose wounds stream grease paint, staggers over the boards, making sweeping gestures and appealing to the heavens and the hissing audience before finally expiring across the form of him for whom we grieve.

As improbable as it may seem, we have it on good authority that when Henry's men arrived on the bloody scene, they found the sow slumped across the man. They rolled her off what they thought was his corpse and discovered that he was still breathing. This revelation did not fill them with delight.

There would have been some in that circle who felt that he had got what was coming to him. Earlier that very day, a man identified only as "Allen of Mohave notoriety" had spotted Hugh "dodging along the forest alone" and had told a companion that he hoped Glass ran into a grizzly — it would serve him right. Wish had proved prophecy, and who was there to object? Yet Glass had not received his true comeuppance — he remained alive and was therefore a burden. That was just like old Hugh: damned near dead, he was still causing trouble.

The only comfort was in the obvious fact that he could not last long. He had sustained "not less than fifteen wounds, any one of which under ordinary circumstances would have been considered mortal." Among others was a tear in his throat from which blood gurgled every time he breathed. Glass had been, as trapper Daniel T. Potts succinctly put it, "tore nearly all to peases." Yet despite the certainty that he was finished, they felt compelled to sew up his wounds. Even in the howling wilderness, proprieties must be observed.

The battle with the grizzly had occurred late in the day, and so with night coming on they made camp nearby, no doubt fully expecting that in the morning they would find the issue nicely resolved. But dawn arrived without a neat resolution. The man's chest still rose and fell.

According to Edmund Flagg, who interviewed one or more members of the expedition, "a litter was constructed from the boughs of trees, and during that day and the succeeding one he was borne onwards, as a corpse upon a bier." He was carried on the shoulders of men walking through "thickets of brushwood, dwarf-plum trees, and other shrubs indigenous to a sandy soil." Glass experienced "new agony at every step of their uneven forward trudging." This went on for several days, maybe as many as six, until they came to a large stream in the middle of a grove of trees. Henry ordered a halt, and "here a conversation was holden, and it was resolved that Glass should be left with two of his companions, Fitzgerald and Bridges [*sic*]."

Matters were a bit more complicated than that. Major Henry had
had Hugh carried along for quite a distance, but he was not getting
any better, and by slowing down the expedition he was putting
everyone in jeopardy. These men were deep in Indian country, and
they had recently fought the Arikaras (also known as Rees). Glass,
in fact, had received a leg wound in the engagement, but it had not
hampered his movement — or theirs. So it was necessary and right
that they should leave him. The major called for volunteers to remain behind and care for him, but none came forward, owing either
to Glass's unpopularity or to the proximity of savages. Henry
sweetened the pot, offering "an extravagant reward"; this may
have been eighty dollars, as Philip St. George Cooke would have
it, or three or four hundred dollars, as others say. Either way it was
a goodly sum. "Still," writes John Myers Myers, Glass's modern
biographer,

> there was no subway rush of takers. The two who agreed to stay with
> Hugh didn't have to fight for the chance — a thing to be plunked in
> their favor. If they came to regret their decision, they were gritty to
> make it; and the sigh of relief breathed by the men who didn't speak
> up, but heard them do so, can all but be heard today.

Fitzgerald was unquestionably one of the volunteers, and the
other, according to Flagg, was Jim Bridger, a boy in his late teens.
These two watched the other eight men depart. Perhaps they experienced a peculiar sinking feeling as the last of the pack horses
trotted out of sight. Myers imagines that in that moment danger
"was around them like a smog — smelled and felt but not seen; and
they had no ally but a man thought to be dying."

What Hugh Glass had to say about these events is not known.
Indeed, how aware he was of them is debatable. If he was conscious, he would have been distracted by pain, but it is likely that
he was in a coma. His slipping into unconsciousness may have given
Henry the opportunity to leave him. One school of thought holds
that he had been comatose ever since the mauling. Sage and Ruxton
are two who subscribe to this view. Others have him take that
bumpy ride in the litter conscious but unable to speak because of
the wound in his throat.

Days passed as Fitzgerald and Bridger waited. Flagg, with an
attitude colored by the knowledge of coming events, expends all his
sympathy on Glass and has none for these two uneasy volunteers:

But what a situation! A man languishing under fifteen frightful wounds thousands of miles from all surgical succour — surrounded by roving savages — almost destitute of the necessaries of existence, and in the care of two lawless men whose interest it was that their patient should, as soon as possible, cease to live.

Myers is only slightly less judgmental. He suggests that the two men became like buzzards, "without having that bird's genial feelings toward the dead." Glass was now their enemy. "Every time he breathed again, he gave Indians time to ride that much nearer; and from that awareness to the suspicion that Glass was conspiring for their downfall would be no great jump of illusion for a couple inching toward a nervous breakdown apiece."

Yet who among us would have stayed behind to risk the Sioux and Ree just to bury a fatally injured companion when he finally got around to giving up the ghost? And for forty dollars, or even two hundred dollars, the equivalent of a year's wages? These men did, and they kept their commitment for four . . . or five . . . or six days. How many of us could have held out so long? Glass got neither better nor worse — he just *lingered,* maddeningly, unnervingly. How long could he last? How long could their torment go on?

Fitzgerald, the adult, talked the teenaged Bridger into giving up the vigil. The youth might have had trouble admitting his fear and turning tail and running. An older man would know that you could not win every fight, that in poker sometimes you just threw in your hand and left the table.

It was what they did next — at Fitzgerald's insistence — that brought them lasting disapprobation. They took nearly all of Glass's possessions, including his food, knife, and firearms. On the frontier such items were too valuable to be buried with the dead or, in this case, left with the dying. If Fitzgerald and Bridger left them behind, the Indians might find them, God forbid. Furthermore, the two white men needed Glass's belongings to establish their veracity and, not incidentally, claim the reward: leaving them would constitute an admission that they had not lived up to their part of the bargain. If Glass was dead, where were his guns?

So they took them. To keep them from the hands of savages, for their own use later on, and, most of all, to shore up their lies, they took them.

George Yount told Orange Clark, an Episcopalian minister, that Hugh was conscious during these deliberations and that, though dumb, he used gestures to plead with the thieves to leave him his weapons. This is too much: that man with those dreadful wounds, his clothes caked with blood, breath rasping in his throat, silently imploring his brothers not to rob him of his only means of sustenance and protection — and being rudely denied. It is better to believe that he was comatose.

The subconscious directs the beating of the heart, controls the lungs. The subconscious is also capable of listening, comprehending, and remembering. So if he was in a coma, Glass still may have heard how his fate was decided. After his perfidious confederates had abandoned him, he may have lain in his suspended state for as many as four or five days. Did his subconscious during that time serve up any scrambled bits of memory? Did he review the stages of his life to discover how he had come to be destitute and forsaken in the howling wilderness?

He awoke beside the stream. He drank clear water and plucked buffalo berries from the bushes that grew along the stream's edge, mashing them between rocks and swallowing the mush. He slept, awoke, drank, ate, and then slept again. He grew stronger. Once he awakened to find a huge rattlesnake beside him. Happily the reptile had just swallowed some creature and was groggy with digestion. Glass brained it with a stone. His recently departed caretakers apparently having been too queasy to frisk his body, he was in possession of a razor. He probably used the blade to cut off the rattler's head and skin the body, and then he pounded its flesh between rocks. He ate this pulp mixed with crushed berries and water. He slept again.

At some point in his recovery he swore an oath of vengeance: not only would he survive, but he would take his revenge on those who had left him. The day came when he had grown strong enough to begin to carry out this promise. He could not walk, mind you — he could only crawl — but he set off. Fitzgerald and Bridger had followed Major Henry's trail, but the rough, rising terrain prevented Glass from taking the same course. He needed a reliable supply of fresh water, anyway, and so he would follow along beside the stream until it fed into the Missouri River. He would go, in the direction opposite that taken by his betrayers.

Washington Irving, who heard the story of Hugh Glass around a prairie campfire, has it that Hugh *floated* down the stream, eventually reaching the mouth of what Irving's informant incorrectly identified as the Mississippi, where he found a "forked tree," which he mounted like a bronco and rode on "the current of the mighty river" until he reached the fort at Council Bluffs.

On that first day, pushing and pulling himself along, struggling to go just a few dozen yards, Glass would have been grateful for such a means of conveyance. He had 350 miles to go to reach Fort Kiowa, and he was going to have to do it an inch at a time.

Day after day he crawled onward. He endured the rain, the wind, and the cold. He ate berries. He used sharp stones to dig up edible roots "which he had learned to discriminate while sojourning with the Paunees." Sometimes he came across the carcasses of buffaloes. The meat always had been devoured by predators and scavengers, but he split the bones with rocks to get at the marrow.

His luckiest moment came after a pack of wolves cut a bison calf out of a herd. Glass hid and watched as the young beast was dragged down: "He permitted the assailants to carry on the war until no signs of life remained in their victim." Then he moved in, flourishing the razor or a stick as best he could, probably emitting a few croaking sounds, trying to scare the wolves from their meal. No such sorry spectacle could drive them from a fresh kill, of course, but why did they not attack him? They are shier and less aggressive than tall tales and hunters' stories would have you believe; so they did not attack him, but neither did they abandon the carcass.

Glass needed that food.

According to Flagg, he used a razor and a flint to strike a few sparks to ignite some dry leaves and "set fire to the grass. This maneuver was successful — the wolves were put to flight, and nearly the whole of the calf fell into his hands." This is a wonderful bit of woodsmanship, one any Boy Scout would be proud to have accomplished, and it is possible, but Cooke offers a likelier strategy: Glass waited until their hunger was appeased, and they were willing to be impressed enough by his feeble show to quit the carcass.

Either way, Hugh finally got something substantial to eat.

Myers writes that the wolves

> had performed the service of partially skinning the animal, leaving Glass free to batten on flesh tender enough for his convalescent throat.
> The abiding need of one who had lost as much blood as Old Ephraim had let out of Hugh was food with bottom enough to put it back. Dripping with gore, the chunks he ripped from the young buf-

falo were just behind a blood transfusion in the immediacy with which they joined forces with his system. With his arteries flush for the first time since his terrible encounter, he was now on the way to rising from all fours.

Miraculously, he had improved while denying himself the rest supposedly indispensable to a graveside case. Except for a festering back wound, which he couldn't get at and clean out, the great rends in his body were mending, in spite of the fact that the energies needed for healing had so largely been diverted to the uses of creeping forward. This he had done at a progressively faster rate — so that he was reeling off marches of two miles a day even before the wolves gave him this chance to get off his hands and knees.

He stayed by the calf for several days, eating and continuing to regain his strength, and then he was off again, this time walking upright with the help of a staff, which he also used to club any small hapless, succulent creature that came his way. "The starveling who could crawl a scant two miles a day had been replaced by a walking man who could cover that much in an hour. And his pace quickened with every sun which saw his torn muscles better knitted by his renewed bloodstream."

His erect posture made him more of a target for Indians, who could see him at a greater distance. Somewhere near the Missouri he made a detour, apparently to avoid Sioux raiding parties. They were in the area to steal food from the Arikaras, and Hugh passed several hastily abandoned villages. At one of these he encountered a couple of dogs left behind by their masters, and he managed to kill and eat one of them.

Before long he met up with Sioux. Luckily for Glass, this particular group, because it included women and children, was peaceable. As a recent historian put it, "Domestic of mood, they took a kindly interest in one who showed so many signs of having lately tangled with the foe most respected by the savages of the Plains." Cooke finds them more generous than idly curious or impressed: "[Glass] was discovered by a small party of Sioux Indians. These acted toward him the part of the good Samaritan. The wound on his back was found in a horrid condition. It had become full of worms! The Indians carefully washed it and applied an astringent vegetable liquid."

They carried him either by horse or "bullboat" to Fort Kiowa. His arrival was sometime in early October. Rufus Sage tells us that one morning residents of the fort opened the gates to find Glass standing there, emaciated, half-naked, and covered with wounds and running sores. It was as if he were a ghost come back from the land of the dead. "But sensations of pity and commiseration quickly succeeded those of surprise, and the unhappy sufferer was conveyed within doors and received from the hands of friends that careful attention his situation so much required." They found his story of misfortune to be "thrillingly interesting," and they nursed him back to health.

No doubt his tales met with excitement and rapt attention, but after only a few days of care, he set off again. The men who had betrayed him were not at the fort, after all, and so having equipped himself with goods — and weapons — he boarded a mackinaw boat that would take him on the first leg of his journey to Fort Henry, at the mouth of the Yellowstone River. "His great object, it may be readily conjectured, was to meet the two wretches he was so much indebted to."

At about the same time, John Fitzgerald, Moses Harris, and another man deserted Major Henry's post and started making their way to Fort Atkinson, which was below Fort Kiowa. Glass and one of the men he had sworn to kill were on a collision course.

But it would not be that simple. Hugh and the five or six French traders on the boat worked their way north slowly, hampered by the cold and the current. On or about November 20, Glass was put ashore. He may have been delegated to go hunting or he may have chosen to leave the traders at that point. They were nearing the Mandan Indian village that was their destination, and staying with them any longer would have constituted a detour. Hugh was used to walking by now.

What happened shortly after he set off on foot has caused more than one writer to remark on his singular good luck. The mackinaw was rowed into an Arikara ambush. Those Frenchmen not killed in the first fusillade fired back, but "the Indians rushed upon their victims, and the war club and tomahawk finished a work that had been so fearfully begun."

Glass was unaware of these events, but after walking only a few miles he ran into a smaller band from the same tribe. Their chief was Elk's Tongue, and thus they had been among the Indians who had fought Henry's men the previous summer, in which engagement Hugh had been wounded. He did not have time to inquire as to their pedigree or marvel over the extraordinary coincidence of meeting up with them again. He ran for his life.

He was on foot and less spry than he had been before the bear chewed on him, and they were on horses. Yet the predictable end to the race did not occur, because one or two Mandans fortuitously appeared on the scene. Their tribe was presently in conflict with that of Elk's Tongue, and so they were only too happy to snatch the enemies' prize away from them. Glass was pulled up onto a horse and taken to the Mandan village. He "was well received, for the announcement of his presence was naturally accompanied by the story of his escapes, which naught but the greatest bravery could have accomplished; and nothing is better calculated effectually to engage the interest and admiration of Indians."

They escorted him to Fort Tilton. He did not tarry there long. In fact, his eagerness to find Fitzgerald and Bridger was such that he left the post the same day he arrived. The Rees had besieged Tilton, forcing Glass to slip away under cover of darkness. He crossed over to the east bank of the river to avoid having to run another footrace, and set off again for the Yellowstone.

Had he rested up a few days, he could have saved himself a lot of trouble, because Fitzgerald and his two companions actually stopped at the fort. They did not linger either, one of them perhaps fearing that Hugh might be forced to come back, but quickly shoved off again. Before long they, too, were ambushed by some of Elk's Tongue's followers. These mountain men were luckier than the French trappers had been: they seized their firearms, plunged into the river, and swam to the far shore. The Indians took everything in the canoe but left it unguarded, and that night the three white men stole it back and resumed their voyage.

While this was happening, Hugh was resolutely making his way north.

> He was without a solitary companion for this long and perilous journey — his sole conveyance was his feet and his sole defence against savages and wild beasts his rifle — besides the weather had become severely cold, and snow lay on the frozen soil for the most part of his route a foot in depth!

Not long ago he had crawled and walked about 350 miles armed with only a razor, but now he had, in addition to a rifle, a knife, a small ax, a kettle, a flannel shirt, leather leggings and moccasins, and even a cap. He must have felt immensely wealthy, or at least at the height of wilderness fashion.

It is sometimes assumed that Glass headed right for Major Henry's *new* fort on the Big Horn River, but John Myers sensibly points out that Hugh would have thought the major was still at the post he had built on the Yellowstone and toward which he had been headed when Glass had had that disagreement with the she-bear. Henry and his men had indeed proceeded there and were soon joined by Fitzgerald and Bridger, but the Blackfeet had proved to be too pesky and desirous of the white men's horses. The major moved to a new site a hundred miles away, on the Big Horn.

Since leaving Fort Kiowa, Glass had traveled about 300 miles by river and then walked another 450 miles to arrive at — a deserted post. "Henry [must have] left some trail marker, showing the general direction he had taken," Myers writes.

> That's all that Glass could have had to go on, though, for the Major didn't know that he was going to set his course for the "little horn" when he started up the Yellowstone. All wayside traces being hidden by snow, Hugh might have doubted his ability to track down a party somewhere in a never-before-visited wilderness; but he strode ahead.

The word "dauntless" does not even begin to describe Hugh Glass. He had left Fort Kiowa on about October 10, and he had been on foot since November 20. He located the new Fort Henry on December 31. A New Year's Eve party was in progress, and some of the revelers, having had a drop or two to drink and having been told that Glass was dead, took him for a ghost. Cooke has it that before reaching the post itself, there to startle the assembled drunks, he ran into a party of presumably sober hunters who, nevertheless, had to touch him to believe he was real. These doubting Thomases then so barraged him with questions that it was a while before he managed to wedge in one or two of his own and learn that Fitzgerald was no longer with the company.

James Hall remarks with wonderful understatement that Glass was disappointed at the news. You can understand that. You row a boat upstream for 300 miles, get chased by savages, walk another 550 miles through snow with the intention of killing a man, only to discover that he is gone . . . and, yes, you too might emit some mild expression of regret.

There was one small consolation: the worst malefactor might have escaped for the moment, but the lesser evil, the unfaithful youth, had not.

The Reverend Orange Clark, who would have known about such

things, tells us that Bridger had been plagued by a guilty conscience ever since abandoning Glass. Now, with the man before him as if come back from the dead, the youth was transfixed with terror. His face and form so perfectly expressed his horror that it gave even Hugh pause. "Glass was unprepared for such a spectacle," and he was struck dumb by it for several moments. He leaned upon his rifle and thought things over. "The more guilty object of his revenge had escaped; the pitiful being before him was, perhaps, but the unwilling and over-persuaded accomplice of his older companion." Eventually Glass roused himself and decided "upon the revenge which sinks the deepest upon minds not wholly depraved, and of which the magnanimous are alone capable; he determined to spare his life."

Still he could not let the boy off that easily. He afflicted him with a sermon that Cooke transcribes this way:

> Young man, it is Glass that is before you; the same, that not content with leaving, you thought, to a cruel death upon the prairie, you robbed, helpless as he was, of his rifle, his knife, of all with which he could hope to defend or save himself from famishing in the desert. In case I had died, you left me to despair worse than death, with no being to close my eyes. I swore an oath that I would be revenged on you and the wretch who was with you; and I ever thought to have kept it. For this meeting I have braved the dangers of a long journey; this has supported me in my weary path through the prairie; for this have I crossed raging rivers. But I cannot take your life; I see you repent; you have nothing to fear from me; go, you are free; — for your youth I forgive you.

This speech is admirably theatrical and seems modest enough considering all the speaker had endured, but it is a bit long and stiff. The Reverend Mr. Clarke offers a briefer and more theological verson of Glass's remarks: "Go, my boy. I leave you to the punishment of your own conscience and your God. If they can forgive you, then be happy — I have nothing to say to you — but don't forget hereafter that truth and fidelity are too valuable to be trifled with."

Indeed they are, and if this young man was *the* Jim Bridger, he remembered the lesson well for the rest of his life. Whether or not he was is debatable. Aficionados of history are like sports fans whose favorite players can do no wrong, whose transgressions are denied outright, overlooked, or at least minimized. Even as a lad, the great Jim Bridger could never have left a man in the wilderness, his admirers insist. No, the Bridger in this story is some other, lesser fellow who unfortunately happened to have the same name. Perhaps — but he could have been *the* Jim Bridger, and there are those who think he was.

Whoever he may have been, Glass's admonition that he "go" was rhetorical: in this weather even bears perferred to sleep warm in their caves, and Hugh, having been strolling around in it for several months, knew why.

Yet he was not content to unroll his blanket beside the fireplace and rest until spring. Fitzgerald was still alive.

Near the end of February, Henry found he needed to send dispatches to his employer, General William Ashley. The major tried to find volunteers, once again offering a "great reward." At first he encountered a lack of "willingness to undertake a passage through a region infested by wandering hostile Indians at such an inclement season; but, no sooner was the enterprise proposed to Glass, than he, at once, acceded to the terms." It goes without saying that the letters were to be carried to Fort Atkinson, where Fitzgerald was now in residence.

Four other men were induced by the reward to accompany him, and the little expedition set off on February 29, 1824. They followed the course of the Powder River and then crossed the Platte. When the thaw set in, they stopped to construct bullboats.

They proceeded without incident (or at least none so horrendous as to be worth recalling) until they came to the site on which Fort Laramie would later be built. There, at the juncture of the North Platte and Laramie Creek, they found an Indian encampment. Incredibly, these hostiles were Arikaras. Worse still, the whites mistook them for Pawnees and accepted their invitation to smoke the pipe in the chief's lodge. One of the mountain men stayed behind to guard the boats and firearms, which, not wanting to offend the hospitality of their hosts, they did not take with them.

No sooner had they sat down with the Indians than Glass realized the truth. "These are Pickarees," he cried, and he and his companions burst out of the lodge and sprinted for the river.

The Rees cut them off from their boats. The guard, whose name was Dutton, pushed off in one of the craft, firing his rifle as he did. His four comrades dived into the river and swam to the other side, where the Indians caught up with and murdered two of them. Glass, who managed to elude his pursuers and conceal himself among some boulders, witnessed the butchery.

He stayed hidden as long as his enemies hunted for him. "Versed in all the arts of border warfare, our adventurer was able to practice them in the present crisis, with such success as to baffle his bloodthirsty enemies; and he remained in his lurking place until the search was abandoned in despair.''

Marsh, the fifth white man, eventually managed to meet up with Dutton, and they continued on to Fort Atkinson, where they sorrowfully reported the deaths of Hugh and the others.

For the second time in a year, Glass's demise was prematurely announced, and for the second time in a year he found himself alone and without a gun in Indian country. Yet these circumstances were no cause for despair. "Although I had lost my rifle and all my plunder," James Hall reports him as remembering, "I felt quite rich when I found my knife, flint and steel in my shot pouch. These little fixin's make a man feel right peart when he is three or four hundred miles from anybody or any place." He detoured away from the Arikaras and then took another four-hundred-mile jaunt, which by now must have seemed to him nothing more than mild exercise. Eventually, still carrying the letters meant for Ashley, he arrived at Fort Atkinson, and there at last he found John S. Fitzgerald.

A satisfying conclusion to this tale would include the death of that villain, either speedily or slowly, depending upon the strength of your stomach and the depth of your indignation. History, alas, rarely offers real justice or neat solutions.

Fitzgerald was still on hand at the post because he was *billeted* there, having enlisted, as Dale Morgan has established, in the Sixth Regiment on April 19, 1824. Never has the United States Army served a recruit better. The bureaucrats in Washington's War Department would have frowned on a commander who allowed one of his soldiers to be murdered by a civilian inside the fort's walls. The officer in charge was unwilling to see his career adversely affected by a mountain man's vengeance, however just. He brought Fitzgerald before Glass and required him to return his rifle and listen to what must have been an extraordinary tongue-lashing, but that was the end of it. Well, not quite: the men of the Sixth Regiment, having heard the story of Hugh's trials, passed the hat for him and filled it with three hundred dollars. That, added to the reward Henry had paid him to act as messenger, constituted a sizable sum in those days. So when Glass walked away from the post, he was a richer if not wiser man.

How much he learned from his experiences is *not* controversial.

Pirate John Lafitte *(center, with cutlass)* orders the decks of a prize cleared with a cannon. It was an atrocity such as this one that caused Hugh Glass to escape the band and set off into the American wilderness. (Copy print courtesy of Library of Congress)

He was as stubborn in refusing to let his ordeal change the course of his life as most other survivors. "One would suppose," wrote Edmund Flagg in 1839, echoing sentiments we have heard before, "that the hardships undergone by Glass would have effectually taken from him all desire, ever again to try his fortunes in the wilderness. But it was not so. . . . A trading party was formed to go to Santa Fe, and with it went Glass."

What a life he had led! He had been a sailor for so many years that Myers thinks he had earned a captaincy before his vessel was captured by a lieutenant of the famous buccaneer, slave trader, and hero of the Battle of New Orleans, Jean Lafitte. Hugh, being strong and having useful skills, was luckier than many other prisoners: he was given a choice between joining the band and being killed. He sailed under the black flag until some particularly dastardly deed committed by the pirates so appalled him that he refused to serve with them any longer. He and a fellow rebel were slated to be carried back to Campeachy to hear Lafitte's judgment, but knowing what it would be, they jumped ship off the coast of Texas while their captors were distracted with carousing. They swam two miles to shore, carrying a few stolen goods for use as barter with Indians, but they lacked firearms.

An easy hike in several directions would have taken them to settlements; unfortunately, they were ignorant of geography and preoccupied with avoiding the cannibalistic Karankawas, whose territory this inhospitable land was. So they struck out on a northwesterly course and walked all the way to what is now Kansas before falling into the hands of unfriendly Indians. These were Wolf Pawnees, who had the uncongenial custom of sacrificing their captives to the Morning Star. Glass's companion was stuck full of resinous pine slivers that were set ablaze. Hugh was slated to meet the same fate, but he won over the chief with a last-minute gift of vermilion and was adopted into the tribe. He remained with the Indians for a long time, getting a graduate school education in wilderness living to match the undergraduate one he had received walking to Kansas. When his tribe visited St. Louis to receive presents from William Clark, the superintendent of Indian affairs, the white Pawnee took the opportunity to slip away.

Glass saw Ashley's newspaper advertisement in the *Missouri Republican* calling for one hundred men. He joined up and so had his first experiences with the Ree and got to shake hands with Old Ephraim.

With the money he received at Fort Atkinson after his confrontation with Fitzgerald, he bought into a trading partnership that took him to New Mexico. He had been out there a year when a misunderstanding between his party and a small band of Utes resulted in his being struck with an arrow that lodged near his spine. None of his companions had the skill or nerve to perform the delicate surgery required to extract it, and so Glass traveled seven hundred miles with the arrowhead in his back until he located a trapper with gumption and a steady hand. The fellow cut out the arrowhead with a razor. The wound had become seriously infected — Hugh's flesh was "swollen and inflamed to an astonishing degree" — but the old man was hard to kill.

He recovered, went back to trapping, and hired himself out as a hunter, for which he became so celebrated that for a time the heights on which he tracked bighorn sheep were known as Glass' Bluffs.

In the winter of 1832–33, he was camped along the Yellowstone collecting beaver pelts. One day he and some other trappers were crossing the ice near the mouth of the Big Horn when they were ambushed — by Arikaras. This time Hugh's luck failed him, and his marksmanship and toughness were not enough. He was murdered along with two other men.

"He had his failings," one mountain man who knew him admitted, "but his fellow trappers bear testimony to his honor, integrity and fidelity. He could be relied on."

It is an epitaph many of us would be proud to have for our own.

By the way, one tradition has it that on the day he died, Hugh Glass was out hunting bear.

CHAPTER 18

A Certain Illusion, a Trick of Light

The Stefánsson Polar Expedition of 1913

On January 17, 1912, Robert Falcon Scott reached the South Pole, which would have been an even more extraordinary achievement had not the Norwegian explorer Roald Amundsen got there first, just a month ahead of him. Having stayed in the tent the Norwegians left behind, Scott and his four associates started back to their base camp, but they never made it. They died in a blizzard just eleven miles short of safety. They had staggered forward as long as they could, dragging a heavy sledge with them, and when Scott realized that they were doomed, he wrote letters to friends and colleagues praising his comrades for their nobility and self-sacrifice. He spoke of himself as a man already dead, but in these letters and the journal he kept there is no hint of self-pity. Near death his thoughts were on his family and the families of the men with him. The final words he was able to write were these: "For God's sake look after our people."

During the Last March, as it is known, Scott had large quantities of opium pills distributed so that each man might commit suicide if he chose to do so. Though they all were suffering terribly from frostbite and exhaustion, no one took an overdose of the drug. One man, Titus Oates, was in worse shape than the others, and realizing that he was slowing them down, he begged them to leave him in his sleeping bag and go on. They would not hear of it. At their insistent encouragement the poor fellow stumbled on. Then, after they had camped for the night, he announced he was leaving the tent. Even though his dying would offer the only chance they had of reaching the depot, his compatriots tried to dissuade him. "I am just going outside," he finally told them, "and may be some time." He disappeared into the storm.

"We knew it was the act of a brave man and an English gentleman," Scott noted in his journal. "We all hope to meet the end with a similar spirit, and assuredly the end is not far." He wanted it known that "Oates' last thoughts were of his Mother, but immediately before he took pride in thinking that his regiment would be pleased with the bold way in which he met his death. We can testify to his bravery. He has borne intense suffering for weeks without complaint, and to the very last was able and willing to discuss outside subjects. He did not — would not — give up hope til the very end. He was a brave soul."

A year and a half after the members of Scott's party died, the *Karluk* was frozen into Arctic ice. What happened to the people aboard her did not have the element of classic tragedy found in the fate of Scott's party, but neither did it have the nobility. In moments of danger some of the *Karluk*'s men would act selflessly, to be sure; others, though, thought not of their parents or their comrades but of themselves.

Students of exploration examining the story of the *Karluk* have pointed out that since it is customary to assign the leader of an expedition the credit for whatever is achieved, so is it appropriate to assign him the responsibility for its failures and losses. From such a proposition the famed polar explorer Vilhjálmur Stefánsson would have demurred. Indeed, he used his considerable communications skills to deny that he was in any way to blame for the fate of those who sailed with him on that ill-starred vessel.

In his youth Stefánsson was a rancher and a cowboy on the "wild land" prairies of North Dakota. Expelled from his state university "because the faculty felt that the student body was on the verge of a mutiny, and . . . they thought I was the spark most likely to start a blaze," he ran for state superintendent of education on the Democratic ticket and earned a bachelor's degree from the University of Iowa. He studied comparative religion at Harvard Divinity School, paying his way by working as a reporter for the *Boston Transcript*. His intention was to become a "field investigator of anthropology in tropical Africa," but he was offered the chance to join an Arctic expedition instead, and he took it.

The ship on which he was sailing to meet the other members of the expedition was wrecked, and he found himself stranded on polar shores. Rather than appeal to local officials for help, he chose to live among Eskimos as a "combination guest, student, and pauper." For months he devoted himself to learning their customs and traditions until he could live, hunt, eat, and speak like one of them. Thus in later years he could be "just as independent of . . . the bases of white men's supplies as are the Eskimos themselves."

In 1908 he embarked on a four-year expedition during which he successfully lived off the land. He discovered a previously unknown tribe of "Blond Eskimos" (Copper Eskimos), explored an immense amount of uncharted land, and amassed an enormous quantity of valuable information about Arctic geography, flora, and fauna.

In 1913 he set off on another expedition, this one lasting five years. In the process he explored and mapped "one hundred thousand square miles of unknown polar territory . . . adding three large and several small islands to the maps of the region." He made no more northern forays after this, devoting himself instead to promoting his belief that the Arctic was not a barren, frozen wasteland but a "friendly" place that should be exploited commercially. He edited journals, wrote many articles and books (including four for children), lectured extensively, taught college courses, acted as an adviser to Pan American Airways and the U.S. government, and collected, catalogued, and indexed perhaps the finest and most extensive library of materials on the polar regions that has ever been assembled.

Although he wrote a number of volumes about his experiences in the north, he steadfastly refused to glamorize the perils he survived. "An adventure is a sign of incompetence," he once said. "Everything you add to an explorer's heroism you have to subtract from his intelligence." Yet he was not modest about what he considered to be his accomplishments, nor was he reticent about accepting accolades for them. He was decorated with Iceland's Knighthood of the Order of the Falcon. He was presented with honorary degrees from Dartmouth, Harvard, and a score of other universities. He was awarded "coveted, prestigious medals" by nearly a dozen geographic societies and explorers' clubs located around the globe.

If a single honor stands out from the rest, it would be the Hubbard Gold Medal given to him by the National Geographic Society in 1920. Present at that ceremony in Washington, D.C., were three of the greatest polar explorers of that or any age. Besides Stefánsson, there were Major General Adolphus W. Greely, who in 1882 had reached a higher latitude than any previous explorer, and Admiral Robert Edwin Peary, credited with being the first man to reach the North Pole. Greely, who presented Stefánsson with the medal for his achievements during the expedition of 1913–18, praised the "idealistic spirit and . . . geographical importance of the discoveries made by Vilhjálmur Stefánsson." Referring to his own advanced age and that of the other two surviving members of the Greely International Polar Expedition, he said, "Appreciative of Stefánsson's endurance of hardships, recognizing his ability in devising new methods, his courage in testing such methods, and his standing as a typical Arctic explorer, the members of the Greely Expedition, who are about to die, salute him."

Peary was himself a dying man — he had only a few months to live — but, defying his doctor's orders, he attended the ceremony in what would prove to be his last public appearance. In his speech he praised Stefánsson's "invaluable" contributions to the knowledge of the Arctic and said he was "perhaps the last of the old school, the old regime of Arctic and Antarctic explorers, the worker with the dog and the sledge, among whom he easily holds a place in the first rank." The audience greeted these sentiments with applause that was both thunderous and heartfelt.

Had a dramatist written the scene, it would have been just at the moment the medal was presented and the crowd was on its feet that the eleven ghosts would have entered the room, the shades of the *Karluk*'s dead, shuffling in single file, bodies bent forward as if against the wind, white spots on their translucent limbs, indicating where in life the frost had seized them, and one, the last in line, displaying a wound where once an eye had been. They had been part of the expedition of 1913, too, and they had been abandoned by Stefánsson, and so they had died. They would have wanted to be present, to hear their names read out from the podium, their deeds and the manner of their dying enumerated, and their eulogies sorrowfully delivered. Then the poor ghosts, comforted by the knowledge that their memories were as honored as their leader's triumphs, would have returned to the netherworld.

In the real world, apparitions are not welcome at festivities where their appearance might disturb the laureled guest. To recall the dead on such a momentous occasion would cast a pall over the proceedings and raise questions about the honoree. Doubts are never welcome where self-satisfied men toast one of their own.

In Greenock, Scotland, that year, there was a thirty-two-year-old schoolmaster named William Laird McKinlay who could not forget the tribulations of those who sailed on the *Karluk*. Service on the Western Front in the Great War had not dislodged the memory that gradually took on the character of an obsession. For more than five decades he would compile, in the words of Magnus Magnusson,

> a dossier on Stefánsson's Arctic ventures. He read every scrap of evidence he could lay his hands on, corresponded with the survivors and the relatives of the dead men. He acquired copies of the diaries of the victims to add to his own carefully kept log, along with all the official reports and correspondence from the Canadian National Archives. For more than half a century he has studied and analyzed, checked and cross-checked every word published by Stefánsson, [Robert] Bartlett and the great explorers of the day.

In 1976, at the age of eighty-eight, McKinlay wrote his own account of what happened to the *Karluk* and the men who served on her. "The record must be put straight," he said. "I owe that to the memory of my dead comrades, and to Captain Robert Bartlett, who saved my life."

The *Karluk* never should have been sailed into Arctic waters. Steel icebreakers could have broken through the floes or withstood being frozen into the winter ice, but the *Karluk* was not built for such conditions. She was a nineteenth-century wooden barkentine constructed for fishing (her name is Aleutian for "fish"), and converted into a whaler in 1889. When the price of oil fell she was left idle. Her one virtue for Stefánsson was that she was cheap: he bought her for $10,000 and had another $6,000 worth of repairs hurriedly made on her.

Budget should not have been a significant factor in preparing for a polar expedition: cutting corners could cost lives. For Stefánsson, however, it was crucial. He had wanted to go north to continue his studies of the Eskimo and ensure his place in history by exploring the landmass Peary thought he sighted as he struggled toward the Pole. (Unfortunately, Peary was in error; the landmass did not exist.) Needing $75,000 to fund his expedition, Stefánsson secured a total of $45,000 from the American Museum and the National Geographic Society. He approached the Canadian government for the remainder of the money. Ottawa's politicians saw an opportunity to indulge in chauvinism and assert their country's bid for sovereignty over northern territory while at the same time verifying the existence of valuable mineral deposits. They gave lofty speeches about patriotism and insisted that the other two backers withdraw so that Canada would not have to share any of the glory. The one thing they did not do was properly fund the enterprise. Thus Stefánsson ended up spending $16,000 on the *Karluk* when he should have spent a substantially larger sum on a proper vessel.

Captain Bartlett understood the danger. He privately predicted that the ship could not withstand being frozen in the ice, and he went so far as to send Stefánsson a scathing appraisal of her; he agreed to take her out of port only on the condition that she not winter above the Arctic Circle.

Under the circumstances, Stefánsson should have delayed the expedition for a year and sent Bartlett in search of another vessel. He did not. He was frantic to get things under way. He may have feared that during the delay someone else would find Peary's island first and steal his glory. He was not a good organizer and did not have the experience to plan an undertaking of this magnitude. His arrogance would not allow him to admit this, of course. Anyway, he was an anthropologist, not a sailor. What did he know of the hazards of the Arctic Ocean?

Bartlett knew them well enough: he had been on two previous polar expeditions with Peary in the *Roosevelt,* a ship especially and exactingly designed to withstand ice pressure. Despite all the careful foresight, she had sustained crippling damage on the first outing and without his skillful seamanship would surely have sunk. Thus, why he was willing to set sail on the *Karluk* remains a mystery. He had been hired at the last moment, after the first skipper — who had bought the vessel and chosen the crew — had bowed out. Bob Bartlett was a true adventurer who had survived two shipwrecks and had made a vast number of northern voyages. As soon as he returned home from one arduous episode, he was prepared to leave on some new journey. A telegraphed invitation was all that was necessary to start him packing his gear. So perhaps he could not resist an offer from the renowned explorer, and no doubt he trusted his own abilities and good luck.

The disharmony began even before the expedition set off. It was obvious to the recruited scientists that preparations had been made hurriedly and with the kind of confusion that haste brings. The plan, such as it was, was unsatisfactory, and they were particularly worried about the provisions made for food, clothing, and the establishment of bases of operations. Stefánsson, who did not arrive at the point of departure until the last moment, had been making statements to the press which some of those who had been to the Antarctic with Sir Ernest Henry Shackleton found disturbing: he had indicated in exclusive interviews that the *Karluk* would proceed as far north as possible, where he expected that she would be crushed.

The malcontents expressed their concerns, but he turned them aside as impertinent and disloyal and indicated that they had no business questioning him. His attitude was such that at least some of his subordinates took to calling him "his lordship" behind his back, and a few men anxiously wrote letters that might be used as evidence if disaster befell them.

On July 26, 1913, the *Karluk* sailed from Port Clarence, Alaska. On the first of August she was struck by a blizzard (a month before such storms usually began at that latitude), and the next day she encountered sea ice. Bartlett spent four days trying to find a way through the pack and then recommended they turn back while they could, but Stefánsson would not hear of it.

Before long the vessel was frozen fast. McKinlay could not help being

> fascinated by the scene. The ice was much broken up and rough, with scarcely a level patch of any extent. The multitude of hummocks of varying size and height had weathered throughout the summer so that their surfaces were clear of snow and all their edges had been smoothed and rounded. Their shapes were infinite in variety and they gleamed and glistened in every conceivable shade of blue. It was like being in some gigantic sculptor's-yard, stacked as far as the eye could see with glistening marble blocks cut in a million fantastic shapes. As people do when confronted with great sculpture, I had the irresistible urge to touch as well as look. We left the ship and cavorted about on the ice for hours.

Not everyone was so entranced. Most of the sailors were unnerved or angry. They had signed on for what was essentially a ferrying operation and certainly not to winter in the Arctic; now they indulged in "wild talk" and "spoke quite openly of deserting at the first opportunity." (The selection of personnel seems to have been as haphazard as the other preparations and was clearly not made with the idea that they would have to spend a grueling year in the North: included in the company were at least two alcoholics, several thieves, and a drug addict who brought along his paraphernalia.)

As the days went by, the men relieved their boredom by going hunting, at which, of course, the Eskimo guides were particularly adept. They had already set aside a considerable supply of seal meat when, on September 19, Stefánsson announced that the next morning he was setting off on a ten-day caribou hunt. "This came as a surprise to some of us because not long before he had told us that in northern Alaska the caribou (North American reindeer) was practically extinct."

Bartlett apparently took his superior at his word — that he really was going hunting and not deserting the *Karluk* — but in retrospect others have not. Harold Horwood, Captain Bartlett's biographer, points out that "it was a curious hunting party" in that Stefánsson was taking along his personal assistant, his photographer, an anthropologist, and two Inuits. He also requisitioned a substantial amount of supplies and twelve or fourteen of the best dogs. "It looked more like an exploration expedition than a hunting trip, and that was what it became."

Stefánsson was a vigorous man who hated inactivity, and it would be said by at least one survivor that once the ship was icebound he lost his appetite, wandered about her aimlessly, and expressed the fear that her being held fast might mean the end of the enterprise. Richard J. Diubaldo, Stefánsson's biographer, notes that the Royal Northwest Mounted Police suggested in a report that his decision to go hunting at that moment was suspicious: "Stefánsson appears to have left the *Karluk* just in time." It is also true that Stefánsson's reputation would rise or fall with the success of the venture and that he had a sizable financial stake in it: he had already sold rights to the story of the expedition to magazines and newspapers around the world. So important were these rights to him that he had taken the precaution of getting the Canadian government to award them to him in writing and to require that "every man should agree neither to publish any written article nor to give lectures within two years from the return of the expedition, except on special permission given by [its] leader." (Since scientists, as Diubaldo observes, "depended on publication to establish or enhance their own professional status" and therefore might object to being stifled for so long,

Stefánsson did not bother to inform them of the prohibition until they were aboard the *Karluk* and at sea.)

How long would readers of magazines and newspapers want to read about the life on board an ice-locked ship? "I had made up my mind," Stefánsson wrote in *The Friendly Arctic,* "that the *Karluk* was not to move under her own power again, and that we were in for a voyage such as that of the *Jeannette* or the *Fram,* drifting for years, if we had the luck to remain unbroken, eventually coming out towards the Atlantic, either we or our wreckage."

On the afternoon of September 20, he posed for newsreels taken by his photographer and then departed. Two days later a storm arose, and the next morning the ice split between the vessel and the coast. "We were being carried away from the land in the grip of the gale-swept ice-pack, moving west at the rate of thirty miles a day, leaving an ever widening expanse of Arctic sea between us and our leader."

He "never saw the ship again or showed the least interest in her," Horwood contends. "In fact," counters Diubaldo, "Stefánsson indulged in some grievous soul-searching over the *Karluk*'s disappearance and there is strong evidence to suggest that he wished he had never left her." Biographers generally develop a strong identification with their subjects — it is a natural hazard of the profession — so it is hardly surprising to find such a marked disagreement between two honest scholars.

In 1927, the celebrated explorer himself described how, while the Canadian government was affirming his decision to proceed,

> the newspapers were saying that the entire complement of the *Karluk* had perished, that my plans were unsound, and that the expedition had failed. Editors especially, who presumably had been through high school, were asserting that all the knowledge ever gained in the Arctic was not worth the sacrifice of the life of one young Canadian.
>
> I am one of those who think the fighting of the Great War worthwhile not so much to attain what was attained as to prevent what has been prevented. But I never could see how any one can extol the sacrifice of a million lives for political progress who condemns the sacrifice of a dozen lives for scientific progress. For the advance of science is but the advance of truth, and "the truth shall make you free."

In Scotland, William McKinlay, who had drifted on the *Karluk,* been marooned on Wrangel Island, *and* had fought in the First

World War, read those words in *The Friendly Arctic* and was wounded by them. He might have wanted to add the caveat that it was one thing to die for a patriotic crusade or for the furthering of truth; it was another to lose your life because of the disorganization, arrogance, and ambition of one man: "We felt not so much like soldiers sacrificing ourselves to a great cause, as lambs left to the slaughter."

Bartlett quickly made preparations for both wintering the *Karluk* in the ice and abandoning her in an emergency. Battered by storms, embedded in an ice floe that was nearly two square miles in size, she continued to drift on a serpentine west-northwesterly course. Once away from the Alaskan coast, the men witnessed the spectacular collisions of ice fields.

> When the adjoining floes raced together, the weaker floe would be pounded into pieces sometimes as large as a house, which would pile one on top of the other into huge ridges, then collapse and roll about as if they were light as feathers; or one large floe would crack, the crack would open a few yards, the two pieces would come together again, one would be pushed under the other, and the upper one would be heaved higher and higher until, as it neared the vertical position, large chunks would break off and roll, rumbling and tumbling amid the crashing devastation.
>
> The noise was deafening: thunderous rumbles far away, then not so distant, then nearer still; coming from all directions; rending, crashing, tearing noises; grating, screeching; toning down to drumming, booming, murmuring, gurgling, twanging — all the sounds of a gigantic orchestra. If only I had been a musician. What a theme for a great symphony! I might have out-Wagnered Wagner.

Even when the floe that held the *Karluk* collided with ice driven by the Japanese current, in what seemed to mean the certain destruction of the wooden ship, McKinlay felt no fear — only "awe and wonder at the gigantic forces that were at work." The vessel was not crushed, although the pressure ridges formed by the impact came quite close to her.

In accordance with Captain Bartlett's orders, a fuel dump was established on the ice and several snow shelters were built. The Eskimo woman Kiruk made waterproof boots from sealskin, but there was not enough time for her to make cold-weather wardrobes for twenty-five people, so Bartlett set everyone to sewing fur clothing. He insulated the ship by having snow piled high around her hull and ice blocks put on her decks.

One ongoing problem involved the dogs. Stefánsson had taken so many of the best ones that the men would have "serious transportation difficulties" if forced to march to safety. Therefore all of the remaining canines were given careful, even lavish care. They had to be tethered on deck, however, and the close quarters resulted in frequent fights. On calm days they could be transferred to the floe, where there was enough room to keep them apart, but whenever the ice began to crack or break up, the dogs were hurriedly brought back on deck, "where they kept up a continuous howling day and night." Once the ice shelters were constructed, the dogs were moved into two of them; one housed the healthy animals, and the other served as a hospital for the wounded. Even then the trouble did not end among these tough creatures. Therefore

> we got the Eskimos to dig separate kennels out of a huge snowdrift close to the starboard side of the ship, and in these we isolated the hoodlums, the militants of canine society. We never did manage to eliminate dog fights. As soon as a yelp, or a series of yelps, announced the start of a scrap, every dog on the loose would bear down on the scene. It was a free-for-all until one unfortunate would go down, and then every other dog concentrated on him. The outcome was at least a serious surgical case, at worst another dead dog. In one fight two brother bobtails fought shoulder to shoulder against the rest of the pack until both were fatally injured. After the first died his brother lay on deck, howling day and night until he too succumbed to his injuries.
>
> The howling and barking of the dogs was the only break in the black, icy silence that surrounded us. As the days passed without hope of release, we turned more and more in on ourselves, ever more dependent on the warmth and comfort inside the ship, and increasingly aware of the imperfections and deficiencies of the *Karluk*.

To keep their minds off the predicament as much as possible, Bartlett organized a chess tournament, the winners receiving a box of cigars Stefánsson had brought along to give to the Mounties. To celebrate Christmas, he organized a sports competition that included sprints, an obstacle course, long jumps, and shot-puts. (The men had already built a ski slope on which they could make downhill runs.)

At the same time the captain wisely decided to reduce the rations somewhat, although "being a Newfounder" he did not cut back on

Captain Robert Bartlett, skipper of the *Karluk* (Photograph by Lomen Brothers, Nome, Alaska)

their tea drinking. Some sacrifices are just too painful to ask anyone to make.

Bartlett was probably the only member of the expedition who understood the extent of the perils that lay ahead. Yet he maintained an equanimity that calmed most of his subordinates. He could be a hard-bitten leader when he had to be, but wherever possible he used praise and encouragement as motivators. Ironically, his casual, friendly air caused those scientists left behind by Stefánsson to distrust him. They were educated men from respectable families, and, of course, they had been to the Antarctic with Shackleton; their notion of a leader was someone who was aloof and, well, who *looked* the part. Captain Bartlett eschewed a uniform in favor of baggy sweaters and old pants. When the crisis came that required him to assert his authority, make decisions, and enforce them, he would not be found wanting: he would drive his men before him with a menacing manner until they reached safety, but by then the scientists had long since defected, gone off on their own — and died.

The floe that held the *Karluk* had become a part of the vast sea ice of Arctic winter. On the morning of January 2, 1914, the slow destruction of the ship began. McKinlay was awakened at about four A.M. by a

curious sound, like the strumming of a banjo, just outside my bunk on the port side. Raising myself on my elbow, I put my ear close to the ship's side. At times it was a distinctly musical note, then it became a discordant noise; then silence. When it struck louder than before and the door of our cabin shuddered, the explanation dawned on me. It was the ice crushing and raftering (forming pressure ridges) some distance away. I lay awake listening until about six o'clock, fascinated by the extreme delicacy of the note which such a fearsome condition of things could produce. When I got up about eight-thirty the sounds were closer, but nothing could be seen in the darkness, not even at noon in the mid-day twilight. I prayed that it might not come any nearer.

For several days the noise continued unabated, and then one morning there was a change: now it was more martial than musical; it alternated between the sound of distant gunfire and the beating of a drum. These noises gradually grew louder and louder. One or two of the men became silent and withdrawn, but the rest turned with a vengeance to their tailoring: "As the twanging, drumming, omi-

The *Karluk* frozen in the ice, shortly before she was crushed (Copy print courtesy of Bill Dewald, Medfact, Inc.)

nous ice sounds got louder and nearer we sewed, sewed, sewed."

Shortly before five A.M. on January 10, McKinlay was once more awakened, this time by a harsh grating sound followed by a shudder that shook the whole ship. Beginning at her bow was a narrow, two-hundred-yard-long crack in the ice running in a northwesterly direction. As the day went on, the crack widened to one foot and then to two feet. Bartlett had everything on the vessel that might be of use taken off. At about 6:45 P.M. a point of ice pierced the *Karluk*'s port side, making a hole ten feet long below the water line. Now the pressure increased and the hull was crushed, "her pumps and pipes shattered, her timbers splintering upward like the shell of a . . . nut" broken with a nutcracker.

The skipper ordered all hands to abandon ship. They lowered themselves down her sides and crawled into the igloos. He alone was left on board. He would not go down with her, but he would stay with her as long as he possibly could.

As the hours passed, he sat in the galley playing a wind-up Victrola with a bell speaker. Other explorers had made the mistake of taking such luxury items with them on their sledges during their long, desperate retreats. Inquisitive Eskimos had easily been able to follow the trails of these doomed men, marked as they were with discarded silverware and fine china. There would be no such foolishness for Captain Bartlett's men: as he finished listening to each of the 150 records in the collection, he threw it into the galley fire. When he came to Chopin's *Funeral March,* he put it aside. Now and then he would go down into the engine room to see about the water level, but most of the time he sat near the warm fire, listening and thinking.

He was a curious fellow. Tough and resolute, he was also a lover of poetry and music. Once, on an earlier day, McKinlay had happened on him reading a book about gardening. Bartlett asked him if he grew roses, "and then we sat, in the midst of limitless ice, with between sixty and seventy degrees Fahrenheit of frost outside, in perpetual darkness, numberless miles from the nearest garden, talking about roses."

At 3:30 P.M. the ice opened up and the vessel began to settle. Bartlett put the *Funeral March* on the Victrola. "When the water came trickling along the upper deck and began splashing into the hatch I ran up and stood on the rail. Slowly the *Karluk* dipped into a header. When her rail was level with the ice I stepped off." He watched her going down in thirty-eight fathoms of frigid sea. Chopin's dirge could still be heard — and then a puff of steam arose as the galley fire was extinguished. He pushed back his hood, baring his head in a sign of respect, and called out, "Good-bye, old girl!"

He retired to his igloo and, not having lain down for a day and a half, fell into a long sleep. When he awoke he found that solid black ice had formed over the grave of the ship. He was responsible for twenty-two men, the Eskimo woman, and her two children, and he was unwilling to have them remain where they were, vainly waiting for rescue. He intended to establish food caches in a line of camps in the direction of Siberia during the winter, and before the ice broke up in the spring, he would use the depots to supply a march to land and safety.

On January 21, he dispatched a party led by First Mate Sandy Anderson to make a camp at Berry Point, Wrangel Island. From the beginning, the mate's party ran into rough ice and deep drifts. They were forced to spend the first night and part of the next day — sixteen hours — in their hastily built snowhouse, while outside a storm raged. Eventually they were able to resume their march, but after a time they encountered a wide lead, or opening, in the ice. They unhitched the dogs, threw them over it, and pulled the sledge across. Their feet became frozen, and Bjarne Mamen dislocated his knee trying to stop a dog fight. He had to ride on the sledge as dead weight. They slogged on in the bitter cold. Their stove ceased to work, and so they had no heat when they rested at night. One day they crossed a lead eight and a half feet wide, only to find another, bigger one beyond it. They had to wait until it froze over. As they got closer to the isle, they realized it was not Wrangel but Herald Island, some forty miles farther east. They had gone off course, but the problem was not the extra distance they had traveled: Herald was "almost unapproachable, ringed by cliffs, surrounded by constantly running ice, and totally barren of all life." Three miles short of the island, they were stopped by open water. They camped beside it to wait for the ice to close, and they sent Mamen, the two Inuit guides, and the dogs back to Bartlett at "Shipwreck Camp."

Mamen and the Eskimos returned safely to make a report to the skipper, but the other members of the party were never seen alive again. They were "four young men with no grand ideas about exploring the Arctic, or finding new land," wrote William McKinlay, "just four sailors trying to follow orders."

Fifteen years later, the *Herman* visited Herald Island, and her crew found a badly torn tent and pieces of a broken sledge, as well as four human skeletons. The identities of the deceased were confirmed by the initials on the stocks of their rusty guns: Sandy Anderson, Charles Barker, John Brady, and A. King. "They had made it ashore," Harold Horwood tells us, "in spite of cliffs and running ice, perhaps already wet and freezing when they landed, and they had died there."

After Mamen's return, the men at Shipwreck Camp built a fire in the futile hope of guiding in Anderson and the others. Over the course of a week, a whaleboat, a ton of coal, a cask of alcohol, a case of oil, and several cases of gasoline were burned.

Even as Mamen was giving his sad report, the scientists staged a small mutiny. They announced that they were taking a sledge and their share of supplies and dogs and were setting out on their own. Bartlett argued with them: none of them had experience traveling on Arctic sea ice; it would be exceedingly difficult to move a sledge over the ice because of its continual cracking, shifting, opening, and "piling up in fantastic ridges." Nothing he could say would convince them. They knew how a commander should comport himself — and dress — and they put no credence in what this sloppy-looking fellow had to say. They had long distrusted his leadership and had openly challenged it at least once. He had faced them down that time but was unable to do so now: they were not his crewmen, after all; they had signed on to carry out experiments for the great Stefánsson.

In the end, he could do nothing but require that they write him a letter absolving him of responsibility for their fate. Then, having assured them that they would be welcomed back if they were unable to make it, he issued to them food for fifty days, a sledge, dogs, a tent, a stove and fuel, and a hundred rounds of ammunition. The four men (led by surgeon Alistair MacKay) embarked on the fifth of February to the encouraging cheers of their comrades.

A few days later, the skipper dispatched two relief teams to Herald Island in a futile attempt to locate the mate's party. The first had to turn back, and the second, consisting of Ernest "Charlie" Chafe and two Eskimos, could only get close enough to the isle to study it through binoculars. They saw no signs of life.

On the return journey, they met the doctor's party. Three of the men were hauling the sledge, and the fourth was staggering two miles behind, feet and hands frozen, and "half-delirious from his suffering." This was anthropologist Henri Beuchat; he was convinced that he would die and bitterly regretted leaving Bartlett's command. Chafe tried to convince him and the others to come back to Shipwreck Camp, but they would not; they were bound for Wrangel Island. They accepted some seal meat and trudged on. Resuming his own march, Chafe hit upon their outbound trail and, following it in reverse, found it littered with discarded mittens, shirts, and waterproof boots. "Their sleeping bags had been soaking wet and it seemed they had been in the habit of going to bed without even removing their boots, which probably accounted for Beuchat's condition."

Captain Bartlett was stunned when he heard about the plight of the doctor's party, but there was nothing he could do for them. A heavy gale was brewing, and the area that would have to be searched was too large for so few men and dogs. Anyway, from what Chafe said, it was pointless to risk other men's lives: the obdurate four were undoubtedly already dead.

"I suspect that they died of exhaustion," Bartlett wrote fourteen years later.

> They were used to the Antarctic plateau which is level; but not to the terrific chaos of the Polar Sea. I picture their sledge breaking as Peary's sledges so often broke, their dogs getting weaker, and frostbite hindering their work. For none was skilled in the handling of dogs or protection of their clothing and equipment in Polar Sea conditions. All this comprises a technique that takes years to learn.

For six weeks the skipper had his men carefully establishing a chain of camps and learning how to travel over sea ice. On February 19, Bartlett dispatched two advance teams for the push to Wrangel Island. These consisted of four men and five dogs for each heavy-laden sledge.

Five days later the main party set out: nine people with seven healthy dogs and several injured ones. One man carried in a sack around his neck the ship's cat, Nigeraurak. The skipper had given firm instructions as the *Karluk* was sinking that the animal was not to be forgotten, and in the months ahead, while the men would know much hunger, no one proposed eating the cat; he was "the only member of the expedition to survive the whole affair sleek and unscathed." Kiruk's two small children, Helen and Mugpi, ages five and three, also benefited from this attitude: they were always given full rations no matter how little the white men had to eat.

The main party trekked twelve miles the first day, passing camps one and two, and slept that night in summer tents. The temperature was forty degrees below zero. McKinlay thought it was the coldest night he had ever spent, and he was fearful of getting frostbite. He remembered the advice he had been given on how to prevent it: "Wriggle your fingers and toes and wrinkle your face. Give your ears an occasional rub." He followed the prescription, but he was lying huddled beside the skipper, who finally growled, "If you can't be still, boy, get out." McKinlay lay quiet for a time and then went out into the snow to stomp around, "trying to induce some warmth in my limbs."

The next day they arrived at camp five, having made eighteen miles. Kuraluk, Kiruk, and their two children were already ensconced in the igloo, so the white men built one of their own. They drank hot tea into which they threw sugar and chunks of frozen milk. They slept with their damp socks on their chests so that their body heat would dry them. Sometimes they were awakened by the sounds of the ice breaking, "grinding, crushing and raftering." One crack split the floor of Kuraluk's igloo down the middle, and he dragged his children out before it could open farther and deposit the little ones into the frigid water. They moved into the white men's shelter.

One morning Bartlett and the others were hitching up the dog teams when the two advance parties arrived. Their leaders reported to the skipper that the route to Wrangel Island was blocked by a series of pressure ridges that reached heights of up to a hundred feet and ran as far as the eye could see. Faced with this impenetrable barrier, they had elected to go back to Shipwreck Camp. Bartlett was appalled: there was no hope of being rescued from the old camp; the only prospect for them there was miserable death. He asked them what they intended to do once they reached Shipwreck. "Their rather sheepish replies showed that they hadn't thought so far ahead, and he raged at them for their folly in risking the loss of all they had achieved up to that point."

He told them to fall in line, and he led everyone forward to the pressure ridges. He found that the disheartened men had hardly been exaggerating the difficulty: the ridges, or rafters, ranged in height from twenty-five to one hundred feet and blocked the way to

Wrangel. There was no way around them, so the skipper decided on the spot that they would go *over* them, dragging their sledges with them. They would make a road across the rafters, chopping at their sides with pickaxes and using the resulting loose ice like gravel to form grades and fill in the troughs. Some of the men must have thought he was mad and more than one believed they could never do it, but no one dared tell that to Captain Bartlett. Later even he would admit that it was as hard a job as he ever had to do in his life. Still, he drove them to it and worked beside them.

Sometimes we had to get the sledges up on a ridge fifty feet high with an almost sheer drop on the other side. When we came to such rough places we would harness all the dogs to a sledge and all of us who could get a hand on it would help push the sledge. When we got the sledge up to the top we would run a rope from it to another sledge down below and as the first sledge went down the other side it would pull the second sledge up.

They believed that the ridges covered three miles, and maybe it is just as well that they did not know that the real distance was closer to eight miles. While most of the men continued making the road, John Hadley, Chafe, and McKinlay were sent back to Shipwreck for more supplies. Once, while Hadley and Chafe were scouting ahead, McKinlay heard the dogs barking and turned to see a polar bear just fifteen yards away. The Scottish schoolteacher was transfixed by the sight.

He began to move in an arc, keeping a constant distance

from the dogs, which were harnessed to the sledge. I suppose I should have rushed for the rifle on the sledge, but it never entered my head. I stood only a few feet away, fascinated by the movements of this beautiful creature. My only previous acquaintance with polar bears had been at the Edinburgh Zoo, and I have always loved to watch them moving around, swinging their massive heads. Now I had no thought of the danger from those huge paws. I just stood admiring the to-and-fro motion of his head, the dainty footfalls as he pirouetted around like a ballet dancer.

Hadley, who was a more practical sort, "burst on the scene," grabbed a rifle, and killed the bear, leaving McKinlay to grieve over its beauty.

They saw and shot two more bears on the way back to Bartlett. One appeared as McKinlay was feeding the dogs: he turned and found the bear facing him across the sledge. "I had only to stretch

William Laird McKinlay on Wrangel Island cleans out his cup with eiderdown in preparation for a meal of blood soup. (Permission and copy print courtesy of George Weidenfeld & Nicolson, Ltd.)

out my arm and I could have touched him on the nose." Again he should have reached for a rifle, but he did not. Once more it was Hadley who made the shot. When they cut up the bears, they found their stomachs empty except for pebbles. The thought that he might have filled the belly of one of these hungry monsters did not give the schoolteacher a moment's pause: "I felt rather sad. I knew the bears were dangerous, and I also knew our lives might depend on our being able to kill them. But they were such magnificent animals. I hoped we would never kill one except for self-protection or for food."

Looking at the rafters, McKinlay contemplated the fate of the doctor's party:

> MacKay, Murray, Beuchat and Morris must have been in the center of those immense ridges as the gale piled them higher and higher against the immovable miles of land-locked ice. That area would be like some nightmare storm at sea, in which waves rising to a hundred feet and more would be made of solid ice, crashing and tumbling down in pieces as big as houses.

Bartlett led the expedition on toward Wrangel. Past the high rafters were smaller ones, but these they could get around. They fought their way forward until, shortly after noon on March 12, the Inuit Kataktovik, who was breaking the trail, cried out, "Nuna! Nuna!" They had finally reached land — they were on Wrangel Island. The men shouted and hugged one another and danced. "We were almost wild with delight," Chafe remembered later.

> No more open leads, no more midnight alarms! In their gladness men dug through the snow so they might touch the earth with their hands, or pick up a pebble from the frozen ground. There was no sign of vegetation . . . except for the mountains that reared their lofty summits inland . . . there was little change in the eternal whiteness.

They collected driftwood for fuel and built a shelter out of ice blocks with tent canvas for a roof. They searched for tracks of game but found precious few. It was clear that the island was nothing more than a "temporary refuge": polar bears and seals might be had, and in the summertime there would be birds, but it was a place rarely visited by ships, and if they were not to starve slowly, they would have to save themselves. Bartlett had planned to lead them all to Siberia, of course, but most of them were not capable of a further, arduous trek, one "far more dangerous than anything they had attempted so far." Someone would have to go for help, and that someone would be Bob Bartlett. He took along the unmarried Kataktovik, and the urgency he felt was such that they set off in the midst of a snowstorm on March 18.

Less than a mile from "Shore Camp" they were "assailed by increasing blasts of the northwest wind, which swirled the drifting snow about us and prevented our seeing more than a hundred yards." They pushed on anyway. The wind grew in violence, and they were nearly blinded by the snow. They built igloos to sleep in at night, and during the day they tried to watch for traces of the lost parties; they sighted only a raven and a lemming. When they encountered ridges, they worked their way around them or climbed over them. The runners on their sledge broke sometimes, and they had to stop for hours to fix them. When they came to wide leads, they went in opposite directions to find a place to cross. They threw the dogs over them, bridged the sledges, and jumped themselves. If a lead was too wide for bridging, they used a floating ice cake as a ferryboat. Hardly had they crossed one lead and started out again than they were confronted with another one.

Repeatedly the sledge broke through the young ice, wetting the supplies and sleeping gear and terrifying the dogs. The hungry canines chewed on their harnesses and freed themselves. The men lured them back and tied their mouths shut whenever they put them to work. Once the whole dog team broke away from the sledge and ran in the direction of Wrangel Island; Bartlett, afraid they might go all the way back, followed behind with a tin of pemmican (dried meat mixed with fat and other nutritious ingredients), which he pretended to be opening. Eventually they stopped and came slowly toward him. When they were close enough, he grabbed the rope. Once captured, they clearly expected to be beaten; he just hooked them up to the sledge and pushed on.

The men killed two bears and two seals; they fed the dogs as much as they could without making them sluggish. On March 30, after thirteen days of travel, they sighted Siberia through binoculars. The next day Kataktovik told the skipper that his people believed that Siberian Inuits were fierce and hostile to strangers and would certainly kill any Alaskan Inuits who fell into their hands. Bartlett, suffering from snow blindness, tried to comfort him as they crossed onto land ice. They put on their snowshoes and made a trail with their pickaxes.

On April 5 they sighted igloos and, the skipper leading the way, met up with "Chukches." These Inuits proved to be effusively hospitable and took the strangers into a dwelling that "smelled worse than any Greenland igloo I have ever been in, which is saying a good deal." Kataktovik inhaled happily.

They had traveled more than two hundred miles in a little over two weeks and were in need of rest, but Bartlett, worried about the food supply on Wrangel Island, felt compelled to keep going. The Bering Strait was more than four hundred miles away, and because the Chukches had so few dogs and could not part with more than one or two, the journey was made using the same weary dog team that had come all the way from Shore Camp. Along their route the two men repeatedly encountered Inuits who willingly shared with them what they had; such cordiality, observed the skipper, was "merely typical of the true humanity of these . . . kindly people."

On April 25, thirty-seven days and nearly seven hundred miles from Wrangel, Bartlett and Kataktovik arrived at East Cape. The next schooner for Nome was not scheduled to depart until early June, and Bartlett was searching for another ship when he came down with protein poisoning, the result of having for so long subsisted largely on pemmican. His legs and feet swelled enormously, and he developed a severe throat infection. While he was ill, he was visited by Baron Kleist, the Russian supervisor of Northeastern Siberia, who invited him to travel with him by sledge to Emma Harbour, the closest Siberian port to the Alaskan coast. Sick as he was, Bartlett readily accepted. (No longer in need of a hunter and guide, he said good-bye to Kataktovik, thanking him profusely for all he had done.)

The journey through "wild country" took six days. Upon arriving at the port, Bartlett tried to locate Captain C. T. Pedersen, skipper of the *Herman* and, incidentally, the officer whom Bartlett had replaced on the *Karluk*. Bartlett gave messages to several Chukches, hoping one would find Pedersen. On May 21, the *Herman* sailed into Emma Harbour. Bartlett boarded her immediately, and she sailed for Nome, which proved to be ice-locked. He managed to get ashore at St. Michael on May 27, but the wireless station there was closed. He appealed to a U.S. marshal who had served with Peary, and the station was opened. The operator, however, refused to send the emergency message to Ottawa without being paid in advance. Bartlett, who had no money and must have been a little crazy with frustration, got the marshal to intervene again. The telegram finally went out. He later dispatched additional messages urging that the United States and Russia help in rescue efforts. The Canadian government released an announcement of his surfacing in Alaska, and he became an instant celebrity. He received congratulatory telegrams from all over the world and was inundated with inquiries from the press. The advertising department of an American magazine, working up a tobacco ad, even asked permission to use a photograph of him smoking a pipe.

Bartlett's only concern was rescuing his people. He managed to get permission to sail to Wrangel on the U.S. revenue cutter *Bear,* but the ice would not be open until the end of July at the earliest. He made his way to Nome in June, nonetheless, and buttonholed the master of every northbound schooner that passed through, asking them to stop by Wrangel.

The *Bear* embarked on July 13. On August 24 she encountered ice packs. For several days her captain tried to find a way around or through them, and then, only twenty miles from Wrangel, he was forced to turn back to Nome for more coal. Bartlett was "wretched" and inconsolable. (All the more so after he learned that a Russian icebreaker had gotten within ten miles of the island on August 4 when, the First World War having broken out, the crew received orders to sail south immediately.)

On September 8, returning from Nome and still seventy-five miles from Wrangel, the *Bear* met the schooner *King and Winge.* Bartlett studied the figures on her deck with binoculars. Eventually he recognized McKinlay, Chafe, and the Eskimo family. He ferried over to the ship, and his first question was "All of you here?" They told him that six others were on board, but three men had died before they could be rescued. Bartlett could think of nothing to say. He had no hope that any of the mate's party or the doctor's party would be found alive, but "it was an especially bitter blow to learn that three of the men whom I had seen arrive at Wrangel Island had thus reached safety only to die."

Two of the three fatalities resulted from protein poisoning, and all of the survivors on Wrangel were stricken with it. Their limbs became swollen, and they experienced rheumatic pains. They were listless and weak. As the malady advanced, the afflicted suffered from severe depression. The first man to die was George Malloch.

In the days before he succumbed, he simply lost the will to live. "Malloch is certainly a peculiar specimen," Bjarne Mamen wrote in his diary on May 15. "He told us today that he couldn't see any point in going out and wasting his strength and provisions when nothing could be done. He believes that it does a man good to lie inside all the time without moving." Two days later Mamen added another entry:

Malloch is now beyond hope. I expect he will die any moment. He lost consciousness at ten o'clock and from that time we couldn't get a word from him. At five-thirty he stretched his legs and drew his last breath, to great relief for Bob and me. I cannot describe how sorry I feel about his death, but I thank my Heavenly Almighty Father that he had such a quiet death without too great pain. He has suffered pain, though, since *Karluk*.

Mamen himself would live for only another eleven days. The last words he wrote were these: "I for my part cannot stand it staying here any longer."

Most of the men thought the bear meat they sometimes ate was responsible for their affliction, but McKinlay noticed that his symptoms grew worse after eating the tinned pemmican that Stefánsson had chosen as the basic food supply for the expedition. "The pemmican was not only insufficient as a ration but led to illness, both of men and dogs," Stefánsson explained to the readers of *The Friendly Arctic*.

This does not mean that there was anything poisonous about it. It is merely an illustration of the generally accepted fact that a diet consisting almost entirely of protein leads to "protein poisoning," which is poisonous in only the sense that illness results because the kidneys are overtaxed with trying to excrete the excess of nitrates. This leads to nephritis or derangement of the kidneys, of which a common symptom is swelling of the body, beginning usually at the ankles.

Thinking the matter over, Stefánsson judiciously concluded, "Our pemmican makers had failed us through supplying us with a product deficient in fat."

As the decades passed and McKinlay went on gathering evidence on the *Karluk* debacle, he came into possession of Admiral Peary's *Secrets of Polar Travel*, in which the illustrious explorer praised pemmican as the only food one can eat twice a day, 365 days of the year, and have the last mouthful taste as good as the first. And it is the most satisfying food I know. I recall innumerable marches in bitter temperatures when men and dogs had been worked to the limit and I reached the place for camp feeling as if I could eat my weight of anything. When the pemmican ration was dealt out and I saw my little half lump about as large as the bottom third of an ordinary drinking glass, I have felt a sullen rage that life should contain such situations. By the time I had finished the last morsel, I would not have walked round the completed igloo for anything or everything that the St. Regis, the Blackstone, or the Palace Hotel could have put before me.

The *Karluk*'s survivors had found their pemmican barely edible, but what troubled McKinlay about Peary's remarks was his addendum:

Next to insistent, minute, personal attention to the building of his ship, the Polar explorer should give his personal, .constant and insistent attention to the making of his pemmican and should know that every batch of it packed for him is made of the proper material in the proper proportion and in accordance with his specifications.

McKinlay, who had buried at least one victim of protein poisoning and had tried to keep animals from digging up the body, had underscored that sentence. Stefánsson had devoted considerable time to selling the expedition's story in advance but had given little or no attention to the quality of the food its members would have to subsist on.

Undoubtedly the illness affected them psychologically. For most of them it was mysterious, defying any rational explanation. As the summer wore on, they were faced with the prospect of spending another winter on the ice. They became querulous, accusing one another of theft, hoarding, wasting precious ammunition, and shirking work. Bartlett had made them pull together as a team, but he was gone and so was the spirit of unity. They cursed one another over the allocation of biscuits, threatened to kill one another over missing socks. "I know it all sounds ludicrous," McKinlay wrote sixty-two years later,

and anyone sitting at home with a well-stocked larder will find it difficult to appreciate the angry passions that were aroused. But it must be remembered that we were a very small isolated community with barely enough food to last two months, and [had] many more months, perhaps another year to go, before relief might come. There was a feeling of every-man-for-himself in the air.

Some of the men became cheats in that when they had a successful hunt they did not share what they had shot. Several men stole food. This went on even after the men had divided themselves into small parties and moved to camps scattered about the island in order to increase the hunting opportunities.

One day when I was alone in our tent I heard footsteps outside and looking through a small hole in the wall I saw Chafe and Breddy helping themselves to our soup. Breddy then handled the birds in our store, and when I checked on them they were one short. I said nothing, and when Hadley and Kuraluk returned with forty-three crowbills we divided them as usual in the proper ratio.

McKinlay tried to promote harmony among the men, but they were by turns edgy, irascible, and furious. Ironically, given the discord and conflict, the last death on Wrangel Island was apparently not a murder but a suicide. On the morning of June 25, McKinlay was awakened by the sound of a single shot. Breddy, who had been one of the *Karluk*'s firemen, was found dead in his tent with a Mauser revolver beside him. A bullet had passed through his right eye and brain, exiting above his left ear.

An inquest was held on the spot, and Breddy's things were examined in the presence of everyone. McKinlay's compass and some other stolen articles were found. It may be that Breddy was beset by guilt and shot himself, but the death was suspicious. The usual method of killing oneself with a firearm is to put the barrel against the temple or in the mouth; to have a high-velocity bullet strike the eye is especially unpleasant to contemplate. And Breddy was a *thief* who had been stealing not just food, as others had, but the few pathetic objects of sentiment they possessed, things that might have taken on an inordinate value. In writing his book, McKinlay was careful to tell his readers where each man was when the shot rang out — in other words, to establish alibis for the suspects — but since he was asleep in his tent at the time, he was relying on their statements. He attributed Breddy's death to suicide or an accident, but he may have had his doubts because he entitled the chapter describing the incident not "Breddy's Suicide" but "The *Shooting* of Breddy" (italics mine).

Perhaps the fireman's death was cathartic. It did not bring the men together or end their squabbling, but no one else died, violently or otherwise, after Breddy's shooting.

Rescue came on the seventh of September. Kuraluk spotted the ship, and Hadley fired his revolver to attract the attention of the searchers. When the survivors saw a party of men disembark and move across the ice, they immediately began cooking the remainder of their fish. This was not a hospitable gesture: as hungry as they were, they were not going to leave food behind. "We didn't rush out with glad cries to meet the men who trudged up to our tents. We were shy and too dazed to speak." A "cinematograph" cameraman had come along on the *King and Winge* in hopes of getting a story, and he followed the *Karluk*'s men about, filming them as they stumbled here and there, "gathering our bits and pieces together." They left the tents standing and posted conspicuous notes on the poles telling other would-be rescuers that they had been found. (Another vessel stopped by Wrangel soon afterward.)

> We staggered out across the ice for the last time. We were sure we could walk unaided the three miles to the ship, but the cameraman insisted that each of us should be supported by two of the ship's company. I think it made a better picture.

On board the *King* they were told that the world was at war, but they could not grasp the meaning of this revelation. They soaked themselves in hot baths and put on new clothes.

> We mooned around, or lay down on beds of skins spread on the deck. We got up again and drank coffee in the galley, where the coffee pot was kept continuously bubbling on the stove for our special benefit. We smoked and smoked. We lay down again, got up again, drank more coffee. Sleep was impossible.

The captain of the *King* set a course for Herald Island to make a final search for the mate's party, but winter was approaching, and the ice had become "solid and impenetrable." The ship turned south until she encountered the *Bear*, with that anxious, familiar, and rumpled figure on the deck.

The Royal Geographic Society awarded Robert Bartlett the Back Grant for his leadership of the survivors of the Stefánsson expedition. Among other honors, he also received the Hubbard Medal of the National Geographic Society for traveling farther north in 1909 than any previous explorer had.

Less than a year after disembarking from the *Bear*, Bartlett became captain of the *Bonaventure*, one of the new ice-breaking ships, and went off on a seal hunt. For the next thirty years he continued to sail and explore. During World War II he did surveying work and supplied military bases for the Allies. His last command ended in 1945, when he was seventy years old. Living in New York, he wrote magazine articles and debated retiring from the sea permanently. Before he could make a decision, he contracted a "spring cold." Too active to bother with bed rest or to be properly treated, he developed pneumonia, and he died on April 28, 1946.

He is buried beneath a simple headstone in a churchyard in Brigus, Newfoundland.

Vilhjálmur Stefánsson had long since been given up for dead when he returned to civilization in 1918, having spent five years on the ice. Like many another fabled character, he had the chance to read his own obituaries. The islands he discovered after leaving the *Karluk* have proved to be among the last landmasses to be added to the maps of the globe. How many lives this is worth I leave to the reader to judge.

He never went north again himself, but thereafter he did participate in at least two commercial ventures in the Arctic. Both were failures. One involved the establishment of a trading colony on, of all places, Wrangel Island. Stefánsson was still trying to show that the Arctic was a friendly place, imminently habitable and economically inviting. To this end, he had four white men and an Eskimo seamstress named Ada Blackjack put ashore on Wrangel on September 16, 1921. Two of the men were inexperienced and quite young, neither having reached his twenty-first birthday; the other two had been north before, and one of them, incredibly, was Fred Maurer, who had been a crewman on the *Karluk*. Left for what was expected to be a period of up to two years, they were given six months' worth of food supplies; they would supplement this meager diet by hunting and fishing. When the *Donaldson* arrived at the island in mid-August 1923 with a relief party, the men were all dead. Facing starvation, three of them, including Maurer, had tried to walk to Siberia and had died on the ice. The fourth succumbed to scurvy while being looked after by Ada Blackjack. She was the only survivor brought back to Nome.

Stefánsson tried to suppress the actual causes of the deaths of his colonists, supposedly to spare the feelings of their families. In *The Adventure of Wrangel Island* he tried to put what had happened in the best possible light, as he had sought to do with the debacle of the *Karluk* in *The Friendly Arctic*. In the latter book, in McKinlay's estimation, he "gave an inaccurate account of the *Karluk* affair, subtly putting blame for all the mistakes and disasters on everyone but Vilhjálmur Stefánsson." This time he intimated that the four men had died because they had failed to carry out his instructions.

He was not a meticulous planner or a careful organizer, and he surely did not prepare for every eventuality. He relied upon his instincts, skills, and ability to improvise. Unfortunately these qualities were not readily transferable to his subordinates — at least not without the kind of lengthy training for which he had no time.

On August 26, 1962, Vilhjálmur Stefánsson died, having suffered a stroke. He was eighty-two years old and had only recently finished the first draft of his autobiography, which was his twenty-fourth book. He is buried in Pine Knoll Cemetery, Hanover, New Hampshire.

"After years of friendly dealing with the ice," he once wrote, "seeking my food upon its surface or at its margin, walking upon it by day and camping upon it comfortably at night, I am as much at ease on its floating cakes as the Swiss are among the Alps that horrified Hannibal's generals."

At the conclusion of *"Karluk": The Great Untold Story of Arctic Exploration,* William Laird McKinlay, recalling his service as a volunteer in the First World War, had this to say:

> Not all the horrors of the Western Front, not the rubble of Arras, nor the hell of Ypres, nor the mud of Flanders leading to Passchendaele, could blot out the memories of that year in the Arctic. The loyalty, the comradeship, the esprit de corps of my fellow officers and of the men it was my privilege to command, enabled us to survive the horrors of the war, and I realized that this was what had been entirely missing up north; it was the lack of real comradeship that had left the scars, not the physical rigours and hazards of the ice pack, nor the deprivations on Wrangel Island.

In 1927, Roald Amundsen, who, in contrast to Stefánsson, was efficient and thorough at planning and equipping his expeditions, made a pointed remark in his autobiography that might stand as an epitaph to the sad story of the *Karluk:*

> Some adventurous spirits, seeking a fresh thrill in the North, may be misled by this talk about the "friendliness" of the Arctic and will actually attempt to take advantage of this "friendliness," and venture

into those regions, equipped only with a gun and some ammunition. If they do, certain death awaits them. . . .

It is difficult for men living in comfort in civilized countries to realize the harshness of the Arctic, so the "Friendly Arctic" has given to many an entirely wrong impression of the care, experience, equipment, and planning necessary to merely stay alive in the far North. I have had men express astonishment at the elaborate preparations made by me to carry abundant food in concentrated form for use on my expeditions. They have been led to believe that a march to the North Pole is little more than a light-hearted hunting expedition, upon which one leisurely advances across the ice, stopping occasionally to kill something to eat and wandering on his way with no cares about to-morrow's food.

CHAPTER 19

Maine Tarzan
Joseph Knowles in the North Woods

At twilight a man stumbles awkwardly through the darkening, dense jungle. He is William Cecil Clayton, a young Englishman. He had been a passenger on a ship when the crew mutinied, took control of her, and set him and the other passengers ashore on the African coast. Clayton, separated from some of his fellows in misfortune, is searching for them.

His movements are not unobserved. In the trees above him an ape watches and wonders. On the ground a dozen paces from him, a black-maned lion moves stealthily on a course parallel to his own, stalking him. Clayton does not hear the big cat until it roars, and then, horrified, he turns to face it. He is transfixed by the sight of the beast creeping toward him. There is no hope; there can be no reprieve. In an instant he will be ripped by fangs and claws.

The lion hunkers down, tenses to pounce.

Clayton hears the twang of a bowstring and sees an arrow strike the big cat's hide. The animal roars in pain and leaps for him. Clayton throws himself out of its path and turns to face it once more.

From out of the trees a half-naked giant of a man drops onto the beast's back. He slips his right arm around its neck and stands, pulling it upright. The lion is roaring and pawing the air. The huge man's left hand holds a knife; he plunges it into the cat's side over and over again.

The animal sags, sinks to the ground.

Its killer stands on its corpse, throws back his head, and bellows in triumph. It is a sound that generations of little boys will attempt to imitate. *Eh-wa-au-wau-aoooow!*

The young Mr. Clayton has become the first human being to glimpse . . . Tarzan of the Apes.

For most of us, our image of the mighty lord of the jungle is derived from the dozens of movies that were rather loosely adapted from the adventure books of Edgar Rice Burroughs. In particular we think of barrel-chested Johnny Weissmuller woodenly delivering such positively Shakespearean lines as "You Jane, me Tarzan."

Burroughs's character is much more urbane and sophisticated than the one portrayed by Weissmuller on the silver screen. He is literate, multilingual, and an interested visitor to European capitals and American cities. Being the heir to Lord Greystoke's title and property, he can live the life of a wealthy aristocrat in an English manor. Instead he voluntarily *chooses* to dwell in the hostile jungle.

Burroughs never traveled to Africa, and so as a writer he was not constrained by an awareness of reality. As a result, the jungle he depicted sometimes lacks a certain degree of . . . accuracy. (It contains tigers as well as fruit trees indigenous to the Americas, among other improbabilities.) It is, nonetheless, a fearsome place filled with merciless wild beasts and cannibalistic tribesmen; even the colony of carnivorous apes that adopted the baby Tarzan, and over which he now rules, has numerous cruel, cannibalistic members. Thus Tarzan forever finds himself beset by danger — or rescuing some hapless soul who has stumbled into jeopardy.

If Burroughs overstated the perils of the "fierce" African bush with its supposed "hundred unknown dangers," his vision was in keeping with one of our common notions of the "untamed" wilderness: it is a dark and malevolent place fraught with hazards and populated by vicious creatures and evil men. Ironically, our *other* common wilderness image is of a safe, sweet place, an Eden regained.

The latter conceit has been traced by the eminent scholar Leo Marx as far back as the Roman poet Virgil's *Eclogues*. Many Elizabethan explorers of the New World had perpetuated the notion describing the landscapes they saw in distinctly Edenic tones. For them the uncolonized America was "earth's only paradise," a virginal garden of "incredible abundance" populated by "gentle, loving, and faithful" Indians. Captain Arthur Barlowe, for instance, who voyaged to Virginia with Sir Walter Raleigh in 1584, reported that he "found shole water where we smelt so sweet and so strong a smell, as if we had been in the midst of some delicate garden abounding with all kind of odoriferous flowers." The place where he and his men first came ashore was

> so full of grapes, as the very beating and surge of the sea overflowed them, of which we found such plenty, as well there as in all places else, both on the sand and on the green soil of the hills . . . that I think in all the world the like abundance is not to be found; and myself having seen those parts of Europe that most abound, find such difference as were incredible to be written.

It is hardly surprising that inhabitants of such a paradise would be innocents. Their gentle dispositions were in marked contrast to those of residents of foul European cities. Indians, in the opinion of planter Robert Beverley, who wrote the *History and Present State of Virginia* in 1705, had been neither

> debauch'd nor corrupted with those pomps and vanities, which had depraved and inslaved the rest of mankind; neither were their hands harden'd by labour, nor their minds corrupted by the desire of hoarding up treasure. They were without boundaries to their land; and without property in cattle; and seem'd to have escaped, or rather not to have been concern'd in the first Curse, *Of getting their bread by the sweat of their brows.* For, by their pleasure alone, they supplied all their necessities; namely, by fishing, fowling and hunting; skins being their only clothing; and these too, five sixths of the year are thrown by. Living without labour, and only gathering the fruits of the earth when ripe, or fit for use. Neither fearing present want, nor solicitous for the future, but daily finding sufficient afresh for their subsistence.

Of course, some early settlers would come to dissent from the suggestion of both an idyllic landscape and the affability of those prior residents whom they were seeking to supplant. Even some of the aforementioned Elizabethan voyagers had unhappy experiences in the New World and described it as a "hideous and desolate wilderness, full of wild beasts and wild men," "the most dangerous unfortunate, and most forlorn place of the world," and "this hideous and hated place."

These two contradictory images of the wilderness have never been reconciled, but the one that presents America as a land of limitless abundance and its forests an unthreatening Eden would soon become dominant on both sides of the Atlantic, and even into the twentieth century it would continue to exert a profound influence on the imaginations of painters and poets, philosophers and common people alike. As the woods have been cleared and the landscape cultivated, the nostalgia for the forest has grown. We long for a simpler, unencumbered existence, one free of bosses and bureaucrats, petty regulations and restrictive laws. For some it is enough to dream of owning a farm and working the land, but others wistfully see themselves as, say, bush pilots in Alaska.

Either way, many of us who are restive on city streets or suburban avenues assume as some New World visitors did that nature is benevolent. This is hardly realistic, but it buttresses our fantasies nonetheless. "Nature never did betray / The heart that loved her," William Wordsworth asserted, and an extraordinary number of otherwise sensible people have picked up this preposterous sentiment, repeated it, and — more dangerously still — believed it.

One of those who did is the man who comes forward now, at the place of our rendezvous, shaggy, leaning on a staff, clad in a bearskin and very little else. Do not be alarmed by him. Painter, trapper, hunting guide, and splendid charlatan, he is Joseph Knowles, late of Wilton, Maine, and the Dead River region.

On October 4, 1913, Joe strode out of a Canadian forest at a point fourteen miles south of Megantic, Quebec. His hair was long and matted, and his beard was bushy and tangled. He was wearing the hide of a bear he claimed to have clubbed to death and skinned with a sharp stone. His feet and calves were protected by moccasins and leggings made from the skin of a deer whose neck he said he broke with his bare hands. (Edgar Rice Burroughs would have approved: Tarzan dispatched lions and apes alike by breaking their necks with a self-taught full nelson.) He carried a bow and arrows he had made himself, and hanging at his waist was a knife fashioned from the horn of a deer.

When Knowles struck the Canadian Pacific railroad tracks, he began following them toward Megantic. Almost immediately he encountered a fourteen-year-old girl. She did not run from him despite his wild appearance; she did not even seem to be frightened. Possibly such sights were common then, north of the border, but more likely she recognized him. Certainly the railroaders who came along shortly afterward knew who he was: one of them was more than happy to lend him the train fare so he could ride to town in comfort. Having just hiked more than seventy miles from his camp in Maine,

Joe was tired, but he had no chance to let the rhythm of the wheels beneath him lull him to sleep. For hardly had he sat down than his car was filled with well-wishers who hurried from all over the train to shake the hand of the "Primitive Man" from New England. A few miles down the line, ten thousand people had gathered to greet him. Here and in the States were reporters and photographers eager to get at him, politicians anxious to honor him, and mobs of people assembled just to see him — and to tear at his clothes for souvenirs.

Three months before, nobody had heard of Joseph Knowles, but on this fall day he was a famous and beloved man. Eight weeks in a forest had transformed an obscure artist into a national hero and a truly modern celebrity.

Several journalists in the last decade have made the connection between Burroughs's creation and the bearskin-clad nature buff Joe Knowles. They have applied to Knowles such appellations as "Yankee Tarzan" and "Tarzan of the Maine Woods." They have noted with a discernible tinge of regret, however, that the first novel about the lord of the jungle was not published until *1914,* a year after Joe had climbed aboard that Canadian train. Knowles therefore could not have gotten his inspiration from a certain very imaginative writer. Still, they say, there was something in the air back then. Darwin's ideas were gaining wide circulation, and Teddy Roosevelt's presidency had ended only four years previously.

There was indeed something in the air that could have given Knowles the idea of stripping off his clothes and heading into the bush. Joe knew enough about evolution to devote a chapter of his book, *Alone in the Wilderness,* to examples of the survival of the fittest in nature. And how could he have failed to be influenced by the energetic Mr. Roosevelt? Having been a sickly child afflicted with asthma, the young T.R. put himself on a vigorous program of exercise and went out west. He came back with a rugged physique and a love of the outdoors. He was a vociferous, lifelong advocate of strenuous activity. A devoted hunter and rancher, he was also a committed conservationist. During his administration, 194 million acres were set aside for parks or otherwise protected from commercial exploitation, and he is credited with having created the first wildlife preserve.

It is hardly surprising, then, that a back-to-nature movement was flourishing. It may have been this that gave Joe the idea for his experiment — or it may have been Edgar Rice Burroughs after all. Because while the novel did not appear until 1914, a shorter version of it was published in the October 1912 issue of the pulp magazine *All-Story.* (It was also reprinted serially in the *Evening World.*)

Perhaps someone left a copy of *All-Story* in the Vermont tavern where Joe lifted a few every now and then, telling tall tales of his days as a trapper and guide and of the year he lived with the Sioux and Chippewa Indians up in Michigan. On the other hand, the idea might have been the brain child of Michael McKeogh, a scheming free-lance newspaperman and friend of Joe's, who was always on the lookout for a good yarn and a fast buck.

Anyway, when Knowles came to write *Alone*, he left out the part about the bar and the tall tales; he said only that one day in October of 1912, while he was living in a secluded cabin on a Vermont mountain, the idea came to him. He was just finishing a painting of a moose when, adding a dab of color to the canvas, he "began to wonder how many people would notice that particular bit of color, which, from a standpoint of faithful portrayal, was as important as the eye of the creature itself. From this thought my mind wandered on to the realization that the people of the present time were sadly neglecting the details of the great book of nature."

Joe forgot the brush in his hand. In a moment of inspiration worthy of Hollywood, he understood what he should do: he knew about the woods, and he would put that knowledge to use for the benefit of mankind. Modern life was a sham. People were living false, "artificial" existences and were too dependent upon luxuries. He would show them that it was possible to live harmoniously with nature — even in a wilderness, without tools or a single scrap of clothing.

When he came down from the mountaintop with this revelation, his drinking buddies at the hotel bar in Bradford scoffed. It was not until the next summer that he and McKeogh saw a chance to parlay Joe's revealed truth into a pocketful of money and a shot at lasting fame. A newspaper circulation war was raging in Boston between the *Post* and William Randolph Hearst's *American.* Knowles and McKeogh first approached the *American,* but while none of Hearst's papers was renowned for scrupulous regard for fact and judicious presentation of news, the editors unaccountably turned down the boys from Bradford. The *Post,* on the other hand, was losing the circulation war, and its editors quickly saw the intrinsic worth of the project. To contribute to the sum of human knowledge and at the same time rake in a pile of loot has ever been irresistible.

The setup was a simple one. Knowles would live for two months in isolation, and he would record his adventures on birch bark with the charcoal of burned sticks. Each week he would leave one such crude report in a secret cache; it would be retrieved by a local guide and delivered to the cabin where McKeogh would be staying. McKeogh would then expand Joe's message into a feature-length article for the Sunday *Post*. The interest in the stunt was so great that the stories were syndicated to more than forty newspapers across the country.

(Joe was never so crass as to reveal just how much he received from the *Post* and the other newspapers, of course. Do we know what Pasteur's profit was from his discoveries in immunology? Who has asked to see Jonas Salk's tax returns?)

It was raining on the morning of August 4, 1913, as Joseph Knowles came to the end of a logging road near King and Bartlett Lake. Around him gathered invited guests — hunters, sportsmen, and friends, as well as at least one official photographer to record the momentous occasion. As Joe dramatically disrobed, the photographer snapped away. The pictures show a lantern-jawed, stern-faced, barrel-chested man, powerfully built if a bit beefy at five feet nine and two hundred pounds. Wearing a sort of jockstrap for modesty's sake, he smoked a last cigarette, shook hands all around, and then, pausing only once on the crest of a hill to turn back and wave, he strode vigorously into the forest.

He spent the first day exploring along the shore of Spencer Lake. So interested was he in his environment that it was late afternoon before he thought to build a fire, and by then the daylong downpour had soaked the woods so thoroughly that his attempts were unsuccessful. In the night the temperature dropped and the rain continued, so that to keep warm he was forced to run back and forth across a little clearing in a spruce thicket. Whenever he grew tired and his breathing labored, he sat on the wet ground with his naked back against a tree. These rest periods were necessarily short, and by morning he felt as if he had run and walked many miles.

The temperature rose as the day went on, but the hard rain did not abate. Joe continued his explorations, his great excitement overshadowing his hunger. Coming upon Lost Pond, he was so taken with the scenery that "I wanted to put my hands in my pockets to

RIGHT: Joseph Knowles strips before going into the Maine woods and (BELOW) comes out sixty days later. Knowles claimed that the photograph taken as he emerged from the forest was authentic, but obviously it has been touched up. Note the trees in the background and his costume's bear claw. (Copy prints by Larry Rubens, Audio-Visual Services, Kent State University)

enjoy the picture better, but I didn't have any pockets to put them in. Nothing in that view escaped me that day. I saw the sky, the trees, and the opposite shore.''

He still was unable to get a fire going, and the second night was a restless repetition of the first. The sun came out the next morning, and in its warmth he slept off and on through much of the day. He awoke hungry. Searching near the "burnt lands," he found bushes of blueberries and raspberries. Having sated himself, he quickly peeled birch bark from trees and made two baskets in which to store the fruit.

He built a "rude" shelter, using sticks for a frame and covering them with fir boughs, moss, and bark. And then at last he succeeded in making a fire out of sticks and bark.

Joe had imagined that he would "live in primitive luxury," dining on wild duck and goose, venison and fish, wild onions and roots and berries. Pickings were slim at first, however. He was forced to rob a swimming otter of a trout by yelling and throwing rocks at the startled creature until it released its catch and fled. In desperation he moved into the marshes and brained a few frogs, but their legs were not a delicacy for him. Eventually he learned to catch trout by wading into a big pool and driving them into shallow water, where he could grab them with his hands. He chewed on spruce buds and bark and ate roots. He caught partridges with a slip noose made of bark. (Some of the birds were so fearless that when he approached them with the noose held out before him on a stick, they would obligingly thrust their heads into it. Those less accommodating he shot with the bow and arrows he made.)

The woods were a continuing education. He watched industrious beavers with approval and became distant friends with a red doe and her albino fawn. Animals could immediately gauge a man's intention, Knowles decided. This mother and her young knew instinctively that he meant them no harm, and so they did not fear him. Chipmunks played at his feet and foxes took no notice of him. When he saw two bears pursuing an injured deer, he followed as closely as he could, fascinated by the drama being played out in the forest. After the deer was killed he rushed the two bears, driving them away from the carcass.

If people could only learn the lessons of the wilderness, he thought. So much of what they believed to be essential in their daily lives was really superfluous. Salt, for instance: at first he missed

being able to put salt on the trout; yet he soon reached the conclusion that sodium chloride was nothing but a luxury. After several
days he did not miss it at all. Then there was the matter of cigarettes: he manufactured a couple of smokes out of squaw bark and
whitewood leaves, but after these were gone he felt no craving,
despite his having been a heavy smoker.

Nevertheless, living in the woods had its problems. His feet and
legs were scratched as he moved through the brambly bush. He
made moccasins out of bark and leggings out of witchgrass, but
these weedy garments and footwear wore out rather quickly.

A greater problem soon presented itself. He was faithfully notching his calendar stick, marking off the days until his experiment
would be over, but the growing number of notches also indicated
the coming of fall. The nights were getting noticeably colder, and
he had no blanket or warm clothing. He knew that it would be
necessary for him to kill a bear. This was a difficult task with a rifle
— but with the bow and arrows fashioned out of hornbeam slivers?
He would have to call upon his time among the Chippewa and
Sioux: "A deadfall was impractical, so my plan was to build a
combination pit and deadfall, much after the plan of the Indian way
of trapping grizzly bears in the West."

It took three days to complete the trap. He baited it with "stale
fish." Three nights later a young, small black bear fell into the trap.
But it was one thing to catch a bear; it was another thing to kill it.

Knowles broke away some of the sticks that formed the roof of
the pit and stepped back, raising a hornbeam club. The opening was
big enough for the animal to get its head through but not big enough
to allow its easy escape. As the bear thrust its nose out, Joe took a
"vicious swing." He missed, but the animal became enraged and
frantic. It was leaping and clawing. Its head came through the opening again, and Knowles brought down the club squarely on top of
it. The bear disappeared into the hole. Joe lifted the club and waited.
He believed that "you can't kill a bear by hitting him over the head.
You must strike him on the nose." He was unhappy with this rather
cruel method, but when the animal's front paws appeared in the
opening, he bashed them. The bear cried in pain and fell back.

Knowles widened the opening a little more and stuck a leafy tree
limb into it to distract and further infuriate his quarry. The bear's
muzzle came out, and Joe landed a blow to the side of it. The animal
toppled over and was still.

Knowles cautiously poked the carcass with a stick. The bear was dead. He suddenly felt weary and decided to put off the arduous job of skinning it until the next day. He went back to his camp, pleased with what he had done. "I think every man who has accomplished something a bit bigger than the ordinary things of his daily routine has a right to feel proud. It is part of his reward."

It took him all the next day to skin the bear with a sharp stone. In the twilight he bathed in a pond, washing his cramped, scratched hands and easing the aching muscles in his back and arms. He had been in the woods less than three weeks, but he was healthy and in possession of shelter, fresh water, a warm bearskin, and a variety of foods. The only essential he now lacked was sturdy protection for his feet and legs. . . .

When, some days later, he saw a spikehorn buck, it was feeding on bottom grass in the pond. Knowles was downwind, in a spruce thicket. If he left his hiding place, the deer would escape, so it was necessary to drive it toward the thicket. Joe threw a stone over the animal's back and into the water. The splash started it moving in his direction. The noise of the second rock brought it close to him. Joe seized its forelegs, and the buck went down. Knowles dropped onto its back, grabbed its horns, and gave them a quick twist. The deer's neck snapped.

Before long, Joe had made chaps and moccasins, punching holes in the deerskin with the sharp point of a horn and lacing it with rawhide.

There was no small amount of skepticism when the Sunday *Post* published Knowles's account of the wrestling match with the buck, and once back in civilization, he was at pains to gather testimony from hunters and outdoorsmen to verify that, yes, it was quite possible to kill a deer in this fashion. Believing that all woodland creatures had souls and being sensitive to the complaints of animal lovers, he felt compelled to express regret for what he had done: "I want to apologize for killing the deer in that manner," he told the readers of his book, "but, under the circumstances, it was the only way I had. I needed the skin badly."

What Joe did not need was the interference of the Maine Fish and Game Commission. His reports of killing the bear and deer had outraged these bureaucrats, and a number of them fanned out through the forest, seeking to arrest him for hunting out of season. When Knowles learned of their search (presumably through a

note from McKeogh), he was indignant and bitter. He had applied
for an exemption long before he had begun the experiment, but the
paper shufflers had never gotten around to considering his request.
Now, like small-minded bureaucrats of every time and place, they
were determined to punish him for ignoring their rules.

Well, let them come in force and seek him where they would.
They would never catch Joseph Knowles or subject him to the
indignity of being brought out of the wilderness under arrest. Thereafter Joe kept on the move, avoiding his enemies by never staying
too long in one place.

At the same time, however, he was in the throes of a *genuine*
crisis, one that was ongoing and increasingly excruciating. It had
begun on August 13, his birthday. A sentimental man in a sentimental age, his thoughts that day were of his mother. She was from a
remote province of Canada, and she had been the one to teach him
about the forest and the animals. Her husband had been disabled in
the Civil War, and she had supported the family. She picked berries
in the summertime and walked six miles to the village to sell them.
She wove baskets, made moccasins, and took in work. She was,
thought Joe, the most courageous person he had ever met. (After
his stay in the woods, Knowles, the dutiful son, made a pilgrimage
to his mother's house in Wilton. He brought along a photographer
and, wearing his bearskin, posed with her: this muscular man in his
shaggy outfit, standing before a small, wizened woman dressed in
black, her hair pulled tightly into a severe bun; she is shaking hands
with and staring intently into the face of her beloved, middle-aged
boy.)

Throughout his birthday, then, he dwelled on memories of his
family and a youth spent traveling the world as a sailor. He found
himself becoming lonely. In the days and weeks that followed, this
feeling grew, until he was quite miserable "without the sound of a
human voice, or the contact of a human being, and [knowing] that
there wouldn't be either for two whole months."

Isolation seems to have greatly stimulated his imagination. Each
evening just at twilight he would be tormented by recollections:

> The torture always commenced with pictures of my friends and those
> I loved best coming into my mind. My heart was with them. I would
> dream of them as their faces rose before me in the firelight. When
> finally I dropped off into a troubled sleep, I would keep right on
> seeing them in my dreams.

Time and again those mental spells were almost too much for me. At those times I would vow that I would leave the forest on the very next day.

He remained in the woods, but the psychological struggle did not abate. It reached a peak when he became sick. He awoke one night, aching all over and suffering from chills and fever. In a disoriented state of mind, he wondered if he was going mad. In the morning he set out for the King and Bartlett camps. As he went, he debated whether to give up the experiment and enter one of the camps or merely settle close enough to them so that if he went out of his head the lumberjacks would "find me, sooner or later, and take care of me." But as he neared the camps, he decided to stick it out for at least one more night. He lay down and fell asleep. He awakened in darkness to the sound of a dog coming up the trail. It was an Airedale terrier that Joe knew. The canine was excited to find him and, after wiggling and dancing around, lay down beside Joe. In the morning both the fever and the dog were gone.

Knowles, hating above all to be called a quitter, went back into the woods. Thereafter, whenever he became depressed and tempted to give up, he always managed to hold off the impulse: "I would agree with myself to stick it out one day longer. Another night would come, with its terrible mental battle. 'Just one more day,' I would say again; and thus the days went slowly by."

This was the vast and unexpected irony: he could subsist easily on a diet of berries and water; he could endure the cold and ignore the rain; he could sleep happily on the hard ground and break the necks of deer with his bare hands; but he found solitude almost unbearable. "If I could have had just one human companion in the wilderness I would have been perfectly contented away from the luxury of the world. Human companionship is the greatest luxury I know of."

But the extent of Knowles's deprivation would soon become a controversial issue. First there was the matter of Allie "Tripe" Deming. This shrewd trapper found employment, it would later be charged, by knocking on the door of McKeogh's cabin and asking, "Where's Joe?" When McKeogh appeared nonplused, Deming allowed as how he had been hiding in the bushes and watching the cabin for three days. He had observed a man who bore a remarkable resemblance to Joseph Knowles showing up promptly at mealtimes.

McKeogh was an unabashed admirer of perseverance and grit, and any man who could lie in the mud and endure insect bites for seventy-two hours just to see who was getting three square meals a day was exactly the kind of fellow any crack reporter would want on his team. McKeogh hired Deming on the spot, giving him the prestigious position of guide at the princely sum of $2.50 per diem. Deming was pleased to be working but felt the remuneration was a bit stingy. Why, the fact that he had nestled in the weeds for three whole days, getting chewed on, seeing what he saw, showed the caliber of fellow he was. McKeogh doubled his salary without batting an eye.

Of course, McKeogh already had a guide, and the cabin was getting awfully crowded. The first guide was allowed to return to his home in Farmington, but just so he would not suffer any hardship, he was kept on the payroll at full salary. The arrangement could not help but please him. "Normally loquacious," as Gerald Carson describes him, "he maintained a no-comment posture when the topic of Knowles and his Superman exploits was introduced."

Deming was not the only enterprising soul with an interest in the now-famous "Original Nature Man." Once Knowles got back to Boston, a reporter for the Hearst's *American* began an exposé. He charged that Joe's bearskin had a couple of bullet holes in it and had been purchased for the inflated sum of twelve dollars, which was almost double the going rate. Knowles was not only a fraud but a bad businessman to boot. As for his much-vaunted combination bear pit — why, a kitty cat could have gotten out of it. There would even be rumors that not only did he eat in the cabin but — oh, horror! — he lived in it as well.

The people on the train that October day knew nothing of these controversies, and neither did the ten thousand souls waiting for him at Megantic. Even if they had, it might not have mattered to them. The North American public wanted to believe in Joseph Knowles and his woodland feats. He was a great hero for them, one whom they embraced fervently and unquestioningly, and they would hear no criticism of him.

You already know that as the Canadian Pacific car rolled toward Megantic, it quickly filled with well-wishers come to shake the hand and slap the back of their new idol. Questions, congratulations, and expressions of sympathy and concern gushed from these excited fans. For a man who claimed to have been two months without hearing the sound of a human voice, the noise must have been deafening.

There were Canadian and U.S. flags flying in Megantic, and its streets were packed with people craning their necks and shoving one another just to get a look at the Primitive Man. The mayor was on hand, as was at least one member of Parliament, and, of course, there were all those reporters, photographers, and newsreel cameramen jockeying for position. Also in the crowd were four Maine game wardens, come not to arrest Joe but to act as an honor guard to escort him home.

The mayor delivered some extravagant words of praise, and then Knowles was hustled off to the Queen's Hotel before the crowd could get at him and "tear the skins from my body." He stripped off his costume, settled himself on a soft mattress, and ordered a dinner of "fried salt pork, potatoes and tea." He also urgently borrowed a cigarette, although the man who had supposedly just been living the pure life and who would sternly lecture his readers on the evils of smoking could hardly admit to such a carnal craving: "When I collected my thoughts I saw that I was smoking a cigarette. I don't remember taking it or lighting it. Someone just shoved it into my hand."

Clamor and crowding would be the norm for Knowles in the days and weeks ahead. He made slow progress on a circuitous route to Boston. There was an adoring throng at Kingfield, and in Farmington the local paper likened his grand entrance to the return of a conquering Roman general: "Never has there been in this section the arrival of a visitor, be he ever prominent, whose advent has so nearly approached triumphal entry." Six hundred people greeted him at his hometown, where he marched at the head of a noisy parade. Thousands more stood in the streets of Lewiston, shouting his name as if he were a war hero: "Three cheers for Joe Knowles, who fought and won!"

The one sour note was sounded in Augusta, where, despite the assurances of the wardens who had traveled to Canada, the fish and game commissioners lay in ambush. The Original Nature Man was marched to their office, scolded, and fined a total of $205.00 for five offenses, including one of especially stinging pettiness: "making a fire without a license."

The folks at Portland more than made up for the insults of the riled bureaucrats. The throng numbered ten thousand, and the Cumberland County Angling Association threw him a whopping banquet at which politicians and local dignitaries vied with one another to pay tribute to him. The city's mayor praised him for demonstrating that "modern man is the equal of the man of the Stone Age." For once Joe seems to have suffered the briefest spasm of modesty. "Any man in good condition and with some knowledge of the woods could do it," he told the celebrants. "In fact, I would wager twenty thousand dollars that I could take six men into the woods and provide, for two months or more, food and clothing for them using the same methods I did for myself."

There were banquets and receptions everywhere Knowles went. Administrators closed schools so that children could take advantage of the once-in-a-lifetime opportunity to see in person the celebrated Primitive Man, and he might have suffered permanent hearing loss from the blare of the parade bands. When he boarded a train in Portland, bound for Boston, his smoking car immediately filled with well-wishers. The men peppered him with questions, and the women were sympathetic or flirtatious. One lady worried that he had suffered from dyspepsia in the forest, and another "confided shyly that she had prayed for him every night."

The workers at the United Shoe Machinery plant had telegraphed a request that he wave at their trackside factory as his train rolled through Beverly, Massachusetts, and Joe, standing on the rear platform of the car, was more than happy to oblige. At each station along the route, still more eager admirers were waiting, and to please them he would slip into his bearskin. He was reluctant to make speeches (where was the money in that, after all?), but he was willing to deliver some pithy pronouncements along these lines: "It was survival of the fittest that gave us this great country of ours."

On October 9, Bostonians gave him the biggest welcome of all. Twenty thousand flooded the streets around North Station. Photographs of the scene conjure up the clichés that compare crowds to vast and ever-moving seas. Clad in his bearskin and moccasins, Knowles rode in an "auto parade" that crept toward the *Post* building on Newspaper Row. He waved, and the crowd surged against the police lines, frantic just to touch him or shake his hand. A number of women — remember, now, this is 1913 — actually tried to climb into the car with him.

A reception was held in his honor at noon on Boston Common. He mounted a grandstand with what the *Transcript* termed the "quick, graceful movements of a tiger." Appearing to be genuinely touched, he thanked everyone "from the bottom of my heart."

Gerald Carson estimates that altogether about two hundred thousand people "welcomed Joe Knowles home. Even the World Series had to take second place to the wilderness hero." But the interest in him had hardly subsided. At three P.M., he arrived at the Harvard gymnasium, where he was examined by Dr. Dudley Sargent. The physician, who had given Joe a pre-experiment physical, found him in "the pink of condition, if ever a man was." He had lost eleven pounds, and his height had unaccountably increased one tenth of an inch; Sargent's tests showed that he was measurably stronger and that his lung capacity had increased remarkably. Summing up, the doctor compared Knowles to a renowned strong man: "Sandow was perfect in strength and development; Knowles is perfect in strength and development, but probably has the staying power of three Sandows."

As Joe was being tested and measured, his costume was being examined by Harvard anthropology students. Meanwhile, as Lois Lowry reports, "Radcliffe College girls, apparently indifferent to anthropology, created a near riot outside the gym as they attempted to get a glimpse of the man himself in his natural state."

They were not the only young ladies eager to have a look at him. Sargent next led Knowles to his very own academy — Dr. Sargent's Physical Training School for Women — where four hundred female students were anxiously waiting.

They sang a song dedicated to the wondrous Primitive Man. Sargent then peeled the bearskin from Joe's upper torso, exposing him to the waist. Knowles's skin, he told his rapt pupils, was "perfect, as a result of wind, weather, and sunlight." And just to prove the point, the four hundred girls were allowed to file past him in "awed silence" and one by one touch that nonpareil epidermis.

All in all, it must have been quite a day for Joe.

He was praised as the "hero of the twentieth century." The students in Harvard Square sent up a wild cheer when he walked through. The mayor of Boston and the governor of Massachusetts met with him in their respective offices and questioned him solicitously. A clergyman speaking from the pulpit allowed as how more could be learned from Knowles's woodland sojourn than from a sermon. The head of the economics department at the Massachusetts Institute of Technology also felt compelled to draw a lesson from the Original Nature Man's adventures: Joe might not have been well capitalized in the way a businessman would want to be, but his "was the capital of the true cave man, consisting of the knowledge of woodcraft and a manual ability to make tools and clothing which then become his capital." These were all wonderful accolades, of course, and they might go a long way toward making up for the deprivations of the forest, but what, oh what, was there for poor Joe, this middle-aged bachelor, after the caresses of all those soft, moist, hesitant hands? What was there left for him?

Well, there was money.

On October 10, just one day after he had heard the sweet song of Dr. Sargent's virgin Training School girls, this advertisement appeared in the *Post:*

KNOWLES
MAN OF THE WOODS WILL VISIT
THE FILENE MEN'S STORE
THIS AFTERNOON

He will come in his woodland attire, composed largely of skins and bark, and will go through the process of evolution from the primitive to the modern man.

This process will include barbering, manicuring, chiropody and complete outfitting in new and fashionable clothes from our men's shops.

The friends of Mr. Knowles, old and new, can pay their respects to him while in the Filene store.

He may be found on the second floor (reached by escalator just off Washington Street) about 2 P.M. to 3 P.M.

Sometime on that very day, shorn or unshorn, Joe signed a contract for a twenty-week lecture series and vaudeville tour. (For the latter he reportedly received an impressive $1,200.00 per week.) He already had a contract to write *Alone in the Wilderness*. But that, of course, was precisely the question: had he indeed been alone? Even as the honors were being heaped upon him, there were those nagging doubts. As a matter of fact, hardly had he left the forest when people began to ask him — innocently or maliciously — if it was really possible to break the neck of a deer with one's bare hands or kill a bear by clubbing it in the face.

Knowles reacted testily to the slightest hint that he might be a fraud and, as we know, gathered those numerous testimonies from hunters that what he said he had done most assuredly could be done. Yet the rumors could not be squelched. Then came the *American*'s exposé. The *Post*'s editors learned of it at the last moment and obtained an injunction to halt the publication of the story. They were too late to stop the shipping of the bulldog edition, and so while most Bostonians might not know of the charges against the Primitive Man, a fair number of early risers did.

Furious, Joe announced he was suing the *American* for a whopping fifty thousand dollars. He strode onto the stage of the Tremont Temple and demanded that anyone who could prove him a fraud come forward right then. No one in the audience moved, but he was not mollified. He announced that he would go back to Maine to show the world that you could kill a bear with a club and skin it with a sharp stone.

A suitable candidate was duly shipped by boat from Prince Edward Island to Portland, where its crate was loaded on a railroad car for the journey to Bigelow Station. Knowles was waiting for it at his bear pit near Lost Pond. With him were a notary public and three or four other men to act as witnesses. Also along was a fifteen-year-old boy named Helon Taylor. He would later become superintendent of Baxter State Park, and in the summer of 1973, Mr. Taylor, then in his mid-seventies, would recall what happened for Wendell Tremblay of the *Maine Sunday Telegraph*. Taylor helped the men muscle the bear into the pit. It weighed about two hundred pounds — just the size of the one Knowles claimed to have killed — but since it was winter now, the poor beast was sluggish and dopey:

> It was the middle of December with ten or twelve inches of snow on the ground in some places. The bear wasn't doing very well. He'd had a long trip and wanted to hibernate but we got the bear into the pit, which wasn't very deep — about up to my waist. Joe killed it quickly with a club. He then dug around until he found a sharp piece of shale and in less than ten minutes he had the hide off one of the bear's legs. We were all impressed.

This brave spectacle might have sufficed to preserve the Original Nature Man's reputation for history, except for what Taylor and the other witnesses found after its conclusion.

I'd read all the stories about Joe in the papers and believed every one of them but on our way out of the woods we went by Lost Pond and everyone noticed a nice, tight, little log cabin up at the far end. It had only been there a few months, the peeled logs hadn't even started to change color.

Now, Lost Pond was where Joe had said that he'd spent quite a bit of his time while he was in the woods and when the members of this bear hauling party asked Joe about the little camp, he said he didn't know it was there. Out behind it was a pile of beer bottles and tin cans about four feet high.

Lost Pond is small and almost round. I don't think there was one spot on the shore from which you couldn't see that camp. Joe was lying to us. I lost all faith in him right there.

I never saw Joe's bow or arrow or any of his tools, but I did see his basket. It had two bullet holes in it. That had bothered me before, but the Lost Pond camp clinched it. He was a fake.

The opinions of teenage boys notwithstanding, the notary made his declaration, and Knowles embarked on his vaudeville tour in triumph.

Alone in the Wilderness came out in December 1913, only about two months after Joe had come out himself. It contains relatively few details of his day-to-day existence in the forest, but the author filled 295 pages with his observations about life, the Boy Scouts, his mother, his past, and his philosophical attitudes toward art and nature. At the end of the book he presented a proposal that he thought was of "international importance and magnitude." He would establish a College of Nature, where young men could dwell for a time to learn the secrets of the woods and how to live a simple life.

Alone in the Wilderness proved immensely popular, despite the digressiveness and murky thinking of its author. Three hundred thousand copies were sold. Even *The Nation*'s book reviewer had high praise for it, albeit he complained about Joe's grammar and diction and his conclusions, which "are set forth in a disorganized, slapdash manner, and, when related with the author's intentions regarding his future, are fatuous."

Nothing ever came of the chlorophyll college, but eleven months after the start of the Maine experiment, Knowles was at it again. In late July 1914, he went into the Siskiyou Mountains of Oregon. This time he was sponsored by a Hearst paper, the *San Francisco Ex-*

aminer. WILD BEASTS ROAR INVITATION TO JOE KNOWLES, one *Examiner* headline read. He was once more scheduled to spend sixty days in the wilderness, and just so there would be no hint of scandal, this time he was accompanied by two naturalists.

Alas, it was not to be. After Joe had been wandering around in his G-string for only a week, Austria had the temerity to declare war on Serbia. The kaiser, afraid of being upstaged, hurriedly declared war on Russia, and before long Britain and France had entered the fray. Knowles went from being first-page news to last-page news overnight. What was the use of conducting a Man versus Nature test if no one cared about the outcome? Joe put on his pants, collected his professors, and walked back to town.

Some twenty-four months later, he tried it once more. This time his sponsor was yet another Hearst paper, the *New York Journal.* The world was a far more jaded place than it had been in 1913, however, and a sixty-day Tarzan in a jockstrap would hardly raise an eyebrow after two years of the Great War. A new gimmick was necessary. This was found in the person of Elaine Hammerstein, "the beautiful society leader and well-known actress," as the *Journal* introduced her to its readers. She was to be the "Dawn Woman" to his "Dawn Man," and after a week of receiving his instruction in wilderness living, she was to go with him into a wooded region of Essex County. The reporters loved it, and Miss Hammerstein may have enjoyed the attention much more than she did learning about edible roots and making fires by rubbing two sticks together. Knowles thought so, anyway. She seemed to lose a little more of her enthusiasm each day she attended his noncredit single-pupil school of nature.

Still, she insisted to reporters that she was game to try.

Stewart H. Holbrook describes how "boozy cameramen shot the pretty girl in all sorts of semi-Dawn attire; and they also snapped Joe in all his Cro-Magnon nakedness." Having missed their chance in Boston, the Hearst chain pulled out all the stops. Editors were unwilling to risk the treachery of understatement. The would-be Tarzan and Jane were given a two-headline sendoff. KNOWLES HURLS DEFY AT GRIM NATURE! was one lead; the other blared, DAWN GIRL SLIPS NAKED INTO DARK FOREST! That must have caused a few coffee cups to rattle around Sunday-morning breakfast tables. Of course, there was never any need to worry over Miss Hammerstein's honor: her mother had been along from the start. In fact, Mrs. Hammerstein had been at her daughter's side from the first moment she met the Primitive Man.

"Tango teas, Broadway, and matinees are a far cry from the absolute of the great woods," the Dawn Girl inscribed on a piece of birch bark left for a *Journal* correspondent. Possibly just a little too far — within a week Elaine and her mother slipped back to their convenience-filled home on Riverside Drive.

"She just couldn't take it," Joe said mournfully. This time around, reporters had had little interest in him, pushing past him to get to the young woman. Without her he would be relegated to the back pages once more. There was nothing for it but to put on his pants again and go home. He packed his bearskin in mothballs — this time for good.

Joseph Knowles put aside his charcoal sticks, bear-hair brushes, and wild-berry paints and went back to using manmade art supplies. His landscapes, drawings, and murals remained in demand for the rest of his life. His celebrity had seen to that.

He drifted out to the Pacific Northwest, eventually settling on the Washington coast near a place appropriately called Seaview. He built a shack out of what he told visitors was timber from the hulls of wrecked ships.

In 1920 Fred Lockley, a correspondent for *American Magazine,* was hiking between Ilwaco and Long Beach when he came upon the rustic shelter and a curious figure standing before it, hanging split salmon on a line to dry. Feeling that he had seen the odd fellow somewhere before, Lockley engaged him in conversation. Joe was not reticent about revealing his identity: "I used to be more or less in the public eye before the war," he admitted quickly. He was still his old self, railing against an effete culture, bragging about his exploits, and promoting his vision of a benevolent nature. He never could stand to be in a city for very long, he said. He always heard the call of the wild echoing down the mean streets, and when he could bear no more of the "sordidness and futility" of urban life, he would strike out for the forest.

Time and again I have entered the woods both in Maine and out here on the Pacific coast with the clothing I had when I was born. Naked and without a manmade thing, I depend upon Nature, who, if we will but realize it, is our friend and protector. The moment you have left the haunts of man, the high cost of living and all such other artificial problems vanish. We have gone stale by living within brick walls and by depending upon steam heat and push buttons. Our woodcraft instincts have atrophied through lack of use.

Why should a white man lost in the woods in the winter lie down and freeze, when a savage will live on the fat of the land? What do I do first when I leave so-called civilization? I arrange to get something to eat; then some place to sleep, and then something to wear. It is all so simple that I cannot see why so many people make a mystery of it.

He rambled on in this fashion at considerable length, giving a great deal of instruction in the art of wilderness survival. Lockley did not mind; he was as gullible and admiring as most newspaper readers — and reporters — had been seven years before. He did learn one fresh piece of news: the longtime bachelor had finally tied the matrimonial knot. Whether or not Mrs. Knowles traipsed through the brush in her pale altogether beside her nude Primitive Man was a matter about which Mr. Lockley failed to inquire. History is ill served by witnesses who allow their modesty to restrain their curiosity.

Before Lockley resumed his march, Joe was at pains to tell him how much he enjoyed living the simple life beside the sea. For the moment, at least, he felt a profound sense of contentment, although, of course, wanderlust might strike him at any time; he was not willing to say he would nevermore roam, that he had finally reached port. Who knew when the "lure of the far horizon" might stir in him again? Until then he would be here, smoking fish for his wife to can for the winter.

"I don't know whether the public has forgotten Joe Knowles, the nature man, or not," he remarked with apparent indifference to the reporter from *American Magazine*. But, of course, in this he was being uncharacteristically modest. His fellow citizens never did forget him. All the rest of his life he received fan letters from those who remembered his wilderness exploits, and many a tourist managed to find his oceanside shack. They all wanted him to recount the old adventures, but after a time he seemed to grow weary of it. He eventually refused to answer the letters, and he would not retell the old tales for fawning visitors. The origin of this reluctance has never been satisfactorily explained. Perhaps, like modern celebrities, he became annoyed with the intrusions and the repetitive, often silly, and thoughtless demands. Or perhaps the reiteration of worn deceptions became too burdensome.

He was more cooperative with professional writers. They had once helped make his fortune, and they knew the rules, although even with them he tended to avoid detailed descriptions of the old days.

The war and the Great Depression had made them a more jaundiced group. Following the lead of Stewart Holbrook, they now were inclined to write about Joe with a whimsy and a wink, but their cynicism was always tempered with what seems genuine affection. Indeed, the discerning Mr. Holbrook was no more immune to Knowles's charm than anyone else. In 1936, he made his way to Joe's home in Seaview, where the "wild Pacific breakers pound his door yard and high tides surround his studio, [and] where he paints and does etchings." He found Knowles, then sixty-nine years old, to be "hearty" and "jovial." Joe professed to harbor no lingering animosity toward those who had once sought to debunk his exploits, and looking back over his life, he had only two regrets. One involved his failure to bring off a planned theatrical entrance into Megantic, and the other had to do with the abrupt termination of his second sojourn in the forest: "I'm still sorry I didn't manage to catch a bear cub, up there in Maine," he told Holbrook wistfully. "It would have been a knockout — parading out of that timber a-leading a bear like a Scottie. It's just about the only regret I have. . . . That and that goddam war breaking out when it did."

In 1973, Helon Taylor thought that there was something else unfortunate about those wilderness adventures: "Joe was a great woodsman," the retired park superintendent said. "I'm sure he could have done everything he said he did. My big regret is that he didn't. And I don't know why. I guess he was just too lazy. Isn't it too bad."

But the Primitive Man had sold a lot of newspapers, and so journalists, who were always looking for a gimmick to boost circulation or a story to fill two columns on a slow day, were inclined to be more charitable. Joe in his bearskin outfit was, thought Stewart Holbrook, "Steve Brodie, Nellie Bly, and Stanley-and-Livingstone all rolled into one."

If he was drinking beer in a cabin when he said he was running naked in the rain, whom did he hurt? He inspired a lot of youngsters and changed the way many adults perceived the wilderness. He drew attention to the back-to-nature movement and told Americans in dramatic terms that they were too dependent upon technology, too fixated upon luxury, too oriented toward materialism; he showed that they could simplify their lives and find meaning in that which was natural and free. If he could do all this and put some money in his pocket at the same time, where was the harm?

Joseph Knowles died at the age of seventy-three in Seaview, Washington, on October 22, 1942. The Associated Press carried the news of his demise nationwide. One of his home-state papers, the *Portland Press Herald,* wrote a gentle obituary that glossed over all those ancient charges of chicanery. The headline read, JOE KNOWLES, WHO CONQUERED MAINE WOODS HAZARDS, DIES. Another headline in the same paper termed him the MAINE WOODS VICTOR.

The Original Nature Man would have been pleased.

The Sands' Glorious Prisoner

Antoine de Saint-Exupéry
Down on the Libyan Desert

Clark Gable is a black market-eer, amassing a vast fortune and lounging in bordellos while half a million men die for a cause. Humphrey Bogart is content to manage his saloon and fence stolen goods while the Nazis overrun Europe. Harrison Ford is a graverobber, stealing the religious artifacts of ancient cultures for pay. Ours is the age of the antihero. We distrust the self-sacrificial; the principled have no attraction for us. We prefer the wealthy — and if they get their loot dishonestly or dishonorably, so much the better.

It was not always so.

The debacles of amateur explorers diminished the public's enthusiasm for polar ventures and for the explorer as hero. Perhaps it was just as well: the politicians and presidents of geographic societies who had to fund the expeditions — and the many rescue missions that sometimes followed — were disenchanted, too, and turned to dispassionate scientists and steady, methodical professionals. How could such cautious types enthrall the collective imaginations of entire nations? Yet there is ever a need for heroes, and the vacuum was quickly filled by a new one: the dauntless, daring, solitary aviator.

Any number of men and women were responsible for the emergence of this new hero. Combat pilots, barnstormers, and airmail fliers won the admiration and even the adulation of people all over the world, fixing in their minds the notions of the pilot as the last real adventurer and the sky as the last realm of unfettered freedom, a permanent frontier — boundless, infinite, and pure.

The Great War was the stage on which the aviator made his grand entrance. Combat pilots thought of themselves, or would come to be thought of, as the knights of the air. On the ground, soldiers lived in foul trenches for years at a time, fought over narrow strips of terrain, gassed one another, and charged machine guns, but aviators with scarves for plumes soared through the heavens, far above all the mud and mad carnage. Hell, when they went into battle, they *dueled* one another.

Mustered out after the armistice, many of the military fliers came home, bought surplus Jennies for a few hundred dollars, and took up barnstorming. They buzzed towns and landed in farmers' fields. They drew crowds with their "aerobatics," and then collected a dollar each from the rubes for a few minutes' ride in the sky. With other barnstormers they formed "flying circuses" and put on shows. They became adept at publicity and, in an intensely competitive profession, self-promotion. That was what you had to do: you got people excited about flying and got them to remember your name, or you got into another line of work. You made them gasp and point, or you bought yourself a pair of bib overalls and found a job in a factory.

To keep the crowds coming back, barnstormers had to devise new and ever more spectacular stunts. They looped the loop, hung by their toes on trapezes swinging under fuselages, and walked on wings — or roller-skated or rode bicycles on them. Sometimes they sewed parachutes out of hotel bed sheets, but all too often they wore no parachutes at all. When they lost their grip or their feet slipped or the wind snatched them away, they died. If their aircraft caught fire, they jumped, preferring the fall to the flames. Their planes stalled and went into nose dives, crashed into buildings, collided with other aircraft, or had wings torn off by tree limbs and church steeples. The list of dead daredevils is eloquent in its disheartening length.

The likelihood of death should have ended barnstorming, kept the crowds away, caused the fliers to quit — but it did not. Too many gawkers came just in the hopes of seeing an accident. As for the pilots, you could not go aloft and do the things they did if you had any reasonable fear, any self-doubts. You had to believe in your skills and reflexes and in your luck. Besides, the sky was exhilarating freedom. Those who toiled on the ground were ants to those among the clouds.

Other forces were working to make the aviator the last sovereign and the heavens the final terrain of freedom. Carrying the mail by plane meant livelihoods for pilots and profits for new companies. Entrepreneurs saw the possibilities of commercial flight for shipping goods and transporting passengers. War heroes like Captain Eddie Rickenbacker, America's "Ace of Aces," and celebrity fliers like Charles A. Lindbergh became executives of airline companies and promoted aviation through speeches, articles, books, and publicity-generating flights.

Governments and private parties offered prizes to open up new routes or cut time on the old ones. Here again pilots showed a shrewd ability to promote themselves and aviation. Consider Charles Lindbergh. We think of him as a shy man, extremely uncomfortable in the glare of publicity — but that was after he became famous. Certainly the extraordinary attention given him by a voracious press and an adoring but demanding public made him uneasy, yet he was a man who knew how to command attention and what to do with it once he got it. After all, his early days of flying had been as a barnstormer, and he had rakishly billed himself as "Daredevil Lindbergh"; but more revealing was his solo flight to Paris. He had flown the Atlantic ostensibly to win the $25,000 Orteig Prize, and to claim it he had only to set down his aircraft anywhere in France. He might have landed, in other words, as soon as he reached the coast, but, despite having been aloft for thirty-three hours and having flown nearly 3,500 miles, he elected to proceed to Paris, where a huge crowd and not a few photographers and newsreel cameramen would be waiting.

Thus by the age of twenty-five he had become a confidant of kings and presidents, European aristocrats and American industrialists. He was also undoubtedly one of the most famous men in the United States — indeed, in the entire Western world. The flight across the Atlantic won him the Distinguished Flying Cross, the Congressional Medal of Honor (the first time it had been awarded for a "feat unconnected with war"), two million fan letters, a ticker-tape parade watched by four million people, and lasting acclaim. His books were bought, his words were given rapt attention, and, the ultimate accolade, he was portrayed on the movie screen by Jimmy Stewart. All of this was his essentially because he had managed to remain off the ground for thirty-three and a half hours straight.

Nothing he did the rest of his life tarnished his reputation or affected his standing with the American public. That he was duped by the Nazi high command and became a leader of the misguided isolationist movement mattered not at all. He was a living embodiment of the aviator as hero, and his exploits fed the public's infatuation with flight. He had his share of crashes, of course, perhaps the worst of which was a midair collision from which he had to parachute to safety, but these mishaps did not diminish his admirers' enthusiasm for aviation or result in their affixing a codicil of caution to his legend.

Ironically, for many fliers the numerous and terrible accidents they suffered, like the scars on the faces of professional hockey players, served only to enhance their fame and add to their glory. One thinks of Rickenbacker, for instance, who, despite all his accomplishments as a wartime pilot and peacetime entrepreneur, would probably come to be best known to his contemporaries for two of the plane crashes he survived. The first of these occurred in 1941, while he was a passenger on one of his own airliners. The fog was thick, and the plane slammed into the side of a hill. Rickenbacker was pinned in the wreckage and was lying underneath the corpse of a flight attendant. His pelvis, left elbow, and left knee were shattered, a half-dozen ribs were broken, and one eyelid was torn in half so that the eyeball lay on his cheek. He took charge of the survivors nevertheless, and for the next nine hours he comforted and cajoled them, sending some of the ambulatory injured for help and keeping others from lighting matches in the fume-filled fuselage.

Less than eighteen months later, while still recuperating from the first accident, he was in a second one. While Rickenbacker was on a secret wartime mission for the United States government, his aircraft ran out of fuel and went down in the Pacific. Although he was a civilian and, at fifty-two, a good deal older than most of the servicemen in the rafts with him, he once again took charge. He gave orders, conducted prayer meetings, rationed supplies, and kept the castaways from giving up. Many of the survivors would attribute their having made it to "Captain Eddie's" leadership.

The twenty-two-day ordeal so contributed to his renown that Rickenbacker's book about it became a phenomenal best seller, and he was touted as a presidential candidate. So undaunted was he by these disasters that, just a few years after the second crash, he sold his beloved Indianapolis Speedway so that he could give even more time to convincing the public of the safety of flight.

This is something we have encountered before and will again: the resolute refusal of the survivor to learn from his ordeal and change the pattern of his behavior to avoid further misfortunes. As with sailors of earlier centuries, this may bespeak in the aviator a cavalier attitude toward fate or a denial of reality, or it may mean that most pioneering pilots had no other marketable skills and so felt themselves trapped. Yet celebrities like Lindbergh and Rickenbacker, whose sudden fame assured them wealth and job security while they were still young, continued to fly. The writings of the onetime airmail and test pilot Antoine de Saint-Exupéry were so successful that he could easily have settled down to a life before a typewriter, but he refused to do this. His psyche was bound inextricably to flying. No matter how many times he crashed or how many of his comrades died in crashes, he would not forsake what he felt to be his calling. The lasting, numerous accident-related injuries he suffered were such that as a middle-aged man he was extremely uncomfortable sitting in a cockpit, yet he went on doing so. When the Second World War broke out, he twice volunteered to serve in air corps; each time his friends, concerned for his welfare, tried to have him grounded, he pulled strings to keep his assignments. Thus he pursued his vocation ardently and faithfully until his plane went down for the last time.

If the aviator has become an authentic twentieth-century hero, he has also become the quintessential modern survivor. And if early fliers possessed the commitment to remain at their occupations, no matter how many of their friends and colleagues vanished from flights never to be seen again, so their bravado is reflected even in contemporary recreational pilots who insist on going aloft despite the statistics on small-plane accidents.

"In moments of danger," Saint-Exupéry wrote, "a man does not think of himself." He might have added that what he himself thought about was his duty, his comrades, and his family. For him a flier had a calling that was almost religious in nature. To lose one's nerve, to abandon aviation out of fear for one's safety, was tantamount to sacrilege.

In his life he had a number of opportunities to test his philosophy, and he never found it wanting. He experienced his first serious accident in 1923, when he was only twenty-two years old: his aircraft ran out of fuel and crashed near Paris. His skull was fractured, and he was carried unconscious to a hospital. He awoke believing that he had died and studied his strange surroundings with curiosity and detachment.

Ten years later, he was a test pilot of an amphibious plane that slammed into the sea and sank, carrying him down with it. He would have drowned in the submerged fuselage had it not been for an air bubble trapped in the cockpit. Yet all he said about the near-fatal accident was this: "Nothing is intolerable. I thought one day I was going to drown, imprisoned in a cabin, and I didn't suffer very much."

In 1938 he was again in a terrible crash, although this time he did not escape serious injury. He and his mechanic, André Prévot, were on a pioneering flight from New York to Cape Horn when their aircraft went down. Prévot had his leg broken and was knocked unconscious. Saint-Exupéry was even more badly hurt: he received a concussion, multiple skull fractures, a cracked shoulder bone, a broken wrist, and facial lacerations. So extensive was the damage to his left arm that he had great difficulty keeping the doctors from amputating it. His convalescence was a long one, and he never fully recovered.

These are only the highlights of his experiences as a downed aviator. Just how many times he found himself stranded in the Sahara, where nomads murdered Europeans or held them for ransom, no one has ever ascertained. Certainly Saint-Ex, as his friends called him, never kept count. It did not matter how many times you crashed; what mattered was the freedom of flying.

The repeated brushes with death, far from frightening him, actually seemed to give him a feeling of ease and a reaffirmation of his existence. He had long since given up conventional religion, but in these moments he sensed, as he said of yet another near-fatal accident, "a new undefinable intelligence"; he glimpsed a "world from which one does not often return to describe." Recalling the serenity with which his beloved fifteen-year-old brother accepted terminal illness, he wrote, "One does not die . . . There is no more death when one meets it. When the body breaks apart, the essential is revealed. Man is only a knot of relationships."

Airmail pilots were tough individuals in a hazardous occupation. In the early days, planes sometimes literally fell apart in the sky. The wind tore off their wings, and cyclones and tornadoes dashed them to the ground. Pilots made navigational errors, became lost, and ran out of fuel. They bailed out in snowstorms thousands of feet above the unseen and unknown terrain. Mechanical problems forced them to land, and if their craft did not crack up or slam into trees, they repaired them as well as they could and took off again. (Saint-Ex was required to study airplane mechanics before he was allowed to fly mail for his first employer; the knowledge would come in handy on more than a few occasions.) Aviators greeted these unhappy prospects with casual shrugs. Theirs was the studied indifference of those for whom risk is, if not routine, at least familiar and expected.

Thus Saint-Exupéry was hardly overstating the case when he claimed that pilots were a rare and singular breed. He cited, for example, his great friend Jean Mermoz. Mermoz had become a "prisoner of the Andes" when his aircraft was forced down on a plateau some twelve thousand feet above sea level. For two days he and his mechanic searched for a way to climb off the plateau, but they could find no path on its sheer sides. In desperation they "played their last card":

> Themselves still in it, they sent the plane rolling and bouncing down an incline over the rocky ground until it reached the precipice, and went off into the air, and dropped. In falling, the plane picked up enough speed to respond to the controls. Mermoz was able to tilt its nose in the direction of a peak, sweep over the peak, and, while the water spurted through all the pipes burst by the night frost, the ship already disabled after only seven minutes of flight, he saw beneath him like a promised land the Chilean plain.

Saint-Exupéry collected survival stories such as this one from fellow aviators. They seemed both to have increased his sense of awe toward those with whom he flew and to have heightened his mysticism. Like the tales that sailors preserved in oral traditions and chanteys, they inspired him and provided him with practical information valuable during his own ordeals. One story in particular would come to be profoundly important to him. It concerned another close friend, Henri Guillaumet, who had also gone down in the Andes. When Saint-Ex was wandering in the Libyan desert, he would remember the things Guillaumet told him of his experience in the mountains, and they would play a crucial role in shaping his behavior.

Guillaumet had run out of fuel in a snowstorm and crashed as he tried to set down his ship. He dragged himself out of the cockpit, but the wind was so strong that he could not stand. He dug a cave in the snow and waited for two days and two nights until the storm blew over. Then he started to make his way out of the mountains. He was at an altitude of fifteen thousand feet, and the temperature was twenty degrees below zero. Without climbing gear or boots or provisions of any kind, he had to crawl down sheer vertical walls of rock. His hands and feet quickly became torn and bloody, and he lost feeling in them; he was forced to cut his shoes open ever wider because his frozen feet kept swelling. On the less steep slopes his worst moments came when he fell. Each time he lay in the snow, he felt an overwhelming desire to give up and fall asleep.

"Amid snow," he told Saint-Ex later,

> a man loses his instinct of self-preservation. After two or three or four days of tramping, all you think about is sleep. I would long for it; but then I would say to myself, "If my wife still believes I am alive, she must believe that I am on my feet. The boys all think I am on my feet. They have faith in me. And I am a skunk if I don't go on."

As he staggered forward, Guillaumet fought against pain. He tried to focus on other things, but pain always intruded. He found that recollections of movies and books were the best distractions. "But the film and the book would go through my mind like lightning, and I'd be back where I was, in the snow. It never failed. So I would think about other things."

Once he fell flat on his face — and gave up. He told himself that he had done his best and could not make it. He was relieved to feel himself falling asleep . . . but then he thought again of his wife. If his body was not found, the law would prevent her from collecting his insurance for four long years, and she would be penniless for all that time. His dying there would mean that the waters of the spring thaw would wash his corpse into a crevasse, where it would disappear forever. But fifty yards ahead of him was a rock; if he could reach it and prop himself against it, his body would be spotted after the snows were gone. His wife could collect the money if he made it to that boulder. He got to his feet — and went on for three more days and two more nights.

Not long before the conclusion of his ordeal, he sensed that he was near death.

> I could tell by different signs that the end was coming. For instance, I had to stop every two or three hours to cut my shoes open a bit more and massage my swollen feet. Or maybe my heart would be

going too fast. But I was beginning to lose my memory. I had been
going on a long time when suddenly I realized that every time I
stopped I forgot something. The first time it was a glove. And it was
cold! I had put it down in front of me and had forgotten to pick it up.
The next time it was my watch. Then my knife. Then my compass.
Each time I stopped I stripped myself of something vitally important.
I was becoming my own enemy! And I can't tell you how it hurt me
when I found that out.

What saves a man is to take a step. Then another step. It is always
the same step, but you have to take it.

I swear that what I went through, no animal would have gone
through.

With nothing to eat, after three days on my feet . . . well . . . my
heart wasn't going any too well. I was crawling along the side of a
sheer wall, hanging over space, digging and kicking out pockets in
the ice so that I could hold on, when all of a sudden my heart conked.
It hesitated. Started up again. Beat crazily. I said to myself, "If it
hesitates a moment too long, I drop." I stayed still and listened to
myself. Never, never in my life have I listened as carefully to a motor
as I listened to my heart, me hanging there. I said to it: "Come on,
old boy. Go to work. Try beating a little." That's good stuff my heart
is made of. It hesitated, but it went on. You don't know how proud I
was of that heart.

The Chilean authorities had told the other French pilots that it
was pointless to search for their comrade because the Andes never
gives up its dead, but after five days and four nights Guillaumet was
found alive. His skin had been badly burned by the glare of the sun
on the snow; he was shriveled and "shrunken into an old woman."
Back among his friends he sat on a cot, panting for breath. His feet
were dead weights and his hands were useless.

When Guillaumet fell asleep, Saint-Exupéry remained by the bed
watching him. Guillaumet's face was "splotched and swollen, like
an overripe fruit that has been repeatedly dropped on the ground."
He twisted and thrashed in his sleep, unable to be at ease:

> When you turned and stirred on the pillow in search of peace, a
> procession of images that you could not escape, a procession waiting
> impatiently in the wings, moved instantly into action under your
> skull. Across the stage of your skull it moved, and for the twentieth
> time you fought once more the battle against these enemies that rose
> up out of their ashes.

Saint-Ex studied the restless, sleeping form. Guillaumet had
shown tremendous courage in the Andes; however, what was most

admirable about him was not his bravery but his commitment — to his profession, his comrades, and his family. To be a man, thought Saint-Exupéry, is to feel "responsible for that new element which the living are constructing and in which [one is] a participant. It is to feel shame at the sight of what seems to be unmerited misery. It is to take pride in a victory won by one's comrades. It is to feel, when setting one's stone, that one is contributing to the building of the world."

Five years later it would be Saint-Ex's turn to crash and thus test again his courage and his commitment to life and to those he loved.

It would happen while he was attempting to break the record of ninety-eight hours, fifty-two minutes, for the Paris–Saigon run. Such races were fairly common then, and the French government had encouraged this one with a prize of 150,000 francs. The only stipulation was that the record be broken by December 31, 1935. Saint-Exupéry had received the financial backing of the newspaper *L'Intransigeant* in return for promising to write an article about the flight. He had had hurried modifications made to his beloved Simoun airplane (which he seems to have won in an earlier competition), but the weather in late December prevented takeoff until the twenty-ninth. At dawn Saint-Ex and Prévot set the Simoun rolling down the runway.

Late at night, three and a half hours out of Benghazi, they began to wonder if they were off course. They should have been approaching the Nile Valley, but a cloud cover prevented their seeing any landmarks. After four hours and five minutes in the air, Saint-Exupéry took the Simoun into a slow descent in the hope that they would slip beneath the clouds and be able to spot the Nile River or the lights of Cairo or *something* from which to get their bearings. The altimeter read twelve hundred feet, but he dared not descend further. The clouds hid the horizon. He decided to take the plane out to sea — if they were not already over the water. Saint-Ex pressed his face against the window and peered down. "I was a man raking dead ashes, trying in vain to retrieve the flame of life in a hearth."

The two men glimpsed the lighthouse at the same time. It was nine hundred feet below them. . . . An instant later, traveling at 170 miles per hour, their aircraft slammed into the earth. It should have blown up in that first second, but it did not. Prévot was calm as he waited for immediate death, but Saint-Exupéry was tense with expectancy: they were about to vanish into a "resplendent star." And yet the seconds ticked by and they remained alive. Still skidding across the desert floor, the Simoun shuddered and shook and then began to spin; it was a bomb that did not explode.

"Jump!" Saint-Ex cried. They dived through a shattered window and found themselves standing sixty feet from the fuselage. Each man ran his hands over his body, feeling for injuries and wounds, but there were none. Prévot had banged his knee on the emergency pump — that was all.

They walked back in the furrow created by the plane. It ran for more than 250 yards. Their ship had stayed together because the surface of the desert was not fine sand but round, black pebbles, "which had rolled over and over like ball bearings beneath us. They must have rained upward to the heavens as we shot through them."

While Prévot disconnected the batteries to prevent a fire, Saint-Exupéry leaned against the motor and assessed their situation. The lighthouse had been an illusion, a "winking decoy," an "invention of the night." They were nowhere near the sea. They had come down somewhere in the middle of the Libyan desert, with 250 miles of sand between them and civilization, no matter which direction they went.

Prévot sat down beside him and said, "I can't believe that we're alive."

Saint-Ex did not reply. He switched on his electric torch and walked slowly away from the Simoun, studying the terrain as he went. He changed directions repeatedly, keeping "my eyes fixed on the ground like a man hunting for a lost ring. Through the darkness I went, bowed over the traveling disk of white light." He returned to Prévot with gloomy news: he had not seen a single sign of life. In the accident all the water containers had burst, and the earth had immediately soaked up the water. The only liquid remaining was a pint of coffee and half a pint of white wine, the only food a few grapes and an orange. Saint-Exupéry knew that these supplies would not last them more than five hours if they attempted to trek across the desert, and he had once been told that a man down on the Libyan sands could not last nineteen hours without water.

They crawled into the cabin and waited for the dawn. Saint-Ex could not sleep; he kept thinking about their predicament:

We didn't know where we were; we had less than a quart of liquid between us; if we were not too far off the Benghazi–Cairo lane we should be found in a week, and that would be too late. Yet it was the best we could hope for. If, on the other hand, we had drifted off our course, we shouldn't be found in six months. One thing was sure — we could not count on being picked up by a plane; the men who came out for us would have two thousand miles to cover.

Prévot must have been having similar thoughts, because he suddenly remarked that it was too bad they had not crashed properly and thus had a quick end to things. Once the sentiment was voiced, they both realized that it was too soon to give up. They had to pull themselves together. There was at least a slim chance that they would be found, and an oasis might be nearby. They agreed to set out in the morning and walk all day. If they found nothing, they would return to the fuselage by nightfall.

Having a plan was comforting. Saint-Exupéry happily lay down to go to sleep.

My weariness wrapped round me like a multiple presence. I was not alone in the desert: my drowsiness was peopled with voices and memories and whispered confidences. I was not yet thirsty; I felt strong; and I surrendered myself to sleep as to an aimless journey. Reality lost ground before the advance of dreams.

In the morning they walked in an easterly direction. This was an irrational choice. Convinced now that they had flown far enough to have crossed the Nile, they were certain that the proper course lay to the west. But when they struck out that way, Saint-Ex had felt a vague foreboding. The sea should be to the north, but he did not want to go that way, either. Guillaumet had gone east and had escaped from the Andes, and so Saint-Exupéry and his mechanic would go that way, too: "In a confused way the east had become for me the direction of life."

Everywhere they looked, the desert was covered with that layer of black, glistening pebbles. They glinted like metal scales and made the dunes shine as if they were covered in coats of mail. "We had dropped down into a mineral world and were hemmed in by iron hills." The aviators scraped their boots as they walked to mark a trail that they could follow to return to the Simoun.

They had been marching for five hours when they struck what appeared to be a riverbed. After walking beside it for some time, Saint-Ex suddenly realized that they had long since ceased to mark their trail. Their Thermoses were back at the ship, and if they were to live they would have to find it. They doubled back, working at an angle until they intersected their tracks. Then they strode forward again, being careful to leave a trail.

The heat assaulted them, and they saw mirages — most often sheets of water that appeared and disappeared quite suddenly. At the end of the sixth hour, they calculated that they had marched twenty miles. They struggled up the highest dune they could find to survey the surrounding terrain for signs of life.

> At our feet lay our valley of sand, opening into a desert of sand whose dazzling brightness seared our eyes. As far as the eye could see lay empty space. But in that space the play of light created mirages which, this time, were of a disturbing kind, fortresses and minarets, angular geometric hulks. I could see also a black mass that pretended to be vegetation, overhung by the last of those clouds that dissolve during the day only to return at night. This mass of vegetation was the shadow of a cumulus.
>
> It was no good going on. The experiment was a failure. We would have to go back to our plane, to that red and white beacon which, perhaps, would be picked out by a flier. I was not staking great hopes on a rescue party, but it did seem to me our last chance of salvation. In any case, we had to go back to our few drops of liquid, for our throats were parched. We were imprisoned in this iron circle, captives of the curt dictatorship of thirst.
>
> And yet, how hard it was to turn back when there was a chance that we might be on the road to life! Beyond the mirages the horizon was perhaps rich in veritable treasures, in meadows and runnels of sweet water. I knew I was doing the right thing by returning to the plane, and yet as I swung round and started back I was filled with portents of disaster.

They drank the last of the coffee and the wine when they reached the Simoun. They wondered how long they could stay alive. Only twenty-four hours had passed since the crash and already their thirst was terrible.

They built a pyre out of pieces of wing. They poured gasoline on it and added bits of metal with a magnesium coating, which gave off a white light as it burned. They watched the flames rise and hoped someone would see them. Studying the fire, Saint-Exupéry told himself that it constituted not only a call for help but a message of love as well. He and his friend were crying out for water, to be sure, but they were also begging for the communion of fellow human beings. A fire in the distance could only mean that another man had seen their pyre. They strained to see such an answer — but there was none.

Saint-Ex imagined he saw his wife's face in the flames; he looked into her eyes, "under the halo of her hat." She seemed to be questioning him and looking at him with yearning. He tried to reply, to communicate with her. . . .

He realized that Prévot was weeping and attempted to console him with the inexorableness of fate: if they were done for, they were done for. But Prévot was not "bawling" for fear of death. He was thinking only of his family, of the grief and loss they would suffer. Saint-Exupéry understood. He imagined he heard the "cry that would be sent up at home, that great wail of desolation — that was what I could not bear." Their being lost was hurting their loved ones. Raging, he felt that he needed to save his family as a rescuer would people who were drowning.

The fire died down, and squatting over the embers for warmth, he promised that he would not readily accept death, that he would escape for the sake of those he loved.

At dawn they wiped the dew off the wings with a rag and wrung it out. There was only a spoonful of liquid — water mixed with paint and oil — and it nauseated them. This "banquet" did not seem to improve Prévot's disposition at all. He casually remarked that at least they had a gun. Saint-Ex flared and turned on him. This was no time for despair. Anyway, dying of thirst would be no more complicated than being born. But Prévot was not brooding or sorrowful; he merely recognized with a cold dispassion that suicide might become necessary.

Saint-Exupéry had to admit that he, too, had already eyed the leather holster. It was not an emotional response for him, either, but a rational one: "Pathos resides in social man, not in the individual; what was pathetic was our powerlessness to reassure those for whom we were responsible, not what we might do with the gun."

They decided that Prévot would stay with the aircraft that day and prepare another signal fire in case a search plane came over. Saint-Ex would go out again, reconnoitering for an oasis. He set off soon after daybreak with his hands in his pockets, "like a tramp on a highroad." He thought that the chances of Prévot's fire being seen were slim indeed. The searchers would have a vast expanse to cover. To them the men below would be little more than two dots among "the thousand shadowy dots in the desert." No doubt they were looking for them along their planned route, and Saint-Exupéry was now firmly convinced that the Simoun had been carried far off that.

He had been down in the desert before, of course, quite a few times. But that was in the Sahara, which he loved. "I had spent nights alone in the path of marauding tribes and have waked up with an untroubled mind in the golden emptiness of the desert where the wind like a sea had raised sandwaves upon its surface. Asleep under the wing of my plane I have looked forward with confidence to being rescued the next day. But this was not the Sahara!" The humidity there was 40 percent, while in the Libyan desert it was 18 percent. After less than a day without water in this place, a man's

> eyes fill with light, and that marks the beginning of the end. The progress made by thirst is swift and terrible. But this northeast wind, this abnormal wind that had blown us out off our course and had marooned us on this plateau, was now prolonging our lives. What was the length of the reprieve it would grant us before our eyes began to fill with light? I went forward with the feeling of a man canoeing in mid-ocean.

The night before, Saint-Ex had set snares before some burrows he had found. Now, as he went on his way, he checked them, but they were all empty. He wondered about the creatures who lived beneath the ground. They were fennecs, he was sure, long-eared sand foxes no bigger than rabbits.

He came on the track of one of them and decided to follow it. He was in the desert with fewer than twenty-four hours to live and yet he could not stifle his curiosity. He actually

> marveled at the pretty palm formed by the three toes spread fanwise on the sand.
>
> I could imagine my little friend trotting blithely along at dawn and licking the dew off the rocks. Here the tracks were wider apart: my fennec had broken into a run. And now I see that a companion has joined him and they have trotted on side by side. These signs of a morning stroll gave me a strange thrill. They were signs of life, and I loved them for that. I almost forgot that I was thirsty.

Eventually Saint-Exupéry found their feeding ground, their "pasture." Shrubs were sticking out of the ground a hundred yards from each other, and attached to the twigs of every one were small golden snails. Here was something else to wonder at:

My fennec did not stop at all the shrubs. There were some weighed down with snails which he disdained. Obviously he avoided them with some wariness. Others he stopped at but did not strip them of all they bore. He must have picked out two or three shells and then gone on to another restaurant. What was he up to? Was he nurseman to the snails, encouraging their reproduction by refraining from exhausting the stock on a given shrub, or a given twig? Or was he amusing himself by delaying repletion, putting off satiety in order to enhance the pleasure he took from his morning stroll?

The tracks led to a hole in which he lived. Doubtless my fennec crouched below, listening to me and startled by the crunch of my footsteps. I said to him:

"Fox, my little fox, I'm done for; but somehow that doesn't prevent me from taking an interest in your mood."

When at last Saint-Ex wearily resumed his march, he was soon wounded by mirages. The first appeared to be a man standing in the near distance. It proved to be a large rock. Next he saw a sleeping Bedouin, but as he stooped to awaken him, he found the prone form was a tree trunk. He was startled. A tree trunk in the desert? He touched its surface and discovered that it was made of black marble.

Straightening up I looked round and saw more black marble. An antediluvian forest littered the ground with its broken tree tops. How many thousand years ago, under what hurricane of the time of Genesis, had this cathedral of wood crumbled in this spot? Countless centuries had rolled these fragments of giant pillars at my feet, polished them like steel, petrified and vitrified them and indued them with the color of jet.

I could distinguish the knots in their branches, the twistings of their once living boughs, could count the rings of life in them. This forest had rustled with birds and been filled with music that now was struck by doom and frozen into salt. And all this was hostile to me. Blacker than the chain-mail of the hummocks, these solemn derelicts rejected me. What had I, a living man, to do with this incorruptible stone? Perishable as I was, I whose body was to crumble into dust, what place had I in this eternity?

He felt dizzy. The sun burned on him, glinted on the marble as if oil had been smeared on its surfaces. The desert was a gigantic anvil against which the sun hammered. He staggered on under the blows.

He saw another apparition, this one of an entire caravan moving along the horizon, and he cried out to it. He had to calm himself, talk to himself reasonably and out loud, to keep from running after it. Nothing was real in the desert, he said.

Now he saw a cross on a hill — but this must be real. He had studied a map by firelight the night before. On it had been marked a monastery, and nearby were permanent wells. The huge cross had been planted by Dominicans as a signal to those lost and dying on the sands. He would reach the gates of the monastery and pull on the bell rope. The monks would hurry out and pump water from the well and give him a great feast! He was trembling with joy.

But there was no cross on the hill and no monastery. He fought to keep back his tears.

He heard the sound of the sea and realized it was over the next dune. Then he saw a city on another dune and had to tell himself these were more illusions.

Of course I know it is a mirage! Am I the sort of man who can be fooled? But what if I *want* to go after that mirage? Suppose I enjoy indulging my hope? Suppose it suits me to love that crenelated town all beflagged with sunlight? What if I choose to walk straight ahead on light feet — for you must know that I have dropped my weariness behind me, I am happy now. . . . Prévot and his gun! Don't make me laugh! I prefer my drunkenness. I am drunk. I am dying of thirst.

Twilight sobered him. Suddenly he realized how far he was from the Simoun. In the fading light the illusions disappeared. "The horizon had stripped itself of its pomp, its palaces, its priestly vestments." He cursed himself for having wasted so much time. The darkness would soon hide his tracks, and so because of his foolishness he might not be able to find his way back to the aircraft that night. By morning the wind would have swept the sands clear of his footprints, and he would not know what course to take. Perhaps then he should just go forward; forget about Prévot and the plane and strike out for the sea. . . . But how far away was it? He might die long before he reached it. Prévot would be waiting — and, who knows, he might have been found by a caravan.

Saint-Exupéry decided to return to the plane. But first, standing on the empty sands, he shouted desperately for help. His voice was so hoarse he could do little more than croak, and he felt ridiculous. It did not matter. There was no one to hear his absurd cries.

He went back the way he had come.

Hours later, he saw the glow of the fire his worried friend had built to guide him in. It took him another hour of laborious trudging to bring him within fifty yards of the ship. He could see Prévot beside it and — he stopped dead in amazement — two Bedouins were with him. They were leaning against the motor, and all three of them were talking. They had not even noticed Saint-Ex. He was exhilarated, and his heart beat wildly. What a fool he had been to strike out that morning! How wasted his effort had been! If he had stayed with Prévot he "should have been saved already."

He cried out a greeting and went forward. The Arabs, startled, turned toward him and stared. Prévot left them and came to meet him. Saint-Exupéry babbled happily about their being saved by the Bedouins, and Prévot caught his arm and looked at him uneasily. Then he whispered reluctantly, "There are no Arabs here."

Saint-Ex felt tears fill his eyes.

They tore a parachute into six triangular sections, spread them out on the ground, and anchored them with stones to keep the wind from blowing them away. Then Prévot unhooked a fuel tank: they hoped to catch the morning dew on the pieces of cloth and store it in the tank. While he was working on the tank, he happened to find an orange, which he divided in half and shared. Saint-Exupéry lay by the fire, contemplating the "glowing" fruit. "Here we are, condemned to death," he thought, "and still the certainty of dying cannot compare with the pleasure I am feeling. The joy I take from this half an orange which I am holding in my hand is one of the greatest joys I have ever known."

He lay on his back and sucked on the orange and counted the shooting stars. In that moment he felt completely happy.

> For the first time I understood the cigarette and glass of rum that are handed to the criminal about to be executed. I used to think that for a man to accept these wretched gifts at the foot of the gallows was beneath human dignity. Now I was learning that he took pleasure from them. People thought him courageous when he smiled as he smoked or drank. I knew now that he smiled because the taste gave him pleasure. People could not see that his perspective had changed, and that for him the last hour of his life was a life in itself.

In the morning there were copious amounts of dew on the parachute sections; the men ended up with nearly two quarts of liquid in the metal tank. It was yellow-green in color, but Saint-Ex thought it quite lovely. The first drink of it nauseated him horribly. He was sure that mud would be more palatable. It was positively poisonous.

Prévot was walking in a tight circle with his eyes on the ground;

he appeared to Saint-Exupéry to be looking for a lost object. Just then the mechanic vomited, but he kept moving even while he retched. A moment later the pilot's stomach contracted so violently that he fell to his knees and dug his fingers into the sand, and then he was retching, too. For a quarter of an hour they both suffered dry heaves, and for a long time afterward they were nauseated.

They never knew whether their reaction was caused by the magnesium lining of the tank or the sizing in the parachute cloth, but either way their experiment with catching dew was over.

Also at an end were any delusions about being found by aerial searchers. However slim it might be, their only hope was to walk out. That was how Guillaumet had escaped from the Andes, and that was how they would get out of this place. Pilots had a deeply ingrained belief that a downed man should always stay with his plane because it was the larger object and therefore easier to spot. But if they remained where they were, they were dead men. There was nothing to do now but walk until they dropped. The sun came up as they started off.

"If I were alone in the world," Prévot said, "I'd lie down right here. Damned if I wouldn't."

Both felt that it was their families, not they, who were "shipwrecked." It was their loved ones who were fearful and grieving and brutalized by anxiety and dread. So the pilot and the mechanic walked toward these helpless "lost" ones, just as Guillaumet had before them. And they went east as he had, although they believed that their course would carry them deeper into the desert.

They hurried as if something were chasing them. Saint-Exupéry kept his eyes on the ground so that he would not see the excruciating mirages. The sun beat down on his head and seemed to be cooking his brain.

At twilight he realized that he could remember nothing of the day. All through it they had continued to feel pursued: there was a "wild beast stalking us, had us in its power. I could feel its breath in my face, could feel it lick my face and hands." He knew they should walk through the night as planned, but they agreed to make camp instead. He was sure he could last for only another five or six miles. He thought ruefully about how earlier in the ordeal he had walked those many miles, but now his strength was nearly gone.

Suddenly Prévot saw a lake. Saint-Ex told him he was mad, but he insisted. Mirages were a product of the sun, and now it had set.

The lake was real. It was only a twenty-minute stroll away. He was going to get a drink.

Saint-Exupéry lost his temper at the other man's mulishness. "Go ahead!" he shouted. "Take your little constitutional. Nothing better for a man. But let me tell you, if your lake exists it is salt. And whether it's salt or not, it's a devil of a way off. And besides, there is no damn lake!"

But Prévot, determined and glassy-eyed, had already left. He was in the grip of an irresistible obsession, Saint-Ex knew. He was like a somnambulist, and somnambulists were capable of walking into oncoming locomotives. He would not come back even when the lake disappeared. He would continue on until he dropped. "He was somewhere, and I was somewhere else. Not that that was important."

Saint-Exupéry lay face down on the ground, trying to write an imaginary letter for posthumous delivery. He had no saliva in his mouth and could not remember when he had last been able to spit. His lips were stuck together as if by glue, and they were covered with a thick crust. Yet he could still swallow, and his eyes had not filled with that bright, fatal light.

He rolled over onto his back. The moon in the night sky above him looked much larger than it had the night before. He thought of Prévot again and then found himself at sea. He was stretched out in a chair on a deck of a ship bound for South America. He was being carried along without any effort on his part.

He wondered dazedly over the fact that Prévot had not returned. Not once had the mechanic complained about their plight. "That was a good thing. To hear him whine would have been unbearable. Prévot was a man."

Then he saw the light. Prévot had lost his way and had turned on his electric torch. Saint-Ex had no light, no beacon for him, but he stood and shouted at him — even though he knew that his friend could not hear him. Then he saw a second light . . . and a third. It was a rescue party searching for him! He shouted, but the lamps did not come toward him. He knew he was not hallucinating. He was sane and clear-headed and calm, and there were men just five hundred yards away. He yelled and yelled, but they could not hear him.

Now, for the first time in the whole ordeal, he gave in to panic. He tried to run, managing only to stagger forward, screaming for the searchers to wait for him even as they moved farther away. He was "tottering, tottering on the brink of life when there were arms out there ready to catch me!" He stumbled on screaming, and then he heard an answering shout. He could not draw a breath, and he was strangling, but he went on until he saw Prévot, and then he fell face down.

"Whew!" he said to his friend as soon as he could speak again. "When I saw all those lights . . ."

And Prévot asked him, "What lights?"

The lamps were just another illusion. As for the lake, Prévot had pursued it for a half hour without ever getting any closer to it. Each time he took a step toward it, it retreated an equal distance. Yet he still insisted it was real.

"You're crazy," Saint-Exupéry told him indignantly. "Absolutely crazy. Why did you do it? Tell me. Why?"

"I felt I had to find some water," Prévot said meekly. "You . . . your lips were awfully pale."

Saint-Ex's anger died. He felt as if he were awakening from a deep sleep, and he was very sad. The lamps were real, he told his friend who had tried to get him a drink from an elusive lake. There were three of them, and there was no doubt . . .

Prévot was silent, unwilling to dispute a man as doomed as himself. Then, after a long time, he said quietly, "Well, I guess we're both in a bad way."

The night was cold. Saint-Exupéry had discarded his waterproof during the march that day. Light as it was, it had been a burden. Now, however, he could have used it as a blanket. He stood up and stamped his feet and suffered a violent fit of trembling as a result. His teeth chattered uncontrollably, and his muscles twitched. How ironic it was: he had always been nearly impervious to the cold, and now he would die of it.

The freezing wind swept over the unbroken surface of the desert "like a troop of cavalry across open country. I turned and twisted to escape it." There was not a rock or a tree behind which he could huddle. He kept standing up, lying down, and then standing up again. He felt he was being beaten by the wind as if by the broad side of a sword. He fell to his knees and held his head in his hands. To end his life in the sunlight, chasing his illusion, was an acceptable way to die, but to be lashed to death by a bitter wind . . .

He rose uncertainly and staggered over the sand. He did not know where he was. Prévot's voice jolted him back to reality. He swung around and headed toward his friend. An attack of hiccups convulsed him, and his whole body was shaking. He understood that he was very close to death. He fell on his knees near Prévot. They had brought along a first-aid kit, and now the dying pilot removed from it a bottle of pure ether. Fumbling, he opened it and took a sip. The liquid cut his throat like a knife blade.

He dug a trough in the ground and lay in it. He threw handfuls of pebbles over his body until he had buried everything but his face.

Prévot managed to find a few twigs and to build a pathetic fire, but it soon went out. A grave in the sand was not for him; he tried to keep warm by walking in a circle and stamping his feet.

Saint-Exupéry thought that his throat was closed, and he knew that was a "bad sign." Yet he was feeling better. Indeed, he was experiencing a serenity, a peace borne of hopelessness. He drifted off again into a reverie.

> So long as I lay absolutely motionless, I no longer felt the cold. This allowed me to forget my body buried in the sand. I said to myself that I would not budge an inch, and would therefore never suffer again. As a matter of fact, we really suffer very little. Back of all these torments there is the orchestration of fatigue or of delirium, and we live on in a kind of picture-book, a slightly cruel fairy tale.
>
> A little while ago the wind had been after me with whip and spur, and I was running in circles like a frightened fox. After that came a time when I couldn't breathe. A great knee was crushing my chest. A knee. I was writhing in vain to free myself from the weight of the angel who had overthrown me. There had not been a moment when I was alone in this desert. But now I have ceased to believe in my surroundings; I have withdrawn into myself, have shut my eyes, have not so much as batted an eyelid. I have the feeling that this torrent of visions is sweeping me away to a tranquil dream; so rivers cease their turbulence in the embrace of the sea.
>
> Farewell, eyes that I loved! Do not blame me if the human body cannot go three days without water. I should never have believed that man was so truly the prisoner of the springs and freshets. I had no notion that our self-sufficiency was so circumscribed. We take for granted that a man is able to stride straight out into the world. We believe that man is free. We never see the cord that binds him to wells and fountains, that umbilical cord by which he is tied to the womb of the world. Let man take one step too many . . . and the cord snaps.
>
> Apart from your suffering, I have no regrets. All in all, it has been a good life. If I got free of this I should start right in again. A man

cannot live a decent life in cities, and I need to feel myself live. I am not thinking of aviation. The airplane is a means, not an end. One doesn't risk one's life for a plane any more than a farmer ploughs for the sake of the plough. But the airplane is a means of getting away from towns and their bookkeeping and coming to grips with reality.

Flying is a man's job and its worries are a man's worries. A pilot's business is with the wind, with the stars, with night, with sand, with the sea. He strives to outwit the forces of nature. He stares in expectancy for the coming of dawn the way a gardener awaits the coming of spring. He looks forward to port as to a promised land, and truth for him is what lives in the stars.

I have nothing to complain of. For three days I have tramped the desert, have known the pangs of thirst, have followed false scents in the sand, have pinned my faith on the dew. I have struggled to rejoin my kind, whose very existence on earth I had forgotten. These are the cares of men alive in every fibre, and I cannot help thinking them more important than the fretful choosing of a nightclub in which to spend the evening. Compare the one life with the other, and all things considered this is luxury! I have no regrets. I have gambled and lost. It was all in the day's work. At least I have had the unforgettable taste of the sea on my lips.

I am not talking about living dangerously. Such words are meaningless to me. The toreador does not stir me to enthusiasm. It is not danger I love. I know what I love. It is life.

The sky was glowing faintly. Dawn was coming to the desert once more. He extended one arm out of his grave and felt a piece of parachute cloth that they had laid out the night before. There was no moisture on it. He was dully confused: dew should have fallen. He heard himself say, "There is a dry heart here, a dry heart that cannot know the relief of tears." He could still speak. There was hope — and just a little time left. He stood up. "We're off, Prévot," he told his friend. "Our throats are still open. Get along, man!"

During the cool morning hours they hurried as much as they could, knowing that once the sun was high they would not be able to walk further. They dared not stop to rest. They had ceased to perspire, and it was as if the wind, with its "soft and treacherous caress," was drying the blood in their veins.

As they went on, Saint-Exupéry heard a rasp begin in his throat. Before long it would become a cough that would signal the end. Now he started to see spots. That was another sign: when they became flames he would lie down, finished. He had a horrible taste in his mouth, but he was no longer hungry. "Thirst had become

Antoine de Saint-Exupéry, recently rescued, points out to his wife where he was downed in the Libyan desert. (Permission of AP/Wide World Photos)

more and more a disease and less and less a craving. I [realized] that the thought of water and fruit was now less agonizing than it had been. I was forgetting the radiance of the orange, just as I was forgetting the eyes under the hat-brim. Perhaps I was forgetting everything.''

Their legs were giving out. Despite the imperative to keep moving, they had to stop and sit. These breaks soon were occurring every five hundred yards. They wanted to lie down but knew that they had better not. They would never get up again.

The landscape was gradually changing around them. Firm yellow sand was replacing the rocky, steely surface they had walked on for so long. A mile ahead were dunes on top of which grew scruffy vegetation. It was becoming a "golden desert" much like the Sahara Saint-Ex knew and loved. "It was in a sense my country."

They were slowing down; their strength was fading. They had to stop now every two hundred yards.

> The previous day I had tramped without hope. Today the word "hope" had grown meaningless. Today we were tramping simply because we were tramping. Probably oxen work for the same reason. Yesterday I had dreamed of a paradise of orange trees. Today I would not give a button for paradise; I did not believe oranges existed. When I thought about myself I found in me nothing but a heart squeezed dry. I was tottering but emotionless. I felt no distress whatever, and in a way I regretted it: misery would have seemed as sweet to me as water. I might then have felt sorry for myself and commiserated with myself as with a friend. But I had not a friend left on earth.
>
> Cries of despair, misery, sobbing grief are a kind of wealth, and we possessed no wealth. When a young girl is disappointed in love she weeps and knows sorrow. Sorrow is one of the vibrations that prove the fact of living. I felt no sorrow. I was the desert. I could no longer bring up a little saliva; neither could I any longer summon those moving visions toward which I should have loved to stretch forth arms. The sun had dried up the springs of tears in me.

They both felt the change at the same moment, and they looked at each other. It was a ripple of hope moving through them, Saint-Exupéry thought, like a faint breeze over the surface of a lake. He sensed life stirring in the desert. They looked about them and saw footprints in the sand. "We had wandered from the trail of the human species; we had cast ourselves forth from the tribe; we had found ourselves alone on earth and forgotten by the universal migration; and here, imprinted in the sand, were the divine and naked feet of man!''

They saw traces of where two men had stood together and a camel had knelt. A caravan was somewhere nearby. They could not wait to be found. They had little time left. Soon enough they would be coughing. They pushed on.

Suddenly Saint-Ex heard a cock crow. Guillaumet had told him that near the end he had heard cocks in the Andes, and train whistles, too. It was another death sign. . . . But Prévot had heard it, too. Then Saint-Exupéry saw three dogs chasing one another. He pointed them out to Prévot, but the mechanic did not see them. They were not there.

Both the fliers did see the Bedouin on the camel, however, and they shouted and waved at him together. They laughed in mad joy, but he did not hear them. He was only thirty yards away; their voices would not even travel that far. His animal carried him slowly and unknowingly on until he disappeared behind a sand dune. "The man was probably the only Arab in this desert, sent by a demon to materialize and vanish before the eyes of us who could not run." But, no, he was not alone. Here was another man moving in front of them. Their shouts were whispers, so they waved their arms wildly, thinking that their "monstrous signals" must be filling the sky. The Bedouin was looking in the opposite direction. And then he very slowly turned his camel to the right until he was coming directly toward them. He was like a god who creates life with a single glance, who glides across the sand as if on water.

He put his hands on their shoulders, indicating that they should lie down. He gave them water in a basin, and they drank it like calves. They were so greedy for it that repeatedly he became alarmed and pulled first one and then the other back from the basin. But each time he let go of them, they shoved their faces into the water once more.

Water, thou hast no taste, no color, no odor; canst not be defined, art relished while ever mysterious. Not necessary to life, but rather life itself, thou fillest us with a gratification that exceeds the delight of the senses. By thy might, there return into us treasures that we had abandoned. By thy grace, there are released in us all the dried-up runnels of our heart. Of the riches that exist in the world, thou art the rarest and also the most delicate — thou so pure within the bowels of the earth! A man may die of thirst lying beside a magnesian

spring. He may die within reach of a salt lake. He may die though he
hold in his hand a jug of dew, if it be inhabited by evil salts. For thou,
water, art a proud divinity, allowing no alteration, no foreignness in
thy being. And the joy that thou spreadest is an infinitely simple joy.

You, Bedouin of Libya who saved our lives, though you will dwell
forever in my memory yet I shall never be able to recapture your
features. You are Humanity and your face comes into my mind simply as man incarnate. You, our beloved fellowman, did not know
who we might be, and yet you recognized us without fail. And I, in
my turn, shall recognize you in the faces of all mankind. You came
towards me in an aureole of charity and magnanimity bearing the gift
of water. All my friends and all my enemies marched towards me in
your person. It did not seem to me that you were rescuing me: rather
did it seem that you were forgiving me. And I felt I had no enemy left
in all the world.

The pilot and the mechanic were put on a camel, which they rode
for some three hours. When they could no longer bear to ride, the
Arabs made a camp so that the two Frenchmen could rest while
they went for help. That evening, a party of armed Bedouins arrived
in a car and took Saint-Ex and Prévot on a half-hour ride to the
home of a Swiss engineer who managed a soda factory beside some
saline deposits in the desert. He treated them with great compassion
and arranged for them to be taken to Cairo. They were in soft beds
by midnight.

I awoke between white sheets. Through the curtains came the rays
of a sun that was no longer an enemy. I spread butter and honey on
my bread. I smiled. I recaptured the savor of my childhood and all
its marvels. And I read and reread the telegram from those dearest to
me in all the world whose three words had shattered me:
"So terribly happy!"

PART IV

THE CHARMS OF
SOLITUDE

Whoever travels in wartime must expect risks.
— Eddie Rickenbacker

There was no one to blame in Diane's death. She was the
victim of circumstance. She was also a casualty, perhaps, of
the "return to nature" trend. We read the *Whole Earth Cat-
alog,* we hear about communes living off the land, we watch
the Apple family on the tube finding a meaningful life in a
return to native Iowan soil, and we think we are regaining
our lost innocence. We think we can escape doomsday by
concerning ourselves with ecology and the preservation of
natural beauty. We promote the sentimental view of a benevolent nature which can solve our problems and make us better men. We yearn for Walden Pond, and forget that one can
drown in Walden Pond.
— Ted Morgan

CHAPTER 21

Risk and Recreation
A Chronology

The globe has grown small, as if constricted by its spinning. Once the Spaniard described most of it as the Unknown World and feared that Drake would find his way in it. In this century our emissaries have traveled to every part.

The outer borders have all been reached, their wavering outlines traced. Oh, there remain vast patches where few ever go, but their sizes and shapes have been defined by our needs. The jungle is encroached upon by the plantation. The desolate mountain is a national park. The forest has become a designated wilderness area, where the use of motorized vehicles is restricted.

The oceans are still broad and vast and empty, it is true, but they are thickly webbed with shipping lanes. The sky above is criss-crossed with flight corridors.

Seldom is anyone marooned these days, and certainly not for anything like four years. For the modern Selkirk, six weeks is a long time. Castaways still drift, of course, but rarely for months and months. A few days or weeks is closer to the norm.

This is not to say that contemporary survivors do not undergo ordeals as dramatic as those of previous centuries, or that they do not suffer as greatly, only that their suffering is usually not so prolonged.

The Second World War acted as a catalyst for change. There were more planes in the sky, more vessels on the sea. The combatants of each nation hunted their enemies' air forces and navies with great dedication: one way to hamper an opponent's ability to fight and thus ensure victory would be to bring down enough of his planes, sink enough of his ships. The fighter and the anti-aircraft gun, the submarine and the destroyer, all did their deadly work. In a conflict involving numbers of technologically advanced nations, plenty of people are bound to be in need of rescue.

If there were more *opportunities* for combatants to be lost, Allied military commands made strenuous efforts to ease the plight and bring about the rescue of those downed in the jungle or adrift on the ocean. Many service personnel attended government-sponsored survival schools, and their planes and ships were supplied with survival equipment, the design of which had evolved just as the strategies for search and rescue operations had. Alterations were made as the experiences of downed or castaway individuals became known. Thus not merely were inflatable life preservers employed (which, years later, would come to be equipped with signal lights), but also superior life vests that buoyed up the wearer more effectively. (These Mae Wests, as they came to be known popularly, in honor of the bosomy movie star, soon included pouches containing flares.) Rubber rafts were increasingly weighed down as designers tried to prepare for any eventuality: hand pumps and repair kits for slow leaks, dyes to be spread on the sea to make location from the air more likely, first-aid kits, tinned water and food, fishing lines and hooks, Very pistols and flares to which were attached small parachutes so that they would linger in the sky longer, disassembled paddles, and survival manuals.

(These could be hilariously inappropriate: in one instance castaways entertained each other by reading from detailed instructions for existing in the *jungle*, until the joke soured and they tore up the booklet and threw it overboard. Somehow they had not been provided with similar printed matter dealing with the problems of being adrift on the ocean, although they were fliers whose missions routinely took them far out over the Atlantic.)

During the war certain units and area commanders were specifically assigned to the task of air and sea rescue. The cessation of hostilities did not mean the end of such specialization any more than it signaled a diminishing of interest in improving the survivor's chances of coming back alive. Although I have not focused on rescue efforts in these tales, most lost people are diligently sought for. Helicopters, light aircraft, amphibious planes, destroyers, merchant vessels, yachts, Jeeps, off-the-road vehicles, snowmobiles, and even horses are among the means of transportation routinely used in ocean and land searches.

Many wilderness areas now boast trained and practiced rescue teams. In addition, individuals with specialized skills act as volunteers: mountain climbers, hikers, handlers of tracking dogs, Civil Air Patrol members, and even Boy Scouts work alongside sheriffs' deputies, park rangers, and National Guardsmen.

The prolonging of the survivor's life and the efforts to improve the efficiency of the hunt have sometimes been facilitated by the research of inventors and scientists. During the Korean War, for example, pilots were supplied with portable two-way radios to broadcast their locations. Combat fliers in Vietnam were issued radios, considerably miniaturized and more reliable to boot. Today, in addition to conventional voice radios, many light aircraft are equipped with transmitters that automatically send out a locater signal onto which searchers can lock. Life rafts now have canopies to prevent their being swamped by heavy seas and to protect their occupants against bad weather.

Too often, however, the inventions and improved search techniques are for naught. Rafts tip over, and their carefully selected contents spill into the ocean and promptly sink. Radios inexplicably fail to work, or bad weather interferes with their signals. Wilderness areas are so vast that hundreds of man-hours of searching do not turn up lost hikers. Snowmobilers noisily whiz close by the shouting, stranded hunters they seek. Heavy cloud covers prevent search aircraft from taking off. Stormy seas inhibit rescue vessels from reaching sinking hulks. Thick jungles hide the lost from those flying overhead. Planes drone over or ships sail by the unnoticed individuals, specks in the vast landscapes or oceans' surfaces.

Many of the survivors in the preceding tales came to be in their predicaments because of economic reasons: they were seeking gold or booty or profitable trade in new lands when they came to grief. The prototypical modern survivor is not an explorer, a soldier, or a sailor, but a hobbyist. He sails on the sea or walks into the wilderness — or flies over them both — not because he is after wealth but because he has already attained a relative degree of it.

This, too, is traceable to the war. The victorious nations (soon to be joined by the vanquished) embarked on peace with vibrant economies. The ranks of the middle and upper-middle classes expanded while working hours declined. In the Great Depression, those lucky enough to have jobs often worked six days a week or even seven, but by the 1950s, employees had two days a week off. Wages went up, and auto workers purchased Chris-Crafts and off-the-road vehicles; executives bought yachts, Piper Cubs, and, later, Lear jets. At the same time the federal government was opening up millions of acres for parks. In the 1960s, a generation that distrusted technocracy desired to "get back to the land." A few moved to farm communes, but many more bought hiking boots and backpacks.

A healthy economy not only provided more people with increased income and leisure time but also lowered the cost of certain goods. One no longer had to be a wealthy European aristocrat or have the backing of corporations to afford mountain-climbing gear — or plane fare to reach a place to climb.

As the result, then, of the expansion of the middle class and the increased wages of skilled workers, many of the postwar survivors described here will not be professional adventurers or military or naval personnel; rather they will be people like us, out on a lark, in pursuit of . . . fun. Theirs will not be a defect of temperament like Selkirk's or a prissy sense of decorum like Philip Ashton's, but a failure to gauge the serious implications of what seem to be innocuous decisions. In a sense, misjudgment has replaced the unseaworthy ship as the cause of distress.

To enter into danger ignorantly has become a civil right in the latter half of the twentieth century, and the bold privateer has been transformed into a weekend boater.

I have organized the stories that follow into a chronology, and in recounting each of them I have provided only a brief setup of the situation, then have gone on to tell the tale.

The myriad ways we discover to endanger ourselves and the inventiveness that we employ to put ourselves at risk are a tribute both to our endless resourcefulness and our determined refusal to learn the most elemental lessons of nature.

For all that, you will see over and over again the will of the human animal to preserve his life and the ingenuity and clarity of the mind focused on survival. It is a compelling and heartening sight.

October 12, 1942 *The destroyer* DUNCAN *is sunk in a battle with the* TOKYO EXPRESS *not far from Guadalcanal.*

The *Duncan* had been struck by forty or fifty shells, and the three senior officers had been killed or knocked into the sea. Responsibility for ordering the abandoning of the burning ship fell to the chief engineer, Lieutenant Commander Herbert R. Kabat. The exercise was complicated by the availability of only two lifeboats, the others having been burnt or thrown overboard some days before to aid the survivors of another sinking. As many of the wounded as could fit into the rafts were lowered over the side, and word was passed to the rest of the crew that they would have to make do with life jackets.

There was no panic. In fact, the men prepared to disembark with such a distinct air of casualness that Kabat and the other officers had to urge them to hurry. Many of the sailors took the time, nonetheless, to locate whatever might be useful in the ocean or on an island, including inflatable mattress covers and aluminum cans. Kabat found two such powder cans himself and tied them together with a piece of line in the hope "that their buoyancy might help to support me in the water." He slipped off his shoes and trousers, put on a kapok life jacket, and dropped over the side.

His first hours in the sea were tranquil.

> The water was cool, but not cold. Towing my powder cans, I paddled clear of the ship as fast as I could. When I seemed far enough away in case she exploded, I lay back in the water, resting. I could hear the voices of the men calling back and forth to one another, but I could see no one — nothing but the blackness of the water, the *Duncan* burning steadily, and the dark mass of land several miles away. If I hoped to swim to that island, I would have to save my strength.
>
> I now began to notice the stars crowding the clear sky. The battle seemed remote and long past. The quiet and easy motion of the water began to relax some of the tautness within me. Surely the daylight would bring planes and rescue ships. We had only to move toward land and wait. I tied the rope to my life jacket and, pulling my cans behind me, swam slowly on my back toward the unknown island. Several times waves rolled over my head and I fought back the water, gasping. Frequently I stopped to rest, to judge my distance and direction. The land seemed no closer. The night was a long one.
>
> I thought I had never seen a more beautiful dawn. The bright color swept up quickly after the first glimmer, clear pink and rose and a line of green. A feeling of relief surged through me. Here was light and increased warmth and possibility of rescue.

He could see the islands clearly now: there were three of them, the closest being Savo Island. Eight hundred yards to his right were two men on an inflated mattress cover, and another man floated four hundred yards to his left. He heard a buzzing that grew steadily louder until high in the southern sky he saw a formation of some

150 aircraft. He told himself that on their return flight, some of the planes would be flying lower, and their pilots would spot the *Duncan*'s men and radio their location. He lay on his back, "relaxed, appreciating the clean formation of the planes against the sky, judging their number."

It was at this moment that he felt a "scratching, tickling sensation" on his left foot. Startled, he lifted it out of the water and saw blood pouring from it. He scanned the ocean's surface and found just ten feet to his left the brown back of a shark. For an instant he did not believe it; then his mind filled with panicky questions.

Would he keep going or would he turn and come back? Had he deliberately attacked me, or had he only brushed against my bare foot accidentally? What weapon could I use? I had no knife. I had thrown away my pistol because of its weight. I had nothing — nothing but my bare hands and feet.

The real fear did not hit me until I saw him turn and head back toward me. He didn't rush. His five-foot body, breaking the surface of the water, came in a steady direct line, effortless and deadly. I kicked and splashed tremendously and this time he veered off past me, not frightened, not hurrying.

Now I grabbed my powder cans and thrust one under each knee to keep my feet up. I yanked at my life jacket, raising it to lift my body further out of the water.

All the time I followed him with my eyes. He went about twenty feet and swam back and forth.

I shouted to the man to my left, "Have you got a knife?" There was no answer.

The shark was going to come in. Every muscle in my body tensed for the attack. He waited, as if he knew the terrible toll of waiting on the victim. With a great effort I yelled to the men far off to my right, "A shark! Have you a knife? A knife?"

Then he turned to make the attack. He came in from the same angle toward my left. I raised my right arm, holding it up as I watched him come and trying to control myself. When he was almost upon me, I thrashed out, kicking and splashing. I brought my fist down on his nose with all my force again and again. He was thrust down into the water about two feet. He swam by and I saw him go out and stay there, waiting.

Kabat checked his limbs for wounds, and he found that all he had lost was a piece of flesh out of his left hand. He shouted over and over again to the men on both sides, "A shark! A shark's eating me! Have you a knife?'' Finally the sailors understood and responded with hand gestures: no, they did not have a knife.

Commander Kabat now began to conserve his energy. While the shark kept his distance, he must remain silent and nearly motionless so that when the attacks came he would have the strength to fight. At the same time he wondered how long he could keep it up. If the shark persisted, eventually Kabat would tire, and he would be a defenseless, inanimate object in the wide sea.

For fifteen minutes he floated, watching, and then the shark started in again, once more at an angle to his left. He steeled himself to meet the murderous assault.

> When his head was almost upon me, his jaw plainly visible beneath, I brought my fist down across my body and managed to hit him on the eyes, the nose. The flesh was torn from my left arm. He passed me and as he did so I could feel the movement of his great body against me.
>
> My whole mind and body now centered on the battle against annihilation, as if I were an animal fighting off a stronger, larger beast. At intervals of ten or fifteen minutes he would ease off from his slow swimming and bear directly toward me, coming in at my left.
>
> Only twice did he go beneath me. Helpless against this type of attack, I feared it most, but because I was so nearly flat on top of the water, he seemed unable to get at me from below.
>
> Each time he attacked on the surface I could hit him, but each time he took another nip out of me. After an attack I would raise my feet and arms to see what I had left. The big toe on my left foot was dangling. A piece of my right heel was gone. My left elbow, hand and calf were torn. If he did not actually sink his teeth into me, his rough hide would scrape off great pieces of my skin. The salt water stanched the flow of blood somewhat and I was not conscious of great pain. The physical shock of the encounter served to keep that in check for a while.

In the midst of one scuffle, as Kabat called it, the lid came off one powder can, and it quickly filled with water and sank. He tried to grab it before it disappeared, but he could not. He shifted his body so that both knees draped over the remaining can.

At some point in all this, the *Duncan* sank. During a lull the commander looked over to where she lay burning, as he had so many times, and she was gone. He felt a kind of sorrow at not seeing her go down.

He lost all track of time. He did not know how long he had been fighting — though, of course, it seemed like forever — and he did not know how much longer he could continue. Each assault took some energy from him, weakened him just a little more. His strength was slowly being drained away. "The constant hitting with my right fist made the muscular ache in my arm more painful than my wounds."

He heard planes, saw a dozen of them flying low and directly over him. He waved frantically and shouted. He observed several of the pilots waving their white scarves at him. Then the shark was back, and Kabat was savagely pounding at him with strength renewed by hope. He had been seen; there would be help. . . .

As I lay there watching, I looked up and, suddenly, there was a ship approaching. Was it American or Japanese? I had no idea who had won the battle. Squinting my eyes against the brilliance of the sun which was now high in the sky, I finally made out that it was a U.S. destroyer. It drew closer. I saw a boat pull away. They were coming for me. First the men nearer to them. Then me. Then me.

I turned my eyes away with a great effort, to watch the shark. When I could look back again their boat was nearer. I yelled and shouted, but they were still too far away to hear. Then the lifeboat was within a couple of hundred yards, full of survivors. I tore off my undershirt and waved it wildly. The boat turned and I was sure no one had seen me. I kept yelling. Then I controlled myself, feeling that they were only going back to the destroyer with that boatload. They would be back for me. I only had to wait a little, to fight once more. They would come back, I was certain.

I saw the boat return to the ship and disappear on the far side. In numb silence, I saw the ship get [under way]. She [had] hoisted in her boat. She came in my direction at high speed. I screamed again and again.

She passed me. No one had seen me, leaving me to the shark.

In the excitement I had forgotten the shark. Now he was upon me before I was ready. I fought him off, swinging my arms, hitting blindly. I turned and whirled and struck. As he swam away, I lifted my left leg. He had torn out the flesh in the thigh so deeply that the bone was exposed.

Kabat's leg was bleeding profusely. He started to tie his shirt around it as a tourniquet, but he felt so very tired and his fingers were clumsy, fumbling. He gave up the effort, realizing that a tourniquet would cause his leg to become numb, which would hamper his ability to use it in battle. The loss of blood was making him groggy. . . .

He despaired and desired only to slip out of his life jacket and sink beneath the waves. It would be a quick and painless death. His fingers touched the fastenings . . . it would be so easy just to die. In the depths there would be no horror, no gaping, tooth-filled jaws slowly chomping him to death, a piece at a time. Yet he did not give up: "the body will keep on fighting even when the will is going, and even a small man has tremendous strength in desperation."

An aircraft flew low over him. He was dazed and confused. He tried to wave, but it took too much energy. The shark came at him again, and he fought automatically, without thinking. Then he lay back in the water and stared at the sky.

When he finally raised his head, he saw a destroyer coming toward him. He decided later that the ship's crew probably noticed the plane diving over his position. He waved his shirt at the vessel. Floundering about in the ocean, he pulled the powder can out of the water, hoping it would catch the light of the noonday sun.

He dropped the can and began waving with both arms. He shouted. Then a dreadful anxiety seized him: "Perhaps I was only seeing things. Or again, maybe they would not see me. There were men on the forward part. Why didn't they wave back? They were coming right toward me. Perhaps they would run me down and never know I was there."

Kabat was relieved to see a man wave back. Indeed, the fellow was so excited that he waved both arms, too.

I started to paddle furiously. All my strength seemed to come back, and I thought I was swimming toward them at a great rate. With those strong strokes, I thought, any moment now I would be bumping into the side of the ship. I stopped and took a look. I had made no headway whatever.

The men on the deck were cheering. They had seen the shark. Usually, if a man is in the water, the procedure is to tie a line to a strong swimmer and send him out, but they obviously could not do that. As I paddled futilely, I heard a zing close to my head and looked up again. Five or six men were lined up on the deck above me with rifles shooting at the shark.

A terrible fear of being shot to death in the water, when rescue was so near, swept over me. With each zing of a bullet, I screamed and pleaded and cried out to them to stop. The shark was too close. They would hit me first.

The firing stopped, and a boat came toward him. He felt hands grip him, felt himself being dragged over the gunwale. He flopped

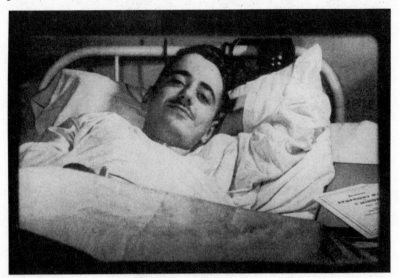

Lieutenant Commander Herbert R. Kabat recovers in a hospital after his bare-fisted battle with a shark. On the bed beside him is the sheet music for a Beethoven symphony. (Permission of *The Saturday Evening Post*)

into the bottom of the craft and vomited. He heard a voice comforting him, saying repeatedly that it didn't matter. He asked about the others in the sea, had they all been rescued? He asked for morphine, and he saw an officer bend over him, heard him say, "Herb, you're all right now. You're all right now, Herb." By odd coincidence, the man was an old friend from Jersey City.

A sailor tied a tourniquet around his leg, and someone gave him morphine. He saw his friend's face above him. "Other men in the water," Kabat managed to say as the drug took effect. There were words said in reply, but he could not understand them. . . . He slipped into unconsciousness.

Lieutenant Commander Herbert Kabat spent fourteen months in various hospital ships and medical facilities. He lost no limbs, but his body bore the deep scars of his ordeal. Still, as he wrote in the *Saturday Evening Post* in 1944, he felt himself to have been "fortunate, amazingly fortunate.

"One thing I do know. The human body is a wonderful mechanism. It will fight against great odds and take terrible punishment. It can call up strength you never imagined it possessed. Men on every battlefield and ocean must be discovering this and feeling the same surprise and wonderment that I did."

November 13, 1942 *On the second day of the four-day Battle of Guadalcanal, the cruiser* JUNEAU *is sunk, resulting in a loss of 560 men. Another 140 sailors climb into life rafts or congregate in the water around them.*

Seaman Allen Clifton Heyn, gunner's mate, second class, had been about to relieve another sailor on the 1.1 stern gun. The man was still wearing the phone set, and Heyn saw his mouth drop open. An instant later a torpedo struck at midship. The explosion slammed Heyn against a gun mount and knocked him out cold. When he regained consciousness, oil was falling in such a quantity that he thought it was rain.

Heyn later recalled the scene for a debriefing officer:

There was smoke and there was fellows laying all around there and parts of their gunshields torn apart and the fantail where I was was sticking almost straight up in the air. It was so slippery that you couldn't walk up it and guys that was still able to climb over the side couldn't walk up. They were crawling over the side and holding on the lifeline trying to pull themselves further aft and jump over. And they were jumping over and bumping into each other.

It was still so smoky and all, you couldn't quite see and I was still hazy and I knew I had to get up and get off of there. I was afraid the suction would pull me down. When I went to get up, I felt this pain in my foot and I couldn't get my foot loose from the shield or something, it fell down on top of my right foot across the instep of it and I couldn't get loose. It was only a few seconds, and the water was closing in around the ship and there was just this little bit of it left. And I knew that I had to get off but couldn't and there was a lot of kapok life jackets laying around deck.

I grabbed one of them in my arms and held it. I didn't even put it on, and the water closed in around the ship, and we went down. And I gave up, I just thought that there wasn't a chance at all, everything just run through my head. And you could see all [the] objects in the water, all the fellows and everything and after we were under the surface I don't know how far but the sheet of iron or whatever it was, it was released and my foot came loose and then the buoyancy from the life jacket brought me back to the surface.

The oil was two inches thick on the sea, and all around Heyn swirled blueprints, drawings of the *Juneau,* and many rolls of toilet paper. He was groggy and unable to see anyone else around him. He wondered dully if he was the only one who had made it. He put on the life jacket and began paddling around.

A doughnut life raft popped up out of the ocean in front of him. He had just gotten a grip on it when he heard a man cry for help. It was a boatswain's mate, second class, who had worked in the *Juneau's* post office. His leg had been blown off, and he could not swim. Heyn pushed the doughnut over to him and helped him into it.

Other survivors soon made their way to the raft and climbed or were pulled in. "Everybody was kind of scared at first," Heyn remembered. "Some of them couldn't swim, they were afraid they'd lose their grip and drown."

A number of B-17 Flying Fortresses flew low over the water, and the pilots waved to the men, giving them the hope — a false one, as it turned out — that they would soon be picked up.

The *Juneau,* which had sustained crippling damage before being hit by the torpedo that sank her, had been part of a makeshift convoy of five ships, all of which had been put out of commission and had withdrawn from the battle. The survivors in the doughnut thought they might be picked up by one of the other vessels. The ranking officer of the convoy, however, had decided that with a submarine in the area, a rescue operation was too risky, and he gave orders that the ships were to keep sailing. The *Juneau's* men saw the masts disappear over the horizon.

Late in the afternoon it rained heavily. Although the visibility was poor, every few minutes one man or another would call out that he could see a vessel, but all the reports were false. When the rain stopped, Heyn's raft was joined by two others. Each of them was a circular float with netting over the doughnut hole. They were designed to hold large numbers of men, but these three were badly overcrowded with survivors, most of whom were at least partially immersed in the water.

> I should say there was about 140 of us when we all got together. Some of them were in very bad shape. Their arms and legs were torn off. And one of them, I could see . . . his skull. You could see the red part inside where his head had been split open, you might say torn open in places. They were all crying together and very down in the dumps and wondering if anybody was ever going to pick them

up. And they thought, well, at least tomorrow there will be somebody out here.

And that night, it was a very hard night because most of the fellows who were wounded badly were crying and, you know, groaning about their pains and everything. They were all in agony. And in the morning this fellow that I said that had his head open, his hair had turned gray just like as if he was an old man. It had turned gray right over night.

Everybody had so much oil on them, their ears and eyes would burn and the salt water would hurt so much that you couldn't hardly look around to see if anybody was there. You couldn't recognize each other unless you knew each other very well before the ship went down, or unless it was somebody that you'd recognize by his voice. So all these rolls of tissue paper were floating around there. If you unrolled them, in the middle they were dry and we'd take that and wipe our eyes out with them and ease the pain a lot and wipe our faces off a little.

Lieutenant Blodgett, the *Juneau*'s gunnery officer, took charge. He thought that land was nearby and was determined that they paddle to it. The sailors formed the doughnuts into a line and tied them together. The ablest men got into the first two, straddled the floats, and paddled. They worked in shifts throughout that day and the night that followed, with Blodgett navigating by the stars. Yet they did not seem to make any progress. The rafts just did not move very well in the sea.

On the third day, a Flying Fortress dropped a rubber lifeboat some distance from them. They could see it occasionally when it rose on the crests of high waves. They wanted to retrieve it because its design made it move better than the ones they were in; with it they might be able to make more progress. Some men were going to swim for it, but sharks were spotted in the water. In the end Heyn and some others detached one of the doughnuts and paddled over to it. They triggered its self-inflating mechanism, and one of them paddled it to the other rafts while the rest returned in the doughnut.

Most of the castaways agreed that the best use for the new boat would be to house the seriously wounded; at least they would be dry there. The several uninjured sailors who had already climbed into it, however, had other ideas.

It was towards evening now, and there were three men in this rubber raft. They hollered back to us that they had decided to go for land, that it would be better that they go for land and send us help. But all these fellows that was on the doughnuts who were very sick and wounded didn't want that. They wanted to be put in the rubber raft and all stay together. They felt, well, it was much easier there than it was on the doughnut. And why should those three go in that rubber raft and leave us here? It looked like we would just be goners that way, that's what it looked like. Everybody figured that anyway.

Well, they said they were going anyway, so they unsecured this line and they paddled off. And all these fellows that was hurt bad was hollering for them to come back but they kept going.

A few of those left behind were even more desperate to reach shore. Wooden planks floated around the doughnuts; the men held on to these and swam away. One of them realized after a time that he would not make it, and so he returned to the rafts, but Heyn never saw any of the others again; presumably they drowned or were taken by sharks.

Heyn estimated that there were now only fifty of the *Juneau*'s men left alive. Some of them did not have shirts and were suffering terribly from sunburn. Those, like Heyn, who still had their clothes fared much better, he thought, because the oil had soaked into the cloth and afforded them an extra measure of protection.

On the fourth day the sea turned rough, and the rafts became detached from one another. The twelve men in Heyn's doughnut tried to keep it close to the others, but the waves drove them away.

Before long the deprivations began to affect them mentally. When aircraft would fly over, a few of the more rational men would wave at them and try to get the attention of their crews. The seamen who had become disoriented, however, would castigate the signalers, telling them to ignore the planes because the military did not want to save them and meant to leave them on the ocean to die. Heyn was not one of those to despair, being certain that only the continued fighting was preventing the dispatching of a vessel to pick them up.

They knew we were there, I knew that, so when they could send a ship they'd come. Some of the guys was kinda disappointed and pretty low in mind so they sorta gave up. There's one fellow, he was a gunner's mate from the *Juneau*, second class. Well, he kept swallowing salt water all the time and he'd let his head fall down in the water and swallow it and he'd begin to get very dopey and dreary. He couldn't help himself at all so I held him up. I held him in my arms, his head above the water as much as I could, and I held him that way all afternoon. Toward night he got stiff and I told the other fellows.

I said, "Well, how about holding him a while? I can't hold him, I've got all to do to hold myself." And they said they wouldn't do it, they were arguing and fighting among themselves a lot. And I said, "I felt his heart and his wrists and I couldn't feel any beating." I figured he was dead and I said to them, "Well, I'm going to let him go."

And George Sullivan, the oldest brother of the Sullivans, he said to me, "You can't do that." He said, "It's against all regulations of the Navy. You can't bury a man at sea without having official orders from some captain or the Navy Department or something like that." And I knew he was delirious and there was something wrong with him and all, but they wouldn't let me let him go.

I said to them, "Well, you hold him," and they wouldn't hold him. So it went on that way for a little while. His legs were hanging down in the water a little way below mine when a shark bit his leg, bit his leg right off below the knee. He didn't move or say anything. That was enough for me. I figured, well, I'm going to drop him. There isn't any sense holding a dead man. So we took his dog tag off, this one fellow did, and said a prayer for him and let him float away.

At night it was so cold for the fellows who didn't have no clothes, we'd try to huddle them among us to keep them warm under the water. The sharks kept getting worse in the daytime, and you could see them around us all the time. We'd kick them with our feet and splash the water and they'd keep away. But at night you'd get drowsy and you'd kinda fall asleep and you wouldn't see them coming. As night went on they'd come and they'd grab a guy every once in a while and bite him. And once they did, they wouldn't eat him altogether, then they'd just take a piece of him and go away and then they'd come back and get him and drag him away and drown him. He'd scream and holler and everything but there wasn't anything we could do to help.

The weather was causing the raft's canvas to tear, and the netting was wearing out. Afraid the doughnut would fall apart, the men busied themselves repairing it: "We were trying to secure it together all the time."

That night a man announced that he was going to swim for land. Heyn and the others repeatedly dragged him back into the raft, but eventually he got away from them. He had made only fifty yards when a shark grabbed him, "and that's the last we seen of him."

And then the fellows got kind of ideas that the ship was sunk under us, sitting on the bottom. You could swim down there at night and get something to eat and all them kinda things, and I was beginning to believe them. They said they could see a light down there and this one fellow kept saying, "If it's down there what are we staying up here for, let's go down there and get something to eat then." So I said, "You show me the way down there." So he dives under water and I went after him and I never did find nothing down there, no hatch or anything like he said was there. And I got my sense again and I knew what I was doing and I didn't believe him anymore.

The fifth day was coming up then. There were only two or three guys gone but things were getting pretty bad. The guys were fighting among themselves. If you bumped into one of them, he'd get mad and holler at you. And they did talk a lot about home and what they were going to do, and a lot of them said if they could get on an island, they'd stay there, they'd never go back to the Navy. They didn't want to see it no more. And they were mad that they were left out there in the water. It wasn't fair that they should be left like that! The ships went off and didn't pick them up.

The men without shirts were in agony. Heyn thought their skin looked as if it had been scraped with a razor. Some of them were saying that they would rather drown themselves than endure anymore. After dark, George Sullivan announced that he was going to take a bath. He stripped and went into the ocean, swimming a little way from the doughnut. Heyn thought that the whiteness of his body "flashed" and attracted the shark. . . . The sharks took two other sailors that night as well.

On the morning of the sixth day, with the sea rough, a gull landed on the raft. The men grabbed for him, but he took off. He returned, however, and this time he was caught and his neck was wrung. There were only three or four men left to share the small carcass.

We just floated in the water and talked together and the sharks kept bothering us all the time. We'd keep beating them off and try to keep away from them, and the planes flew over all the time again. But they didn't pay any attention to us.

Well, another night went on and the next day, this gunner's mate, second [class], his name was Stewart, he said that there was a hospital ship there and we were going to go over to it. There were three of us — him, me and another fellow — and he said that we should swim over to it and leave the doughnut. We didn't know whether to or not. You hated to leave it there because you knew if you got in the water, you were gone. So he dove in the water and swam off and he just kept swimming out over the water and he wouldn't turn around. You could see the sharks going after him and he swam and kicked and swam. And he hollered to us to come and get him with the raft, to paddle towards him but he kept swimming the other way. We paddled towards him and he finally got tired. He turned around and came towards us and he got back before the sharks got him.

But that night it got cold again. He had thrown all his clothes away and he didn't have a thing and he wanted me to give him my clothes. But I said no, there's no sense to that. And he said, "Well, then I'm going down to the ship and get a clean suit. I got a lot of them in my locker. " He also said, "I got a case of peaches in my gun mount."

Several times Heyn talked him out of swimming down to the *Juneau,* and to keep him warm he set Stewart between himself and the third man, a Mexican-American whose name Heyn did not know. Before long, however, Stewart decided that he had had enough of hardship and the cold. He went into the ocean and swam until the sharks found him.

Now there were only two of them left. They spent the day talking and securing the raft.

We were at each end with our feet kinda up in the water so we could fight the sharks off better. That night we got sleepy and we dozed off, I guess, because a shark grabbed him and tore his leg off below, just jaggedy like. And he complained, he said to me that somebody was stabbing him with a knife. I said how can anybody stab you out here? There's nobody but us two.

And he swore at me and called me all kinds of names and said I had to get him to a doctor. I guess I was delirious, because I was paddling and paddling in the water there. I didn't know where I was going, I was just paddling, trying to get him to a doctor. Well, finally he screamed and hollered and he came over to me and I held his arm and then I could see what it was. I knew that he had been bit by a shark and I held him and the shark came up and it just grabbed him underneath and kept eating him from the bottom and pulling on him. Well, I couldn't hold him anymore. The sharks just pulled him down under the water and he drowned. Well then, that's all that happened, it seemed like the night would never end.

The next day I just floated around some more and it went on like that for the next couple of days and in the morning of the last day, which was the ninth day, I began to get delirious myself. I see these guys come up out of the water. It looked like to me that they had rifles on their backs and I'd holler to them and they said they were up there on guard duty. They'd come up from each hatch on the ship. Well, I asked them how it was. And they said the ship was all right, you could go down there and get something dry and eat. So I said to them, well, I'll come over there by you and go down with you. Well, I swam over to them and they just disappeared. I went back. I done that twice. Each time they disappeared when I got there. And then my head got clear and something told me just to hang on a little longer.

seek the bad for our very lives. On our last flight from India we took off into a pea-soup fog, and a few minutes out of our base the monsoon rain was flooding down the windshield in torrents. At twelve thousand feet the rain turned to snow. We couldn't see our wing tips. That meant we were safe. As well as the Japs like pot shots at our unarmed and always overloaded transports, no self-respecting combat pilot would fly in weather like that. With another few thousand feet, we'd be over the hump and the worst would be behind us.

Rosbert was comfortable with this sort of mission, being a veteran of Chennault's Flying Tigers and the China National Aviation Corporation, but his copilot was distinctly uneasy. Charles "Ridge" Hammel was a "past master" at desert flying, having been a pilot for Pan American's "Africa Corps," but he remained tense during each flight over the mountains until he felt certain that the heavy-laden C-47 would clear the highest peak on their route. As the aircraft rose above twelve thousand feet, he smiled with relief. "We're okay now," he told Wong, their Chinese radio operator. "Another thousand feet and we'll be clear of the hump. Another hour and you'll be home!"

But while Ridge was turned toward Wong, Rosbert saw a thin film of ice form on the windshield and then spread to the wings. The film quickly thickened into a layer six inches deep. The plane began to lose altitude. Ice now formed on the inside of the windshield and all the windows. The men could not see outside. Rosbert put one bare palm and then another against the glass until he melted a two-inch hole in the ice. They were passing through a cloud, and then suddenly it opened, and there was a peak directly ahead.

"Look out!" I yelled. "There's a mountain!" Grabbing the controls, with my eye still glued to the tiny opening, I swung the ship violently over into a bank. We missed the face of that cliff by inches. Then my heart stopped. A huge dark object swept by. A terrible scraping noise tore under the cabin; an explosive crash struck right behind me; the engines raced into a violent roar. Something stabbed my ankle, an intense pain shot through my left leg. Then, suddenly, we were not moving. Only the falling snow broke the silence.

I don't know how long I sat there before I heard Ridge's voice. It seemed to come from far away. "Get out of that thing before it catches fire!"

I heard my own voice answer, "Come on back in. You'll freeze to death out there."

My shocked brain told me the ship wouldn't burn. Both engines

had been torn off when we hit. The cabin was intact, except for the
radio station, which was crumpled like tissue paper. Wong lay
sprawled in the aisle behind the cockpit. I struggled out of my seat to
reach him. I held his wrist; there was no pulse. I put my arm under
him, and a broken neck dropped his head back between his shoulders.

Ridge huddled against the rear bulkhead. He was badly cut about
the face and hands. Little rivers of blood dripped down on his flying
jacket, and he was holding his left ankle. His right eye was closed
and the swollen flesh around it was already discolored.

I struggled to stay conscious. Nothing seemed very real. I tried a
step, but my left ankle turned under me. The pain almost took my
breath away. I looked down. I seemed to be standing on my leg bone,
and my foot was lying at a right angle to it. Holding on to the roof
supports, I swung myself down beside Ridge. For several minutes we
just lay there looking at each other.

The silence was broken by Hammel. "What happened?" he
asked.

To the obvious question Rosbert gave the obvious reply: "We hit
a mountain." He was thinking, *This is a crazy conversation. Things
like this don't happen. You hit a mountain at 180 miles an hour,
and that's that.*

They prayed, thanking God they were alive, and then took stock
of their situation. The C-47 was lying at a thirty-degree angle, and
the weather outside was bitter. Rosbert's leg was throbbing, and
"even the slightest movement [sent] shocks of sickening pain
through my whole body." Hammel's ankle was also injured, but he
was mobile. (It would turn out that Hammel's ankle was only badly
sprained, but Rosbert had a fracture.)

Ridge Hammel worked his way over their jumbled cargo of machinery and dug whatever was useful from the back of the plane,
including parachutes and six tins of emergency rations. Bringing
those few precious supplies forward was a chore: the distance to be
traversed was only twenty-five feet, but the steep angle at which the
aircraft rested combined with the chaos of the cargo area meant that
it took him an hour to reach Rosbert.

The two exhausted men spread out the chutes and lay down upon
them. They fell into a sleep troubled by pain and nightmares.

In the morning the snow had stopped, and they went out to gasp
at the beauty of the picture-postcard snow-covered peaks. They
saw, too, that had their plane slid for just another fifty feet, it would

have been crushed "like an eggshell" against an "ugly, jagged peak." The aircraft's stopping where it did was miraculous.

The night before, they had reminded each other that the "first rule of a crash is to stay by the ship," but a two-foot layer of snow now blanketed the fuselage, and more would be falling. Aerial searchers would never spot the wreckage. They were sixteen thousand feet high in the Mishmi Mountains on the frontier of Tibet, and if they were going to get out alive they would have to *walk* out. Far below them lay a timber line where two ridges met at an angle. There might be water there, they decided, a river that would lead them to a village. It was at least five miles away down a steep slope, but it looked like their best chance.

They could not start out immediately, however, because of their injuries. They spent five days resting, recuperating, and debating which route to take and what goods they should carry along. They located a gallon of soft-drink syrup and mixed it with snow for refreshment. They found a deck of cards on Wong's body; they would play gin rummy "until we were exhausted, would sleep for a few hours, then start all over again." They told each other about their childhoods, swapped war stories of fighting in Burma and North Africa, and "recited navigation lessons" — anything to keep their minds off the heavy odds against their survival. At dawn on the sixth day they started out.

> We knew we had to make it down to [the] timber line before dark, because we could never live through a night on that unprotected slope. Our injured ankles turned under at every step, and we began to flounder. The slope was so steep that we kept falling, and the struggle to get on our feet again would sap every ounce of strength we could muster. In four hours of almost superhuman effort we had covered scarcely two hundred yards. It was hopeless. We just managed to get back to the shelter of the plane with the last streaks of daylight.
>
> Gripped with despair, we lay awake most of the night. We had only one full emergency meal left between us. We had to get down the mountain. But how? Finally, from sheer fatigue, we dozed off. I was awakened by Ridge, who was prying up one of the extra boards used to reinforce the floor. A sled! Now we were riding the crest of hopefulness again. Why hadn't we thought of that before? While it was still dark we pried the braces off the side of the cabin and made splints. We tore our parachutes into strips, bandaged our ankles, then set the splints and wrapped yards of the silk around them until our injured legs were fairly stiff. What was left we wrapped around our

hands and feet for protection from the cold, except for two long runners which we used to strap ourselves to the sleds. By daylight we were on our way.

We literally flew for the first hundred yards, but when the slope flattened out, the ends of the boards plowed deep into the soft snow. The struggle to get off, pull them out, set them flat, pile on, and get started again was almost as difficult as our walking had been.

They tried to lighten their load by jettisoning most of the things they had brought along, but it did not help. They continued to use their sleds, however, until Hammel slammed into a rock and went sprawling down the slope, rolling fifty yards before he came to a stop. Watching him tumble, Rosbert had an idea: he rolled until he reached his friend. Thereafter they slid down inclines on the seats of their pants, holding their feet in the air. When they could not slide, they rolled. They often managed to travel forty or fifty yards at a time. They were stopped just short of the timber line by a slope

that was almost five hundred feet straight down. If getting out of the plane alive was a miracle, we both felt it would take another miracle to get down to the bottom alive. Because Ridge had a little better control with his sprained ankle than I had with my broken leg, he took the risk first. I watched him hurtle downward in a cloud of snow and suddenly disappear. I heard him scream. The most welcome sound I ever knew in my life was Ridge's voice, breaking that awful silence. It sounded weak and far away. "It's okay, but it's rough. Come on down." I slid over to the edge, took a deep breath and shoved with my good foot. Finally, I hit solid earth with a crunching jolt. As I lay there, afraid my back was broken, I heard the sound of rushing water. Just before darkness settled, we reached a stream in a steep-walled gorge.

They located a small cave and huddled in it, wet and worn out. They tried to make a fire with twigs and all the scraps of paper they had in their pockets: passports, address books, licenses, and even Rosbert's photographs of his wife. The captain decided darkly that he and Ridge were destroying "every tangible bit of evidence we possessed to prove that we had a home, a family, a country." The destruction was meaningless, anyhow: the wood was too wet to ignite.

They took off their soaked outer clothes and hung them up to dry. They crowded together for warmth and slept fitfully.

The next day they followed the river's course as best they could, climbing over difficult mountain terrain thick with undergrowth.

For three days we crawled up and down those tortuous hills, taking one half bite of our last remaining ration at daylight and dusk, huddling together on the ground at night. Near the end of the eighth day we had to turn back to the river. The peaks were too steep to climb. We struggled over and around the boulders, half in, half out of the water, until suddenly, the river dropped off into a series of steep falls. It was impossible to go forward. On both sides the walls of the canyon were almost vertical. We were at the end of our strength. We had spread one day's normal emergency minimum over eight days, but had swallowed the last bit of it that morning.

They sat together, staring bleakly at the wall of rock, until Hammel spied a thick vine hanging into the canyon. They tested it, then pulled themselves up, hand over hand, to the top. Once there, they found a trail marked by notched trees. Feeling they were close to help, they staggered on for three more days "through the brush, over boulders, up and down the hills, looking for those all but indistinct marks."

They had an "intense empty feeling" in their stomachs that soon turned into a constant dull ache. Always on the lookout for something edible, they sampled almost everything they saw that had stems or stalks. Rosbert found a piece of fruit that looked like a mango but tasted awful: "It seemed as if someone had struck me a blow in the mouth. I retched horribly and rolled on the ground in agony." Despite his reaction, Hammel took a bite. He vomited, too. The men were glad to have tried the fruit, however: it made their stomachs "numb" for several days. "Even starving as we were, we could not bear the thought of food."

On the thirteenth day they came to a fork in the trail. One path ran west toward Burma and India, where their base was. The other ran to the east, farther into the mountainous terrain of Tibet. Rationally they should have turned westward, but they went east instead.

They walked for an hour and came to a clearing. In the midst of it were the charred remains of a hut. In the afternoon they saw prints of a child's bare feet in the mud. Just before dark they came over a hill and spied a thatched roof.

The hut, made entirely of bamboo, stood on stilts about four feet above the ground. The door nearest us was securely latched. So was the center door. When we got no reply to our knock at the last door, Ridge threw himself against it and we sprawled inside. It was so dark and the air was so thick with smoke that we could scarcely see. A big pot was boiling over an open fire in the center of the room. Then we made out the huddled forms of two very old women to whom six nude, wild-looking children were clinging. At the sound of our voices, they appeared to be even more frightened. We finally tried our few words of Chinese. [Using] gestures, we tried to tell them that we were fliers and only wanted food, but the children kept pointing to the old ladies' eyes. One, we learned, was totally blind, the other almost so.

The children later gave us each a gourd. But instead of ladling out the food, one of the women simply picked up the boiling-hot cooking pot in her bare hands and passed it around while each of us, and then the six children, scooped out a gourdful of the food. Ridge and I were so impressed with this witchery that, starving as we were, we momentarily forgot all about eating — until our gourds got so hot we had to set them on the floor. Almost immediately, with hot food inside and the hot fire outside, we rolled over on the hard bamboo floor and went sound asleep.

Eighteen hours later the hundreds of wood ticks we had attracted in our wanderings chewed us awake. Sunlight was streaming through the open door and some of the smoke had cleared. The faces and bodies of the women — such as showed outside the aged, ragged blanketlike cloth they wore draped over one shoulder and around their middles — appeared to be encrusted with a lifetime's exposure to dirt and wood smoke. Their hair was long and coarse, and around their heads each wore a wide metal band.

On the third day after the arrival of the Americans, two of the older children left the clearing and returned before dark with three men "who stepped right out of the Stone Age." Their long, matted hair hung down to their shoulders, and they had broad, flat foreheads and noses. They wore earrings made from silver coins and necklaces of beads, animal teeth, and more coins. Sleeveless leather jerkins and loincloths were their only clothing; they did not wear shoes on their wide, strong feet. Each man carried a "long sword-like" knife on one hip and a fur-covered pouch on the other. Like the other Mishmi the white men would meet during the next month, they were "cheerful, hospitable, interested little men."

The Americans used elaborate gestures to explain that they were "flying men" who had hit one of the mountains and now desired only to return to their own people. Throughout the recitation, the Mishmi smiled and nodded their heads as if they understood exactly what the strangers meant, but Hammel and Rosbert suspected that they were utterly bewildered.

When the white men's gestures ceased, the inevitable scene occurred: "Finally they could resist no longer. They had to feel our clothes, try our shoes, run the zippers up and down the front of our flying jackets amid roars of gleeful laughter, blink their eyes in childlike amazement when we let them turn on our flashlight, listen with ever widening eyes to the ticking of our watches."

Word spread of the wondrously entertaining guests with their intriguing paraphernalia. That evening two more men arrived to view them. They drew from their pouches eggs, a sweet potato, and a handful of rice, which they offered as gifts. They also invited the Americans to accompany them back to their own settlement. Willing to try anything that might put them in contact with the outside world, Rosbert and Hammel nodded their acceptance of the invitation.

The Mishmi visitors removed their long knives, tugged their pouches around to their stomachs, and lay down to sleep. The following day's journey took eight hours because of the Americans' injuries and fatigue. Rosbert doubted it would have taken the Mishmi more than two hours to traverse the same distance had they been alone.

At the end of this painful trek was another, albeit much larger, hut. Hammel and Rosbert managed to stagger inside the door, and then, aching and exhausted, they collapsed on the floor and fell into a deep sleep. They awoke to find that while they had slept their hosts had carried them into another room and laid them on a pallet.

Seven men and fifteen women lived communally in the shelter. Also present were innumerable children — "Ridge and I never did get all [of them] counted."

There, in that primitive smoke-filled hut, deep in the heart of the Himalayas, Ridge and I held court for two incredible weeks, receiving scores of these long-haired, leather-jerkined, bare-legged men of the Stone Age. Their implements were cut from wood or stone and, from what we could learn, they had never heard of Chinese or Indians, let alone Americans. After days on the trail and in their smoke-filled huts, we were as dark-skinned as they. It was not until Ridge felt strong enough to walk and had gone out in the rain that the natives discovered we were white. It produced some awe, at first, and then a curiosity which expressed itself in sly, quizzical looks from all except the children.

To entertain them Ridge and I repeated, over and over again, our gestured description of our flight, our crash, and the display of our clothing and equipment.

Anticipating that they might be in the mountains a long time, they endeavored to learn their hosts' language but were able to master only about two hundred words. They found that the Mishmi

had many peculiar customs, but their one characteristic which never ceased to startle us was their imperviousness to certain kinds of pain. The men would sort through the red-hot coals with their bare hands to find a tinder with which to light their pipes. One of them, trying to get us to unwrap the bandages from our ankles to see what was under them, rubbed his hand over his own ankle in a gesture. For the first time, apparently, he discovered a large round bump, like a cyst, on his ankle bone. He simply drew his knife, sliced off the bump with one deft blow and, with the blood streaming down his foot, returned the knife to the scabbard and kept right on talking to us as though he had simply brushed away a fly.

What work was done was managed by the women. The men, for the most part, sat about the fire, which the women tended, conversing with the most raucous laughter, smoking their long bamboo pipes, into which they would stuff dark, stringy, home-cured tobacco. I had never smoked before, but I became an inveterate tobacco fiend with the pipe they made for me. We began to smoke opium, not only because it was expected of us but because we thought it might help us to sleep. It did not have the slightest effect on us. Later, we were told that, had we stopped smoking and then started again, we might have become addicts.

One evening an unusual visitor appeared, sporting a wide bamboo hat and carrying an ancient flintlock on his shoulder. He was an elderly trader, and he brought with him two bearers carrying enormous bags of what appeared to be red sand but which was, in fact, salt. Unlike everyone else Rosbert and Hammel had met, he actually had some familiarity with Caucasians, having met one or two in the course of his life. He viewed their story in sign — "which by now had become a mechanical routine" — and offered to take them with him on his travels.

They estimated that it would be the better part of a week before their ankles would be strong enough for them to keep up with him but indicated they would follow after him when they could. The old man was obviously disappointed and tried to console himself by getting them to give him their one pencil, "which we used for one of our stock demonstrations." They were unwilling to part with it since it was their only means of writing the messages that might bring about their rescue, and so they gently refused, even though the old man came back to them several times asking for it. Eventually he gave up and set off into the night with his porters.

A few days later, a strikingly handsome youngster arrived, sporting an impressive set of earrings and a necklace of large silver coins. He was the trader's son, and he came bearing gifts in the form of a chicken, a little tea, and some rice. These he presented with an elaborate show of generosity, and then "he, too, evidenced a peculiar interest in the pencil." Rosbert placated him by tearing off a corner of his flight map and inscribing a message for the boy's father on it: WE ARE TWO AMERICAN PILOTS. WE CRASHED INTO THE MOUNTAIN. WE WILL COME TO YOUR CAMP IN FIVE DAYS.

The boy snatched the paper from the captain's hand and hurried away. The men decided that he had wanted the note for a souvenir, and they could only hope that he would return at the appointed time to lead them to his father.

He was back at noon on the fourth day. They could see that he had made a long march in a great hurry and that he was very tired, but he was wearing an intriguing, enormous grin. He sat cross-legged before them and ceremoniously produced presents — four eggs — one at a time from his pouch. Then with a theatrical flourish, he left the hut for a moment, coming back with an envelope.

It was a standard India state telegraph form sealed with wax. With hearts beating like trip hammers, Ridge and I clawed the envelope open. It contained a message from Lt. W. Hutchings, the commanding officer of a British scouting column then about four days' march away. He was sending rations by the messenger, and a medical officer with aid would follow shortly.

Ridge and I were delirious at the good news. We hugged each other and cried like a couple of babies. The boy explained to our houseful of hosts and hostesses, and they, too, joined in our jubilation, heaping more wood on the fire, breaking out bamboo stocks of some alcoholic corn drink and dancing and shouting about the room. In an hour or so, the porters arrived with the supplies, and we shared cigarettes, matches, salt, and tea with everyone in the hut. The matches and white salt they put in their personal treasure pouches, the tea they brewed, and the cigarettes they smoked with a religious ritual, deeply inhaling each little puff. It was daylight before any of us in the hut slept. It was a night to celebrate.

The medical officer Lieutenant Hutchings sent was Captain C. E. Lax. He had taken two days longer to traverse the same route than the native messengers had. Though weary from the trip, he immediately examined his new patients. He diagnosed their injuries, deciding against trying to reset Rosbert's ankle until he could be taken to a hospital, and then he treated their numerous cuts, bumps, and bruises. He also told them that they were the first white men to come into the area and that "had it not been that the British column, because of the war, had penetrated even as close as four days' march, we might never have been found."

The doctor's plan was to set out the next morning for the nearest British camp, using native porters to assist the injured Americans. Arrangements would then be made to get Rosbert and Hammel back to their unit.

Long before dawn, Ridge and I were urging the doctor to start. Such a swift change of fortune had unsettled us a bit, and we both confessed to a heavy tug at leaving these strange people who had been so kind and so hospitable to a couple of strangers who, dropping suddenly out of another world, had been taken into their family and treated as brothers through these many days. We divided among them everything we had — the pencil, the flashlight, everything out of our pockets, and then borrowed all the silver coins the captain had, in an effort to express our appreciation. They, too, seemed to regret our going, and accompanied us to the edge of the clearing as Ridge and I, leaning on the shoulders of the two native messengers, followed the doctor down the rocky trail.

It took sixteen more days of hiking to get out of the mountains, but hiking on a full stomach, resting at night in shelters on grass pallets, swathed in blankets. Over tough places our little native helpers, who weighed fifty pounds less than either Ridge or I, carried us, resting in a sling swung from their foreheads. Up the sides of cliffs, along boulder-strewn river beds, on cable-slung bridges that Gurkha engineers built ahead of us over monsoon-fed raging torrents, these little men led or carried us until, finally, we reached the crest of the last mountain range. There, below us, in a lovely green valley on the banks of a great river, lay a little British frontier station, a sight as welcome as the skyline of New York.

Rosbert and Hammel were transported by truck to their base in India. Ridge remained there, recuperating for a month before he resumed flying. Rosbert, on the other hand, was immediately flown back to Seattle to have his ankle reconstructed by a specialist. There he was reunited with his wife, Marianne, who had never given up hope that her husband would be found alive. A singer in a band, she had for some time been performing a song written in her honor: "I'll Be Waiting."

January 31, 1944   *An Air Transport Command plane runs out of fuel near the Florida coast and crashes into the ocean.*

The three-man crew had braced themselves for a wrenching impact, but the aircraft belly-flopped with hardly a jolt. As water poured into the fuselage, Private First Class Hubert Elsie inflated a rubber raft, pushed it through a side door, and climbed into it along with the other two crewmen, Captain Bill Hart and Lieutenant Paul Madden. They carried with them a parachute bag into which Elsie had thrown some tools, emergency gear, and a few supplies.

They scrambled to assemble two oars as the inflated lifeboat was bounced and spun about by heavy swells. No sooner had they gotten the pieces together, however, than they became nauseated and dropped them to retch.

Madden would later recall that he

> had fished in choppy seas before, but I had never had a feeling like that. It was as if we were trying to get rid of not only any food we had in us but our insides as well. I was careful to be sick in the water. I was afraid that if we got anything on the raft it would draw sharks; and if, in my spasms of sickness, I accidentally made a mess on its rubber surface, I washed it off.
>
> The raft was taking in a dangerous amount of water and, sick as we were, we had to get out the collapsible bailing bucket and go to work. But the least effort, such as bending over, made us violently ill all over again, and left us sweating and trembly until another attack of nausea hit us. Between spells, I tried to congratulate Bill upon his landing and tell him what a swell job he'd done and how we owed it to him that none of us had broken legs or cuts to make matters worse.
>
> We could see the ship with its wing and tail lights shining — we had come down around ten-thirty at night — but try as desperately as we could, we couldn't work our way back to it. Using the oars sent us off into other spells of violent retching. We kept within sight of the plane's lights for about twenty minutes. Then, all at once, they were gone. Seeing them go left me with a stunned feeling, a sense of being lost and lonely more intense than I had ever imagined such a feeling could be.

Elsie lost an oar over the side, and Madden, wanting to preserve the other one, disassembled it and stowed it with the supplies. They could not control the course of the boat, anyway. It skidded over the waves like a cake of soap, Madden thought. It would rise on the crest of a swell and then plunge into the trough on the other side, only to rise again on the next one.

Sea water soaked their clothes and filled the bottom of the raft. They spent that first night alternately bailing and napping. The hours passed slowly, and the night seemed endless.

When the sun finally rose, it was hazy and obscured by clouds. "Hell's bells," Hart complained, "all night I dreamed of taking off my clothes and drying them out, and what do we get? A sun with hospital pallor."

They still felt seasick, and so they ate nothing that day. In the compartments in the walls of the raft they found five cans of water, fourteen tins of emergency rations, a sea anchor, a small air pump, two sails, and several cans of sea trace, a yellow-green signal dye to be spread on the water.

They inflated the boat's seats with the pump and spent most of the day seated under the sail, trying to stay dry, but the spray soaked their backs, and they shivered. Madden would come to regret the inactivity of those hours. They should have taken the time to secure the food and supplies, tying the compartment bags to the raft with shroud line. It would be a tragically costly error, one born not of laziness but of optimism. The fliers believed they would be picked up very quickly, probably before the day was over. In reality the boat would not be found for eleven days.

> We took our first drink of water early in the afternoon. We hadn't got to the point of limiting ourselves to a certain amount, because we were still clinging to the illusion that we'd be rescued promptly, so we drank what we wanted. In the afternoon our stomachs didn't feel quite so wobbly, and what with our first drink and Bill's cigarettes — he found two packs his leather jacket had protected from water, and lit them with matches kept in a watertight container — we perked up and even began to joke. Before long, we were launched on one of those "If I had my choice of somebody to spend time with on a raft, who would I choose" discussions. Bill thought Hedy Lamarr might be a cozy raft mate. I held out for Ginny Simms, but all Elsie wanted was a fine, solid body of rock-ribbed land to cling to.

Madden, an ardent Catholic whose sister was a nun, got out a rosary she had sent him. Throughout their ordeal he would pray regularly, and he urged the others to do the same.

> After a while, darkness came down again, and we faced the fact that we'd have to spend another night on the raft. We decided to keep one man on watch. We put the sail over us as a blanket, and Bill and I tried to doze off while Elsie took the first watch. We lay on our

sides, huddled together. There wasn't a single moment during our time on the raft when we weren't touching one another. When one man made a move the other two knew it instantly. We were continually damp — the covering over us made it very steamy and sticky. I felt as if I were smothering, and occasionally I poked my face out to breathe.

Toward morning, Elsie woke me and pointed out a light on the horizon near the water. We wanted it to be a lighthouse so badly instead of a star that we convinced ourselves its color was different from the other stars. When we roused Bill he was skeptical, but even he thought it might be a light of some kind. He said, "Let's yell," and we all yelled together. Then gradually the light began to rise into the sky, and we knew we were wrong. Afterward, thinking about how we had yelled like that out there to call a lighthouse keeper, when there was no one to hear us, we felt foolish.

The sun warmed them, and they spread their leather jackets out to dry. Their spirits rose, and they ate parts of two tins of rations and divided a fruit bar. (Hart placed Madden in charge of the food because he had taken courses in a survival school.) Madden cut shroud lines to tie the parachute bag to the seat, but he still did not secure the boat's food supplies or the gallon-and-a-half vacuum bottle of water they had brought from the plane.

At ten o'clock in the morning, they sighted a C-47 or C-46 flying west. They fired several flares and took off their Mae Wests and waved them, but the aircraft flew on. Long afterward Madden would reflect that "to those in the plane, which was flying at a couple of thousand feet, we were only a dancing speck in the distance."

They were disappointed but told themselves that the appearance of the aircraft was a hopeful sign. Later in the day a PBY (U.S. Navy patrol flying boat) flew near, but again flares and the waving of Mae Wests failed to attract the crew's attention.

To cheer up his fellows, Madden wrapped a length of parachute around his body and did impersonations of Katharine Hepburn and Mohandas Gandhi. To the great amusement of his audience, he nearly fell overboard "giving my all as Hepburn in *Morning Glory*." The men talked about their families and the jobs they had held in peacetime. They discussed flying, and they worried aloud about how their mothers would feel when they heard they were missing.

In midafternoon the wind picked up and the temperature dropped. They put on their jackets and finished one of the cans of rations.

After dark Madden doled out some crackers and half a tin of cheese mixed with meat; he put the other half in his pocket. The food made them thirsty, and so "we drank conservatively from one of the emergency water cans — each one of which held about half a pint. Bill was bothered by thirst more than Elsie or I; from the beginning his system seemed to need more moisture than ours."

The violence of the ocean increased.

As we headed into our third night, it became very rough indeed. Angry-looking swells lashed at us wickedly, and there was more stinging salt spray than we had felt before. The waves seemed to take hold of the raft and give it a shove, as if a hand were pushing it. We could almost feel it skidding over the water in a series of sudden rushes, and it gave us a queer and shaky sensation.

Elsie was on watch when the boat capsized for the first time. Hart and Madden woke to find themselves swimming. The three men fought to turn the raft over; finally it seemed to come alive and flip over by itself. Hart screamed, and Madden swam over to him. Elsie was already trying to help. The two men grabbed Hart by his belt and pushed him up until he could flop into the boat. Hart turned and drew Madden in while Elsie pushed, and then the two officers pulled in the enlisted man.

We lay there and panted like dogs after a hard run on a July day. After a while, it occurred to us to see if we had lost anything. The vacuum bottle was missing. Bill had taken a drink out of it just before we capsized, and hadn't had a chance to put it back. Then we made a discovery that sent our hearts downward under our ribs — the rubber compartments, with the exception of one which held the patching equipment to repair the raft, had torn loose, and by that time were on their way to the bottom of the sea. Our legs knocking around in the bottom of the raft had loosened them and, with the raft upside down, the weight of the things in them had finished tearing them off.

We had also lost our fishing tackle and the large and small sails that would have kept us dry. All the food was gone, with the exception of the little I had in my pocket, and one ration can that I had put into the parachute bag. We still had the emergency water cans under the seat, and while fishing around in the patching equipment we found a little book called *Survival in the Jungle*. Looking back at it now, that book seems a comedy touch. It didn't then. We took turns reading it and making sarcastic comments on it, until Bill finally became so disgusted with it that he tore it up and threw it into the sea.

Hart felt bad about having forgotten to put the vacuum bottle back into the bag. All three of the men upbraided themselves for not tying the sail to the boat and for not carefully securing the compartments.

Then they noticed that the oar and the sea anchor were gone. Captain Hart explained that he had screamed for help because his leg had become entangled in the anchor's rope, and he had felt himself being pulled under.

We were shaken by our losses and weak from that first capsizing, but after that, when we saw a rough wave coming, we threw our weight to that side to keep us from going over. However, in spite of all we could do, we capsized once more that night. This time we had no help from the waves in flipping the raft right side up again. When at last we made it, Bill had swallowed so much water that he was too knocked out to help himself, and I had to pull at him hard while the water yanked hungrily at his body. When, finally, we all got in, we lay there, completely bushed. The waves had slapped us around, and we were cold and emptied of strength. But we couldn't lie there long, because, as bad as we felt, it would have been ever so much worse if the raft had turned over again, and we had to do what we could to keep that from happening.

In the morning Madden dug out of his pocket the half tin of cheese and meat. Salt water had gotten to it, and only one other can of food remained. Madden divided the contents of the open tin three ways. Hart said he did not want any of it, and the other two tried to talk him into eating, but in the end Madden and Elsie shared the ration. They gagged against the sea salt but kept the food down.

The heavy swells and cold weather continued through the day. In the afternoon a PBY flew over, but Hart's red parachute flare was not seen. They talked about the plane for a long time after it was gone. "I think we should have fired the flare earlier," Hart said. "I bet that pilot would feel bad if he knew how close he came to us." The ordeal was beginning to take a toll.

On the fourth night, my wrist watch was the only one still running, and the other two kept asking me what time it was, and trying to get me to look at its luminous dial. They'd made up their minds it was about two in the morning, when it was actually only eight or nine o'clock. Finally I stopped telling them the time, and just shoved my wrist out for them to see, because I knew it would be so much earlier than they thought.

Most of the time, the waves were so rough we had to bail. In the beginning, I hadn't been so ambitious as Bill and Elsie about bailing; Bill hadn't wanted any water to stay in the raft at all. But by the end of the fourth day, things were reversed. He didn't display as much interest in bailing, and I had a terrific urge to wield the bucket. I grew to count on it to give me something to do and to pass the time — especially at night.

In the darkness they whiled away the hours fantasizing about what they would do when they were rescued. Hart promised to take them to a Turkish bath and buy them a massage, a steam bath, "and all the trimmings." Then he would stand them to a round of creamy milk shakes so thick they would have to be eaten with spoons. He recalled a meal he had been served at a hotel, how the waiters had repeatedly filled his glass with water.

"Lay off, Bill," Madden pleaded. "You're driving me crazy."

But Elsie chimed in with a recollection of a wooden rain barrel on his folks' New York State farm. He used to stick his head into it up to his ears and drink and drink and drink. . . .

The topic changed to the Hollywood film *Action in the North Atlantic,* in which a German submarine torpedoes a ship and the survivors spend eight days on a raft. The men remembered how much healthier the actors looked during their cinematic ordeal than they felt themselves to be.

"That Humphrey Bogart is tops," Hart admitted, "but maybe we're just sissies."

A plane flew directly overhead on the afternoon of the fifth day. The castaways fired more flares, waved Mae Wests "like windmills," and shouted desperately. "Come on, you!" Madden cried out in despair. "Don't turn away like the other one did." But the aircraft sped on. Hart cursed wildly, alarmingly, and Madden tried to calm him by suggesting that the pilot was on a mission that would bring him back over the same course again. The next time he would surely spot them.

Captain Hart's slowly deteriorating physical and mental health was evident again at twilight. Lieutenant Madden proposed that they eat the last tin of rations and finish off a can of water opened earlier in the day. He unsealed the food tin to find it contained a large bar of chocolate wrapped in layers of paper. He carefully unwrapped the bar and divided it in half, saving half for the next day and cutting the remainder into three pieces. But Hart irascibly refused to consume his share.

"Bill, you've got to eat it," the lieutenant pleaded. "You'll be in bad shape if you don't."

But Hart remained adamant. "The hell with it," he said. "It's too heavy. I'm thirsty now, and having my mouth gummed up with chocolate would drive me nuts."

Elsie and Madden managed to swallow the candy.

I made a confession to the others that day. I said, "Don't get sore about this, but once, a long time ago, I told somebody I wouldn't mind going out on a raft and spending a few days on it, just for the experience." I made it plain to them that I hadn't wished it, but that I'd had it in my mind, and even the fact that I'd thought about it at all was bothering me and I had to get it off my chest.

The admission offered Madden little relief, however, and he continued to dwell on his mistakes and misdeeds, especially the time he burned up all his sister's clothes by setting her closet on fire. Hart, too, was feeling remorse: "Boy, when I'm saved, I'm going to mend my ways," he would say over and over again.

Sometimes in conversation one of the men would say, "*If* I'm saved," instead of "when," and the other two would invariably upbraid him: "What do you mean, *if?*"

By now Hart was constantly complaining of thirst, and he talked a lot about his pet theory that the best place for storing water is inside the human body. "It doesn't do much good to try and hold water in a container," he would say. "A doctor told me once you couldn't do anything better than store it inside yourself." Having offered the argument, he finally got to the real point: "Well, fellows, let's have what's left of it."

They made a ritual of their last drink of water. The captain brought out the tin, unfastened the stopper, and passed it to his lieutenant. Madden was painfully aware of just how small a container it was. He knew that there was only enough for him to take just a sip.

But that drink tasted better to me than any other drink I'd ever had in my life. Perhaps knowing I wouldn't have any more for a long time, maybe never, made me feel that way about it. Then I passed it on to Elsie. He drank his share and looked away from us. Whatever was in his face, he didn't want us to see it. Bill took the can and drained it. When he was done I cut the lid off and pressed down the rough edges. The inside of the can was waxed and still wet, so I rubbed my fingers over the wax and sucked them.

That night — I marked the days off on the rubber fabric of the raft with a stub of pencil; four down strokes, then one stroke crossing them out, for the fifth — the sea made the raft buck like a bronco and kept us awake. We had to keep sliding from one side of the raft to the other to keep it from going over, and we were forced to bail continuously. We ran into a bit of rain that night — a skimpy, tantalizing shower, barely enough to wet our mouths.

Madden made a distress signal out of an empty water tin by carefully inscribing a message into it with his penknife: 3 MEN ALIVE HELP. He cast it overboard and then cut open two of the other empty cans, carefully turning the edges down with pliers. If there was a hard rain, the tins could be used to catch water, and, anyway, it gave him something to do.

The next morning the aluminum cans served as mirrors in which they could see the deterioration of their faces and bodies. Madden was conscious of the drastic changes in all their appearances, but he was most disturbed by Hart's decline. As the days went by he became thinner and thinner and his cheekbones more and more prominent.

Elsie had curly, sandy hair and a ruddy complexion. Ordinarily, he was chubby, but lack of nourishment made his neck shrink and melt away, until, after a while, it was thin as a small boy's neck. The lack of food drained our fat away and we had begun to look dehydrated and hollow-eyed. Our beards had begun to sprout, and we were wild-looking. Elsie's nose was burned by the sun, and since Bill's hair was sparse, I was afraid he'd get a bad burn, so I gave him the bandanna I'd worn on my head after I'd lost my cap being seasick the first night. Bill had a peaked look. He showed the effects of what we were going through more than either Elsie or I, but he still had his chin up and kidded me about my beard.

"Paul," he said, "you could get a job posing for holy pictures, the way you look."

On the morning of the sixth day a wave flipped the boat, scattering the men across the water. They struggled against the heavy swells to return to it, then wrestled to right it. When at last this was done, Hart's strength was gone. He was unable to help the others climb in. Madden and Elsie managed to pull themselves in and fell to the bottom, weak and dizzy. They had to rest for a few moments before they could gather the strength to haul Hart's dead weight in after them.

Madden felt as if "my bones had turned to water, and my muscles twitched and jumped." He was dazed and semiconscious, as was Elsie. But Hart, who had swallowed great quantities of salt water both in this dunking and in previous ones, was in the worst shape. Before long he was delirious. Slyly, trying to hide it from the others, he downed an imaginary tin of water. He asked someone whom only he could see, "What time is that fellow going to show up?" Then he added, "It's time we got that message. . . . We've got to get in shape, if we're going out tonight on a date."

He turned furious, belligerent. Glaring wildly at his subordinates, he raged, "I would have to go and get two bozos like you two to get stuck with in the middle of nowhere."

Madden could see that his eyes were not focusing properly. Hart complained of the sores on his spine and buttocks caused by the salt water and the rubbing of the fabric against his skin, and he announced that he was going to walk away from them, walk across the water. Madden managed to talk him out of it.

Now Hart tried to peel pieces of rubber from the seat, wanting to eat them as food. More ominously, he pulled a machete out of the parachute bag and put it down beside him. Madden did not attempt to reason with him; he just calmly took the weapon away and put it back in the bag. Hart did not protest; he only looked at his copilot in that hazy way of his.

Madden and Elsie were both experiencing lung problems; they felt as if great weights were hanging under their breastbones. Madden was also plagued with a dry, racking cough. They had finally gotten Hart to lie down when the raft flipped over again. The two of them managed to right it once more, but by that time Hart had drifted ten yards away. Elsie swam to him and held him up while Madden pushed the boat over to them.

> They clung to one side, while I held on to the other. Bill kept going under at intervals. He couldn't hold his head up, and when Elsie lifted him to the surface again, he came up with his eyes open; sea water was streaming from them, and they were staring at us unseeing. His mouth was open too. It was almost impossible to bring him into the raft, but we got him in at last, and I took my jacket off — as did Elsie — and we spread them over him.
>
> Once more we persuaded him to lie down with his head back. His eyes rolled upward until you could see only their whites. The color was drained out of his face, and he looked shockingly pale. We cast about desperately in our minds for something we could do to help him, so I brought out some sulfa pills — the water had made a paste

of them — and said to him, "Bill, you've got to take some of these."
But he wouldn't swallow them, and while I was trying to get them
between his lips, he bit down on my finger so hard that I yelled in
agony. He must have thought that my finger was food. Certainly he
wouldn't have done a thing like that in his right mind.

After all the earlier banter with Hart about religion, Madden now
discovered that Elsie was a fellow Catholic. They said the rosary
together for their captain. He lay in the bottom of the boat, mumbling and groaning. Madden, who had been an altar boy, thought
his mutterings sounded like a Latin prayer.

About eight-thirty that night Madden checked Hart and found that
his pulse was very faint and his skin cold. He asked him if he had
ever been baptized, but Hart could not reply. The captain was
clearly near death. Having been taught by priests that where there
is a question about whether a dying person has been baptized, a
layman should perform the rite himself, Madden sprinkled sea water
on Hart's head, intoning, "In case thou aren't already baptized, I
baptize thee in the name of the Father, and of the Son, and of the
Holy Ghost." Fearful that he had not done it right, he repeated the
baptism.

A short time later, Hart sat bolt upright and cried out Madden's
name. His eyes rolled down into their normal position, and he
smiled. He slumped against Madden, who first grabbed him to keep
him from falling over and then checked for a pulse. There was none.
He slipped his hand inside the captain's shirt, feeling for a heartbeat, but felt nothing save "icy-cold skin."

We had tried to prepare ourselves for Bill's death. Elsie and I had
held whispered conferences at our end of the raft in which we had
agreed that he wouldn't be with us long. There was something about
him, a sort of indescribable look that told us that nothing we could
do for him would do much good, but now, just sitting there looking
at him with life gone from his body, I felt as if I were drowning in
black depression, and it seemed unbearably sad that he would never
kid Elsie any more about his big feet or be able to take that job in
India after the war or even light up a cigarette and drag on it with a
blissful look on his face.

I guess it's not according to the Book, but I made a little speech to
God in my mind about him. It was as if I were giving him a reference,
so those where he was going would know all about him. It went
something like this: "His full name and rank is Capt. William E. Hart.
He is a captain in the Army of the United States. He came in as a

first lieutenant in 1942 and was later promoted to captain. He has
served as an instructor in Reno, Nevada, and Homestead, Florida,
and he is check pilot to the squadron we belong to. He has done his
best to make me a better flier, quizzing me from time to time as to
what I would do in this emergency or that emergency. Now he's
making an emergency landing he's never made before. He is a good
Joe, and we hope he gets a break.''

They could not bring themselves to drop his body over the side.
They tucked it under the seats, resolving to keep it with them as
long as they could. They sat for a long time in silence, and then
Elsie wondered aloud how long it would be before they died, too.
Madden would not let him dwell on it: "Let's not worry about it. If
we're going to die, we're going to die.''

They did not lie down to sleep that night. Not wanting to crowd
against the corpse, they sat up, thinking and talking a little.

In the morning their minds were still on Hart. They kept looking
at his body, recalling things he had said and done. How, on the
fourth day, he had organized a contest to determine which of them
had the prettiest feet and had been the winner by acclamation. They
remembered jokes, genial arguments, and bits of wisdom. . . .

They talked about what to do with his corpse. The festering sores
on their buttocks and backs made them want to shift their positions
from time to time, but it was difficult to move around without stepping on Hart's body or kicking it. To put their feet on it made them
uneasy. It was therefore time to bury him.

They said the rosary again and prayed that what they were doing
was "the decent and honorable thing by Bill.'' They took off his
heavy flight jacket but left the rest of his clothes on. They weighted
his corpse by tying a section of parachute to the feet and filling it
with most of the tools Elsie had brought from the plane. They had
difficulty getting the body over the side of the boat, and after they
did, it floated briefly and then slipped beneath the surface at an
angle. They saw no sharks and "somehow that made us feel better
about it.''

In the evening, having been without water for so long, Elsie
"brought up the advisability of drinking waste water from our
bodies.'' Madden had been told in the survival course that it was
best to drink urine only after boiling the impurities out of it, something which it was obviously not possible to do. They drank it anyway, mixing in chocolate shavings from their last cube to make it

"less repellent," but they were still nauseated. They agreed to give up the idea for another twenty-four hours.

The raft capsized three times that night. We thought it might be easier not having Bill to hold up in the water and boost back into the raft, but, actually, it didn't help any; just getting ourselves back in took every morsel of strength we had left. We didn't get any sleep at all. During the night, Elsie kept thinking he heard train whistles, but I couldn't hear them, so [he] decided it must have been his imagination playing tricks. That night was really hell. Even with the distraction offered by the roughness of the sea and the constant bailing, it seemed unending. We'd think it must be three or four in the morning, and it would be only nine or ten at night.

To pass the time, I tried to get Elsie to talk by telling him about some of the things that happened to me when I was stationed in Alaska. I told him about shooting geese up there, and how a pal and I got into pursuit planes and showed off for some girls by flying in formation under a bridge, and how the general caught us and grounded us for three weeks.

Elsie wasn't much of a talker. I had to pull the words out of him. He'd been a fireman in peacetime, and I asked him if he'd seen any good fires. "Yes," he answered, "we had some pretty good ones."

There was a long pause, and I asked, "What were they like?" And after another interval of silence, he told me about a big, oily one that had sent up great clouds of greasy smoke.

On the eighth day the ocean became calm again, and the men wanted to take off their clothes to dry. Their zippers were corroded, and the tabs cut into their swollen fingers. Madden finally pulled them down with pliers.

Their sores looked terrible. Elsie had one that appeared to be gangrenous. They took turns applying mosquito oil to the wounds — it was the only salve they had.

In an effort to stabilize the boat, they dangled a leather jacket over the side. The lining attracted fish, including baby sharks, and Elsie baited fishhooks with sheepskin, using copper wire for a line. None of the fish bit, and the men cursed them wearily. They cut off their insignia with the idea that the bright colors might serve as lures, and when they did not, they pulled the peeling skin from their lips and put it on the hooks. The skin floated away in the water.

Finally, after all the ideas had failed, I tried to knock off a fish with a machete. I hung over the side with my arms wet up to the shoulders and slapped at passing fins with the knife. I managed to hit one and drew blood, but he went down quickly out of my reach. I couldn't have been thinking too clearly, for my first and almost overpowering impulse was to go right down after him, but I managed to restrain myself.

At dusk they put on their clothes, and when it got dark they fell into a fitful sleep. They awoke to find the boat rocking wildly. A shark was "playing tag" with them, swimming around and under the raft. Elsie proposed going after him with the machete. Madden, worried about would happen if the shark became enraged, talked him out of it.

On the ninth day they experienced a series of storms broken by occasional calms. They chewed on seaweed, doubting it would be nourishing but hoping it would ease their pangs and the "cottony" taste in their mouths. It did not: it only made them feel worse. They did find a small crab in the bottom of the boat, however, which had come in with the weeds. They ate it while its legs still wriggled.

We hoped that when night came on, it would be calmer, but the seas showed no indication of easing off, and it began to look as if we were in for a storm. When it came, the waves were like houses towering above us and obscuring the sky. They were so tremendous that our amazement at them almost overcame our fear. It was like sitting in on a fantastic movie in a nightmare. It was impossible for us to comprehend how waves could get that high. I'd flown over mountains, and those waves reminded me of some of the mountains I'd seen from the sky. For a while they seemed to come from every direction, beating in from all quarters and head-on too.

Toward the end of that tenth night, we capsized three times. Fortunately, each time we upset, we came up close to the raft. The sheepskin jacket hanging over the side seemed to help pull it right side up. And even with the waves mountain high, we managed to get back in. But each time we felt weaker and weaker. Even with all that welter of sound and the frightening display of the sea's fury, our eyes were so heavy that it was impossible to keep them open. Once I opened them just as a wave hit Elsie's end of the raft. It threw him up into the air, still in a sitting position, his eyes open in a shocked expression, and dropped him into the water. He came up right next to the raft. Then the sea, having taken him away, became whimsical and, as I reached over to help him in, a wave banged him on the bottom and threw him up into my outstretched arms.

For a moment, in all that churning helter-skelter of wetness, a brief sharp rain beat down so hard and so fiercely that when Elsie and I held our faces to the sky with our withered mouths wide open, it stung our skins severely. It hurt our eyeballs through the lids, even with our eyes closed. We each got a small mouthful. Just as we got over the first blissful thrill of having moisture soaking into our tissues and began to think of trying to bring out receptacles to catch it in, it stopped off short, as abruptly as it began.

Toward morning, when we capsized again, I thought, *I'm never going to get back.* Panic grew inside me, and I told myself, *This is it.* But gradually I worked my way back to the raft and hung on until I regained my breath. Elsie waited until I was strong enough to climb back in alone, then I helped pull him in after me. It was impossible for him to make it by himself because of his weight and weakness.

Large waves broke over the boat, flooding it and forcing the men to bail "like crazy people," but eventually they discovered that some water in the bottom added to its stability.

Elsie was hearing train whistles again, and when they slept, he dreamed of an island resort for castaways, called Joe's Place. There the food was delicious and plentiful, the fruit juice ice-cold, and the beds incredibly soft. He talked of Joe's Place in his sleep until Madden, fearing he was losing his mind, questioned him closely about the resort.

Did he really think he was there?

"No," said Elsie, "I just dreamed about it, but I feel sure there is a place like that somewhere."

Madden did not find the answer reassuring, but he was having hallucinations of his own. He kept dreaming of a gondola sliding up beside the raft. In it were waiters who tapped him on the shoulder and pointed to a French café on a nearby shore. "Won't you come over and join us?" they asked politely.

Madden decided to be tolerant of Elsie's little fixation.

On the morning of the tenth day the sun came out, and the castaways stripped and sunbathed. They tried to spear fishes with the machete. But as Madden lay draped over the rim of the boat, a new and uncontrollable urge seized him. He stuck his head into the ocean and filled his mouth with salt water, but he managed to stop himself from swallowing, gargling instead.

Elsie was watching him with grave concern. "You want to be careful of that," he warned him. "You know what it will do to you."

His obsession with staying alive had turned this normally taciturn flier positively loquacious. "Look at the things we've missed in life," he urged his lieutenant. "You're a lot younger than I am, and

you've got all your life ahead of you. Me, I want to get married.
When I get out of the army, I'm going to look around for a nice,
clean girl. I've had a lot of things just within my grasp, and I've let
them slip by. When I get married, I'm going to buy a farm and go
fishing and hunting.''

Madden's mind was on his family, particularly his mother, who
was gravely ill. He worried that the news of his death would kill
her.

> The thought came to me that, perhaps, if we both died, we would
> meet. But I hated knowing I must be causing my family worry and
> concern.
>
> Neither of us broke down during these discussions, but once when
> I was thinking about the gang at home and about my brother's chil-
> dren and my sister's child, my throat worked and my eyes burned
> and I had to stop thinking about them. Something seemed to tell us
> that it was best to keep certain things to ourselves — things that hit
> us hard — like how we felt about missing the plane on the fifth day,
> and the thought of those close to us back home.
>
> More and more, our thoughts were turning to food. Hunger seeped
> through us, filling every corner of our bodies. We talked about
> whether we could suck any nourishment from the leather of our jack-
> ets, and we spent hours looking the raft over, cataloguing the things
> we had with us that we might possibly put into our mouths. We tried
> chewing our leather jackets, but they were so saturated with salt that
> the pleasure of feeling our teeth bite down on something didn't make
> up for the unpleasantness of the taste. The hunger feeling was not
> exactly a pain; it was a sensation inside the stomach that gradually
> became more insistent, until it was the most important thing in the
> world — even more important than being rescued. It was a sort of
> tight, crampy feeling; ironically, very much like the feeling you have
> after you've eaten too much. There was a kind of dull soreness, as if
> you were enormously distended and someone were pressing against
> you. We'd lost so much flesh that the weight of our Mae Wests resting
> upon us was almost insupportable. But we had to wear them con-
> stantly because of the treacherous waves, and I sat for long periods
> of time with my folded arms supporting mine to ease its weight from
> my belly.

He kept thinking about the last meal he had eaten before takeoff.
He lovingly dwelled on each course: the big steak, french-fried
potatoes, peas, salad, and vanilla ice cream. The steak had been so
large he had not been able to finish it, and now in his mind it grew
to truly gigantic proportions; it became browner on the outside and

rarer on the inside; he saw its juices, smelled its aroma. . . .

The two men ripped buttons from their uniforms and put them into their mouths in an attempt to stimulate their salivary glands but disagreed on whether the strategy worked. Madden tried eating quinine tablets but found them too bitter to swallow. He washed out his mouth with salt water.

The boat had started leaking air on the second day, and they had had to inflate it regularly with a small hand pump. Now, as they grew weaker, this light chore became more exhausting. After just a few strokes Madden had to stop and rest. Even the mildest exertion quickly left both of them gasping for breath.

They hung their legs over the side and washed their faces with sea water, using a compress from the first-aid kit as a washcloth. They combed their hair and tidied their clothing.

Before sunset, Elsie began to talk about his imaginary train whistles and locomotive sounds again. He was so intense about it, he almost made me think I heard them too. So I got a whistle out of the parachute bag, and said, "We'll give out with three dits, three dots and three more dits to spell out SOS and see what happens." I blew three shorts, three long ones, then three more shorts. When Elsie tried it, he made his dashes too long, and his dots too short, and I had to tell him, "Elsie, get your dashes a little shorter." But even the slight effort of blowing tired us so tremendously that we gave it up and just sat there together. Then, after a while, he said, "I still hear those train whistles," and we'd do it all over again.

We must have looked funny, whistling out there in all that water, with no one to hear us. Then we thought we heard the sound of a motorboat, and we yelled in our cracked voices, but the motorboat was a delusion too.

That night around ten o'clock, I was awakened once more by a shark. He was nosing around the sheepskin jacket hanging over the side. Then he'd give a flip of his tail and duck under the raft. Finally, I became fed up with his antics and waited until he came in once more. My left foot was swollen so badly that I had taken that shoe off, and this time I belted him on the side with it. Little incidents had taken on tremendous importance in my mind, and for a few seconds the whole world was made up of a bitter contest between me and that shark. The blow with the shoe chased him under the raft, and I kicked him there when I felt him under the rubber. Afterward, I thought of how foolish I'd been, as I might have punched a hole in it.

The ocean was choppy on the morning of the eleventh day. White-caps surrounded them, and the wind flung salt spray into their faces.

The danger of the boat's capsizing brought Elsie out of his stupor. Agitated, he repeatedly warned Madden that they were in jeopardy, but the copilot could only stare at him dully and wonder how he could care about anything, even getting dumped in the sea. Besides, there was nothing they could do about it.

The raft did go over, and the two men fought to right it. When at last they succeeded, they were exhausted and trembling. Madden tried to pull himself back in, but he could not. He worked his way around to the far side of it, where Elsie was clinging. He told the private that he did not think he had the energy to climb in, but he would make one more attempt — and if he succeeded he would try to pull him in, too. Madden managed to get his body over the rim, and then a wave turned the boat over, dumping him into the ocean again.

It took a long time for them to right it once more.

It seemed as if I had been in water boiling around me all my life. The parachute bag with the various objects Elsie had put into it was hanging overside. I worked myself up until I got my legs around it, and by sitting on it and holding onto the side of the raft, I managed to stretch out and grab hold of the carbon-dioxide canister that we'd used to inflate it. With the other hand, I held the shroud line that ran around the raft's edge. With these two I managed to get my body over and into it. I lay there as if dead. Finally I sat up, and crawled over to the side of the raft and tried to help Elsie. Seizing him, I pulled, putting everything I had into the effort.

Elsie did not move. The two men looked at each other, and Madden was struck with how deeply the other man's eyes had sunken into his head. Elsie said, "Paul, I don't know how you ever got in."

"Come on," Madden replied. "You've got to get in before you lose too much strength."

"I just don't think I can do it," the man in the ocean said softly.

The problem, Madden decided, was Elsie's leather flight jacket. It had absorbed so much water that he estimated it weighed thirty or forty pounds. "Elsie," he said, "let's try to unzip your sheepskin jacket. It's holding you down."

The two men fumbled with swollen hands at the zipper, eventually managing to work it lower. Getting him out of it was no less difficult.

I lay over the side of the raft, with the water butting my shoulders and chest, trying to pull him out of the jacket. But each time that I thought I had it off him, his hands would slip and he'd grow panicky, and we weren't getting anywhere.

I was trying to shift my balance a little to work more effectively when I heard him say, "I'm going, Paul. It's no use."

A wave splashed into my eyes, blinding me. I must have slackened my grip when the salt made my eyes burn intolerably, for in the second or two that elapsed before I could see once more, Elsie was five or six yards away. He went down as quickly as if a weight had been attached to him.

I lay there, half in the raft and half in the water. One part of my mind told me to go down after Elsie, but another part seemed to keep me from what would have been a suicidal effort. I knew I'd never be able to get back into the raft again if it went over. I'd just have to cling to its side until I let go and dropped down into the sea to join Elsie or a shark ripped me to bits. Instinct took over my actions and by inches I fell back into the raft.

I lay there with the water sloshing over me, not even bothering to bail, and said all the prayers I knew.

Alone now, Lieutenant Madden began slipping in and out of a dreamlike state. He returned to the French café and saw a table heaped high with food. A huge bowl of fruit stood in the middle of it, surrounded by dishes of olives and carrots. Seated around the table were his friends and family. A waiter approached him and invited him to join the others. Still hallucinating, he decided he had been put in this predicament as a test "to see if I was on the level with the world." He awoke feeling "all the pangs of a condemned prisoner who has had a reprieve held out to him, only to have it snatched away."

It was a nightmare, he told himself, though its vividness continued to disturb him. He tried to get hold of himself, to clear his brain, but soon he was off again. This time he saw a basket of oranges float up to the boat. The fruit was as cold as if it had just come out of an icebox. He hauled the basket in, and he and Elsie began devouring the oranges, skin and all. After a while they "got choosy" and peeled them before putting them into their mouths. Having eaten nearly a dozen each, they were satiated, but the magical basket held still more fruit. They filled the parachute bag and stuffed oranges into their pockets. There was yet one more in the bottom of the basket. Madden and Elsie agreed to share it by way of celebration.

So vivid was this dream that Madden awoke with the taste of oranges in his mouth. He shook his head, trying to clear his brain again, afraid of the fantasy's effect on his sanity. His mind was go-

A jaunty Lieutenant Paul Madden is on the mend after eleven days on a raft. (Permission of *The Saturday Evening Post*)

ing. Not only was he hallucinating, but he was experiencing black-outs as well. Even when conscious he was stupefied. He looked at Elsie's Mae West and thought, *There's a packet of sea trace in that, and I might as well use it.* He opened the package, dropped its contents into the ocean, and watched with dull fascination as the chemical spread.

He took a novena leaflet from his wallet and prayed. The prayer, to be said for nine days, had been sent to him by his sister from the convent, and he had been praying for eight days in a row. He said the novena and then turned the tattered and water-stained card over to read the other prayers printed on the back. He was so clumsy and weak, however, that a slight breeze blew it from his fingers. He was just feeling for the card under the water when he looked up and saw a tanker 150 yards away.

It was a mirage, he told himself, no different from Elsie's train whistles; another dream like the French café and the basket of oranges. Those oranges . . . he saw the basket float to the boat again, devoured the fruit with Elsie beside him once more . . . they did not bother to peel them until they each had had nearly a dozen . . . stowing the rest in the bag and their pockets . . . savoring that last celebratory one . . . Elsie alive and well with him, not drifting from the raft alone, in despair, sinking like a stone . . .

Madden looked up and saw the ship again. He spotted an American flag, heard alarm bells ringing. He watched the tanker sail past, thinking the crew had not seen him, and then she drifted back in his direction. He saw a boat being lowered and thought, *If they had only come an hour and a half sooner, they could have saved Elsie.* While he waited for rescue, he tried to figure out why he had been spared and not Elsie or Hart, but he could make no sense of it.

Sometime during the previous hour I'd put my weight on one side of the raft with my legs hanging over one side. The men at the tanker's rail started to yell at me to get my legs up, because there were sharks swimming around. But my head was dull, and the idea they tried to get across to me didn't seem very important. When the lifeboat reached me, a big husky fellow wrapped me in a blanket and lifted me in his arms and put me into the lifeboat. The tanker's crew pulled the lifeboat up on davits, and afterward pulled the raft up too.

Somebody unclasped my hands and removed my rosary. I didn't know I was holding it, and I looked down to see what they were up to. In an hour and a half since Elsie had died, I had wrapped it through my fingers so tightly that it was cutting into the flesh.

Brought on board the vessel, the emaciated Madden had further cause for reflection on his fate. This was, he learned, the only time the tanker had traveled this route without being part of a convoy, and as a result, she was far off course and four hours behind schedule. Then, too, that day was the first time in ten days he had used the sea trace, and he had dumped it just in time for the ship's crew to see it. "I don't want anyone to think my experience gave me a religious complex," Madden wrote, but he attributed his being found to the prayers said by him, his family, and friends.

He was told that when the yellow-green streak was first sighted, the American captain suspected that it might be a trap. He had been warned of just such a possibility, but a plane had flown over the tanker not long before, and he thought that the pilot might have had to bail out. It was only because of that aircraft that the captain risked his ship.

> When they got a good look at my face through the binoculars, they knew I hadn't been down any couple hours. To me all these things will always seem more than a series of coincidences.
>
> I asked whether we were in the Atlantic Ocean or the Gulf of Mexico. They told me I was in the Atlantic, and I answered, "That's good. Now I'm all set for combat." They didn't know what I was talking about, but what I really meant was this: I had been a wild pilot, fond of flying a hot plane and doing such forbidden things as buzzing towns and airports, but now I knew I'd never be wild again. All that had been beaten out of me by the sea, and I wanted the chance to prove that I could be steady and dependable.

May 13, 1945 *At three o'clock in the afternoon, a Douglas C-47 carrying sixteen servicemen and eight servicewomen crashes into a mountain in an area of New Guinea known as Hidden Valley, where no white man has ever been before. Nineteen die in the crash, and four of the five survivors are seriously injured.*

Before takeoff, WAC Corporal Margaret "Suzy" Hastings had first chosen a seat behind the pilot's compartment but had moved back to the rearmost seat because it offered a window with a better view. She wanted to get a look at Hidden Valley: pilots who had flown over it told of giant natives who were headhunters and cannibals; their women were all "Dorothy Lamours in Blackface." Yet the land these people inhabited was said to be carefully cultivated and watered with irrigation ditches. Corporal Hastings was anxious to see for herself, and some of the others on board shared her excitement. "Isn't this fun!" shouted Private First Class Eleanor Hanna as the engines revved up.

In less than an hour, the C-47 had crossed the Oranje Mountains and had swooped to a height of only three hundred feet above the valley's well-cultivated fields. Hastings glimpsed "a cluster of round huts with thatched roofs" just as the plane started to climb. The man sitting next to her was Lieutenant John S. McCollom. He suddenly gave a violent start and shouted, "Give her the gun and let's get out of here." For an instant Hastings believed he was joking. As the aircraft hit the treetops she thought, *I'm going to die, this is the time. But I won't die.* She found herself bouncing, bouncing, bouncing — and heard explosions like gunfire. The C-47 smashed into a mountain. Fire was scorching her face and hair. She could not move because someone was holding her tight around the waist. The diminutive corporal, who was only five feet tall and weighed less than a hundred pounds, broke that "viselike grip" and crawled on her hands and knees out of the wreckage.

She stood up to hear a man call her name. It was McCollom, who had emerged without a scratch. They saw that the tail of the aircraft had broken off from the rest of the fuselage. Both pieces were now engulfed in flames. The front end had borne the brunt of the impact, and only one person who had been in it lived through the crash; being in the rear had saved her and McCollom's lives.

They heard a woman cry, and McCollom raced back into the burning tail section; he emerged in a moment, dragging her, then plunged back into the fire and brought out another woman. One of them was Eleanor Hanna, who had thought the flight would be a lark.

A man staggered from the front of the plane. He was Technical Sergeant Kenneth Decker. His hair was matted, and a gash on his forehead exposed his skull. While it was not immediately evident to the others, he had also been badly burned and had suffered a broken arm. Dazed and unsteady, he mumbled over and over how this was a "helluva way to spend your birthday." (It was his thirty-fourth.)

The fire was spreading, moving closer to the little party of survivors. McCollom took charge of them, and, carrying Hanna, who was clearly dying, he led them to a ledge twenty-five yards away.

Hastings realized she had lost her shoes, and her right foot was cut and bleeding. Although she felt no pain yet, her legs were burned and the left side of her face was blistered. Her eyebrows and some of her hair had been singed, too.

> We had crashed at nine thousand feet and already we were chilled to the marrow. Now the daily rain of New Guinea began to fall, and soaked clothing added to our miseries. McCollom made repeated trips to the plane to see what he could salvage. Never once did he let us know the agony he was enduring. In that funeral pyre was his twin brother, Robert.
>
> He found emergency life rafts and stripped them of everything we could use: big yellow tarpaulins, small tins of water and hard candies, and a signal kit. He put the tarpaulin over the other two girls, gave Eleanor a little morphine, and then, exhausted, crawled under another tarpaulin with Decker and me. I guess you have to share the kind of paralyzing accident we had before you can realize that under such circumstances you cease to be two men and a woman. We were just three human beings bound together by a will to live.

At dawn McCollom knelt by Hanna and found that she was dead. He carefully wrapped her body in a tarpaulin and laid it underneath a tree.

The survivors did not talk about the death, one more added to so many, nor did they weep. Perhaps it was the stoicism of their wartime generation: McCollom, who had been so close to his brother Robert that they were known as "the inseparables," displayed no outward signs of grief through the long ordeal; Decker insisted on doing his part of the work despite his many injuries — and, indeed, for a long time did not even reveal that he had been severely burned.

They drank a little water, took vitamin pills, and ate hard candy. Decker and the two women were shaking uncontrollably from shock. It was agreed that they would rest where they were until the next day and then make their way down the mountain. Hastings wondered if she could make the trek without shoes but kept her doubts to herself.

A search plane flew over, and McCollom tried to attract the pilot's attention by flashing a mirror from the signal kit, but the canopy was too thick. They would have to get to a clearing down below to be seen. The knowledge that they were being searched for cheered them, nonetheless.

> As usual mist and rain began to close in on the mountain in midafternoon. I crawled under the tarpaulin with Laura. She was terribly restless. Not even the morphine we gave her quieted her. I dozed a

while, and when I woke up, Laura was so still it frightened me. I
screamed for McCollom. He came over and felt her pulse. He didn't
say a word. He just got another tarpaulin and wrapped her in it, then
laid her down beside Eleanor.

Laura Besley, a dark, pretty young woman, had been Hastings's
friend, and they had often double-dated together. Now she, too,
was dead, but Maggie Hastings, burned and in shock, was intent
upon her own preservation. "I ought to have felt terrible grief for
this dear friend," she later wrote candidly. "But all I could think
was: 'Now her shoes belong to me.'

"McCollom lighted a cigarette and gave me one. He stayed with
me till it was light. No night will ever again be as long as that one."

They went down the slope in the sunlight, carrying what supplies
they could. McCollom was in the lead, and Decker brought up the
rear. The jungle clawed at them and constantly snagged Hastings's
hair, which hung more than halfway to her waist. The men were
having to stop to disentangle it, so she told McCollom to cut it off.
He hacked at it with his pocketknife until it was only an inch and a
half long.

They went on through gullies and torrential streams and past
roaring waterfalls. Once their way was blocked by a twelve-foot
drop. McCollom seized a vine and swung out and over the waterfall
before letting himself down. He called out, ordering Maggie to follow, and she hurried to do so, not letting herself think about the
danger. When Decker was standing beside them, he joked about
Johnny Weissmuller.

At midday they heard rescue planes, but the canopy was too
dense for them to see the aircraft or for them to be seen by the
searchers. They were standing in a stream, exhausted, their bodies
numb with the cold. Their only hope lay below. They walked on.

That night they camped in the jungle, and in the morning they had
hard candy and water for breakfast. Hastings fantasized about hot
coffee. Her feet, legs, and one of her hands were infected, and she
was having trouble keeping up with McCollom. She was "half blind
with tears." She tried to hide it from the men, but once, when the
lieutenant got too far ahead of Decker and her, she cried out hysterically that "McCollom has gone off and left us, and he's got all the
food, and we're going to starve to death!"

To get her moving, Decker assumed the role of a callous drill
sergeant. "The least thing he called me was a piker and a quitter. I

was so mad I wanted to kill him. But I got to my feet and stumbled
on downstream. No one knows better than I that I owe my life to
McCollom, and it shames me to the core to think that even in
hysteria I doubted him for a moment."

For five hours that morning they waded downstream, and then
McCollom pulled himself up an eight-foot bank. "Come on," he
called, "this is it!" The other two followed, and finally all three lay
sprawled, panting in the sun.

An hour later a search plane passed overhead. They scrambled to
spread out the yellow tarpaulins and saw the aircraft circle back and
the pilot dip his wings. "We, who were so tired we could scarcely
stand ten minutes before, now jumped up and down. We screamed
and waved our arms."

The men joked that one of them would have to marry Maggie to
give their experience the storybook finish. Hastings joined in the
joke, and they were still laughing when they heard what sounded
like a pack of dogs barking. They knew the sounds were being made
not by animals but by human beings. They remembered the tales of
seven-foot-tall cannibals. . . .

McCollom had his two subordinates stand facing the noise and
holding out what pathetic gifts of friendship they had — hard candy
and a jackknife. He told them to smile. They saw heads popping out
from behind trees, and their smiles grew wider. A hundred men
came out of the bushes, each carrying a stone ax. The Americans'
grins grew positively maniacal. The warriors stopped only fifteen
feet from them, and their chief spoke to them . . . and then he
smiled, too.

McCollom shook the man's hand and tried to make nervous small
talk, none of which, of course, was understood.

> We suddenly realized that the natives were more afraid of us than we
> of them! Far from being seven feet tall, they averaged about five and
> a half feet. And certainly they didn't look very fierce. Their clothing
> consisted of a thong around their waists, from which a gourd was
> suspended in front and a huge tropic leaf hung, tail-like, in back. All
> but the chief, whom McCollom nicknamed Pete, wore snoods made
> of heavy string hanging from their heads down their backs. In these
> snoods they tucked anything they had to carry — even tobacco, the
> coarse native leaves which they rolled into short green cigars.
>   Pete and his followers had the biggest, flattest feet we'd ever seen.
> And some of his boys smeared themselves with a smelly black grease
> to make themselves look even blacker.

Hastings brought out a compact, and perhaps inevitably the tribesmen were entranced by their images in the mirror: they were "gurgling and chattering like magpies when they saw their own faces." Suddenly, her legs too weak to support her, Corporal Hastings sat down, and the natives gathered around her. She was self-conscious about her appearance: swollen nose, eyebrows and lashes singed off, half her face black from burns, and her hair standing up in short tufts. "I was a sight, all right, guaranteed to fascinate only savages or interns."

McCollom tried to indicate the injuries she and Decker had sustained and received only grunts in reply. The tribesmen soon left, but before they did so they carefully returned all the presents they had been offered.

The next morning an army aircraft dropped supplies, including cans of tomatoes and jungle kits containing medicine, bandages, and knives. There was also a radio, over which Lieutenant McCollom reported their condition.

They promptly set about treating one another's injuries. Hastings's legs and feet had "big, evil-smelling, running sores" that were gangrenous. But this was no time for hysteria, she thought, and she and McCollom put medication on them and wrapped them in bandages.

They had not the skill to sew up Decker's head wound, and when he revealed the severe, gangrenous burns on his back, they were appalled. They were astonished to think of the pain he had been enduring without complaint. Maggie set about cleaning and medicating his injuries.

By twilight Decker and Hastings had both taken a turn for the worse. He was barely able to move, and she was sick and feeble. She thought that if help did not come soon Decker might die, and her legs would have to be amputated.

Despite their problems, in the morning they informed the army by radio that medics should not be dropped in their area because of the hazardous terrain. They did not want anyone to die in an attempt to treat or rescue them.

> That afternoon Pete came to call and brought his wife. Mrs. Pete wore the snood-shopping-bag arrangement around her head, but neither she nor any of the women used ornaments. All they wore was a G-string woven of supple twigs. They were graceful, fleet creatures, and as shy as does.

We were all dog-tired by the time McCollom got us settled for the night. But we hadn't been in bed an hour when we were surrounded by Pete and his followers. They held out a pig, sweet potatoes and some little green bananas. "They want to give us a banquet," McCollom groaned.

We tried to make them understand that we were sick and exhausted. Pete, who must have had a wonderfully understanding heart in that wiry black body, comprehended at once. He clucked over us reassuringly and herded his followers home.

The next afternoon an aircraft flew over, dropping more supplies (Hastings accumulated absurd amounts of cosmetics before she was rescued) and announcing that two medical paratroopers would make a jump a few miles away. In short order the medics were walking down the trail. They were Filipinos, Corporal Rammy Ramirez and Staff Sergeant Ben Bulatao.

They quickly set to work retrieving supplies from the jungle, building the first fire the survivors had had — and making hot chocolate. Then Bulatao, known as Doc, of course, began treating the injured. It took two hours for him to clean and dress Decker's scalp wound and two more to treat (by flashlight) his gangrene. Corporal Hastings was given care as well before they all turned in.

In daylight Bulatao again worked on Decker's infected back and discovered that the sergeant's right arm was broken at the elbow. Ken Decker dealt with his pain stoically, an attitude Hastings emulated when her turn came again: "I was determined to be as good a soldier as Decker. For hours Doc worked on me and I didn't make a sound, but I was yelling bloody murder inside all the time. Still, my heart felt lighter. Decker would get well and I wouldn't lose my legs."

Feeling better the next day, she wanted to take a bath. The Filipinos carried her to a secluded spot and left her with the "soldier's universal bathtub," a helmet filled with water. "I took off my pants and shirt and started to bathe. But all at once I felt as if I were not alone. I looked around, and there, on a neighboring knoll, were the natives. I never could figure out whether they were goggle-eyed at the queer rite I was performing or at a skin so different from theirs."

That week a nine-man Filipino rescue team parachuted into a valley some forty miles away. Three men were left there to build huts and a glider strip while the other six marched to the survivors' camp. On Friday, May 25, they arrived led by six-feet-four

Captain Cecil E. Walters, who made his entrance singing "Shoo-Shoo Baby" at the top of his lungs.

On Sunday an army aircraft dropped twenty crosses, one Star of David, and a set of twenty-one dog tags for use in burying the crash victims. As the markers were set up and a tag hung over each, a plane circled, broadcasting funeral services over the radio. Three chaplains — Catholic, Protestant, and Jewish — each read a service. On the ground the three survivors silently grieved.

> When Doc finally announced, on June 15, that Decker and I could travel, we said our farewells to Pete and his men. The term "savages" hardly applies to such kind, friendly and hospitable people. The greatest miracle that befell McCollom, Decker and myself, aside from our escape from death in the crash, was the fact that the natives were good and gentle. As we left, they followed us down the trail weeping.
>
> I started out on the forty-five-mile trek to the glider strip with a chipper confidence that melted in thirty minutes. The steady infantry pace set by the paratroopers was too much for me. We crawled over fallen logs, hopped from tree stump to tree stump, wallowed in mud. By midday, I was so lame and in such agony I wanted to shriek. Decker was equally bad off. But neither of us would give in. We knew it was impossible for the others to carry us out over that jungle trail.
>
> Surely the followers of Moses when they came upon the Promised Land saw no fairer sight than that which unrolled before us when we stood on the last height overlooking the Big Valley of Shangri-la. It was a beautiful, fertile land, ringed by giant peaks of the Oranje Mountains. A copper-colored river wound through the valley's green length. There below us, clearly marked, was the glider strip, and a small, neat U.S. Army camp. The three paratroopers who had stayed behind had obviously worked like beavers.

They entered the camp to the accompaniment of boogie-woogie piped down by the radio operator of the aircraft overhead. Hastings was led to a "boudoir" consisting of a thick grass bed with a yellow nylon parachute canopy and a rug made of chute bags. A bathtub had been fashioned from waterproof ration cans.

The Filipinos traded with tribesmen using assorted shells dropped in for that purpose. They purchased, among other things, seven pigs. The runt became the pet of the camp and was nicknamed Peggy in Hastings's honor (Peggy being a nickname for Margaret).

The day after her arrival, Corporal Hastings led a party on a visit to the nearest native village. At its border, the way was blocked by

Kenneth Decker, Margaret Hastings, and John S. McCollom after their rescue. Note the scar on Decker's forehead. (OPPOSITE) Hastings, whom *Life* magazine dubbed "Suzy of Shangri-la," in a New York hotel room after her return from New Guinea. (Permission of UPI/Bettmann Newsphotos)

a dignified old man. Suzy did her best to be a 1940s-style vamp. "I pouted, as prettily as I knew how, batted what few stubby eyelashes I had left, and cooed, 'Aw, Chief, don't be mean.' "

He relented and allowed her and three of the men to go in.

I met the chief's wife that day. We liked each other instantly. Again it was a case of the understanding heart, for neither of us was able to understand the other's language.

I visited the queen often after that. We would sit in the communal room where the women did the cooking, and munch hot sweet potatoes. Her Majesty did not think much of my GI clothes. She wanted me to swap them for a G-string of woven twigs such as those worn by herself and her ladies in waiting.

One day when I was visiting the queen, I absent-mindedly ran a

comb through my hair. She was enchanted. Half the village gathered
round and I combed my hair until my arm was tired.

Every piece of equipment we had in camp fascinated the natives.
Yet they wanted none of it. They would use a good GI axe or jungle
knife when working for us. But they reverted to the stone axe the
minute they had anything to do for themselves. They were too smart
to permit a few chance visitors from Mars to change the rhythm of
centuries.

On Thursday, June 28, a glider sailed into the valley and settled
on the strip. The pilot announced, "This express takes off in thirty
minutes." Everyone raced to pack their souvenirs: the stone axes
and bows and arrows for which they had bartered shells. "The
natives understood that we were going. Tears streamed down their
faces. I knew I was losing some of the best and kindest friends I
would ever have. I blew my nose rather noisily, and discovered that
McCollom and Decker were doing the same."

There was one last bit of danger. A C-47, the *Leaking Louise,* power-dived into the valley and hooked the glider's line success- fully, but the towrope dragged through the trees at the far end of the strip. This reduced the *Louise*'s speed to just over a hundred miles per hour, which was slow enough to stall a C-47 and send it crashing into the jungle. The pilot managed to keep the engines going, although the glider brushed against a treetop. (He would subsequently be recommended for a Distinguished Flying Cross for his action and would say vehemently, "I wouldn't do it again for a dozen of them!")

One of the cargo chutes used to mark the strip was snagged by the glider as it took off. The nylon repeatedly slapped against the thin body of the ship, tearing a two-foot-wide hole in it, running the entire width of the fuselage. The passengers peered down through it to watch the terrain pass below.

The trip took ninety minutes. McCollom, Decker, and Hastings disembarked after forty-seven days in the bush. Photographers were waiting to snap pictures of them looking slim and casual; Maggie clutched a sheath of arrows. "I realized," she wrote later,

> more fully than ever how lucky I had been to survive the crash with such men. Each, in his way, had suffered far more than I. Back on that mountainside, a white cross marked the grave of McCollom's twin brother. Ahead of Decker stretched long weeks of hospitaliza- tion for his many injuries.
>
> I thought gratefully of Captain Walters and his Filipino paratroop- ers who were still in Shangri-la. And, as I walked away from the glider, into my old life once again, I thought of the twenty-one back on the mountain peak under the little white crosses and the Star of David. Only then could I weep.

In the years after the war, a few people continued to be intrigued by the story of the three survivors and the valley of Lavani. Twice expeditions were mounted in an attempt to reach it by foot, but both failed.

Then, in 1954, a twenty-eight-year-old Australian geologist named John Zehnder came out of the jungle to Port Moresby to announce that he had penetrated into the magical region while leading a large expedition prospecting for minerals. For two months he had strug- gled through the interior. Hostile tribesmen sometimes shot at his party with bamboo arrows, but he was able to win over other na- tives with gifts of seashells, mirrors, and beads. One elderly man told him of a valley high in the mountains that could be entered only through a pass; in it were said to dwell people with white skins.

Zehnder was on a commercial mission and had no time for folk tales. Not many days after the conversation, however, while climbing in a thirteen-thousand-foot mountain range, he saw a cleft between mist-shrouded peaks. Inside the pass he soon met up with a large party of muscular warriors wielding stone axes, bows, and arrows. They seemed poised to attack when their leader cried out. Zehnder realized from the man's gestures that what had stopped the assault was the color of his skin. Soon he was surrounded by laughing tribesmen reaching out to touch him. They led him to a hut that housed a shrine — "a collection of apparently sacred objects" — composed of a piece of a yellow life raft, a burned and mangled propeller blade, a can of corned beef, a lipstick case, and a lock of blond hair.

Zehnder spent several days exploring the area. He was initially puzzled because the valley into which the C-47 had crashed was said to be fifty miles long, fifteen miles wide, and nine thousand feet above sea level; yet this valley was at seven thousand feet and was only sixteen miles long and fourteen miles wide. He solved the mystery by discovering that there were actually *two* valleys linked by a narrow trail; the larger one lay just beyond the one he had first discovered. More to the interest of his employers and perhaps to the detriment of his hosts, he found traces of gold, iron, oil, and uranium.

It was the revelation of this potential wealth that might prove the undoing of a generous people who had declined the gifts of modern axes and knives because, in the estimation of Margaret Hastings, they did not want "the rhythm of centuries" altered. For, as John E. Carlova predicted in the February 1955 issue of *The American Mercury*,

> Soon there will be many other white men returning — government patrols, scientists, geologists, oil and mineral company field researchers.
>
> Anthropologists particularly consider Lavani a fertile field for research. Mineral exploitation companies intend to lay out air strips in the hidden valleys and delve deeper into those traces of gold, oil and uranium.
>
> Whether the lost people of Lavani like it or not, they are about to be whisked thousands of years through time — from the darkest Stone Age into the middle of the atomic age.

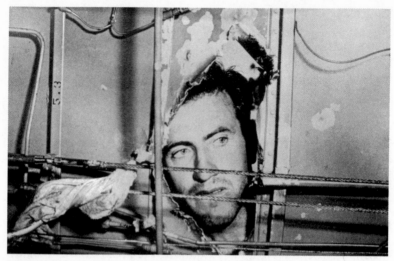

Lieutenant Louis Zamperini peers through damage done to his bomber's fuselage by anti-aircraft fire. On a subsequent mission his plane would crash, and he
would be cast away and made a POW by the Japanese. (A U.S. Air Force
photograph)

September 9, 1945 *A year after the War Department has declared
him dead and issued an official death certificate, Louis Zamperini
is found alive in a Japanese prison camp.*

Before the war Zamperini had been a track star at the University
of Southern California, and he had run the mile in the 1936 Olym-
pics. He subsequently served in the Army Air Corps as a bombardier. On May 28, 1943, while Zamperini was on a search mission
for a downed crew, his B-24 crashed and sank in the Pacific some
two hundred miles from Palmyra Island. Trapped in the cabin, he
went down with the plane.

At a depth of forty feet he inflated his life belt, forced open a
window, and rose quickly to the surface. Two other men also escaped from the wreckage: Lieutenant Russell A. Phillips and tail
gunner Staff Sergeant Francis P. McNamara. The three climbed
into two rubber rafts that had risen to the surface and lashed them
together. Their only supplies were six pounds of chocolate and a
small quantity of water in emergency cans. They would be adrift for
nearly seven weeks.

Their water was gone after only forty-eight hours. In the weeks that followed they drank rainwater and managed to catch two small fish. Twice Zamperini reached into the ocean, seized yard-long sand sharks by the tail, and flipped them into the lifeboats. (The men found that except for the livers, which they removed with a pair of pliers, these fish were inedible.) They also caught four albatrosses and three small birds that "lit innocently" on their rafts.

As time went on the famished Phillips and McNamara insisted that Zamperini cook elaborate, imaginary meals for them, "describing the preparation of each dish, even to the exact quantity of each ingredient." As Zamperini would recall in his autobiography more than a decade after the ordeal,

> Food had long since passed from the realm of reason and had become an obsession. Quite seriously, when the time for a meal came I would "prepare" the proper lavish dishes for Mac and Phil. It was no joke. The look in their eyes and the greedy silences with which they listened to my meticulous preparations showed only too well. So we had gnocchi, chicken *cacciatore,* omelets, steaks smothered in mushrooms — all the things I learned to make in my mother's kitchen. No steps could be eliminated: "You forgot to grease the skillet," they would remind me, or, "What about the butter, don't you need butter in the gravy?"
>
> Though we dwelled on such feasts in our waking hours, strangely it was not this kind of food which occupied my dreams. Through the latter floated garbage, scraps — the things which had been so flagrantly wasted before and which consequently seemed more available now.
>
> It was the same with sleep: we did not think of luxuriating in a soft bed or on green lawns. Rather, we ached for the more believable assurance of a rough, rock-strewn plain. I even dreamed at one time of the sheer joy of falling asleep in a splinter-filled woodpile; at least it would be solid and I could reach out at night to grasp something earthly rather than simply groping up into a black night or a phosphorescent sea. It would be a pleasure just to touch one thing which was not wet or encrusted by this eternal, waving, spewing, crawling web of water.

On the twenty-seventh day the boats were strafed by a Japanese plane. Initially believing the Betty bomber was a B-25, they had signaled it with a mirror and their last flare. Even as the aircraft circled low overhead and they could see its red insignia they were deluded: it was the new symbol for the Pacific Air Transport Command, they told each other. The plane made its first run, and her bullets spurted across the ocean's surface and cut through the rafts.

Mac cried out that the B-25's crew was "signaling" them, but Zamperini finally understood.

"Signaling? What kind of a signal is it to shoot holes through you?"

As the next run began, the men slipped into the water. It was filled with sharks that had been trailing the boats for some time, but the castaways had no choice.

As the bomber rose again, Phil and Mac were so weak and disheartened that Zamperini had to help them back into a raft. It was clear that they would not be able to climb out and in again. They would have to remain in the boat during subsequent attacks. When the bomber came on, Zamperini plunged into the ocean alone.

Under the surface, I could see the bullets penetrate to a depth of two or three feet, then slow up and drift away slowly into the darkness below. From my position under the raft I could also see that they were coming right through its fabric.

Those poor guys up there must be riddled, I thought the first time I saw this, but when I surfaced and reached over the side to shake them we found that the bullets had miraculously skimmed past them by inches, once between their legs, another under an armpit!

As the strafing continued and my splashing around the raft became more violent, the companions of our long journey, the wolves of the sea, arose from their deep lairs. First I tried to scare them off by remembering the instructions given at the survival school in Hawaii. I grinned, showing my teeth, opened my eyes wide — trying to display everything white I had. Then I made quick movements as they approached closer. When that failed and the monsters began to roll for their attack as they came, I pulled myself out of their way at the last minute by tugging on the rope attached to the raft — fighting, at the same time, the strange current which flowed past and which had carried us along on its swell during the past weeks.

Finally, even this did not deter the silent, gliding gluttons and it became a matter of pushing myself away with my foot or hand against their nose as they rolled. Trying to coordinate my time under the water so that neither the Jap plane nor one persistent shark would have a clear shot at me was an ordeal beyond terror, beyond even a clear comprehension so that words might tell of it.

By now the rafts were full of holes, one completely deflated and the other half-submerged. When I rose, gasping to the surface after the next pass of the shark, the other two boys were lying in the submerged raft watching the Jap plane circle for the next pass.

"Lie still," I shouted to them. "Try to make them think you're dead."

The strategy may have been partially successful: on that next pass the Japanese did not fire, but on the following one they dropped a depth charge. The bomb did not explode. After a few more runs, the Betty flew away.

Zamperini climbed back aboard to find the other two men uninjured. Using a repair kit, they patched the boats as best they could.

A few days later Mac began to hallucinate. Zamperini brought him around by threatening to "report him." But on the thirty-second day he was clearly failing. He asked the other men some questions about death, "questions for which we had no good answer." Finally he asked Zamperini in a hoarse whisper, "How long will I last?"

"I think you'll die during the night," the bombardier told him gently.

"Yes, sir," the young man softly replied. "I think you're right, Lieutenant Zamperini."

And he was exactly right.

At dawn the bombardier recited the Lord's Prayer over the body and then delivered a half-hour eulogy. He prayed once more before slipping the emaciated corpse over the side.

Actually, the difference between Mac and ourselves at that point was only a matter of a heartbeat. We were so wasted and corroded by the constant washing of our [bodies] that our flesh was almost transparent. When we scratched ourselves we could almost tear the skin. Beneath its scarlet, waxy surface the bones were clearly visible. The thing we wanted most was water, but our stomachs were so shrunken that they could hold only a half pint at a time. Had it not been for the frequent rains we certainly would have dried away in the middle of the world's greatest moisture. Our food intake spaced itself further and further apart, as we weakened.

Yet, the closer we approached the reality of death, the stronger grew our hope and faith that we would live. We continued our rasping attempts at singing; we joked as we ate our imaginary meals; most of all, we prayed, believing.

Looking at each other ruefully, we estimated our weight at about seventy pounds. We each had a long stubble of a beard and the last bird I had caught had filled mine with lice, which I had washed off with difficulty. All there was left for us through the interminable days was to ride through the occasional storm, slopping back and forth in the half-floating raft, then scoop and pump it dry, exhausting ourselves in the process, and lapse back into our thoughts of God, food, and home.

In the sixth week the two men began to see more Japanese aircraft. A storm struck, and when their boats rose on the crest of a wave, they glimpsed land ahead. They were too drained to experience elation.

"Say, Phillips, there's an island over there," Zamperini said dully.

Phillips looked in the direction his companion indicated. "I'll be darned," he replied.

They drifted on and paddled as much as their strength allowed. A second gale struck, carrying them inside a lagoon of what proved to be the Marshall Islands. They had been at sea for forty-seven days.

Found by a Japanese patrol boat, they were treated reasonably well and turned over to military authorities at Wotje. They were cared for by a kind Japanese physician, allowed to sleep on mattresses, and given decent rations. Their luck continued to hold until they were transferred to Kwajalein. Here the camp guards poked at their prisoners with sharp sticks and made them sing and dance for their entertainment. They threw balls of rice at them, forcing them to scramble over the dirty floor for the food.

The prisoners were sent to Truk and put on board a transport destined for Japan. On the ship guards searched Zamperini and found in his wallet a clipping of an advertisement for war bonds. The item featured a drawing of him in running togs, and the text trumpeted his accomplishments as an athlete in the "last Olympic games ever held" and as a bombardier who had participated in the first air raid on Wake Island. The discovery of the keepsake earned Zamperini a savage beating by a mob of drunken sailors. Repeated blows to the face broke his nose, and to set it he was forced to hold the broken bone in place for several weeks until it healed.

On Yokohama, the Japanese made him run against well-fed soldiers, despite the fact that he was weak and weighed less than a hundred pounds. Sometimes they bribed him with food to throw the races. At other times the races resulted in beatings whether he won or lost, although a win triggered a special fury in his assailants.

At Omura there were more beatings and punishments, the most savage inflicted by Sergeant Watanabe Mitsuhiro, whom the prisoners called The Bird. The descendant of a wealthy and socially prominent family, Mitsuhiro specialized in inflicting the most degrading humiliations on his prisoners. He had Zamperini and other men do pushups over a latrine until, exhausted, they fell face down in it. He repeatedly lined up the American officers and made each enlisted man — there were ninety-eight of them — strike every officer in the face with his fist. If a blow was not hard enough, the deliverer was beaten with a club and forced to hit the officer over and over again until The Bird was satisfied.

"As each man struck an officer, The Bird would say 'Next!' and that got to be the horrid chant which was all we heard or knew of what was going on," Zamperini told Robert Trumbull of the *New York Times*, who found him in Yokohama. "Next, next, next — like the tramp of feet."

The officers urged the men to strike hard the first time; it actually meant that they were hit less often. Anyway, reasoned Lieutenant Zamperini, "we'd rather be struck by our own enlisted men than by those dirty Jap hands. It was worse to watch a beating than to take one, for eventually you fell unconscious and knew nothing about the prolonged beating and kicking of your senseless body."

When Zamperini was shifted to Naoetsu, he was relieved at the thought of escaping the cruel Mitsuhiro, but he soon found that the sergeant had been transferred there, too. The Bird's sadism and fury continued undiminished until the end of the war. Zamperini and some other prisoners had been plotting to murder him, but he managed to slip away, escaping not only their retribution but a war crimes trial as well.

A month after the Japanese surrender and almost twenty-eight months after his bomber had crashed, Louis Zamperini was brought home. In his ordeal he had not merely endured but prevailed. Yet he did not feel triumphant. "If I knew I had to go through these experiences again," he told Robert Trumbull, "I would kill myself."

December 9, 1948   *Seven crewmen of a C-47 transport are stranded after their plane crashes on Greenland's bleak south coast.*

Flying in an eighty-mile-per-hour windstorm, the aircraft lost power in both engines, and the pilot pancaked her onto a frozen plateau 7,700 feet above sea level. The temperature was forty degrees below zero, and the men quickly set to work protecting themselves against the weather. They built three snow houses, each about ten by fourteen feet. They made the roofs out of parachutes and used the C-47's power plant for lighting. Air force planes dropped them survival supplies.

Air force officers did not anticipate any problems rescuing the men since they had had plenty of practice: in one day alone during the war, two B-17s and six P-38s had gone down in the same area. In this instance, however, one plan after another failed. Winds increased to one hundred miles per hour, and no attempt could be made for three days. Then the first B-17 to land swerved out of control on the rutted ice and went into a snowbank; two more men joined the seven already comfortably established.

Four days later a C-54 released a glider with a two-man crew for an air-to-ground pickup. As the tow plane caught its pickup line, the glider broke through the surface crust, the line snapped, and the ship became bogged down. Its pilot and copilot brought the number of stranded to eleven, and the air force dropped more clothing and food as well as heaters, fuel, and a plywood shelter. The gale continued unabated.

The men climbed into the glider several days later, and this time it was successfully lifted off the ice. Just fifty feet above the ground, however, the towline broke, and the glider drifted down to earth. Its occupants struggled back to their shelters.

A week later another glider was landed, loaded, and lifted off — and its towline broke, too. Now thirteen of the military's best were trudging back to their dwellings. The air force dropped more supplies, including clothes, whiskey, playing cards, magazines, a Christmas dinner of roast turkey and pumpkin pie, and even a Christmas tree. The downed fliers were able to exchange season's greetings with their families via radio.

At this point the *navy* dispatched an aircraft carrier from Norfolk, bearing helicopters capable of making the rescue. Facing the ultimate humiliation, air force brass frantically ordered ski-equipped planes and brought in an Arctic pilot experienced in emergency cold-weather operations.

His help was not needed. Exactly nineteen days after the first crash, Lieutenant Colonel Emil Beaudry and Lieutenant Charles Blackwell landed a ski-equipped C-47 on the ice. Knowing the air force's track record, the maroons had already prepared bunks for these two, but thirty-eight minutes after landing, the transport plane was ready for takeoff. "We faced into the wind," remembered Blackwell, "counted noses, checked the engines and took off."

When the fliers landed in New York, they were treated to a heroes' welcome. Politicians slapped their backs, and reporters swarmed over them. Billeted in a midtown hotel, they took in shows and toured the sights. (In the hotel lobby, one young woman bounded up to a glider pilot, handed him a piece of paper, and wished him a happy new year. She was his ex-wife, and the paper was a court summons "charging him with desertion.") When the hoopla subsided after a few days, the men returned to duty in Greenland.

July 11, 1951 *A man falls overboard from a racing sloop shortly after dawn during the annual Los Angeles to Honolulu yacht race.*

Ted Sierks, forty, had leaned out over the side of *L'Apache* to make repairs on her broken boom tackle when a wave caused her to roll, and he was dumped into the water. He swam for the stern of the cutter and lunged for a line dragging behind it but succeeded only in injuring his hand.

His friends threw him a life preserver, but by the time they brought the sloop about, Sierks was out of sight. He could see the top of her tall mast, but in the choppy sea they could not spot him. They searched for hours, but the current had carried him away. They sent out a "Man Overboard!" distress signal, and six other yachts converged on the area, followed by four destroyers, three destroyer escorts, an escort carrier, and even a B-17.

Ted Sierks knew he was far out of the shipping lanes, and so he had little hope that he would be picked up. He estimated he was nearly 900 miles from Honolulu and 2,400 miles from San Pedro Harbor. The ocean was vast and empty. He drifted on it, praying and thinking.

I calculated the chances against me as, conservatively, a million to one. I pulled off my heavy rubber boots and dragging pants; in my long woolen underwear I felt no colder but a lot lighter. The ring buoy bobbed on the waves and jerked my shoulders ceaselessly. Whitecaps smacked me in the face. Blood from my fingers and wrists oozed out into the water. That, I suppose, is what attracted the shark.

The first I knew of him was when he shot up from below and made a pass at my feet, hanging white and water-soaked below me. I saw him in the split second's time to jerk my feet out of his path. He did not flash on by me though, and as I kicked out to try to frighten him away (the way they tell you to in books) I actually barked my shins on his rough hide. He whisked away to make another pass.

How I did what I did next, I'll never know. But I hardly had any choice. When the shark came circling back after me, I made a pass at him with the knife that, by God-given fortune, I had had in my belt when I went overboard. He came so close and so slowly that I actually got the knife into him, right near the backbone. It slowed him enough so I could grab him by the tail and get in another sharp stab. This time he thrashed over onto his back to get his underslung jaws at me, but he also exposed that pale, vulnerable underbelly. One slashing stroke of the knife ripped it open. A gushing swirl of blood and he was gone. He did not come back.

Knowing that the blood would quickly attract other sharks, Sierks hurriedly swam away.

With the immediate danger past, he became conscious of his predicament. Immersion in the cool water had turned his skin a cadaverous white. His body ached all over, and he was exhausted. With night falling he kept drifting into sleep, his head dropping down on the life preserver.

In waking moments he reflected on matters both inconsequential and profound. "I thought about how I was messing up the race for a lot of people," he told a reporter for *Time* magazine later. "I thought about the time I had wasted in my life."

In the darkness he prayed the Lord's Prayer for what he was certain was the last time. When he came to the word "trespasses" he substituted the phrase "my life's trespasses." Then he let his head go down again, putting his face into the water, accepting death. . . .

He heard a voice shout, "Don't give up, you weakling!"

He straightened up, coughing and gagging. Ahead of him he saw the sky glowing and wondered dumbly what was causing it. Then he realized that the source of light was a parachute flare. Searchlight beams were skittering across the ocean's surface just a mile away.

"Those are the few moments I remember most clearly of all; the last prayer, the angry, noisy sea, the choking, panicky sensation as the water gets into the lungs, that voice I was sure I heard, and then the brilliant light in the sky. It was an eerie thing, out there as I was in the middle of the measureless, timeless sea."

His life preserver was equipped with light. Sierks flashed it on and off, but the signal was not seen by the men on the ships or in an airplane that flew overhead. It was nothing more, he thought, than a firefly in a canyon.

A wave drove him under the surface and doused the light.

Two rescue vessels were sailing toward him on a crisscross pattern, searchlights working. They came abreast of him, just two hundred yards away on either side. They both sailed on.

An hour later he spied another ship, this one sailing straight at him. He "alternately yelled and cheered. On she came until I could make out distinctly the line of her big bow slicing through the waves." Only six hundred feet from him, she turned and sailed downwind.

He told himself that in the morning the vessels would return, and in daylight he was sure to be spotted. The prospect of rescue kept him awake. Phosphorescent jellyfish swam up from the depths to sting his feet. A pilot fish approached, and Sierks slashed at it with his knife, driving it away.

Shortly after dawn the ships did reappear, and several came very near him, but again he was not seen, and they soon sailed off.

I did not have time to get discouraged though, for despite the fact that I had once been ready to resign myself to drowning, I still could not give in to the sharks. Now two more came into view. The first was a big ten-footer, and he swept at me belly up, trying to swipe off my feet with his gaping jaw. I yanked them out of the way and got my knife into him once. He did not come back. The other one looked to be about eight feet long. And he was more patient. He sat there in the water just out of reach, gliding slowly in toward me whenever my head drooped a little. This was when the metal light attached to the ring buoy, though it had not brought my rescue, saved my life just the same. I looped my feet up onto it, and when the shark struck, his great teeth clanked against the hard metal. He swam off and kept his distance.

U.S. Navy experts were certain that no man could live more than thirty-one hours in those waters. The ships were therefore ordered to abandon the search at 2 P.M. As the hour approached, the captain of one of the vessels, the destroyer escort *Douglas A. Munro*, offered a fifty-dollar reward to the first man to sight the castaway.

By 1:45 Ted Sierks had given up. He had stayed awake all night on watch the night before he had fallen overboard, which meant that by now he had been awake for nearly forty-eight hours. The lack of sleep, the battles with sharks, his struggles to swim in the sea, and his frustration and disappointment at not being found had all taken their toll: once again he accepted death; he was no longer willing to fight to keep his head out of the water.

It was literally at this last moment that I saw the two destroyer escorts, steaming along slowly, headed for home but still searching.

Yachtsman Ted Sierks poses with the two *Munro* sailors who rescued him. They are Rene Cortez *(left)* and L. Peoples. (Permission of UPI/Bettmann Newsphotos)

This time I was right in line with their course. This time they could not possibly pass me by.

They came so close that I could see the whole ship's company lining the rail and searching the surface of the ocean. But they did not see me. I shouted across the narrow stretch of water at them. A man on the foredeck of one of the ships [the *Munro*], scanning the sea in the opposite direction, heard me. He spun about and looked straight in my direction. Then I knew they had finally found me.

It was hard for me to believe. Here the two ships came, right up alongside me. A man stood ready with a line. A rope ladder snaked down the side of the nearest ship. The line whirled out across the sky and plopped down in the water right next to me. I grabbed it and they pulled me toward the ship. Even after my ordeal I was a little surprised to find I was too weak to climb the ladder. A sailor plunged in beside me and hoisted me into the arms of two others who started to haul me up the ladder. As my legs swung out of the water one last rolling wave came in and climbed up the side of the ship. It missed me by a few inches and fell back with an angry splash as I was hoisted up the swinging rope ladder to the ship's deck and safety.

Thus as it turned out a *Munro* sailor was able to collect fifty dollars from his skipper. Surrounded by smiling seamen, Ted Sierks posed for photographs at the vessel's rail with the life preserver about his neck and his knife clenched in his fist. He spent the better part of a month recuperating in a Honolulu hospital. He wrote an article for *Life* magazine: "Don't Give Up, You Weakling!" and gratefully donated the fee to the recreation fund of the *Douglas A. Munro*.

"Now that I've been rescued," he remarked to one reporter, "I figure there must be a reason. There must be something for me to do. I'll have to try and find out what it is."

July 15, 1957 *Three weeks after the air force has officially declared him dead, Lieutenant David A. Steeves encounters campers in the Sierra Nevada Mountains.*

Steeves reported to authorities that his T-33 jet trainer had exploded on May 9, and he ejected at thirty-three thousand feet. He came down in California's Kings Canyon National Park, one of the most isolated and rugged areas in the continental United States.

> I landed on the only rock that was bare of snow for miles around. I sprained both ankles and tore some ligaments when I landed. I lay there trying to recover. How long I don't know.
>
> I couldn't walk. My ankles were swelling rapidly. I had nothing to eat, no candy bar, nothing. My survival kit went down with the plane. All I had was my revolver; pictures of my wife and daughter; some identification cards; paper money; a few stick matches and a couple of half-used packets of book matches; my pipe but no tobacco; my fountain pen and a mechanical pencil.

He built a fire and remained near it for three days. Then, although the snow was six feet deep and he was wearing only a summer uniform, Steeves began crawling and then walking painfully through the 11,400-foot-high Dusy Basin and down out of the mountain range.

The first day he made only a quarter of a mile, but as his ankles grew stronger he was able to move more rapidly. "There was nothing but snow and ice," he told park rangers after he had reached safety. "For fifteen days I didn't have a bite to eat. It was just ice and snow the whole time."

As he reached the lower elevations he occasionally stumbled onto campsites, where he found parts of discarded books and magazines. A book might begin on page 55 and stop in the middle, but he read it, anyway. Once he found a cookbook, which he read three times, studying the illustrations longingly and planning elaborate menus.

Lieutenant David A. Steeves at the Cedar Grove
ranger station (Permission of AP/Wide World
Photos)

He read a magazine piece on how to survive in the Arctic; it was
interesting but not useful: "By the time I read it I was [at] a lower
altitude, the temperature was seventy-five or eighty degrees, and
the weather was fine."

On the fifteenth day he wandered into Simpson Meadow. He
broke into a shack but found only a can of beans and a can of ham.
"Luckily there were some fishhooks and line in the cabin. In the
next few days I caught some trout in the stream nearby [actually
the Kings River] and ate them." During the ensuing weeks he enlarged his diet to include grass snakes, dandelion greens, wild straw-
berries — and venison. He "rigged a deadfall" by strapping his
cocked revolver to a sapling near a salt lick. A few days later the

gun went off, but Steeves did not hear the report. Predatory animals had eaten half the carcass by the time he checked the trap. He cooked what was left and husbanded it for twenty days.

Knowing he "could not last much longer," he set out for Granite Pass, but the spring thaw had turned the Kings River and its tributaries "into swollen torrents." Steeves was forced to return to Simpson Meadow, where he remained until June 30. On that day he climbed through 16,600-foot-high Granite Pass and walked nine miles to Granite Basin. There he met outdoorsmen who were on a fishing expedition. "I don't know how to explain the way I felt when I saw these men. All I can say is they supplied me with food and showed me a great time." Having cooked him a steak, they put him on a horse and escorted him to a ranger station.

The heavily bearded twenty-three-year-old pilot had been alone for fifty-four days and had lost thirty pounds. In starting fires he had burned all of his identification papers and all but one of his photographs: "The only thing I saved was a color snapshot of my wife in her wedding gown." At the beginning of his ordeal "I didn't know if I was going to make it," he remarked to journalist Lawrence E. Davies. "As time went on, I began to develop faith. I'd never been a very religious man but this faith in God grew stronger and stronger. That, plus the love of my wife and child, drove me."

Lieutenant Steeves became an instant celebrity. *Life* magazine printed a photograph of him eating his first full meal at Cedar Grove in Kings Canyon. The air force trumpeted him as a hero and announced his appointment as a survival-school instructor; Vice Chief of Staff Curtis LeMay proudly posed for photographs with him. Steeves made guest appearances on television and radio shows on both coasts. Arthur Godfrey engaged a suite for him and his wife at a swank New York hotel and did not bat an eye when the young couple ran up a $600 bill in five days. The manufacturer of electric shavers paid Steeves $1,250 for shaving off his beard on TV. A publisher contracted to have his story ghost-written by Clay Blair, Jr., and the *Saturday Evening Post* bought the magazine rights to the tale for $10,000. The *Post*'s editors sent Blair into the Sierra with Steeves, where, with the help of a guide, they retraced his steps. After the trip, however, the *Post* canceled the contract, citing "discrepancies" in his account.

Others soon began to doubt Lieutenant Steeves's story. While some local people, including the guide, unhesitatingly believed him, the area's sheriff flatly questioned that anyone could survive in the range for fifteen days without food. Blair let it be known that he was troubled, among other things, by the good condition of Steeves's boots after a walk of twenty-five miles or more in the snow.

Wilderness experts were bothered by the fact that the lieutenant, who was wearing only summer-weight clothing when he walked out of Dusy Basin, had left behind some of his matches and a parachute that he might have used as a blanket. Then, too, the oxygen mask, parachute harness, and other gear he had abandoned were in surprisingly good shape for having been in the snow for two months and then through a thaw. Finally, the tree against which he had built his Dusy Basin fire was charred only a foot above the ground, not six feet above it, as should have been the case if the fire was built before the thaw. As for his elaborate animal trap, they pointed out that deer in the park are so tame that they are easily approachable by man.

No one doubted that Steeves had spent fifty-four days in the Sierra Nevada, but where had he spent them? One theory was that he had landed near Simpson Meadow to begin with and had stayed there until conditions improved. Then he had made his way up to the more remote Dusy Basin to establish a camp.

Life magazine, which had originally marveled at his feat, sent reporters and photographers up into the mountains to dissect the case. (They even took pictures of obliging deer.) The editors published a photograph of Steeves posed in front of the $3,700 Jaguar he had bought a few months before the crash, at a time when he was earning only $6,000 a year in pay and living with his wife and child in a trailer.

Air force officials told the press that they were disturbed by the fact that a thorough search of the mountains had failed to turn up the wreckage of the $125,000 jet.

In the midst of all the controversy, Steeves's twenty-one-year-old wife, Rita, announced that she had asked for a separation. She refused to make her reasons public, although she insisted that they had nothing to do with "the whole adventure in the mountains." Steeves seemed baffled and hurt by what was happening to him. "Look, I've lost everything in the world — my wife," he complained to a journalist from *Time* magazine. Gesturing toward his new gray Jaguar, he added, "What have I got with all this publicity? I've got a nice car. I'm lonesome as hell."

As the media lost interest in the story, the military investigation continued, but the young lieutenant was sticking to his version of events. "They can't disprove my story," he insisted to the *Time* reporter. "How can they? Are they going to interview the animals? Things happen miraculously to people in this day and age. I don't have anything to hide."

March 7, 1960 *The mystery of the* LADY BE GOOD *is finally solved, seventeen years after the plane has disappeared.*

At approximately 1:45 P.M. on April 4, 1943, the B-24 took off during a sandstorm from a base in Soluch, Libya. It was one of twenty-five aircraft making the Naples bombing run that day. Mechanical failures, many of which were caused by the sandstorm, forced some of the planes to turn back, but the *Lady Be Good* was one of those that proceeded to the target. Darkness had fallen by the time the bombers arrived, however, and so the mission was aborted. The aircraft broke formation, and each set off alone for Libya. The *Lady* did not return.

A routine search was made at the time of the disappearance, and after the war more thorough searches were conducted along the

In a souvenir photograph taken shortly before the crash, the crewmen of the *Lady Be Good* clown for the camera. *From left:* Staff Sergeant Vernon L. Moore, Second Lieutenant Hays, Second Lieutenant John S. Woravka, Staff Sergeant Guy E. Shelley, and Technical Sergeant Harold J. Ripslinger.

The fuselage of the *Lady Be Good,* found in the desert seventeen years after the crash (A U.S. Air Force photograph; Copy print courtesy of *Life* magazine)

Mediterranean coast, where it was presumed the bomber had gone down. When no traces were found, authorities concluded that the plane had crashed into the ocean.

In May of 1959, a British oil prospector came upon the *Lady,* crashed deep in the desert and eerily preserved by the dry air. The fuselage contained edible rations, canteens of potable water, and a Thermos of drinkable coffee. Fatigue uniforms and flight gear hung in their proper places, and guns and ammunition were carefully stowed. But there was no sign of the servicemen who had been on board. Further examination showed that the compass and one engine still worked. (American military technicians visited the crash site and removed the plane's instruments for further study.)

Air force search teams combed the area and found arrows made from rocks and parachutes, indicating that the crew had walked in a northwesterly direction. Desert experts had doubted that the men could have traveled more than thirty-five miles on foot, but the trail ran for some fifty-five miles before petering out.

The following February another oil man, American James W. Backhaus, discovered the bones of five of the fliers. Along with the bodies were, among other things, a khaki sweater, a flight jacket, shoes, pieces of parachutes and harnesses, an empty canteen, and a diary that had been kept by one of the victims, Second Lieutenant Robert F. Toner. With it and the evidence in the fuselage, investigators were able to piece together the last days of the doomed men.

The pilot, First Lieutenant William J. Hatton, was inexperienced (as were the other crew members) and in the bad weather had overshot his base by some five hundred miles. He was probably misled as the result of a tail wind that pushed his aircraft to much higher speeds than his indicator showed. Running low on fuel, Hatton had shut down three of the four engines to conserve gasoline, but in the end the fliers were forced to bail out. They did not try to land the *Lady* with its radio and precious supply of food and water because they thought they were over the sea. Instead they jumped; once on the ground they assumed that they were near the coast. "This tragic mistake," observed the editors of *Life* magazine, "created a false hope which was to haunt them to the very end."

Eight of the nine men came down about fifteen miles from the crash site but did not search for the plane, presumably believing it had been smashed to pieces or burned. A spent ammo clip indicates that they fired off rounds to rally together. (The ninth man, bombardier Second Lieutenant John S. Woravka, failed to join the others and was never seen again.) They then hiked northwest toward Benghazi, an impossible 450 miles away. They desert through which they walked was so arid and unsupportive of life that not even Bedouins visited the area.

They marched on, leaving in their wake markers, empty canteens, and shoes. By day they hid under parachutes to escape the sun and the 130-degree heat, and by night they walked. They rationed their water supply and took regular rest breaks. They crossed seventy miles of desert in a week.

The editors of *Life* magazine noted that

If there had been a way out this heroic effort would have saved them. There was none. The perverse fate which had made them miss their airbase held them to the end. For, unknowingly, they and the *Lady Be Good* had come down on a broad plateau in the midst of a vast expanse of desert which the Arabs know — and do not enter even on camel back — as the Sand Sea of Calanscio. They did, unbelievably, reach the dunes of the plateau's edge. Because the dunes there resemble those they had seen along the Mediterranean, they probably thought they had made it. The three strongest, Sergeants Moore,

A pair of shoes discarded in the desert by one of
the *Lady*'s crewmen (A U.S. Air Force photograph)

Shelley and Ripslinger, went ahead for help. The rest, now too weak
to walk, waited. They died, probably on April 12 when Toner made
[the] last entry, eight days after the *Lady* had set out. The three men
who went for help never returned. Their bones, like the wreck of the
Lady Be Good herself, will probably lie forever in the desert.

The entries in Toner's diary are laconic; yet, written with a thick
pencil, they tell with a simple eloquence the story of the airmen's
last days:

> *Sunday, Apr. 4, 1943*
> Naples — 28 planes — things pretty well mixed up — got lost re-
> turning, out of gas, jumped, landed in the desert at 2:00 in morning,
> no one badly hurt, cant find John, all others present.

> *Monday 5*
> Start walking N.W., still no John. a few rations, ½ canteen of water,
> 1 cap full per day. Sun fairly warm. Good breeze from N.W. Nite
> very cold. no sleep. Rested & walked.

Tuesday 6
Rested at 11:30, sun very warm. no breeze, spent P.M. in hell, no planes, etc. rested until 5:00 P.M. Walked & rested all nite. 15 min on, 5 off.

Wednesday, Apr. 7, 1943
Same routine, everyone getting weak, cant get very far, prayers all the time, again P.M. very warm, hell. Can't sleep. everyone sore from ground.

Thursday 8
Hit Sand Dunes, very miserable, good wind but continuous blowing of sand, every[one] now very weak, thought Sam & Moore were all done. La Motte eyes are gone, everyone else's eyes are bad. Still going N.W.

Friday 9
Shelly [*sic*], Rip, Moore separate & try to go for help, rest of us all very weak, eyes bad, not any travel, all want to die. still very little water. nites are about 35°, good n. wind, no shelter, 1 parachute left.

Saturday, Apr. 10, 1943
Still having prayer meetings for help. No sign of *anything,* a couple of birds; good wind from N. — Really weak now, cant walk. pains all over, still all want to die. Nites very cold. no sleep.

Sunday 11
Still waiting for help, still praying. eyes bad, lost all our wgt. aching all over, could make it if we had water; just enough left to put our tongues to, have hope for help very soon, no rest, still same place.

Monday 12
No help yet, very cold nite

On May 15, 1960, two British oil prospectors found a sixth body. The identity of the dead man was not clear because two sets of papers were in the pockets of his uniform. One of these belonged to Technical Sergeant Harold J. Ripslinger, the other to Staff Sergeant Guy E. Shelley. Whoever he was, he had walked thirty-eight miles after leaving Toner and the others, still on a northwesterly course toward the Mediterranean, and he died alone in the arid Sand Sea of Calanscio.

January 17, 1960 *A sixty-foot landing craft in which four Soviet sailors have been practicing attacks against "the enemy" is swept out to sea off the northern coast of Japan.*
The storm struck the Russian-held Kurile Islands on January 17,

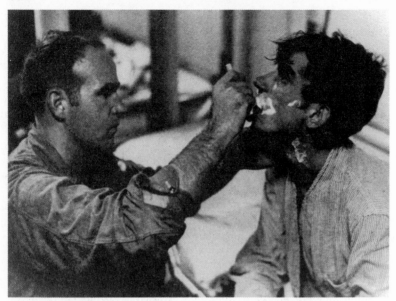

U.S. Navy corpsman Dale Davis gives Soviet Master Sergeant Victor Zygon-
schi his first shave in forty-seven days (A U.S. Navy photograph)

and the men drifted for forty-nine days. They soon ran out of fuel.
Unable to catch fish and making no effort to capture sea birds, they
were reduced to eating leather. They did not keep regular watches
or fabricate a distress signal to attract passing ships, though they
saw at least three.

"The weather never abated," recalled Private Philip Poplavski.
"The waves smashed and pounded. We got almost no sleep. Each
time we awoke, we were surprised to be alive. But we felt we were
too young to die."

The only provisions they had were three cans of dried beef, a loaf
of bread, a bottle of vodka, and three canteens of water. "Our water
soon ran out, but there was much rain," Poplavski explained. "We
rationed the vodka, but it finally went, too. And last of all, our food.
Those last few days we were eating the leather thongs of the tops of
our boots."

A thousand miles from where they started — and nearly that far
from the nearest landfall — a plane from the U.S. carrier *Kearsarge*
spotted them. Picked up by helicopters with slings, the castaways

asked to be returned to Russia, but the carrier stayed on course for San Francisco. The landing craft, although considered a hazard to navigation, was left afloat because the U.S. Navy was unwilling to sink a Russian vessel in peacetime.

On the American ship the Soviet sailors, who had lost twenty-four to thirty-five pounds each, received not only medical care but specially prepared Russian meals. In San Francisco they were presented ceremonial plywood keys to the city, given new clothes, "filled with Cokes," and taken on a tour of the sights in a city-owned car.

They were flown to New York, accompanied by two beefy Soviet security men and a woman doctor. After a few days' rest at their embassy's quarters at Glen Cove, Long Island, they were booked aboard the *Queen Mary* (in tourist accommodations, of course). In Paris they were given a "crushing welcome" by French reporters, who fired questions at them in French and broken Russian. They appeared startled and confused but "neat in their American clothes." They were rescued by bouquet-bearing Soviet embassy staff, who formed a flying wedge and spirited them away.

Arriving in Moscow aboard a Soviet airliner, they found three thousand people waiting to greet them. "We want to thank the Soviet government and the Communist party for educating us in such a way that we were able to do what we did," their appointed spokesman, Junior Sergeant Arkhan R. Ziganship, told the crowd. He and his three fellow survivors had exchanged their U.S. civilian garb for new uniforms and boots, but they still seemed dazed by their celebrity. Suddenly the mob surged through the police lines and swarmed around them, cheering wildly.

Even before the huzzas stopped, teams of Russian artists were turning out posters and planning murals of the young men. Songs and poems were being composed in their honor. Books and a motion picture extolling them as "representative of the typical Soviet man" were soon in the works.

While the Soviet government was effusive in its formal thanks to the United States for the rescue, the Russian press found in the experience of the four young men a great propaganda victory. Their lack of discipline was ignored, and their optimistic attitude was contrasted favorably to that of the crewmen of the *Lady Be Good,* who, it was pointed out, all wished to die after a week in the desert, according to the recently discovered Toner diary. Crowed *Pravda,*

"In the exploit of the four Soviet men, like the sun in a drop of water, the features of the Soviet way of life are reflected." The youth newspaper *Komsomolskaya Pravda* added, "Through the stormy night, battling in Stygian darkness across the thundering ocean, four simple Soviet lads bore aloft the torch of bravery. Soviet people are a special alloy!"

September 23, 1962 *On a flight between McGuire Air Force Base, New Jersey, and Frankfurt, Germany, a Flying Tiger Line Super-H constellation loses power in three engines and is ditched into the North Atlantic. The passengers are military personnel and their dependents; all told, seventy-six people are on board.* *

The plane was at an altitude of 21,000 feet when Captain John D. Murray had the first indication of trouble. "I got a fire warning on Number Three engine. I shut it down, feathered the prop, and shot a bottle of fire extinguisher into it. Eight minutes later an overspeed condition developed in the Number One propeller."

That engine was shut down, and Murray took the aircraft to a lower altitude and changed course for the closest airport, at Shannon, Ireland, more than nine hundred miles away. He had the chief stewardess, Betty A. Sims, reassure the passengers that Super Constellations were designed to fly on two engines. Nonetheless, flight attendants helped passengers into life jackets, collected their shoes and sharp objects, and briefed them on ditching procedures. The women were told to remove their stockings and tie them around their waists to provide a handhold for anyone helping them while they were in the water.

Some of the paratroopers joked about which of the stewardesses they wanted to be cast away with on a raft. The women kidded, too, as they distributed blankets and pillows to cushion the crash shock. Sims put a soldier in charge of each emergency exit. Other men were given responsibility for the five deflated lifeboats.

Everyone remained calm, and most were optimistic that the plane would reach Shannon. Some continued to read paperback books or, like Lieutenant Colonel George H. Dent and his wife, went on playing cards — "I was winning the [cribbage] Championship of the

---

*Among the passengers was Senior Sergeant Peter A. Foley, who subsequently interviewed his fellow survivors and wrote two accounts of what he and they went through. Although the crash and its aftermath received wide media coverage, my recounting of events is based almost entirely on Foley's work.

North Atlantic," he said later. But several women sat quietly weeping. "I know we are going to fall down," one of them kept whispering. "I know it."

The Number Two engine sputtered, and Dent looked out the window to see it "emitting hunks of carbonized fire, some of them the size of a fist." An alarm sounded, and then, according to Sergeant Foley, the engine "stopped with a thud you could both hear and feel."

Captain Murray calmly instructed the passengers over the intercom to "get ready to ditch," and he steered the Constellation into a spiral descent. The lights were shut off so the passengers' eyes would be adjusted to the darkness outside. Betty Sims raced down the aisle, repeating the ditching instructions one last time. The other stewardesses checked seat belts, even though the plane was dropping fast, and then someone yelled for them to sit down, too. Prayers were being said.

"As I took my seat," stewardess Carol Gould told Foley, "I remembered I hadn't had time to take off my stockings. I pulled up my skirt, but when I realized all those guys around me were looking, I just couldn't do it. So I fastened my seat belt and braced myself, and then I was praying. There's a friend of mine who was killed in an accident. I was talking to him. I don't know why."

Captain Murray could see the whitecaps very clearly in the landing lights. "I got down a little below 110 knots, picked an oncoming swell, chopped Number Four and dropped the plane to hit what appeared to be a relatively level spot between swells."

Sergeant Foley, a reporter for *Stars and Stripes,* describes the impact:

> People were thrown forward as some of the seats broke loose. My seat stayed put, and I braced for a second impact, which we had been told to expect. But it never came. I realized I was unhurt, so I unbuckled my seat belt and started to think about getting out of the plane. All I could see were shadows. It was dark, really dark. People began struggling out of their seats. Water was already pouring in from the bottom of the plane. I could sense an undercurrent of terror, but no one panicked. There was a little bit of talk: "Keep calm . . . keep it moving . . . don't get excited."

The Constellation's officers came out of the cabin and took up their ditching stations. Navigator Samuel Nicholson pushed a raft out the rear door, and when it did not open, he jumped into the ocean and swam after it, finally catching up to it twenty-five yards from the sinking fuselage. He inflated it, climbed in, and began pulling people in after him.

While the others were abandoning ship, Murray, who had forgotten his flashlight in the cockpit, went back for it. By this time Sergeant Foley had made his way to an emergency exit.

Another soldier and I yanked out the escape hatch next to us and dropped into the water. I tried to get my life vest inflated, but I couldn't. I was carried by waves toward the rear of the plane. It had sunk so deep that my head was level with the top of the fuselage. I decided not to waste any more time on the life jacket and began to swim. The waves buried me a couple of times. People were all around me. There were cries of "Where are the boats?" But no rafts were in sight. It was dark and windy, and giant waves were pitching us around.

I thought I felt a wing under my feet. It was the tail. Then a wave slammed me against the antenna. It's strung from the top of the forward cabin to the top of the tail. I threw my left arm over it. I scraped the arm and it hurt. I thought it was a good time to rest for a moment. I kept telling myself not to panic. Once you panic, you've had it.

After a few moments I realized it was calm. I kept waiting for a wave to break over me. Then I realized the plane was sinking and I was under water. I let go and swam slowly to the surface.

I was tired, dead tired. How easy it would be to quit fighting the sea and get it all over with. It would be so easy to die. Just stop fighting for half a minute. I shook my head, realizing this was a hell of a way to go.

Then I spotted a raft. It was just a shadow and it seemed a long way off. I managed to swim over to it and held on to a rope. I got my head up far enough to see inside, but I couldn't get in. I asked for help. Someone said he didn't have the strength. Then he grabbed my arms and somebody else pulled me in by the seat of my pants.

Private George V. Brown was still in the ocean. He had a deep head wound. A woman grabbed his shirt and life preserver and, in her panic, was pulling him under the water. "I got free and shouted to her to take it easy," Brown said. "Suddenly there was a raft. When I got into it I felt blood all over my face. I started hauling other people in."

Although four boats had been thrown from the Constellation, the survivors found only one of them. It quickly became overcrowded. Foley discovered he was unable to move: someone was lying across his ankles, and someone else across his thighs. He saw an injured man lying near him; because water was in the raft, a woman had to hold up his head to keep him from drowning. The sergeant saw a "tangle of arms and legs" everywhere he looked. As more and more people climbed aboard, the water rose up around his shoulders.

Captain Murray reached the boat with a woman beside him. They held on to ropes. Bleeding profusely from a gash in his head, he was weak and nearly blind. Someone called out, "Can't you find another raft? There's no more room."

"I've got a woman," he gasped in reply, and the two of them were pulled in, the last to get on board.

A few people were burned, and some others had broken bones or internal injuries. Many more were suffering from shock. An air force medical officer, Captain Juan Figueroa-Longo, was in the boat, but it was so packed that he was unable to treat anyone and could only call out advice: any sort of cloth could be used as a compress to stop bleeding, he shouted, and everyone should cup their hands over their mouths so that they would breathe warmer air.

Colonel Dent, the cribbage player, was six feet from his wife. He knew from her weak voice that something was wrong, but he could not get to her; he could only cry out words of encouragement.

Sergeant Foley writes in the *Saturday Evening Post* that

> This was not just a raft out in the cold, though. It was a horror. It was hard to realize at the time, because we were so numb with shock and fear, but remember that this was a fifteen-foot-wide raft designed for twenty-five people, and there were fifty-one of us in it. It was a cold, clear, starry night, and we were about five hundred miles from land, with no idea how soon anybody would find us. And we were being tossed around by huge waves. There were groans as the raft went up a wave, spun crazily around, and came down almost vertically. Some people were vomiting. We were jammed so tightly that every time the raft moved somebody would be rubbing against somebody else. There were cries of pain as the soggy clothing chafed and burned the tightly packed survivors.
>
> The biggest waves kept sloshing water into the raft, and soon it was dangerously near sinking. Navigator Nicholson kept urging, "Bail, bail! Bail if you want to live."

Despite the overcrowding, a few of them managed to bail with caps and wallets.

After a time they heard a plane circling overhead, but the crew could not see them in the dark. Many people were asking Nicholson where the nearest ship was. The only one he knew about was ten hours' sailing-time away, but he did not want to discourage them, so he told them she was four hours away — and there might be others even closer.

Someone asked if anyone had a flashlight to signal the aircraft. Murray did, but his arms were pinned so that he could not get it out of his pocket. Those around him managed to shift away long enough for him to pull it out.

The crew of the MATS C-118 soon spotted the signal and swooped low over the boat, dropping a red flare to mark its position. In the glow of the rosy light, Carol Gould looked about her and was aghast.

> When the first flare dropped it was like daytime on the raft. It was good — but also it wasn't. I could see everyone around me and they were all bloody. And the water in the raft was turning a sickening red. George Brown was bleeding so badly from the big gash in his head that I knew something had to be done. I looked around for something to make into a compress. Then I thought of my slip — it was only a half-slip. I took it off and made a compress out of it and put it on his head. Then a wave washed it off. The only way to keep it there was to hold it. He blacked out a few times. We both prayed.

Private Joe Hofer and his wife, Carol, who were on opposite sides of the boat, tried to boost morale by shouting out corny jokes and leading sing-alongs. The survivors sang "The Battle Hymn of the Republic" and "Side by Side" before the cold dispirited them, and they turned instead to reciting the Lord's Prayer in unison.

By now there were a number of aircraft circling and dropping flares. One paratrooper repeatedly claimed to see a ship's light on the horizon, but it always turned out to be a flare or an optical illusion. His false reports bothered a number of men, and they kept telling him to shut up.

The moon came up, and some of them thought it was a vessel, but that unfounded hope soon faded like the rest. One person and then another would give in to despair, saying that they would never be picked up alive. The rest would hurry to reassure them, reminding them of the planes overhead. Navigator Nicholson always joined in, telling them that a ship was close.

It was the navigator who first saw the rescue vessel. "After we had been in the water about three hours, I saw a constant light on the horizon," Nicholson told Foley. "I kept it to myself for a while. I hated to say it was a ship and get a lot of hopes up falsely. But the light was underneath one of the stars in the lip of the Big Dipper. When it continued in the same place, never flickering, I was sure, and I told them that a ship was coming."

Everyone "stretched and craned" to see the vessel, which at that point was nothing more than a small, steady glow on the horizon. Sometimes when the lifeboat plunged into the troughs of waves, the passengers lost sight of the ship, but then they would rise again and see her searchlights sweeping across the ocean's surface. Hofer directed the flashlight toward their rescuer and sent signals until the searchlights found them. The survivors shouted for joy, and Foley thought he could actually feel the light on his body.

Suddenly the vessel began to back away, and someone shouted, "It's a Russian ship and they aren't going to pick us up!" The *Celerina* was not Russian but Swiss and was simply maneuvering to get between the raft and the wind. As she came alongside, the survivors cheered so wildly that the freighter's captain incorrectly assumed that no one was injured.

With waves now up to twenty feet high, the sea was too rough for launching of boats, so the sailors threw out a line. But we were a rough target, lurching around on the waves. It was many minutes before someone finally managed to catch the rope and hold on. We were made fast to the side of the *Celerina,* and three rope ladders were lowered.

The waves were so high that one minute we'd be looking at the crew on deck, and the next moment we'd be below the ship's water line. A few soldiers had enough strength to catch the rope ladders, however, and they climbed up to the rail. Captain Murray grabbed a ladder, but fell back into the sea. A sailor came down and hauled him back into the raft. Other sailors started helping the rest of us up the ladders.

It took more than an hour to get everyone off the raft. When about twenty people had been taken off of it, Colonel Dent was finally able to reach his wife. He lifted her up, spoke to her and tried mouth-to-mouth artificial respiration. "It was too late," Dent later said. "I don't know how you know these things, but the moment I turned around and saw her, I knew she was dead. Dead people are dead."

Two of the sailors lifted her body into a hammock which was raised to the deck. The lifeless forms of two servicemen also were lifted to

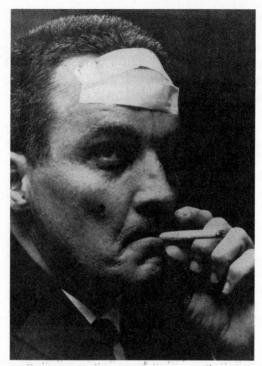

Captain John D. Murray, the last survivor pulled
from the sea (Permission of *The Saturday Evening
Post*)

the ship. No one had been aware that these three people had died
during our five-hour ordeal on the raft.

It was early morning, but still dark, when a sailor pulled me onto
the deck. I said I was all right, then fell on my face. Somebody caught
me and helped me into the crew's mess, where I was given warm
clothes and a jolt of whiskey. I couldn't pick it up. A sailor poured it
down my throat. It felt wonderful.

There was no doctor on board the freighter. Although Captain
Figueroa-Longo was himself ill and had lost his glasses, he set about
treating the injured. Carol Gould and the wife of the Swiss captain
acted as his nurses. He quickly found that some of the survivors
had sustained broken bones and internal injuries. Many more had
second-degree burns "aggravated by the constant chafing of their
clothing as the raft buffeted them about." Virtually everyone was

suffering from shock and exposure. The Swiss sailors slept in chairs so that the Americans could sleep in their bunks.

The Constellation's survivors had assumed that many of their missing fellow passengers and crewmen had climbed into the other lifeboats, but the other three were picked up empty. Seven bodies were recovered, but the corpses of eighteen others were never found, including that of Betty Sims, who had worked so hard to prepare the passengers for ditching. Her death was made more poignant by the fact that she had only recently been married and had tendered her resignation. After ten years of flying, she was on the last flight she was scheduled to make as a stewardess.

In all, twenty-eight of the seventy-six who were on board the Constellation when it went down were lost.

Four days later the *Celerina* docked at Antwerp. The air force arranged a flight to Frankfurt for those who were willing to get right back on a plane. Peter Foley noted proudly that no one refused the offer: "All of us agreed we had no objections to flying again, any old time."

June 4, 1969 *A Cuban refugee stows away in the landing-gear well of a Boeing 707 during a nine-hour flight from Havana to Madrid.*

Armando Socarras Ramirez, seventeen, was told by a friend how to stow away without being crushed by the retracting double wheels. He had planned to make the escape with him and another friend, Jorge Perez Blanco, sixteen. But only Socarras and Blanco dashed to the airliner from their hiding place in the tall grass beside the runway, the other man having backed out at the last moment.

"Jorge helped me into the right landing-gear well, then ran off to get into the left one," Socarras later explained. When the plane took off and "I saw the wheels coming, instinctively I huddled myself even further than I imagined possible and I grabbed some cables."

Sometime during the flight, Perez fell to his death. Aviation experts speculate that this may have occurred when the pilot lowered and retracted the gear once the Boeing had become airborne, in response to a warning light indicating something was wrong in the well, or perhaps when he lowered them again prior to landing in Madrid.

Socarras was wearing only lightweight clothing. "Little by little I felt cold, sleepy and had great pains in my ears. I must have fallen

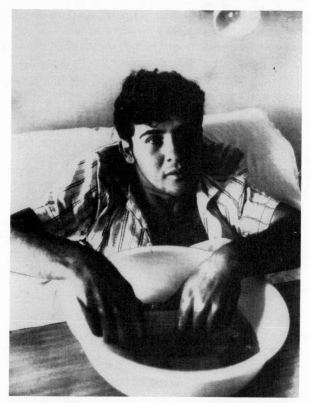

Cuban stowaway Armando Socarras Ramirez soaks his fingers in a solution for the treatment of frostbite. (Permission of AP/Wide World Photos)

asleep. I don't know anything more. I know I woke up once thinking it was terribly cold.''

At thirty thousand feet the temperature fell to forty degrees below zero. His freezing to death was not the only danger: the insufficiency of oxygen might have asphyxiated him, and the plane's rapid climb to the high altitude could have given him the bends. Doctors who examined him suggested that he may have survived by going into a state of hibernation. By this theory, he experienced a hypothermia similar to that used to reduce the body's need for oxygen during open-heart surgery.

When Iberia Airlines Flight 904 pulled up to the ramp at Barajas

Airport, an unconscious Socarras, his clothes covered with ice, fell from his perch onto the tarmac at the feet of startled mechanics. Taken to the Gran Hospital de la Beneficencia, he had his limbs soaked in warm water to overcome frostbite. His temperature was ninety-three degrees, and he was suffering from shock and exposure. He was often incoherent or extremely disoriented when speaking to physicians and nurses. Sometimes he talked as if his friend Perez had occupied the right landing-gear well with him instead of the left, and he did not always give the same answer when asked how old he was. A reporter who sneaked past guards to get an exclusive interview found the young man's thinking so disordered that he could not write a story.

His doctors expected that a prolonged oxygen deprivation might have seriously damaged his brain, heart, kidneys, and liver, but after a week of treatment, Socarras's hearty appetite had returned, and he was talking of moving to New Jersey.

As he recovered Armando Socarras Ramirez continued to experience minor memory lapses. "I have some uncles living in New Jersey and maybe they will help me," he told reporters from his hospital bed. "I am upset now that I do not remember their address, but it will come to my mind pretty soon, I'm sure. I had planned to escape from Cuba and come to Spain in order to get in touch with them."

On July 25 he flew to New York's Kennedy Airport for a "tearful reunion" with one of his uncles, Elo Fernandez, of Passaic, New Jersey. At a press conference Socarras, whose entry into the United States had been sponsored by the International Relief Committee, explained that he left Cuba because "I was not in agreement with the government. I was not inspired with it. There was no future there at all for me. I was looking for a new world and a new future."

As for his risky adventure in the landing-gear well: "If I was in the same situation, I would do it again. I was not cold at first. Then my clothes froze, and I became unconscious. I was unconscious during most of the trip."

June 5, 1971 *Trapper Ronald Woodcock becomes lost in the wilderness of northwest British Columbia. The nearest settlement is Hazelton, 125 miles away.*

An experienced woodsman, Ron Woodcock actually made his

Ron Woodcock *(left)* some years before he became lost in the Canadian wilderness (Permission of R. Woodcock)

living working for a railroad. The previous winter a fire had destroyed his uninsured home, and he was forced to put his wife and six children into a rented house. He hoped to recoup his losses by trapping beaver. In April he took a leave of absence from his job and had a bush pilot drop him off at Damdochax Lake.

His base camp was an old cabin built by telegraph linemen before the turn of the century. At the end of May, after a few days' visit to an outlying camp in Groundhog Pass, where he emptied his traps and skinned his catch, he tried to take a short cut back to the cabin and became lost. "Around three o'clock I knew something was wrong. I had run into landmarks I had never seen before." He realized that he might never find his way back to his camp. His best chance was to follow a nearby creek in the hope that it would lead him to the Skeena River, which he could then follow south toward Hazelton.

He had a rifle, fifteen rounds of ammunition, a sleeping bag, an ax, and a cigarette lighter, but the only food he was carrying was a little rice and dried soup.

The weight of the pelts he had brought along was a problem. He was in good condition, but he was forty-eight years old, and he had a long way to go. It was hard to abandon them after "I'd spent two months catching them," but they were too big a load to lug very far. Reluctantly he walked away from them.

There was no path to follow, the undergrowth was thick, and he had to climb one hill after another. Piles of fallen trees formed barriers he had to work his way around.

He shot and ate wild game: a woodchuck, a grouse, and two moose. Each time he shot a moose he would camp for several days, cooking and eating the meat. Then he would set off again, carrying about twenty pounds of meat with him.

The day after he had shot one moose, a grizzly bear appeared, drawn by the smell of the carcass. The grizzly was huge: he was nine feet tall, and Woodcock thought he must have weighed over a thousand pounds. The bear did not see him, so intent was he on the moose, and Woodcock shot him in the neck. The grizzly went down, crippled by the bullet. Needing to save his ammunition, Woodcock did not finish him off but waited for him to die. After four or five hours the animal was still alive, and it was getting dark. Woodcock put a bullet into his brain.

On the fourteenth day he came upon the Skeena River. It was too deep and swift for him to cross, so he followed alongside it: "I knew it would eventually take me out someplace." A few days later he found himself at a fork where another wide river joined the Skeena. He could not cross either one, so he worked his way upstream beside the second river, heading north when he needed to go south.

When a rainstorm struck, he built a shelter and a pallet out of spruce limbs. For several days he stayed in his sleeping bag, listening to the rain, thinking about his family and about how much he had to lose if he did not make it to Hazelton.

When the storm ended, he resumed walking. Finally he came upon a windfall: there was an island in the river, and a tree had fallen between it and the shore. He strode across the tree and made a bridge to the far shore out of small tree trunks. He was headed south again.

By the end of the first month he was entirely out of meat, soup, and rice. Thereafter he ate only vegetation — squaw weeds, skunk cabbage, and ferns. He was losing weight and slowing down. No longer could he stay on the move for anything like ten or twelve hours a day.

One morning he stumbled on a downed, rotting telegraph pole, the remnant of an abandoned line. All the poles had long since fallen, but if he could stay on the trail the linemen had made, it would lead him to Hazelton. He cut a walking stick and moved forward cautiously feeling for the hardness of the packed earth of the trail, trying to distinguish by touch the difference between it and the looser earth on either side. He detoured around bogs and other barriers. Again and again he lost the trail, and then he would "wander through the bush [until] eventually I'd hit it again." Once he lost it for two or three days, but he kept searching, trying to be patient and thinking of his family.

His clothes were ripped and torn by the undergrowth, and he was so thin that to hold his pants up he had to rig his rifle sling as a suspender. One of his boot soles came loose, and he tied it in place with a piece of string. The mosquitoes swarmed about him, but the black flies were worse: they would "just take a chunk right out of you." He had little energy, and he needed to stop frequently to rest. Climbing grades was a debilitating struggle for him, and he was able to make only four or five miles a day.

On the fifty-fifth day he could find only cranberries to eat. The seeds lodged in his intestines and gave him terrible cramps, forcing him to lie down each time they came on.

In the early afternoon of the fifty-seventh day, he staggered out of the woods onto a dirt road. A car passed him and stopped. The men inside were returning from a day of fishing and were amazed at the sight of him. He could not speak well enough to make himself understood. One of the men gave him a piece of paper and a pencil. He wrote that he needed a drink of water. They had none and gave him a beer instead. Now he scribbled a polite request that they take him to his mother's house in Hazelton.

What did his mother say when she saw this tattered, gaunt apparition? "She said she knew I'd come home sometime."

Ron Woodcock had lost seventy pounds and was suffering from malnutrition, exposure, and an intestinal disorder. He convalesced for two weeks in a hospital, and it was many months before he fully regained his strength. The next year he went trapping again in the very same wilderness in which he had been lost for so long.

October 1, 1971   *Two Americans are dumped into frigid Missinaibi Lake in northern Ontario after a sudden storm capsizes their canoe.*

The men, Don M. Campbell, forty-two, and Gerald L. Julius, twenty-eight, were experienced outdoorsmen. They had come to the lake to photograph ancient Indian picture writing (known as pictographs) for a film that Campbell was putting together.

On an overcast and rainy day they went out on the water to scout possible locations. In their excitement they failed both to take along basic survival gear and, as was Campbell's habit, to leave a note beneath the windshield wiper of their van telling where they had gone and when they would return.

Fourteen miles southwest of their camp, at a place known as Fairy Point, they found a whole series of drawings on a rock face. As they sat in their craft examining their discovery, the prevailing wind blew a storm down on top of them.

Don Campbell would later write,

> My first indication of danger came when a savage gust of wind hit us broadside. Its force snapped some dead limbs from trees that grew on top of the cliff. The wind was followed instantly by a wave three to four feet high. And while we were wallowing in the trough of that wave, a bigger one slammed into us broadside.

The canoe capsized.

We had spilled at a remote, exposed spot on the lake. The wind and waves that hit us had more than ten miles of open water over which to build force, and Missinaibi's canyonlike surroundings had funneled the storm directly upon Fairy Point. Even if we had seen the storm coming, we couldn't have run for shore at that point. The rock wall offered no handholds, and the waves might easily have beaten us unconscious on the rocks.

They were not wearing life jackets, and the life cushions had been swept away. Campbell managed to grab a paddle that floated by, and Julius seized a six-gallon gas can. They each clung with one hand to the small part of the bow that remained above water, the rest of the craft being held under by the weight of the outboard motor. Both were wearing heavy clothes — long underwear, over-alls, and lined jackets — but they did not try to strip these off. The "savagely churning waves" would have made removing them diffi-cult.

Campbell's hip boots had filled with water and come off, but Julius still had on his hiking shoes. These had been a problem in the first moments, he told Campbell, but he did not notice their weight anymore.

Waves four to six feet high broke over their heads as the canoe drifted. Having swallowed a lot of water, Julius quickly began to experience stomach cramps. Their hands soon became numb and nearly useless, their limbs heavy and slow. They felt their strength draining away, and their minds became dull and confused.

Twice Campbell went under the boat, attempting to detach the motor, but the lake was so cold that he could not stay immersed long enough to succeed. Julius tried to swim for shore, but the waves were too big. He struggled back toward Campbell, who swam out and stretched the paddle toward him, pulling him in after he grasped it.

After an hour and a half the wind began blowing them toward a rocky point. They held on to the craft as it was carried toward safety — but then the wind shifted and they went right past the point.

"The wind isn't going to blow us to shore, is it?" Julius called out. He was no longer able to hold on to the canoe.

Straddling the keel, Campbell held him tightly against the bow with the paddle, gripping one end of it and thrusting the other through the handle of the gas can, so that its length pressed across

Julius's torso. For another hour they stayed with the craft as it drifted north, and then Julius said he would rather take his chances swimming for shore than die helplessly in the middle of the lake. Campbell saw that Julius's face had turned purple and knew they had both reached the limit of their endurance. He told him that he would come along.

> Communication was at all times difficult. The wind snatched our words away, and even with our faces only inches apart we could barely hear each other. Our jaws were so cold that they hung slack. We couldn't get our lips together to form sounds properly. Thus, we could establish no definite plan for our attempt to swim for shore.

It was Campbell's intention that they each hold on to an end of the paddle as they kicked, using the gas can between them as a buoy. Before he was ready to start, however, Julius pushed off alone. Campbell took a grip on both ends of the paddle and swam in pursuit of his friend, but the can slowed him, and the wind pushed him in another direction.

For several minutes Julius swam strongly and then rolled over on his back to float. Campbell was sure he was going to make it.

> He seemed much stronger than I was, and I was convinced that he would get to shore and I wouldn't. As I rose on a wave, I saw him spit water. Then, as he rose to the top of a wave, he turned face-down. When he dropped into the trough, he sank from sight.
>
> Jerry was gone. He had made no struggle, had shown no panic. At that moment I imagined that if drowning was like that, it couldn't be too bad.
>
> Mentally I was already in bad shape from our ordeal. And when Jerry slipped beneath the waves my mind really went haywire.
>
> "He's just playing tricks on me," I thought. "He's holding his breath and he'll reappear somewhere soon."
>
> I began looking all around in the waves for him, but even as I looked I knew that it was crazy.

Campbell wanted to let go of the can and sink down into the lake too, but he forced himself to go on. In twenty minutes he reached the shore, not far from where his friend had drowned.

At the water's edge Campbell let go of the can and discovered that he could no longer control his limbs. He had to lie still because when he tried to push himself up and crawl on his hands and knees he simply crashed back down on the rocks. His wrists and elbows would not support his weight. He rested awhile and then reached for a rock and pulled himself forward, but after dragging himself only a few yards, he blacked out.

When he came to, he tried to think what to do. He estimated that the van and campsite were at least thirty miles away, through rugged and wild country. He was sick and exhausted, and he had no shoes, food, or matches. He did not think that he could make it on foot. His only hope was the canoe.

Without the weight of the men, the bow was riding much higher in the lake, and the wind was pushing the craft along so fast that it was already far beyond Campbell. He would have to follow the shoreline as best he could until he caught up with it and it came within reach.

Using the paddle as a crutch, he began to hobble from tree to tree, grabbing limbs to pull himself along. He fell frequently. Many times the undergrowth blocked his path and forced him to turn away from the shore. In one respect he was lucky: his feet were still so numb that he could not feel the sharp stones and sticks he stepped on.

At last he found himself parallel to the boat, but then he looked down and saw that he was completely naked.

While working my way through the bush, trying to catch up with the drifting canoe, I had unconsciously removed all my clothing. I stopped and forced myself to calm down. I would need clothing for warmth, and my car keys were in a pocket of my trousers, so I retraced my steps for about half a mile and retrieved all my clothing.

I dressed and again struggled through the bush to catch up with the canoe. By then I wasn't sure if I was ahead of or behind it. Finally I spotted it out in the lake and worked my way through the bush until I again was ahead of it. I found a rocky point that jutted into the lake fifteen or twenty feet, and went out on the rocks to wait.

He thought it was about three P.M. The wind had died down and the waves were smaller. Sometimes the sun broke through the clouds. Campbell lay down. *I'll just sleep here in the sun a little while,* he thought, and dozed off. But in that state between waking and deep sleep, it came to him that he should stay alert until the boat drew close. He awoke and sat up.

When the craft came near the shore, Campbell stripped off his clothes, took a piece of twine that had been a belt for his rain pants, and tied one end of it to a dry cedar log to use as a buoy. Going back into the water was one of the hardest things he had ever had to do, but in he went. He swam to the boat, finding the going much easier without his clothing.

His fingers were so numb that it was hard for him to tie the twine to the bow, and when he finally managed to do so, a large wave struck the craft, slamming the bow into his groin, knocking the wind out of him, and driving him beneath the water. Once more he thought he would not live, thought that he would die there, but he fought back to the surface.

When I had recovered from the blow, I worked my way to the end of the log and began to tow the canoe to shore. My progress was slow and exhausting, but finally my feet touched bottom. When I turned to look, the canoe was still out in the lake; the twine had snapped. I knew that I had to swim right back out to get the canoe or I would never again have the strength or the heart for it.

I turned around, pushed the log into the water, and headed out again. This time I stuck my finger through the canoe's bow ring and swam slowly for shore, pulling the half-submerged craft behind me.

The stern of the canoe began to drag on bottom about fifteen feet from shore. I worked about two hours trying to get the water out. First I had to pry the sunken craft partly out on the rocks. Then I used the paddle to splash out enough water so that I could pull it farther up on shore. The canoe was about half emptied when a big wave came along and filled it again. I had to start all over. When I could reach the motor, I removed it from the stern and dragged it up on the rocks.

At about five P.M. Campbell set out for Fairy Point. He was going against the wind, however, and could make little progress. He lay down in the bottom of the boat to wait for the wind to die down, and he fell asleep.

He awakened in darkness to find the air was nearly still. Once more he struck out for the point, but though the lake was calm, he was so weak he was barely able to work the paddle. He could exert himself for only ten or twenty seconds at a time.

It took him four hours to reach the point, but once he rounded it a slight breeze was at his back, and he made better progress. He felt stronger and was able to work the paddle for a minute at a time before slumping over in exhaustion. Through the night he alternately paddled and slept, gaining strength as he went, until he was able to paddle a half hour at a stretch.

He arrived at the cove where their camp was shortly after four A.M.

As I walked from the lake toward the van, I sensed something wrong. Our tent was down. I unlocked the van and turned on the headlights. Then I could see that the bears had ripped into the tent and had torn and mangled all our gear. Rain had soaked nearly everything that the bears had not ruined. At that moment, even though I had found my way back to camp and eventual safety, I was nearly overwhelmed by the situation. The bear raid, which I would have laughed off at any other time, was the straw that nearly broke my back.

Sick, exhausted, and aching all over, I chose the drier of the two sleeping bags, crawled into the van, and tried to sleep. Then I became violently ill and vomited water and blood throughout the rest of the night.

In the morning Campbell loaded the canoe on the van and drove south until he saw a radio antenna above the trees. He turned onto a road and found a shack maintained by the Department of Lands and Forests. Campbell radioed the police, who directed him to a hospital and set up a search for Gerald Julius's body.

The next day the corpse was found in fifty feet of water, only fifteen feet from shore. Fully clothed except for one glove, it was in a relaxed position, and there were no signs of struggle or panic. Authorities believed that he had passed out before he sank below the surface. In the words of his friend, "The long hours of immersion in cold water and the strain of swimming fully clothed through turbulent waves toward the tantalizingly near shoreline must have drained the last bit of endurance from him."

Thinking over his ordeal on Missinaibi Lake, Don Campbell concluded that it was a result of

unforeseen incidents, such as the unnoticed approach of the storm and the capsizing in front of high cliffs that prevented us from swimming ashore before the cold water had weakened us. Our predicament was worsened by the motor-laden, vertically floating canoe that offered little support and would not be blown or pushed ashore, and by the loss of the untethered life cushions and lack of life jackets. It was the absence of simple survival items such as shoes, waterproof matches, emergency food and a compass that forced me to re-enter the lake, again risking death, to retrieve the canoe instead of hiking out to safety.

These circumstances might have been only a nuisance at another time or place, but they killed when woven together at Missinaibi Lake on that nightmarish day in October.

Ours may well be the story behind many of the unwitnessed and unsurvived tragedies that have occurred on wilderness waters. I hope that others might avoid a similar tragedy.

December 24, 1971 *A Lockheed Electra carrying ninety-two passengers and nearing the completion of a short flight between Lima and Pucallpa, Peru, flies into a storm, is struck by lightning, and breaks apart in midair.*

Strapped into a seat by the window was a petite seventeen-year-old girl named Juliane Koepcke; beside her was her mother, Marie. Juliane was looking out through the glass when she saw a flash of light and heard a loud noise — and then flames were spreading across the right wing. She turned to her mother and heard her say, "This is the end of everything."

"An instant later," Juliane wrote in *Stern* magazine, "there was a hefty concussion and I found myself outside the plane, flying apart from it, still strapped in my seat. I can remember turning over and over in the air. I remember thinking that the jungle trees below looked just like cauliflowers. Then I lost consciousness."

She came to after three hours and heard the sounds of birds singing and frogs croaking. She was still buckled into her seat, which was now lying on the forest floor, but the seat next to hers was empty. She called her mother's name, but there was no answer. Her right shoulder hurt from what turned out to be a broken collarbone; she was scratched, bruised, and badly cut on her right arm and foot.

She unstrapped herself and got out of the seat. Walking around slowly, carefully, a few steps at a time, she looked for her mother or any of the other passengers. She was dazed, and because she had lost her eyeglasses, her vision was blurry. She saw no one, but she did find some candy and little Christmas cakes. She ate the cakes but saved the candy for the days ahead. When it grew dark and rain began to fall, she climbed under the seat and tried to sleep.

The canopy overhead was lush and thick, making it unlikely that she would be spotted from the air. If she was to survive, she would have to reach civilization on foot. Luckily she had some experience in the outdoors: her German-born parents were both scientists, her mother being an ornithologist and her father, Hans, an ecologist. Thus she had spent considerable time in the jungle while her parents did their research, and having just graduated from high school, she was shortly to go to West Germany to study zoology herself. While other girls her age went on dates or to parties, she collected marine specimens on the beaches of Lima.

Her father had told her that if she ever became lost in the forest she should walk downhill until she found water and then follow it downstream until she reached a settlement. On Christmas morning she picked up a stick to use as a staff and began working her way down the slopes and through the thick undergrowth. She was dressed in the clothes she had worn to her confirmation two weeks earlier, and the bushes tore her frilly dress. Her white high heels often sank into the mud. She lost one shoe and limped on with the foot bare; then the other shoe was gone as well. Thorns tore her feet, which turned black and blue.

She rested every midday, traveling in the mornings and afternoons to avoid the worst of the heat. The zipper on her dress had broken, and when the sunlight broke through the canopy, it burned the skin on her back.

During the early going she sometimes heard helicopters and airplanes that were searching for the Electra, but the jungle hid the wreckage. After the third day she heard them no more.

Once she happened on another section of the Electra's seats lying face down, and she turned it over. Beneath it were the corpses of three teenage girls. They were black with flies. She staggered on.

Before many days had passed, she came to a stream, and she followed it until it fed into a swift-flowing river. Whenever fallen trees blocked her path, she waded or even swam in the water, although she feared that the blood from her wounded feet would attract piranhas. Leeches attached themselves to her skin and sucked her blood. Hordes of insects attacked her and laid their eggs in her bites and wounds, and she felt the larvae crawling under her skin. She saw a few wild animals, and sometimes small crocodiles slithered off the shore and into the river.

Remembering the lessons her parents taught her, she worried less about "big animals" like "ocelots, jaguars, and tapirs" than "snakes, poisonous spiders, and ants." On the move, she constantly probed the ground with her staff to locate and discourage serpents. Each time she found armies of marching ants in front of her she made a hasty detour. "Nights in the jungle were scary. There was always a rustling somewhere: snakes? There was something crawling over my legs: a tarantula? I slept fitfully."

She picked wild fruit and licked the skins, but she did not eat any for fear of being poisoned. She thought of killing toads and eating them, but though she knew that some would be poisonous, she did not know which ones to avoid. She recalled throwing away one of the small cakes she had found on the first day because it was wet and smelled bad; now she wished she had eaten it, anyway. She kept going, sucking pieces of candy as she went.

On the tenth day she found an empty hut by the shore, with salt and kerosene inside. She put a little salt on her tongue. With a splinter of wood and some kerosene she tried to clean the insect larvae out of her skin. That was the worst thing about the walk, she would decide in retrospect: not the hunger or the sun or the thorns and bushes or the mud, but the worms moving around beneath her skin.

She lay down on the floor and slept lightly. "I kept listening for human voices. But I heard only the screaming of monkeys and the screeching of parakeets." In the morning three Indian hunters burst into the hut, which was one of several they had built for camps. They mashed fruit into pulp for her to eat and offered her farina, sugar, and more salt, "but my stomach was a lot less uncomfortable than my insect bites." One man poured gasoline over her: "I counted thirty-five worms that came out of my arms alone. The men helped me take another ten out of other parts of my body." They washed her with salt water and put salve on her wounds.

At dawn the next day they set off with her in their canoe. They brought her to the hut of an Indian woman who, upon catching a glimpse of the girl's face grossly swollen from insect bites, bloodshot eyes, and limbs "pocked with worm lesions," screamed that she was a demon and chased them away. Juliane could not blame her: "I was a living nightmare." The men navigated the canoe for seven and a half hours to the small settlement of Tournavista, where there was a doctor.

The next day an American woman pilot named Jerrie Cobb landed at the Tournavista airstrip and then flew Juliane to the American missionary station at Yarinacocha, near Pucallpa. Her father was waiting for her there. It had been eleven days since she and her mother had climbed aboard the Electra in Lima.

Using the girl's information, searchers flew to the crash site, hoping to find other survivors. There were none. A dozen people, scattered through the forest, had actually lived through the crash itself and had stayed where they landed, waiting to be found. None of them lived more than ten days. Had the girl not chosen to walk out of the jungle, her body would have been carried out with the rest.

Juliane Koepcke, who was suffering from exposure and exhaus-

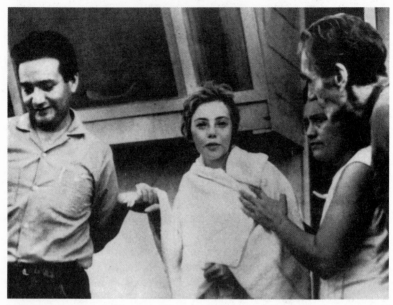

Juliane Koepcke is led from the Tournavista medical clinic, where she received initial medical treatment. (Photograph by Harold Sells, Jr.)

tion, slept deeply for a period, but as she recovered and grew stronger, she began to dwell on her mother's death. Indeed, the deaths of all ninety-one passengers seemed so senseless, and she could see no reason why she of all the others would survive. Never very religious, she now read the Bible almost obsessively. One day a visitor said to her, "You can be thankful that God saved you." She answered, "Yes, but why me? And why not my mother?"

January 24, 1972 *Two hunters capture a fifty-six-year-old man who has been hiding out in the jungles of Guam for twenty-eight years. He is Sergeant Shoichi Yokoi of the Japanese Imperial Army.*

When American forces took Guam in the summer of 1944, after a month of fierce fighting, several hundred of the nineteen thousand Japanese troops stationed there chose to escape into the forests rather than surrender. Among them was a band of ten men that included Sergeant Yokoi. The ten soon split up to elude capture, and Yokoi and two others went into the Talofofo River District. They dug a cave in a bamboo thicket, but after a few months it was clear that the available food supply would not long support three people. The other two moved, and Yokoi visited them occasionally over the years.

Alone, Yokoi spent his days hiding in the cave; to make it more homey he strewed the floor with leaves and put together a coconut oil lamp. Under the cover of darkness he foraged for food, gradually enlarging his diet to include wild nuts, mangoes, papaya, breadfruit, pigeons, snails, and rats. Having been a tailor's apprentice before the war, he made "burlap-like" suits from the fiber of tree bark, sewing them together with needles he fashioned from nails; he carved buttons out of wood. He walked on sandals made from coconut husks, from which he also fashioned belts. His calendar was a tree trunk that he notched at each full moon, and he built fires by rubbing sticks together. Though he learned from a leaflet in 1952 that the war was over, he never gave up his determination to avoid capture and hold out until the Imperial Army returned: "We Japanese soldiers were told to prefer death to surrender." Over and over he reminded himself that "I am living for the Emperor and for the spirit of Japan."

In 1964 he went to visit his two comrades and found them both dead. Medical authorities speculate that they died of malnutrition.

When Yokoi was captured by hunters and brought to Guam Memorial Hospital, the examining doctors were surprised to find that he was quite fit, other than suffering a mild case of anemia. His first question was "Tell me one thing quick — Is Roosevelt dead?"

At the hospital Yokoi learned that he had been declared dead in 1944 and had been posthumously promoted from private to sergeant. He had never heard of television or the atom bomb, although he had a vague notion of what a jet was: "Those strange planes whose wings are all swept back." Informed that the Japanese government had chartered one for his return that would have him home in three hours, he stared incredulously.

News of his existence electrified Japan, and Yokoi became an instant hero. Newspaper editorials lauded him, and politicians vied to top one another in singing his praises and awarding him honors. Private citizens donated thousands of presents, including electric blankets and lifetime passes to hotel baths. Job offers and marriage proposals poured in. Gifts of money soon totaled $80,000. (Yokoi's back pay amounted to $129, to which the government added $340 as a "token of sympathy." His military pension came to $432 a year.)

But the sergeant seemed baffled by his celebrity and a little regretful of his impending return to society. "Maybe I should have stayed in my cave and died," he remarked to newsmen. "But since I am going home, my goal will be to see my family, then live in solitude and meditation high atop a mountain."

He flew to Tokyo on February 2, 1972. The sight of Mount Fuji through the aircraft window caused him to cry: "My handkerchief was soaked with tears while I thought of my country." He was greeted at the airport by a cheering, weeping, waving crowd of five thousand. "I have returned with the rifle the emperor gave me," he told them, dabbing at his eyes. "I am sorry I could not serve him to my satisfaction." Looking around he added, "Little did I dream that Japan had achieved such a remarkable advancement in civilization."

When he drove to his hometown of Nagoya, cheering onlookers lined the highway, waving paper Japanese flags. Cars clogged the roads around his family's house, and vendors were selling corn on the cob and balloons. A large throng cheered him as he emerged from the automobile. Politicians assisted him as he walked up the gravel drive, and they hovered close by while, with tears streaming from his eyes, he examined the inscription on the memorial his mother had erected to his memory. (She and his other close relatives were all dead.)

Not everyone appreciated the carnival-like atmosphere and the acclaim Yokoi was accorded. Some residents pointed out that fifty men from the village had gone off to war, and thirty-six had been killed. Why was such a fuss being made over one survivor? Dissenting voices were being raised elsewhere as well. Some people saw his devotion to the emperor as antiquated and embarrassing and his willingness to stay in the jungle for so long as absurd and even dangerous: for them he symbolized the fanatic militarism of the old regime.

Still others, though, were intrigued by the Rip Van Winkle aspect of his life and the unique perspective it gave him. "Putting aside his fear of always being sought and [his] loneliness," said university student Koji Ito, "I guess he might have discovered real affluence in a life remote from civilized society. When he . . . gets to know about contemporary Japan, I want to ask him which of the two he would think was really affluent."

■   ■   ■

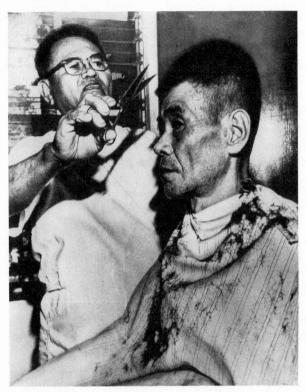

Sergeant Shoichi Yokoi gets his first professional haircut after twenty-eight years in the jungle. (Permission of AP/ Wide World Photos)

When the man *Time* magazine dubbed Rip Van Yokoi got to know modern Japan, he found it spiritually impoverished. He had trouble coping "with all the changes that have happened in my country" and found them "tough to accept." He was unhappy that Hirohito had been humanized: "Perhaps the emperor has ceased to be a living God to other people, but to me he remains a sacred person." Yokoi was glad that the widespread poverty of prewar Japan had been eradicated, but "what a price to pay! The glories of nature that I used to know have all disappeared. Instead up in the sky we have this thing called smog. On earth cars are killing people faster than war. The jungle of Guam may be the most peaceful place there is."

Children had become "spoiled brats" who now seemed "to make it a profession to defy the authority of parents," he complained to a

Time correspondent who looked him up after he had been home seven months. Improved diet had made the young big and strong, but "mentally they are so soft that what they need is a good stretch in the barracks. I would call for the restoration of the old conscription."

Inflation alarmed him too. "Before the war, I could have had a perfectly satisfying evening out on a mere ten-yen note. Now you might spend ten thousand yen and the geisha will still say no." He was afraid to resume his old occupation. Prices so staggered him that he doubted he could competently haggle over the cost of a suit.

Most disturbing of all were modern women. They were "monsters" whose virtue was "all but gone from them" and who screeched "like apes." They wore miniskirts, dyed their hair, painted their nails, and used so much purple eye shadow that they looked like ghosts. Before the war women were "everything that made life blissful for men — virtuous, obedient to commands from menfolk, lovely to look at, gentle and retiring." The type of woman he had dreamed about all those years in his cave seemed to have disappeared from his homeland.

It was not that he wanted to go back to the old days, he insisted to the *Time* reporter, but that he longed for a Japan "halfway between then and now, a combination of prewar Japan without its militarism and postwar Japan without its *kogai* [environmental disruption]."

By the time he expressed this wish, most of his countrymen had already forgotten him. Other heroes had stolen their attention and adoration, especially the members of the 1972 Japanese Olympic gymnastic team. The sergeant's neighbors were tired of hearing his opinions. Some of them wondered why, if he was such a good soldier, he had not committed hara-kiri when Guam fell. Others muttered that he looked down on them "and seems convinced that nobody else suffered during the war."

Ironically, it was his disdain for his countrymen that had kept him alive all those years in isolation. His early life had been unhappy, and he was made to feel inferior. On Guam he had the chance to show that he was superior to everyone else in his capacity to endure suffering: "I had an extra tough childhood. So many people were harsh, cruel or downright brutal to me. By sticking to the jungle, I actually sought to vent my spite on all these people by remote control; I had to become somebody who could look down on these fellows to even the old score. And I think I have.''

Shortly after he was interviewed by the American journalist, Shoichi Yokoi's fortunes changed. He met Mihoko Hatashin, forty-four, who could only be described as an old-fashioned Japanese girl. After just three dates they were in love. "We can now communicate with each other by eyes," she said to a reporter, "though we don't talk to each other very much." They were married in early November in a Shinto ceremony at the Atsuta Jingu shrine near Nagoya. Bride and groom wore traditional costumes and sipped sake. Then they retired to the house he had bought with some of the money his countrymen had donated, and she prepared him a meal of eggs and *miso shiru* (soybean soup).

They let it be known that they would be honeymooning on Guam.

February 29, 1972 *Near midnight, medical secretary Carole Taylor is trapped beneath her car on the grade of a deserted road in Montreal.*

Carole Taylor had been trying to push her automobile, which was stuck in the snow, when she fell, and one of the wheels ran over her legs. Beneath the snow the road was unpaved, so that the slow spinning of the wheels caused the vehicle to sink lower and lower and rest ever more heavily on her body.

Her right leg and right arm were immobile, but she could move her left leg slightly, and her left arm was free. During the night the car shifted several times, each time bringing the rocker panel higher up her torso until it rested on her chest and chin and seriously impaired her breathing.

The exhaust pipe was burning both of her legs. Her right leg and arm became numb, and she feared gangrene would set in. An immense pain in her back gradually spread throughout her body. The sound of the motor so close to her head seemed to be intensifying in volume, and it alarmed and maddened her. She tried to stall the motor by packing snow into a hole in the tail pipe but managed only to burn her hand.

As the hours passed she had to fight against panic and despair. She remembered reading of a boy swimming alone and drowning, a family burned up in a fire, a woman who had died trapped in an automobile that had run into a ravine.

Although lacking in "deep religious convictions," she prayed, trying to make a deal with God, promising to really believe in him, and then, more wildly, to be good, to quit smoking . . . if he would get her out of this situation. She tried to make herself fall asleep, but the engine kept her awake. She realized that the object that she had thought was a rock and against which she had been kicking with her left leg (to keep the circulation in it) was actually her right leg. She tried to end her agony by twisting her head and neck so she could inhale exhaust fumes, but the wind blew them away from her, and she succeeded only in increasing her pain.

At about three A.M. she heard a truck and saw the red lights outlining its body. "It was useless to yell, so I talked to the truck: 'Please, you've got to come closer. Look at my headlights. See me? Come now! I can't wait any longer. Now!' "

The vehicle sped on, and soon she was gripped by terror. She began to scream, "Help! Help me! Selby Street! Selby Street!" After a time she fell silent, exhausted.

She wondered if, when her corpse was finally found, it would be understood what she had endured. She imagined what her head would look like, exploded by the weight of the car. She tried to let the sound of the motor lull her to sleep and prayed to God to make her unconscious and let her die.

At 4:16 A.M. she heard the sound of another vehicle and saw the flicker of headlights. The lights disappeared but then returned stronger than before. An automobile was coming closer. Beneath her car, buried in snow, she feared she would not be seen. She slowly raised her left arm and began to wave. She heard a door open and the crunch of snow beneath shoes — and she was found.

Two young police officers on routine patrol had departed from their usual route to drive down a deserted dead-end road. One of them radioed for help while his partner knelt by her face and asked how she felt.

"I felt paralyzed, and my body hurt terribly. I wanted to say, 'Grateful,' but I couldn't move my mouth."

Carole Taylor was hospitalized for more than a week and convalesced for another month. For months thereafter she experienced weakness in her right leg. She often thought of how the policeman told her that he did not set out with the intention of going down that street, and that when he reached it he turned down it without thinking about it. "His unconscious impulse," she says, "will never let me stop wondering."

October 20, 1972 *On the island of Lubang a Filipino police patrol stumbles on two men stealing from a village. The bandits open fire with .25 caliber rifles, and in the exchange that follows one man is shot eight times and killed, but the other, wounded only in the leg, seizes the dead man's weapon and escapes into the jungle.*

The body is identified as that of Private First Class Kinshichi Kozuka of the Japanese Imperial Army.

When it was evident that American forces would retake the Philippines, the islands' military commander, General Hirobumi Yamashita, sent Second Lieutenant Hiro Onoda to Lubang. "Stay there until the Imperial Army comes back again," Yamashita ordered. "You are a clever young man. We'll need you one day to teach the Japanese army how to survive in the jungle."

Onoda started out with a band of seventy-five men, but as the decades passed, their number was reduced by illness, skirmishes — and even surrender, although Onoda forbade it. "We were afraid of the commander," one deserter later told journalists. "We knew he would not hesitate for a minute to kill us if we tried to desert. He made us clean and polish our guns twice a day. He even made us polish our bullets." The passing of the decades did not in the least diminish Onoda's obsession with discipline: Private Kozuka's worn clothing had been carefully mended; his fingernails were clean; and his hair was closely cropped in accordance with the old regulations.

Onoda was a wily and elusive guerrilla. He and his men never stayed at one campsite for more than a few days, and he was careful to see that their traces were obliterated when they moved on. When they raided villages they would set fire to crop fields or huts to distract the villagers while they made off with whatever they could steal.

If the news of Shoichi Yokoi electrified the Japanese public, word of Onoda and Kozuka outraged it. Many people felt that the government had not done enough to locate and bring in the two men and other "war stragglers" like them. (Authorities have never been able to account for some 3,500 soldiers assigned to the Pacific Theater.) Officials at the Welfare Ministry were quick to point out that they had conducted extensive ground searches and leaflet drops, noting that found on Kozuka's body was a surrender poster specifically addressed to him.

Nevertheless, a special effort was made to bring in Hiro Onoda. Ten thousand new leaflets were printed up, and officials, family, and friends were flown into the Philippines along with the inevitable mob of journalists and photographers. Through megaphones and loudspeakers dignitaries shouted over and over, "Your mission has been completed. It has been successful. Please come back." Onoda's own older brother, Toshio, a Tokyo physician, knelt in the mud and, weeping, called out for "Hiro-chan . . . Hiro-chan." Yet the stubborn lieutenant, who would then have been fifty years old, made no reply. "He must hear us," his sister complained, "but why won't he answer the call of his own brothers?"

Major Yoshimi Taniguchi, Onoda's instructor at the Nakano Military School, who had also come to search, recalled General Yamashita's praise of the young man and his orders to him; he doubted that he would ever come out. "He is naturally a very suspicious man," he explained.

Another former comrade shared the major's doubts. "Even if I went into the jungle and was able to meet him," commented Sergeant Yokoi, formerly of the forests of Guam, "he probably would not come back. The Imperial Army told us never to come back."

Some thought that the lieutenant might be better off where he was: Japan had changed radically since the war, adopting much from Western culture. "It would be a severe shock for Onoda to return to present-day Japan," a member of the search party said to a *Newsweek* reporter. "It would be better to leave him alone on this island where it is still 1945 for him."

January 28, 1974 *A newly converted Newfoundland fishing schooner founders in a storm her first night at sea. On board are Captain Cyril LaBrecque, his wife, four crewmen, and Hap, the captain's Labrador retriever.*

As the result of what transpires during the next eleven hours, LaBrecque will be tried on two counts of manslaughter and gross negligence. The prosecution will be recommended by the commandant of the Coast Guard, and it will be the first trial of its kind in over 130 years, the last being that of Alexander William Holmes.

As the waves battered the *Sadie and Edgar*, twenty-one-year-old Michael Riker went down into the forecastle, found water pouring in, and saw his suitcase float off his bunk. He hurried back on deck to alert the captain. The pumps were manned.

The bowsprit snapped off, and the foremast fell over the side, beating against the hull, as journalist Michael Levitt would describe it, "like a berserk battering ram as the schooner wallowed in the heavy seas." LaBrecque declared an emergency and, since he had no working ship-to-shore radio on board, fired off flares. In the rain and the fog of that winter night the flares were not seen.

To increase the chances of other distress signals being spotted, the captain headed the *Sadie* toward shore but in the process ran her aground a shoal. "In a minute or maybe two minutes, the boat hit the rocks sixty times," LaBrecque told reporters from his hospital bed. "Then we got [her] off and away from the rocks to fairly smooth water and dropped anchor." By now he had fired off all his flares, and the schooner was taking on water "everywhere." He was certain she was doomed.

He gave the command to abandon ship, and a sixteen-foot outboard runabout and an eleven-foot skiff were lowered. Everyone scrambled into the runabout, which pulled away, towing the skiff behind it, but after just a few moments its motor stopped. First Mate Valentine Bach tried frantically to restart it.

Soon they heard the sound of breakers. Bradford Blakely, twenty, climbed into the skiff and tried to row the two craft away from the surf. After struggling for nearly an hour, he asked for someone to relieve him.

"I think he was lonely," judged LaBrecque. "No one wanted to be in the smaller boat alone." The captain attempted unsuccessfully to get somebody else to row, and then he himself took over for Blakely. Mrs. LaBrecque found a penlight in her purse. She gave it to Bach, and when he turned it on, the light revealed water rising in the bottom of the runabout.

Paul Sagarino shouted, "No kidding, this thing is sinking!" Everyone stood up at once, causing it to capsize and spill them into the ocean.

The dog started to head for shore, then turned and swam to the skiff instead. Witnesses disagreed on how he got in. One testified that he "climbed in over the shoulders of two crewmen clinging to the small boat"; another said that the sailors boosted him in.

At the time, LaBrecque was rescuing his wife, who was floundering in the water beside the craft. "Peggy was being choked by her fur coat, so I took the coat off and helped her in. Then I turned around and the dog was in. This was a shock to me since I had no intention of pulling Hap in the boat."

Michael Riker's life jacket did not fit him properly, and he was struggling to keep his head above water. His legs were numb, and he was "very tired, cold, and scared." He shouted that he had to get into the skiff, but LaBrecque told him there was no more room.

Riker pulled himself over the gunwale, anyway. "When I was half-way in, Mr. LaBrecque gave me a hand to help me in the rest of the way."

By now Valentine Bach had reached the boat. He "grabbed the transom and held on for the next eleven hours." Someone tied a line to him and Blakely. LaBrecque secured Sagarino with a belt, but it was removed when he complained that it hurt him. Mrs. LaBrecque bailed with the only container she could find, her cosmetic bag, and her husband rowed the skiff to keep it headed into the waves. He estimated that he rowed fifteen miles that night.

While it was dark and the sea rough, it was impossible to rotate the men in the ocean into the boat and have the others take a turn in the cold water. To try to do so would have caused the little craft to tip over, all the survivors agreed in court. But in the morning the sea became calmer, and still LaBrecque did not order a rotation.

"Mr. LaBrecque said he had to admire the way the boys were taking it," Riker remembered. He quoted him as saying, " 'If I got in there I couldn't last more than ten or fifteen minutes.' I asked Mr. LaBrecque whether rotation was possible. Once again he said there was no way to rotate. No effort was made to try."

The captain's failure to make such an attempt was hotly debated at the trial. Even his friend Valentine Bach, who testified on his behalf and who was the only experienced sailor among the crew, was forced by the prosecutor to admit rotation "probably" could have been accomplished after dawn. But LaBrecque, who took the stand in his own defense, was adamant. "It was still rough. Everyone was stiff, and it was necessary to row the boat. I asked Mr. Riker to row the boat, but he wouldn't answer me."

Riker's allegations against the captain were particularly damning. He had begged him to cast the dog overboard and bring Sagarino and Blakely into the skiff. "I yelled, 'We can't leave them in the water!' They pleaded for rotation."

LaBrecque initially told the jury he could not remember the two men making any such request, but on cross-examination the prosecutor reminded him that Riker's account had been corroborated by Bach.

"Was there any time during the evening that they asked to get in?" he questioned LaBrecque.

"They did," admitted the captain.

"You didn't let them in, did you?"

"No."

The long hours in the cold water began to tell. First Paul Sagarino announced that he was "going home." He swam away. They rowed after him, and his friend Michael Riker reached over the side and grabbed him. "I shook him," recalled Riker, "slapped him and screamed at him."

Next Blakely lost his mind. He sang songs and babbled incoherently.

LaBrecque told the others that Blakely "has had it, and it doesn't look like Paul has much more time." His judgment was quite correct: very soon both men were dead.

Their dying compelled the third man in the water, Valentine Bach, to act. He pulled himself over the transom and lay half in the boat and half out of it. He remained in that position for thirty minutes, then slid all the way in.

Sometime around noon the survivors spotted an oil tanker, the *Providence Getty,* on the horizon. LaBrecque rowed for her. Blakely's body was still tied to the skiff, and Riker held Sagarino's corpse by the hood of the dead man's sweat shirt. Peggy LaBrecque got a "round hand mirror" out of her purse and gave it to Michael Riker. "Mike flashed it. We waved and he flashed like mad. All of a sudden they gave us a honk."

Friends and relatives of the deceased expressed much outrage over the captain's dog having stayed in the boat while two young men were left in the ocean to die. LaBrecque, who was small, slim and fifty years old, testified that he tried to throw the dog out twice, but since the animal weighed about ninety pounds, he was too heavy for him to lift. Had other men grabbed the dog, the animal's panicky thrashing would have upset the skiff.

Rotation was not the only issue raised at the trial. The lack of a working radio was debated, as was the seaworthiness of the *Sadie* and the advisability of setting out so early in the year.

LaBrecque's attorney, John F. McMahon, argued that his client should be accounted a hero for saving four lives, instead of being condemned for failing to save all six. In a summation reminiscent of that given by David Brown in a Philadelphia courtroom 133 years before, he asked the jurors to

put yourselves in that boat. Turn out the lights in this room. Add noise as ferocious as the storm at sea made. Have your boat climb

Outside a New Jersey courtroom, Captain Cyril LaBrecque is congratulated by his wife after his acquittal. (Permission of AP/Wide World Photos)

waves to the heights of this ceiling, up and down, rolling side to side, imagine this continuing twelve hours.

It was under those conditions that Mr. LaBrecque functioned. [The boat had] a capacity for three people. He wanted everyone to survive, but he wouldn't and couldn't jeopardize the boat. To do so would have cost the lives of all.

The jury voted to acquit the defendant on all charges. The jury foreman explained to reporters that the two men who died were adults and had chosen, after all, to sail with LaBrecque. Another juror added, "Given the weather and the waves, any attempt to move around in the boat would have caused it to capsize."

The dog, who had been eleven years old at the time of the wreck, died of natural causes before the trial began.

April 26, 1976 *A small plane crashes near the crest of a peak in the Sierra Nevada Mountains. On board are Lauren Elder, Jay Fuller, and his girlfriend, Jean Noller.*

They had set out for a daylong excursion to picnic in Death Valley; now their Cessna was smashed against a steep granite incline. A bone in Lauren's left forearm was broken, and one of her legs was gashed to the bone. Her mouth felt full of gravel, but she spat out pieces of teeth, not stones. Jay had a deep wound on his head, and when the blood on his face dried, it gave him the appearance of wearing a hideous mask. Jean was the most seriously injured: her face had been severely lacerated, and she was slumped unconscious in her seat.

Lauren and Jay got her out of the aircraft and laid her on the ground. She had lost her rubber sandals, and Lauren was disturbed at the sight of her naked feet, which "seemed horribly vulnerable." (They had all dressed for a springtime outing, not for a night above the snowline.) Lauren took off her own warm socks and put them on the feet of the insensible woman, who, after a few moments, opened her eyes, groaned, and went into convulsions. Lauren and Jay tried to get her back into the Cessna, but her movements were wild, and her friends were too weak.

Jay radioed distress signals and activated the ELT (Emergency Location Transmitter) while Lauren held Jean. The woman's body was jerking violently, causing her to slide down the sharp angle of the slope, dragging Lauren with her. Jay returned and tried to help hold Jean. He and Lauren were both so debilitated that eventually they had to let her go. They were too stunned and distracted to grieve.

For a time after the crash, Lauren and Jay had experienced a physical numbness, but now they began to feel stiff and achy. Jay complained of a terrible pain in his abdomen; he seemed dazed, lethargic, and confused. A veterinarian by profession, he was an amateur pilot, yachtsman, and athlete. Lauren had always known him to be self-confident and decisive, but now she realized that if they were to survive, she would have to take charge.

Although the sun was shining, the temperature was near thirty-two degrees Fahrenheit, and when it dropped at night they might freeze to death. They needed to build a fire. Lauren dragged out of the plane everything that would burn, including scraps of paper and the cardboard carton from the case of beer they had brought along. She used the Cessna's cigarette lighter to ignite these items, but in the oxygen-thin air the fire burned poorly. She emptied a beer bottle and crawled under the aircraft to where the fuel tank was leaking. She filled the bottle with gasoline, crawled out, and threw the fuel on the fire. She found more bottles, and she and Jay drank the beer to prevent dehydration.

So the routine was set. I had a line of bottles waiting under the plane, the last one spilling over before we could burn the full bottles. I would take one for me and one for Jay and, crawling over him, go back to take my turn sending a steady stream [of fuel] into the rocks, to be rewarded with flames that threw off a wonderful heat.

Darkness had moved up from the valleys. We might have been out on a dead planet out in space, the cold and the dark were that complete. There was no moon; the only light came from the fire. I could not imagine being without that light and that heat. The cold to our backs was bitter.

Jay's aim was much better than mine. He seemed to have more control of the gasoline. He could throw a stream into the fire, then let the flames get low before spurting a new stream into them. Sometimes he waited so long that I became alarmed and called to him; but always, at what seemed the last possible moment, he would send a jet of gas and it would flare up again.

The fire was capricious. After a while I learned that I could sit back and rest for five minutes or so before returning for another bottle. I focused on those minutes, concentrated on them when I began to feel weary, so that I could gather the energy to make another trip. I would sit as close to Jay as I could, feeling the heat [on] my face and the cold behind me, and I would think: *One more trip, then another and another.* And then I would say to myself: *Think only of the next one, no more.*

Sometimes the bottles caught fire and had to be thrown away before they exploded; at other times Lauren and Jay spilled gasoline, setting themselves on fire, and had to beat out the flames. Once Lauren felt herself cracking up. She chanted a mantra, but the sound of it disconcerted Jay. She tried talking to him to calm herself but realized she was rambling on and on about nothing. She sang gospel songs, but they all seemed to be about death. In the end, high on that windswept peak with the darkness of the freezing night all around, she quietly crooned lullabies — and was soothed.

After one of her trips to the fuel tank, she inadvertently sat on a rock that had recently been set afire. She found it marvelously warm and realized that they could use stones as a source of heat: they could put them into piles and set them ablaze, and they would function like radiators, gradually releasing their warmth. She cried out her idea to Jay and started stacking medium-size rocks together. "Help me," she pleaded with him. "The more we can heat up, the better off we'll be. Don't you see how important it is?"

In her account of the ordeal, Elder writes that Jay just

lifted himself on one arm, the way he did when he had to throw gas
on the fire. For a minute I saw him make what seemed to be an effort,
but then he sank back against the door. He had moved very little
since the fire had started, and that was five or six hours ago.

My anger spilled over. "Look," I spat out at him, "the least you
can do is keep your hands in your pockets or under your armpits.
You're all spread out, which means you're losing body heat. The
least you can do is take care of yourself, damn it."

I was nagging and I hated it; Jay hated it too. Every time I told him
to do something he would grunt. The sound would say, as clearly as
anything, "leave me alone." I wondered why I couldn't just let him
be. Why did I feel so compelled to remind him, over and over again,
to take care of himself?

I managed, finally, to get about two dozen rocks into a pile. The
wind was rising in earnest now, and it was all we could do to keep
the gas trained on the pile of rocks. There was no longer a steady
flame; the wind put the fire through crazy paces, tossing whirlwinds
of flame into the air and blowing them out.

Lauren's idea worked extraordinarily well — until Jay let the fire
go out. She was under the plane filling bottles when she saw it
flicker, and she yelled for him to attend to it, but he did not. She
tried to restart it, but the cigarette lighter no longer worked because
the Cessna's battery had died. It seemed to her in that moment as if
there was no light left in the world.

The only heat they had for the remaining night hours was a pile
of hot granite stones. Lauren decided that they would retain their
heat longer in the tail of the aircraft. She suggested to Jay that they
pile them there and then climb in themselves. She got him to agree,
but in order to draw this or any other response from him, she was
now having to repeat herself several times; when he did reply, his
voice was always expressionless. As she groped in the dark for the
rocks, he made no move to help. She felt the pain in her hands,
smelled her flesh being singed. She bit her lip and kept working.
The hotter the better, she thought. Her fingers were becoming
charred and smashed, but she told herself that this was the price
she had to pay to stay alive.

I curled into the bottom of the cone [-shaped tail] with the rocks I
had gathered: one at my head, several at my feet, one for my bottom
and another for my back, and one tucked warm into my stomach, my
arms and hands wrapped around it.

For the first time in what seemed an eternity I felt almost comfortable. The rocks had warmed my aluminum nest remarkably well. The wind whistled outside, but it seemed removed. I was snuggled in like a squirrel, and it wasn't bad at all.

She called out to Jay to crawl in with her, but he did not answer. She drifted into a long reverie that was not broken until she heard him bump against the exterior of the baggage door. She asked him to pass in more stones, but he ignored her and climbed into the front seat of the aircraft, hugging a warm rock to his stomach. Resigned, she went out into the cold and gathered more stones. She added the six biggest ones she could find and, when she climbed back in, noticed immediately the additional warmth.

She lay curled in a fetal position, thinking about Jay. She felt responsible for him — a feeling she resented. She could not understand why he would make no effort to help them survive. They had made a pact soon after the crash that they would get through the night together, but he was not keeping the bargain.

She called to him to lie down next to her, and after a while she felt the fuselage vibrating as he made his way over the seats. She thought about how graceful he had always been, and now he was awkward and stiff. She saw that he had lost a shoe, and she warned him about frostbite, but he irritably cut her short.

He was thrashing around, trying to get comfortable, knocking his elbow into my cheek and my head, pummeling me with his knees. The plane rocked as he thrashed about. I had visualized us curled up together, our bodies curved to share the heat of the rocks and of each other, cradled together like spoons. I should have known better. Jay tossed and turned, pushing me to get himself into a position in which he was extended rather than curled up. I could do nothing except wish with a passion that I had not asked him to join me, that I had left him in the front of the plane by himself.

I grunted and Jay moaned. Our arms and legs were hopelessly tangled. I could feel the plane tilt and shift with his clumsy movements. I was terrified. "You've got to stop this," I yelped. "Stop it right now! You're going to kill us!"

When he had finally settled down she told him that they could not allow themselves to go to sleep, that they had to keep talking and nudging each other to prevent their dozing off. "All we have to do is make it through this night," she said. "I'm sure everything is being put in motion right now. It's just a matter of waiting for the light. At dawn they'll come looking for us."

She fantasized about the coming of the sun, but with the first lightening of the sky, they looked out the windows and saw swirling snow. A blizzard would mean that no rescue attempt could be made, that the air would not warm them this day, and that they faced another night on the mountain. Jay howled and began to thrash about. "I've got to get out of here," he cried. "I've got to do something." She tried to reason with him, but he only grew more frenzied. He kicked and pounded on the metal sides of the compartment with "strong, blunt blows." He twisted and turned, trying to escape the fuselage, and his movements caused it to rock back and forth. Afraid he would dislodge it and it would fall off the mountain into the valley far below, and furious at being so often if inadvertently kicked, Lauren hit his back with her fists. "I hit him again and again, bringing both fists down on him, meaning to hurt." *Damn you,* she thought. *Damn you for making me do this to you, making me hurt you.* Desperately she demanded that he be quiet, that he shut up and lie still. He remained agitated, so she moved as far away from him as she could. *It can't get worse,* she told herself. *It can only get better.*

After a few moments he came to rest, fell silent, and died. She went to tend his wounds — his hands were torn and bloody — and felt that his flesh was cold. The stones having lost all their heat, his corpse was already freezing.

> I looked at his face, at his staring eyes, and I thought that now he was out of the cold.
> *So,* I said to myself, *that is how it is.* I had never seen anyone die before. I did not know that it was so — easy. Jay had been talking to me and then he was dead.
> His death surprised me; it did not frighten me. Instead, I was filled with a kind of wonder. Jay looked as if all the hurt and turmoil were over, all the worry and the not knowing. He looked as if he had managed to end the struggle. It would be so very, very nice to be out of the cold. And it would be so easy.

She lay down beside Jay's legs and tried to keep herself warm, moving her limbs and wriggling her toes and fingers to avoid frostbite. She thought about how the searchers would find her when the weather cleared, frozen in a fetal position, how her mother would grieve, and how much she wanted to do with her life.

She stirred, pulled Jay's warm socks off his feet, and put them on. While she was doing this the sun came out. (She would find out

later that there had never been a storm; what the two of them had
seen through the windows was loose snow blown about by strong
winds.) Her thinking was distracted, but after a time she came to
the conclusion that she had better climb down the mountain to the
desert below. (In this she was correct: Jay's ELT had not been
properly maintained and so was not functioning. The emergency
radio signals he had sent had not been picked up, and he had not
bothered to file a flight plan before taking off. Aerial searchers
would not spot the wreckage until just before nightfall, and so it was
not until the following day that climbers reached the crest. By that
time, without the means for making a fire, Lauren would have been
dead.)

She climbed to the crest of the mountain and started down the
slope on the other side. The wall was steep, almost vertical, and
she had to work her way diagonally across its face, moving in a
spiderlike fashion, "balancing myself on the ice crust, punching
through it with my hands and feet." Her arm hurt and her hands
were raw and ghostly pale; she smashed them into the snow anyway. Her fashionable boots were uninsulated and high-heeled; she
drove the toes into the wall of ice. She did not look up or away from
the surface right in front of her; to do so would have been to see
how hopeless her task was and to realize how small she was, how
"infinitesimal in the vast, cold quiet."

There were rocks that obtruded through the snow, and each time
she reached one she clung to it, resting. She always pushed on with
a "peculiar energy." The fatigue of yesterday was gone.

At last the slope lessened, and she found she could sit down on
the ice and slide from rock to rock. She cried out in exhilaration
and scooted along. By midmorning she was able to stand up and
walk. She broke through the crust often, and her boots filled with
snow. She gave up trying to empty them: they would only fill again.
As the slope became yet more gradual, she slipped into a rhythmic
walk. Iridescent lights played across her clothing, wide ribbons of
colors at once charming her and making her anxious that she was
going snowblind. When the colors disappeared, however, she was
disappointed.

She sat down on a large stone to rest, lifted her eyes — and saw
a row of redwood houses in the distance. She ran toward them, fell
into a drift, crawled out, and ran again. As she grew near them, she
saw a man on the deck of one of them, wearing a white robe and

doing stretching exercises. The sight of him brought her up short. She called out to him that she had been in a plane wreck, that she needed help. He did not answer. A large black cross was hanging around his neck. . . . She realized that what she was looking at was not a man but a statue. . . . There were sled tracks in the snow where children had been playing, and she could hear laughter coming from the houses. She hurried to the nearest of them — and found it was a boulder. She touched its rough surface and all the illusions vanished.

Bitterly she realized how much energy she had wasted and how far she had detoured from the shortest path down the mountain. She made herself push on. The mirages that her mind had created were a kind of cosmic joke, she decided, and she wondered how many more such pranks were ahead of her.

The snow gave way to a stony landscape occasionally broken by sagebrush or a pine tree. Whenever she felt the need to rest she would climb on top of a boulder and let the sun warm her. She fell sometimes now: her boots were not meant for wilderness hiking. She struck a dry streambed, and though it meandered, she climbed into it and followed its course. She saw a Mexican in loose white clothes working on the hillside above her and called out to him first in English and then in Spanish. When he did not respond, she knew "he was another fiction." As the hours went by, she saw a middle-aged woman doing sketches of wildflowers . . . a man in gray trousers and a green sport shirt hanging over a cliff . . . a housing development with a blond man on a porch . . . and a rancher's wife gathering watercress in a stream. Each vision instantly elated her, and each let her down. She always went on, trying to pick her steps, humming folk tunes to cheer herself up.

The streambed suddenly ended in a dry waterfall. A sheer granite wall dropped to the canyon floor a hundred feet below. She howled in grief and was "shocked at the bleating anguish I heard in my own voice." "Help!" she shouted. "Please somebody help me!" Time passed and she calmed down. She knew she had come too far to retrace her steps. Lying on her stomach, she inspected the wall. "There was a series of narrow ledges at ten-to-twenty-foot intervals. . . . So the drop was broken . . . into sections." She took off her socks and boots, tossed them onto the first ledge, and then eased herself over the side, feeling with her toes for a hold on the granite.

Monkeylike, I began to move down the cliff. One bad choice of footing and I would fall. I could feel it, the terror of coming loose from the wall, of falling free, of breaking on the rocks below. *Oh God, don't think about it,* I told myself. *Concentrate on not reaching too far, not getting all spread out.*

I realized that something extraordinary was happening. This part of the climb had not been easy, but it was infinitely more perplexing — and exciting. I couldn't seem to make a wrong move. Something was happening between my body and the face of the dry waterfall. They seemed to understand each other.

I had known this feeling before. I had it sometimes when I was surfing. I would catch a big wave and ride it on and on, sensing that I was part of the sea. I didn't have to think or even to make an effort. We just flowed together, my body responding without any command. And it happened to me at other times — the best times when I was jumping a horse. Then everything was so finely balanced that I knew I could do no wrong, that whatever move we made together was right. But I could not believe that I had this feeling on a sheer granite cliff in a mountain wilderness.

I studied each drop, then threw my boots over the side and followed them down. I concentrated, thinking only of the rock and each move. I reached for a niche with my right toe; it was there. Everything was working. It was hard, but there was a kind of rhythm to it. The one thing I knew not to do was look up; that would undo me.

The climbing wearied her, and she gradually lost her self-assurance. Her hands and feet grew clumsy. They became more cut and bruised, and she had to keep rubbing them to get the circulation going. But moving sideways as she had on the icy slope that morning, she eventually reached bottom. She picked up a stick to use as a staff and set off again. She resumed her singing and fantasized about sitting in a car with the heater on and her toes resting on the carpet.

She encountered more mirages, each one as apparently real as the last, and then came to a real stream. As she followed it the landscape became bright and colorful and the air fragrant. Her first portent of civilization, the first indication that her ordeal was ending, was a pile of manure on a path. She told herself not to be fooled, that it might be another illusion, but it was not: "I had never seen anything so gorgeous. I kicked it with my foot. That's what it was: genuine, one-hundred-percent horse flop. Praise the Lord!"

It was perhaps one of the few times in human history that a pile of dung caused anyone to weep hysterically for joy.

■   ■   ■

Lauren Elder's travail had not exactly come to an end. She followed the path to a parking lot (she had stumbled into a bighorn sheep preserve). From there she wandered into the desert, looking for a town, became lost, and walked in a circle. She saw still more mirages — bicyclists, Mexican farm hands, young men in a Jeep, and so on — and she believed each was real and so suffered repeated disillusionment. At dusk the headlights of automobiles moving in the distance led her to a road which she followed, hoping to reach a town. She attempted to flag down passing motorists, but none would stop.

Long after dark she finally arrived in Independence, California, but here again no one would assist her. This was not unfounded small-town xenophobia on the part of residents: Charles Manson had been arrested nearby, and while he was detained in the Independence jail awaiting transfer to Los Angeles for the Tate–LaBianca murder trial, a number of his female followers had shown up and hung around the town. Now here came this young woman, dirty, disheveled, barefoot, blood on her clothing, her skirt torn, and talking dazedly, as if on drugs. She wandered from one end of Independence to the other, stopping at motels to ask for a room, adding immediately that she was penniless and needed money to call her boyfriend. Eventually one alarmed clerk telephoned the police after she left his motel office, and a deputy sheriff found her in the lobby of an old hotel, trying once more to get a room.

"Is your name Elder?" he asked. When she nodded, he told her, "Well, now, we've been looking for you. Let me help you, dear." In that moment she knew that she had been waiting to hear those words for what had seemed a very long time.

She was taken to a hospital in Lone Pines, thirteen miles away. The sergeant who drove her there was kind enough to run the car heater the entire journey.

The autopsy done on Jean Noller revealed that she had died from brain damage and hypothermia. Jay Fuller had also died of hypothermia, aggravated in his case by hemoperitoneum: his stomach pain had been the result of massive hemorrhaging. Doctors explained to Lauren Elder that his uncharacteristic apathy and listlessness were classic symptoms of hypothermia. Lauren's wounds were sewn up, but the broken radius in her arm had to be rebroken and set with a metal plate. One happy note was that her feet had been only mildly frostbitten.

Lauren Elder *(right)* and actress Blair Brown pose on the set of a movie being made about Elder's ordeal. (Permission of AP/Wide World Photos)

Her father, an aircraft company executive and retired test pilot, flew up to Lone Pines in a small plane to bring his daughter home, but she was reluctant to fly again so soon. She chose to stay in the hospital for the better part of a week, recovering slowly and sleeping between clean sheets. When she went back to her apartment in Oakland, California, she drove.

December 20, 1979 *A young couple living in a remote cabin on the western coast of Alaska are forced to attempt to make their way out of the wilderness by kayak.*

Roger Lewis and Denise Harris had agreed to re-open an abandoned gold mine for its owner in return for a share of the profits. The owner had promised to fly out to the mine a few weeks after their arrival to pick up ore samples and replenish their supplies. But after nearly two months had passed without the appearance of a plane, they were down to their emergency food rations, and winter was closing in.

The nearest outpost was a lumber camp sixty miles away by water. They loaded the kayak with camping equipment and what supplies they had left and, along with their mongrel dog, Nuka, set out. They paddled out of "Nuka Bay," down through a strait, and into the Gulf of Alaska, following the coast of the Kenai Peninsula. Their little craft rode with only about "three inches of freeboard" above the water's surface. Sometimes the swells rose high, terrifying Denise and making the kayak seem "tiny and vulnerable." Yet they paddled on for the better part of a week, beaching the craft at night and putting up a tent.

They had gone some thirty-six miles when, late on the fifth day, a storm arose. Eight-foot waves forced them ashore. They pitched their tent a hundred yards from the water's edge, against the base of a cliff. Through that evening and the next day the tempest raged, and the surf moved closer to their camp. By midafternoon it was less than ten feet away. They "tore the tent down as fast as we could," and, leaving it with their other gear on the sand, climbed fifteen feet up the cliff and nestled among boulders. "I put a foam pad under us," Roger explained to journalist Jim Rearden, "and we wrapped a couple of blankets around us, then sat huddled together. Rain splattered [us from] above. Then we started to pray." The rain soaked them, and Roger decided to go down to the shore for a plastic sheet to use as a tarp.

Denise protested, but he returned to the sand — and was engulfed by an enormous wave that slammed against the side of the cliff. He swam, still holding on to the plastic sheet. "Bubbles came in front of my face, and I gagged on the salt water. I swam toward the shelter and grabbed Denise's legs to shove her [higher]. As the water receded I yelled, 'Get out of here.' " Another wave struck, and he pushed her ahead of him and followed with the dog slung under his arm. The three of them spent the night shivering under a blanket and the plastic sheet.

When the storm eased, the couple found that the kayak had been broken in two and most of their supplies had been carried away. They were fortunate in that they still had an ax, some food, blankets, warm clothing, and a gasoline stove, but they could not find wood with which to make a fire to dry their clothing and sleeping bags. Their world seemed to consist solely of "rocks and ice and snow." They stayed on the cliff for four days, "trying to get dry." Each evening they would light the stove for just a few minutes, crouching above it, holding their wool shirts over their heads to keep in the warmth. "That was the best time of the day," Roger would decide, "the only time we had heat. We couldn't open our eyes, and we had to lean to one side to breathe because the gas fumes were so strong." To keep their feet warm, Roger cut up a metallic space blanket and made pouches for them to wear.

On December 27 Roger was on the beach trying to figure out how to repair the kayak when he looked up to see Nuka sitting near the tent. He called to her. Nuka appeared and ran up to him — but the "dog" by the tent had not moved. It was, Roger suddenly realized, a wolf. He raced to the tent, yelling for Denise to hand him his rifle. The wolf loped away to where the couple had strung a makeshift clothesline between kayak paddles, and he pulled a sweat shirt off it. While he was tearing at the sweat shirt, Roger shot him just behind his front leg. He went down and rolled to the edge of the hill, still alive. With only a few cartridges left, Roger did not want to shoot a second time. He was digging a rock out of the snow with which to brain the animal when the wolf got up and ran down the steep hill and across the beach, "gushing blood all the way."

Roger followed, wading through tide pools and climbing over rocks until he found the wolf crouched, growling fiercely, between two boulders beside the gulf. Intimidated, Roger decided to wait until his quarry was weakened by further blood loss. But as he waited the tide began to come in, and, fearing it would carry the wolf away, he went back to camp for the ax and a knife. When he returned to the shore a large pool of blood had accumulated beside the wolf, but he seemed as strong as ever and was still snarling fiercely.

Roger moved in, and the wolf lunged at him. He backed up, took aim with the rifle, and fired — just as a wave struck him from behind. The shot missed. He put the rifle down and collected an armload of stones. He threw them until one struck home, and the animal turned his head away. Roger sprinted forward and hit him with the ax. Even after this blow the wolf was still twitching, so Roger held his body under the water for a couple of minutes. . . . They cooked the meat that night, frying it with lots of salt and pepper.

They had been hoping to be spotted and rescued by a plane, but now Roger decided that "if a wolf could get to where we were, we could travel inland to where it had come from." They would walk out of the wilderness.

They set out on December 28, carrying everything they had in a pack and a duffel bag. Disaster struck almost immediately: heading up a steep slope following the wolf's trail, Denise slipped and lost her grip on the pack. It slid down the incline and dropped into the gulf. Roger wanted to dive in after it "but [I] realized that I probably couldn't recover the pack, swim to the beach, get ashore and be in any condition to carry on." They had lost all their food and matches, a wool blanket, a mattress pad, the stove, and the tent.

There was nothing to do but go on. Before long they had lost the wolf tracks and decided to climb Gore Peak, fourteen hundred feet high. Partway up a sheer cliff, Roger, clinging to a ledge by just two fingers, slipped. He fell thirty feet, struck a snow-covered slope, and began sliding. Ahead of him was "a five-hundred-foot sheer drop to a jumble of rocks. I moved across the icy slope faster and faster. I knew I was dead, and I thought about Denise being left alone. I spun around to my back and dug my heels in, slid another six or seven feet, and stopped. I could hardly believe it."

He was badly bruised but had not broken any bones. Painfully inching his way up again, he came upon the wolf's trail, and he and Denise followed it the rest of the day, moving along the edge of a sheer cliff. By nightfall they had reached a stand of timber. Their clothes were wet, and without the stove they were unable to dry them. They took off their boots as they did each evening, and using fishing line as thread, Denise sewed a sort of wolfskin bootie into which she could put her feet while she slept; Roger donned the "space blanket booties" and covered them with wool socks. To keep from sliding down a steep incline he dozed with his legs wrapped around a tree trunk; Denise was stretched out on a narrow rock ledge. "The sea boomed and rolled almost directly beneath us."

The next day they worked through hip-deep snow, and that night they made a shelter and beds out of spruce boughs, cutting them with a Swede (bow) saw. As Roger described it for Jim Rearden,

> We established a routine. We put the foam pad down, and our boots next to the pad. Nuka would usually circle our feet a few times and plop down, then we'd get our feet warm on her fur. We didn't know at the time that it was a mistake to thaw our frozen toes and then allow them to freeze again [the] next day. Once our toes were frozen we would have been better leaving them frozen. Alternate freezing and thawing caused much more damage.

In the morning they set off again. As he dragged the heavy duffel bag, Roger fantasized incessantly about candy and pastry, "especially the German chocolate cake that Harold makes in the Seward Bakery. I'd tell myself as I took a step, 'This is for that cake.' I'd reach out and plow through another five feet of snow."

Eventually they got off the peak and found themselves on a beach, where, much to their relief, there was no snow. They camped in a spot with plenty of driftwood, but, maddeningly, they still were unable to start a fire. They tried using the plastic lens of a ruined flashlight to "condense sunlight, but it wouldn't focus to a sharp enough point."

When it was time to go they went along the beach, but after less than a mile it ended, and their way was blocked by the sea. The only possible route lay over a frozen waterfall 150 feet high. They would have to leave their dog behind and climb it like primitive mountaineers. Roger used his knife to cut hand and footholds.

> I chipped one hole at a time, and stepped and pulled myself up, chipping hole after hole, with Denise following slowly. I dragged the duffel bag attached to my wrist. By about one o'clock in the afternoon we were about one hundred feet up. It was a warm day, with the sun on the ice, and it was slick because the surface was melting in the sun. The higher we got the thinner the ice became, until only an inch covered the rocks. There was no way for me to cut a foot or handhold.
>
> I looked frantically for something to grab, noticed the adjoining snowfield, and dug into that. But there was just a small crust of snow and ice, with loose snow underneath. It was risky. I would get into it and slide maybe four or five inches wherever I put my foot. Each step might have been my last. I crept closer and closer to a pencil-diameter bush sticking out of the snow, about twenty feet away.

Behind it about five feet was a bigger bush, and I knew if I could reach that I'd make it the rest of the way.

I was about ten feet from the bush when I heard Denise scream and turned to see her fall. She bounced off the first rocks and shot down the waterfall, and for a few moments I lost sight of her. She then reappeared on the beach, crumpled, and I saw her hit the rocks there. She had fallen the entire 120 feet, bouncing and sliding.

For a moment Denise thought that she had died, but then she saw Nuka near her and rose painfully to her feet. She had broken no bones in the fall, although she was badly bruised and scratched. She was also frightened and crying.

"Roger," she called, "please come down and help me. I can't climb back up there."

"I can't come back down there," he shouted in reply. "It took us all day to climb up here, and I have the duffel bag here. You *have* to climb back up."

"I'm tired and I'm hurt, and I can't climb anymore!" she yelled.

"You'll die there," he told her, "and I am not going to come back down."

In the end she started up the ice wall again. On the first ascent she had been wearing mittens she had fashioned from a blanket, but she had lost them in the fall, and now her fingers were terribly cold. Sixty feet up she slipped and fell once more, banging into the very same boulder she had hit on in the first fall. This time she was certain she could not make it. "Roger, throw me down my clothes. I'm going to stay here. I'm going back to that beach and die there."

Roger was adamant: he would neither try to make his way to her nor throw her spare clothing or a blanket. He could not descend carrying the bag, and if he left it hanging on one of the bushes and then they could not get up to it again, everything they had to help them survive would be gone. Their only hope was for Denise to make the ascent.

She put her fingers and toes into the lowest ice holes and lifted her weight. . . . She was weak from lack of food, and she ached from the falls. . . . Her hands became bloody . . . blood just "poured from [them], and they hurt terribly, but I heard Roger above, urging me on. 'Come on, you can make it,' he kept saying."

He reached out his hand to her and joyously helped her the last few feet. They made it to the small bush and the larger one and then the trees beyond.

That evening they heard Nuka barking in the distance — and the answering howls of wolves. The calls back and forth went on for much of the night, and Roger was certain that the wolves would kill the dog. He and Denise were sorry to have left her, but they could not carry her up the waterfall. She had been a cheerful presence, tireless and frolicsome. "While we slogged through snow like snails, she often ran ahead and around us, playing. She would run off a ways, and come back as if to say, 'What's keeping you slow-pokes?' " Now she would be dragged down and torn apart by sharp teeth.

At dawn she miraculously appeared at their camp. The three of them set out once more. They walked up steep inclines and across icy plateaus. Day after day they went on, hungry, losing track of time, doubting that they would make it, thinking that all this effort and pain was for nothing. Their toes were black from frostbite, and neither Roger nor Denise could sleep for a half hour without waking to scream in pain. They tried to get hold of themselves, to steady themselves with prayer, but it was very hard to do.

Roger went into a severe mental decline. Throughout much of the ordeal he had been the strong one, but now he became dispirited. He was pale and looked "hollow" to Denise. This was, she thought, like watching him die. "We were totally empty," she told Rearden, "and when we talked, it sounded like an echo. There seemed to be no substance to our bodies. We were so weak that we couldn't talk loudly, and we were so tired that we talked very slowly."

But if they were both suffering intensely, Denise was finding an inner strength even as Roger was giving up. After more than a week without food, he pointed out that they had three cartridges left. "Denise," he said, "it's been a couple of weeks since we lost the kayak, and a couple of months since we've seen people. I don't think anyone is looking for us, and, well, look at what's ahead. We'll never make it. I hurt from the tip of my toes to the top of my head, and everything in between, and it's getting worse. I think we should use the three bullets on ourselves and Nuka."

She would not hear of suicide: "No, Roger. I'm going to get out of here if I have to crawl all the way. I want to see my mother again."

The words stung him, and he told her he would go on, too, but secretly he was still certain they were doomed. They progressed very slowly, only a mile or two a day — sometimes only half a mile. Nevertheless, on the twelfth day they arrived at Sunday Harbor, and they awoke the next morning to a fantastic sight. As the sun came up and struck the snow-covered peaks, the light changed from purple to pink to orange. As weak as they were, they could yet be awed by such a "majestic" spectacle. They lay beneath their blanket and watched the show. When it was over, Roger found that there

> was about two inches of frost from the ocean spray on top of the blanket, and it creaked off in big chunks when we pushed the blanket back. By then I couldn't stand up in the morning. My body would be cramped and cold — we were still wet — and during the night I kept my arms crossed with my hands inside my clothes and next to my shoulders. Denise slept curled up to my back as close as she could get.
>
> That morning, as on others, I would get my hands out first, gradually pulling them out and working them slowly. Then I'd look for something to grab so I could pull myself up on my feet. I simply couldn't stand up. My toes were on fire, and I hurt more or less all over. Once I was standing and finally had my balance I would pick up my hip boots one at a time, knock the snow and frost off the top, and shake the frost and snow from the inside.
>
> Then I had to do the worst thing in the world. I had to push my hurting feet down those dark passages and into those frozen hip boots, one at a time. I'd balance on one foot, slide my leg down, and then stomp to get my foot [in] all the way. Have you ever had to stomp a frozen foot inside a frozen boot? It was pure agony. And, of course, I had to do it with each foot. Once my boots were on I'd tie the tops up to my belt with string by jerking them tight and tying a couple of half hitches.
>
> Then we'd fold the blanket and the foam pad and put them into the duffel bag, stick in the Swede saw and rifle, then close and buckle the bag and hoist it on my shoulder. Then we'd look at each other and say, "Let's go for it."

Roger's decline in mind and body continued. He would walk along mumbling to himself. On one occasion he suddenly asked Denise what would happen if she woke up some morning to find him dead. Startled by the question, she answered that she would die beside him. But while he was growing weaker, she was growing more determined. She had to see her mother again and tell her how much she loved her. "I'll keep on even if I have to crawl on my knees," she told Roger when he suggested that they give up. "So what, no lower legs. Can still have babies. Go to the movies. Lots of things. I'll crawl if I have to."

Once more he passively acquiesced, but he was not always willing to cede leadership to her. One day he told her that it was necessary to kill and eat Nuka. She knew he was right and nodded in agreement. He felt he could not spare a bullet — "I guess I'm going to have to stab her with my belt knife." He called the dog, and obediently she came. She climbed into his lap, tail wagging. Denise sat beside Roger and held Nuka's head. Roger drew his knife with one hand and touched the dog's chest with the other, feeling for her heartbeat. "I'm sorry, Nuka," he told her, and drove the blade in. She yipped and struggled . . . and died.

At that moment, Roger noted, a most remarkable thing happened. "I had used my Buck knife to chip ice, to cut branches, and for all kinds of things. When I used it to kill Nuka the blade broke, right at the widest part."

They skinned and gutted her, cutting out her heart and liver, thinking these would provide "the most energy." Roger gagged on the first bite and could not swallow a second. He put the heart down and walked a little distance from the bloody scene and sat down. Denise called to him, but he told her to leave him alone for a bit. He thought, *It has finally come to murder. I've murdered a good friend. I hurt all over. None of this makes any sense. We aren't going to be found. Why go on?*

While he meditated in despair, Denise was cutting the meat off the dog's hindquarters. She carried the rest of the body down to the water's edge to be taken away by the tide and then went to where Roger sat. He turned away from her, unable to look at Nuka's hide. "That little dog had been so cheerful, so full of energy, so full of life. Killing her was just too much for me."

But Denise knew that they needed the food if they were going to go on, and they needed the fur to keep their feet warm. "As hard as it was to eat the little bit of Nuka that we did, I know it helped give us energy to make it to where the helicopter finally picked us up."

When they saw the first chopper it was two o'clock in the afternoon of the nineteenth day, and Roger was standing on a cliff overlooking Taylor Bay. They had just made camp when a Coast Guard helicopter flew across the water. Frantically they yelled and waved, and it came right over them . . . and kept on going.

This seemed to Roger to be the final blow. "I just didn't care anymore. I had had no hope anyway." (He and Denise later learned that the chopper's crew did not see them because they were looking for their bodies in the gulf. The day before, the wrecked kayak had been spotted by another Coast Guard crew, and it was assumed that the couple had drowned.)

Roger roused himself to make an SOS. He cut spruce bows with the Swede saw and formed them into letters ten feet across. He tied a red sweat shirt to a pole and stuck it in the middle of the *O* in the SOS. Just as he finished he sighted a plane in the distance. He raced to grab the rifle, hobbling desperately on frozen feet, but by the time he got the weapon out, the aircraft was very close. He fired off the last three precious cartridges, not realizing in that moment of elation that the pilot, deafened by his motor, could not hear them. As the Grumman Widgeon passed over, Roger fell backward into the snow, trying to keep it in view. Lying on the ground he saw the plane's wings dip. "I think he saw me, Denise," he cried. She had run out from a stand of timber and was watching the aircraft circle. It continued to circle without dropping flares or otherwise signaling to the couple that they had been seen. As night came on, Roger, cold and "discouraged to death," proposed that they go into the trees and lie down on a bed of branches. But Denise would not hear of it: "I'm not leaving until he goes away or something happens. Why is he flying in circles like that?"

The pilot, Bill DeCreeft, was radioing their location to a rescue helicopter. He had been hired by the mine owner to pick up Roger and Denise at the cabin and, finding them gone, had reported them missing to the Coast Guard, which in turn had instituted the search that had turned up the kayak. DeCreeft had then spent several days trying to find the couple from the air. Having located them, he could not set his amphibious plane down on the bay because of the rocks in the water.

Before long Roger and Denise heard a chopper coming and saw its lights flashing. "After months of not seeing anyone or anything mechanical, it seemed almost like something out of *Star Trek*." Its searchlight found them, and when it was overhead, hovering, a door opened "and people — real people — waved down to us."

A basket was lowered, and Roger was lifted into the craft. When he got on board he wrapped his arms around the burly state trooper who had pulled him in the door "and kissed and hugged him, crying." The helicopter's pilot wanted to burn some more fuel to lighten his craft before taking on the weight of another passenger, and so he circled for a few minutes. Denise, on the ground, thought

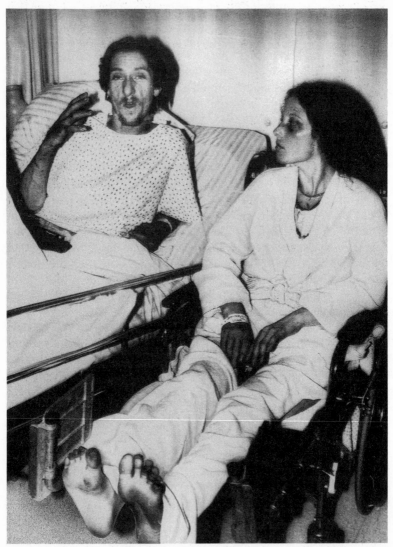

In an Anchorage hospital room, Roger Lewis and Denise Harris describe for a reporter their wintertime trek through a Yukon wilderness. The discoloration of Harris's feet is due to frostbite. (Permission of AP/Wide World Photos)

she was being abandoned and wept bitterly until the basket was dropped for her. "It was so weird being lifted up into the sky. I got up inside and saw a Coast Guard guy and grabbed him so tight and started to cry, saying, 'Thank you, thank you, oh, thank you.' "

Denise Harris and Roger Lewis were fed sweet rolls and then transported to an airfield where Bill DeCreeft was waiting with an ambulance. Not long after their rescue, a series of storms struck the peninsula on which they had been stranded; these would have made further searching impossible, and beyond a doubt Roger and Denise would have died. They were hospitalized for months, suffering from exposure, malnutrition, and frostbite. Denise had lost twenty-five pounds and Roger, thirty-five pounds. They both lost toes or parts of toes on each foot. When Jim Rearden, the outdoors editor of *Alaska* magazine, interviewed them, they were still not able to wear shoes. They were cheerful, however, and were responding well to treatment. They told him that they planned on getting married after they were released from the hospital. "When we were near death," Roger said, "I saw deep inside what kind of person she is. We somehow touched each other's very souls out there, and now I want the commitment of marriage with Denise, and she feels the same way about me."

December 1981 *John Harrison is marooned on the Pacific atoll Palmyra after his trimaran is wrecked in a storm. With him are his two daughters.*

Harrison, a thirty-nine-year-old industrial designer from Vancouver, British Columbia, had perhaps unfortunately named his forty-one-foot boat the *Sisyphus*. In early December she had been struck by a typhoon that was followed by eight straight days of gales. Forty-foot waves broke off her mast, but Harrison, with the help of fuel dropped by the U.S. Coast Guard, managed to bring the disabled trimaran to the atoll. He and his daughters, Micki, twenty, and Kristen, thirteen, then subsisted on fish, coconuts, and provisions salvaged from the wreck. They supplemented their diet with canned goods supplied by Palmyra's only permanent resident, Ray Landrum, a fifty-four-year-old yachtsman turned hermit and self-appointed caretaker of the islets.

Harrison called for help, using Landrum's radio, but Canadian and American authorities proved unsympathetic. The U.S. Coast

Guard was unwilling to rescue the maroons because, as a spokesman sensibly pointed out, they were not in any *danger*. If the lack of drama left American officials unenthusiastic, their Canadian counterparts were daunted by the expense of the operation. When Michelle James, Harrison's ex-wife and the mother of the girls, appealed to Ottawa authorities, bureaucrats estimated that the rescue would cost $7,000 to $12,000. They explained to her, as she put it, that they "have a certain budget they allow each year for rescues of Canadian citizens. They tell us that this would eat up one twelfth of the entire budget."

When governments are unimaginative or excessively parsimonious, private citizens must intervene. Lawrence Friend, of Scottsdale, Arizona, who was cruising in the area, volunteered to sail his thirty-three-foot sloop, the *Friendly*, to Palmyra and take the three maroons home. He set his course on December 29, but the next day a ham operator relayed a message from John Harrison, declining the offer. "They want an aircraft to pick them up," a Coast Guard spokesman told an Associated Press reporter. Harrison and his elder daughter had been perfectly willing to sail again, but Kristen had had enough of boats. As her father explained in a radio transmission, she "was so traumatized by the recent sailing trip she doesn't want to get in a sailboat." If the only way off the atoll was on a yacht, she seemed to feel, she would just stay where she was, drinking coconut milk from the shell and working on her suntan.

Now it was the American officials' turn to be stingy. "He's not drowning, he's not starving, he's on dry land," the Coast Guard's exasperated spokesman, Mark Scire, pointed out to reporters. "Why should the U.S. government spend a hundred thousand dollars to send a military plane down there when he could have got off the island on that boat essentially for free?"

Michelle James was not interested in considering this question. She must have been wondering if she would have to take instruction in parachuting in order to see her daughters again. She set out to hire an aircraft and contacted Fred C. Sorenson, the owner of a charter service and the stunt pilot who had flown the amphibious plane in the film *Raiders of the Lost Ark*. He agreed to undertake this bit of derring-do, this time using an aircraft with *wheels*, in return for $11,500. There was an old airfield on the island, built by the U.S. Navy in World War II, and the Harrisons set out to clear it of brush while Michelle James and some others raised the cash. John Harrison's girlfriend, Jennifer Poapst, and a high school classmate, Gary Clancy, started a formal fund-raising drive, the "Get the Harrison Family Home Trust." By now readers of newspapers all over the Western world were following the drama via AP and UPI dispatches.

This story should end with the prompt return of the Harrisons, but, alas, life is always more complicated than we wish it to be. Sorenson had to scrap his rescue plans when Palmyra's owners, three brothers who resided in Honolulu, required him to post a five-million-dollar bond before landing on their island. Some of Harrison's friends felt that Sorenson wanted too much money, anyway, and thus he found himself "on and off the team at different points."

Meanwhile John and his daughters were living on the disabled *Sisyphus* and working on the airstrip. They had celebrated Christmas day with a dinner of "canned spinach, condensed tomato soup, bread and a can of beets. Dessert — also courtesy of Ray Landrum — was a can of pumpkin."

Things came to a head on January 5, when Fred Sorenson decided he had had enough. "The Canadian consulate in San Francisco had told us to stand by for nine straight days and that money was available for the rescue," Sorenson complained to Malcolm Gray of *Maclean's* magazine. "Then the money wasn't available. We'd put off several other customers for our planes, and with all the waiting around the crew was starting to get down." To save their morale as well as the Harrisons, Sorenson posted the bond and took off on the 2,200-mile round-trip flight between Honolulu and Palmyra.

Back in Hawaii, the three maroons were photographed with huge grins on their faces as they disembarked at the airport. Their good cheer did not seem much diminished by the fact that John Harrison was arrested as soon as he got off the plane. He and his daughters were still beaming broadly as he was led away in handcuffs.

Harrison's marooning on Palmyra had caught the attention not only of millions of idly curious newspaper readers but of banking officials and law enforcement officers as well. Harrison had borrowed $65,000 from the Bank of British Columbia to buy the *Sisyphus* and had fallen behind in his payments. Apparently fearing that his beloved boat would be repossessed, he had sailed her out of the harbor so hurriedly that he had not had time to unload the personal belongings of the three-man crew that had recently worked on her.

Thus while his daughters were being reunited with their mother in California, he was being charged with theft.

There is too much sorrow in life and too little joy. In this case, however, you may leave your handkerchief in your pocket, undisturbed. John Harrison is from all reports a likable man — the arresting officers even treated him to a banana split before putting him into the paddy wagon — and he was not condemned to rot in some dank dungeon. When he had left the *Sisyphus* at the atoll, he had abandoned many of his own possessions, but he had brought along the belongings of the crew. Thus he was allowed to plead nolo contendere to a reduced charge of theft and was sentenced to a year's probation.

All three of the Harrisons were safely home at last. The owners of Palmyra Atoll found that their property was undamaged and were no doubt greatly relieved. Ray Landrum presumably was happy to return to his uneventful solitude, even if his supply of canned goods had been somewhat depleted. Only Fred Sorenson seemed to be bemused by the whole business. He had been paid two thousand dollars plus expenses for his work, and he could not help thinking of an earlier and more lucrative assignment. "Making *Raiders of the Lost Ark* was a lot easier than this," he told Malcolm Gray. "Nobody had to worry about legal problems."

There is no end to such stories as these. They just go on and on. In March 1982, for instance, not long after I had begun my research on survivors, a young man named Carl McCunn had himself flown into a Yukon wilderness. He did not bother to make firm arrangements to be picked up, and by August he was worried and hoped that a plane would fly overhead. His food supplies were dwindling, and he was supplementing his diet with fish he caught in a lake and rabbits he snared. As winter set in, the wolves began to raid his traps, and he was starving and running out of fuel for his stove. "Am burning the last of my emergency Coleman light and just fed the fire the last of my split wood," he noted one day in his diary. "When the ashes cool, I'll be cooling along with them." He then wrote out a will. "They say it doesn't hurt," he added, and shot himself.

In the summer of 1983 a young man named Karl Bell was hiking in California's Bear River Canyon when he fell into a deep ravine.

Bell, a Marine lance corporal on leave and a self-described "dumb jerk that got lost," broke his ankle in the fall. For a few days he ate nothing and was obsessed with memories of the time he worked in a restaurant — "I thought about all that food." Such recollections were not his only torment: ants continually crawled all over him. "I'd smack them, and then I started eating them. . . . They didn't really taste that good." They were not very nutritious or filling, either. His only other food being moss, he lost seventy-five pounds before, near the end of his fifth week in the ravine, he found a climbing piton and a rope. He used them to haul himself back up to the trail from which he had fallen. Thereupon he passed out, but he was discovered by two other hikers.

Eighteen months later, at the end of January 1985, Russell Scott and his older brother, James, were taken from their Hawaiian home at gunpoint by three men who had been paid $150 to kill them. The men took the brothers out to sea in a boat, murdered James, and shot Russell twice. He jumped or fell into the water and stayed afloat for fifteen hours, guarded by dolphins, until he was rescued by fishermen. The only thing that kept him going, he told journalists as he lay in his hospital bed, was the "will to get back and get the people convicted that killed my brother."

On March 3, 1985, the crew of a tugboat sighted a rubber raft floating in the Atlantic, seven miles off the coast of Nantucket. In it were four commercial fishermen whose sixty-seven-foot trawler had sunk in "rough and freezing seas." They had floated for two days, subsisting on water and five bags of cookies. "Everyone did plenty of praying and eating Chips Ahoy chocolate chip cookies," recalled the captain, Joao Medeiros. "Without God and the supply of cookies, I don't think we would have made it. The cookies saved us. They're good and we had to watch out that we didn't eat them all because we didn't know how long it would be before somebody spotted us."

Two and a half months later, the skipper of a commercial fishing vessel sighted the partially submerged hull of a twenty-eight-foot powerboat. Tangled in the wreckage was the corpse of a young woman. Nearby was "something orange. It was moving. It seemed to have someone in it. Someone alive." That someone proved to be a nine-year-old girl who had been asleep when the boat capsized. Five adults and one other small child had drowned, but the girl, Desiree Rodriguez, had clung to a piece of wreckage for twelve hours. When rescued, said First Officer Mark Pisano, who pulled her to safety, "she was just about worn out and I am not sure she knew what was happening right then. But she was still moving, still trying to swim toward the boat. She was great!"

Before a week had gone by another survivor story surfaced, this one rather bizarre and oddly reminiscent of Sergeant Yokoi's. Soviet authorities announced the discovery of a World War II deserter from the Red Army who had been hiding out in a pigsty since 1944. Because deserters had been treated harshly by the Russian military during the war, a frightened Pavel Navrotsky had forced his wife to bring food to his hiding place for forty-one years. He was finally found, ragged, unkempt, and filthy, by villagers, after his wife died. Meeting strangers for the first time in four decades, his only question was "Will I be punished?"

A few months later Nelson McIntosh set out on what he thought would be a routine ninety-minute boat ride between two islands in the Bahamas. He had not taken along a radio or any provisions, other than two cans of beer. A storm struck, disabling his craft. He drifted for seven weeks, catching rainwater in an ice cooler and hooking an occasional fish, which he ate raw. He lost a hundred pounds, and he would not let his picture be taken in the hospital because "I don't look like I should."

On May 14, 1986, the *Pride of Baltimore,* a 136-foot reproduction of a nineteenth-century clipper ship, sank in a gale 240 miles off the coast of Puerto Rico. Four crewmen drowned, and eight others climbed into a lifeboat. There had not been time to send off a distress signal, and because she was on a routine voyage, no provision had been made for daily radio contact with the mainland. Thus no search was instituted for the ship or her crew. Without weights for their lines, the survivors were unable to catch fish, but they did pull seaweed from the water. "It played havoc with our stomachs," twenty-eight-year-old Scott Jeffrey remembered later, "but it was a psychological boost. You were putting something in your mouth." The castaways sang songs and comforted each other as they drifted. At various times one person or another would break down under the pressure. "It happened to all of us . . . but when it did, you had seven other people there to put their arms around you and tell you it was going to be okay." After five days on the ocean they were spotted and saved by the crew of a Norwegian tanker.

"The whole ordeal has made me look at things a little differently," Jeffrey told the readers of *People* magazine.

I don't worry so much about the bills or the car insurance. It wasn't a good experience. I lost four friends. I feel a sense of loss, of course, but I don't like to dwell on it. Things could have been a lot worse. The raft leaked, but at least we had a raft. The biggest thing that came out of this, though, was the beauty of the human spirit. There were so many little acts of heroism. If somebody lost a piece of biscuit, seven other people gave parts of theirs. If you were cold or crying, someone would put their arms around you. I have seven friends who saved my life, and we'll always be tied together.

I was supposed to be on the *Pride* for nine months. Then I was going to decide whether to pursue sailing seriously or get out. For obvious reasons, it's just not something I want to do now. I can go back on a boat without any problem, but the desire to make sailing my life — it's just gone.

Not every survivor has been able to think even that positively about his or her travail. "If I knew I had to go through these experiences again," said Lou Zamperini, referring to his days as a castaway and a POW, "I would kill myself." His life in the years following his liberation was as bitter as that remark. He announced to reporters that he would resume his athletic career, even though physicians had told him that the injuries to his legs would preclude competitive running. With his new bride holding the stopwatch, it was soon evident just how right the doctors were.

Since athletics were closed to him, he set out to realize a lifelong ambition to become wealthy. He sought to enrich himself through investments and business deals, but all too often the choices he made were poor ones, or he was swindled.

An alcoholic before the war, he now drank even more heavily. He verbally abused his wife and children. As she saw her marriage failing, Cynthia Zamperini became a born-again Christian and tricked her husband into attending a Billy Graham crusade. Zamperini fled the service but returned the next night and was converted.

He became an evangelist and missionary. Incredibly, he returned to Japan to witness there. He preached at a prison containing war criminals, among them some of the very guards who had brutalized him. When he returned from Japan, Zamperini, once a juvenile delinquent himself, formed a school for what used to be called wayward youth.

John S. McCollom, who crashed into a New Guinea Shangri-la with Margaret Hastings and Kenneth Decker, had a more conventional response to his ordeal. After he was mustered out of the

service in 1946, he took a civilian job working in aviation for the
U.S. military. For thirty years he was stationed at Wright–Patterson
Air Force Base in Dayton, Ohio, and involved in the acquisition of
planes and in their design and development. Upon his retirement
from the federal government in 1980, he took a job as vice president
of special projects for Piper Aircraft in Lakeland, Florida. When he
retired from Piper in the summer of 1984, he became a consultant
to a number of aerospace companies.

His jobs required him to fly on a regular basis. For a year or two
after he returned from New Guinea, this was a problem for him. "I
used to sweat takeoffs and landings. I flew the right wing, if I was
sitting on the right side; I flew the left wing if I was sitting on the
left, checking the engines over there. I'd be flying at night in an
airplane and they'd feather a propeller, and I'd sit up and take a
look and ask the steward to go up and ask the pilot what the hell
was going on." His anxiety continued until one night in 1947, when
he was flying from Edwards Air Force Base to Dayton in a C-47; as
the hour grew late he fell asleep, and the plane flew through a
thunderstorm. He did not wake up and did not know anything about
it until someone told him the next day. Since that flight "nothing
bothers me." Soon thereafter he renewed the pilot's license he had
obtained before the war and for the next thirty-four years he flew
gliders and a variety of light aircraft.

Some years ago, the World War II Glider Pilots' Association had
a reunion in St. Petersburg, Florida. McCollom, Decker, and Hastings were the honored guests. It was the first time since the ordeal
that all three survivors had been reunited — and as it happened, it
would be the last: subsequently Margaret Hastings died of cancer.

For a while after the war McCollom kept in touch with both
Hastings and Decker, calling each of them every May 13, the anniversary of the crash, which is also Decker's birthday. As the years
went by he had less contact with Hastings, although he has remained close to Ken Decker. Every year or two his work has taken
him out to the Pacific Northwest, where Decker lives, and they have
always gotten together.

At the time of the rescue, a photographer had parachuted into the
jungle and taken footage of the three of them, and a few years ago
Decker had the twelve-minute film converted to videotape. He gave
a copy to McCollom. "Every so often we've got to run it for all the
grandchildren," says John. "Show them the 'Young McCollom.' "

That and the annual telephone call are the only times these days that McCollom ever thinks about New Guinea. On the forty-first anniversary of the crash, it was nearly midnight before "I suddenly remembered that I hadn't called my friend Decker to wish him a happy birthday. So [the ordeal] doesn't come to mind too often now."

If you suggest to him that having gone through what he did, some people would have given up flying, he will shrug. For him aviation "is a way of life. I believe in airplanes. They're safe. I've worked on a lot of them; I was running a couple of military programs at the wrong time when we had a few crashes [of experimental prototypes], but that's part of it, I guess, if you are in the airplane business. I've flown the Atlantic fourteen times, and I have flown the Pacific twice, so to me it's just like getting on a bus and going somewhere. Of course, that's dangerous too, I suppose. No, for me, flying is a way of life."

He never went back to that place which imaginative journalists had dubbed Shangri-la. In 1986 he took a vacation to Australia and New Zealand with his wife and some friends. "Everybody kept saying, 'Do you want to go to New Guinea?' I said, 'Why? There isn't anything there for me anymore.'"

Unlike his buddy, Ken Decker has often thought about returning to New Guinea and wishes that he could have when he was younger. Unfortunately, until very recently the area where they were downed remained too inaccessible for tourist travel. "You wouldn't [have wanted] to go back there without the backing that you had in the Army or the Air Force," he explains. "There was no particular accommodations or transportation. It's getting better now . . . but in the early days there weren't."

After he returned to the States from the jungle, he spent six months in a hospital in Vancouver, Washington. He received a medical discharge from the military while he was in treatment, and once released, he re-enrolled at the University of Washington, where he had been a student before his induction. He earned degrees in mechanical and industrial engineering. Following his graduation, he spent fifteen months constructing dams with the Army Corps of Engineers and then took a job with Boeing Aircraft. He was employed by the company for twenty-four years, retiring in 1974. Among other duties, he was involved in the design and production of planes.

His job with the company required that he fly only very infre-
quently, which may be just as well, because going aloft has long
made him distinctly uncomfortable. "I experienced it particularly
on our flight home [from New Guinea]," he says with perhaps just
a trace of humor in his voice. "I don't really enjoy flying anymore.
I used to love it, but I don't enjoy it anymore." He feels that the
1945 crash is certainly at least in part responsible for his change in
attitude. He has not let his uneasiness ground him, however: he has
used commercial airlines for vacations as well as business trips. As
the decades have gone by, the disquiet has gradually lessened. "It's
just a decreasing thing. I've developed a fatalistic attitude about it.
You figure you will make it or you won't make it."

As for the ordeal itself, he rarely thinks of it. He shows the
videotape once in a while, of course, when someone is interested in
it or when "our young cousins [visit] who don't even know about
World War II." The telephone calls from McCollom also serve to
remind him, and he has remained in touch with many of the veterans
of his old army unit and with some of the Filipino soldiers who
rescued him. What comes to mind when he recalls his New Guinea
experience? "Oh, I think about the Filipino paratroopers who came
in to save our necks for us, to help us. Two of them were medics,
and they were great. I see one of them still. He lives not too far
from me. And some of those guys I would like to see. One or two
of them are dead, I know, but the others I would like to see again."

As for the hardship, pain, and suffering he endured in the jungle,
"It seems pretty distant. It's as though it was something I read
about rather than something I went through myself."

John McCollom and Kenneth Decker both were dependent upon
aviation for their livelihoods, but Ron Woodcock earned his salary
working on a railroad. His family would have suffered no real economic hardship if he had never gone back into the wilderness. He
did, though, just as often as he could. If you tell him that there are
people who, having undergone what he did, would never return to
the bush, he will laugh softly. "Yup, it scares quite a few of them.
But trapping is like panning for gold," he says. "It gets in your
blood." It surely must: every year or two he has returned to the
very same area in which he was lost for fifty-six days. Recently,
though, he set his traps in unfamiliar territory. A thick fog de-
scended and lasted for days, rendering him "lost" once more. On
the morning of the sixth day snow moved in, and he knew that if he

did not get out very soon, he never would. He built a fire and in the afternoon was spotted by a search plane. The pilot dropped him some survival chocolate bars and radioed for a helicopter.

Ron Woodcock went home for a few days to rest up — and then went right back into the wilderness. This time he was not so lucky. His right foot broke through the ice on a creek and went into the frigid water below — snowshoe, boot, and all. By the time he was able to get medical attention, all the toes on that foot had to be amputated. The disability meant that he had to retire from his job, but it did not cause him to give up that activity he loves so well. He expects to go trapping again, although he thinks he will find a place a little closer to home.

Woodcock's behavior would not surprise Steven Callahan. On the night of February 4, 1982, while he was on a solo voyage across the Atlantic, his sloop, *Napoleon Solo,* struck a hazard west of the Canary Islands and quickly swamped. Callahan spent the next seventy-six days adrift in an inflated lifeboat. Sharks attacked it, and it was buffeted by storms. He speared fish for food and devoted himself to the endless chore of bailing out his raft. He suffered from painful boils that became ulcerous sores, and by the time he was picked up by fishermen, he had drifted an estimated eighteen hundred miles and had lost fifty-five pounds.

When he had recovered sufficiently to travel, he declined an offer of airfare home, choosing instead to set out for the United States by "hitching" rides on boats. "For me it was much more natural to get on a boat, to get back to the scene that I was comfortable with, than to fly home and sit around and be pampered like I was an invalid and needed nurses." Thus he refused the invitations of solicitous people who would have opened their homes to him so that he might have a leisurely convalescence. "That wasn't for me. I just told them, 'Hey, I've come through the worst part. I just want to get back in shape and start having fun.' I needed control of my life again. As out of control as I was during [the ordeal] itself, at least I had a say over my own decisions. And then I came ashore and found that, as well intentioned as everybody was, I was losing all of that control, and I'm the type of person who can't stand that."

In the year that followed his rescue, his experiences in the raft were much on his mind. He needed to come to terms with the pain, but he was being thwarted in this by the attention of the media. Almost from the moment the fishermen had brought him to the island of Marie Galante, he was pursued by newspaper and television reporters. At first his relief at being saved made him cordial and open. "I was glad to talk to them and was extremely happy the whole thing was over and that it had come out all right in the end." Before long, however, the intrusion of the journalists became oppressive, and he fled to the other side of the island to avoid them — but they tracked him down. When he returned to the States this pursuit continued.

> If you do a successful interview with [one reporter], then suddenly two more people are asking you for an interview. Then there will be four more requests. . . . I was giving a lot of interviews. I got requests from an awful lot of people. . . .
>
> I think on the whole, the media tried to do a good job with my story. And most of the journalists are interesting people in their own right and do a good job. But if you are being interviewed about something which is emotionally meaningful to you, the tendency is — for me anyway — to open myself up, and I would recall a lot of things that were . . . [emotionally draining]. I really felt drained after an interview.
>
> The reporters come around and act like you're the most important thing in the world to them. They really build you up. They'd say, "This [story of yours] really impresses me. It is fantastic what you went through, and it is really important to share this with the public!" And blah, blah, blah. They use you to satisfy their needs and then they're gone. And when they are gone *they* aren't emotionally drained. They've had a kind of fix, and they are on to the next one. After a while, I thought, as much as I liked the individuals involved and appreciated what they were doing, in a way they were like sharks in a feeding frenzy. The sharks devour one victim, and then they go on to the next. . . . And meanwhile the first victim is *gone*.
>
> The reporters would say, "Well, I think you're wonderful, and you're great, give me your story!" And then they were gone. And I was left there no further on with my life or working things out for myself than I had been six months beforehand. So, finally I just withdrew and said, "No, I'm not doing any more interviews."

He wrote a book about his travail, *Adrift,* which made the best seller list in the spring of 1986 and again in the paperback edition the following year. Writing the book was therapeutic for him. Reviewing his experiences and going over a journal he had kept at sea helped him enormously to come to grips with his feelings:

> Keeping the log while in the raft helped me to "remove myself" on one plane from the experience and to recognize, if not enjoy, some

of the amazing things around me — the small miracles and beauty
. . . maybe even the strength in myself. Writing the book was a con-
tinuation of this process: to find beauty, even humor, out of what
was a horrible experience. It gave meaning to the event, rationalized
it, so I could accept the hell of it.

He had a chance to reflect on his own process of adjustment while
he was doing a publicity tour for *Adrift*. He had been invited to
appear on a West Coast television program. "It was a live show
with a live audience. It was what they call a 'theme show.' The
theme for this week was 'Survivors.' " The producers had arranged
for the appearance of Callahan and two other men.

One guy was the survivor of a hostage situation in the Middle East,
where he had been on a plane that was taken over by terrorists. They
killed a Marine, I believe, and threw him out on the tarmac. The
terrorists beat and tortured people and all these horrendous things.

The other guy was in a shopping mall when a small plane crashed
into it. He got his family out and then went back in and pulled people
from the wreckage of the plane and shoppers from the mall.

Both of these guys had psychiatrists with them, who, I presume,
felt that this would be a catharsis for them, a little cathartic exercise.
The guy who had been in the shopping mall seemed very nervous and
shaken even before the show started. The guy who had been a hostage seemed less so — emotionally he was sort of between me and
the other guy. I was just promoting a book. It was quite a different
scene [for me] from what it had been a couple of years before when I
had got burned out by people interviewing me. And now at least I'd
come to terms with it by telling my story in my book; it was kind of
routine.

As the program began, the other two men were seated on the
stage, and Callahan was sitting in the audience. He was thinking
how strange television was because so many of those involved in it
— anchorpersons, producers, and reporters — thought they could
get to the heart of any matter or issue in three minutes.

And this to me was just the perfect example of the worst aspect of
the media. The scene had an almost surreal tone to it. The show
opens, and the audience claps [on cue; they are] being prompted.
They get right into the gory details, and they start pressing both of
these guys for the gory details as though that is what is really important about their experiences.

They got the guy who was at the mall to describe what he actually
did. So he is describing pulling this woman from the wreckage who is
so badly charred that her eyelids are burned off and so is all the hair

on her head; and she was burned over 60 percent of her body or
something like that. A really horrendous scene. And he's sitting
there, and his voice is quivering, and his chin is quivering, and he's
got tears in his eyes, and — it's time for a commercial break! *Clap,
clap, clap, clap, clap!*
   The audience was prompted to applaud, and it was so out of place
that it seemed strange to me. I sat there, and I said to myself, "What
am I doing here? What am I doing being a part of this?" Because I
really don't think that at that point, for him, that he had any business
being there.
   I left. I had another appointment anyway, thank God, and I ended
up leaving the show. I wanted to go up to his psychiatrist and ask
him, "What the hell do you think you are getting accomplished here
with this? I don't think that this is going to help this guy work out
whatever it is he has to work out, to deal with his experience."

Unlike those other two talk-show guests — and many modern
survivors — Steve Callahan is a professional whose occupation has
repeatedly taken him into perilous circumstances and thus, to a
degree, conditioned him to deal with a survival situation. He is a
naval architect and has overseen the construction of a number of
boats. Prior to the wreck of the *Solo* he had participated in many
sailing races, made Atlantic crossings, and undertaken quite a few
other long voyages. He had carefully studied survival manuals and
had collected the essential safety equipment. Even if these things
did not bring him through his ordeal quickly and easily, at least the
process of studying the handbooks and choosing the emergency
gear, in conjunction with his previous experiences at sea, conditioned him mentally. Thus he was better off than someone like
Lauren Elder, who set out for an afternoon picnic in the desert and
found herself on a freezing mountaintop with the corpses of her
friends nearby.
   Since he was prepared for disaster and it did not take him completely by surprise, perhaps it is natural that Callahan did not radically alter his life. He continues to sail and to participate in oceanic
races. If you ask him why he still sails, he will answer with his own
question: "Why do anything?"

   I don't see the point of hiding one's head in the sand to pretend that
   anything is safe. I'm in a pretty safe part of the country [New Eng-
   land]. There aren't any volcanoes here . . . earthquakes are rare . . .
   but every now and then something happens — a tornado touches
   down or there is a fire. People die. I don't see any reason to stop
   what you are doing just because there is a potential for danger.

I have a tendency to think it's normal to sail across the Atlantic, though people disappear doing that. But if I drove racing cars, I'd know people who died in car accidents.

There is something that you get from dealing with high-stress situations, and it is not all negative. It may be frightening at the time, it may be painful, but if you lead a life trying to minimize risk and pain and anxiety, then I think you will miss a lot.

I've somehow been fortunate enough to have been given the opportunity to turn what was a rather bad experience into something that's given me a lot of room for personal growth. If I had never gone through it that would have been great with me, but because I did go through it doesn't mean I should regret having done so. You can learn a lot from terrible situations.

When I lecture to audiences and I say that I still sail today, many people are surprised. But actually it makes sense because in the survival situation itself I found that life is full of paradoxes and dilemmas. Although the sea was a great enemy, it was also a great ally and allowed me to live. It provided for me. It severely tested me, but it also gave me the great gift of seeing a lot of things both within myself and within my relationship to my environment that few people ever get to see.

The passage of time is slowly anesthetizing Steve, as it has John McCollom, Kenneth Decker, and, it seems, every other survivor. In the early days following his rescue, his ordeal was very much on his mind, but gradually he thought about it less and less often. Now it takes specific stimuli to trigger the memories. Each time he draws a bath, for instance, he looks at it and thinks of how he survived for more than two months with less fresh water than is in the tub. Or he will be complaining about one of life's petty annoyances when suddenly he will stop and say to himself, *Ah, gee, you're such an ass. Think about how much better off you are now than you were in that raft.* Or he will visit an apartment and the occupant will apologize for its being such a mess; he will look around at the spaciousness of the place and remember the months he spent in a lifeboat hardly bigger than a coffin.

He never dreams of his ordeal, and when he thinks of it he rarely feels pain. He has built up a "pretty good armor" against the unpleasantness. He senses a change in himself, but he does not claim it is a radical one.

There is a presence within me that I don't think will ever leave that will tell me, "You remember what it is like to starve; you remember what it is like to be really thirsty. So although you are complaining about some little thing, don't take it seriously."

There are other things that may have subtly changed or been strengthened within me. I don't think I'm essentially a different person; I'm the same person. If I had stepped ashore [after being rescued] and suddenly been a different person that wouldn't make sense to me. There was really no reason to step ashore and change my personality.

But on the other hand, there are a lot of things I saw in the experience that strengthened many of my beliefs and perceptions of things — like the paradoxes and the dilemmas of life. Everywhere, in every decision we make, I see a dilemma, and every situation is a paradox. And that became clear to me in the survival situation. In normal life we really don't see the paradoxes and dilemmas; it's much easier to see things as black and white. On the raft there was no decision that I could make that had no negative consequences, no matter how positive it was. In that environment, if it was windy, that meant I was making good progress toward my destination, but it also meant that it was more difficult for me to fish and I was going to get even more wet than I already was, so I'd develop more salt-water sores. Everything was a two-edged sword. That was very apparent to me, and I think I see the paradoxes and dilemmas more now — even in minor decisions.

In all probability the voice Callahan hears cautioning him to remember what he has endured is losing its volume. Eventually, if the experiences of other survivors are any guide, the voice will become so small as to be nearly inaudible. His ordeal, surely the most dramatic and singular event of his life, is even now slipping from his consciousness. It is a photograph that is blurring and losing its color year by year until, at last, after several decades, it may be hard for him to be certain just whose image it is.

Perhaps this is an enigma he would appreciate. Unless you have been transformed by the distress you have been subjected to, you must accept the fact that you will lose its good effects. And yet radical alteration is impossible for most of us. As Steve Callahan himself puts it, life in Western civilization in the latter half of the twentieth century "is not so Zen as that, and it is very difficult to function in our society [having been so transformed] unless you want to join a religious community or something."

What is true for him and for other abandoned souls is doubly true for the rest of us. In the island and the wreck we see our lives mirrored. If a man who was adrift for seventy-six days finds himself annoyed, say, at the length of the line at the bank teller's window, what more can be expected of us?

Most survivors who have come of age since the 1950s do not

claim to find any deep meaning in their travails. Conditioned by popular culture, they report that what they have learned is to live for the moment and to appreciate the little things in life. It is remarkable just how often these sentiments are expressed using these very words. For instance, one recent survivor, referring to an ordeal during which he was very close indeed to dying, explained that "when God didn't let me go, I was sure He had something in mind for me. And now I think I know what it was — learning to really appreciate living. Little things I used to take for granted, I don't anymore. Just getting up in the morning or watching one of [my] boys hook a fish is an unbelievable thrill. I never felt this way before — and it's wonderful."

Did God have Job and Jonah suffer just so they would notice the flowers beside the well-worn path or the play of light in a drop of water? Paul was struck blind on the Damascus road so that he might be able to open his eyes and *see*. Today, sitting atop the ruins of our lives, we do not reconcile ourselves to God, fate, or the laws of the natural universe; instead we find wonder in the petals of roses that push up through the ashes. We do not discover inspiration in the belly of the leviathan; rather we emerge from that enormous digestive tract to pay heed to the phosphorescent fishes that swim near the surface of the vast ocean.

As we kneel on that ancient thoroughfare, the scales having fallen from our eyes, we lift our heads and cannot perceive anything in the bright new light that our popular culture has not instructed us will be there. And this culture teaches us that nothing is of value except wealth and immediate gratification.

The hymn to the survivor — and to the rest of us — must be composed in the present tense because that is all we expect and all we know. The past recedes with the boiling swiftness of the tide, but unlike the tide, it will not return to us. We deny the future as being something we may not know or control, something we fear will end in fire and dreadful rain. With such a condemnation facing us, we seek to exist only in the imperative *now*. But to live for the moment is to be encapsulated in a bubble and to be carried on the blustery wind as if in a frail vessel on the great churning sea. If it is a bubble we choose for ourselves, then we must always wonder when some cruel point — a blade of grass, a cat's whisker — will pierce our transparent globe and send us spinning aghast and rudderless through the empty air.

ANNOTATIONS
BIBLIOGRAPHY
ACKNOWLEDGMENTS

Annotations

Many recent survivors — those born after 1945 — claim that what they have learned from their ordeals is to pay attention to the little things in life. However, some survivors I have talked to raise objections to this observation. A few insist that, like survivors of old, they have found deep spiritual insight; others simply cannot understand why I attempt to find meaning in travails. They look back on what they have been through simply as unpleasant experiences that had to be endured. I can only say that having read hundreds of survivor accounts, I have been struck by how often pre-twentieth-century survivors found God (or at least his providence) in their ordeals, and how rare that sort of profound discovery is these days.

Perhaps it is my love of English literature that has conditioned me to look for psychological change. Protagonists in fiction usually gain insight and understanding from crises, and they are often markedly changed by them. Anyway, the reader should be aware that I am solely responsible for my conclusions and that some survivors will disagree with them.

In quoting texts, I have found it necessary to do some editing — primarily to modernize spelling, capitalization, and punctuation. I have also abridged a few quotations in order to make them more readable and to the point.

I have not attempted to sanitize the stories of all vestiges of prejudice. Many of the early survivors in this book lived in periods of intense religious and/or nationalistic conflicts. To ignore references to such matters would be to change the character of the experiences themselves. Many survivors viewed the inhabitants of strange lands with fear or condescension; these attitudes shape responses, and so I have not attempted to filter or remove them.

Anyone wishing to read first-person accounts of survivors would do well to begin with three anthologies: Charles Neider, *Great Shipwrecks and Castaways;* Keith Huntress, *Narratives of Shipwrecks and Disasters;* and R. Thomas, *Remarkable Shipwrecks.* I have found Neider and Huntress to be particularly helpful; they have been excellent guides, and I could not have written this book without them.

In setting down the annotations that follow, I have not attempted to footnote every fact; the limitations of space obviously preclude this. I have tried to identify my principal sources, acknowledge a few of my many debts, and offer the reader some pertinent asides on matters covered in the text.

Prologue

For sources on Woodes Rogers and Alexander Selkirk, see the annotations to chap. 5.

In *The Great Days of Piracy in the West Indies,* George Woodbury tells us that six weeks after Rogers was wounded he had a "fit of coughing" and "spat out the bullet which had wounded him" (p. 151). This is a remarkable detail, although it is more likely that Rogers had the missile surgically removed, as Alexander Winston states in *No Man Knows My Grave,* p. 212.

Catholic scholars will disagree with my contention that Pope Alexander divided the New World between Portugal and Spain. In fact, in a signed article for the *New Catholic Encyclopedia,* J. B. Heffernan states specifically that the pope's "Line of Demarcation was a logical definition of spheres, and not an attempt to divide the world between two nations." Maybe, but as established by Alexander's first bull, the line ran north and south at approximately 38° west longitude; territory to the west, which included most of what was known of the Americas, was to be under Spanish control, while the tip of Brazil, the East Indies, and any new lands to the east were to be under Portugal's influence. To the layman it surely looks as if the pope meant to divide the *New* World.

Readers interested in the Inquisition and what is sometimes called the European "witch-craze" might read H. C. Lea's formidable and definitive works on these subjects; however, a brief and much less daunting introduction to them is the title essay in H. R. Trevor-Roper's *The European Witch-Craze of the Sixteenth and Seventeenth Centuries and Other Essays.*

In writing of demonology or witchcraft encyclopedias that could function as torture manuals, I was thinking particularly of the *Malleus Maleficarum* (The Hammer of the Witches). This most infamous of the encyclopedias was put together by two Dominican inquisitors in 1486 and thereafter caused a great deal of misery and mischief.

Chapter 1

The story of Pedro de Serrano is anthologized in James's *Providence Displayed,* pp. 159–66. James got the story from Garcilaso de la Vega's *Royal Commentaries of Peru.* I have used the 1688 translation by Sir Paul Rycaut, a copy of which is housed at the Library of Congress, but the tome has been translated and reprinted in a number of modern editions, notably the two-volume set entitled *Royal Commentaries of the Incas and General History of Peru.* Harold V. Livermore is the translator, and he wrote a long and valuable introduction. The material on Serrano is to be found in vol. 1, pp. 27–30; there is a reference to "Serrana Island" and its namesake on

p. 22. Incidentally, Garcilaso de la Vega, whose mother was an Incan princess, his father a Spanish captain, ends his account of Serrano with this afterthought: "After seeing the emperor, Pedro Serrano cut his hair and beard to just above the waist; and to enable him to sleep at night, he plaited it, for otherwise it spread out over the bed and disturbed his rest" (Livermore, p. 30).

Some years ago Robert F. Marx, who describes himself as being an "explorer-archaeologist," visited the Archivo de las Indias in Seville, Spain. No doubt his purpose was to do research relating to his job as the vice president of a company that locates and salvages wrecks, but while there, he found a document entitled "An Account by Master Pedro Serrano of Eight Years Spent as a Castaway on the Serrana Keys in the Caribbean Sea, 1528–1536." He published his translation along with an article in which he describes his visit to the five small cays known as Serrana Bank in the September 1974 issue of *Oceans*. "An Account by Master Pedro Serrano" is so very different in detail from the story in *Royal Commentaries* that it is not possible to merge or reconcile them. In choosing to follow Garcilaso de la Vega's version I do not mean to suggest that what Mr. Marx uncovered is unauthentic; I simply had to choose one or the other, and for a variety of reasons I went with Garcilaso de la Vega. Anyone who is interested in Serrano's adventures, however, will certainly want to look up Marx's article.

"Etiquette" and the other Bab Ballads have been published in any number of editions; the one I used was put together by Gilbert himself in 1897 and published the following year in London by George Routledge & Sons. "Etiquette" appears on pp. 541–46.

Chapter 2

"The True Relation of Peter Carder" was published in Samuel Purchas's *Hakluytus Posthumus, or Purchas His Pilgrimes,* vol. 4, pp. 1187–90.

The fullest modern biography of Drake is *Sir Francis Drake* by George Malcolm Thomson. Another biography is Ernle Bradford's *The Wind Commands Me.* Alexander McKee gives a thorough account of the circumnavigation of 1577–80 in *The Queen's Corsair.*

There was a protracted period late in his life when Drake stayed on land. Some scholars believe that this was an enforced idleness resulting from Queen Elizabeth's blaming him for the failure of the Portuguese Expedition of 1589. Others hold that he remained at home for personal reasons, and Thomson, for one, states flatly that throughout Drake's long career he never fell into disgrace.

Chapter 3

The story of the Poor Englishman appears in *The Voyages and Travels of J. Albert de Mandelslo,* p. 226. On the same page Mandelslo recounts the experience of the Dutch mariner on "St. Helena's Island." The Frenchman's tale is on p. 199.

One oddity about the Mandelslo account is that a portion of it is in the first-person singular and is presented as a monologue that the Englishman directs to Pickman when his rescuers wonder if he is an apparition or demon. In other words, he is trying to convince the master that he is human and therefore should not be summarily thrown into the sea. Some of the seventeenth- and early-eighteenth-century writers who repeat the story render it entirely in the third person, as if they doubt that the monologue was actually taken down verbatim by Pickman or anyone else. Since Mandelslo does not identify his source for the monologue, I have used the James version.

Increase Mather recounts the Poor Englishman's adventures in *An Essay for the Recording of Illustrious Providences*, pp. 64–70. The other sad anedcotes I alluded to are to be found in chaps. 1 and 2, pp. 1–72.

Job is referred to as the "blameless and upright man" in Job 1:1 and 1:8. God speaks to Job from out of the whirlwind, 38:4–13, and Job acknowledges the greatness of his creator in 42:2–6. All biblical quotations are from the Revised Standard Version.

Sarah's speech, which is the last in *J.B.,* comes at the end of sc. 11, pp. 151–53.

Chapter 4

As noted in the text, I have drawn most of the biographical material on the privateering captain from Christopher Lloyd's *William Dampier* and to a lesser extent from his and P. K. Kemp's *The Brethren of the Coast.* The Dover edition of *A New Voyage Round the World* contains useful introductions by Sir Albert Gray and Percy G. Adams.

The corpulent captain who joked about Dampier's being thin was named Swan. The anecdote is related in *A New Voyage,* p. 196. The remark about "being sufficiently weary of this mad crew" is on p. 273. Dampier catalogues his illnesses on pp. 178, 192, and 335. His voluntary marooning and open-boat journey are recounted on pp. 323–37.

In *Voyages and Discoveries,* chap. 5, Dampier relates his adventures in Tonkin. Of his narrow escape from the angry mob, he remarks that "this was the only funeral feast that ever I was at among them, and they gave me cause to remember it: but this was the worst usage I received from any of them all the time that I was in the country" (p. 67).

Dampier had genuine affection for Prince Jeoly and wrote about him at length in *A New Voyage,* pp. 342–48. He was not the sole owner of the boy, having been given only a half interest in him and his mother (who was also ornately tattooed) by a Mr. Moody. The "two painted People" sickened while living with Dampier at the fort at Bencouli; Dampier nursed them "as if they had been my brother and sister, yet she died." Jeoly was so grief-stricken and inconsolable that Dampier quickly had a grave dug

> to hide her out of his sight. I had her shrouded decently in a piece of new callico; but Jeoly was not so satisfied, for he wrapt all her cloaths about her and two new pieces of chints that Mr. Moody gave her, saying that they were his mother's, and she must have 'em. I would not dislodge him for fear of

endangering his life; and I used all possible means to recover his health. [p. 346]

It was Dampier's intention to use his share of the proceeds from displaying the boy to buy his freedom from Moody (who had paid sixty dollars for his mother and him) and "carry him back to Meangis and re-instate him there in his own country, and by his favor and negotiation to establish a traffic for spices and other products of those islands" (p. 347).

Dampier was fascinated by Miskitos and had great respect for them. Throughout *A New Voyage* he frequently digresses on them, making careful note of their customs and abilities. He relates the story of "Moskito Man" Will on pp. 66–68.

De la Mare's humorous, condescending view of the Miskitos is to be found in *Desert Islands and Robinson Crusoe*, pp. 23–24. The source for his remarks is a passage in *A New Voyage*, pp. 16–17. The origin of the tribe's name is thought to be a corruption of the Spanish word for musket. The Miskitos traded their skills for firearms, which they used both to subdue Indian tribes in territories richer in resources than their own and to force them into trading relationships. Thus they obtained goods from the interior of the continent which they could trade to Europeans for still more Western-made goods.

The Miskitos' reputation among privateers for toughness and ferocity can hardly be exaggerated, but by the end of the nineteenth century they had become a peaceful people, many of them converted by Christian missionaries. They are known today for their industriousness, and they earn their livelihoods as lumbermen or fishermen; the turtles the latter catch wind up on the tables of European restaurants.

Ironically, given the Miskitos' history as warriors and their decidedly nonmartial modern tendencies, they have been caught in the crossfire between the Sandinistas and the Contras. In the early days of that conflict, the Nicaraguan government feared the Miskitos would join forces with the Contras or would provide them with haven and food supplies when they crossed into Nicaragua from Honduras on raids. Government authorities therefore forcibly moved many Miskitos out of their traditional homeland and into camps. Some atrocities were committed against villagers by Sandinista troops. As I write these notes, the atrocities apparently have been stopped, and some Indians have made their way back to their land, but other, bitter Miskitos are reportedly fighting on the side of the Contras. Thus my statement in the text that they remain distinct and proud in the home of their ancestors is, unfortunately, not universally true at this moment.

Chapter 5

I have compiled the list of what Crusoe salvages from the wreck from the chapters entitled "I Furnish Myself with Many Things" and "I Build My Fortress." Even with this vast wealth, Defoe's generosity to his character is not at an end because he has a second ship wrecked offshore two thirds of the way through the novel (pp. 182–90). Karl Shapiro's poem "Crusoe" was published in *V-Letter and Other Poems*, p. 49.

There are three standard sources for Selkirk's marooning experience: Edward Cooke, *A Voyage to the South Sea;* Woodes Rogers, *A Cruising Voyage Round the World;* and Richard Steele, *The Englishman* (Dec. 1, 1713); Neider reprints *The Englishman*, pp. 83–86. I have relied most heavily on Rogers and Steele. Cooke was a captain on the voyage, but there are some suggestions that he was a difficult man, a troublemaker. His account is generally held to be inferior to Rogers's; it was also brought out rather hurriedly to steal a march on Rogers: in his introduction to vol. 2, Cooke himself states that having only briefly mentioned Selkirk in vol. 1, he now will digress to give "a fuller account of the man found on the island John Fernandes, in the South Sea, than we were able to give in the first volume, being then press'd to publish it with all possible speed" (pp. v–vi). For the reasons given above and his dubious claim that Selkirk preferred remaining a maroon to sailing with Dampier, I do not entirely trust Cooke and have used his work judiciously.

Rogers's circumnavigation was an exciting adventure, which Alexander Winston describes in highly readable fashion in *No Man Knows My Grave,* pp. 163–217. Rogers's subduing of the West Indian pirates was another remarkable accomplishment, and George Woodbury has several chapters on it in *The Great Days of Piracy,* pp. 136–99. The Seafarers' Library edition of *A Cruising Voyage* has a long and thorough introduction by G. E. Manwaring; it contains much useful information on the voyage and Rogers's life. The only complete, modern biography is *Crusoe's Captain,* by Bryan Little.

The two sources for Selkirk's life before and after his marooning are John Howell's little book, *The Life and Adventures of Alexander Selkirk,* and Thomas Wright's biography, *The Life of Daniel Defoe,* pp. 10, 164–74, and 230–33. I have used all these sources in putting together this chapter.

In *The Harleian Miscellany,* vol. 5, pp. 402–6, editor William Oldys presents what is supposed to be Selkirk's autobiography ("written by his own hand, and attested by most of the eminent merchants upon the Royal Exchange"), but it is obviously a melange of Rogers, Cooke, and Steele. Through the centuries there have been rumors that Selkirk kept a journal while marooned, and some of Defoe's detractors have claimed that the novelist bought or stole this document from the Largo native. The implication is that there is hardly anything creative about *Robinson Crusoe,* that it is nothing more than a thinly veiled autobiography of Selkirk. This is absurd because there is no evidence that Selkirk ever wrote a journal; neither Rogers nor Cooke mentions such a valuable and intriguing work, and the former maroon would surely have showed it to his rescuers. Yet even such an admirer of Defoe as Thomas Wright repeats the error: he identifies the owner of the house where the meeting supposedly took place and provides a photograph of the residence.

Selkirk's ordeal was important for Defoe because it radically altered the plot of his novel. Until he read *A Cruising Voyage,* he had conceived of *Crusoe* as a picaresque tale of a wanderer. A good short essay on Selkirk and Defoe is the afterword to the Signet Classic edition of *Crusoe* — "Robinson Crusoe: The Man Alone" by Harvey Swados. Defoe was influenced by other survivor stories, too; see Secord's *Narrative Method*, pp. 29–34, and Moore's *Daniel Defoe*, pp. 222–28. Moore calculates the distance Defoe moved Greater Land on p. 223.

Alexander Winston describes the ordeal of Simon Hatley and establishes the connection between his killing an albatross and the use Coleridge made of the incident for "The Rime of the Ancient Mariner" (pp. 197–201). He is also quite clear and concise on the problem of scurvy for European voyagers (pp. 167–68) and states that Rogers's afflicted men "stared feebly as they were hoisted up through the hatch" (p. 184).

Walter de la Mare's enchanting book provides a good history of Más á Tierra and its reluctant inhabitants (pp. 22–30, 128–30, 140–42, 186–88). Today the island has a small population of fishermen. Several years ago a British author moved there in order to write a book about the place. His intention was to live alone like Selkirk, and he was dismayed to discover not only that there were other residents but that they were hospitable to the point of intrusion. He left in a huff.

Chapter 6

In writing of the deaths of pirates, my principal source was Defoe's *A General History of the Pyrates*. I have supplemented this with Philip Gosse's *Pirates' Who's Who*. Among the many interesting recountings of the deeds of pirates are Patrick Pringle's *Jolly Roger: The Story of the Great Age of Piracy* and Edward Lucie-Smith's *Outcasts of the Sea: Pirates and Piracy*.

I have based the body of the chapter on Ashton's narrative, which has sometimes appeared under the title of *Ashton's Memorial: An History of the Strange Adventures and Signal Deliverances of Mr. Philip Ashton*. A recent edition was brought out by the Peabody Museum of Salem. The American Imprint Series includes the *Boston News-Letter*.

Charles Ellms has a chapter on the life of Edward Low in *The Pirate's Own Book*, pp. 228–35. But the best single source is Defoe, who has chapters on both Low and Spriggs. Howard Pyle wrote about Low in "Buccaneers and Marooners of the Spanish Main," *Harper's New Monthly Magazine*. The article is illustrated with engravings made from Pyle's drawings and is worth looking up for them alone. Pyle's two "papers" on the buccaneers were reprinted in the February and March 1985 issues of *American History Illustrated*.

Chapter 7

The Just Vengeance of Heaven Exemplified was published in London (1730) and then in Philadelphia (1748) by William Bradford (Evans No. 5980). It does not seem to have been anthologized widely, presumably because of its homosexual theme. (Neider, however, does include it in *Great Shipwrecks*, pp. 121–35.)

Chapter 8

I based my observations about the persecution of homosexuals on scattered references in a number of texts that appear in the Bibliography.

There are two excellent secondary sources available on Marguerite: Arthur P. Stabler's *The Legend of Marguerite de Roberval* and Elizabeth Boyer's *A Colony of One: The History of a Brave Woman*. Stabler, who is a professor of French, has an interest in the literary treatments and adaptations of the story, while Boyer, a lawyer and a feminist, focuses on its biographical and historical contexts. Stabler provides a useful comparison and textual analysis of the contemporary accounts. Boyer devotes a chapter to a study of each of the principals in the case; she also provides translations of Thevet's accounts. I have quoted from these translations in the text.

As far as I am aware, no complete English translation has been made of the Belleforest account. (Stabler gives only a partial translation, rendering just the most relevant passages.) I have a microfilm copy of "The Story of the Generous Heart," *Histoires tragiques* (catalogued under the title *The French Bandello*), which was provided to me by the Folger Shakespeare Library. The story appears in vol. 6, pp. 70–123. My French is not such that I am willing to provide the reader with my own translation, and I have quoted from Stabler's translation in the text.

Boyer downplays Roberval's religion as a motive for the marooning and uses legal documents to show that he was financially hard-pressed. Belleforest says that Roberval and Marguerite were brother and sister, a fact that would make the marooning all the more appalling, and Thevet has their relationship as being that of uncle and niece, but Boyer establishes that they were cousins.

On the subject of Saguenay: Cartier was looking for a sea route to Asia and found mainland Canada instead. Like every other explorer to the New World, it would seem, Cartier's charge was that he convert the Indians and bring home wealth, but on his second expedition he was also instructed to "discover certain far-away countries." Admiral Samuel Eliot Morison, in *The European Discovery of America: The Northern Voyages,* seems to believe that Cartier learned of Saguenay during his first voyage to Canada in 1534, from a clever Huron chief named Donnaconna. Cartier either kidnapped two of the chief's sons or bribed them into returning with him to France. He reunited them with their father on his next expedition (1535–36) but carried them back to France once more — one way or another — along with their father and seven of his followers. So far as is known, none of the Indians ever saw their homeland again; nine of them died within five years of arriving on the continent, and the tenth, a little girl, has, as they say, disappeared from history. Donnaconna converted to Christianity and became such an embroiderer of the legend of the land of pale-skinned warriors that Morison calls him "the publicity agent for the mythical Kingdom of Saguenay" (p. 430).

See Morison for more on the Saguenay legend, especially p. 415. See also John Bartlet Brebner's *Canada: A Modern History,* pp. 20–21. The land Donnaconna described was inhabited by pygmies, men who could fly, others who had only one leg, and still others who could neither eat nor digest. Anthropologists and "reporters" for supermarket tabloids alike must mourn the fact that the place does not exist. Readers who become interested in the legend will want to consult *A Collection of Documents Relating to Jacques Cartier and The Sieur De Roberval* by H. P. Biggar. The following documents are relevant: 75, 89, 90, 101, 112, 119, 124, 126, 127, 130, 131, 132, and 164.

I have relied most heavily on André Thevet's account. Boyer, who also makes extensive use of his work, calls him the "major chronicler" (p. 5). She characterizes Roberval as an "unstable man" driven over the brink by Marguerite's affair into "insensate tyranny" (p. 87). She has visited the island, and she devotes a chapter to a description of it, pp. 121–29. For her speculations about the lovers' confrontation with Roberval, see pp. 2–3, 117, and 269. She points out that the flame from the barrel of the arquebus might have set the wooden ship on fire (p. 3).

Belleforest is the source for the mocking speech Roberval delivers when he condemns the lovers to the isle. Some students of Marguerite's story will object to my having used it because of its clear implication that she was already pregnant when she was marooned; it is unlikely that she would have been pregnant at this time and certainly her pregnancy would not have been obvious to others. I have quoted the passage nevertheless, because it so clearly demonstrates Roberval's indignation and cruelty.

"When the lions and other wild beasts . . ." is from Queen Marguerite's *Heptameron*, p. 210. Stabler thinks the queen may mean either sea lions or wildcats rather than the kings of the jungle, which would have had to make a long swim from Africa in order to dine on the poor damsel (p. 20, n. 26).

Both Stabler and Boyer feel that the cause of the death of the child was his mother's inability to lactate because of her diet. Stabler is uncertain about Thevet's chronology of the story: Marguerite may not have been on the island two years and five months because "the entire area is ice-bound from October through April at least, and any fishing vessel would long before the autumn have sought the safety of its home port for winter" (p. 17).

According to Gerald Sandford Graham in *A Concise History of Canada,* "Roberval's effort at colonization was a fiasco, and he was fortunate to reach his homeland again, in the summer of 1543, with a cargo of 'fool's gold' and stones like diamonds, subsequently shown to be worthless" (p. 44). Cartier, who had the good sense to desert his captain and go back to France at the first opportunity, took home a similarly worthless cargo.

Morison writes that Roberval "was killed in a religious riot in Paris in 1561" (p. 454). Stabler's study of relevant documents leads him to conclude that it was 1560 — "or at the earliest late in 1559" (p. 24). Boyer, citing a genealogy of the captain's family, states that he died in 1560 (p. 262, n. 19).

Stabler identifies the isle of Marguerite's confinement as being one of the Harrington group (pp. 25–27), but goes no further than that. Elizabeth Boyer's investigation revealed it to be Hospital Island. When she visited the place, she was shown around by residents, and her book includes quite a number of her color photographs; among them are several of the cave in which, according to a local oral tradition, the lovers resided for a time, presumably until they finished building their shelter.

Queen Marguerite states that the fishermen took Marguerite de la Roque to La Rochelle. Samuel Eliot Morison tells his readers that she settled in Montron in Picardy (p. 447). For Boyer this is one of a number of inexcusable and careless errors Morison makes in telling Marguerite's story and is evidence of his sexism and that of a number of his colleagues: "The many-times-repeated mistakes of the major historians who have recorded this episode at all, have caused me, as a feminist, to conjecture that since a notable exploit by a woman was involved, it was not considered to be worthy of serious research" (p. 269). She fixes the place of Marguerite's post-marooning residence as Nontron in Perigord (p. 136).

I have not used Morison as a source for Marguerite's ordeal, but since I do cite him with regard to Saguenay, Cartier, and the make-up of Roberval's expedition, perhaps I should say that, to my knowledge, his research has not been challenged with regard to these matters, and other, presumably less prejudiced historians (Brebner, for instance) confirm it.

Chapter 9

In *Anson's Voyage,* L. A. Wilcox offers a highly readable recounting of the expedition. The book includes a helpful biographical note on Lord Anson's life (pp. xii–xv). Oliver Warner's *Great Seamen* has a biographical sketch (pp. 38–57).

In quoting from the *Narrative of the Honorable John Byron,* I have had to do more editing than on the account of any other survivor. Byron's paragraphs are very long and usually include several different and often unrelated topics. I have found it necessary to alter his grammar and break up his paragraphs into smaller ones.

Wilcox calculates that eighty rebels sailed in the longboat from Wager Island but that only thirty survived to reach the Rio Grande on the coast of Brazil. He describes the later adventures of Campbell (p. 59). My principal source for biographical information about John Byron, his son, and grandson is *Lord Byron,* by Paul G. Trueblood.

Chapter 10

Keith Huntress reprints a contemporary narrative of the loss of the *Earl of Abergavenny* on pp. 133–37. Huntress, an English professor at the time of the publication of his book (he has since retired), provides a long and quite valuable introduction in which he traces the influence of particular narratives and disasters on British and American literature. In the brief introductory remarks to the *Earl* account, he shows the impact of the wreck on William Wordsworth (pp. 131–32). The three poems Wordsworth wrote about his brother's death are "Elegiac Stanzas," "Elegiac Verses," and "To the Daisy." I have reproduced the seventh and eighth stanzas of "To the Daisy."

All the quotations from *Don Juan* are from Canto 2. The specific verses I have quoted are numbered as follows: "even the able seaman, deeming his" — 33; "who, with sense beyond his years" — 35; "But man is a carnivorous production" — 67.

"The Remarkable Shipwreck of the Sloop *Betsy*" was reprinted in R. Thomas's *Remarkable Shipwrecks*, pp. 118–30.

Chapter 11

"The Yarn of the *Nancy Bell*" is from *Bab Ballads*, pp. 101–5. The Walt Whitman poem is "I Sit and Look Out"; it was written in 1860.

Richard Clarke's narrative was published in Richard Hakluyt's *Principal Navigations, Voiages and Discoveries of the English Nation*, pp. 700–701.

Chapter 12

For more on the earliest manifestations of cannibalism, see Reay Tannahill, *Flesh and Blood: A History of the Cannibalism Complex*. In her introduction she notes that human bones found in Stone Age caves or other habitation sites show signs of cannibalism. Such evidence exists for the Peking man, which suggests "not only that he was prepared to eat his fellows when the hunting was poor, but that he ate them without much more compunction than he ate deer, otter, or wild sheep" (p. 3).

She argues nonetheless that "people-eating can never have been a regular feature of the diet" (p. 7). The practice presumably declined after human beings formed small communities, because eating one's neighbor might have unfortunate social consequences: "But since [the earliest farmers] had chosen to live in communities they were bound by the very rules that made community living possible. The basically practical ban on killing and eating the family had to be extended" (p. 17). She traces the development of the taboo in chap. 1, pp. 19–34.

In writing that the dead are not always wholly interred when the burial party is famished, I was thinking particularly of the persistent reports — always denied by the Soviet government — that the besieged citizens of Leningrad resorted to cannibalism to survive. See Harrison Salisbury, *The Nine Hundred Days*, for the grim particulars (pp. 452–53 and 474–76).

Brian Simpson's observation on the lack of moral objection to the custom of the sea is to be found on p. 122.

Several books have been written about the Andes incident, the best known of which is *Alive!* by Piers Paul Read. A second book is mentioned below, but there is yet a third study, *Survive!* by Clay Blair, an American journalist who has written for *Life* and other magazines. Mr. Blair has made something of a specialty of chronicling survival adventures.

Canessa and Vizinting both granted interviews to *Newsweek* magazine reporters. The resulting story, "Deliverance," tells how Canessa convinced his companions to think of human flesh in terms of protein and gives the Vizinting quote of which I have made so much (p. 27).

"Air Crash Survivors: The Troubled Aftermath," *Time* magazine, describes at least one of the ghoulish pranks (p. 53). The same article includes an analysis of the phenomenon of psychic numbing. The phrase seems to have been coined by psychiatrist and author Robert Jay Lifton. He explains that survivors simply "cease to feel." Tannahill's elucidation of psychic numbing is to be found on p. 175 of *Flesh and Blood*.

For information on the Andes survivors' manufacture of the pleasant fiction that they had subsisted on chocolate and cheese, see "8 Survivors of Crash Picked Up in Andes," *New York Times*, Dec. 24, 1972; "Cannibalism After Air Crash Reported," *New York Times*, Dec. 27, 1972; and *Newsweek*, Jan. 8, 1973. This last source traces the indignation of the young men's relatives.

For the press conference, see "Survivors of Andes Air Crash Admit Dead Saved Their Lives," *New York Times*, Dec. 29, 1972, and "70 Days Battling Starvation and Freezing in the Andes . . ." Jan. 1, 1973.

Packer spelled his first name Alferd, but some writers have used the more traditional spelling. Three interesting biographies have been written about him: Robert W. Fenwick, *Alfred Packer: The True Story of Colorado's Man Eater;* Paul H. Gantt, *The Case of Alfred Packer, the Man Eater;* Ervan F. Kushner, *Alferd G. Packer: Cannibal! Victim?*

For the use of the *Mignonette*'s dinghy as a fund-raising device, see Simpson, p. 80. He reproduces a photograph of the craft (ill. 7, following p. 130).

In the author's introduction to *The Place Where the World Ends: A Modern Story of Cannibalism and Human Courage*, Richard Cunningham says that when he approached the survivors he learned that they "had signed a contract forbidding the release of any information." In the context of the introduction, the implication is obvious that the exclusive contract was with Read. In his acknowledgments Read writes, "I was given a free hand in writing this book by both the publisher and the survivors" (p. 10). The dedication page is signed by all sixteen survivors, who state, "We decided that this book should be written and the truth known because of the many rumors about what happened in the cordillera. We dedicate this story of our suffering and solidarity to those friends who died."

The almost bizarre review quotes from the various publications are taken from the cover of the paperback edition of *Alive!*

Newsweek followed up the Andes story in the June 30, 1975, issue ("Alive and Well," p. 11). "Opened many doors" is the phrase of an editor or reporter. By the time the article had been written, Parrado had made a two-day trip on horseback to the crash site to put up a plaque in memory of his loved ones.

At least two different accounts purportedly written by John Dean have been published. The first is *A Narrative of the Shipwreck of the "Nottingham Galley"* (1711; Evans No. 2863). Except for the preface, this version is written in the third person, and Dean is referred to throughout as the Master. There have been at least five editions of this account, and Miles Whitworth is credited with being the editor.

The second account is *A Narrative of the Sufferings, Preservation and Deliverance of Captain John Dean and Company* (1722). There are also several editions of this version; it was reprinted in William Shurtleff's *Distressing Dangers* (1727; Evans No. 2960). This is written in the first person. Neider, for one, accepts this as the authentic version, and I have used the Shurtleff text in my rendering of the ordeal. Dean frequently pauses in his recitation of events to deliver ornate lamentations, but I have generally abridged quotations to remove them.

By the way, a third version exists — *A Relation of a Remarkable Shipwreck, After a Shipwreck of Uncommon Distress* — which was collected in Cotton Mather's *Compassions Called For* (1711; Evans No. 1506). It is simply a rather severe abridgment of the first version.

I have a photocopy of Langman's *A True Account of the "Nottingham Galley,"* which was provided to me by the Rare Book Room of the Library of Congress.

Simpson's remark about competent officers is made on p. 177.

Bligh wrote two accounts of the mutiny and the open-boat journey. The first was published in 1790; the second, much expanded one, in 1792. The New American Library has published a Signet Classic edition of the latter version (*The Mutiny On Board HMS "Bounty"*) along with an excellent afterword by Milton Rugoff. He writes of the mutineers' dubious character on p. 229. For more on Dean's later career, see Huntress, p. 6, and Simpson, p. 116.

Chapter 13

Simpson describes the sinking of the *Mignonette* and the murder of Richard Parker in chap. 1 and the trial of Dudley in chap. 9 of *Cannibalism and the Common Law*.

Cicero's moral puzzles are to be found in book 3, chap. 23, of *De officiis*. John Higginbotham translates the first dilemma as a choice between a "valuable horse or a valueless slave" (p. 169). Walter Miller in an older translation renders it as a "high-priced horse or a cheap and worthless slave" (p. 363). The other phrases are Miller's translations (p. 365).

I have been unable to locate an English translation of *Observationem medicarum* in this country. An early Latin edition is in the collection of the Johns Hopkins medical school library. In "The Judgment in the *Mignonette* Case," an article published in *The National Review*, 1884–85, Sherston Baker quotes the relevant passage, gives a partial translation, and analyzes the incident in light of the *Mignonette* case (pp. 707–8).

"You Seamen Bold; or, The Ship in Distress" is anthologized in John Ashton's *Real Sailor Songs*, p. 125.

In writing of the *Euxine* tragedy, I have used the survivors' depositions, photocopies of which were furnished me by the British Public Record Office. The file is No. MT 9/101/M257/75. The file contains correspondence and other documents that I have not seen, but Brian Simpson, who did research at the Public Record Office, shared his notes on this material with me. Anyone wishing to know more about the case would do well to begin with Simpson's chapter on it; see especially pp. 176–94. The survivors variously corrupted the victim's name in their depositions, but Simpson has seen the ship's articles in which the man may have signed his name as Franco Gioffey (pp. 179–80). The Harrington letter was published in a Singapore newspaper and reprinted in Simpson (p. 181). Simpson cites fears that an acquittal would seem to approve actions that would have had the effect of "quickly reducing the life expectation of ships' boys" (p. 189).

The Melancholy Narrative of the Distressful Voyage and Miraculous Deliverance of Captain David Harrison was brought out in London in 1766. Only sixty-seven pages long, it is still available at several U.S. libraries. It appears in the Neider anthology. C. Fox Smith, in *Adventures and Perils of the Sea,* reprints an anonymous account, apparently written by one of the crew, which states that the black was David Harrison's own slave, that *two* of the crew died on the rescue ship, and that Flatt "was restored to perfect health, after having been so near the gates of death" (p. 380).

Chapter 14

Brian Simpson's *Cannibalism and the Common Law* is replete with examples of the problems of sailors, particularly in chap. 5, "The Custom of the Sea."

The case of Alexander William Holmes is taken up in the next chapter, but according to a trial transcript, he said, "Lie down, every soul of you, and be still. If they make so many of us on board, they will steer off another way, and pretend they have not seen us" (I, p. 362, n. 8).

Captain Ball, who picked up Holmes and the other castaways and who burned his ship's longboat to keep them warm, was paid for the craft and the cost of feeding the survivors, but he does not seem to have been given any *reward* for saving more than two dozen lives.

For "Skipper Ireson's Ride" see *The Poetical Works of John Greenleaf Whittier,* vol. 1: *Narrative and Legendary Poems,* pp. 174–78. I have abridged it by beginning at the second instead of the first verse and omitting the fifth and sixth verses.

I have used two sources in putting together the true story of Ireson: John W. Chadwick, "Marblehead," *Harper's New Monthly Magazine;* and Samuel Roads, Jr., *A Guide to Marblehead.* These authors disagree on several matters, only one of which seems crucial to me: Roads has it that, finding his crew resolutely "would not endanger their lives for the sake of saving others, Skipper Ireson proposed to lay by the wreck all night, or until the storm should abate, and then go to the rescue of the unfortunate men. At this they also demurred, and insisted on proceeding on their homeward voyage without delay" (pp. 47–48). Chadwick, on the other hand, reports that the skipper went below believing that his order to lay by the wreck all night would be obeyed. Having no way of discerning which is correct, I chose to follow the Chadwick version, which is the earlier of the two.

Chadwick relates the "cowed him to death" conversation on pp. 187–88. He is also the source of Flood's later life (p. 187), and the judgment that the old man's house was in one of the "queerest corners of town" (p. 186).

The Narrative of the Shipwreck and Sufferings of Miss Ann Saunders was published in 1827. In 1983 it was reproduced on microfiche by University Microfilms International.

What the circumstances were for the original publication of John Kendall's account I do not know. The first mention of the account that I am aware of is in R. Thomas's collection (1850). Huntress remarks favorably on Saunders's heroism but reprints Kendall's version of events. Huntress also has this to say: "One wonders about the future career of the indomitable Ann Saunders, and about some putative husband of hers, successor to the unfortunate James Frier. What were his thoughts, of nights, when he lay by her in their quiet English bed, with that right arm about him?" (p. xviii).

And what were hers?

Chapter 15

The version of "The Sorrowful Fate of O'Brien" that I have used is anthologized in James N. Healy's *Irish Ballads and Songs of the Sea,* pp. 61–63. I have not reprinted all the verses by any means: the song is both long and very specifically detailed.

Brian Simpson tells the story of young O'Brien's death on pp. 130–39.

In putting together the story of the *William Brown* I have used articles from the *London Times,* the *New York Herald,* and the *Philadelphia Public Ledger.* The most valuable source was the British Public Record Office's file on the case, No. FO 27/634. The Public Record Office provided me with a photocopy of the file. It contains the depositions of the survivors, the results of the official investigation, and the correspondence of government bureaucrats. I have also made extensive use of two distinctly different transcripts of Holmes's trial. The first is to be found in *Federal Cases, United States* v. *Holmes,* Case No. 15,383, pp. 360–69. This transcript, reported by John William Wallace, should be available in every law school and legal library. (I refer to the *Federal Cases* transcript by the roman numeral *I.*)

The second transcript is published by Fred B. Rothman & Co. of Littleton, Colorado, and it is one of a series that bears the general title *Trials.* The transcript is No. 249; its title is the *Trial of Alexander William Holmes, One of the Crew of the Ship "William Brown," For Manslaughter on the High Seas.* The version I have seen is on microfiche; it is a photocopy of a typescript that includes many misspellings and typographical errors. It is 118 pages long (and is referred to by the roman numeral *II*). The reader desiring to locate it may have some trouble doing so, as it is housed, so far as I am able to determine, in only a half-dozen libraries in this country, all of these associated with law schools. Nowhere in the transcript is the reporter identified, although I assume he is Mr. Wallace.

I have made use of the two transcripts because, despite the fact that they frequently overlap, each contains crucial bits of information and testimony that the other lacks.

One of the minor problems in piecing together the story is determining how many people were on the ship before the wreck and how many survived it. Sources disagree over the numbers. For instance, Harris listed nine sailors and thirty-two passengers as being in the longboat, but he left out at least one name — that of Jane Johnson, who was present not only in the craft but in the courtroom as well, where she testified about what she had witnessed (II, pp. 46–49). Early in her testimony Bridget McGee also gave an accounting of the occupants of the craft (II, pp. 7–8), and she included at least two names not on the captain's list; at the same time she appears to have forgotten the name of one of the survivors Harris mentioned. Unable to resolve this and other questions, I have written the chapter using my best estimates of what the various numbers were.

The remarks of George M. Dallas are found in I, p. 363; David Paul Brown's, I, p. 365. Brown's statement is reproduced in II, p. 77.

Chapter 16

Mosby ordered that the seven Union soldiers be hanged, and five were, but the other two escaped, presumably with the help of sympathetic guards. Evan S. Connell, in his wonderful biography *Son of the Morning Star: Custer and the Little Big Horn,* notes that there is doubt that it was actually Custer who had the six rebels executed. *Some* Union officer was responsible, and Mosby was certain he knew who it was. He had the Yankees strung up as close to Custer's headquarters as he could, with this note affixed to one of the bodies: "These men have been hung in retaliation for an equal number of Colonel Mosby's men, hung by the order of Gen'l Custer at Fort Royal. Measure for Measure" (Connell, p. 118).

Brian Simpson observes that Tom Dudley was released on May 20, 1885, "exactly a year and a day after the voyage of the *Mignonette* began" (p. 288). Simpson tells a number of stories that involve the death of apprentices, but as noted earlier, his main focus is on the *Mignonette* case, and in chap. 10 he traces the later lives of those who were involved. Dudley's biography after his release from prison is found on pp. 288–95. The author with the remarkable imagination is Donald McCormick (*Blood on the Sea*).

Given the ongoing interest in the *Essex,* there have been any number of uses of the story, among them a recent novel about Pollard by Henry Carlisle, appropriately entitled *The Jonah Man.* Chase's narrative has been republished many times. (The Library of Congress owns six early editions; the one published by W. B. Gilley in 1821 is available on microfilm.) A useful edition is *The Wreck of the Whale Ship "Essex,"* edited and with a prologue and epilogue by Iola Haverstick and Betty Shepard. The prologue tells much about the Nantucket whaling tradition, and the epilogue, of course, relates the rescue and later lives of the survivors. Readers who would like to know more about the *Essex* tragedy might want to consult Thomas Farel Heffernan's *Stove by a Whale: Owen Chase and the "Essex."* Heffernan is a professor of English and a Melville scholar. His book is an invaluable resource that includes all of the then-known accounts. (Thomas Nickerson's was found in a trunk in an attic a few years after the publication of *Stove by a Whale.*) Heffernan deals with Melville's and other literary figures' interest in and use of the story. He has done considerable research into the lives of all the survivors — especially Chase and Pollard.

Rear Admiral Charles Wilkes recalled his meeting with Pollard in his *Autobiography,* pp. 168–70. (In setting down the conversation so many years after it had taken place, the admiral misremembered the captain's name as being Potter.) The exchange having to do with lightning striking is on p. 169. Heffernan expresses his surprise at Wilkes's question on p. 148.

I have used the Signet Classic edition of *Moby Dick,* which includes an afterword by Denham Sutcliffe. The "Lee Shore" is a very short chapter — I have quoted all but the first sentence (pp. 115–16).

In *Herman Melville: A Biography,* Leon Howard has written a highly readable account of the novelist's life. Melville wanted to be a school-teacher and actually found a position after he disembarked from the *St. Lawrence* (p. 28). Then as now it was not a lucrative calling, and so he went back to sea. While on the *Acushnet* he met Owen Chase's son William Henry, questioned him about his father, and borrowed from him his copy of his father's narrative (p. 45; see also Heffernan, pp. 160–62). For the rest of Melville's voyages, see Howard, pp. 48–82. The *United States* sailed very close to Greater Land so that those on board could get a look at Selkirk's abode (p. 81).

The famous opening lines of *Moby Dick* can be found on p. 21 of the Signet Classic edition.

In talking about men learning the sailor's trade when they were quite young, I was thinking again of Alexander Holmes: the court reporter observed that "he had followed the sea from his youth" (I, p. 362), and his lawyer, with just that touch of hyperbole for which attorneys are renown, said that "from infancy . . . [he] had been a child of the ocean" (I, p. 365).

My generalization about economic conditions is admittedly a very broad one, but I might point out by way of illustration that before he reached his twenty-first birthday Melville had lived through two serious depressions (1819 and 1839) and the financial panic of 1837.

In chap. 45 of *Moby Dick,* Melville tells of the *Essex* and actually quotes from Chase's book (pp. 206–7).

Henderson Island is only one hundred miles from Pitcairn, and Thomas Heffernan speculates on what would have happened had the castaways known of the existence of the latter isle and managed to reach it (p. 85–87).

Chase and the other survivors believed they were on Ducie Island, another in the Pitcairn group, but students of the *Essex* tragedy are certain that the castaways arrived on Henderson (see Haverstick, pp. 109–13). Heffernan also holds to this position and gives a history of both islands (p. 77–87).

George Bennet set down his recollection of Pollard's tale in *Journal of the Voyages and Travels by the Rev. Daniel Tyerman and George Bennet, Esq.* The London edition was published in two volumes in 1831; the material on Pollard is in vol. 2, pp. 24–30. Pollard's offering to shoot anyone who touched Owen Coffin and the boy's resigned reply are found on p. 28; the captain's lament, on p. 29.

Pollard, by the way, broke off his recitation of grim events for a moment, saying, "But I can tell you no more — my head is on fire at the recollection;

I hardly know what to say" (p. 28). Owen Chase suffered from severe headaches all the rest of his life after the sinking of the *Essex;* this affliction was apparently so severe and widely known that it was remarked upon in his obituary in a Nantucket newspaper: "He always complained of pain and difficulty about his head, from that time [November 1820] to his death, particularly so after a long voyage" (Heffernan, p. 144). It will be recalled that he complained of the pain in his head to his cousin, Phoebe Chase.

Melville did not believe that Chase authored the *Narrative,* and Heffernan has done some historical detective work to try to identify the ghostwriter. Thus my saying that Chase wrote a narrative of his experiences will likely be faulted by knowledgeable readers. I would not dare challenge the great novelist or the eminent professor, but certainly Chase worked very closely with whoever set down his story, and no one has questioned the fundamental authenticity and accuracy of the *Narrative,* so perhaps I may be excused for not digressing on the problem of a co-author or ghostwriter.

My main source for the later lives of the *Essex* survivors was Heffernan's *Stove by a Whale.* The author says that Pollard and Chase "were Bulkingtons in behavior if not in motive" (p. 119), and he recounts the traditions about Chase's madness on pp. 143–44. Owen's son, William Henry Chase, went to sea, of course, where Melville met him. Charles Frederick, who had been raised in the Chase household despite being the illegitimate son of Owen's third wife, also went to sea. The evidence is not entirely clear, but it seems that at least three other *Essex* survivors became captains in their own right.

In 1876 Melville published "Clarel: A Poem and Pilgrimage in the Holy Land." The copy I used is found in *The Works of Herman Melville.* The Jonah quotation is from vol. 14, pp. 148–49; "Him they picked up . . . ," p. 148.

Silvio Pellico was an Italian nationalist and patriot who, in the early 1820s, was arrested by Austrian authorities and sentenced to death. His sentence was later commuted to fifteen years, and he served eight years under terrible prison conditions before being released in 1830. Two years later he published his autobiography, *Le mie prigioni* (My Prisons). The editors of the *Dictionary of Italian Literature* write that "the message of the memoirs is one of patient suffering without rancor toward the narrator's Austrian captors. As the book opens Pellico declares in retrospect that all his years of incarceration have not proved humanity to be so evil, intolerable, or unworthy as he had once imagined" (p. 391).

I have quoted from the last ten verses of "The Rime of the Ancient Mariner."

Chapter 17

John Johnston died in the Los Angeles Veterans Hospital on January 21, 1900. The cemetery where he is buried is located not far from what is now Beverly Hills. For more on his life, see *Crow Killer* by Raymond W. Thorp and Robert Bunker.

Denis McLoughlin has an entry for John Colter in his delightful book *Wild and Woolly: An Encyclopedia of the Old West,* pp. 107–8. A lengthier introduction to Colter's life may be found in vol. 8 of Hafen's *Mountain Men.* The essay is by Aubrey L. Haines (pp. 73–85).

Jim Bridger outlived two Indian wives — a Flathead and a Ute. His third wife, with whom he had two children, was a Shoshone. Bridger was a teller of tall tales, and not a few outlandish yarns have been attached to his legend. A brief, careful reconstruction of his life was made by Cornelius M. Ismert for an article ("Jim Bridger") in Hafen's *Mountain Men,* vol. 6, pp. 85–104.

The aficionado of western lore is sculptor Jamie Ely.

The name mountain men gave to the grizzly is apparently derived from the Bible: "Ephraim is joined to his idols; let him alone" (Hosea 4:17).

It is surprisingly difficult to assemble a list of the grizzly's capabilities as a predator. I suspect that this is due to the fact that in modern times, abetted by scientists and naturalists, we have developed a new respect and sympathy for animals. We see them now as being independent of ourselves rather than as creatures whose identities are defined by our needs and their relationships to us. At least one writer has suggested that because of the grizzly's attributes he is a more appropriate symbol of the United States than is the bald eagle. While I am unwilling to enter into that debate, there is no doubt that the bear is highly intelligent, possessed of a keen memory, and not aggressive toward man. He deserves the title of Monarch of the West. The reader may wonder why, if I feel this way, I have related a series of anecdotes showing the bear to be such a fearsome creature. As a practical matter, lacking an eyewitness's account of Glass's mauling, I needed to demonstrate how terrible it must have been and thus to emphasize the man's determination to live and seek revenge.

It is obvious that even given our new respect for such animals as the grizzly, we must keep them apart from us. Explorers wandering through the wilderness unfortunately could not do this and suffered as a consequence. As I wrote about the bears, I could not help but recall meeting a young woman some years before who had been savagely mauled by a grizzly. Her lasting injuries were more terrible than I care to describe. Surely we should respect Old Ephraim and do no harm to him . . . but we should also take care to leave him to his idols.

Some of the sources I have read in gathering material about bears are listed below. None of the authors will appreciate what I have done with the information. (Incidentally, a number of scientists now dispute the mountain-man tradition that female grizzlies were fiercely protective of their young. Hugh Glass, of course, would have begged to differ.) Readers wishing to know more about grizzly bears might consult the following: Bessie Doak Haynes and Edgar Haynes, eds., *The Grizzly Bear: Portraits from Life;* Frank C. Craighead, *Track of the Grizzly;* Jack Olsen, *Night of the Grizzlies;* Walter J. Schoonmaker, *The World of the Grizzly Bear;* F. M. Young and Coralie M. Beyers, eds., *Man Meets Grizzly.* There are also three relevant magazine pieces: Schoen, Miller, and Reynolds, "Last Stronghold of the Grizzly," *Natural History;* Thomas McIntyre, "American History: Grizzly," *Sports Afield;* Jim Merritt, "A 'Turrible' Animal," *Field and Stream.*

For my purposes, the best single source was F. M. Young's essay "The Characteristics of Bears," published in the anthology he and his granddaughter put together.

There are various tall tales associated with Kit Carson's meeting the two bears. Edward S. Ellis in *Kit Carson* says that the grizzlies climbed the tree after Carson, who was forced to cut off a branch and beat them over the head with it. There is a widely held belief that adult grizzlies cannot climb trees; however, I have seen a few reports by hunters and amateur naturalists who have gone deep into wild territories and claim to have seen grizzlies doing just exactly what they are not supposed to be able to do. Carson did not mention that they climbed the tree in his autobiography, although he wrote that one of them "made several attempts at the tree in which I was perched" (p. 38). The animals eventually became discouraged and went away.

The story of Captain Williams's axing of a hungry grizzly may be found in David H. Coyner's *Lost Trappers: A Collection of Interesting Scenes and Events in the Rocky Mountains.*

In borrowing from the accounts of Pattie, Thompson, Bell, Irving, and Fowler, I have generally used original sources or twentieth-century reprints, but there is no need to cite them here. Anyone wishing to read them will find that they have all been anthologized by F. M. Young. He tells us how Old Ephraim might hold you "with one arm, while clawing and striking with the other" (p. 20).

The reminiscences of James Clyman were edited by Charles L. Camp and published in San Francisco by the California Historical Society under the title *James Clyman: American Frontiersman, 1792–1881.* For the bear attack on Smith and Clyman's primitive attempt at cosmetic surgery, see pp. 25–26.

Reuben Gold Thwaites reprints Maximilian, Prince of Wied, *Travels in the Interior of North America, 1832–1834,* in vols. 22 and 23 of his collection. For the aristocrat's observations on the grizzly, see vol. 23, pp. 43–45.

I have used the following accounts for Glass's life and adventures: Charles L. Camp, ed., *James Clyman: American Frontiersman, 1792–1881;* Hiram Martin Chittenden, "Miraculous Escape of Hugh Glass," in *The American Fur Trade of the Far West,* vol. 2, pp. 698–706; Rev. Orange Clark, "The Chronicles of George C. Yount, California Pioneer of 1826," *The California Historical Society;* Philip St. George Cooke, "Some Incidents in the Life of Hugh Glass, a Hunter of the Missouri River," *St. Louis Beacon,* Dec. 2 and 9, 1830, and *Scenes and Adventures in the Army;* Edmund Flagg, "Adventures at the Headwaters of the Missouri," *Louisville Literary News Letter,* Sept. 7, 1839, pp. 326–27; James Hall, "Letters from the West, No. 14," p. 215; Aubrey L. Haines, "Hugh Glass," in Hafen, ed., *The Mountain Men,* vol. 6, pp. 161–71; Washington Irving, *A Tour on the Plains;* Dale L. Morgan, *Jedediah Smith and the Opening of the West;* John Myers Myers, *The Deaths of the Bravos* and *Pirate, Paw-*

nee, and Mountain Man; John G. Neihardt, *The Song of Hugh Glass* and *The Splendid Wayfaring;* George F. Ruxton, *Life in the Far West;* Rufus Sage, *Scenes in the Rocky Mountains.* I have a copy of a letter Daniel Potts wrote to his sister, dated Nov. 14, 1825, in which he describes Glass as being "tore nearly all to peases by a White Bear."

With so many different accounts available and lacking a first-person account from Glass, it has been necessary to piece together a version of his travail. Sometimes in the text I have indicated where sources disagree, but at other times I have simply tried to choose what seemed to me the likeliest scenario. In writing my account I have frequently consulted Aubrey Haines's article and the biography of Glass by Myers (*Pirate, Pawnee, and Mountain Man*). Readers wishing to know more about Glass would do well to begin with the latter. I have relied on Myers for Glass's life before and after the bear attack, although saying this does not begin to describe my debt to him. I used him as a guide to most of the various contemporary sources on Glass and followed his lead in writing about Glass. I found Myers to be especially helpful in coming to an understanding of Glass's travels through the wilderness.

Chapter 18

The chapter title has been taken from a novel by Thomas Keneally, *Victim of the Aurora:*

> Forbes-Chalmers was the name of a certain illusion, a trick of light that had caused members of the expedition (Kittery was the first) to report having sighted a man high up on glaciers or far out on the ice of the sound. Forbes and Chalmers were two members of Holbrooke's expeditions of 1908 who never returned from a journey across the sound to study the Taylor Glacier. Steward now gave their names to a phantasm created by light refraction.
> It was the only memorial they had. (p. 38)

The final entries in Scott's diary have often been anthologized, usually under the title "The Last March." The entire journal along with the letters he wrote while dying have been reprinted as vol. 1 of *Scott's Last Expedition,* arranged by Leonard Huxley; see chap. 20, pp. 396–417.

For material about Stefánsson's life I have drawn from the Stefánsson article in the Oct. 1942 issue of *Current Biography,* pp. 801–4, and the lengthy *New York Times* obituary, "Vilhjálmur Stefánsson, 82, Dies," Aug. 27, 1962, as well as from the biography written by Richard J. Diubaldo, entitled *Stefánsson and the Canadian Arctic.*

The list of honors and awards comes from the Stefánsson entry in *Who Was Who in America,* vol. 4, p. 900. See also Diubaldo, pp. 1–2. Gilbert Grosvenor, in his foreword to Stefánsson's *Friendly Arctic,* describes the Hubbard Medal ceremony (pp. xv–xxv). Magnus Magnusson also makes note of the event in his foreword to William Laird McKinlay's *"Karluk": The Great Untold Story of Arctic Exploration,* pp. vii–viii. Magnusson's summary of McKinlay's obsession is on p. xii.

The organization of, preparations for, and early incidents in the expedi-

tion are described by Diubaldo in chap. 4, especially on pp. 58–74. Harold
Horwood relates the story of the expedition in chap. 1 of his biography
Bartlett: The Great Canadian Explorer. For the Canadian politicians' pos-
turing, see Diubaldo, pp. 63–64. Horwood explains Bartlett's own misgiv-
ings (p. 4), and he notes Bartlett's experiences on the *Roosevelt* (pp. 73–77
and 182).

For the concerns of the scientists, see Diubaldo, pp. 80 and 89. In putting
together a narrative of the events of the expedition, I have generally followed McKinlay, with the exception of Bartlett's trip across the Siberian
ice. McKinlay recalled the appearance of the ice on p. 22 and noted the
discontent of the sailors on p. 24. Stefánsson himself admitted in *The
Friendly Arctic* that the caribou was practically extinct and claimed that he
took the poorest dogs and the worst sledges (p. 54). He expressed his
certainty that the *Karluk* would never sail again on p. 50, and he insisted
that the advancement of science was worth the loss of life on pp. 72–73.

Horwood argues that Stefánsson showed no interest in the ice-locked
ship once he was away from her (p. 5), while Diubaldo offers a contrary
opinion but cites the Mounties' report that Stefánsson left the *Karluk* just
in time (p. 82). Horwood makes the analogy between the ship and a nut
broken in a nutcracker (p. 13).

Robert Bartlett wrote two versions of his ordeal. The first was *The Last
Voyage of the "Karluk";* the second account comprises chap. 17, "Ship-
wreck And Death," in *The Log of Bob Bartlett.* I relied most heavily on
The Last Voyage because it is the earlier of the two accounts and therefore
was written while events would still have been fresh in the author's mind.
The captain's description of the last moments of the *Karluk* is from *The
Log,* pp. 266–67.

Horwood tells us that Herald Island was unapproachable (p. 15) and
speculates on the fate of those sent to establish a camp on it (p. 30).

It is Bartlett who explains the difficulty of dragging the sledges over the
ice (*The Last Voyage,* p. 106); he concludes that the men he sent to Herald
died of exhaustion (*The Log,* p. 272); and he characterizes one member of
the doctor's party as being delirious (*The Last Voyage,* p. 134). He also
depicts Kataktovik and himself as being "assailed by increasing blasts" of
wind (*The Last Voyage,* p. 171). He tells of his grief over learning of the
deaths of the men on Wrangel in *The Last Voyage,* p. 314.

McKinlay reprints portions of Mamen's diary on pp. 113–16.

Stefánsson's remarks about pemmican are to be found on pp. 486 and
718 of *The Friendly Arctic.* Peary makes his comments in *Secrets of Polar
Travel,* pp. 78–79 and 83.

It should be stressed that McKinlay does not make any statement indicating or implying that Breddy was murdered — other than the odd word-
ing of the chapter title. It is my speculation that Breddy's death was a
homicide, although I cannot deduce who the murderer was.

For more about Bob Bartlett's activities after the rescue, see Horwood.
I have used Diubaldo's biography in putting together the material on the
famed explorer's later life. Maurer had been critical of Stefánsson's behavior on the *Karluk*'s voyage, so why he consented to be sent by him to

Wrangel is a mystery. For more on this disaster, see Diubaldo, especially pp. 182–83.

In *My Life as an Explorer* Roald Amundsen suggests that Stefánsson's promotion of the " 'Friendly Arctic' . . . is likely to give dangerous ideas to inexperienced explorers" (pp. 228–29). He then proceeds to give a thoroughly damning critique of the notion from which I have quoted twice in the text of my book. Amundsen also debunks what is supposed to be one of Stefánsson's greatest achievements — the finding of the "Blond Eskimoes." He argues that they are simply the second-generation offspring of Caucasian visitors and Eskimo women.

Chapter 19

William Clayton's encounter with Tarzan is described in "At The Mercy of The Jungle," chap. 14 of *Tarzan of the Apes*. Burroughs was a failure at a variety of jobs, including cattle drover, railroad policeman, and law clerk. Out of work at the age of thirty-seven, he penned a novella entitled *Under the Moon of Mars* and sold it to *All-Story* magazine for four hundred dollars. A few months later he wrote a story called "Tarzan of the Apes," for which the same publication paid him seven hundred dollars.

He went on to found the town of Tarzana, California. Such is the continuing interest in Tarzan and Burroughs's other creations that in 1974 alone, Edgar Rice Burroughs, Inc., a privately held company, grossed one million dollars from sale of the books and the licensing of rights to use the Tarzan name. (See "Me Tarzan, Me Rich," by the editors of *Forbes*.) Not a bad return for the work of an author who wrote his first story on the backs of the letterhead stationery of the failed companies he had started. Readers wishing to know more about Burroughs's life and works should begin by consulting Edward T. Ewen's *New York Times Magazine* article, " 'Eh-wa-au-wau-aoooow!' "

Gore Vidal wrote a thoughtful and surprisingly positive essay, "Tarzan Revisited," for *Esquire* magazine.

For more on the idea of the wilderness in western culture and the impressions of the early explorers of the New World, see Leo Marx's *Machine in the Garden: Technology and the Pastoral Idea in America*.

My principal source in putting together the chapter on Joseph Knowles is his own book, *Alone in the Wilderness*. I have also used a considerable number of newspaper accounts of his adventures. These will be identified below, but I would like to express my debt to the authors of three magazine articles whose work I found most useful: Gerald Carson's "Yankee Tarzan" in *American Heritage;* Stewart H. Holbrook, "The Original Nature Man," *The American Mercury;* and Lois Lowry, "Tarzan of the Maine Woods," *Down East*.

Knowles told of his journey to Megantic in chap. 18, "The Inside Story of the Canadian Trip." Gerald Carson suggests that the stunt may have been the brain child of McKeogh, who had "read *Robinsoe Crusoe* and suddenly, possibly recalling Crusoe's man, Friday, began to think enthusiastically about such matters as 'Tuesday: kills bear' and money" (p. 61). For

Knowles's own version of his moment of inspiration, see *Alone in the Wilderness,* pp. 3–5. Photographs of Joe's dramatic preparations to enter into the woods were published in his book. He describes his early adventures in chap. 2, "The First Days in the Wilderness." In chap. 5, "Trapping a Bear," he tells how he dug the pit (pp. 66–67) and clubbed his quarry to death (pp. 69–70). His dubious claim to have killed a deer with his bare hands is made on p. 146. He devotes more pages to his mental anguish than perhaps any other topic; these make up the bulk of chaps. 6 and 7, pp. 79–125.

Gerald Carson relates the hiring of Allie Deming and the premature retirement of the regular guide in "Yankee Tarzan," p. 62. While Carson and Lowry write about Knowles's chicanery with humor and affection, Wendell Tremblay takes a somewhat harsher view, and those wishing a fuller catalogue of Joe's sins than I have provided should locate Trembly's article "And Naked Into the Woods He Went," the *Maine Sunday Telegram,* Aug. 12, 1973.

The Primitive Man's visit to Portland and his being feted at the banquet is chronicled in "Has Won Peculiar Distinction," a very long and comprehensive article in the *Portland Daily Eastern Argus,* Oct. 9, 1913.

In describing Knowles's "triumphant progress" to Boston and his reception there, I have made use not only of his own account (pp. 278–85), but of articles in the *Boston Post, Globe,* and *Herald.* Both Carson and Lowry delightfully sketch the events, and I have drawn from their articles as well. As far as the contemporary reports go, I have found the following *Post* articles to be most helpful: "Knowles Quits Woods Near Megantic Today," Oct. 4, 1913; "Knowles, Clad in Skins, Comes Out of Forest," Oct. 5, 1913; Paul Waitt, "Native Son Knowles Greets His Parents," Oct. 8, 1913; Paul Waitt, "Knowles, Man of the Woods, to Reach Boston This Noon," Oct. 9, 1913; Paul Waitt, "Knowles, the Modern Forest Man, Welcomed by Cheering Thousands," Oct. 10, 1913; "Forest Man Honor[ed] Guest," Oct. 12, 1913. This last story and the others that do not have a by-line were probably written by Waitt. He had a distinctive gift for sensational reporting and had accompanied Knowles on his entire journey from Megantic to Boston.

"Making a fire without a license" is Waitt's phrase. Lois Lowry tells us that one woman shyly admitted that she had prayed for Joe every night (p. 75). The incident is described by Waitt in "Knowles, Man of the Woods."

It is not possible to overstate the adulation with which Joe was greeted wherever he went. A kind of mass hysteria was at work. At the Boston railway station, for instance, where a "mighty throng" awaited Joe, as he prepared to join the parade, "A rush was made for the autos on Tremont Street. Men climbed the wire fences and rushed across the grass. For a time police lost all control. The people seemed mad over Knowles" (Paul Waitt, "Knowles, the Modern Forest Man").

Waitt recounted Knowles's visit to Harvard and the adoration of the Radcliffe girls, but he was presumably too embarrassed by the behavior of Dr. Sargent's pupils to write about it. I have drawn my reference to these excited young ladies from Lowry (p. 75).

The advertisement for Filene's appeared in the Oct. 10, 1913, issue of the *Post.*

In 1973 Wendell Trembly interviewed Helon Taylor, and he published the results in the *Sunday Telegram* article "And Naked Into the Woods He Went." My description of both Knowles's indignation over the charge that he was a fraud and his consequent killing of the sleepy bear comes from Trembly. Another *Telegram* reporter, C. Hasty Thompson, also seems to have interviewed the cooperative Mr. Taylor — or had access to Trembly's notes — because he quoted the park superintendent in writing two articles for the *Sunday Telegram:* "Nature Man's Exploits in Maine Raised Doubts," July 7, 1985; and "Doubters Saw Nature Man as Flimflam Artist," July 14, 1985.

The *Nation* carried a review of *Alone in the Wilderness* in the Feb. 19, 1914, issue.

I used copies of the *San Francisco Examiner* articles in reconstructing Knowles's California sojourn. Stewart H. Holbrook tells the story of Joe's third and last attempt to live the primitive life in "The Original Nature Man," published by *The American Mercury.* Holbrook's irreverent remark about boozy cameramen photographing Miss Hammerstein in semi-Dawn attire is found on p. 424.

The Jan. 1921 issue of *American Magazine* contained the piece by Fred Lockley, "A Modern Cave Man." I suspect that Lockley was actually looking for Knowles, but he writes as if he accidentally stumbled on the old man. After the Wilton native moved out west, Holbrook ran across him working in a new hotel in Longview, Washington; Joe had been commissioned to do a series of murals in the lobby, the theme of which was "Pioneer Scenes in the Northwest." It seems probable that such commissions came his way at least as much because of his notoriety as his skill with a brush. (See Holbrook's *Far Corner: A Personal View of the Pacific Northwest,* p. 7.) Holbrook tells of his interview with Joe at his cabin on p. 425 of "The Original Nature Man." Knowles insisted to Holbrook that he bore those who tried to debunk his feats no animosity, but he added that he would not answer "letters or other queries" about his "Back-to-Nature experiments."

The epitaph was published in the *Portland Press Herald,* Oct. 23, 1942.

Chapter 20

A good general source on the early history of aviation is the *American Heritage Book of Flight.* Don Dwiggins has written a wonderfully anecdotal account of barnstormers in *The Air Devils.* According to Leonard Mosley, the author of *Lindbergh: A Biography,* "Daredevil" Lindbergh "learned how to hang below a wing by his teeth (thanks to a wire hooked from the plane to a harness concealed beneath his flying jacket)" (p. 43). (By the way, "Lucky" was a nickname given to Lindbergh by the press, and it was one he disdained; his friends referred to him as Slim.) Presumably not all barnstormers were so foolish or cavalier as to do without parachutes: early in his days as a flier, Lindbergh even learned to make double parachute jumps; that is, the first chute having opened, he cut it away and fell unrestrained until the second chute opened (Mosley, pp. 40–42).

As for my comment that those who toiled on the ground were ants to those among the clouds, Saint-Exupéry referred to the former as termites or ants.

The Orteig Prize was named for the man who proposed it, Raymond Orteig. (Sources variously describe him as a Frenchman and a New York hotel owner. The two are not mutually exclusive, of course, but I suspect that there is confusion over Mr. Orteig's identity.) The prize was to go to any flier or team of fliers "who shall cross the Atlantic in a land or water aircraft (heavier than air) from Paris or the shores of France to New York, or from New York to Paris or *the shores of France,* without stop" (emphasis mine). Eighteen hundred tons of ticker tape were used in the parade for Lindbergh, and he was offered a total of five million dollars in commercial endorsements. A group of businessmen even proposed giving him one million dollars with no strings attached so that he would not have to cheapen his reputation with commercialism. They were turned down (see Mosley, p. 118).

Mosley describes Lindbergh's midair collision on pp. 57–59.

In writing about Rickenbacker I have used two obituaries: "Capt. Eddie Rickenbacker Is Dead at 82," *New York Times,* July 24, 1973; and "Captain Eddie," *Newsweek.* I have also used, of course, Captain Eddie's autobiography, *Rickenbacker.* Captain Eddie described the first ordeal in chap. 12, pp. 269–85. The wartime travail is the more famous of the two because of its unparalleled media coverage, and the book he wrote about it shortly after he was rescued is titled *Seven Came Through.* A summary of it may be found in the autobiography in chap. 16, 296–339.

For an account of Saint-Ex's first serious accident, see *Antoine de Saint-Exupéry* by Joy D. Marie Robinson, p. 20. She describes his second crash on pp. 76–77. He made the remark about it in *Wind, Sand and Stars;* the translation is hers. For the third crash, see Robinson, p. 87.

Robinson's book is concise and clear, but those who become interested in the French aviator will also want to read *The Story of Saint-Exupéry,* by Marcel Migeo. It is translated by Herma Briffault. Migeo was a friend of Saint-Ex's, and his biography is much more detailed and anecdotal than that written by Robinson. A third source I have consulted is Curtis Cate's *Antoine de Saint-Exupéry.*

New translations of Saint-Exupéry's works have been appearing in recent years, but during his own lifetime his writings were rendered into English by Galantière. The two men were friends and worked closely together, and I have used the Galantière translation of *Wind, Sand and Stars.* The story of the desert crash is to be found in chap. 8, pp. 173–236. All the quotations I have used are drawn from that chapter, with the exception of those otherwise identified.

Saint-Ex writes of Mermoz's travail in the Andes in *Wind, Sand and Stars,* pp. 39–41. Guillaumet was forced to live in his snow cave for forty-eight hours before starting his climb out of the Andes. The ordeal is described on pp. 48–60.

Like his friend Saint-Exupéry, Guillaumet died in harness: in 1940, his unarmed transport plane was shot down at sea (see Migeo, p. 75).

Readers may also be interested in Lewis Galantière's recollections of his friend, "Antoine de Saint-Exupéry," *The Atlantic Monthly.*

Chapter 21

In writing of the improvements in search techniques and survival gear, I did not mean to suggest that World War II marked the beginning of efforts to protect and save survivors. Certainly there were organized, careful searches made for individuals before the 1940s. (The 1937 search for Amelia Earhart was so extensive that it cost an estimated four million dollars.) But in collecting survival narratives I could not help but be impressed with how the war seemed to focus attention on the plights of survivors and to act as a catalyst for change in the materials and procedures used to protect and locate them. To give just one example, after his ordeal, Eddie Rickenbacker brought together the manufacturers of survival gear and coordinated efforts to improve the design of equipment, especially rubber rafts, which came to be known in his honor as Rickenbackers.

Dr. Alain Bombard would not appreciate my repeated references throughout this book to the long-held belief that drinking sea water causes castaways to go insane and die. In the fall of 1962, Dr. Bombard, then a twenty-eight-year-old graduate of medical school, spent sixty-five days adrift in a raft in order to prove that castaways might live almost indefinitely on what the sea provides and that the drinking of moderate amounts of sea water, far from bringing on madness and death, would sustain a survivor. Ideally, according to his observations, sweet water and sea water should be mixed in a ratio of two to one as a way of extending the life of the sweet-water rations. "If you do not have [sweet] water," he told Tony Roberts in 1982, "drink sea water to survive until you can catch rainwater or a fish for squeezing, or help arrives." At the very time Bombard was talking with Roberts, however, the World Health Organization was reaffirming its official position that sea water should not be drunk even mixed with fresh water; thus it can be argued that the matter is still not settled and remains controversial.

The French physician wrote a book about his experience, which, as you might imagine, was not an altogether pleasant one: *The Voyage of the Hérétique.* In addition to the book and Roberts's article, published in *Oceans,* those wishing to know more about him and his ordeal might wish to consult two other articles: "Young Man and the Sea," *Time;* "On a Raft With Food Only From the Sea," *Life.*

1942. Lieutenant Commander H. R. Kabat wrote about his ordeal in "Bare Fists Against a Shark," *The Saturday Evening Post.*

The USS *Juneau.* I have based my account on a declassified debriefing interview with Allen Clifton Heyn on Oct. 28, 1944. The transcript was supplied to me by the Navy Department, but those wishing to read it will find an abridged version published as "One Who Survived," *American Heritage.* After he recovered, Heyn was a gunner and torpedo reloader on a submarine credited with sinking five enemy ships. At the time of the interview he felt that those sinkings, in which he had taken an active part, were just revenge for the *Juneau:* "That's really what I wanted to go out on the sub for," he told Lieutenant Porter. "I don't know, it made me feel awful good when we got them, because one of them was a troop ship and it was full of them. You could see them hanging over the sides and everything" (p. 16). No prisoners were rescued from any of the five.

Samuel Eliot Morison describes the destruction of the *Juneau* in *The Two-Ocean War: A Short History of the United States Navy in the Second World War.* The Feb. 25, 1950, issue of *The Saturday Evening Post* contains a much fuller account of the sinking and the aftermath (including an update on the lives of the few survivors): Robert L. Schwartz, "The Terrible End of the USS *Juneau.*"

1943. Flight Captain C. J. Rosbert told of his ordeal in "Only God Knew the Way," *The Saturday Evening Post.*

1944. Lieutenant Paul Madden's two-part article, "Tragic Voyage," appeared in *The Saturday Evening Post.*

1945. Inez Robb collaborated with Corporal Margaret Hastings for "A WAC in Shangri-la," published by International News Service. It was reprinted in the *Reader's Digest.* Shelly Mydans interviewed all three survivors for "Suzy From Shangri-la," *Life.* I have drawn some details from Mydans, as I have from "New Guinea Adventure," *Newsweek.*

Another useful source is John E. Carlova's "The Lost World of Lavani," *The American Mercury.* Carlova relates Lavani's belated and perhaps unfortunate discovery by the geologist John Zehnder. A recent treatment of the ordeal is to be found in "Deliverance From Shangri-la," chap. 12, of Gerard M. Devlin's *Silent Wings: The Story of the Glider Pilots of World War II.* I did not use Devlin, having only just obtained a copy of it, but it might be a good place to begin for those who want to learn more about the incident.

Louis Zamperini told his own story in his autobiography, *Devil at My Heels,* but I have drawn some material from the Robert Trumbull article "Zamperini, Olympic Miler, Is Safe After Epic Survival," *New York Times,* Sept. 9, 1945. Trumbull interviewed Zamperini when events were still fresh in the lieutenant's mind. I suspect that Zamperini left out of his autobiography some of the unpleasant details he told the reporter, because after his conversion and his subsequent ministry to the Japanese prison guards who mistreated him, he may have wanted to downplay some of their brutality.

1949. The Greenland castaways were given wide coverage by newspapers, but the two best articles appeared in *Time:* "And Then There Were 13"; and "Welcome Home."

1951. Ted Sierks wrote about his ordeal in "Don't Give Up, You Weakling!" *Life.* See also "Man Overboard," *Time.*

1957. The best single source for the ordeal of Lieutenant Steeves is "The Strange Case of the Sierra Survivor," *Life. Life's* photographer even got a snapshot of an obligingly tame deer. I also gathered facts from other articles: "Bad Earth," *Time;* "Return to the Living," *Newsweek;* " 'As It Happened . . . ,' " *Newsweek;* "Certain Discrepancies," *Time.* See also the following *New York Times* articles: "Flier — Lost 8 Weeks In Sierras Survives," July 2, 1957; Lawrence E. Davies, "Lost Pilot Tells of Sierra

Ordeal," July 3, 1957; Edith Evans Asbury, " 'Dead' Flier Joins His Family Here," July 5, 1957; "Flier and Wife Part," Dec. 28, 1957.

1960. My principal source for the fate of the crew of the *Lady Be Good* was "Desert Gives Up Its Secret," *Life*. Another pertinent magazine piece is "Find Strayed Bomber," *Science News Letter*. From the *New York Times:* "Air Force To Study '43 Crash in Sahara," June 5, 1959; "B-24 Recently Found in Libya Took Off in '43 to Raid Naples," June 6, 1959; "Airmen Died in Desert," June 9, 1959; "Search for Airmen Fruitless," June 17, 1959.

For more on the four Soviet sailors, see "Saved At Sea Just in Time," *Life;* "Four Simple Soviet Lads," *Time;* "49 Tortured Days," *Newsweek*. From the *New York Times:* Jack Raymond, "Four Russians Adrift 49 Days Saved by U.S. Carrier in Pacific," Mar. 9, 1960; "Moscow Hails Rescue," Mar. 13, 1960; Max Frankel, "U.S. Navy Rescue Pleases Moscow," Mar. 15, 1960; Lawrence E. Davies, "San Francisco Greets Four Russians Saved at Sea," Mar. 16, 1960; "Khrushchev Hails U.S. for Rescue of 4 Sailors," Mar. 17, 1960; "4 Soviet Sailors Here," Mar. 18, 1960; "Eisenhower Replies," Mar. 23, 1960; "Russians Homebound," Mar. 24, 1960; "Soviet Sailors in Paris," Mar. 29, 1960; Osgood Caruthers, "Moscow Lionizes 4 Rescued by U.S. Ship," Mar. 30, 1960.

Senior Sergeant Peter A. Foley wrote two accounts of the ditching of the Flying Tiger Super-H Constellation. The first, published in the *New York Times* of Sept. 26, 1962, is entitled "Survivor Tells of Plane Ditching: Jokes and Fear, and Then Crash." The second article, upon which I have relied heavily, is "We Ditched at Sea: The Ordeal of Flying Tiger 923," *The Saturday Evening Post*. In the aftermath of the crash, questions were raised about the adequacy of onboard survival gear, and Congressional hearings were held. The following *New York Times* articles are pertinent: "U.S. Plane With 76 Ditches in Ocean," Sept. 24, 1962; Lawrence Fellows, "16 From Airliner Hunted in Ocean," Sept. 25, 1962; Lawrence Fellows, "Atlantic Search in Ditching Ends," Sept. 26, 1962; Richard Witkin, "Ditching Raises Vest-light Issue," Sept. 27, 1962; "4 More in Ditching Flown to London," Sept. 28, 1962; "Stewardesses Tell House Unit Pilots Let Them Fly Airliners" and "Pilot Says Light Saved 48 in Sea," Sept. 29, 1962; Richard Witkin, "Ditching Inquiry Is Told of 'Goof,' " Nov. 15, 1962; Richard Witkin, "Loopholes Cited in Ditching Case," Sept. 16, 1962; Edward Hudson, "Hearing Focuses on Ditching Drill," Sept. 17, 1962.

1969. For more about the Cuban refugee Armando Ramirez, see "The Survivor," *Newsweek*. From the *New York Times:* Richard Elder, "Cuban Hidden in Landing Gear Survives . . . ," June 5, 1969; "Airliner Stowaway Hopes to Get to U.S.," June 6, 1969; "How Much Stress Can the Body Stand?" June 8, 1969; "Young Cuban Takes Easier Flight Here," July 27, 1969.

1971. Ron Woodcock consented to two interviews with me. Where he was uncertain about minor facts, I have referred to Joseph P. Blank's article, "Ron Woodcock's Long Walk Home," *Reader's Digest*.

Don M. Campbell described his ordeal in "Nightmare on Missinaibi," *Outdoor Life*.

Three articles that Juliane Koepcke wrote for the German magazine

Stern were condensed in *Reader's Digest* ("Nightmare in the Jungle"). I have also used several other sources: Robert G. Hummerstone, "She Lived and 91 Others Died," *Life;* Ralph Graves, "A Jungle Search That Ends in Mystery," *Life;* and "The Survivor," *Newsweek.* From the *New York Times:* "Plane With 92 Lost on Peruvian Flight," Dec. 26, 1971; "Missing Peruvian Airliner Believed to Have Crashed," Dec. 27, 1971; "Survivor of Crash Found in Peru," Jan. 5, 1972; "Airliner Wreckage Is Sighted In Peru," Jan. 6, 1972.

1972. The capture of Sergeant Shoichi Yokoi excited the interest of the American public, and a number of articles were written about him. I have used three magazine pieces: "The Last Blossom," *Newsweek;* "Last Soldier," *Time;* "Rip Van Yokoi," *Time.* From the *New York Times:* "Hermit on Guam Says He's Japanese Noncom," Jan. 25, 1972; "Reunion for Japanese Veterans," Jan. 27, 1972; "His War Is Finally Over," Jan. 30, 1972; John M. Lee, "Japan Debates Spirit of War Holdout," Jan. 31, 1972; "5,000 Japanese Welcome Ex-Soldier," Feb. 3, 1972; John M. Lee, "At Home, Japanese Who Hid . . . Says 'I'm Ashamed but I've Come Back,' " April 26, 1972; "A Traditionalist at Heart," April 30, 1972; "The Saga of Shoichi," Sept. 30, 1972.

Carole Taylor's article was appropriately entitled "Ordeal in the Snow," *Reader's Digest.*

Newsweek covered the story of Lieutenant Hiro Onoda in two articles: "Voices in the Wilderness" and "Where It Is Still 1945." From the *New York Times:* "2 Japanese Holdouts Shot in Philippines," Oct. 21, 1972; "Japan's Soldiers Sought in Burma," Nov. 13, 1972.

Onoda did not remain in the jungle for the rest of his life. On March 9, 1974, under the pretense that he would be issued new combat orders, he was lured into a meeting with his former commanding officer, Major Taniguchi, who ordered him to cease operations. Later that year Onoda wrote a book about his experience, *No Surrender: My Thirty-Year War.*

1974. The best single source for the trial of Captain Cyril LaBrecque is the partial transcript published in *Federal Cases,* 419 F. Supp. 430 (1976), especially pp. 432–34. However, readers might begin with Michael Levitt's "Trial by Water," in *Motor Boat and Sailing.* Levitt brings out all of the pertinent facts in the case and quotes extensively from courtroom testimony. The article is clear and straightforward; I found it very helpful as I wrote about LaBrecque. From the *New York Times:* "2 Die, 4 Rescued at Sea As Schooner Hits Shoals," Nov. 30, 1974; "Inquiry Blames Yachtsman In Drowning of 2 in Crew," July 10, 1974; "Captain Indicted In Deaths at Sea," May 21, 1975; "Jurors Chosen in Lifeboat Case Against a Skipper," May 5, 1976; Donald Janson, "Government Rests Manslaughter Case Against Captain Who Kept 2 Out of Boat," May 11, 1976; Donald Janson, "Mate of Sunken Schooner Testifies for the Captain," May 12, 1976; Donald Janson, "Captain Says He Feared Lifeboat Upset," May 13, 1976; Donald Janson, "Lawyer Pictures Captain as Hero," May 14, 1976; Donald Janson, "Schooner's Captain Freed in Death of 2 Off Lifeboat," May 15, 1976.

1976. My sole source in describing the ordeal of Lauren Elder was the book she wrote with Shirley Streshinsky, *And I Alone Survived.*

1979. Jim Rearden interviewed Denise Harris and Roger Lewis while they were recovering in a hospital. The transcript was published in two parts in *Alaska, The Magazine of Life on the Last Frontier,* under the title "We Nearly Froze to Death." Joseph P. Blank also interviewed the couple for " 'We Want to Live!' " *Reader's Digest.*

1981. The best single source for information on John Harrison and his family is Malcolm Gray's article, "Scenario with an Unexpected Twist," *MacLean's* magazine. I have also used the following AP and UPI reports as published in the *New York Times:* "Family Rescued in Pacific," Dec. 7, 1981; "Yachtsman Sails to Aid of Marooned Canadians," Dec. 30, 1981; "Stranded Family Declines Aid," Dec. 31, 1981; "Legal Problems Delay Family's Island Rescue," Jan. 2, 1982; "3 Marooned on Island Arrive in Honolulu," Jan. 6, 1982.

In making brief references to recent ordeals I have used the following articles (many of which were based on AP or UPI reports):

"A Diary of Death in Alaska," *Akron Beacon Journal,* Dec. 15, 1982 (Carl McCunn).

"Marine Eats Ants Five Weeks in Ravine," *Cleveland Plain Dealer,* July 26, 1983 (Karl Bell).

"Man Left to Die at Sea Lives to Seek Justice," *Massillon Evening Independent,* Jan. 31, 1985 (Russell Scott).

"Prayers, Cookies, Save Four," *Massillon Evening Independent,* Mar. 4, 1985 (Joao Medeiros).

"Girl Clings to Flotsam 12 Hours, Is Rescued," *Akron Beacon Journal,* May 30, 1986 (Desiree Rodriguez).

"After 41 Years Hiding in Pigsty, Red Army Deserter Is Discovered," *Akron Beacon Journal,* May 27, 1985 (Pavel Navrotsky).

"Man Adrift in Atlantic Seven Weeks," *Massillon Evening Independent,* Oct. 6, 1986 (Nelson McIntosh).

Jon Nordheimer, "Schooner Survivors Describe Ordeal," *New York Times,* May 21, 1986 (*Pride of Baltimore*).

Saundra Saperstein, "Historical Schooner Lost at Sea," *Akron Beacon Journal,* May 20, 1986 (*Pride of Baltimore*).

Scott Jeffrey, "When the *Pride of Baltimore* Sank, Eight Sailors Got a Crash Course in Ocean Survival," *People Weekly.*

Lou Zamperini wrote of his postwar life in *Devil at My Heels.* John McCollom and Kenneth Decker both consented to interviews with me. I attempted to locate Margaret Hastings, by the way, but was told that she had died several years before. Like her two fellow survivors, her later life was associated with aviation — at least one of the jobs she had was at an airport in New York State.

I interviewed Ron Woodcock twice and had several long conversations with Steve Callahan.

It was survivor James Tobin who remarked about how he had developed an appreciation for the little things in life (S. A. Schreiner, "One Handhold from Death," *Reader's Digest*).

One last observation should be made. My study has focused on people who had been in jeopardy *and* isolation, most of them having been alone for relatively long periods of time. There is another distinctly different kind of survivor, one who has experienced what might be called, for want of a better word, an "instant" ordeal. For example, I once interviewed a man who had been a passenger on a jumbo jet that had crashed immediately after takeoff, coming down just beyond the runway and catching fire on impact. A few passengers died in the crash and in the smoke and flames that followed, but most managed to escape through the emergency exits. Ambulances arrived very quickly, and the passengers were hurried into them and raced to a hospital.

It is my impression that this man and other survivors of such instant ordeals have a much more difficult time coming to terms with their experiences than do such survivors as I have written about. The very brevity of this type of travail seems to be scaring. There is no time to examine and adjust to one's plight, to experience a variety of emotions (including hope), to take considered action on one's own behalf, to reflect on one's life, and, perhaps most important of all, to get past initial terror and learn to function despite fear. Thus, ironically, in terms of lasting psychological and emotional damage, the survivor who finds himself in a strange, empty place may be better off than one who falls into calamity in an urban area. For the abandoned soul, solitude offers the time and opportunity to grapple with horror and to assert one's essential humanity in the midst of distress.

Bibliography

Books

American Heritage Book of Flight. New York: American Heritage, 1962.

Amundsen, Roald. *My Life as an Explorer.* New York: Doubleday, Page & Co., 1927.

Ashton, John, ed. *Real Sailor Songs.* New York: Benjamin Blom, 1972.

Ashton, Philip. *Ashton's Memorial: An History of the Strange Adventures and Signal Deliverances of Mr. Philip Ashton.* Boston: Samuel Gerrish, 1725.

Bailey, Derrick Sherwin. *Homosexuality and the Christian Tradition.* New York: Longmans, Green & Co., 1955.

Baldwin, Hanson W. *Sea Fights and Shipwrecks: True Tales of the Seven Seas.* Garden City, N.Y.: Hanover House, 1955.

Bartlett, Robert A., and Ralph T. Hale. *The Last Voyage of the "Karluk": Flagship of Vilhjálmar Stefánsson's Canadian Arctic Expedition of 1913–16.* Boston: Small, Maynard & Co., 1916.

————. *The Log of Bob Bartlett: The True Story of Forty Years of Seafaring and Exploration.* New York: Blue Ribbon Books, 1928.

Bell, Horace. *On The Old West Coast, Being Further Reminiscences of a Ranger, Major Horace Bell.* Edited by Lanier Bartlett. New York: William Morrow & Co., 1930.

Bennet, George. *Journal of the Voyages and Travels by the Rev. Daniel Tyerman and George Bennet, Esq.* Vol. 2. London: Frederick Westley & A. H. Davis, 1831.

Biggar, H. P., ed. *A Collection of Documents Relating to Jacques Cartier and The Sieur De Roberval.* Ottawa: Public Archives of Canada, 1930.

Blair, Clay. *Survive!* New York: Berkley Publishing Group, 1973.

Bligh, William. *A Voyage to the South Sea.* New York: New American Library, 1961.

Bombard, Alain. *The Voyage of the Hérétique.* New York: Simon & Schuster, 1954.

Boorstin, Daniel J. *The Discoverers.* New York: Vintage Books, 1985.

Boswell, John. *Christianity, Social Tolerance, and Homosexuality: Gay People in Western Europe from the Beginning of the Christian Era to the Fourteenth Century.* Chicago: University of Chicago Press, 1980.

Boyd, Elizabeth French. *Byron's "Don Juan": A Critical Study.* New York: The Humanities Press, 1958.

Boyer, Elizabeth. *A Colony of One: The History of a Brave Woman.* Novelty, Ohio: Veritie Press, 1983.

———. *Marguerite de la Roque, A Story of Survival.* Novelty, Ohio: Veritie Press, 1975.

Bradford, Ernle. *The Wind Commands Me: A Life of Sir Francis Drake.* New York: Harcourt, Brace & World, 1965.

Brady, Cyrus Townsend. *South American Flights and Fighters and Other Tales of Adventure.* New York: Doubleday, Page & Co., 1910.

Brebner, John Bartlet. *Canada: A Modern History.* Ann Arbor: University of Michigan Press, 1970.

Bullough, Vern L. *Homosexuality: A History from Ancient Greece to Gay Liberation.* New York: New American Library, 1979.

Burg, B. R. *Sodomy and the Perception of Evil: English Sea Rovers in the Seventeenth Century.* Caribbean, N.Y.: New York University Press, 1983.

Burroughs, Edgar Rice. *Tarzan of the Apes.* New York: Ballantine Books, 1983.

Byron, George Gordon Lord. *Don Juan.* In *The Works of Lord Byron.* Vol. 9. Boston: L. C. Page & Co., 1903.

Byron, John. *Narrative of the Honorable John Byron (Commodore in a late expedition round the world) containing an account of the great distresses suffered by himself and his companions on the coast of Patagonia.* 2d ed. London: S. Baker & G. Leigh, 1768.

Camp, Charles L., ed. *James Clyman: American Frontiersman, 1792–1881. The Adventures of a Trapper and Covered Wagon Emigrant as Told in His Own Reminiscences and Diaries.* Edited by Charles L. Camp. San Francisco: California Historical Society, 1928.

Carlisle, Henry. *The Jonah Man.* New York: Alfred A. Knopf, 1984.

Carson, Kit. *Kit Carson's Autobiography.* Edited by Milo Milton Quaife. Chicago: The Lakeside Press, 1935.

Cate, Curtis. *Antoine de Saint-Exupéry.* New York: G. P. Putnam's Sons, 1970.

Chase, Owen. *Narrative of The Most Extraordinary and Distressing Shipwreck of the whale-ship "Essex."* New York: W. B. Gilley, 1821.

———. *The Wreck of the Whaleship "Essex": A Narrative Account by Owen Chase, First Mate.* Edited by Iola Haverstick and Betty Shepard. New York: Harcourt, Brace & World, 1965.

Chittenden, Hiram Martin. *The American Fur Trade of the Far West.* 3 vols. New York: Francis P. Harper, 1902.

Cicero, Marcus Tullius. *De officiis.* Translated by Walter Miller. Cambridge: Harvard University Press, 1913.

———. *On Moral Obligation.* Translated by John Higginbotham. Berkeley: University of California Press, 1967.

Connell, Evan S. *A Long Desire.* New York: Holt, Rinehart & Winston, 1979.

———. *Son of the Morning Star: Custer and the Little Big Horn.* San Francisco: Northpoint Press, 1984.

———. *The White Lantern.* New York: Holt, Rinehart & Winston, 1980.

Cooke, Edward. *A Voyage to the South Sea and Round the World in the Years 1708 to 1711.* 2 vols. New York: Da Capo Press, 1969.

Cooke, Philip St. George. *Scenes and Adventures in the Army.* Philadelphia: Carey & Hart, 1857.

Cowper, William. *Poetic Works.* Edited by H. S. Milford. 4th ed. London: Oxford University Press, 1967.

Coyner, David H. *The Lost Trappers: A Collection of Interesting Scenes and Events in the Rocky Mountains.* Cincinnati: J. A. James, 1847.

Craighead, Frank C. *Track of the Grizzly.* San Francisco: Sierra Club Books, 1979.

Cunningham, Richard. *The Place Where the World Ends: A Modern Story of Cannibalism and Human Courage.* New York: Sheed & Ward, 1973.

Daiches, David. *Robert Louis Stevenson and His World.* London: Thames & Hudson, 1973.

Dampier, William. *A New Voyage Round the World.* New York: Dover Publications, 1968.

———. *Voyages and Discoveries.* London: Argonaut Press, 1931.

Dean, John. *A Narrative of the Shipwreck of the "Nottingham Galley," in Her Voyage from England to Boston.* Reprint of 5th ed. Portland, Maine: The Provincial Press, 1968.

Defoe, Daniel. *A General History of The Pyrates, from Their First Rise . . . to The Present Time.* London: T. Warner, 1724.

———. *Robinson Crusoe.* New York: New American Library, 1961.

de la Mare, Walter. *Desert Islands and Robinson Crusoe.* New York: Farrar & Rinehart, 1930.

Devlin, Gerald M. *Silent Wings: The Story of the Glider Pilots of World War II.* London: W. H. Allen, 1985.

DeVoto, Bernard Augustine. *Across the Wide Missouri.* Boston: Houghton Mifflin Co., 1947.

Dictionary of American Biography. Edited by Dumas Malone. New York: Charles Scribner's Sons, 1933.

Dictionary of Italian Literature. Edited by Peter and Julia Bondanello. Westport, Conn.: Greenwood Press, 1979.

Diubaldo, Richard J. *Stefánsson and the Canadian Arctic.* Montreal: McGill-Queen's University Press, 1978.

Dwiggins, Don. *The Air Devils.* Philadelphia: J. B. Lippincott, 1966.

Elder, Lauren, with Shirley Streshinsky. *And I Alone Survived.* New York: E. P. Dutton, 1978.

Ellis, Edward S. *Kit Carson.* Chicago: M. A. Donahue Co., 1899.

Ellms, Charles. *The Pirate's Own Book or Authentic Narratives of the Lives, Exploits and Executions of the Most Celebrated Sea Robbers.* Boston: S. N. Dickinson, 1837.

————. *Robinson Crusoe's Own Book; or, The Voice of Adventure From the Civilized Man Cut Off From His Fellows.* Boston: Joshua V. Pierce, 1843.

————. *Shipwrecks and Disasters at Sea; or, Historical Narratives of the Most Noted Calamities, and Providential Deliverances From Fire and Famine, on the Ocean.* Philadelphia: Thomas Cowperthwait & Co., 1849.

Farr, Finis. *Rickenbacker's Luck: An American Life.* Boston: Houghton Mifflin Co., 1979.

Fenwick, Robert W. *Alfred Packer: The True Story of Colorado's Man Eater.* Denver: Denver Post, 1963.

Fowler, Jacob. *The Journal of Jacob Fowler, 1821–22.* Edited by Elliot Coues. New York: Francis P. Harper, 1898.

Francis Drake, Privateer: Contemporary Narratives and Documents. Edited by John Hampden. London: Eyre Methuen, 1972.

Gantt, Paul H. *The Case of Alfred Packer, the Man Eater.* Denver: University of Denver Press, 1952.

Garcilaso de la Vega. *Royal Commentaries of the Incas and General History of Peru.* Translated by Harold V. Livermore. Austin: University of Texas Press, 1966.

Gilbert, William S. *The Bab Ballads With Which Are Included Songs of a Savoyard.* 3d ed. London and New York: George Routledge & Sons, 1898.

————. *Original Plays.* 2d series. London: Chatto & Windus, 1925.

Gosse, Philip. *The History of Piracy.* New York: Burt Franklin, 1968.

————. *The Pirates' Who's Who: Giving Particulars of the Lives and Deaths of the Pirates and Buccaneers.* New York: Burt Franklin, 1968.

Graham, Gerald Sandford. *A Concise History of Canada.* New York: Viking Press, 1968.

Hafen, LeRoy R., ed. *The Mountain Men and the Fur Trade of the Far West: Biographical Sketches of the Participants by Scholars of the Subject and with Introductions by the Editor.* 10 vols. Glendale, Calif.: Arthur H. Clark Co., 1972.

Hakluyt, Richard, ed. *The Principal Navigations, Voiages and Discoveries of the English Nation.* London: George Bishop, 1598.

Hansen, Chadwick. *Witchcraft at Salem.* New York: New American Library, 1969.

The Harleian Miscellany, or a Collection of Scarce, Curious, and Entertaining Pamphlets. Vol. 5. London: T. Osborne, 1744–46.

Harrison, David. *The Melancholy Narrative of The Distressful Voyage and Miraculous Deliverance of Captain David Harrison.* London: James Harrison, 1766.

Haynes, Bessie Doak, and Edgar Haynes, eds. *The Grizzly Bear: Portraits from Life.* Norman, Okla.: University of Oklahoma Press, 1966.

Healy, James N., ed. *Irish Ballads and Songs of the Sea.* Hatboro, Pa.: Folklore Associates, 1977.

Heffernan, Thomas Farel. *Stove by a Whale: Owen Chase and the "Essex."* Middletown, Conn.: Wesleyan University Press, 1981.

Hibbert, Christopher. *Gilbert and Sullivan and Their Victorian World*. New York: American Heritage, 1976.

Holbrook, Stewart H. *Far Corner: A Personal View of the Pacific Northwest*. New York: Macmillan, 1952.

Hooper, W. Eden. *The History of Newgate and the Old Bailey*. London: Underwood Press, 1935.

Horwood, Harold. *Bartlett: The Great Canadian Explorer*. Garden City, N.Y.: Doubleday & Co., 1977.

Howard, Leon. *Herman Melville: A Biography*. Berkeley: University of California Press, 1951.

Howell, John. *The Life and Adventures of Alexander Selkirk . . . to Which is Added History of the Wanderings of Tom Starboard*. Philadelphia: Hazard & Mitchell, 1850.

Huntress, Keith. *Narratives of Shipwrecks and Disasters, 1586–1860*. Ames, Iowa: Iowa State University Press, 1974.

Irving, Washington. *Astoria: Anecdotes of an Enterprise Beyond the Rocky Mountains*. Philadelphia: Carey, Lea & Blanchard, 1836.

———. *A Tour on the Plains*. Philadelphia: Carey, Lea & Blanchard, 1835.

James, Isaac. *Providence Displayed*. Bristol: Riggs & Cottle, 1800.

The Just Vengeance of Heaven Exemplified. Philadelphia: William Bradford, 1748.

Katz, Jonathan. *Gay American History: Lesbians and Gay Men in the U.S.A.* New York: Thomas Y. Crowell Co., 1976.

Kemp, P. K., and Christopher Lloyd. *The Brethren of the Coast*. New York: St. Martin's Press, 1960.

Keneally, Thomas. *The Survivor*. New York: Viking Press, 1969.

———. *Victim of the Aurora*. New York: Harcourt Brace Jovanovich, 1978.

Kephart, Horace, ed. *Castaways and Crusoes: Tales of Survivors of Shipwrecks*. Oyster Bay, N.Y.: Nelson Doubleday, 1915.

Knowles, Joseph. *Alone in the Wilderness*. Boston: Small, Maynard & Co., 1913.

Kushner, Ervan F. *Alferd G. Packer: Cannibal! Victim?* Frederick, Colo.: Platte 'N Press, 1980.

Langman, Christopher, Nicholas Mellen, and George White. *A True Account of the Voyage of the "Nottingham Galley" of London*. London: S. Popping, 1711.

Little, Bryan. *Crusoe's Captain: Being the Life of Woodes Rogers, Seaman, Trader, Colonial Governor*. London: Odhams Press, 1960.

Lloyd, Christopher. *William Dampier*. Hamden, Conn.: Archon Books, 1966.

Lucie-Smith, Edward. *Outcasts of the Sea: Pirates and Piracy*. New York: Paddington Press, 1978.

McKee, Alexander. *The Queen's Corsair: Drake's Journey of Circumnavigation, 1577–1580*. New York: Stein & Day, 1978.

McKinlay, William Laird. *"Karluk": The Great Untold Story of Arctic Exploration*. New York: St. Martin's Press, 1976.

MacLeish, Archibald. *J.B.: A Play in Verse*. Boston: Houghton Mifflin Co., 1958.

McLoughlin, Denis. *Wild and Woolly: An Encyclopedia of the Old West.* Garden City, N.Y.: Doubleday & Co., 1975.

Manfred, Frederick. *Lord Grizzly.* New York: New American Library, 1954.

Marguerite d'Angoulême, Queen of Navarre. *The Heptameron.* Translated by Arthur Machen. New York: E. P. Dutton, 1905.

Marx, Leo. *Machine in the Garden: Technology and the Pastoral Ideal in America.* New York: Oxford University Press, 1964.

Mather, Increase. *An Essay for the Recording of Illustrious Providences (1684).* Facsimile reproduction. New York: Scholars' Facsimiles & Reprints, 1977.

Melville, Herman. *Moby Dick, or the White Whale.* New York: New American Library, 1961.

———. *The Works of Herman Melville.* 22 vols. London: Constable & Co., 1922–24.

Migeo, Marcel. *The Story of Saint-Exupéry.* Translated by Herma Briffault. New York: McGraw-Hill, 1960.

Milford, H. S. *Cowper: Poetical Works.* Rev. ed. New York: Oxford University Press, 1967.

Morgan, Dale L. *Jedediah Smith and the Opening of the West.* Lincoln, Nebr.: University of Nebraska Press, 1953.

Morison, Samuel Eliot. *Admiral of the Ocean Sea: A Life of Christopher Columbus.* Boston: Little, Brown & Co., 1942.

———. *The European Discovery of America: The Northern Voyages, A.D. 500–1600.* New York: Oxford University Press, 1971.

Moore, John Robert. *Daniel Defoe: Citizen of the World.* Chicago: University of Chicago Press, 1958.

Mosley, Leonard. *Lindbergh: A Biography.* Garden City, N.Y.: Doubleday & Co., 1976.

Myers, John Myers. *The Deaths of the Bravos.* Boston: Little, Brown and Co., 1962.

———. *Pirate, Pawnee, and Mountain Man: The Saga of Hugh Glass.* Boston: Little, Brown and Co., 1963.

Neider, Charles, ed. *Great Shipwrecks and Castaways.* New York: Harper & Brothers, 1952.

Neihardt, John G. *The Song of Hugh Glass.* New York: Macmillan, 1915.

———. *The Splendid Wayfaring.* New York: Macmillan, 1920.

New Catholic Encyclopedia. Edited by the staff of the Catholic University of America. Vol. 9. New York: McGraw-Hill, 1967.

Nickerson, Thomas. *The Loss of the Ship "Essex" Sunk by a Whale and the Ordeal of the Crew in Open Boats.* Nantucket, Mass.: Nantucket Historical Association, 1984.

Olsen, Jack. *Night of the Grizzlies.* New York: G. P. Putnam's Sons, 1969.

Oxford Dictionary of the Christian Church. Edited by F. L. Cross. London: Oxford University Press, 1974.

Paine, Ralph D. *Lost Ships and Lonely Seas.* New York: The Century Co., 1921.

Pattie, James O. *The Personal Narrative of James O. Pattie of Kentucky.* Edited by Timothy Flint. Cincinnati: John H. Woods, 1831.

Peary, Robert E. *Secrets of Polar Travel*. New York: The Century Co., 1917.

Pound, Reginald. *Scott of the Antarctic*. New York: Coward-McCann, 1966.

Pringle, Patrick. *Jolly Roger: The Story of the Great Age of Piracy*. New York: W. W. Norton and Co., 1953.

Purchas, Samuel, ed. *Hakluytus Posthumus, or Purchas His Pilgrimes*. 20 vols. Glasgow: J. MacLehose and Sons, 1905–1907.

Read, Piers Paul. *Alive!* Philadelphia: J. B. Lippincott, 1974.

Rickenbacker, Eddie. *Rickenbacker: An Autobiography*. Englewood Cliffs, N.J.: Prentice-Hall, 1967.

———. *Seven Came Through*. Garden City, N.Y.: Doubleday, Doran and Co., 1943.

Roads, Jr., Samuel. *A Guide to Marblehead*. 4th ed. Marblehead, Mass.: Merrill H. Graves, 1895.

Robinson, Joy D. Marie. *Antoine de Saint-Exupéry*. Boston: Twayne Publishers, 1984.

Rogers, Stanley. *Crusoes and Castaways*. London: George G. Harrap & Co., 1932.

———. *Sea-lore*. London: George G. Harrap & Co., 1929.

Rogers, Woodes. *A Cruising Voyage Round the World*. New York: Longmans, Green & Co., 1928.

———. *Life Aboard a British Privateer*. London: Conway Maritime Press, 1970.

Ruxton, George Frederick. *Life in the Far West*. New York: Harper & Brothers, 1849.

Sage, Rufus. *Scenes in the Rocky Mountains, and in Oregon, California, New Mexico, Texas, and The Grand Prairies*. Philadelphia: Carey & Hart, 1847.

Saint-Exupéry, Antoine de. *Airman's Odyssey*. Translated by Lewis Galantière. New York: Reynal & Hitchcock, 1942.

———. *Wartime Writings, 1939–1944*. Translated by Norah Purcell. New York: Harcourt Brace Jovanovich, 1982.

———. *Wind, Sand and Stars*. Translated by Lewis Galantière. New York: Reynal & Hitchcock, 1939.

Salisbury, Harrison Evans. *The Nine Hundred Days: The Siege of Leningrad*. New York: Harper & Row, 1969.

Saunders, Ann. *The Narrative of the Shipwreck and Sufferings of Miss Ann Saunders*. Providence: Z. S. Crossmon, 1827.

Schoonmaker, Walter J. *The World of the Grizzly Bear*. Philadelphia: J. B. Lippincott, 1968.

Scott, Robert. *Scott's Last Expedition*. Arranged by Leonard Huxley. 2 vols. New York: Dodd, Mead and Co., 1913.

The Sea, the Ship and the Sailor: Tales of Adventure from Log Books and Original Narratives. Salem, Mass.: Marine Research Society, 1925.

Secord, Arthur Wellesley. *Studies in the Narrative Method of Defoe*. New York: Russell & Russell, 1963.

Shakespeare, William. *The Tempest*. Edited by Robert Langbaum. New York: New American Library, 1964.

Shapiro, Karl. *V-Letter and Other Poems*. New York: Reynal & Hitchcock, 1944.

Shurtleff, William. *Distressing Dangers and Signal Deliverances, Religiously Improved*. Boston: Eleazer Russel, 1727.

Simpson, A. W. Brian. *Cannibalism and the Common Law*. Chicago: University of Chicago Press, 1984.

Smith, C. Fox, ed. *Adventures and Perils of the Sea: Being Extracts from the 100-years-old Mariner's Chronicle and Other Sources Descriptive of Shipwrecks and Adventures at Sea*. New York: Dodge Publishing Co., 1937.

Stabler, Arthur P. *The Legend of Marguerite de Roberval*. Pullman, Wash.: Washington State University Press, 1972.

Stackpole, Edouard A. *The Sea-hunters: The New England Whalemen During Two Centuries, 1635–1835*. New York: J. B. Lippincott, 1953.

Stefánsson, Vilhjálmur. *The Adventure of Wrangel Island*. New York: Macmillan, 1925.

———. *The Friendly Arctic: The Story of Five Years in Polar Regions*. New York: Macmillan, 1927.

Stevenson, Robert Louis. *Treasure Island*. New York: Bantam Books, 1981.

Tannahill, Reay. *Flesh and Blood: A History of the Cannibalism Complex*. New York: Stein & Day, 1975.

Thomas, R., ed. *Interesting and Authentic Narratives of the Most Remarkable Shipwrecks, Fires, Famines, Calamities, Providential Deliverances, and the Lamentable Disasters on the Seas, in Most Parts of the World*. Hartford, Conn.: Silas Andrus & Son, 1850.

Thompson, David. *David Thompson's Narrative of His Explorations in Western America, 1784–1812*. Edited by J. B. Tyrell. Toronto: Champlain Society, 1916.

Thomson, George Malcolm. *Sir Francis Drake*. New York: William Morrow & Co., 1972.

Thwaites, Reuben Gold, ed. *Early Western Travels, 1748–1846*. 32 vols. Cleveland: Arthur H. Clark Co., 1904.

Trevor-Roper, H. R. *The European Witch-Craze of the Sixteenth and Seventeenth Centuries and Other Essays*. New York: Harper & Row, 1967.

Trueblood, Paul G. *Lord Byron*. 2d ed. Boston: Twayne Publishers, 1977.

Vestal, Stanley. *Mountain Men*. Boston: Houghton Mifflin Co., 1937.

The Voyages and Travels of J. Albert de Mandelslo. The second part of a volume entitled *The Voyages and Travels of the Ambassadors*. Translated by John Davies. London: Thomas Dring & J. Starkey, 1662.

Warner, Oliver. *Great Seamen*. London: G. Bell & Sons, 1961.

Whittier, John Greenleaf. *The Poetical Works of John Greenleaf Whittier*. Vol. 1. Boston: Houghton Mifflin and Co., 1892.

Wilcox, L. A. *Anson's Voyage*. New York: St. Martin's Press, 1970.

Wilkes, Charles. *Autobiography of Rear Admiral Charles Wilkes, U.S. Navy*. Washington, D.C.: Dept. of the Navy, 1978.

Winston, Alexander. *No Man Knows My Grave: Sir Henry Morgan, Cap-*

tain William Kidd, Captain Woodes Rogers in the Great Age of Privateers and Pirates, 1665–1715. Boston: Houghton Mifflin Co., 1969.
Woodbury, George. *The Great Days of Piracy In The West Indies.* New York: W. W. Norton & Co., 1951.
Wordsworth, William. *The Poetical Works of Wordsworth.* Boston: Houghton Mifflin Co., 1982.
Wright, Thomas. *The Life of Daniel Defoe.* London: Cassell & Co., 1894.
Young, F. M., and Coralie M. Beyers, eds. *Man Meets Grizzly.* Boston: Houghton Mifflin Co., 1980.
Zamperini, Louis, and Helen Itria. *Devil at My Heels.* New York: E. P. Dutton, 1956.

Magazines

"Air Crash Survivors: The Troubled Aftermath." *Time* 101 (January 15, 1973): 53.
"Alive and Well." *Newsweek* 85 (June 30, 1975): 11.
"Alone in the Wilderness." *The Nation* 98 (February 19, 1914): 88.
"And Then There Were 13." *Time* 53 (January 3, 1949): 15.
" 'As It Happened . . .' " *Newsweek* 50 (August 26, 1957): 27.
"Bad Earth." *Time* 70 (July 15, 1957): 18.
Baker, Sherston. "The Judgment in the *Mignonette* Case." *The National Review* (1884–85): 702–9.
Blank, Joseph P. "Ron Woodcock's Long Walk Home." *Reader's Digest* 100 (April 1972): 88.
———. " 'We Want To Live!' " *Reader's Digest* 119 (July 1981): 97.
Campbell, Don M. "Nightmare on Missinaibi." *Outdoor Life* 150 (August 1972): 58.
"Cannibalism on the Cordillera." *Time* 101 (January 8, 1973): 27–28.
"Captain Eddie." *Newsweek* 82 (August 6, 1973): 67–68.
Carlova, John E. "The Lost World of Lavani." *The American Mercury* 80 (February 1955): 15.
Carson, Gerald. "Yankee Tarzan." *American Heritage* 32 (April/May 1981): 60–64.
Carter, Harvey Lewis, and Marcia Carpenter Spencer. "Stereotypes of the Mountain Man." *The Western Historical Quarterly* 6 (January 1975): 17–32.
"Certain Discrepancies." *Time* 70 (August 26, 1957): 15.
Chadwick, John W. "Marblehead." *Harper's New Monthly Magazine* 49 (July 1874): 295–302.
Clark, Orange. "The Chronicles of George C. Yount, California Pioneer of 1826." *The California Historical Society Quarterly* 2 (April 1923): 3–68.
"Communications: Mountain Man Stereotypes." *The Western Historical Quarterly* 6 (July 1975): 181–202.
Corliss, Richard. "Tarzan Goes to Court." *Time* 118 (July 20, 1981): 70.
"Deliverance." *Newsweek* 81 (January 8, 1973): 27.
"Desert Gives Up Its Secret." *Life* 48 (March 7, 1960): 21.

"Died." (Burroughs obituary.) *Newsweek* 35 (March 27, 1950): 61.

Ewen, Edward T. " 'Eh-wa-au-wau-aoooow!' " *The New York Times Magazine* (September 23, 1962): 55–62.

"Family's Ordeal at Sea." *Newsweek* 100 (December 20, 1982): 42.

"Find Strayed Bomber." *Science News Letter* 76 (August 8, 1959): 85.

Foley, Peter A. "We Ditched At Sea: The Ordeal of Flying Tiger 923." *The Saturday Evening Post* 235 (November 17, 1962): 97.

"49 Tortured Days." *Newsweek* 55 (March 21, 1960): 56.

"Four Simple Soviet Lads." *Time* 75 (March 28, 1960): 32.

Fung, Leslie G. "Jedediah Strong Smith: Escapist or Capitalist." *The Pacific Historian* 21 (Spring 1977): 70–78.

Galantière, Lewis. "Antoine de Saint-Exupéry." *The Atlantic Monthly* 179 (April 1947): 133–41.

Goetzmann, William H. "A Note on 'Stereotypes of the Mountain Man.' " *The Western Historical Quarterly* 6 (July 1975): 297–302.

Graves, Ralph. "A Jungle Search That Ends in Mystery." *Life* 72 (January 28, 1982): 2A.

Gray, Malcolm. "Scenario With An Unexpected Twist." *MacLean's* 95 (January 18, 1982): 23.

Hague, Harlan H. "Some Views of the Mountain Man." *The Pacific Historian* 13 (Fall 1969): 81–92.

Hall, James. "Letters from the West, No. 14 — The Missouri Trapper." *Port Folio* (March 1825): 215.

Harris, Denise, and Roger Lewis. "We Nearly Froze to Death." *Alaska, The Magazine of Life on the Last Frontier* (May, June 1980): 20, 11.

Hastings, Margaret, and Inez Robb. "A WAC in Shangri-la." *Reader's Digest* 47 (November 1945): 1.

Holbrook, Stewart H. "The Original Nature Man." *The American Mercury* 39 (December 1936): 417–425.

Hummerstone, Robert G. "She Lived and 91 Others Died." *Life* 72 (January 28, 1982): 38.

Jeffrey, Scott. "When the *Pride of Baltimore* Sank, Eight Sailors Got a Crash Course in Ocean Survival." *People Weekly* 26 (July 14, 1986): 71–72.

Kabat, H. R. "Bare Fists Against a Shark." *The Saturday Evening Post* 217 (November 11, 1944): 17.

Koepcke, Julianne. "Nightmare In the Jungle." *Reader's Digest* 102 (February 1973): 100.

"The Last Blossom." *Newsweek* 79 (February 7, 1972): 30.

"The Last Soldier." *Time* 99 (February 7, 1972): 41.

Levitt, Michael. "Trial by Water." *Motor Boat and Sailing* 138 (August 1976): 31.

Lockley, Fred. "A Modern Cave Man." *The American Magazine* 91 (January 1921): 48.

Lowry, Lois. "Tarzan of the Maine Woods." *Down East* 26 (September 1979): 70–75.

McIntyre, Thomas. "American History: Grizzly." *Sports Afield* 190 (September 1983): 65–106.

Madden, Paul. "Tragic Voyage." *The Saturday Evening Post* 216 (June 10, June 17, 1944): 16, 22.

"Man Overboard." *Time* 58 (July 23, 1951): 50.

Marx, Robert F. "Pedro Serrano: the First Robinson Crusoe." *Oceans* 7 (September 1974): 6.

Merritt, Jim. "A 'Turrible' Animal." *Field and Stream* 111 (February 1987): 52.

"Me Tarzan, Me Rich." *Forbes* 115 (February 15, 1975): 22–23.

Monture, Joel. "The Mountain Men." *American History Illustrated* 16 (April 1981): 22–31.

Morgan, Ted. "The Outing." *Esquire* 82 (November 1974): 164–65.

Mydans, Shelly. "Suzy From Shangri-la." *Life* 19 (July 23, 1945): 30.

"New Guinea Adventure." *Newsweek* 25 (June 18, 1945): 60.

"On a Raft With Food Only From the Sea." *Life* 34 (March 18, 1953): 115.

"One Who Survived." *American Heritage* 7 (June 1956): 65.

Pyle, Howard. "Buccaneers and Marooners of the Spanish Main." *American History Illustrated* 19 (February 1985): 22–25; 20 (March 1985): 42–49.

"Return to the Living." *Newsweek* 50 (July 15, 1957): 26.

"Rip Van Yokoi." *Time* 100 (September 18, 1972): 66.

Roberts, Tony. "Alain Bombard, Crusader for and Against the Sea." *Oceans* 15 (January/February 1982): 5.

Rosbert, C. J. "Only God Knew the Way." *The Saturday Evening Post* 216 (February 12, 1944): 13.

Saint-Exupéry, Antoine de. "An Open Letter to Frenchmen Everywhere." *The New York Times Magazine* (November 29, 1942): 7.

"Saved At Sea Just in Time." *Life* 48 (March 21, 1960): 26.

Schoen, John W., Sterling D. Miller, and Harry V. Reynolds III. "Last Stronghold of the Grizzly." *Natural History* 96 (January 1987): 50–61.

Schreiner, S. A. "One Handhold from Death." *Reader's Digest* 119 (December 1981): 103–8.

Schwartz, Robert L. "The Terrible End of the USS *Juneau*," *The Saturday Evening Post* 222 (February 25, 1950): 22.

Serrano, Pedro. "Account by Master Pedro Serrano of Eight Years Spent As a Castaway On the Serrana Keys in the Caribbean Sea, 1528–36." Translated by Robert F. Marx. *Oceans* 7 (September 1974): 6.

Sierks, Ted. "Don't Give Up, You Weakling!" *Life* 31 (August 6, 1951): 59.

"The Strange Case of the Sierra Survivor." *Life* 43 (September 2, 1957): 51.

"The Survivor." *Newsweek* 73 (June 16, 1969): 69.

"The Survivor." *Newsweek* 79 (January 17, 1972): 39.

"Tackling Nature in the Raw." *The Literary Digest* 47 (September 6, 1913): 394.

Taylor, Carole. "Ordeal In the Snow." *Reader's Digest* 102 (January 1973): 84.

"Two Months a Caveman." *The Literary Digest* 47 (October 18, 1913): 722.

Vidal, Gore. "Tarzan Revisited." *Esquire* 60 (December 1963): 192.
"Voices in the Wilderness." *Newsweek* 80 (October 30, 1972): 62.
"Welcome Home." *Time* 53 (January 10, 1949): 16.
"Where It Is Still 1945." *Newsweek* 80 (November 6, 1972): 58.
"Young Man and the Sea." *Time* 61 (January 5, 1953): 28.

Acknowledgments

Robert Gottlieb accepted as a client an unknown foreigner washed up on wild Midwestern shores, and he proceeded to promote his book and career with utmost diligence and true professionalism. I really appreciate it, Robert. Thanks also to Laura Shapiro and the other folks at the William Morris Agency for watching out after my interests.

Harry Foster is an excellent editor, an insightful wizard with a sharp pencil, and I am most grateful for his help. He followed this project from submission to publication, and he thoroughly edited the manuscript, substantially improving it. But it was his constant enthusiasm for *Abandoned Souls* that I value most of all.

Becky Saikia-Wilson copy-edited the manuscript with extraordinary dedication and painstaking attention to detail. She also did a second line-editing of the manuscript, working carefully to refine, revise, and enhance it. I deeply appreciate her considerateness, patience, and diligence.

Thanks also to Sandra Goroff-Mailly, the publicist for *Abandoned Souls,* and SusanMary Broadbent, Peggy Cerilli, Melinda Koyanis, and everyone else at Houghton Mifflin who contributed to the project.

Sterling Seagrave read an early and woefully misguided draft of this book. His criticisms were cool, precise, and right on the money. *Desperate Journeys, Abandoned Souls* would be a far different and far poorer work without his suggestions and advice. Much thanks, Sterling.

Carson Gibb made his way through the labyrinths of the Library of Congress and the Folger Shakespeare Library, identifying and arranging for prints of illustrations and collecting material on Joseph Knowles, Marguerite de la Roque, and Alexander William Holmes, among other survivors. He also read large portions of this manuscript, making corrections and giving me the benefit of his thoughts and expertise.

Any mistakes of fact or interpretation are strictly my responsibility, but I would like to express my gratitude to the survivors and experts in various fields who read portions of this manuscript and made corrections and suggestions: Elizabeth Boyer, Ron Woodcock, Jamie Ely, Kenneth Decker, John McCollom, John Marion, Lauren Elder, Steve Callahan, Brian Simpson, and Captain Donald B. Millar, USN (Ret.).

This book is built on the accounts of survivors and the work of numerous scholars. Many are identified in the text or the Annotations and Bibliography, but I feel a special debt to the following: Christopher Lloyd for his research into William Dampier and other privateers; George Woodbury and Alexander Winston, for their studies of Woodes Rogers; Arthur P. Stabler and Elizabeth Boyer for their elucidations of the case of Marguerite de la Roque and translations of pertinent documents; John Myers Myers for his reconstruction of the adventures of Hugh Glass; F. M. Young for his tireless collecting of materials relating to grizzly bears; Lois Lowry and Gerald Carson for their demythologizing of Joseph Knowles; and Thomas Farel Heffernan for his thorough study of the *Essex* case. I have also benefited from the work of a number of journalists, including Jim Rearden, Joseph P. Blank, Michael Levitt, Lawrence E. Davies, Malcolm Gary, Sergeant Peter A. Foley, and Clay Blair, Jr.

Early in my research I encountered two anthologies that proved invaluable to me: Charles Neider's *Great Shipwrecks and Castaways* and Keith Huntress's *Narratives of Shipwrecks and Disasters*. These books caused me for the first time to see the possibilities of a study of survivors; Neider and Huntress also were enormously helpful in identifying particular stories and sources. I am most grateful to these fine scholars.

A. W. Brian Simpson deserves special mention. When I read his remarkable book *Cannibalism and the Common Law,* I had already written the chapters dealing with what I call "the delicate question which." But Simpson's book was a revelation for me, not only in terms of specific stories and sources heretofore unknown to me but also in the way in which he handled the subject. *Cannibalism and the Common Law* had a real impact on my thinking. I did not adopt Simpson's point of view, but I rethought my own and rewrote "the delicate question which" chapters accordingly, often adding new introductions and taking a markedly different approach to them. Having made these changes, I reopened still other chapters, particularly those in Part Three, again changing my approach and adding fresh introductory material.

I corresponded with Mr. Simpson, and he patiently answered all my questions, read and corrected perhaps half of my manuscript, directed me to unusual and obscure sources, and generously shared with me his notes on the contents of British Public Record Office files. Thus my debt to Brian Simpson can hardly be overestimated, and I wish to thank him most humbly for his help — and for his book.

A number of photographers provided me with prints for the illustrations that appear in this book. Employees of research institutions gave me access to or permission to use paintings, etchings, and plates from rare volumes. For their cooperation I would like to thank the following: Sarnya Smith, the Bettmann Archive; Sue Hanson, Head of Special Collections, Case Western Reserve University Libraries; Lenora R. White, Curatorial Dept., and Rowland Elzea, Curator, Delaware Art Museum; Anne D. Muchoney, the Folger Shakespeare Library; Geneva B. Politzer, *American History Illustrated;* Larry Rubens, Kent State University; Alex Gildzen, Curator, Special Collections, Kent State University Libraries; Bill Dewald, Medfact, Inc.; Marie Boltz, Administrative Assistant, and Philip Metzger, Supervisor, Special Collections, Lehigh University Libraries; Debra Cohen, *Life* Picture Service; John N. Welch, Administrator, and Jacqueline Kolle Haring, Curator of Research Materials, the Nantucket Historical Association; Steve Pettinga, *The Saturday Evening Post;* Kevin Grace, Assistant Head, Archives and Rare Books Dept., University of Cincinnati Libraries; John Beck, Assistant Special Collections Librarian, Albin O. Kuhn Library and Gallery, The University of Maryland, Baltimore County Campus; Jean Z. Piety, Photoduplication Office, Cleveland Public Library; Alan M. Scherr, Photographer; Simon Cobley, Archivist, George Weidenfeld and Nicolson, Ltd.; Nat Andriani, Wide World Photos, Inc.; Elaine Wittig Border, Photographer; Bryan Corban, Photographer; and Ron Woodcock. I would also like to thank the Department of the Navy and the U.S. Air Force for giving me permission to publish military photographs.

I would like to express my appreciation to the staffs of the Photoduplication Office, Cleveland Public Library; Photoduplication Service, Library of Congress; Photographic Services, National Maritime Museum, Greenwich; Publications Dept., National Portrait Gallery, London; Photography Dept., the Folger Shakespeare Museum.

Thanks to Bob Freedman, Bethlehem Public Library, for his visits to Philadelphia area libraries on my behalf, tracking down newspaper clippings on the shipwreck of the *William Brown* and other disasters and locating a rare copy of *Providence Displayed*.

Thanks also to Elaine Wittig Border and Mary Anne Uitto for the research they contributed to this book. Thanks to Clyde Tolley for sharing his ideas on witchcraft and for visiting on my behalf the William H. Welch Medical Library and the Milton S. Eisenhower Library, Johns Hopkins University. Thanks to David Lindert, M.D., for offering his insights into the physical problems of survivors who are suffering dehydration, and to John Rodgers, M.D., for his thoughtful discussions. Thanks also to Michael Harvan, Ph.D., for listening to my theories about survivors and generally acting as a sounding board. (Hell, Michael, I owe you a lot more than that.)

Many institutions opened their doors to this gypsy writer. I am grateful to the staffs of the following: Library of Congress; Folger Shakespeare Library; Theodore R. McKeldin Library, University of Maryland at College Park; Eisenhower Library, Johns Hopkins University; Paul N. Elbin Library, West Liberty State College; T. W. Phillips Memorial Library, Bethany College; University of Akron Library and Law Library; Brooke County Public Library; Mary H. Weir Public Library; Steubenville Public Library; Enoch Pratt Free Library; Baltimore County Public Library; Cleveland Public Library; Akron-Summit County Public Library; and Nimitz Library, United States Naval Academy.

I would like to express my gratitude to the following institutions which provided me with copies of transcripts, rare books, and other valuable documents: British Public Record Office; Lehigh University; Cleveland Public Library; Portland Public Library; Case Western Reserve University; Rare Book Room, Library of Congress; Folger Shakespeare Library; University of Maryland, Baltimore County Campus; Special Collections, Kent

584   *Acknowledgments*

State University; Wake Forest University Law Library; and Department of the Navy.

Kent State University gave me scholar's privileges. I am very grateful to the librarians of the Reference, Special Collections, and Periodicals departments and the Microform Center. In particular I would like to express my gratitude to Martha Goold, Reference Dept. Supervisor, and Linda Burroughs, Microform Center Supervisor. For their unfailing patience, I am especially indebted to Mary C. Taylor, Microform Center, and Kathleen E. Noland, Assistant to the Curator, Special Collections, Kent State University.

I would like to thank Annie Laird Scott for corresponding with me regarding her father's adventures in the Arctic and his collection of rare photographs. I am grateful to those scholars, journalists, survivors, and relatives of survivors who allowed me to interview them or who corresponded with me. This list is not complete by any means, but among those kind folk are Gerald Carson, Lois Lowry, Elizabeth Boyd, Lauren Elder, Kenneth Decker, John McCollom, Ron Woodcock, Brian Simpson, Paula R. Backscheider, Don M. Campbell, and Louis Zamperini.

For help in dealing with the federal bureaucracy, I owe a debt of gratitude to Bob Welling, Press Secretary for Congressman J. Dennis Hastert, 14th District, Illinois.

A philosophical disagreement with John Marion caused me to write the Headhunter's Casket chapter. John, if every argument I've had with you since W.D.'s Newman class had led to such productivity, I'd have written more books than Stephen King. Thanks for the chapter, John. May you never stop telling me I'm wrong.

Thanks to John Wolf for his encouragement and his willingness to act as a sounding board.

David Chris Galloway located a rare copy of John Howell's biography of Selkirk and arranged for its duplication. An old and loyal friend, he always generously offers lodging when I travel east on research forays. Thanks, Chris; I really appreciate it.

A number of newspapers published queries of mine as I attempted to locate modern survivors. The editors of the following have my gratitude: the *Sabetha Herald,* the *Ottawa Times,* the *Owego Pennysaver Press,* the *Trenton Republican-Times,* the *Cape Girardeau Southeast Missourian,* the *Longmont Times-Call,* the *Murray News Advertiser,* the *Seward Phoenix Log.* I would also like to thank Sarah Rogers of King Features Syndicate for her help.

I would also like to thank Maxine Demchak and Eric Klein for their patient and prompt processing of my many, many interlibrary loan requests. There are many other individuals who provided me with particular documents or information. I regret that the limitation of space does not permit me to specify the exact nature of my debts, but I am no less grateful to Janet Willson and Rosemary Hauswirth, Hazelton District Library; Sally Walker; Judi Kincaid, Harcourt Brace Jovanovich; Paula R. Backscheider, Professor of English, University of Rochester; Betty Wang, El Cajon Library; Harold and Jerre Vanderpool; Elizabeth C. Young; Mrs. Frank Vihtelic; Jeanne Mitchell; Emily DeForest, Kenai Community Library;

Margaret Deck, Seward Community Library; Jane E. Wood, Cecil County Historical Society; Dorothy E. Mueller, Philadelphia Maritime Museum; Sharon Lass Field, Researcher; Don Johnson, Dept. of Libraries, City of Duluth; Nettie Oliver, Librarian, Filson Club; Kay Wisniewski, Free Library of Philadelphia; Anne McDonnell, Kentucky Historical Society; Judy Sheldon, California Historical Society; George H. Haas, Senior Editor, *Outdoor Life;* Margaret Gale, Reference and Library Division, British Information Services; Jacob Leed, Professor, Kent State University; Margot McCain, Maine Historical Society; James E. Woodruff; Kathy Brumbaug; David Ellefsen, Salt Lake County Library System; Barbara D. Smith, Portland Public Library; Mrs. Lorraine H. Schinz; Captain Hackman, Office of Air Force History; Mr. Walker, Naval Historical Center; B. F. Cavalcante, Operations Archives Branch, Department of the Navy; Nora Whelan, Putnam Publishers; and Nathan Lipfert, Maine Maritime Museum.

The staff of the Massillon Public Library and Museum system and the Brooke County Public Library system have been particularly helpful. For their patience and dedication to public service, I would specifically like to express my gratitude to the following librarians: Jane Biehl, Leslie Picot, Eric Klein, Maxine Demchak, Janice Feller, Harriet Hose, Cheryl Jackson, Kim Senft-Paras, Sherie Brown, Pat Grant, Laura Klein, Ruthy Pedrotty, Larry Brown, Shawn Perry, Stephanie Nussbaum, Chris Berens, Michelle Adams, Sue Chu, Dona Reed, Janet Herrick, Winnie Ash, Hilda Pfouts, Ruth Duke, Marcy Holm, Doris Dean, Patsy Clunk, Mitch Reed, James Hale, Dane Jeffries, and Scott Owen. My thanks also go to Betty Gay Myers, Pearl Baker, Marilyn McGowan, and Patty Olszeski. Thanks also to Leslie Wilson and Brenda Momirovic of the Stark County District Library.

And, yes, thank you, too, Millie Cowan — none of the packages got lost, and they all arrived on time.

There are four last acknowledgments I feel compelled to make. Although to the reader some of them may appear frivolous, I swear that I feel each debt to be a substantial one.

In the 1950s or early 1960s, songwriter W. Chadbourne Mitchell adapted an old Child ballad for his group, the Chad Mitchell Trio. The song concerns an English merchant ship, the *Golden Vanity,* which is sailing on the Lowland Sea. Her officers and crew fear that she will be captured by Turkish pirates, and inevitably one day the *Vanity* is menaced by an enemy vessel. The *Vanity*'s captain calls for volunteers to sink the Turk, offering silver and gold as the reward. No one has the nerve or ingenuity to undertake the task until (a modern addition, this) the skipper promises the hand of his daughter in marriage; even with this added inducement, only the lowly cabin boy steps forward. The courageous lad swims to the Turkish ship, sinks her by drilling holes in her side with an auger bit, and heads back for the *Vanity,* calling to the captain to haul him from the sea. But the skipper, valuing his wealth and his daughter's marriageability more than his honor, leaves the boy to die. The *Vanity* sails on — and, with the only valiant soul among them gone, those on board are once more terrified of being captured.

The other song, "And the Waves Roll Out, And the Waves Roll In," was written in the sixties by Shel Silverstein and Bob Gibson. Silverstein was then known as a cartoonist for *Playboy* magazine and is now a best-selling author of poetry for children. Gibson, then as now, is perhaps the finest twelve-string guitar player in captivity. The song is a sailor's "Ghost Riders In The Sky": after a shipwreck, a sinful mariner sinks to the bottom of the ocean, where he sees the skeletons of men drowned long ago. They reach out their bony hands for him and cry out that if he does not change his ways, his fate will be the same as theirs. He floats back to the surface, and by the time he has made it to the shore, what was revealed to him during his ordeal has so altered his features that those who knew him no longer recognize him. The change marks an inner transformation, and he feels compelled to warn unregenerate seamen of what awaits them.

Some ancient, forgotten disaster took the recordings of those songs and everything else I owned or valued in this whole, sorry world away from me. In the many years that followed, as I stood braced and hunched over, laboring at the task of putting the fragments of my blasted life into some semblance of order again, I occasionally lifted my head from the work to find myself humming one or another of those tunes. None of this would be pertinent except . . . except if this book is about anything, it is about the betrayal of trust and the prospects for a kind of secular redemption. So thanks a lot, and keep writing, boys. And I hope that the many extraordinary songs Silverstein and Gibson have written have given them a sense of fulfillment and accomplishment. They certainly have given me much pleasure and cause for reflection.

Which brings us at last to Camille. You sometimes wonder at the depth of the sincerity of an author who acknowledges the contributions of a spouse, especially when the writer is male and the only thing he specifies is that his wife typed the manuscript. Camille Jeanette Leslie did *not* type this manuscript, but she did read every word of every draft of it, offering suggestions and making corrections. To say that this book would have been far different without her help is grossly inadequate, because this book and whatever others may follow after it would never have been *written* without her. For she held on to the dream during the many years that I forsook it, and so it was there when finally, scalded and penitent, I returned to it.

They pay me now, Camille, to wedge adjectives in front of nouns, but I have no words of my own to express my gratitude to you. So I must fall back on a lyric from another Child ballad, this one haunting, lovely, and inappropriate. But that is one thing I know how to fix. It is a song about a lady alone and apprehensive in the night, waiting for her lover to appear. And at last he does, solemn and slow and possessed of a secret I sometimes know to be my own. In a moment her questioning will reveal it, but for now she addresses him with an ornamental endearment and a heartfelt wish. If the irony is stripped from the desire and the endearment is retained for both its form and truth, then the sentiment they embody may be given to you as a gift. It is a gift like a flower passed in belated recognition through the bars of a subterranean window to a child of another country.

A girl from a different realm altogether.

Francis Drake

D. 1-28-1596